ON THE EDGES OF GRAPHIC DESIGN FROM A–Z–∞

PREFACE

On the Edges of Graphic Design from A—Z—∞ brings together the six-year journey of ideas, projects, and questions that have emerged from A—Z. The Berlin-based space for experimental Graphic Design was born out of a desire to create a place where the Graphic Design community could openly express and expand the definitions and boundaries of their field together.

From the beginning, A—Z has been less about presenting finished work and more about offering a platform for experimentation, collaboration, and reflection. It has given visibility to the process, bringing the marginal to center stage, where Graphic Design is understood not only as form-making but also as a way of thinking and engaging with society, and especially as a means of connecting people through this multifaceted approach.

What you will find in this book is an insight into that journey so far, marked by the participation of over 100 graphic designers and artists, as well as thousands of visitors. They have been listening, talking, sharing, thinking, discussing, and creating together in dozens of exhibitions, talks, workshops, gatherings, and numerous other exchanges—all encompassed in a dynamic program reflecting the overarching approach of understanding design as something alive, engaged, and always in the making.

Transferring the intensity of those interactions to the pages of a book was an exciting project in itself. It required a creative concept capable of capturing multiple layers of initiatives beyond a mere chronological account of events. That is why this book portrays A—Z's journey in the form of an alphabetical index that dissects the entire program of the last six years in singular entries, from A—Z.

Pointers at the bottom corner of the pages indicate related entries so you, as the reader, are invited to wander off and become lost in the maze of ideas and inspirations around Graphic Design. By offering non-linear and atemporal ways of reading—and unexpected juxtapositions—we hope to create new connections that map a territory of possibilities in Graphic Design, rather than define it.

The final section shifts the narrative from reflection to projection, offering a glimpse into possible futures for A—Z. We invited 36 designers who had not previously been featured in the space to express their views on Graphic Design. Their responses, ranging from personal to technical, and from humorous to political, present a broad spectrum of what Graphic Design might become and how a space like A—Z can continue to evolve as a laboratory for new thinking and making.

This book is a celebration of the creative potential of Graphic Design. It is dedicated to all those actively involved in the community, as we continue to push and question the discipline. In its intentionally ambiguous, fragmented, and comprehensive way, we hope it will be an inspiring read, and a clear statement of the power of creativity and community in driving Graphic Design to play a relevant role in transforming society.

FOR A DESIGN PERIPHERY
BY JASON GRANT

I began thinking seriously about Graphic Design and the margins in 2011 when a group of my typography students invited designers from around the world to speak at a three-day conference in Brisbane. It was an ambitious event organized entirely by the students (probably compensating for the deficiencies in their typography education). Over the course of the conference, I got to catch up with speakers I knew, and listen to some I'd never met. One of the speakers made a comment that has stayed with me— about a designer's proximity to power. Their theory was that designers on the periphery were impotent, and that what every designer secretly wanted was a seat at the boardroom table. I guess this is a fairly common industry assumption, and yet it was the first time I had heard it argued so directly; unless you're sitting down with captains of commerce, then your designing is ineffectual delusion. It was the first time I heard the claim, but not the last. More recently, Neville Brody insisted:

> How do you make an impact by standing on the fringe? ... you can't stand on the fringe and have impact. You either have to move society to where you are at the center, or you have to move to the center of society. If you're on the outside, you will never change anything.[1]

In the 'change from within' versus 'change from without' debate I'm always with the latter, assuming the former to be just another way of sustaining the status quo. What exactly did Neville hope to achieve by straight-talking with Dom Pérignon or Dunkin' Donuts executives? For me, like many others, Neville Brody was one of the biggest influences on my formative practice: the raw urgency of his Fetish Records album covers; identities for left-wing groups like Red Wedge; and the experimental digital typography of the Fuse project. Though for a 20-year-old designer, it wasn't just the work, it was the idea that design could avoid the choking conventions of commercial design, that a more human and personal language could respond, not just to a commercial client's agenda, but to real social or cultural need.

Contrary to his later endorsement of the center, the Neville Brody of my formative years stood on the fringe and made a real impact there. It's hard though to do this kind of work and remain viable inside the market economy "without also working as a barista", as Neville put it in the same interview. Harder than taking big pay checks from big corporates, for sure. But isn't claiming that it can't be done—or that all the paths to alternative or oppositional practice have been exhausted—just an admission of defeat? Or, as if for most people, marginality is even a choice. Interestingly, those who most loudly make these claims aren't the straight-up uncritical corporate designers, but designers who have migrated stealthily across this treacherous ideological terrain, arriving at a place foreign and hostile to their humble origins.

Definitions of success are subjective. For my studio, Inkahoots, success is avoiding corporate commissions as much as possible. For others, listing Nike, Google, Apple, and the rest as clients is the ultimate measure of accomplishment. Inkahoots's stance might get dismissed as contrary, as naive, utopian, or even as some kind of misplaced moral superiority. But doesn't that verdict require an assumption that the margins are good for nothing, least of all for catalyzing change? That the fringe is a barren and unproductive pipe dream? Are socially focused designers really wasting their talent and effort on the periphery?

In some ways it's harder to measure impact in the margins. Often, Inkahoots isn't selling anything you can count. Sometimes there are no units to shift, no growth to boost, no profits to raise. But because it's harder to quantify (especially without the resources for collecting data and analyzing outcomes) that doesn't mean we can't observe change. Change in people—in what they feel and understand, how they find and connect with each other—is real enough. We're: staging exhibitions and interventions; protesting with our creative labor and our bodies; connecting cash-strapped community organizations to their audience; helping environmental groups avoid visualizing the logic that they exist to resist; amplifying activists' stature, credibility, and clarity; working with artists on hybrid creative systems; supporting local businesses for whom profitability is merely a means to an end; designing platforms for public discourse; defending the weird and the vulnerable; imagining better alternatives ... succeeding and failing ... So many important relationships, communities, and cultures that are dismissed or attacked by the center can be nurtured by the margins.

In the margins you need to be *active*. The center, however, has an irresistible momentum. It's the magnetic, mesmeric logic of the market. It's a current that carries you along. A gravity that pulls you in and holds you down. You don't need to do anything at all. The center breeds and feeds off *passivity*. It substitutes real change with the hectic energy of market dynamics. The margins are breathing space—not a romanticized space free from danger, but a space to actively resist hegemonic harassment. Designers often talk about experimentation and creative risk, but when we're *inside* the dominant culture (and a culture of domination),[2] we're not even aware of the nature and limits of the borders. In the margins, the boundaries can be more clearly recognized and therefore ruptured.

Neville Brody's 'center' is obvious and desirable. Calling something 'marginal' is a dismissive put-down. It's framed as an avoidable deficiency. Marginality, however, is always relative. It's always measured in reference to a contested center. And inevitably they define each other. To claim that social or cultural change only happens from the top down (or the center outwards) is to shrug off history and underestimate the power of both individual agency and collective struggle.

Graphic Design goes where the money is. But when it doesn't, when it draws on counter-capital resources, like community, criticality, mutual aid, solidarity, and love, graphic design can go anywhere. A—Z, a home for graphic design misfits, conceived by Anja Lutz as a way to platform and encourage the discipline's diversity, has expanded the established definition and possibilities of design. Formal, institutional spaces—like the classroom, the conference hall, or the museum—for gathering in person and talking about graphic design are relatively rare. Even rarer are independent spaces that bypass the canon and champion neglected alternatives. A—Z's compact streetfront gallery space on Berlin-Mitte's busy Torstraße has hosted a rich variety of exhibitions and events, celebrating the unconventional and experimental side of graphic design.

Graphic design is online, even when it's not. It's disseminated, discussed, and physically detached, in ways that are both valuable and devaluing. A downside of the decentralizing bias in digital media is physical disconnection; the decline of local, intimate socialization; the loss of spaces for collective and personal engagement. Douglas Rushkoff talks about how the net is useful for reinforcing real-world relationships when those relationships already exist, but because it's a decentralized, networked technology controlled by a central authority, its tendency is always to replace real-world interactions with distant, simulated digital connection.[3] As a kind of congregation of alternative practice, A—Z makes space for physical immediacy, imagination, and productive confrontation.

In bell hooks's essay, *Choosing the Margin as a Space of Radical Openness*, she writes:

> We are transformed, individually, collectively, as we make radical creative space which affirms and sustains our subjectivity, which gives us a new location from which to articulate our sense of the world.[4]

It has never really been a professional designer's priority to "articulate our sense of the world". Here is where the line between design and art has long been poorly drawn. But if 'marginal' can be redeemed as a position worth occupying, generally, and for design particularly, its frontiers of difference can be a fertile space worth fighting for and from. After all, aren't the real visionaries the outsiders who don't wait around politely for a seat at the boardroom table? Is real independence more likely inside or outside routine systems of coercion and control?

As design takes an ever-increasing role in anti-human extractive cultures, counter-hegemonic design practice offers solidarity with the oppressed and strength for the struggle. The margins bear disadvantage and suffering, yet both in spite of and because of this, they're also a site of radical defiance and possibility. But, as bell hooks put it: "one can only say no, speak the voice of resistance, because there exists a counter language."[5] Whether by imposition or by choice, dissenting designers are making a radical creative space, reaching for a new visual language, extending the scope of human expression, catalyzing real connection and common interest—and it's all happening far from the center, in the good-for-nothing margins.

1. Neville Brody on Navigating Graphic Design's Shifting Identity, Emily Gosling, AIGA Eye on Design, 2021.
2. Choosing the Margin as a Space of Radical Openness, bell hooks, Framework: The Journal of Cinema and Media, No. 36, 1989, pp. 15-23.
3. Program or Be Programmed: Eleven Commands for the AI Future, Douglas Rushkoff, OR Books, 2024.
4. bell hooks, 1989.
5. bell hooks, 1989.

JASON GRANT is a designer and co-founder of Inkahoots Design. The Australian studio is widely known for its creative advocacy, activism, and adventurous visual communication. He studied fine art and Graphic Design, and has lectured in design, typography, and art theory at universities in Australia and around the world. He was born in New Zealand, has lived and worked in London, and now lives in Brisbane.

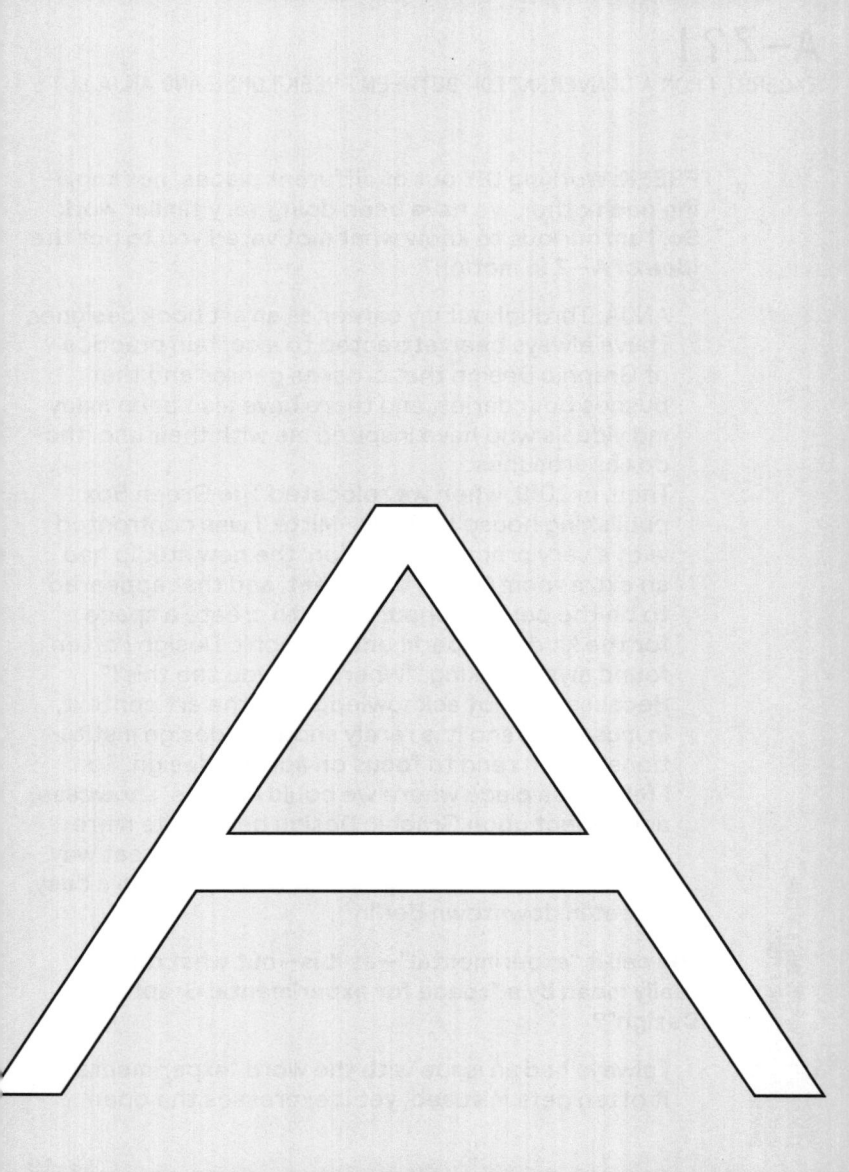

A–Z?!
EXCERPT FROM A CONVERSATION BETWEEN FREEK LOMME AND ANJA LUTZ

FREEK: Working DIY out of different places, not knowing each other, we have been doing very similar work. So, I am curious to know what motivated you to put the idea of A—Z in motion?

ANJA: Throughout my career as an art book designer, I have always been attracted to a certain practice of Graphic Design that crosses genres and that pushes boundaries, and there have also been many individuals who have inspired me with their unorthodox approaches.
Then, in 2019, when we relocated The Green Box publishing house to Berlin-Mitte, I was confronted with a very practical situation: the new studio had an extra room facing the street, and that appeared to be the perfect opportunity to create a space for the kind of experimental Graphic Design I often found myself asking, "Where can you see this?" Because it is not acknowledged in the art context, in museums, and it is rarely shown in design institutions, which tend to focus on applied design. So I felt that a place where we could discuss, showcase, and reflect upon Graphic Design beyond its mere problem-solving and applied realm was a great way to give life and meaning to that nice space on a busy street in downtown Berlin.

You call it "experimental"—as it is—but what do you really mean by a "space for experimental Graphic Design"?

I always had an issue with the word "experimental"; it often gets misused, yet it expresses the open

and speculative nature of the initiative, which I feel strongly about. A—Z is born out of curiosity and questioning, such as "How can we think and practice Graphic Design beyond the applied realm?", "What forms of Graphic Design can arise from its overlap with other disciplines?", "How can predominantly two-dimensional work be experienced in a space?", "How can the design of a space enable connection and exchange?", and so on.
My goal was to create a space that expands the territory of Graphic Design by rethinking its limits and challenging traditional perceptions of it. I can say that A—Z was never meant to be a space for just exhibiting, but also for reflecting. So rather than just being invited to present their work, the designers co-create and co-organize the exhibitions and initiatives, with the overarching mission of exploring new ways of presenting and experiencing Graphic Design.

We can say A—Z has already built its own story: commissioning or supporting new work, fostering cultural exchange between professionals, articulating artistic and cultural gestures, and in some ways advocating this sphere beyond. Are there any experiences on the A—Z floor that are your dearest ones?

There have been many positive and unexpected outcomes that have reassured me to continue with this collaborative approach, and it is also very satisfying to realize how many of the invited designers have seized the opportunity to engage in a new project, or to execute something they had been contemplating for a while ... Another thing that makes me very happy when I look back is realizing the broad spectrum of collaborations—the opportunity we have had to invite and engage with designers from diverse backgrounds, as well as different career stages, ages, and formations. That plurality remains a core value for the space.

Regarding your question, I have always felt strongly about the space as a point for people to come together and connect. These are two good examples of this: the Counter Sessions, a series of one-evening events followed by a bar night, where we could share experiences and interact over drinks. And the *A—Z Collective*, where a group of individuals ran the A—Z program for an entire year. Both initiatives broadened the concept beyond the visual aspects of Graphic Design.

I wonder if you remember any actual situations that really felt rewarding, strong, or just positively weird … Maybe I'm a voyeur, but I'd like to hear at least one of them.

There are so many moments I cherish, but I can pick two. One is a little anecdote about Lucienne Roberts's exhibition. Her approach was to reflect on her personal relationship with Graphic Design, and so she transformed the space into an intimate bedroom set. One night, she decided to stay and sleep in her installation, wearing her exhibition-design matching pajamas. The next morning, I woke her up with coffee and a croissant, and we ended up chatting for about three hours—she in bed, with me sitting next to her, while people walked past the big window, intrigued by the scene.

Another of those experiences that is a dear memory is the first open collective-forming workshop facilitated by Jocelyn Ames. We were high on the community's energy and filled with excitement from all the spontaneous connections that were created. After the workshop, we ended up dancing for an hour to loud music, releasing all that energy. For me, these initiatives highlighted the social and communicative potential of Graphic Design, which I believe is so important.

That's beautiful and very sweet. I think people long for such experiences—or maybe it's just my hopes. It also reveals something about a different way of living, I guess. Would you say there is an ideological impact related to A—Z, or is it more like a fertilizer?

I like the idea of a fertilizer … and of thinking that A–Z inspires other people and projects, that it radiates out … I feel that in an increasingly corporate and technological world—and Graphic Design has been significantly affected and changed by this, as have many other areas—it is essential to keep the space "between", a space in the margins, for unusual practices, for works with lower visibility, subtler nuances, and of course their human and interpersonal dimensions …

I can imagine it must be very satisfying and fun to be doing all of that, but of course, there must have been situations that challenged you personally, or moments that forced you to re-evaluate the whole initiative?

The collective and connecting initiatives I mentioned earlier were all turning points of sorts, where I felt the desire to change the concept or the framing of the space. The idea of *Counter Sessions* originated from a desire to engage more with visitors, beyond their initial visit to an opening, viewing an exhibition, and then leaving. And at another point, when I felt exhausted by being the one who wears the hat, the wish for the collective was born, where the responsibility would be shared. Another turning point was *A—Z Out & About*, where I wanted to be active

A–Z?!

beyond Berlin, and create a program that sends A—Z to manifest and collaborate even in other countries.
So you could say that A—Z in itself is a constant search and re-evaluation of how Graphic Design can stay relevant and engaging. And I am sure there will be more of these turning points driven just by the latest experience, whether that is empowering or challenging. Additionally, it has not been easy to complete the program without ongoing support, whether financial or structural. This remains a challenge, especially during periods when I feel less energetic.

As I try to catch your drift, so to speak, I totally feel your creative and cultural energy, but I can also sense the weight of today's world challenges and how they relate to such initiatives ... Can the creative and artistic energy of A—Z meet any of those challenges? I do not want to sound discouraging or skeptical, so Anja, please empower it: what will come next? And what after that? And where will that go? (I am not planning to copy you, but I would love to hear more about future pathways *laugh*).

On a very positive note, I am incredibly excited about this book, as it will revisit and, at the same time, reflect on and reframe what has been done at A—Z so far. I am even more excited that it will feature new works from 36 international graphic designers who have not been presented at A—Z so far. They are reflecting on the future of Graphic Design, so the questions and investigations continue ...
All these contributions are featured in the $-\infty$ section—a title that you came up with in a previous conversation we had—and will be part of an exhibition at A—Z, continuing to inspire a discussion

around the future potential of the discipline. And some of these ideas might be realized as solo exhibitions afterwards. Depending on when people are reading this conversation, they might already have happened!

Ha ha! Indeed, but that is what books do—and I know that as a publisher.

FREEK LOMME has been working in the field of art, design, and cultural criticism since 2003. Writing, curating, managing direction, artistic direction, art direction, investing, lecturing, tutoring, partaking in boards, and so on. Freek Lomme has been associated with numerous museums, independent art spaces, magazines, schools, and other institutions. He founded Set Margins' publications in September 2022, after having founded and directed Onomatopee from 2006 to 2022. As a support structure, a platform for production, a network and a publisher, Set Margins' exists to frame current impulses from the margin, with particular focus on communication, forms of co-operation, and involved politics.

ANJA LUTZ is a Berlin-based book designer specializing in contemporary art publications, and co-founder and art director of The Green Box, a publishing house for artist books. In 2019, she founded A—Z, a space for experimental Graphic Design, where she has curated more than 25 exhibitions to date.

A–Z COLLECTIVE
COLLABORATIVE STEWARDSHIP OF A–Z

A—Z Collective was a one-year project to create a space for communal practice. The creation of a non-hierarchic, self-organized group of multitalented professionals was motivated by the desire for connection and to explore what collaborative Graphic Design can be.

After an open call for participation, a series of three workshops, *What If ... Explosion, Structures and Tools,* and *Shape-Making,* brought together over 60 designers, artists, students, and open-minded individuals, and resulted in the formation of the collective.

The final multidisciplinary group spent the following year conceptualizing, developing, and presenting several initiatives, exploring forms of collaboration and co-creation inspired by community-building methods such as micro solidarity, liberating structures, and emergent strategies.

Among the public events were three main exhibitions: Sarah Boris's *Exquisite Curiosities* and the participatory format events *Super Collective Market No. 1 Yellow* and *Recipes for Connecting,* both organized by collective members. At the end of the year, a wrap-up workshop, *Happy Ending,* celebrated the project's conclusion.

A—Z Collective members were: Alina Frieske, Anja Lutz, Emily Smith, Eunjung Kwak, Francesco Pini, Gregory Cowling, Ioana Ferariu, Ivana Jecmenica, Kelly Diepenbrock, Lisa Baumgarten, Manuela dos Santos, Pia Steiner, and Sofia Harley.

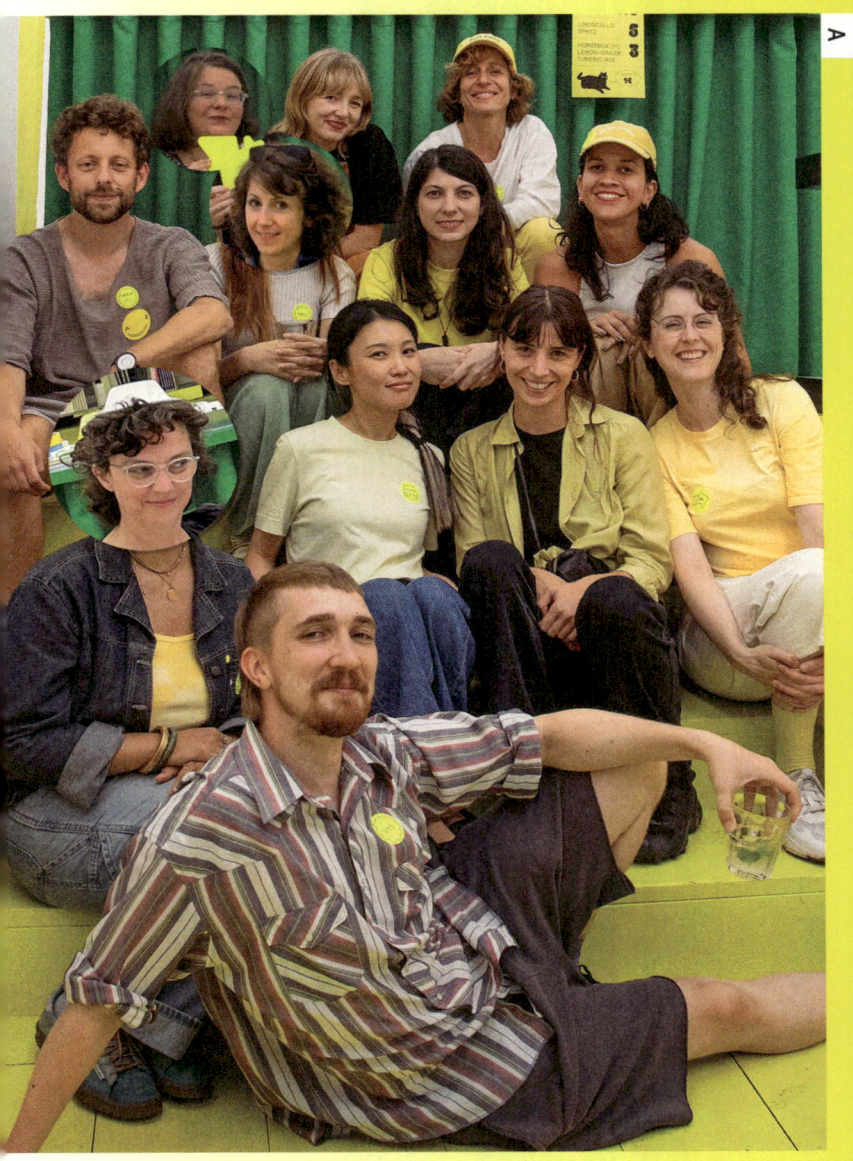

AGORA
OPEN DEBATE HOSTED BY THE RODINA AND PREM KRISHNAMURTHY

In a setup inspired by the Ancient Greek *Agora*, the artists Tereza and Vit Ruller—The Rodina—together with curator and designer Prem Krishnamurthy and A—Z founder Anja Lutz, led an open debate on the notion of creative work, design processuality, project continuity, and precarious work conditions.

In this non-hierarchical open talk, audience members were welcome to share their experiences and impressions on what the production of Graphic Design in capitalism means for them. Visitors could engage in the discussion by writing their questions on stickers and applying them all over the exhibiting space, creating a visual interpretation of the dialogue.

A

ALL MY BOOKS
INSTALLATION BY ANDREAS KOCH AS PART OF *TIME FOR BOOKS*

All My Books presented to the public the work of artist and book designer Andreas Koch, who has designed over 100 art books and magazines over almost 25 years. The exhibition took place under the scope of *Time for Books*.

To overcome the challenge of how one exhibits books, Koch presented and talked about them himself, welcoming two guests at a time to a conversation where he could share his creative process and all elements of the book design practice, surrounded by collages of details and close-ups of several publications on the wall.

Andreas Koch is co-founder of the publishing house permanent and editor of the magazine *von hundert*.

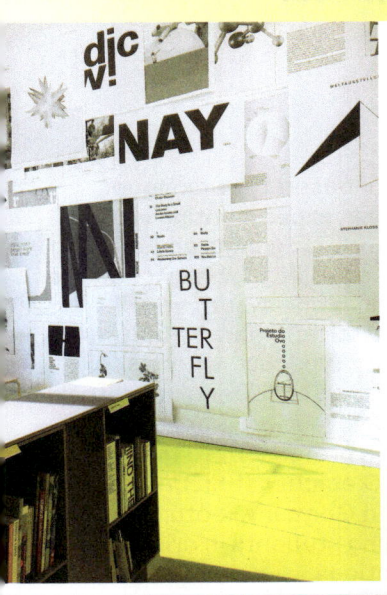
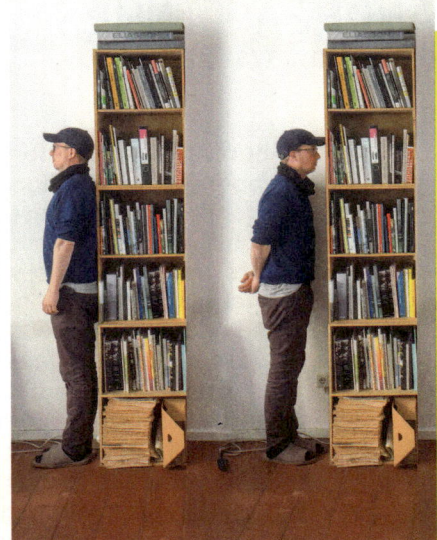

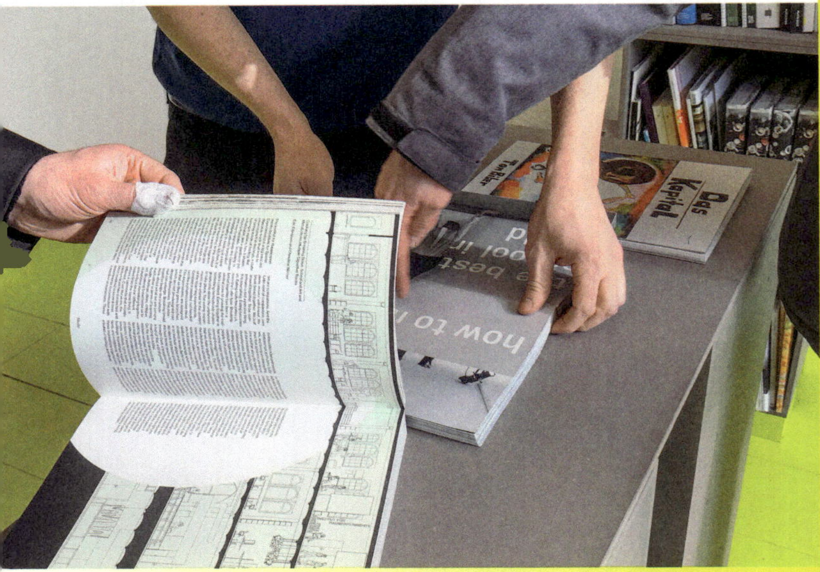

ANDREA TINNES
EXHIBITED ARTIST

Andrea Tinnes is a Berlin-based type designer, typographer, and educator, experimenting with typography, visual research, language, and printing, such as in her continuous project, *Library of Shapes, Texts and Structures*, where she systematically catalogs visual and linguistic elements. Andrea also runs the type foundry Typecuts, where she releases her typefaces, such as Allgemein Grotesk, Retroskop, and Inventar Collection. Since 2007, Andrea Tinnes has been a professor of Type and Typography at the Burg Giebichenstein University of Art and Design Halle in Germany, lecturing, researching, and engaging students in critical and poetic typographic practices.

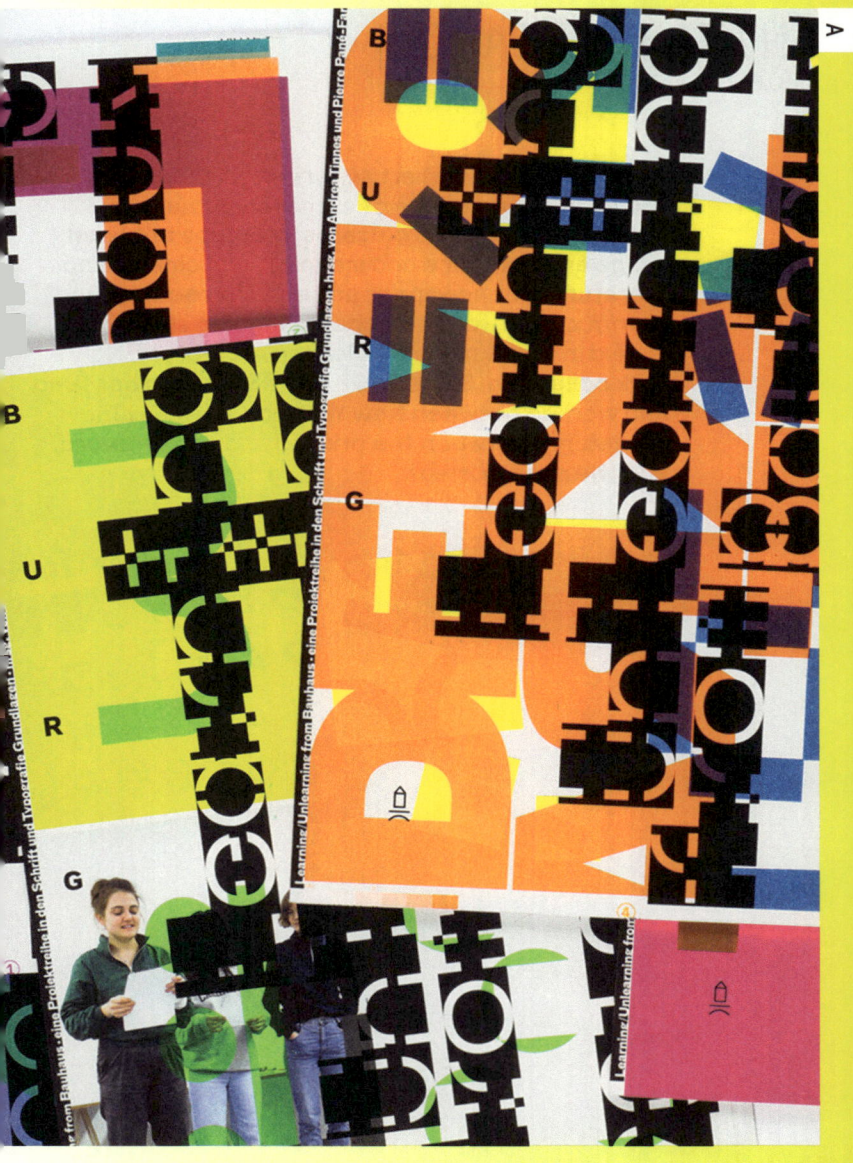

ANITA DI BIANCO
EXHIBITED ARTIST

Anita Di Bianco is an artist, writer, and filmmaker focusing on questions of authorship, the persistence of linguistic patterns, relations between image and text, time and meaning, and cinema and literature. Her newsprint project, *Corrections and Clarifications*, which has been ongoing since 2001, is held in the Museum of Modern Art Library, New York collection. Since 2007, Anita Di Bianco has lived and worked between New York and Germany (now Frankfurt), between the printed and spoken word, and the moving image.

ERRATA
NEWSPAPERS
THE ERROR IS REGRETTED
THE ERROR IS REGRETTED / WIR ENTSCHULDIGEN UNS FÜR DIESEN FEHLER

ember 1984 • A dispatch on day from the Israeli village of Fahm about the activities of Meir Kahane misstated the cal affiliation of a member of aeli Parliament. The legisla- ossi Sarid, is in the left wing Labor Party.

ruary 1984 • A Jerusalem ch Jan. 25 on the visit of cellor Helmut Kohl to the ashem memorial carried ppropriate translation of cal quotation he inscribed man in the register. As it rs in the standard German rather than the King James n.. He draws thee out of ws of anguish, and sets thee mfortable place where there urther oppression."

e 1983 • In several articles ning March 28, The Times ed on a mysterious illness d stricken hundreds of sidents of the West Bank, f them schoolgirls. First s suggested that the illness used by mass poisoning. But and American doctors later ded that the symptoms, ing dizziness, nausea and ches, had been caused by ysteria.

es on April 4, 5, and 26 re- on these medical investiga- but because of the positions lative lengths of the articles, erall effect was greater em- on the charge of poisoning the Israeli rebuttal.

most recent article, on May precise editing resulted omission of previously ed findings by the Centers sease Control in Atlanta ost of the 943 cases resulted nass psychological reaction, isoning.

icle quoted an Arab doctor West Bank who said Israeli s had dismissed him as or of public health services ecause he refused to agree e illnesses had no organic

icle omitted the Israeli ea- on for his dismissal: that he lowed "leftists" to loiter in pitals, that he had discour- e hospitals from releasing oolgirls after they had ted, and that he was trying me the situation.

verage gave more weight Arab charges than to the can and Israeli explanations. was no journalistic justifica- r the disparity.

: Atlanta Journal Constitution Globe / Christian Science r / Dallas Morning News an / Independent / Irish Times Herald / New York Times r / Süddeutsche Zeitung Washington Post / AP

16 August 1982 • An Aug. 11 article incorrectly referred to the American-Israel Public Affairs Committee as "a registered lobby for a foreign government." In fact, the committee represents a coali- tion of U.S. Jewish organizations interested in lobbying for positive relations between Israel and the United States. These organizations and their individual members, and not the government of Israel, pro- vide direction for the committee. Funding comes exclusively from American Jewish sources.

10 August 1982 • On Monday the Monitor incorrectly reported that the Reagan administration has requested $785 billion in 1983 economic aid to Israel, and that Senator Alan Cranston has sponsored an amendment to in- crease that aid to $910 billion. The correct figures are $785 million and $910 million, respectively. The Monitor regrets the error.

7 May 1982 • A dispatch from Israel yesterday gave an incorrect figure for deaths in the occupied territories during the disturbances of the last six weeks. It should have been fifteen.

20 July 1981 • The Monitor regrets a typographical error which occurred in the commentary "Washington's tangle in Lebanon" July 16. The final sentence should have read, "Serious consideration should now be given to a more comprehensive strategy that will openly seek to enlist all major re- gional actors, including the PLO, in an ongoing exchange over the specific issues of territorial control, the ultimate status of the Pales- tinian people, and Israel's right to secure existence."

14 December 1981 • In the Dec. 11 edition, a typesetting error deleted a quotation by President Mitterrand on p 6. It should have read: "Israel has the right to exist. One cannot refuse the means to that existence. It needs security, secure frontiers...
"But in the same way, I will say to my Israeli friends: 'You must recognize the right to existence of the Palestinian people ... And how can you, without falling into illusion and lies say that there could be a Palestinian homeland but with Palestinians forbidden to create and defend the state struc- ture of their choice?'"

4 September 1981 • An article in the Monitor's Aug. 25 issue entitled "Begin and Sadat to revive Palestinian 'autonomy' issue" referred to the autonomy talks as having begun 15 months ago. In fact, the talks started on May 25, 1979, and came to a halt 15 months ago. The Monitor regrets this editing error. •

Gaza or Palestin* or "right of return" or occupied or genocide or "West Bank" or Yemen or occupation or Israel* or ICC or South Africa or Ansarallah or ICJ or blockade or PLO or Hamas or siege or Sabra or Shatila or Lebanon or "Area C" or "march of return" or detention or settler or Nakba

25 June 2024 • An article on Saturday about Iran's upcoming presidential election misstated the composition of the twelve-person Guardian Council. Its members are six clerics and six jurists, not twelve clerics.

24 June 2024 • An article about politics in India said: "Minorities such as Muslims, who number more than 200 million in a popu- lation of nearly 1.5 million, have faced increased persecution and discrimination...". The latter figure should, of course, have been 1.5 billion (Fears Modi will become 'more aggressive' despite loss of majority, 18 June, p30).

21 June 2024 • An article said that the 1958 film Dracula, starring Christopher Lee, was the first time that the character had been portrayed with fangs (Dawn of the undead, 1 June, p58). In fact this had previously been done in the 1953 Turkish film Drakula Istanbul'da (Dracula in Istanbul) featuring Atıf Kaplan.

19 June 2024 • An article on Sunday about the treatment of migrants seeking asylum in Canada misstated the number of migrants who sought asylum there last year. The number of asylum seekers was 29,455 in 2023, not roughly 32,000 in the most recent fiscal year.

An article on Tuesday about Peter Magyar, a conservative opponent of Hungary's prime minister, Viktor Orban, misstated, in early editions, the name of a town at the center of a pedophilia scandal at a children's home. The town is Bicske, not Bicke.

An article on Tuesday about a man accused of orchestrating a failed assassination plot against a Sikh separatist in New York misstated who was present in the courtroom on Monday. The intended target, Gurpatwant Singh Pannun, was not in the courtroom.

A movie review on Friday, in some editions, about "Firebrand" attributed an erroneous distinc- tion to Henry's sixth and last wife, Katherine Parr. She was the only queen to outlive the infamous

18 June 2024 • An article on Sunday about Native American tribes reclaiming land in California referred incorrectly to the Los Angeles Aqueduct. It transports water to Los Angeles from the Owens River, not Owens Lake.

An article on Wednesday about the auction of the earliest known photograph of a first lady mis- identified the material the U.S. Capitol dome is made of. It is iron, not marble.

17 June 2024 • A graphic accom- panying an article showed North Korea as having 501 nuclear war- heads in January 2024; we meant 50 (Global spending on nuclear weapons 'rose by 13% to record $91bn in 2023', 17 June, p2).

16 June 2024 • An article ('When will it be enough?', 8 June, p32) said there was "an international criminal court arrest warrant out for Israel's prime minister Netanyahu". The ICC prosecutor Karim Khan has applied for a warrant, but a decision on wheth- er to grant one has yet to be made.

15 June 2024 • An article on Friday about the number of peo- ple living in the streets and sub- ways of New York City referred incorrectly to the increase in the estimated number of homeless people in the city. It is the most since 2005, when the estimate was conducted in March, and the highest ever recorded since the city began conducting the surveys in January and February, starting in 2006. It is not highest total the city ever recorded.

14 June 2024 • The Palestinian human rights lawyer and au- thor Raja Shehadeh sends some of his journalism to Henry Abramovitch after publication, not "all his journalistic writing to Abramovitch before submitting it" ('All this solidarity from the world – yet nothing has changed', 8 June, Saturday magazine, p55).

An article on Wednesday about a trial in Florida in which Chiquita Brands was found liable for deaths that occurred during the Colombian Civil War misstated the circumstances during which the anecdote of the killing of a girl's mother and stepfather was

ANJA LUTZ
FOUNDER OF A—Z PRESENTS

Anja Lutz is a designer, publisher, and curator based in Berlin, working at the intersection between Graphic Design and art. In the mid-1990s, she initiated the experimental publishing project *shift!*—a series of 17 thematic publications featuring collaborations, and formal and unconventional interdisciplinary approaches to Graphic Design. She co-founded The Green Box publishing house, where she has designed and published over 150 art books since 2007. Anja's artwork *Marginalia*, "An investigation into the anatomy of books" as a series of dissected layouts, was presented in several solo exhibitions around Europe, and published as an artist's book. She has lectured and worked as a Guest Professor for Graphic Design in art academies and universities in Germany and abroad. In 2019, she founded the A—Z Presents initiative, a space for experimental collaboration and transdisciplinary practices in Graphic Design.

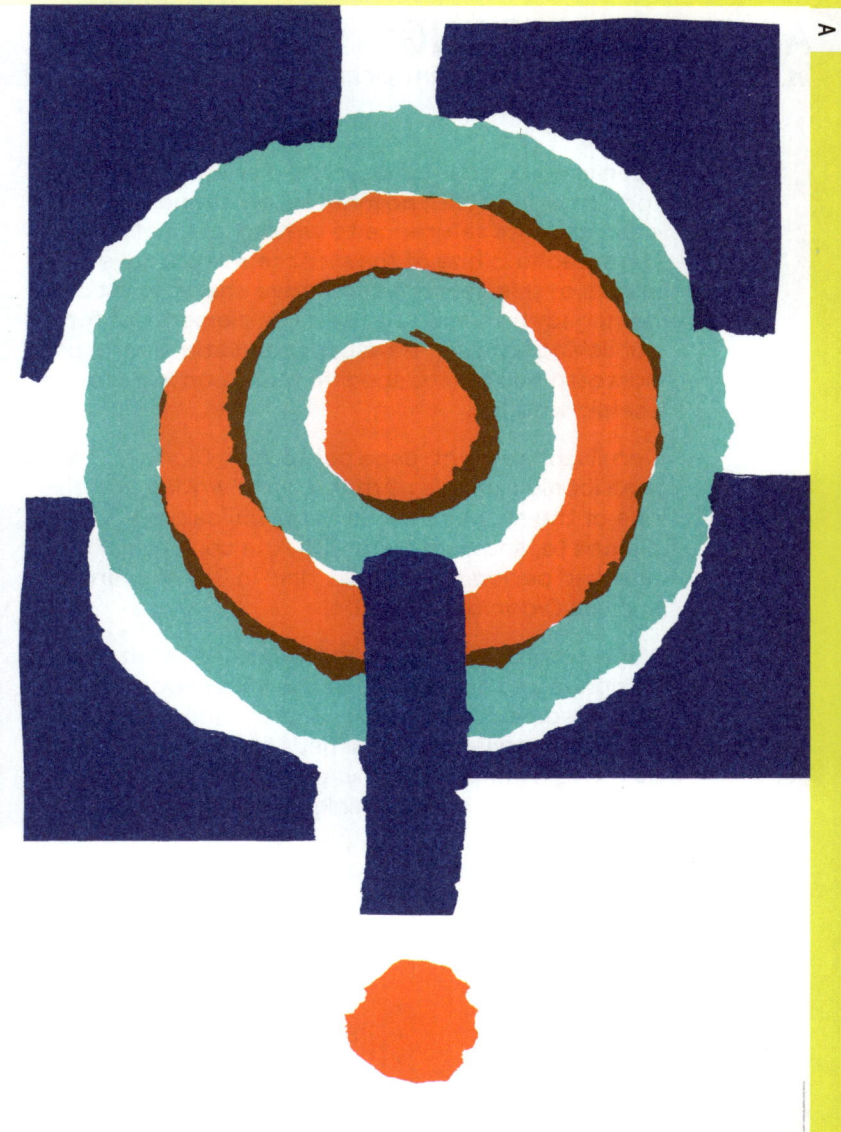

ASEMIC WRITING
DIARIO N° 1 AÑO 1 BY MIRTHA DERMISACHE

Asemic writing can be described as a non-semantic form of writing with no inherent relational meaning other than its reference to writing itself. Mirtha Dermisache is one of the most representative artists of this genre. A distinctive characteristic of her legacy was how she used the elements of formal publishing layouts—newspaper, bulletin, comic, or postcard—to create specific visual contexts for her asemic writings.

Dermisache's eight-page publication *Diario N° 1 Año 1* is an iconic example of that form of writing and also one of the artist's best-known publications. It both alludes to, and contrasts with, the semantically charged periodicals of that time in Buenos Aires, such as *Clarín* or *La Nación.*

A special brochure authored by Regine Ehleiter was designed and distributed at the *Mirtha Dermisache: To Be Read* exhibition at A—Z, providing a comprehensive overview of the artist's life and work, as well as the relevance of asemic writing for contemporary philosophy and critical thinking.

ILLEGIBLE
MIRTHA DERMISACHE
MIRTHA DERMISACHE: TO BE READ
MYSTERIOUS POSTCARD
READING ARTISTS' BOOKS: ASEMIC WRITING

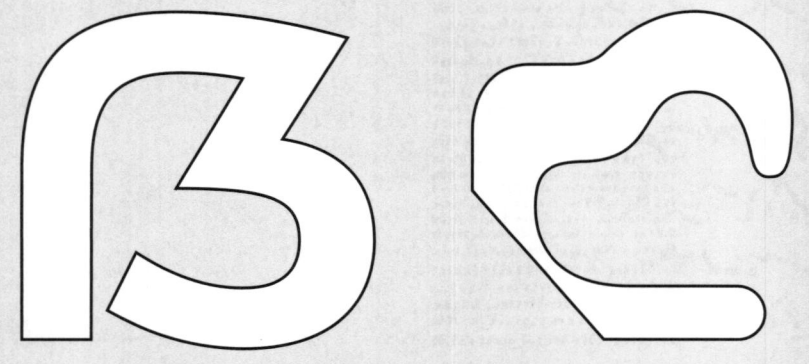

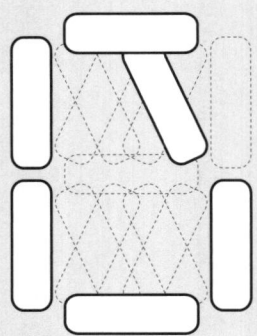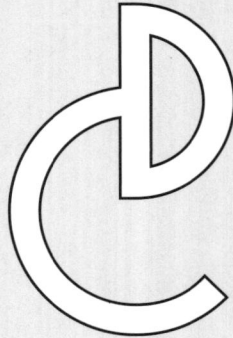

BANANA MUSEUM, SORRY TO SEE YOU SPLIT SO SOON

TALK BY ANNA BROUJEAN AS PART OF *SUPER COLLECTIVE MARKET NO. 1 YELLOW*

Under the series of yellow-themed events as part of *Super Collective Market No. 1 Yellow*, the photographer and visual artist Anna Broujean presented the case of the Banana Museum in California, the US home of over 25,000 pieces of banana-related memorabilia from the last 70 years. Presenting this peculiar place and its collection served as a starting point for Broujean to introduce a reflection upon the importance of preserving design relics, and the challenges faced by such self-funded initiatives.

Anna Broujean is a multifarious artist; her work is stamped with humor and mixes a wide range of media: photography, video, installation, Graphic Design, furniture and wood design, etc. She is the editor of *Club Sandwich* magazine.

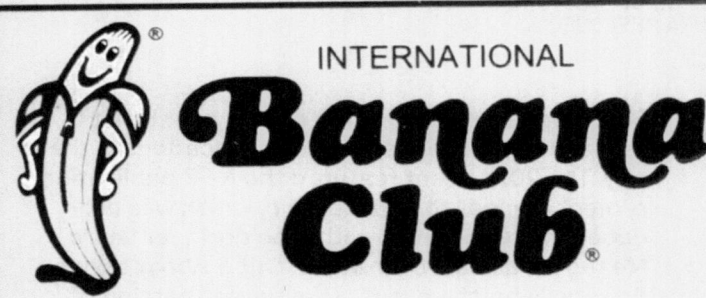

BANANA CLUB® I.D. & DISCOUNT CARD

This card certifies that the holder is a lifetime member of the I.B.C. and is entitled to all rights and privileges. Our purpose is to keep people SMILING, emphasize the positive and promote good health! Exercise your sense of humor today, and go along with all member requests!

B.C. members agree to smile when presenting this card for DISCOUNTS on any product or service and pardons for traffic mistakes! The recipient agrees to go along with all reasonable requests and SMILE! WODDIS!

INTERNATIONAL BANANA CLUB®
www.BANANACLUB.COM
Ken Bannister, T.B. (626) 321-6262

Since 1972 Membership in 27 countries

BARCELONA DESIGN WEEK
RECIPES FOR CONNECTING BARCELONA EDITION IN COLLABORATION WITH LAURA MESEGUER

Barcelona Design Week is a design event that is realized simultaneously in several locations in the city. The 2024 event featured the A—Z publication project *Recipes for Connecting*, which was produced in collaboration with type designer Laura Meseguer as part of the *A—Z Out & About* series. Especially for the event, an extended version of the publication originally conceived by the *A—Z Collective* was created with local designers from Barcelona and exhibited at Casa Bonay, later receiving a special mention from the Premis Ciutat de Barcelona, recognizing its merit in the Design & Fashion category.

Recipes for Connecting Barcelona Edition contributors: Alex Jordan, Andrea Tinnes, Anja Lutz, Anne-Christin Plate, April Gertler, Atipus, Catrin Sonnabend, Cem Eskinazi, Claudia de la Torre, Eider Corral, Emily Smith, Erica Fustero, Eunjung Kwak, Formal Settings, Francisca Torres, Gemma Terol, George Titheridge, Hounyeh Kim, Josepha Conrad, Judy Kaufmann, Judy Smith, Karen Runge, Kristina Wedel, Laia Soler, Lan Kroeger, Laura Meseguer, Lisa Baumgarten, María Carmona, Maria Montes, María Yin, Marisa Lacarta, Mark Bohle, Martí Guixé, Mela Freire, Niklaus Troxler, Orlando, Pol Pérez, Rachael Dunstan, Ramon Tejada, Sarah Boris, Silvia Sfligiotti, Sonia Valentí, Sonsoles Llorens, Susan Ploetz, and Tulah Stanford.

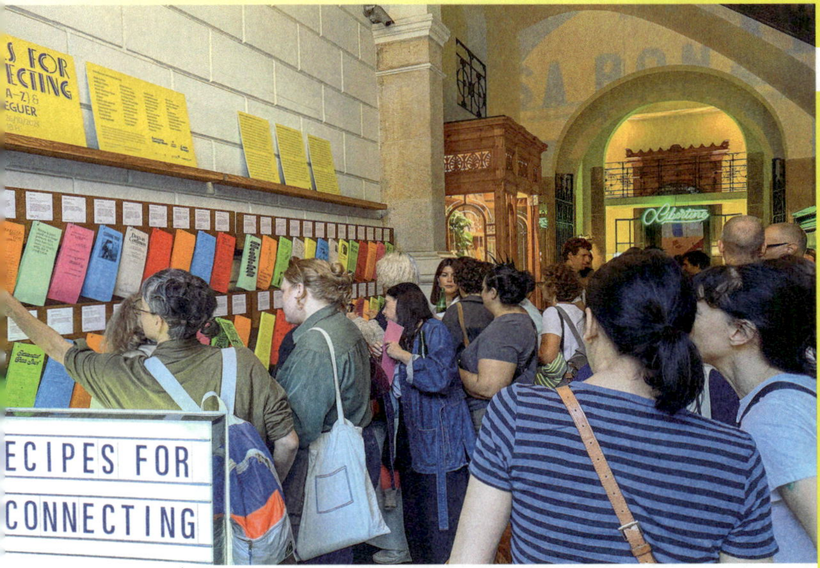

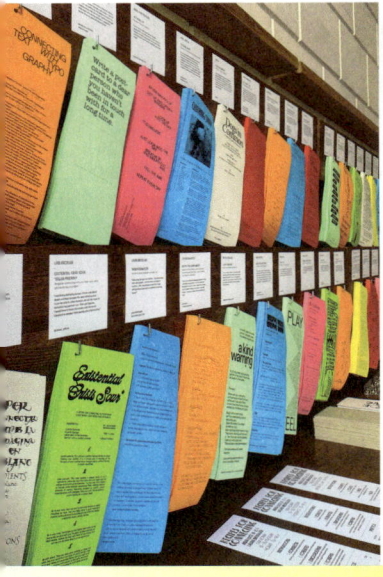
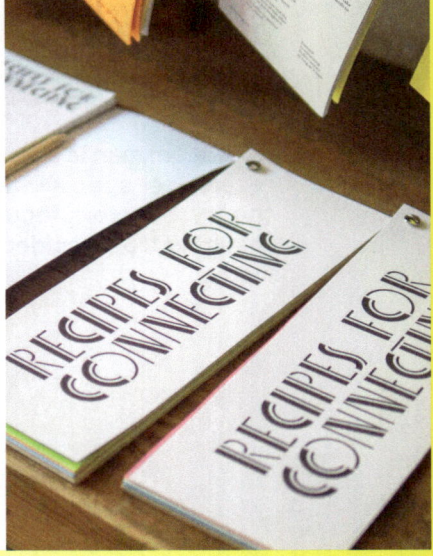

BEHIND THE WHITE SHADOWS

TALK BY ROSA MENKMAN DURING THE *TEMPLATE CULTURE* WORKSHOP

"We can use this 'fog' or 'mi[st]
now universal standards of
So, I am talking about targe[t]
I am present, the more I am
less targetable, I must with[…]
learn to become opaque. In
follow tactics like erasing,
Fog is an instrumental appo[…]
degrees of visibility, clarity[…]

Rosa Menkman is a visual artist, art theorist, and researcher specializing in glitch art and resolution theory. Her work focuses on noise artifacts resulting from accidents in both analog and digital media.

BODIES OF DISCOURSE
TEMPLATE CULTURE
ONLINE VIDEO ARCHIVE

...llegory to deconstruct the
...ntification and locatability.
... advertisements; the more
... wish to be less 'me' and
...w from recognition and
...ntemporary fog, we can
...eting, and disappearing.
...us—it offers varying
...d obscurity."

BINDING YOUR OWN PUBLICATION

HANDS-ON *RECIPES FOR CONNECTING*

One unforeseen outcome of the collective publishing project *Recipes for Connecting* was how much the public at its different venues—from the launch at A—Z in Berlin to the exhibition at *Barcelona Design Week* or at the *Index Art Book Fair* in Mexico City—enjoyed making their edition of the publication by browsing and selecting content and binding it themselves.

The self-binding of insights from the Graphic Design and artist community has proven to be the ultimate connection, enabling collective creativity on all levels. The recipes were designed as elongated half-A4 format in simple b/w print on to varied color paper. The sheets were hung on the wall so they could be read and individually picked up. The binding used one simple book-binding screw, and visitors could finalize their book by adding front and back covers.

The feedback from audiences was consistent: becoming the 'editor' and composing their books in their desired order with their chosen content was an entertaining and reflective task. The wide range of entries written by over 70 contributors enabled the creation of hundreds of unique books with recipes of all sorts, be it for a disaster or a good paella.

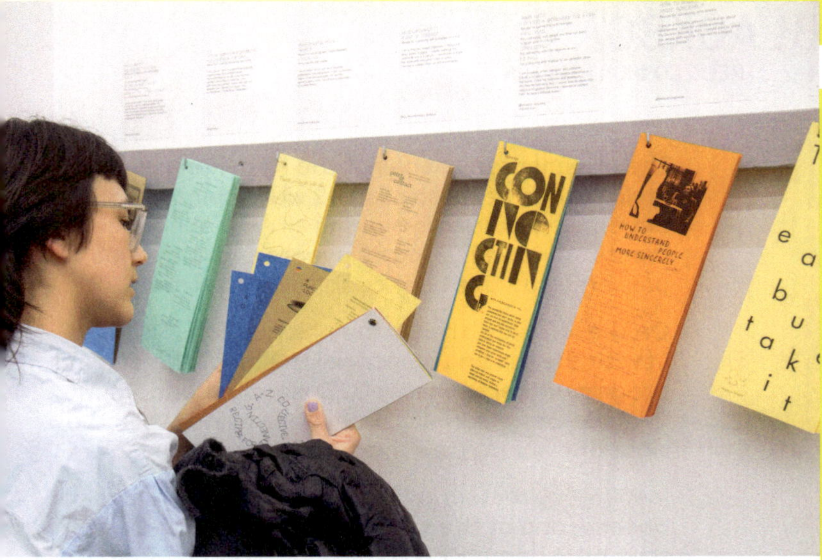

B

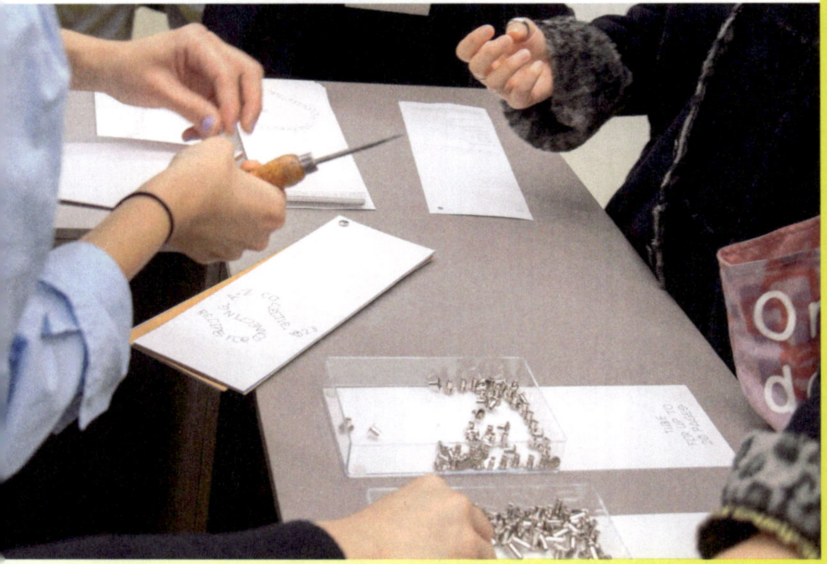

BLACKBOARD
A–Z STREET COMMUNICATION

The ornamented spaces of the Neo-Renaissance style façade at Torstrasse 93 were painted to become blackboards bearing all A—Z announcements, communicating its events and initiatives to passersby on this busy central Berlin street.

On the left side, the prompt "Space for …" is filled in with the guiding curatorial theme of the current program—"Performative", "Collective", and "D.I.Y." Graphic Design are just some examples, while the right one announces the current or next event.

Inspired by restaurant menu boards, these quickly became one of the space's signatures. Over time, they have been filled with hand lettering of different kinds by various contributors, from interns to guest exhibitors.

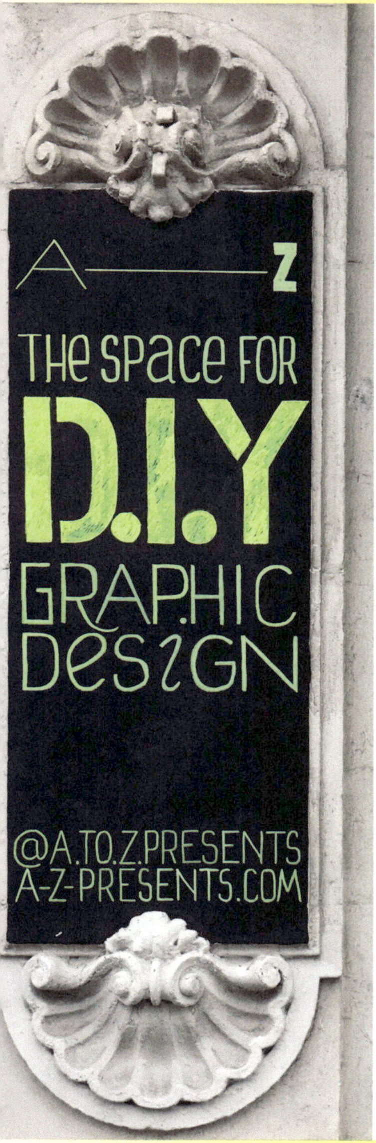

A — Z

THE SPACE FOR **D.I.Y** GRAPHIC DESIGN

@A.TO.Z.PRESENTS
A-Z-PRESENTS.COM

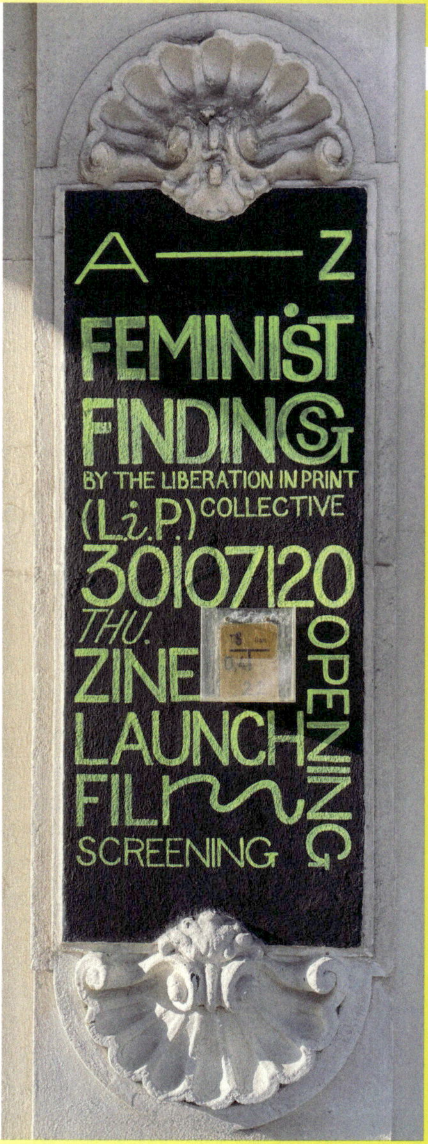

A — Z

FEMINIST FINDINGS
BY THE LIBERATION IN PRINT
(L.i.P.) COLLECTIVE
30|07|20
THU.
ZINE LAUNCH
FILM SCREENING
OPENING

BLUMEN SIND GEIL
EXHIBITION BY TINE MELZER AND MARKUS KUMMER

Blumen sind geil (Flowers are cool) was an exhibition by artist Tine Melzer in collaboration with Markus Kummer. It featured a silver color wall installation combined with framed multiples, displaying flower petals transformed into patterns. The opposite wall exhibited some fragments from the artists' book of the same title, which was released during the exhibition.

An enormous bouquet of mixed flowers was carefully placed by the window of A—Z, greeting visitors with its silent, slow decay. The installation could be described as a philosophical and poetic exploration of the intriguing nature of flowers and gestures that come together on both a visual and linguistic level. "Flowers are cool because they can embody very different meanings. They are products of globalized trade everywhere where people celebrate, praise, seduce and mourn."

At the opening, Tine delivered a lecture full of references to words and images, saying and showing, based on her conceptual and linguistic-philosophical investigations into flowers, introducing her concept of the tilting of meanings and the so-called "aspect seeing", and why this matters.

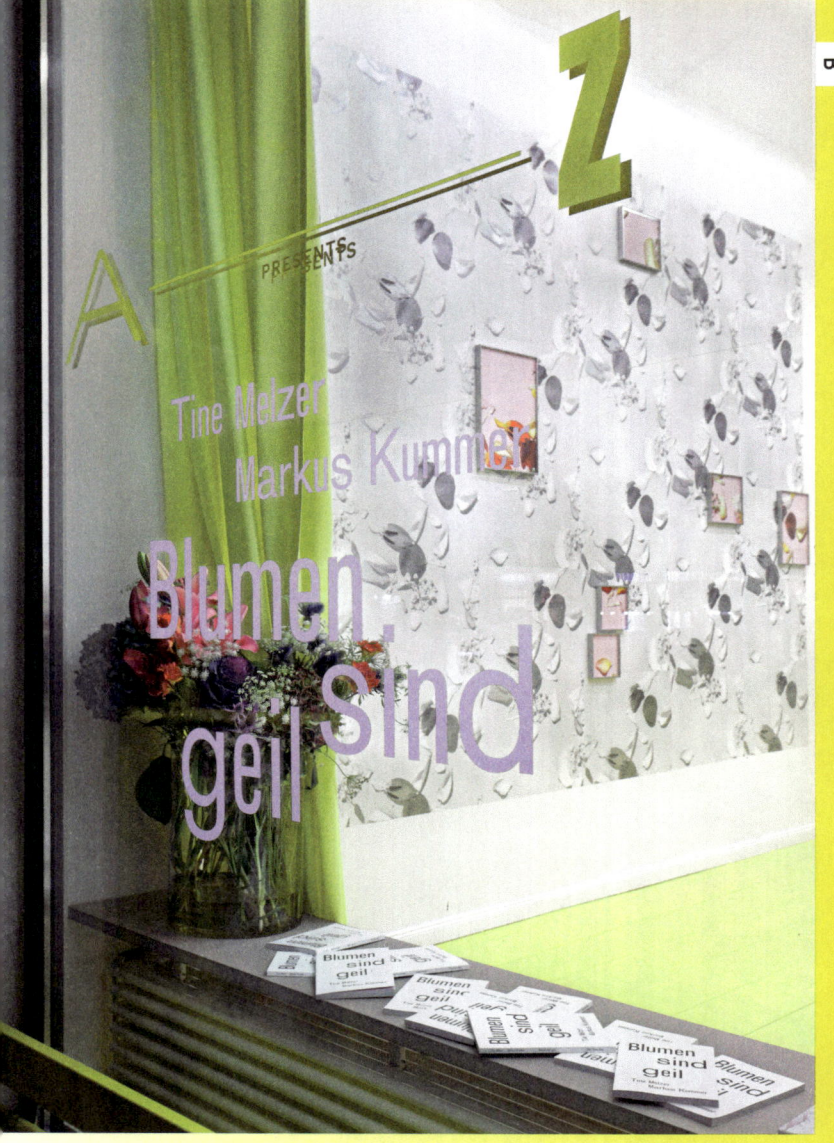

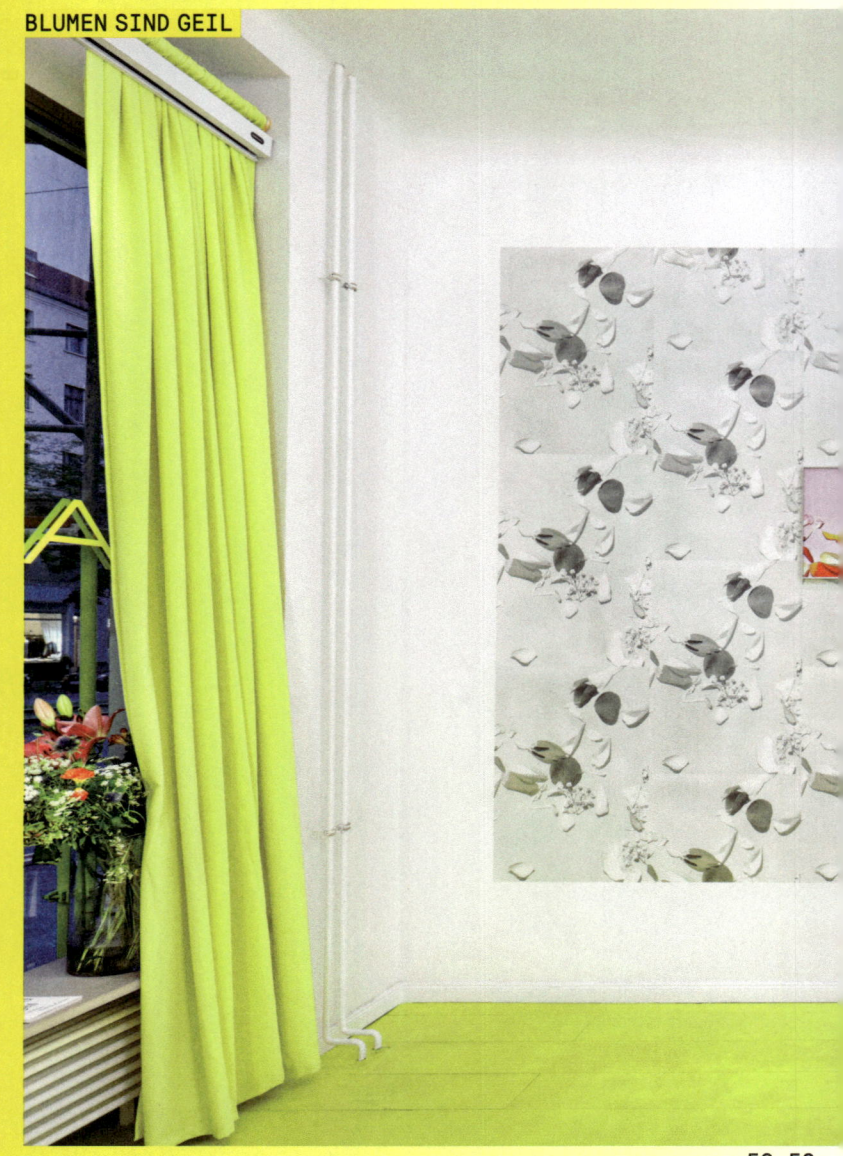

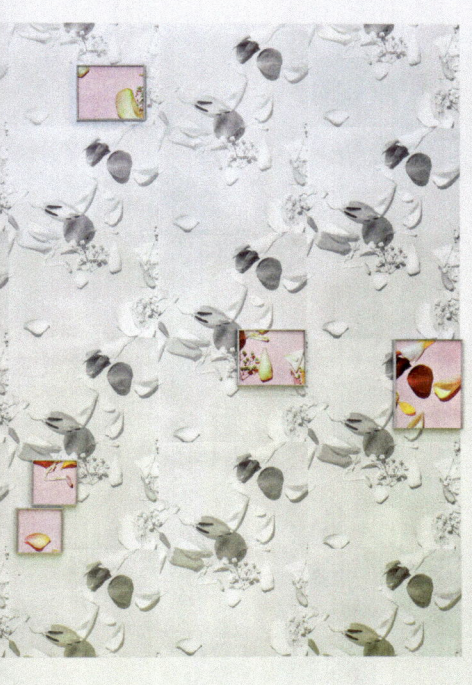

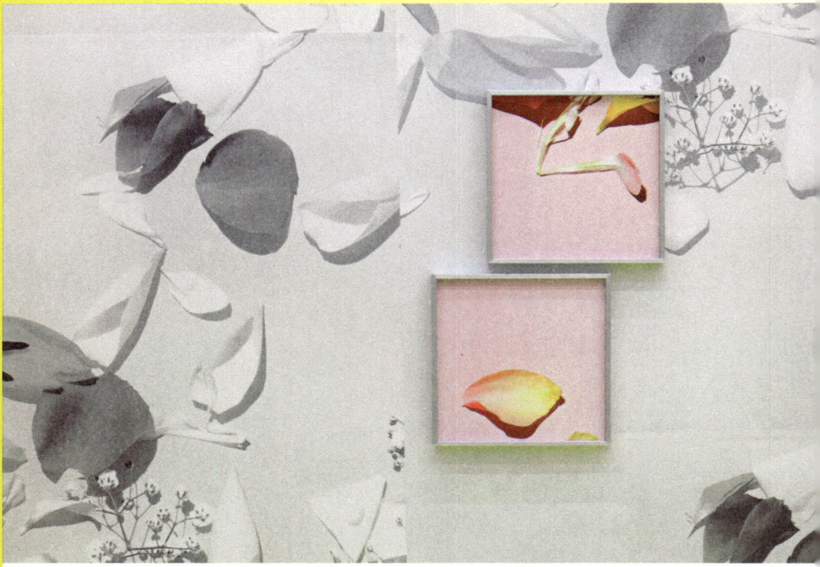

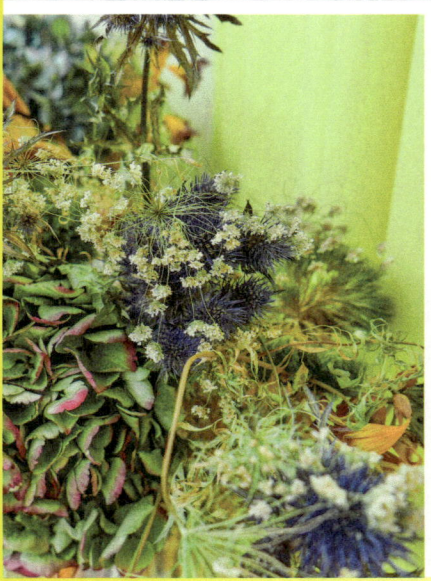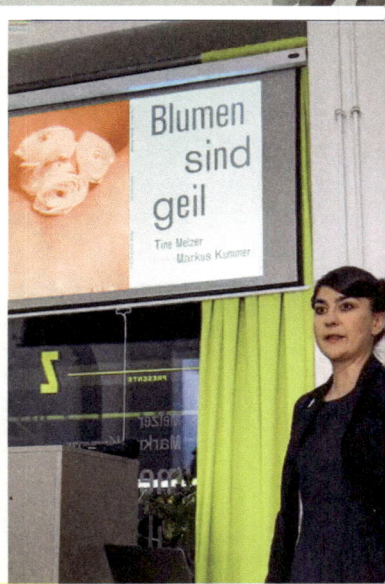

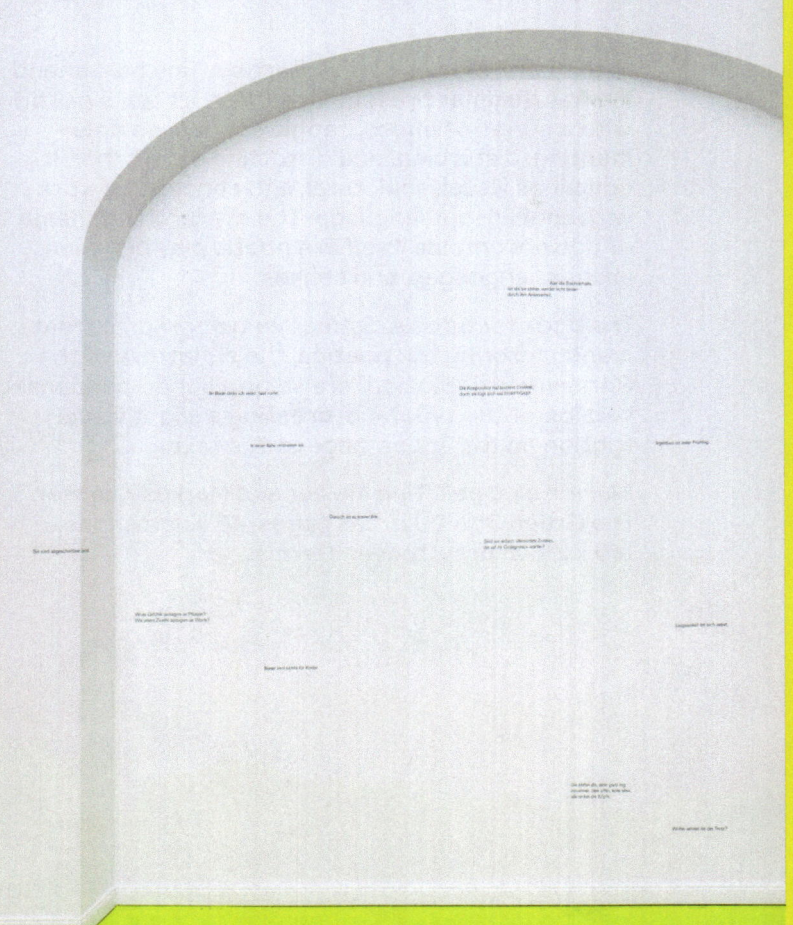

BLUMEN SIND GEIL
BOOK BY TINE MELZER AND MARKUS KUMMER

In the book *Blumen sind geil* artists Tine Melzer and Markus Kummer present literary short texts paired with a series of photographic scenes, complementing, disturbing, and distorting each other. It combines visual, sculptural, and conceptual work with spelled-out language. The overarching theme of flowers unfolds itself in a poetic play between images, languages, and senses.

The book features a distinctive typographic treatment: mirroring the poetics, the six letters of the German word "Blumen" are set in a super-condensed version of the typeface, creating a slight visual friction on the appearance of the text.

Blumen sind geil, Tine Melzer and Markus Kummer, The Green Box, 2021. 128 pages, 46 illustrations, 140 x 210 mm, softcover, German.

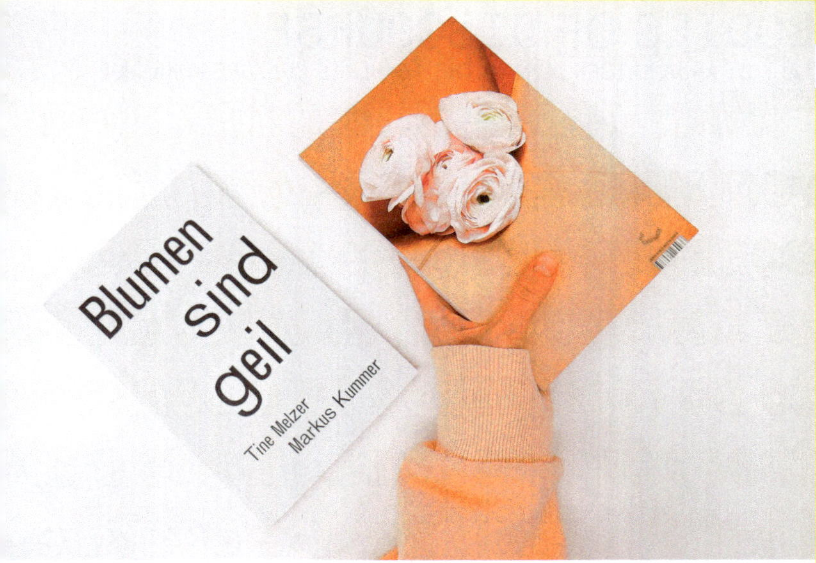

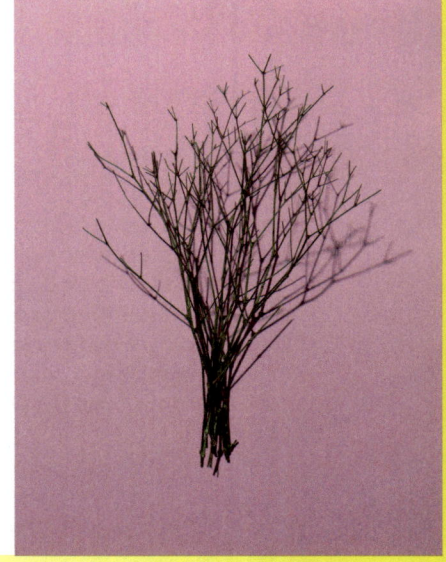

Magnolien machen bereits im Herbst des alten Jahres
die Knospen für das neue. Sie kämpfen sich damit
durch die klirrende Kälte, nur um im Frühling
völlig erschöpft nach zwei Wochen Blust
die ganze Pracht abzuwerfen.
Das ist schlechte Planung.
Das sagt bloß keiner, weil der Natur diese
mütterliche Allwissenheit nachgesagt wird.
Die ist doch auch einfach überfordert.

BODIES OF DISCOURSE
TALK BY ANJA KAISER DURING THE *TEMPLATE CULTURE* WORKSHOP

*"What happens to a face that [
features are there, and from w[
construct was the face recogn[
of the eyes, and at what distan[
to be recognized by a camera o[
these two options. This is a tec[
that decides how the body bec[
remains visible in the end. It is [
parameters of which feature is [
defined as male or female, and [*

Anja Kaiser is a graphic artist based in Leipzig who works in an activist environment. She is the co-author of the book *Glossary of Undisciplined Design*. Her award-winning project, *Sexed Realities—To Whom Do I Owe My Body?*, is a visual platform that mixes technology, corporate concepts, and pop culture to discuss feminism.

BEHIND THE WHITE SHADOWS
TEMPLATE CULTURE
ONLINE VIDEO ARCHIVE

…ad by the camera? What
… or from which customer data
…? What should be the shape
…rom nose to mouth do I need
…ale or female? There are only
…cal process of normalization
…s visible, and which body
…ethod that determines the
…hnologically perceived and
…o gets excluded."

BOOKS ARE BRIDGES
INSTALLATION BY CLAUDIA DE LA TORRE AS PART OF *TIME FOR BOOKS*

How can we still find ways to connect to others? Can books play a role in this connection? From where and to where can they take us? In *Books are Bridges*, artist Claudia de la Torre presented her strategy for uniting people and ideas with participative, open, continuous work that could not exist without some form of contact.

The concept of the exhibition started with de la Torre sending postcards with the phrase "Books are Bridges between ___ and ___", asking people to fill in the gaps. She then used the two-word responses to create sheets of paper, folded and inserted into one another to form a book, where new connections to the word pairs could be formed, resulting in a book that built itself throughout the exhibition, connecting people and ideas.

Claudia de la Torre is a book artist and the founder of the Berlin-based publishing house backbonebooks. She is focused on a flexible, conceptual, and collaborative process of creating publications. In workshops, she shares her knowledge and assists in making highly conceptual and carefully crafted artists' books.

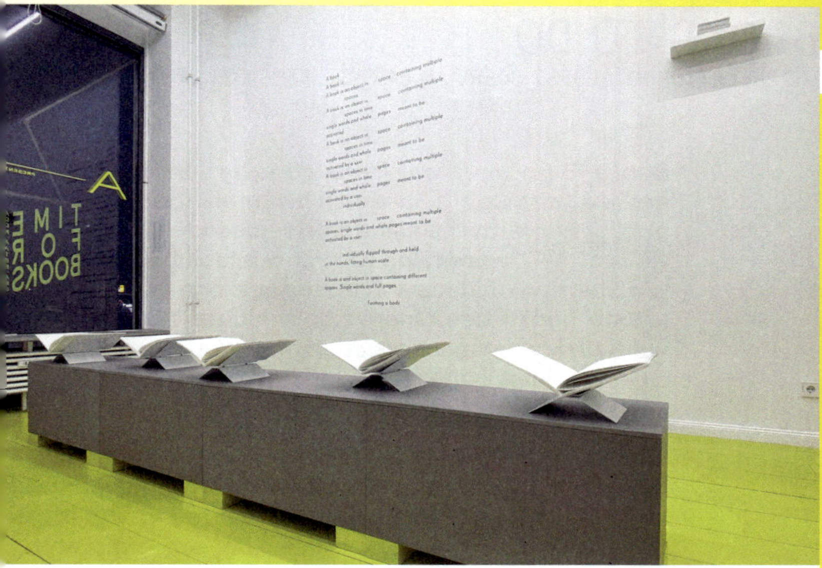

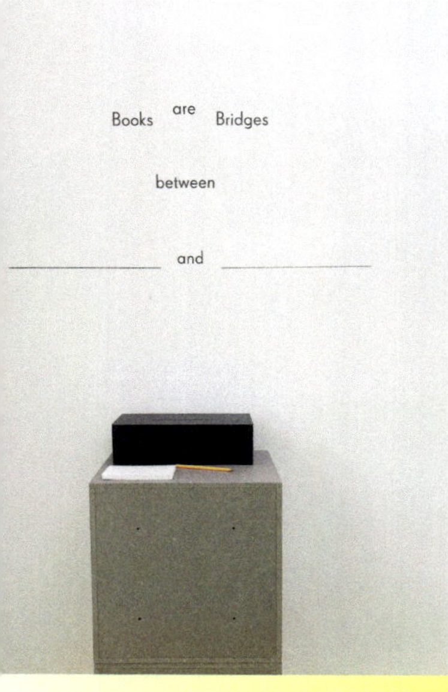

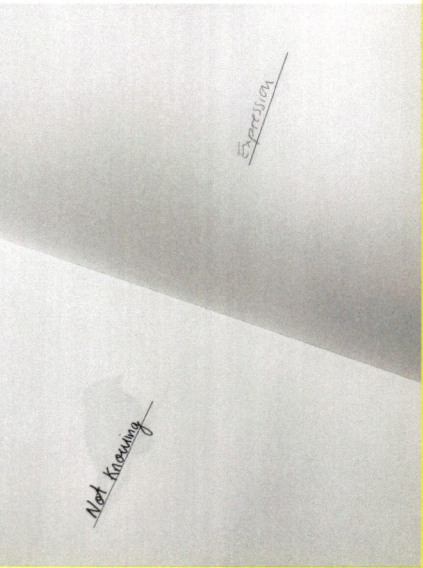

BOOKS TO DO
INSTALLATION BY ALBERT COERS AS PART OF *TIME FOR BOOKS*

Books To Do was a wall installation by conceptual artist Albert Coers based on his "meta-book" publication with the same title released in 2022. The walls of A—Z were filled with possible publications, a collection of ideas and material, alongside some artists' book titles. Coers also exhibited his video work *Du kannst mehr als du denkst* (You can do more than you think), which, like most of his other work, plays with the literal meaning of found book titles.

Albert Coers lives and works between Berlin and Munich, and his artistic work focuses on installations with found objects and language-related material, often thematizing art books in a self-referential and investigative way.

BOOKS TO DO

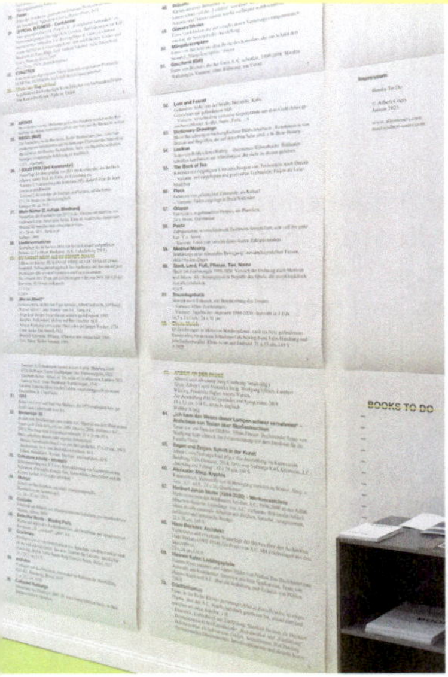

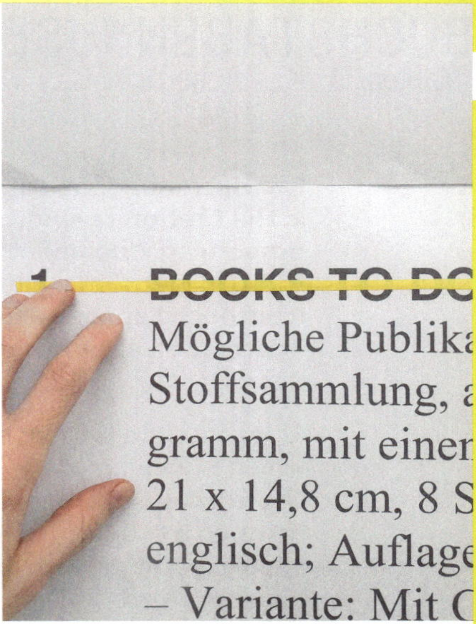

Mögliche Publika
Stoffsammlung, a
gramm, mit einer
21 x 14,8 cm, 8 S
englisch; Auflage
– Variante: Mit C

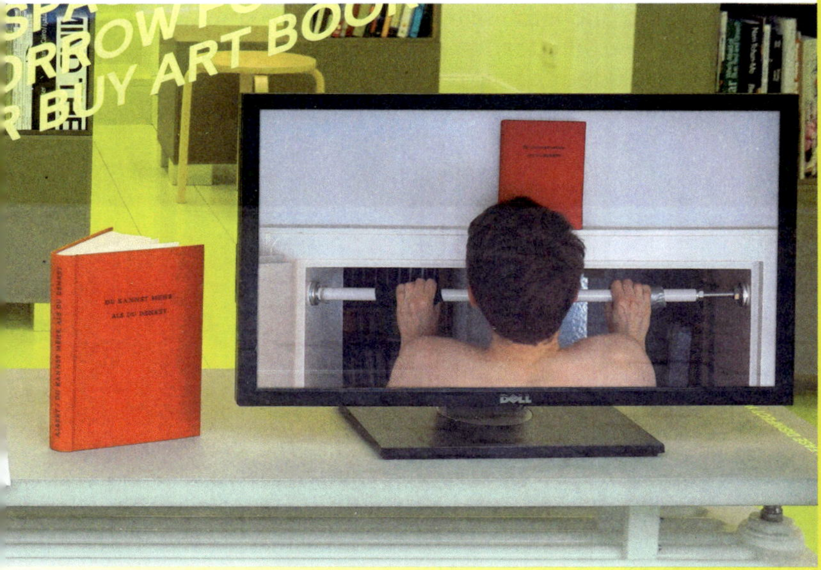

BUCHSTABENMUSEUM
THE MUSEUM OF LETTERS IN BERLIN

The Buchstabenmuseum, the Museum of Letters, is the first of its kind, dedicated to collecting, preserving, documenting, and exhibiting over 3,000 three-dimensional letters and pieces of signage from public spaces and displays, as well as providing information about their origins and their urban history.

Alongside the permanent exhibition, the museum, which is a completely independent initiative, also showcases experimental and thematic exhibitions through a program of special events presented in co-operation with artists, universities, and collaborators.

The Buchstabenmuseum collaborated with A—Z for the exhibition *New Anthems VI (Berlin).* It has also included the original curtain of Flipper Bar in its collection, which was displayed during the *Counter Sessions* events.

FLIPPER BAR
INKAHOOTS
KERNING
NEW ANTHEMS VI – EINE NEUE HYMNE FÜR DEUTSCHLAND

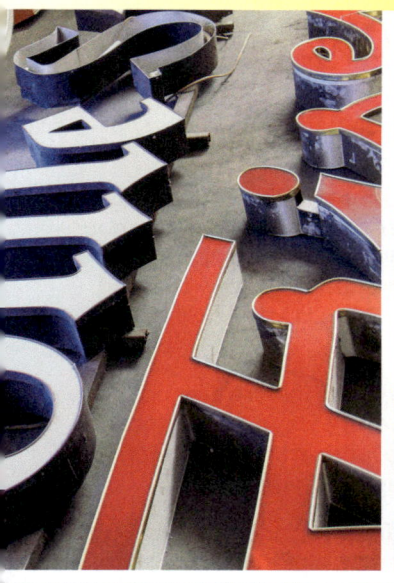
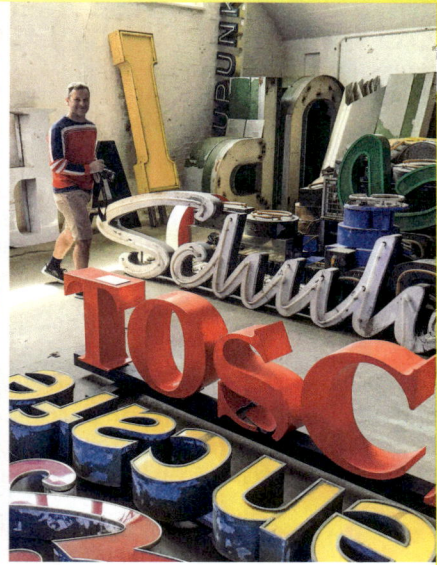

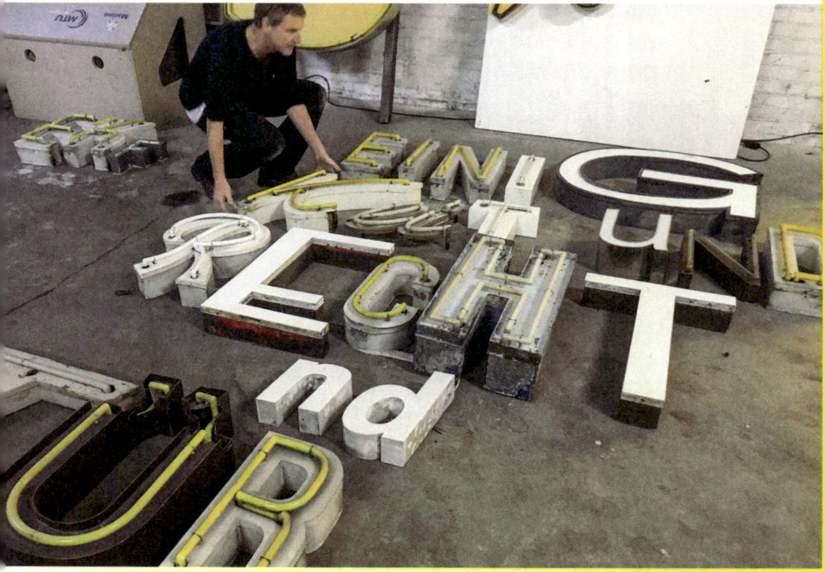

BUTTER BETTER COME

WORKSHOP BY APRIL GERTLER AS PART OF *SUPER COLLECTIVE MARKET NO. 1 YELLOW*

In the workshop *Butter Better Come*, the visual artist April Gertler shared with audience members hacks on how to make your own butter. The experience was part of the series of yellow-themed events connected with *Super Collective Market No. 1 Yellow.*

The family-friendly event was inspired by collective discussions on participatory ways, sustainability, and inclusiveness by collaborating with local creatives from beyond Graphic Design.

April Gertler's artwork involves collage, drawing, photography, performance, and social practice. She founded the art residency program Picture Berlin and is also co-initiator of the independent cultural space WirWir and the nomadic art project *Sonntag.*

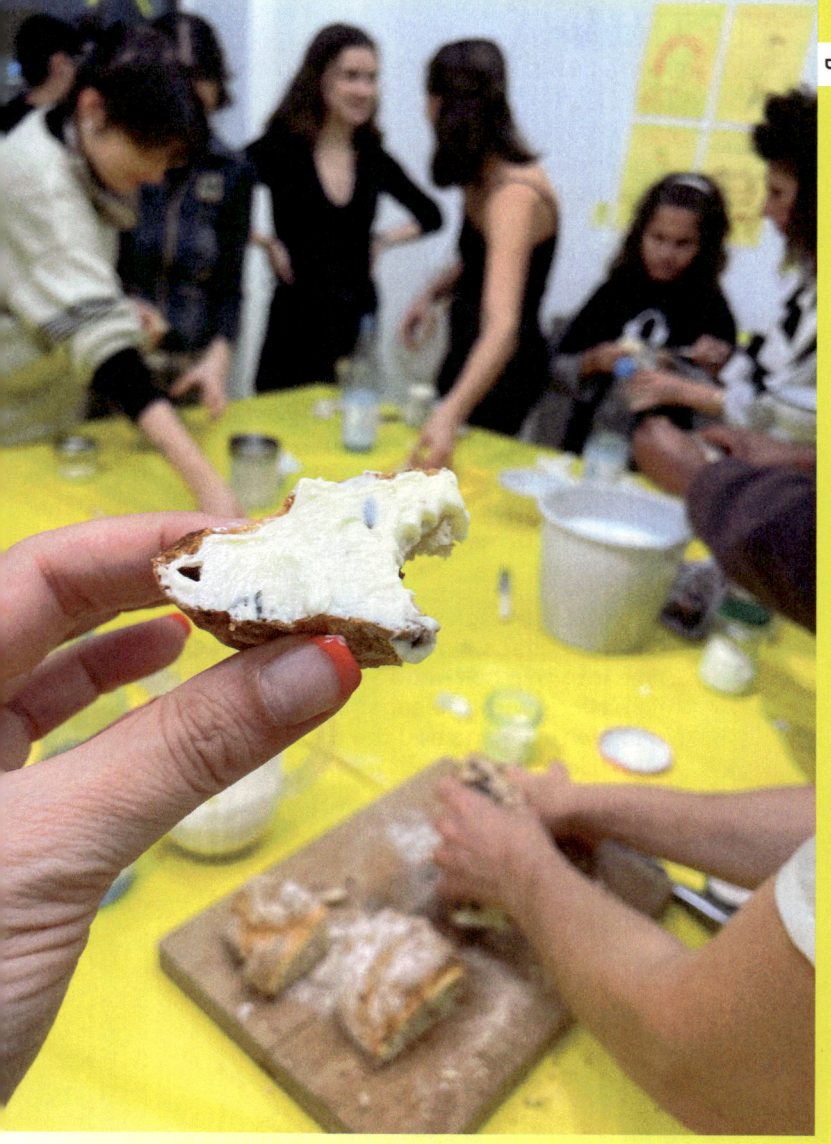

CAIPIRINHA
THE LOVE AND HATE DRINK FROM FLIPPER BAR TO *COUNTER SESSIONS*

Caipirinha, the iconic Brazilian drink, became the one drink served during the *Counter Sessions* series. There is a back story to this: during the early 2000s, when the clandestine Flipper Bar ran weekly in what became the location for A—Z, the caipirinha was the only cocktail the organizers refused to serve due to its cliché popularity in the Berlin night scene at that time.

When the concept of the Flipper Bar was revived to create the setting for the *Counter Sessions*, it was a natural choice and in-joke for caipirinhas to be the only cocktail served after the talks, prepared by the Brazilian-born writer and A—Z collaborator Soraya Guimarães.

Recipe for one glass of caipirinha:
6 cl of cachaça, one lime, and 2 tsp of sugar. Cut the lime into thin half-moon slices. Lightly crush the lime slices with the sugar in a lowball glass. Fill the glass with ice and add the cachaça. Mix and finish with slices of lime.

COUNTER SESSIONS
CYBERFEMINISM INDEX
EVER SINCE THE DAYS OF MRS. GUTENBERG...
FAMILY TREES & SOUND CLOUDS
FLIPPER BAR
INVERSE – A YEARLY RITUAL
YOU NEVER GIVE UP?

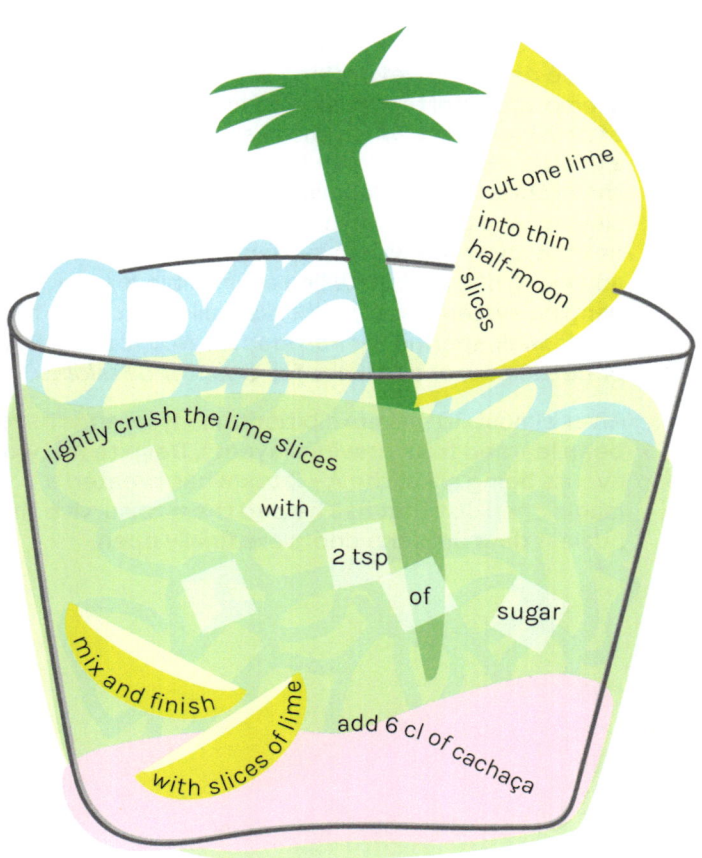

CHECKLIST
BEHIND THE SCENES OF A–Z EVENTS

Behind each new exhibition are long days or even months of preparation through discussions, emails, phone calls, and networking and social media promotion efforts. It is also an incredible amount of physical effort, when the team, interns, guest exhibitors—and one long-term close collaborator, the architect Jens Bauermeister—roll up their sleeves and get ready to do whatever it takes to get the show ready: hammering nails on the wall and fixing displays, installing an invisible magnetic hanging system for *Tape Works*, building frames for *PULP*, wallpapering for *Perhaps It's Not You, It's Me.* or cutting dozens of limes for *Counter Sessions.*

After almost 30 main exhibitions, many lessons have been learned from previous events. Despite no two events being alike, the A—Z team has created a magic checklist that has helped them to survive the busiest days until the doors are finally open.

A————Z

TORSTRASSE 93
D-10119 BERLIN
MAIL@A-Z-PRESENTS.COM
WWW.A-Z-PRESENTS.COM
FACEBOOK: A-Z PRESENTS
INSTAGRAM: A-Z PRESENTS

BEFORE THE EXHIBITION

- Printing of folded card, flyer, poster
- Announcement on website *with image!*
- List of hashtags and links (collaborators, themes, contributors etc.) #azpresents
- Create Facebook Event and Share and Invite
- Inform press (2 weeks before) *NEW PRESS CONTACTS RESEARCH!*
- Update Mailchimp contacts
- Send Mailchimp newsletter (1 week before) including link to FB event !
- Announce on Instagram
- Announce on board on facade
- Order vinyl lettering for windows → *ROCK'N'ROLL LETTERS!*
- Order photographer ✓ *HANS GEORG 3.11.*
- Organize installation of exhibition
- Document installation of exhibition and post

BEFORE THE OPENING

- ~~Distribute and place flyers, posters, etc.~~
- Reminder on Facebook and Instagram
- Wine cooling (& decorating?) *any ideas?*
- Buy a lemon for lemon infused water
- Vacuuming and wiping the floor
- Cleaning window and applying vinyl lettering
- Check exhibits, arrange them cleanly, hang them straight etc.
- Write infosheet and hang on wall
- Set up a bar, little box for donations *OR SUGGESTED DONATIONS?*
- Empty trash, clear the tables, toilet paper in bath
- Camera for documentation (charge the battery)
- For lectures:
  Stool from cellar
  Projection screen
  Projector
  Video camera and tripod (charge the battery)
  Sound recorder (charge the battery)

AFTER THE EXHIBITION

- dismantling, de-installation
- Update board on facade
- Update Website
- Carefully remove the vinyl lettering
- Attach curtain during installation and de-installation

DURING THE EXHIBITION

- Post posts of installtion, details of the exhibition, press news etc. on Facebook and Instagram
- While the Event: 1 person is at the door, 1 person is at the bar and also has a look on the exponats *who is doing what?!*

COLLECTING GRAPHIC DESIGN

ONLINE PANEL WITH CHRISTINA THOMSON, JULIA MEER, AND JENS MÜLLER AS PART OF *GRAPHIC.DESIGNERS.COLLECTORS.* EXHIBITION

The online panel discussion, *Collecting Graphic Design*, held in German, was related to *Graphic. Designers. Collectors*, the first group exhibition at A—Z. The conversation dived deep into the meaning of collecting, with a critical perspective on its institutional practices. Guests shared a privileged insider's view on biases and representativity in collection criteria, and challenges related to digitalization and the inclusion of digital objects.

The panel was mediated by Jens Müller, Professor of Communication Design and Editor of the *A5 Series*, including the title *Collecting Graphic Design*, in dialogue with Christina Thomson, Head of the Collection of Graphic Design of the State Museum of Berlin, and Julia Meer, Curator of the Arts & Crafts Museum—MK&G of Hamburg.

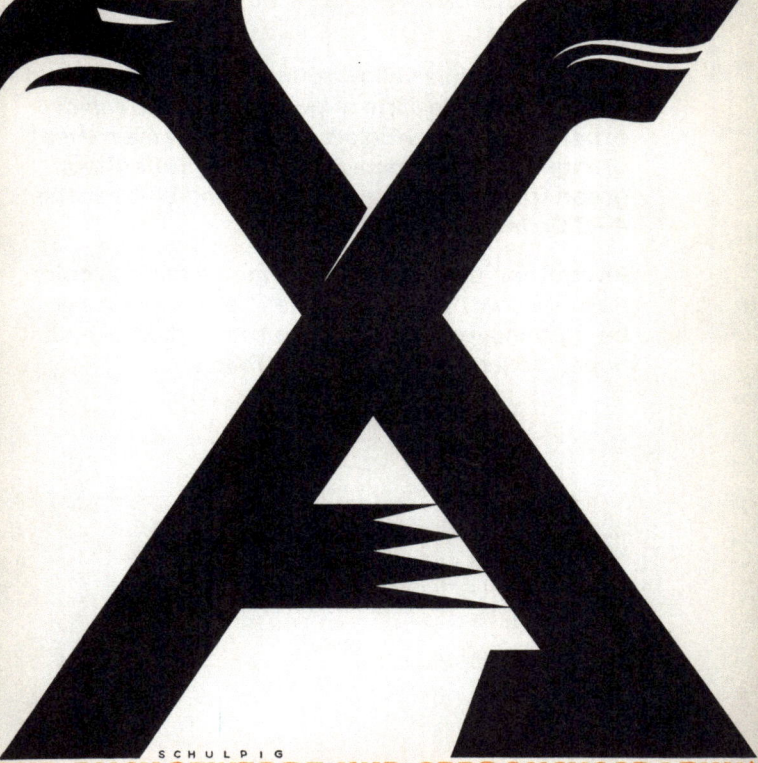

COLLECTING VISITORS
A—Z STICKER COLLECTION

For the exhibition *Graphic.Designers.Collectors.*, in addition to the curious items from all the graphic designers who accepted the challenge of sharing their collectibles, A—Z created its own collection of visitors.

A—Z's distinctive yellow round stickers were used as an alternative form of guest book, and rapidly expanded to other colors at each new main event: orange for *Revealing » Recording » Reflecting*; green for the *Counter Sessions;* and blue for the *A—Z Collective* workshops.

Altogether, these stickers formed a curious color-map filled with people's names before eventually being removed to give space to the next event, *Super Collective Market No. 1 Yellow.*

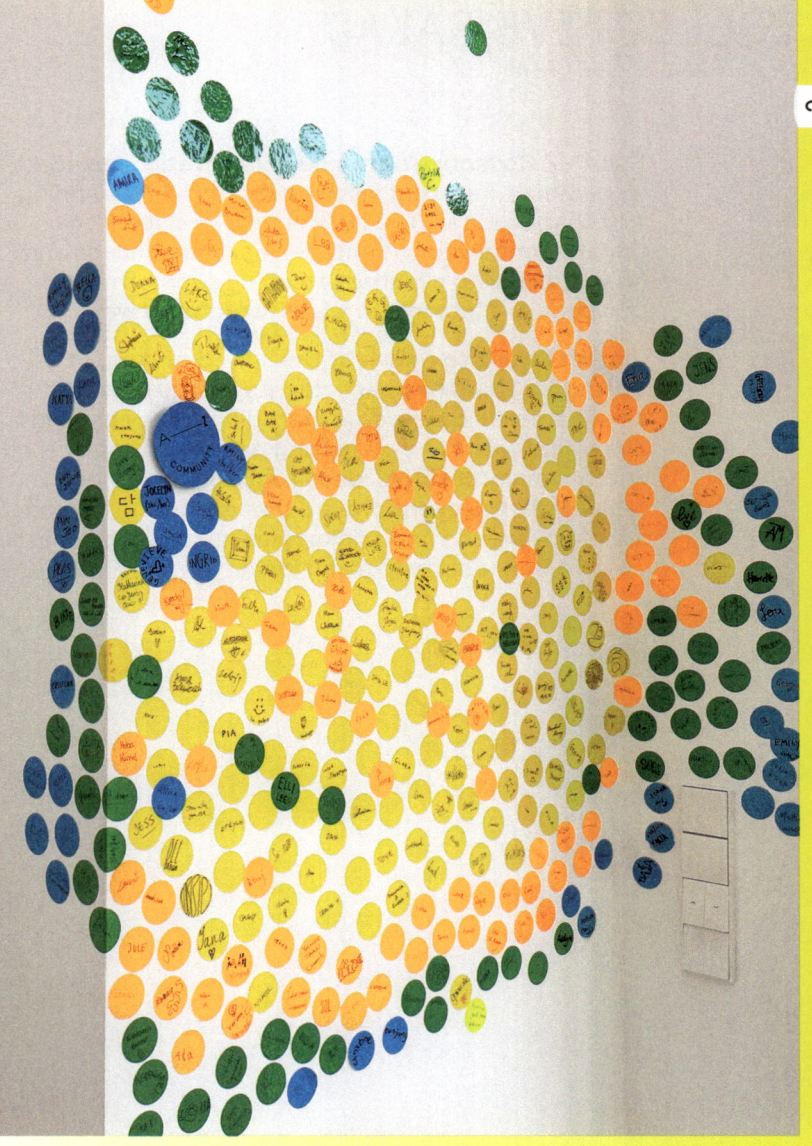

COLLECTIVE SALAD
AN *A–Z COLLECTIVE* GATHERING

The *A—Z Collective*'s intense collaboration included weekly meetings that involved discussions, planning, and sharing ideas. The collective was also intentionally conceived to lighten everybody's minds and hearts, allowing members to enjoy each other's company and interact in a less structured way.

Under the motto "move at the speed of trust", the *Collective Salad* had participants create different salads from all the diverse ingredients they brought. Seasoned with fun connecting games, prompts, and the many creative ideas registered on the tablecloth, the event proved that gathering around a table over food and drinks remains one of the best ways to connect people and ideas.

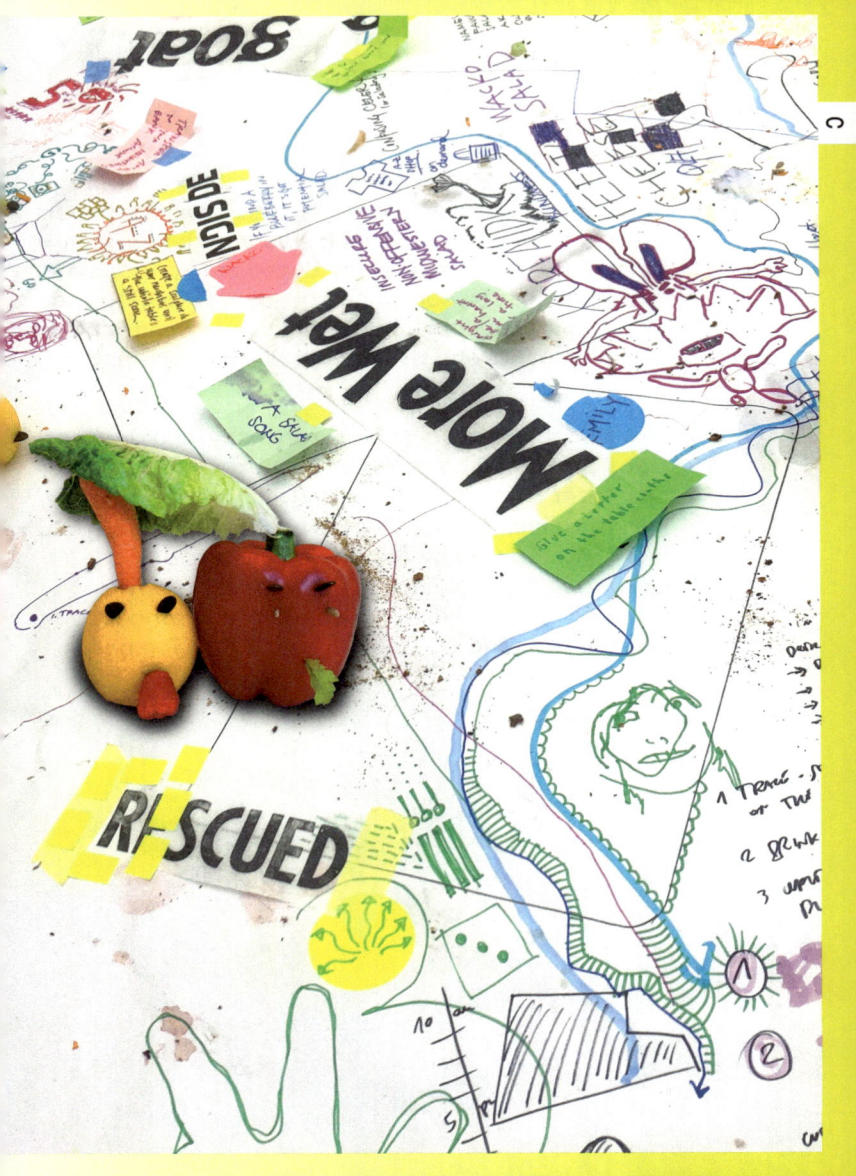

COMMUNITY BUILDING LIBRARY
TEMPORARY LIBRARY OF THE *A–Z COLLECTIVE*

One of the *A—Z Collective* project's foundations was sharing knowledge, which is also available in the form of books. During the one-year initiative, members of the collective contributed publications on topics related to community building to create the Community Building Library, which was accessible to all participants and visitors during the *Recipes for Connecting* exhibition.

This temporary archive featured many inspiring titles that could be browsed or borrowed, such as *Emergent Strategy* by adrienne maree brown, *Nonviolent Communication* by Marshall B. Rosenberg, *Work with Source* by Tom Nixon, *The Art of Gathering* by Priya Parker, *Come Together: The Rise of Cooperative Art and Design* by Francesco Spampinato, and *On Connection* by Kae Tempest.

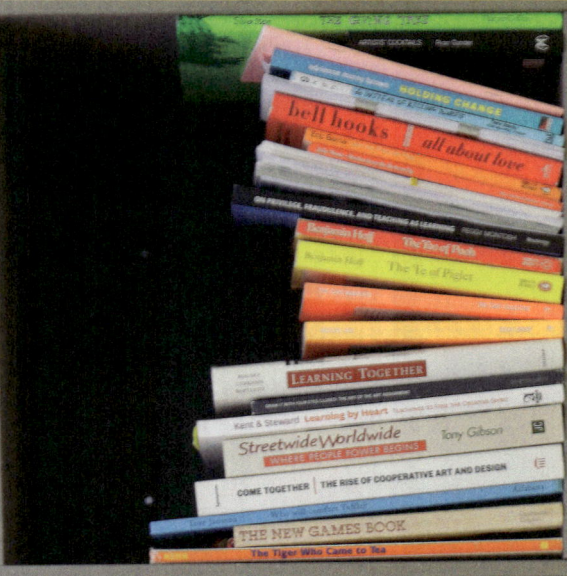
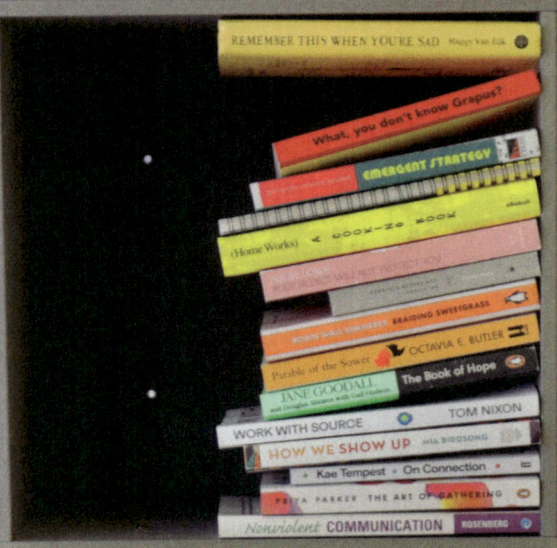

CONNECTING FROM A—Z
COLLABORATIVE FREE FONT DESIGN

Connecting from A—Z was an interactive exhibition project that created one diverse font based on the Latin alphabet. Twenty-eight designers were invited to create the letters and punctuation marks, expressing their artistic style and passion for design as a form of connecting during social distancing imposed by the Covid-19 pandemic.

The making of the alphabet was a chained event. Starting with the letter A, each invitee created the following letter in the alphabet and forwarded their creation to the next designer, in a dynamic and playful experience. The result was a vibrant alphabet of funky letterforms, later printed on yellow cardboard cubes and also used in the index sections of the present book.

Connecting From A—Z is a free font for personal use, downloadable from the A—Z website. The individual letters were created by: Alex Branczyk, Andrea Tinnes, Anja Lutz, Barbara Dechant, Christopher Knowles, Emily Smith, Ferdinand Ulrich, Francesco Pini, Frank Höhne, Franzi Bauer, Georg Rutishauser, Ilka Helmig & Johannes Bergerhausen, Imad Gebrayel, Jason Grant, Johanna Olm, Juliana Toro, Jungmyung Lee, Lucienne Roberts, Mark van Wageningen, Na Kim, Niklaus Troxler, Patrick Thomas, Peter Nencini, Franziska Morlok, So Jin Park, Tine Melzer, and Urs Lehni.

ANDREA TINNES
LETTER CUBES
LUCIENNE ROBERTS
MARK VAN WAGENINGEN
NA KIM
NIKLAUS TROXLER
PANDEMIC
PATRICK THOMAS
TINE MELZER

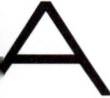

C

ALEX BRANCZYK
Drucken 3000

JASON GRANT
Inkahoots

NA KIM

PETER NENCINI

TINE MELZER

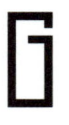
BARBARA DECHANT
Buchstabenmuseum

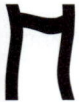
JULIANA TORO

SO JIN PARK

ANDREA TINNES

FRANZISKA MORLOK
Rimini Berlin

GEORG RUTISHAUSER
Edition Fink

NIKLAUS TROXLER

FRANK HÖHNE

FERDINAND ULRICH

EMILY SMITH

LUCIENNE ROBERTS

JUNGMYUNG LEE

PATRICK THOMAS

RK VAN WAGENINGEN
Novo Typo

JOHANNA OLM

ILKA HELMIG &
JOHANNES BERGERHAUSEN

FRANZI BAUER

IMAD GEBRAYEL

"Y"
as in
Yellow Pages
yellow-pages.wtf

URS LEHNI

FRANCESCO PINI

CHRISTOPHER KNOWLES

Z

CONVERSATION PIECES
AN EXPERIMENTAL INVESTIGATION

A—Z continues to be a space for thinking about and investigating experimental practices in Graphic Design in its varied relations with other fields. In this sense, dialogue is a core aspect of A—Z's philosophy, especially dialogue with the Graphic Design community.

This exchange has assumed many formats over the past six years, such as the *Counter Sessions* or in the form of the *A—Z Collective.* A recent experiment is the *Conversation Pieces* series, in which A—Z founder Anja Lutz sets up a one-to-one session with one of her peers to engage in an impromptu dialogue while both participants creatively doodle on a sheet of paper.

There is no planned topic or expectation of results other than exploring how the conversation promotes knowledge exchange and how it manifests itself graphically after the talk is finished—a visual document that abstractively encapsulates the whole interaction beyond words or concepts.

To date, the *Conversation Pieces* has been held with Lucienne Roberts, Prem Krishnamurthy, and Laura Meseguer, who have each engaged in the exchange of views and ideas, doodling, and reacting to their and Anja's thoughts, while expressing themselves on paper.

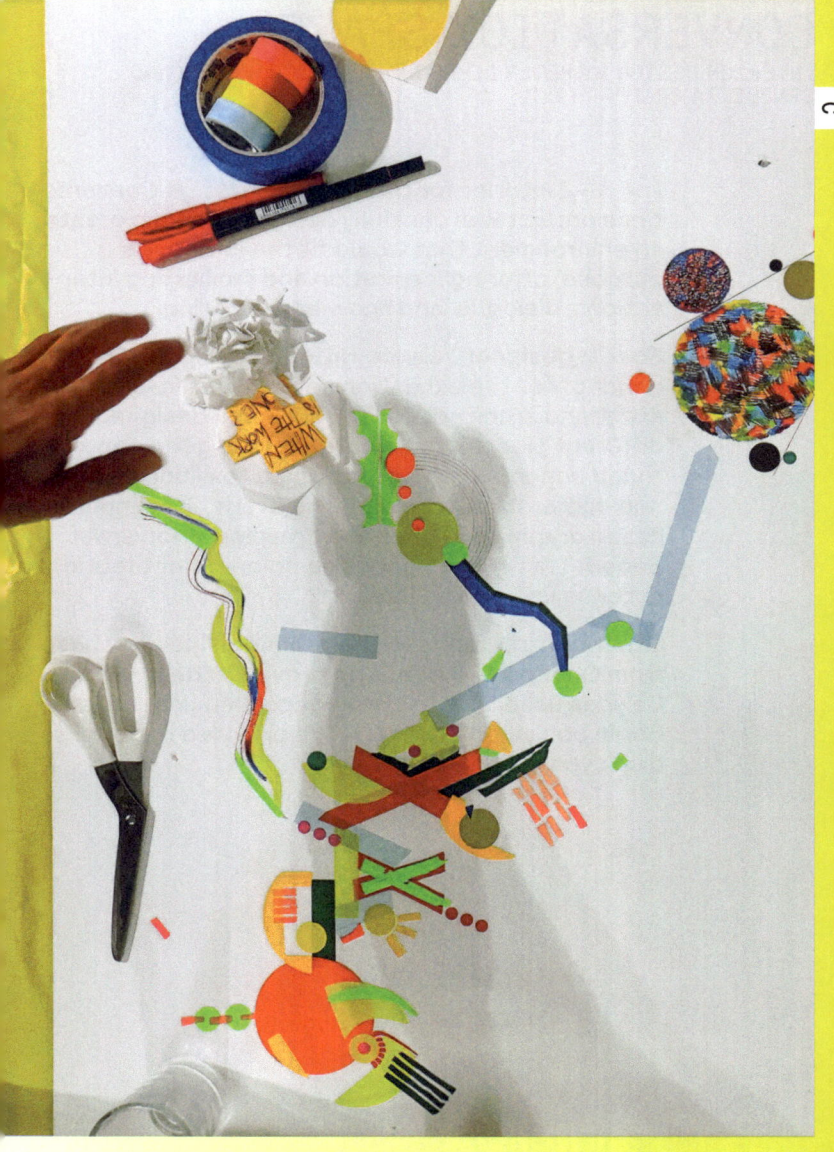

CONVERSATION SPACE

INTERIOR DESIGN BY PETER BEHRBOHM, FABRICE HÖFGEN AND BENEDETTA CRIPPA

The A—Z interior for the *Teaching Design Conversations* project was carefully designed to help create an environment that would fit the initiative's purpose, offering inspiration and facilitating interactions, dialogue, and knowledge sharing.

Spatial designer Fabrice Höfgen developed the concept for the exhibition setting. Berlin-based artist and architect Peter Behrbohm designed different pieces of furniture, including the central round bench, which was designed to allude to the non-hierarchical format of the event. Stockholm-based graphic designer and ornamentation artist Benedetta Crippa signed the colored light fabric curtains used in the interior.

Other contributions to the exhibition include those from Charlotte Rhode, who provided the title font Calyces used in all the project communication, and Berlin bookshop Pro qm, which provided the books displayed in the library.

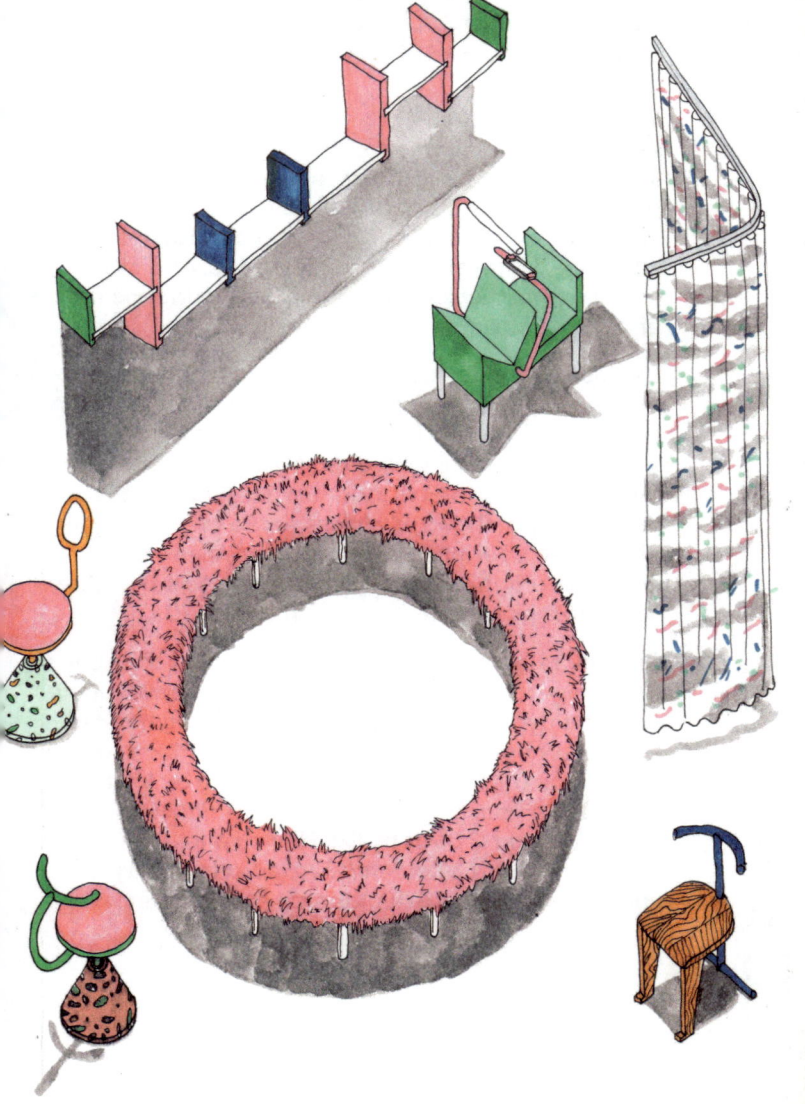

COUNTER SESSIONS
TRANSDISCIPLINARY TALKS OVER THE BAR COUNTER

Counter Sessions was a series of events planned in an open and casual format, aiming at transforming the space into a point of meeting and exchanging ideas, where all happens over the bar counter. This comprised informal talks, discussions, and other forms of interactions exploring the countless facets of transdisciplinary Graphic Design.

The inspiration for the project came from the clandestine Flipper Bar, operating at the exact location between 2000 and 2001. Thus, reproducing the setting, a series of one-evening events were performed around the bar counter, ending in a casual bar night, which would always serve only one type of German beer and Brazilian caipirinhas—the only drink the original Flipper Bar refused to serve due to its clichéd popularity back in the 2000s.

Over eight months, five guests occupied the space, all having in common an interplay of different voices and perspectives rethinking and challenging traditional perceptions of Graphic Design. These were: *Ever Since the Days of Mrs. Gutenberg* by MMS; *Inverse – A Yearly Ritual* by Florian Dombois; *Family Trees & Sound Clouds* by Ilka Helmig and Johannes Bergerhausen; *Cyberfeminism Index* by Mindy Seu; and a final talk and exhibition by Alex Jordan.

CAIPIRINHA
CYBERFEMINISM INDEX
EVER SINCE THE DAYS OF MRS. GUTENBERG …
FAMILY TREES & SOUND CLOUDS
FLIPPER BAR
INVERSE – A YEARLY RITUAL
TORSTRASSE
YOU NEVER GIVE UP?

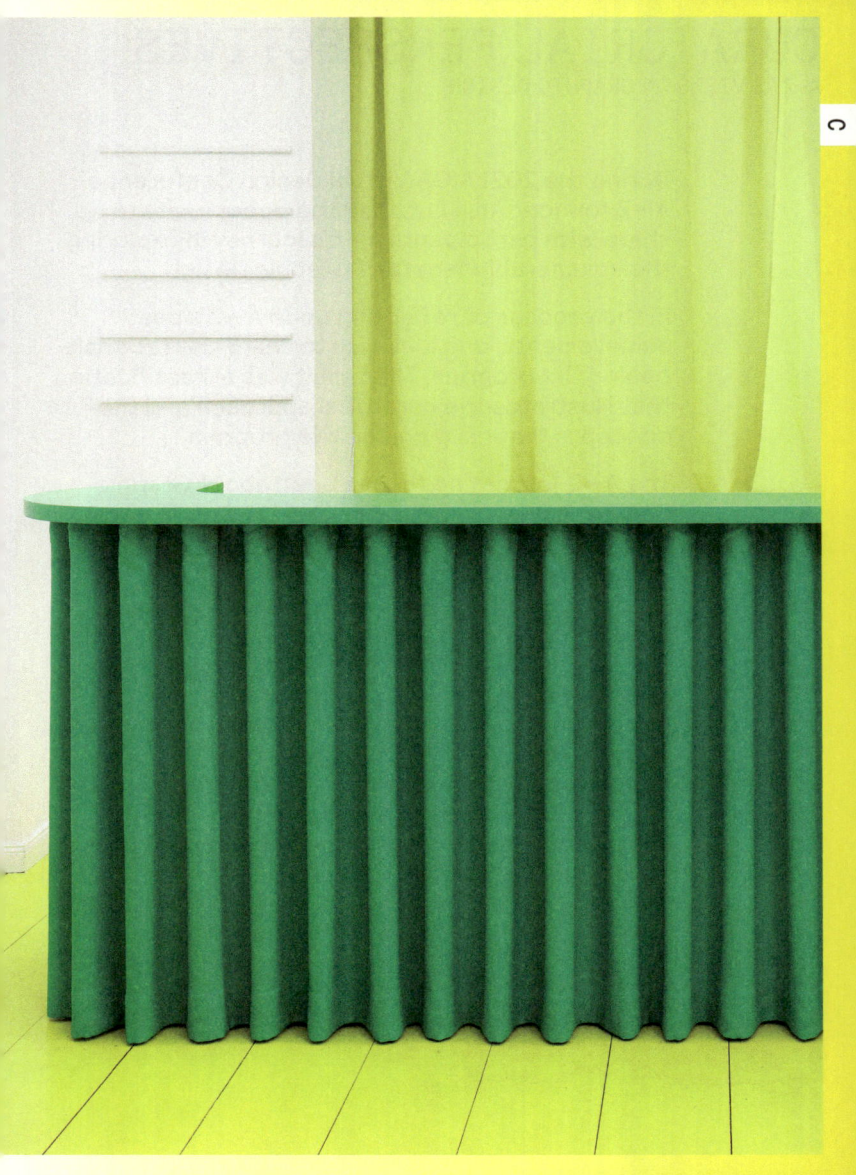

CURATORIAL PERSPECTIVES
A—Z'S VIEWS ON GRAPHIC DESIGN

During the 2021 AIGA Virtual Design Conference, A—Z founder Anja Lutz had the opportunity to share with participants A—Z's journey in exploring the innumerable facets of Graphic Design.

In the process of reflecting upon A—Z's past achievements, one idea was to share the rationale behind the program. The result was a classification that illustrates the curatorial approach and the concepts that have guided the program.

The A—Z journey so far has been about Graphic Design that
… goes beyond the commissioned realm
… branches out into other disciplines
… reflects upon its responsibilities in society
… researches and investigates
… offers an insight into the working process
… relates to personal experiences and needs
… creates a space for community, interaction, and discussion
… looks beyond the Western cultural frame
… helps the weaving of a social fabric
… is aware it is standing on the shoulders of those who came before us

Graphic Design…

- that researches and investigates
- that reflects upon its responsibilities in society
- that offers an insight into the working process
- that goes beyond the commissioned realm
- that branches out into other disciplines
- that relates to personal experiences and needs
- that creates a space for community, interaction, and discussion
- that is aware it is standing on the shoulders of those who came before us
- that looks beyond the Western cultural frame
- that helps the weaving of a social fabric

CYBERFEMINISM INDEX
COUNTER SESSION #4 BY MINDY SEU

The *Counter Sessions #4* featured designer Mindy Seu with an augmented reality presentation of her book *Cyberfeminism Index*. Guiding the audience through the pages and their expanded elements, integrated and exhibited in real-time on the projection, she shared the crowdsourced research process on three decades of cyberfeminism and net art, but also her view and her role as editor and what that means to the publication seen by her as "a highly subjective, biased history of cyberfeminism, a history moderated by me and some other stewards, but primarily through the rules that I created. And a history that is different from History". The book is an ongoing project, available in both online and print forms, published by Inventory Press.

Mindy Seu is a designer and technologist based in New York City and is currently an Assistant Professor at Yale School of Art.

COUNTER SESSIONS
EVER SINCE THE DAYS OF MRS. GUTENBERG...
FAMILY TREES & SOUND CLOUDS
FLIPPER BAR
INVERSE - A YEARLY RITUAL
YOU NEVER GIVE UP?
ONLINE VIDEO ARCHIVE

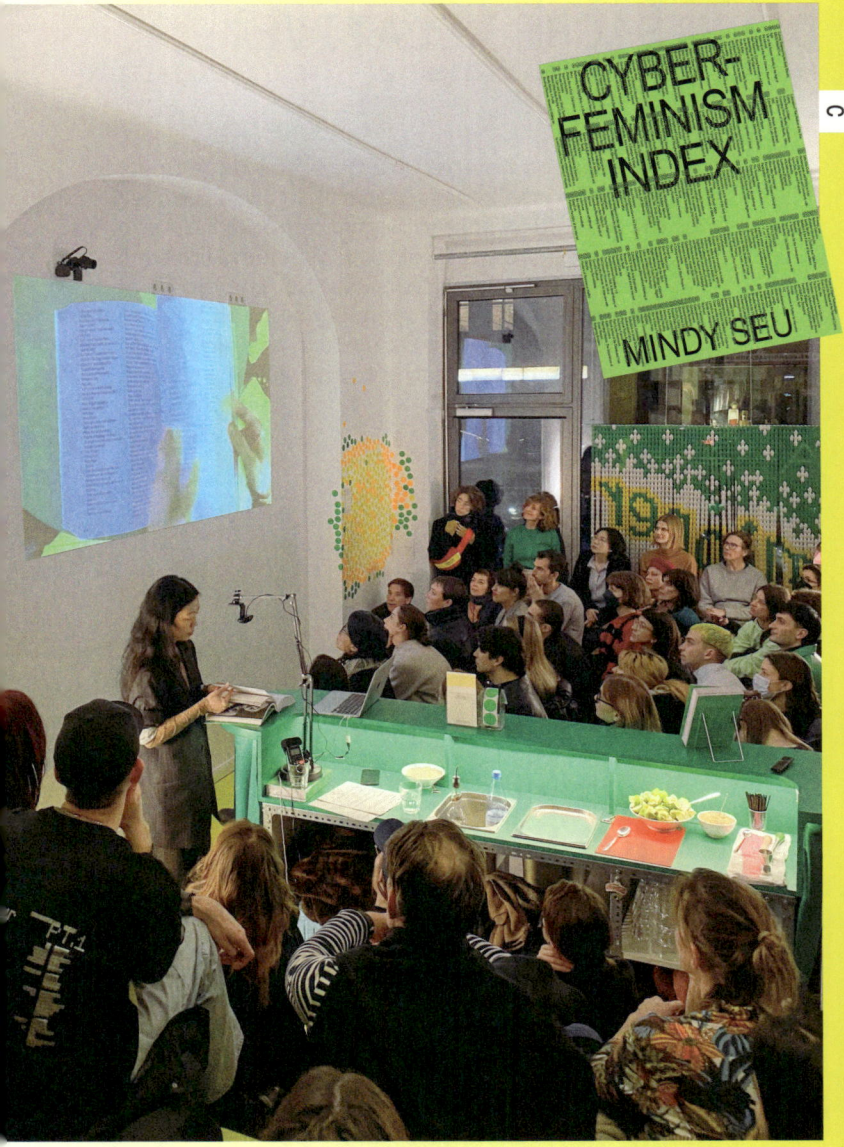

DERMISACHE RELATIVE
TYPEFACE FOR THE *MIRTHA DERMISACHE: TO BE READ* EXHIBITION

Dermisache Relative is a typeface developed by A—Z's former intern Ezequiel Hyon, especially for the exhibition *Mirtha Dermisache: To Be Read.* It combines the font Relative with hand-drawn signs by the artist Mirtha Dermisache. The typeface's different degrees of legibility allowed the creation of animations and texts used in the digital and print communication relating to the event.

ASEMIC WRITING
ILLEGIBLE
MIRTHA DERMISACHE
MIRTHA DERMISACHE: TO BE READ
MYSTERIOUS POSTCARD
READING ARTISTS' BOOKS: ASEMIC WRITING

ABCDEFGHIJKLM
NOPQRSTUVWXYZ

ABCDEFGHIJKLM
NOPQRSTUVWXYZ

ABCDEFGHIJKLM
NOPQRSTUVWXYZ

ABCDEFGHIJKLM
NOPQRSTUVWXYZ

MIRTHA DERMISACHE ▬▬
▬▬ ▬ ▮ ▬ ▬ ▬ TO ▬
E ▬ READ ▬ ▬ . ▬

DESIGN AND SOLIDARITY – HOW CAN GRAPHIC DESIGN BE POLITICAL?

PANEL DISCUSSION WITH MARA RECKLIES, SUSANNE BEER AND SANDY KALTENBORN, MODERATED BY FRANZI BAUER AND TONI BRELL AS PART OF THE *NEW ANTHEMS VI (BERLIN)* EXHIBITION

This panel discussion held in German *Design and Solidarity – How can Graphic Design be Political?* brought together the philosopher Mara Recklies, the designer Susanne Beer from ZOFF Collective, and the activist and designer Sandy Kaltenborn from image-shift for a conversation about how Graphic Design can be political. The talk was mediated by the graphic designer and gender-queer activist Franzi Bauer and the visual artist Toni Brell.

The conversation delved into several questions about socially aware Graphic Design, and how designers, their creations, and even the context and working conditions in which design is conceptualized, are inherently political. A central topic was the collaboration and solidarity present in the participants' design practice, and its role in transforming society.

DESIGN IS…
NEW ANTHEMS VI – EINE NEUE HYMNE FÜR DEUTSCHLAND
POST BRANDING MANIFESTO
YOU NEVER GIVE UP?
ONLINE VIDEO ARCHIVE

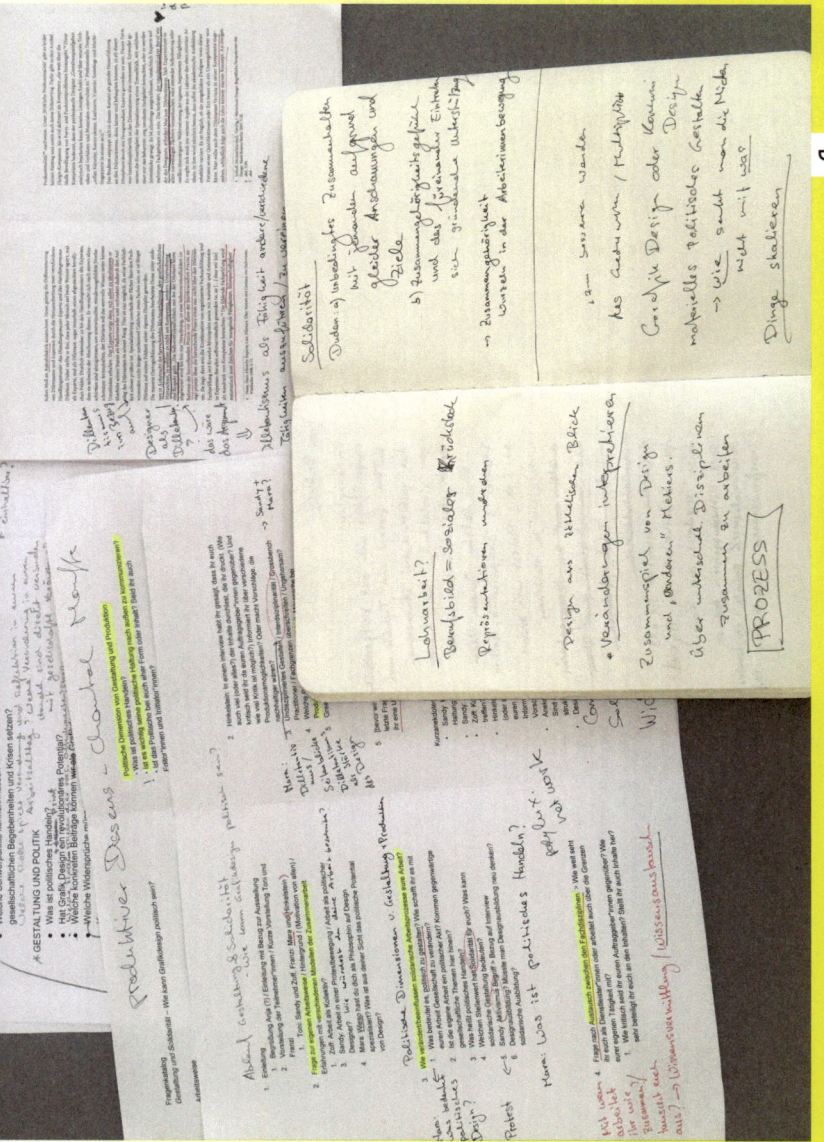

DESIGN IS...
TALK BY PATRICK THOMAS AT THE *PULP* EXHIBITION

"*Design is always a po[litical act,] you like it or not. Des[ign] disproportionately re[flects] society's consumeris[m ... choices I] make as a designer h[ave an impact on] someone else, as a co[nsumer ... Design is] a tool of influence.*"

NEWSPAPERS
PATRICK THOMAS
PULP
ONLINE VIDEO ARCHIVE

ical act, whether
ers are
onsible for much of
Every choice you
consequences for
er of messages and

DO YOU COLLECT GRAPHIC DESIGN?
AN INQUIRY

"Do you collect Graphic Design?" was a question posed to the Graphic Design community with the goal of better understanding how Graphic Design work is perceived as a collectible item, even if it is not necessarily considered a work of art in the traditional sense of what we find in galleries or museums.

This inquiry aimed to understand how to improve awareness of the cultural relevance of graphic works in general, and how that translates into the Graphic Design artworks related to A—Z events and available for sale, such as those by Andrea Tinnes, Niklaus Troxler, or Patrick Thomas.

The research findings showed that very few designers collect Graphic Design, but the vast majority of them do collect something. The variety of topics and objects they collected was so surprising and peculiar that it became the starting point for the *Graphic.Designers.Collectors.* exhibition.

ANDREA TINNES
COLLECTING GRAPHIC DESIGN
GRAPHIC. DESIGNERS. COLLECTORS.
NIKLAUS TROXLER
PATRICK THOMAS
TAKEAWAY GRAPHIC DESIGN

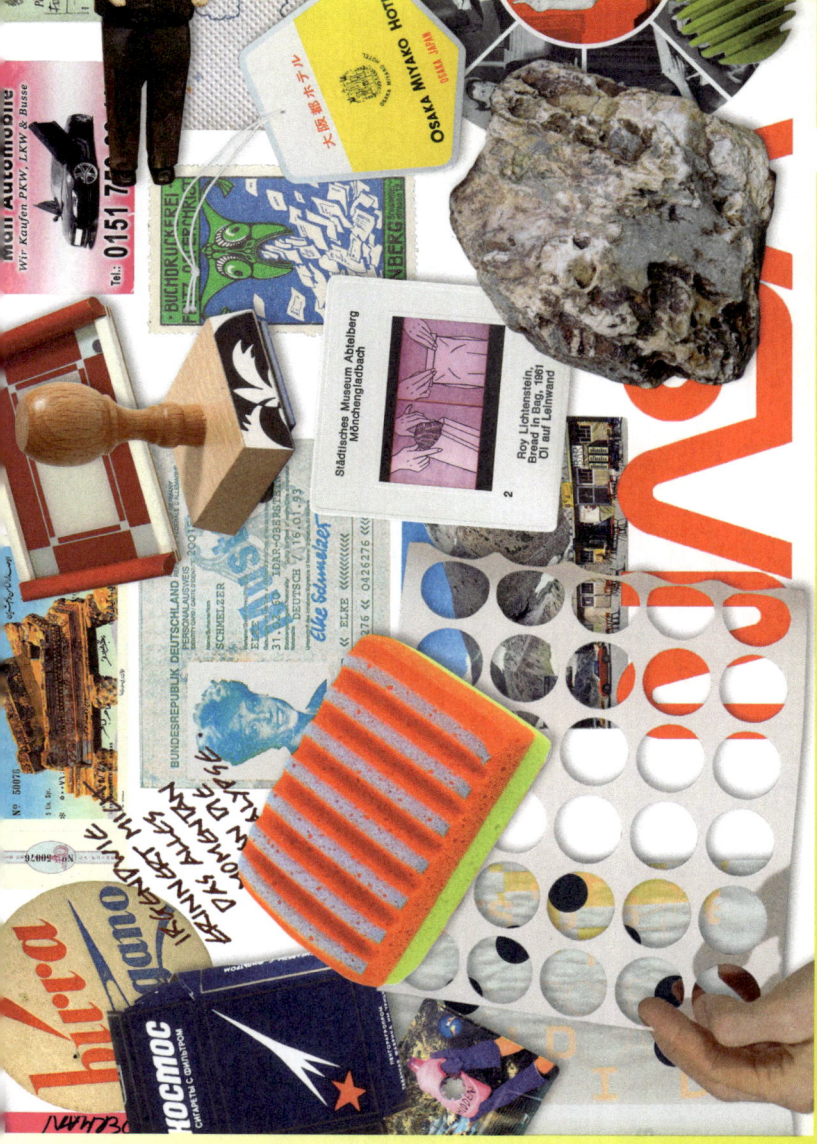

ERRATA

ANITA DI BIANCO IN CONVERSATION WITH FLORIAN WÜST AND
ANNA BROMLEY AT *THE ERROR IS REGRETTED* EXHIBITION

"Every time I had to
the meaning of coll
[newspaper errata]
is just something th
yourself from doing
the accumulation w

ANITA DI BIANCO
NEWSPAPERS
THE ERROR IS REGRETTED
ONLINE VIDEO ARCHIVE

"...t my head around ...ting these things ...decided that it ...you don't stop ...ecause you assume ...build something."

EVER SINCE THE DAYS OF MRS. GUTENBERG...
COUNTER SESSION #1 BY MMS

This first *Counter Session* event was an open conversation about women in Graphic Design throughout history, featuring the names and stories of some of those whose work contributed to shaping the field. The talk also approached questions on collective struggles, research strategies, and history writing today and tomorrow, allowing an understanding of Graphic Design's past, present, and future.

The dialogue was introduced by the design historian Gerda Breuer and the design writer Madeleine Morley, with the design collective MMS as guest. MMS is a Stockholm-based group of graphic designers Maryam Fanni, Matilda Flodmark and Sara Kaaman, who have collaborated since 2012 on investigations and writings on Graphic Design histories from feminist and labor history perspectives.

The panel discussion ended with a workshop open to the public on the traditional technique of marbling paper, led by Matilda Flodmark from MMS, using the group's 2020 book *Natural Enemies of Books: A Messy History of Women in Printing and Typography*.

COUNTER SESSIONS
CYBERFEMINISM INDEX
FAMILY TREES & SOUND CLOUDS
INVERSE – A YEARLY RITUAL
YOU NEVER GIVE UP?
ONLINE VIDEO ARCHIVE

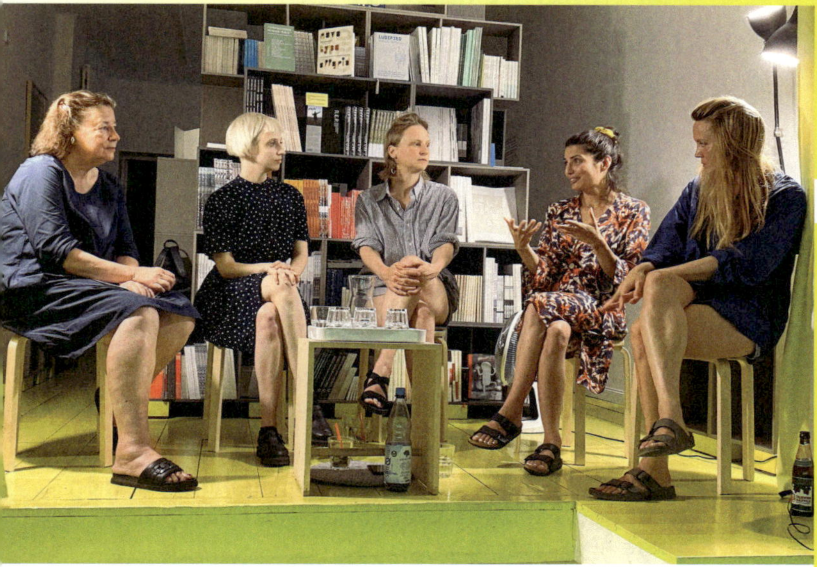

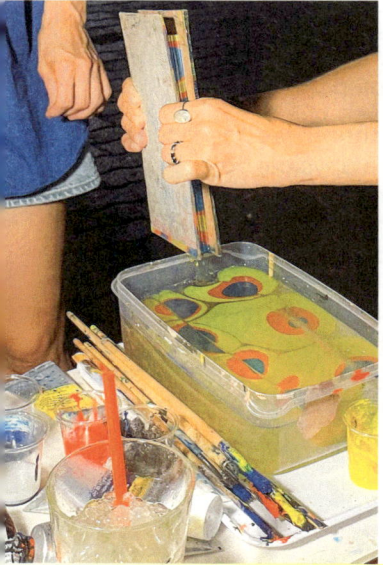
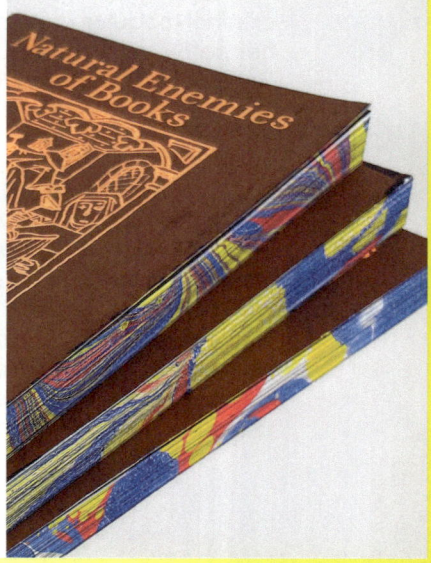

EXQUISITE CURIOSITIES
EXHIBITION BY SARAH BORIS

Exquisite Curiosities was an exhibition by designer Sarah Boris, based on the informal and collective moment of sharing objects, tools, books, artworks, or anything design-related that people had a connection with and felt was of value to submit as an exhibit. Simultaneously acting as exhibitor and curator, Sarah prompted visitors to bring any artwork or piece that "mattered to them" on the opening night, creating an impromptu exhibition based on those contributions.

Aligned with the premise of communal experimentations, *Exquisite Curiosities* was related to the *A—Z Collective* project. The exhibition also showcased some of Sarah's projects, such as the original modular drawings of *Rainbow*, alongside her self-published wordless books, *Le Théâtre Graphique* (2015) and *Rainbow* (2023).

To enter the exhibition, there was only one rule: participants must bring a physical object so others could experience it. This led to the key questions the artist wanted to evoke: "Who can exhibit? Who curates? And what happens to the exhibition when the result is unpredictable?" Among the objects were a Valentine's letter, a dentist's tool, a rare coin, a kaleidoscope …. In a show-and-tell format, each person had one minute to tell the story of their item. Altogether, these portrayed a narrative of treasured curiosities.

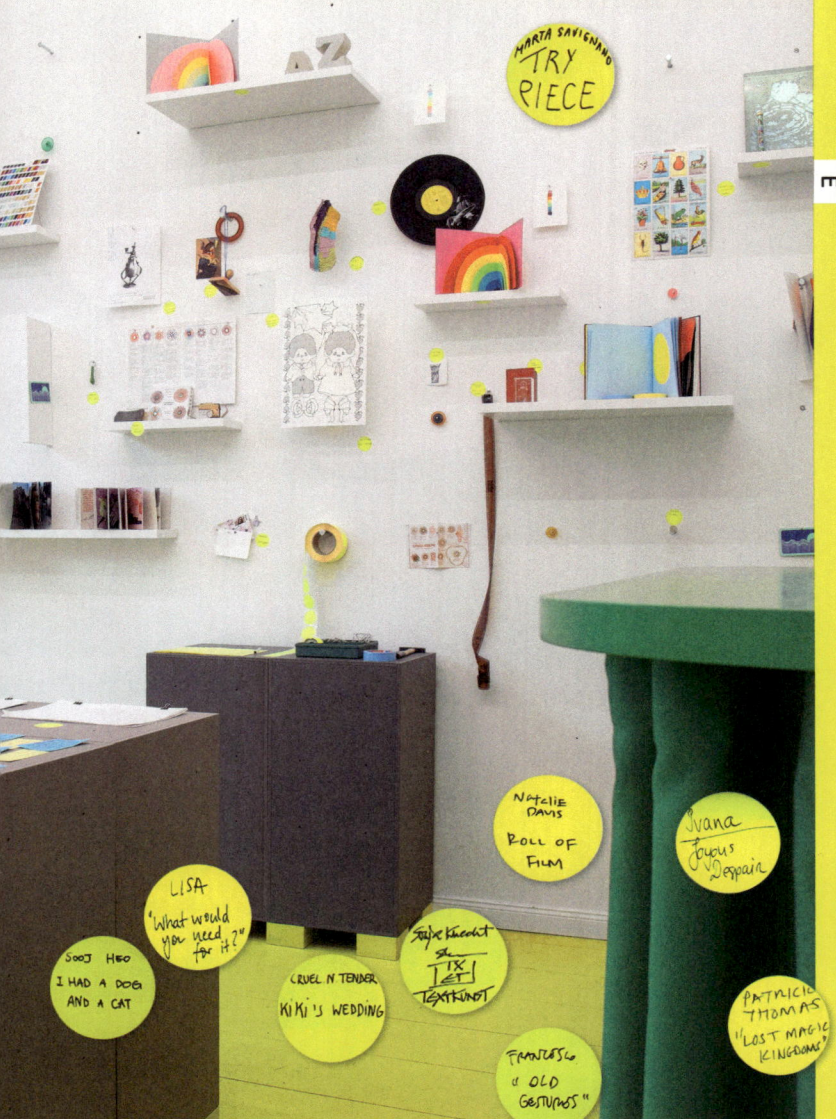

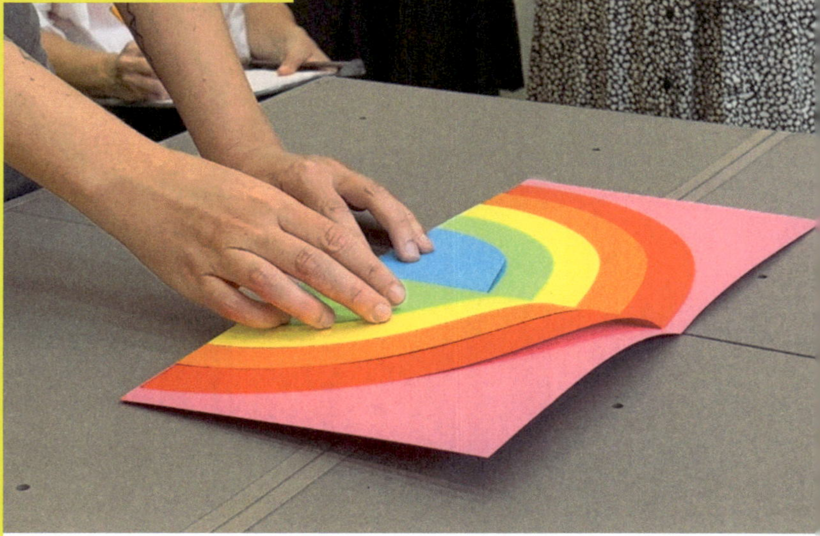

EXQUISITE CURIOSITIES

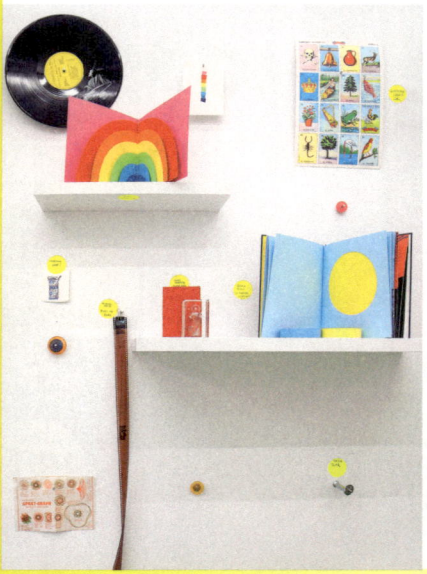
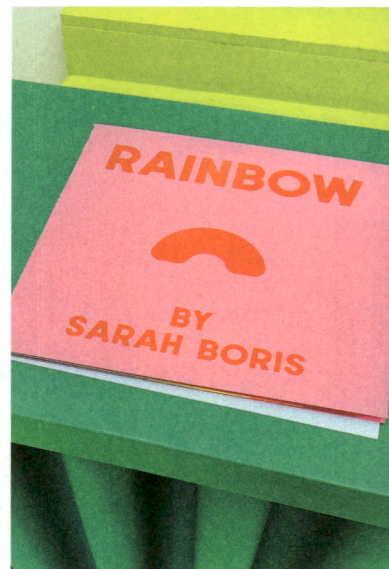

m

EXQUISITE CURIOSITIES

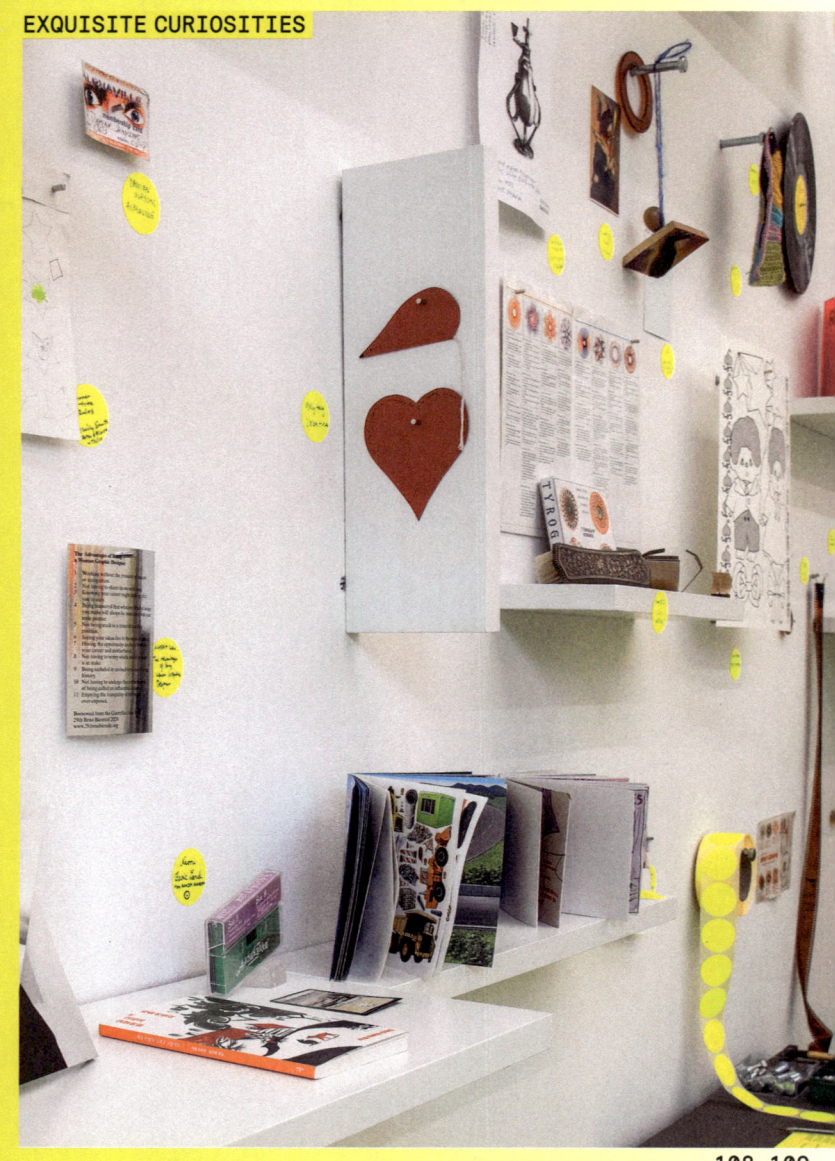

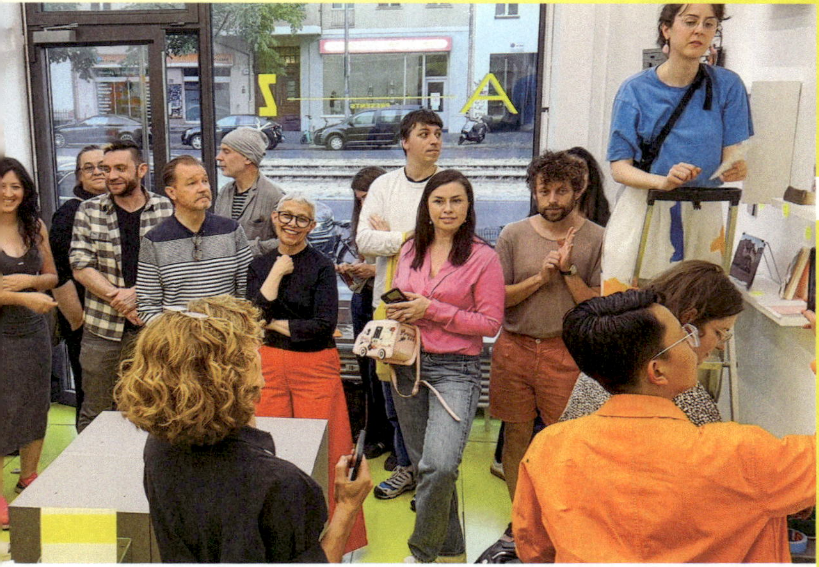

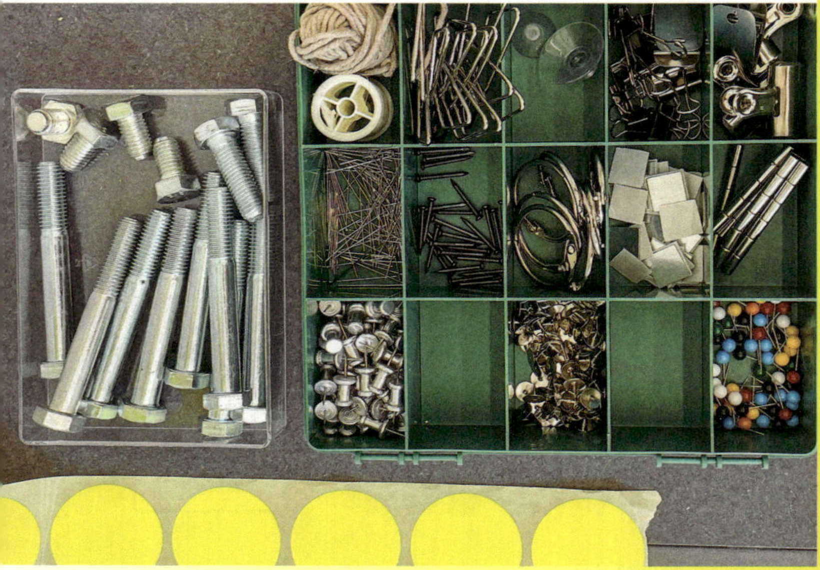

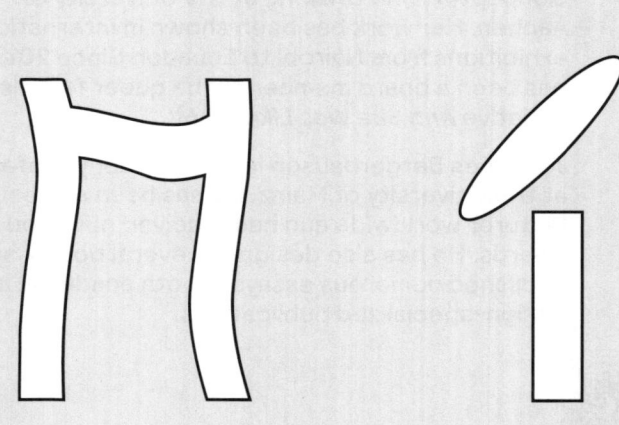

FAMILY TREES & SOUND CLOUDS
COUNTER SESSION #3 BY ILKA HELMIG AND JOHANNES BERGERHAUSEN

Who invented 'writing'? How many writing systems are there in the world? How do they relate to the spoken languages and their sounds? And what would a complete family tree of writing systems look like?

These and other questions on the languages we read, speak and hear were the topic of a visual lecture performed by artist Ilka Helmig, who showed her drawings of the visualization of the aerodynamics of human sounds, and designer Johannes Bergerhausen, who presented the research findings of his projects *The World of Writing Systems* and *Missing Scripts.* Two large posters displayed glyphs of 293 scripts of world writing systems, in chronological and geographical order.

Ilka Helmig is a visual artist and Professor of Visual Conception and Drawing at the University of Aachen. Her work has been shown in international exhibitions from Nairobi to Ecuador. Since 2018, she has been a board member of the queer feminist initiative *And She Was Like: BÄM!*

Johannes Bergerhausen is a Typography Professor at the University of Mainz. He has been a guest lecturer worldwide and has received numerous awards. He has also designed several books, and published numerous essays in both academic and design-specialized publications.

COUNTER SESSIONS
TAKEAWAY GRAPHIC DESIGN
ONLINE VIDEO ARCHIVE

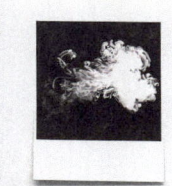
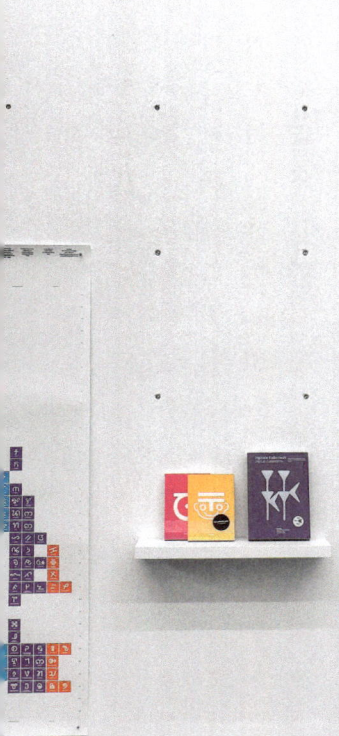
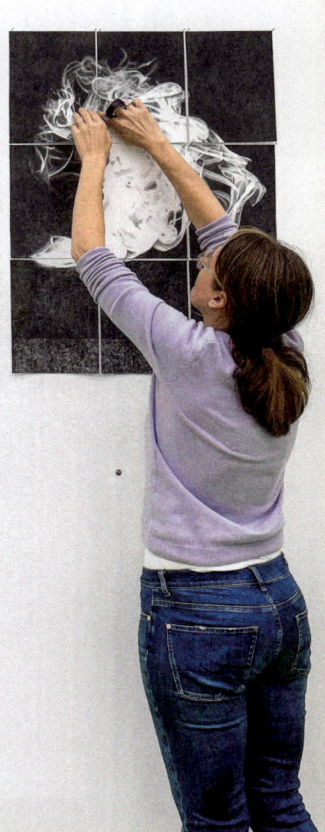

FAMILY TREES & SOUND CLOUDS

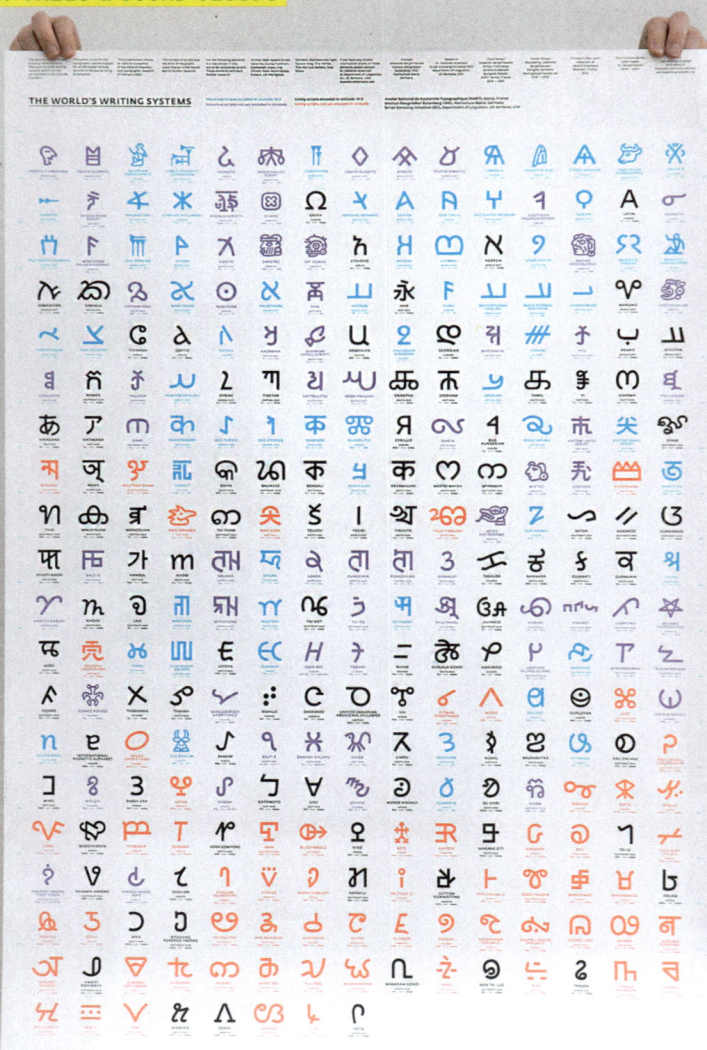

114–115

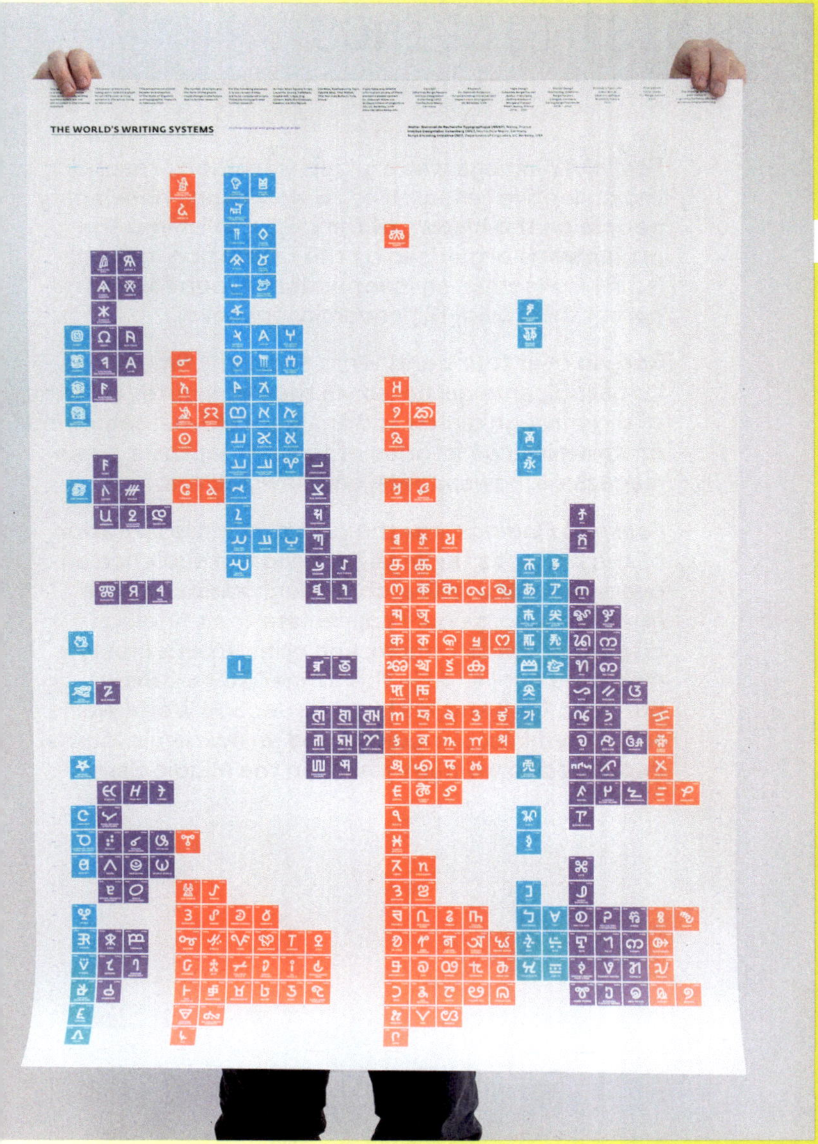

FEMINIST FINDINGS
EXHIBITION BY L.I.P. COLLECTIVE

Feminist Findings was a group exhibition presenting the collective research of 26 womxn and non-binary people on the history of feminist publishing. The project was organized by the Liberation in Print (L.i.P.) Collective, an independent group formed during the Covid-19 pandemic lockdown.

Spread over four continents and many time zones, its participants gathered via their computer screens to dig through digital and analog archives, searching for the missing histories of feminist journals, zines, magazines, newspapers, and newsletters.

Feminist Findings was the first public presentation of the project's findings, offering the audience an overview of the research through various media. At A—Z, visitors could appreciate their findings displayed in video, audio, and print, from a lifestyle magazine published in the former Soviet Union between 1945 and 1991 to pre-Second World War Jewish feminist periodicals and an academic journal dedicated to women's issues in the Middle East.

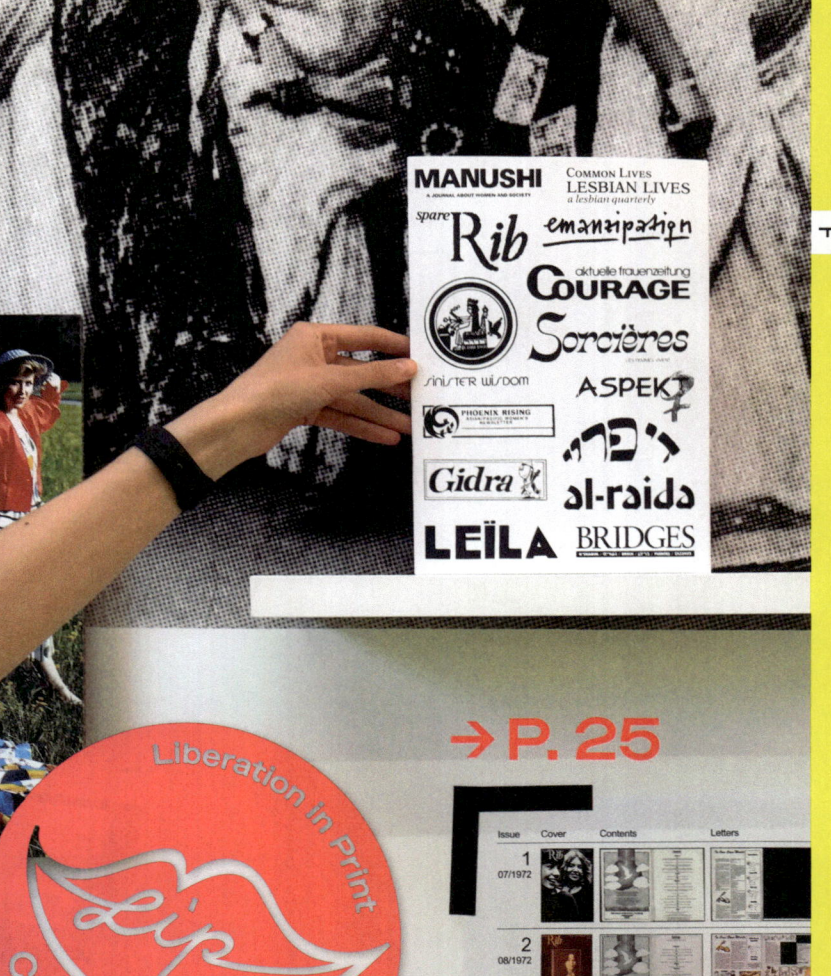

→ P. 25

FEMINIST FINDINGS

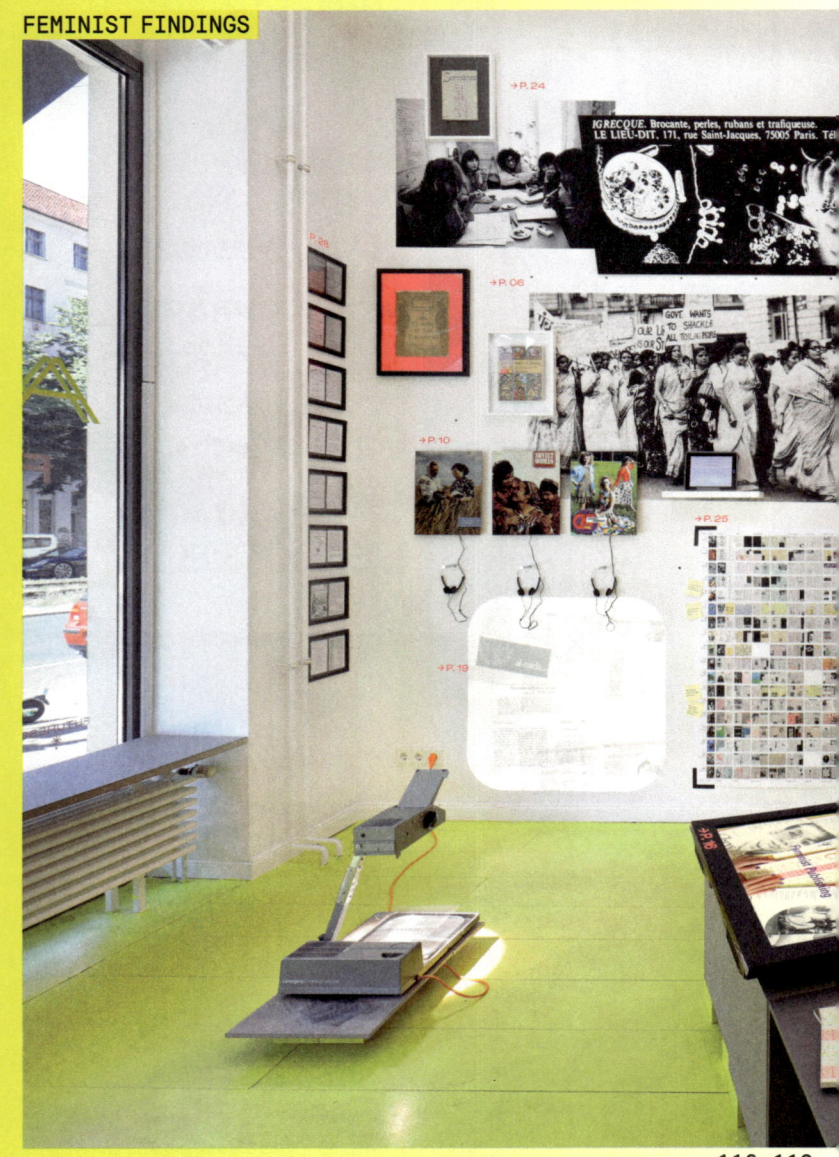

118–119

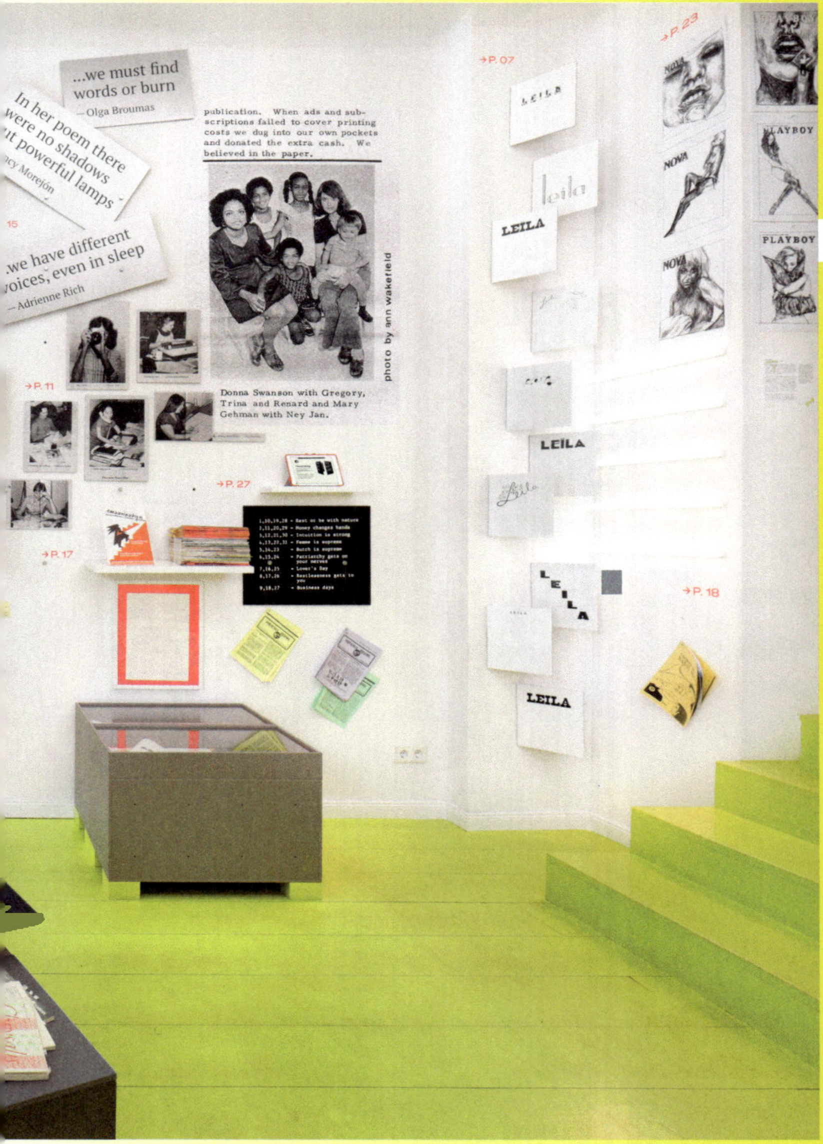

...we must find words or burn
—Olga Broumas

In her poem there were no shadows but powerful lamps
—Nancy Morejón

...we have different voices, even in sleep
—Adrienne Rich

publication. When ads and subscriptions failed to cover printing costs we dug into our own pockets and donated the extra cash. We believed in the paper.

photo by ann wakefield

Donna Swanson with Gregory, Trina and Renard and Mary Gehman with Ney Jan.

→P.11

→P.17

→P.27

1,23,24,28 • East as be with nature
3,11,25,29 • Money changes hands
5,12,21,30 • Intuition is strong
6,15,22,31 • Femme is supreme
5,24,23 • Earth is supreme
6,13,26 • Patriarchy gets on your nerves
7,16,23 • Lover's Day
8,17,26 • Restlessness gets to you
9,18,27 • Business days

→P.07

LEILA
leila
LEILA
leila
LEILA
leila
LEILA
leila
LEILA

→P.23

NOVA
NOVA
NOVA
PLAYBOY
PLAYBOY
PLAYBOY

→P.18

FEMINIST FINDINGS

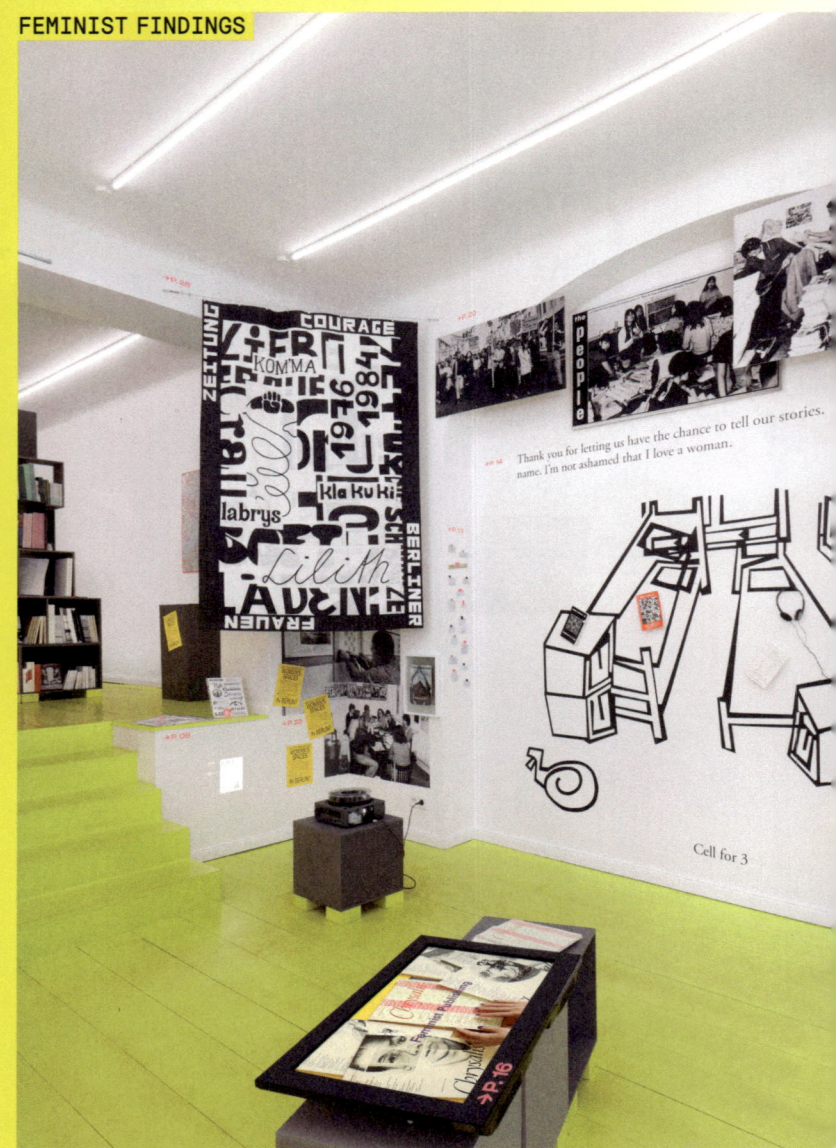

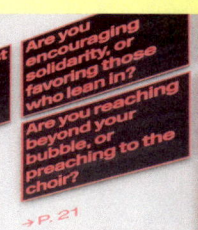
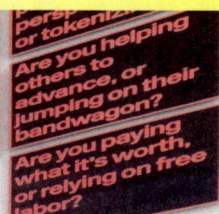

→ P. 21

→ P. 12

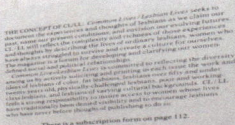

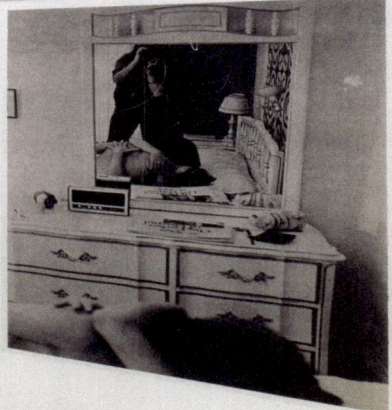

FEMINIST FINDINGS

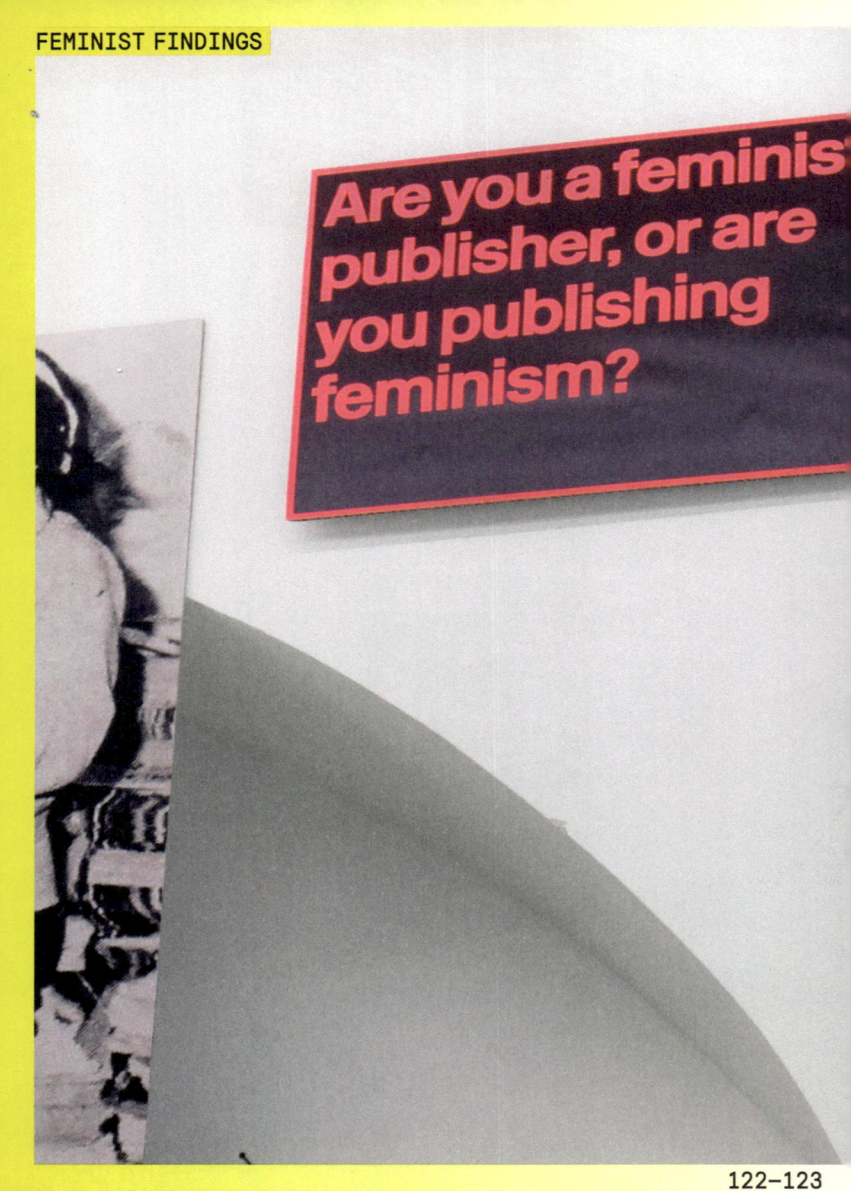

Are you encouraging solidarity, or favoring those who lean in?

Are you reaching beyond your bubble, or preaching to the choir?

→ P. 21

FESTA DEL GRAFISME
A—Z OUT & ABOUT IN PORTBOU, SPAIN

Festa del Grafisme is a collectively organized design festival that has been held annually in Portbou, Spain, since 2008. Its exhibitions, talks, workshops, and social events occupy several locations around the town.

Mere miles from the French border, the idyllic Portbou is known as the site of the philosopher Walter Benjamin's disappearance, as he took his own life when fleeing Nazi persecution in 1940. This tragic event is frozen in time by an impressive memorial by the sculptor Dani Karavan at the location.

A—Z Out & About took part in the 2024 event, which had activism as its main topic, exhibiting the posters from *Time is Running* by Rebellion Riso Posters Collab, a collaboration with Poster Rex, Studio Drucken 3000, and *Slanted*.

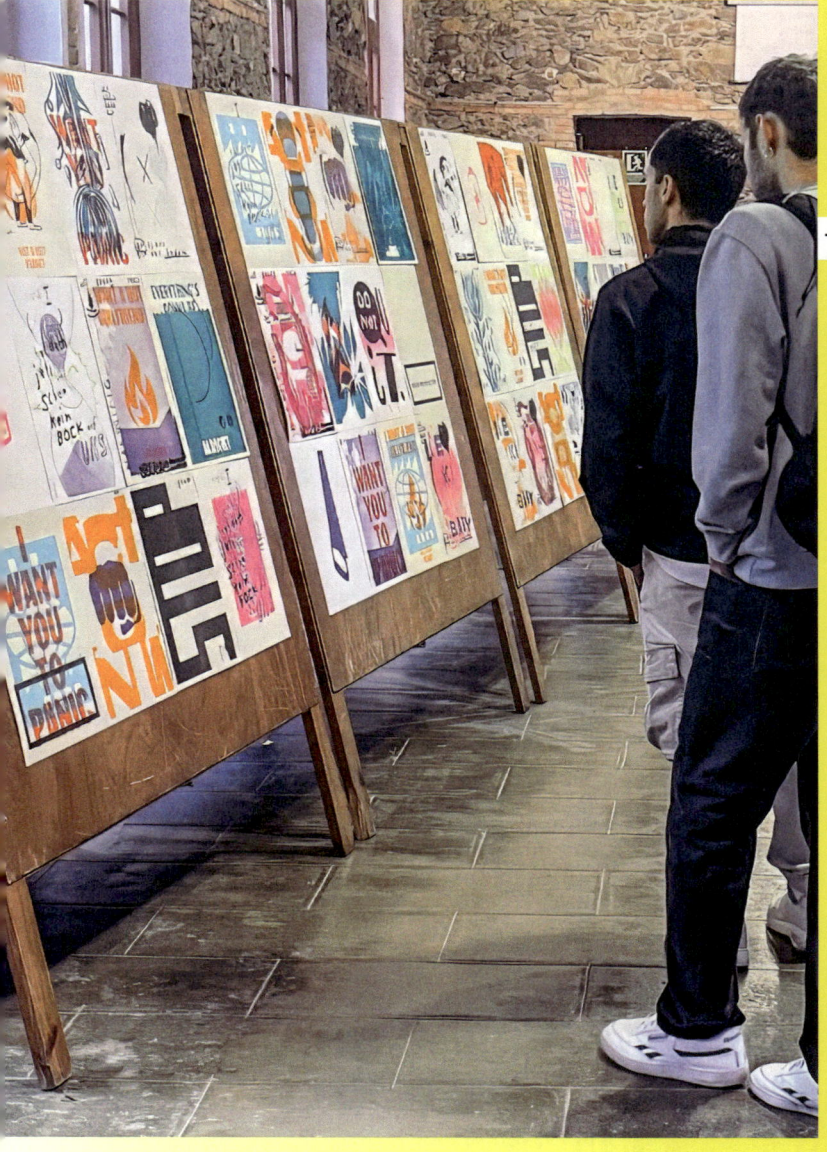

FLIPPER BAR
THE STORY BEHIND THE CURTAIN

During the early 2000s, in Torstrasse 93, in the same building that became the location for A—Z many years later, a clandestine bar ran weekly in the best improvised spirit of the 'wild years' of post-reunification in Berlin. At the Flipper Bar, Anja Lutz and her partner, Jens Bauermeister, would open the doors only on Fridays to welcome friends and passersby, serving drinks and good music played by DJ friends in the after hours.

One piece of that history made its journey to the present: the Flipper Bar curtain, which was crafted from hundreds of PVC interlocking plates brought from a trip to Sicily, and used by Anja to create the pixelated type for the bar name that would hang on the shop window.

At the time, the peculiar typographic curtain caught the attention of David Reinfurt on a stroll through the city in 2001, and it became the topic of an article published on *Dot Dot Dot 5*, a critical magazine on visual culture.

Fast forward in time, the curtain was brought back to complement the inspirational setting for the Counter Sessions series of events in 2022. Coincidentally, this is when David Reinfurt returned to Berlin for the first time since then, just in time to join another bar night.

After the Counter Sessions ended, the Flipper Bar curtain found its forever home by becoming part of the Buchstabenmuseum collection.

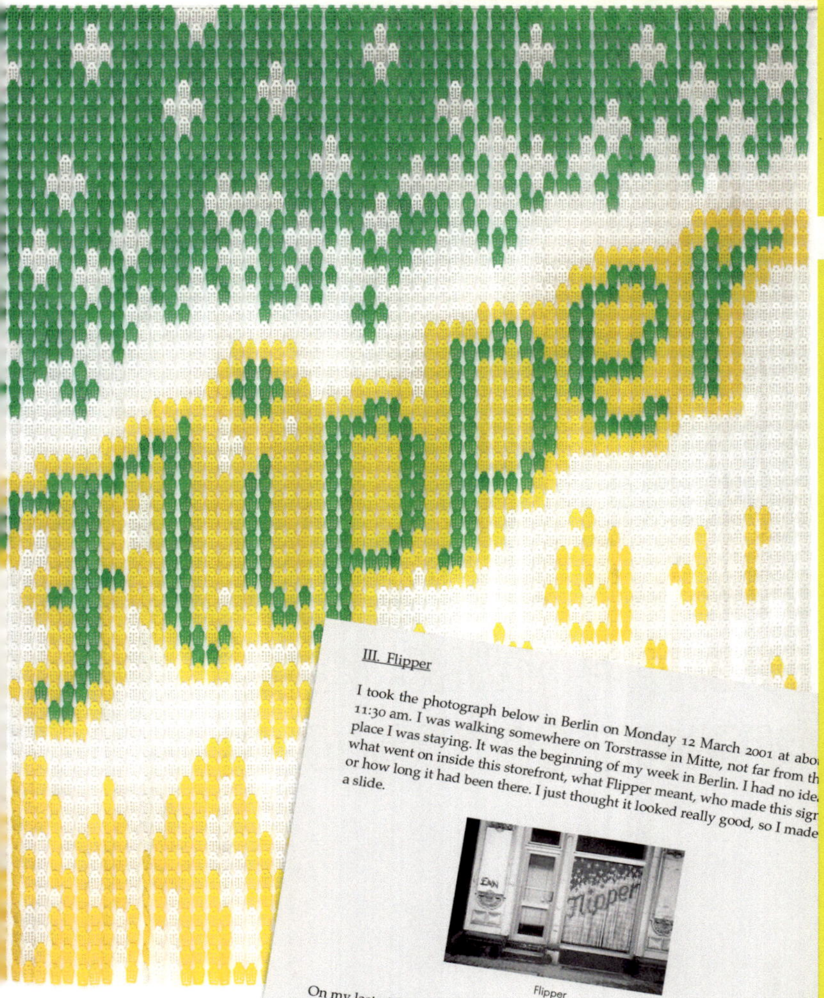

III. Flipper

I took the photograph below in Berlin on Monday 12 March 2001 at abo[ut] 11:30 am. I was walking somewhere on Torstrasse in Mitte, not far from th[e] place I was staying. It was the beginning of my week in Berlin. I had no ide[a] what went on inside this storefront, what Flipper meant, who made this sign or how long it had been there. I just thought it looked really good, so I made a slide.

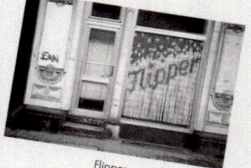

Flipper

On my last night in Berlin, I was set to go to an occasional, not quite legal bar that my American German-speaking friend knew of. The place is run by a graphic designer named Anja Lutz. Anja had started the bar on Friday nights in a vacant storefront. It is called Flipper. I was surprised and amused that it was the place that I had taken a picture of at the beginning of the week. Once inside, I asked about the Flipper sign that I had
earlier in the week and received a lengthy

FLOWERS
TINE MELZER LECTURE AT THE *BLUMEN SIND GEIL* EXHIBITION

"Only the passionate one[s]
there are more names fo[r...]
unless we name them dif[ferently...]
ones over there'. It's simi[lar...]
a few words for the infini[te...]
things, nuances, and son[...]
comparison ... The names[...]
orange, pink, red, violet,[...]
brown, ochre, beige, bla[ck...]

BLUMEN SIND GEIL
TINE MELZER
ONLINE VIDEO ARCHIVE

r botanists know that
ants than necessary,
ently than 'those pink
to colors; we only have
hues and tones, relative
hing that appears in
e limited: white, yellow,
e, turquoise, green,
that's it."

FONT VARIATIONS
TYPEFACE VARIATIONS FOR *RECIPES FOR CONNECTING*

The logo for the project *Recipes for Connecting* was created in different versions. For the Berlin edition, which was also used at Index Art Book Fair in Mexico City, the choice was the typeface Anthony by Sun Young Oh, created from simple straight lines. The text was twisted in various ways so that the letters could touch and connect. Some variations of these twisted lines were used throughout the project, including the different cover designs and announcements.

Barcelona's version used the typeface Sisters by Laura Meseguer, where different shapes and weights of the stencil font connected to form a lively variety of letter shapes.

RECIPES FOR CONNECTING, A-Z COLLECTIVE, 2023

RECIPES FOR CONNECTING

FORMING A COLLECTIVE
PREPARATORY WORKSHOPS FOR THE *A–Z COLLECTIVE*

Before the *A—Z Collective* came into existence, three workshops took place as open gatherings for anyone interested in learning the tools and methods related to collective working and community building. An average of 20+ participants in each round shared their practices in the creative industry, and their desire to explore community experiences.

The first workshop, *What If … Explosion*, focused on collecting communal desires, imaginations, and ideation expertise. The second workshop, *Structures and Tools*, explored experiences on the theory and practice of collective decision-making, decentralized organizational structures, and related concepts. The last session, *Focus: Shape Making*, took inspiration from the mindset of the *Sociocracy 3.0* platform, allowing participants to move from the abstract to the concrete in decentralized calls to action.

This strategy of multidisciplinary gatherings resulted in the final group of people interested in participating in the *A—Z Collective*, formed entirely organically and all committed to working together for an entire year.

Main facilitators: Emily Smith is a designer and educator based in Berlin who is focused on embodied practices and facilitating community building. Jocelyn Ames is a social change facilitator and mediator who supports changemakers to foster belonging, mutual aid, and real-world impact.

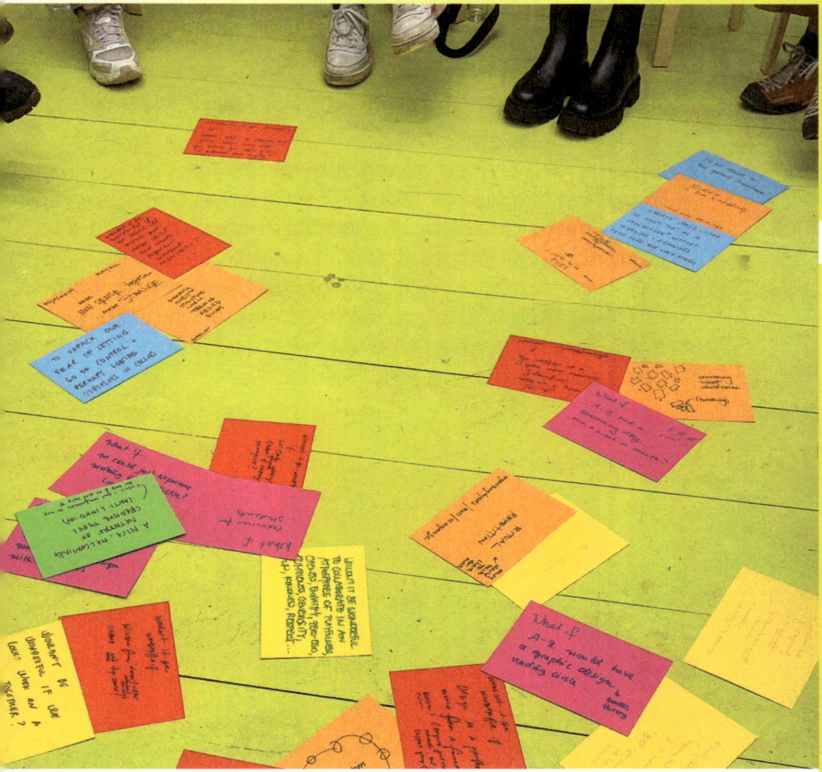

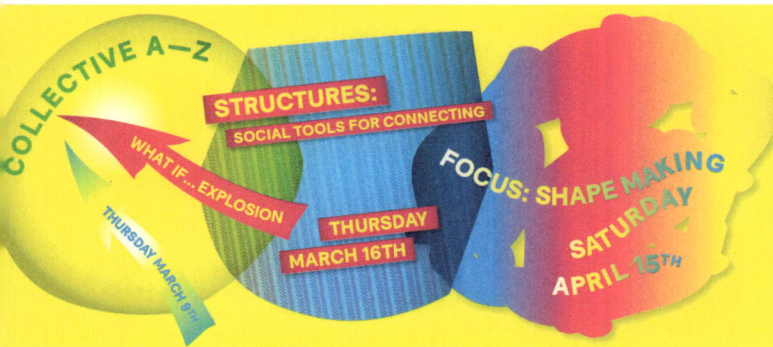

FREEDOM ...
ARTWORK BY CHRISTINE HILL

This hand-lettered artwork by artist Christine Hill hangs on the wall of the A—Z kitchen. A translation of a famous quote by the revolutionary thinker Rosa Luxemburg aligns itself with the core values of A—Z, as a daily reminder not only of the democratic value of freedom and the strength of women in history but also of the need to always listen and be open to embracing different viewpoints.

> **FREEDOM** Is always and Exclusively **FREEDOM** For the one who thinks **DIFFERENTLY**
>
> Rosa Luxemburg

FUTURE VS. PAST
TALK BY MARK VAN WAGENINGEN AT THE *NOVO TYPO OFFGRID BERLIN* EXHIBITION

"I have always been [...] digital because we a[...] century, but I am als[o ...] style, the basic tech[...] if I want to understa[nd ...] or what the future w[ill ...] about the past."

MARK VAN WAGENINGEN
NOVO TYPO OFFGRID BERLIN
NOVO TYPO OFFGRID
ONLINE VIDEO ARCHIVE

two paths: one is
living in the 21st
nterested in the old
ques. I know that
what is going on
be, I have to know

GRAPHIC.DESIGNERS. COLLECTORS.
GROUP EXHIBITION

Graphic.Designers.Collectors. was an exhibition conceived as a giant cabinet of collections and curiosities, where over 30 invited graphic designers presented samples of their collectibles—from poster stamps to toilet paper, fake documents, and queer fanzines.

Through many interesting, funny, and unique ideas of personal collections and their stories, the initiative was inspired by investigating whether, why, and how Graphic Design creations are perceived as art and collectibles. The exhibited objects also offered insights into the designers' work, as the collections assumed inspiration or a conceptual base for their practices. Ultimately, it was up to visitors to relate items to their collectors and their design styles.

The exhibition featured collections from: Andrea Tinnes, Anja Lutz, Anky Brandt, Anna Berkenbusch, Barbara Dechant, Bernard Stein, Franziska Morlok, Fraser Muggeridge, Hala Al Afsaa, Heinrich Müller, Henning Wagenbreth, Isabel Naegele, Jason Grant, Jens Müller, Juli Gudehus, Katharina Sussek, Kinda Ghannoum, Lucienne Roberts, Margaret Warzecha, Markus Etienne, Mark van Wageningen, Na Kim, Niklaus Troxler, Niko Courtelis, Oliver Klimpel, Patrick Thomas, Pauline Clancy, Peter Nencini, Philippe Delangle, Rob Keller, Ronny Duquenne, Sally Alassafen, Sara De Bondt, Sara Kaaman, Sarah Boris, Sarah Illenberger, Sonja Knecht, Sven Völker, and Szymon Stemplewski.

COLLECTING GRAPHIC DESIGN
COLLECTING VISITORS
DO YOU COLLECT GRAPHIC DESIGN?
TAKEAWAY GRAPHIC DESIGN
ONLINE VIDEO ARCHIVE

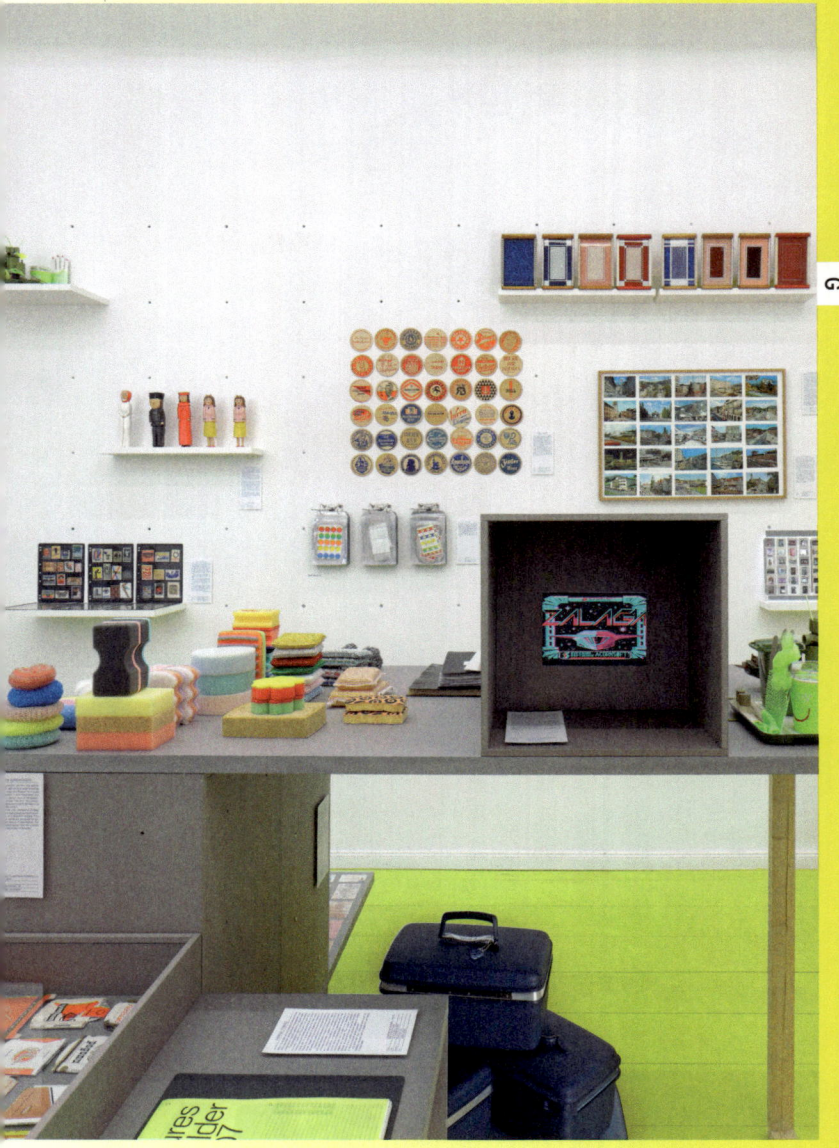

GRAPHIC.DESIGNERS.COLLECTORS.

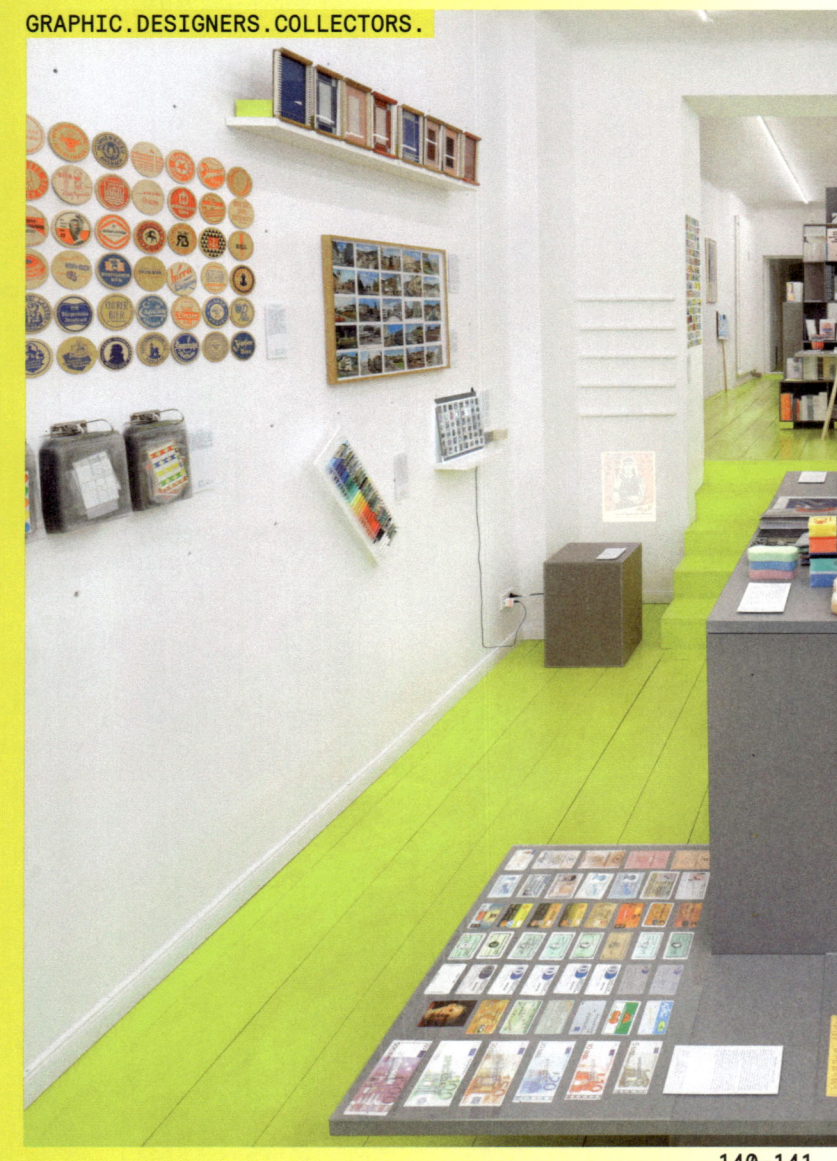

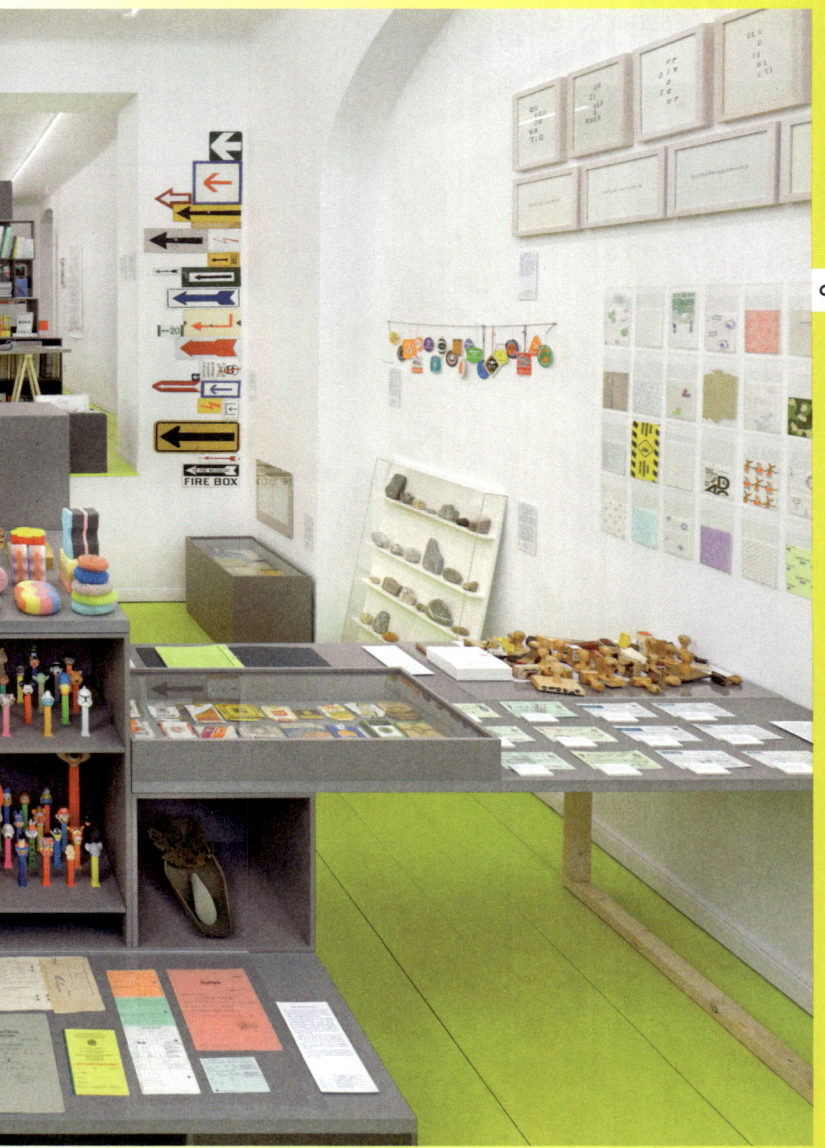

GRAPHIC.DESIGNERS.COLLECTORS.

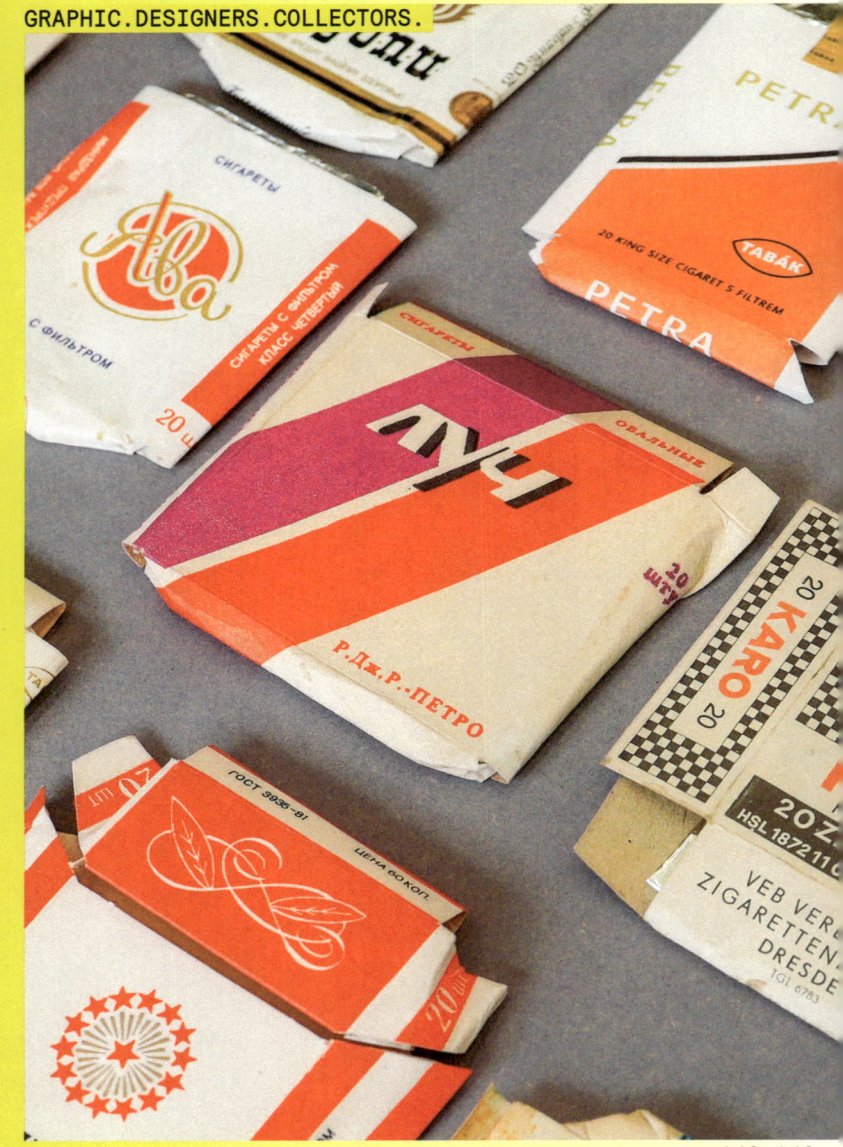

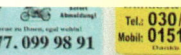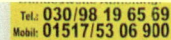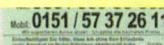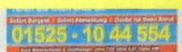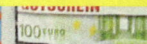
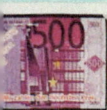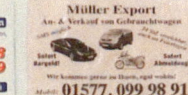
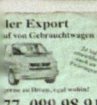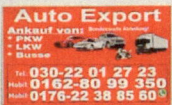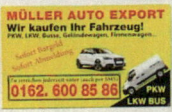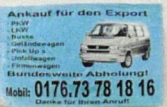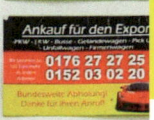
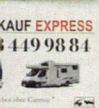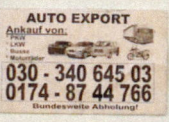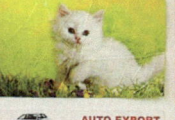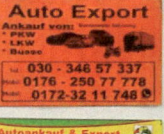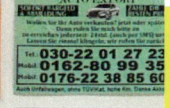
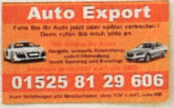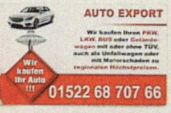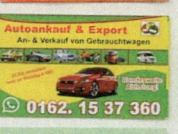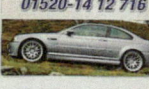
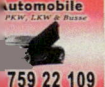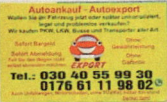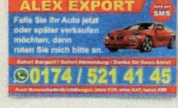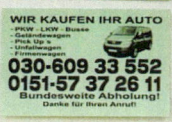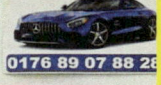
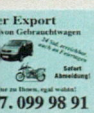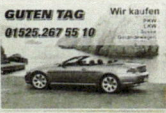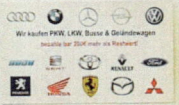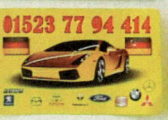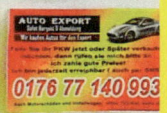
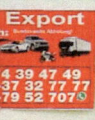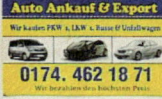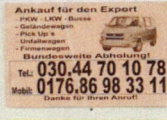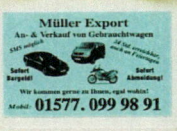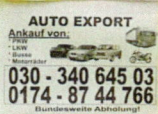
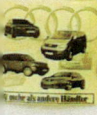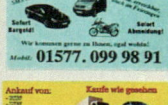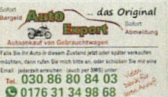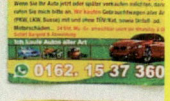
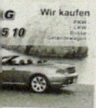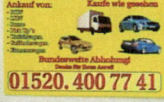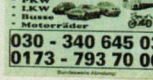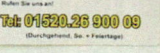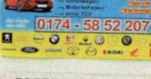

GRAPHIC.DESIGNERS.COLLECTORS.

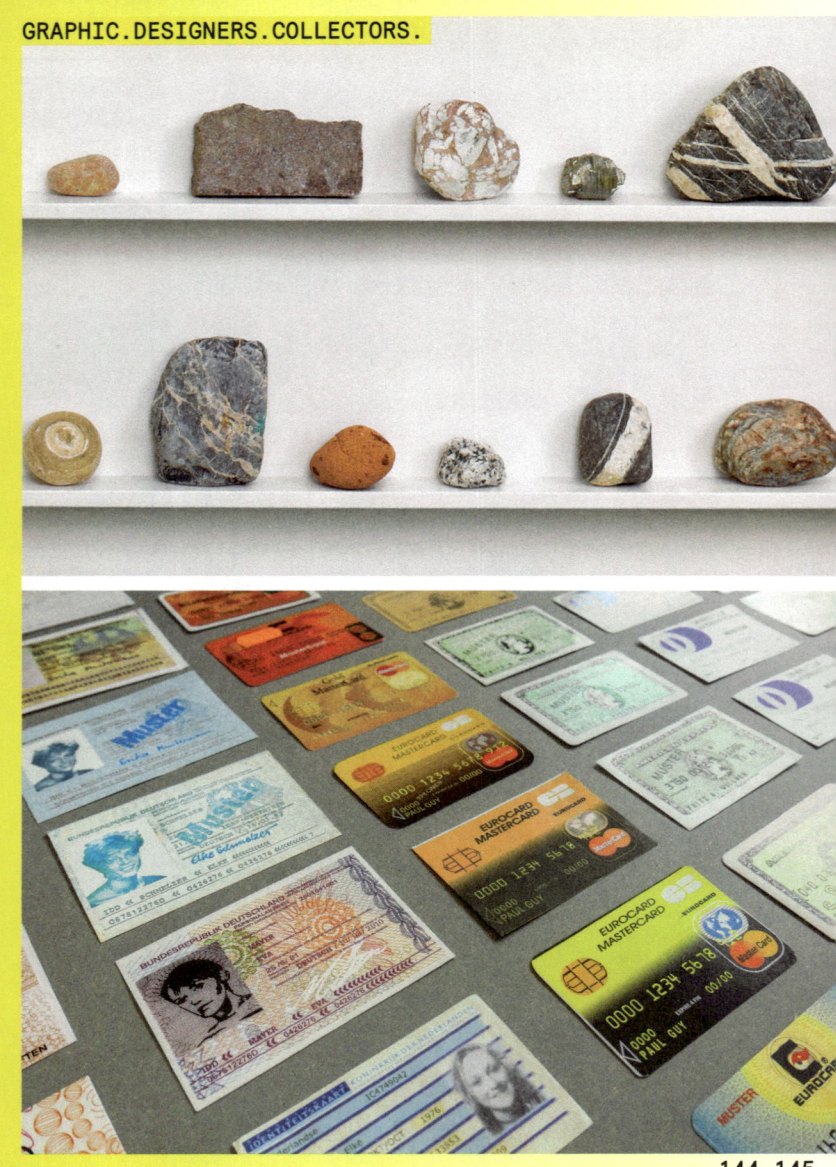

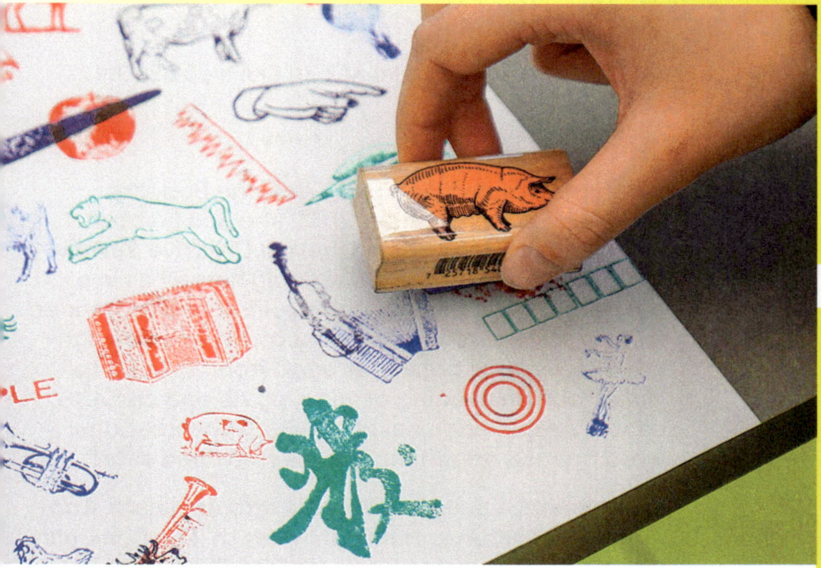

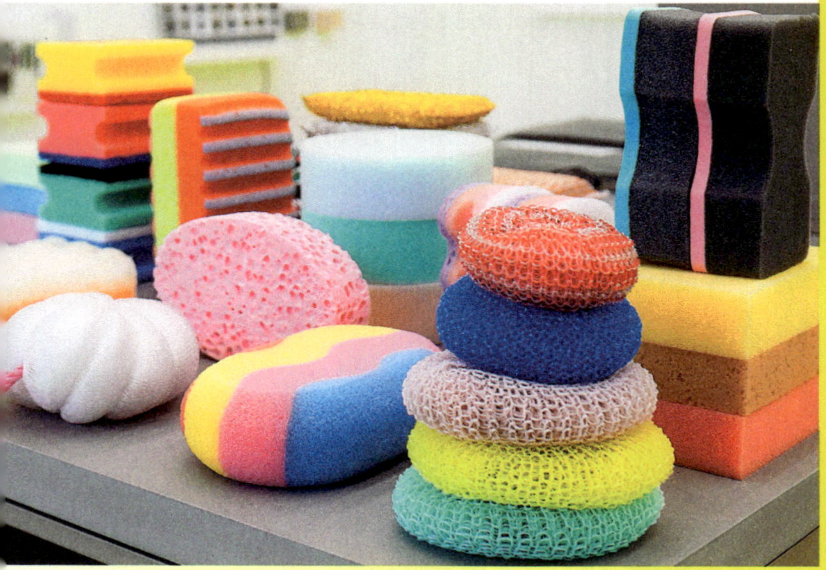

HELLO YOU!
GROUP CONVERSATION ABOUT WOMEN AND AGE IN GRAPHIC DESIGN,
LED BY LUCIENNE ROBERTS

When the graphic designer Lucienne Roberts visited A—Z in November 2021, she had just been interviewed by the design journal *Creative Review* for an issue about age. Describing herself as in a "perpetual midlife crisis", she decided to add 'gender' to 'age' and invited a small group of women designers of several nationalities aged from 22 to 60 to *Hello You!*, an evening of wine, pizza, and conversation. As Lucienne describes it, "Conversations were honest, enriching, empowering, and safe."

Participants: Lucienne Roberts with Anja Lutz, Ann Richter, Constanze Hein, Emily Smith, Eva Dumoulin, Indre Klimaite, Janine Sack, Na Kim, Sibylle Schlaich, Stefanie Rau, and Svenja Prigge.

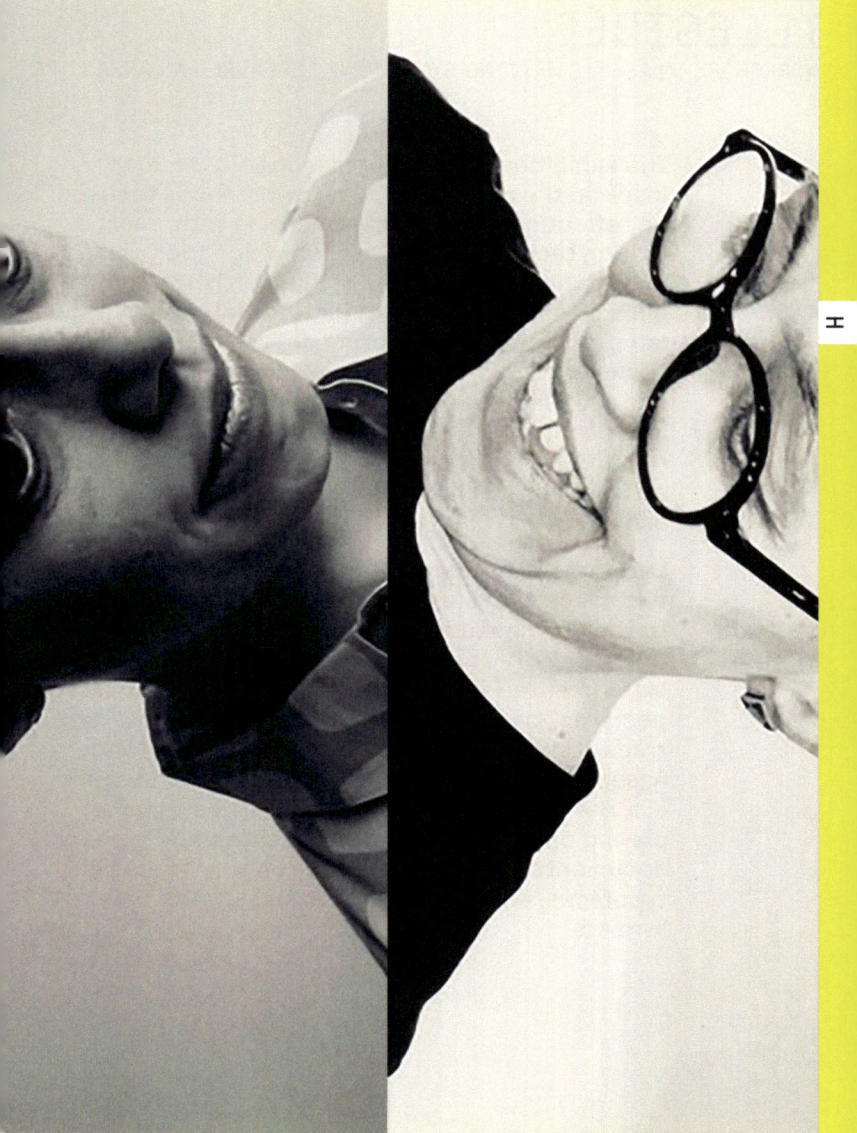

ILLEGIBLE
WORKSHOPS ON ASEMIC WRITING BY ANTOINE LEFEBVRE AND ANJA LUTZ

The exhibition *Mirtha Dermisache: To Be Read* inspired the realization of two workshops focused on reflecting on, and experimenting with, asemic writing techniques. In the first, which took place during the exhibition, the artist, publisher, and curator Antoine Lefebvre (antoine lefebvre editions) led participants in exploring different artistic techniques to create illegible scripts and typefaces, and produce together an asemic newspaper with a layout inspired by Mirtha Dermisache's *Diario N°1 Año 1* and her page work in the catalog *Arte de Sistemas* (1971), both of which featured in the exhibition.

Later on, A—Z founder Anja Lutz offered a related two-week workshop introducing asemic writing to the design students of Burg Giebichenstein University of Art and Design in Halle. Participants experimented with different forms of writing gestures, creating letters from found objects, and translating these experiments into asemic fonts. Assuming the role of editors, writers, and designers, the students created an asemic newspaper, playing on typical formats, structures, and types of documents to communicate by only using illegible typefaces, and the structures and layouts they formed.

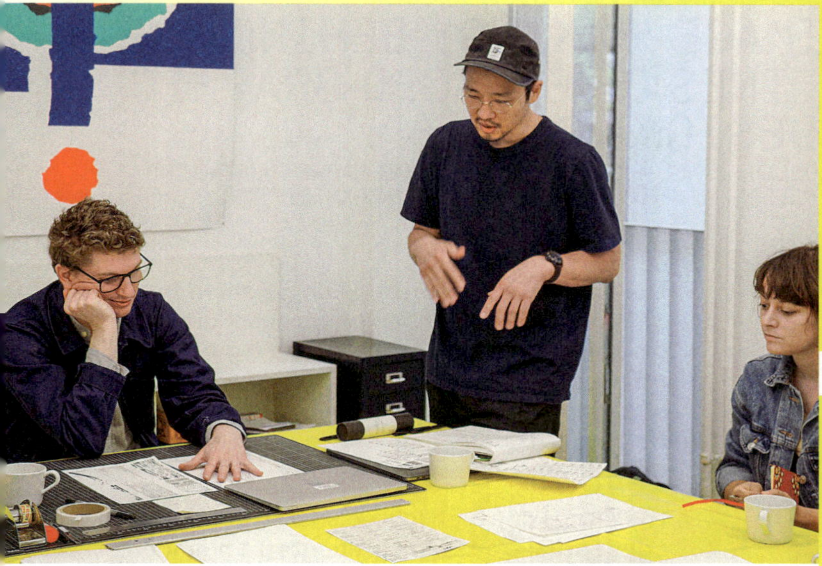

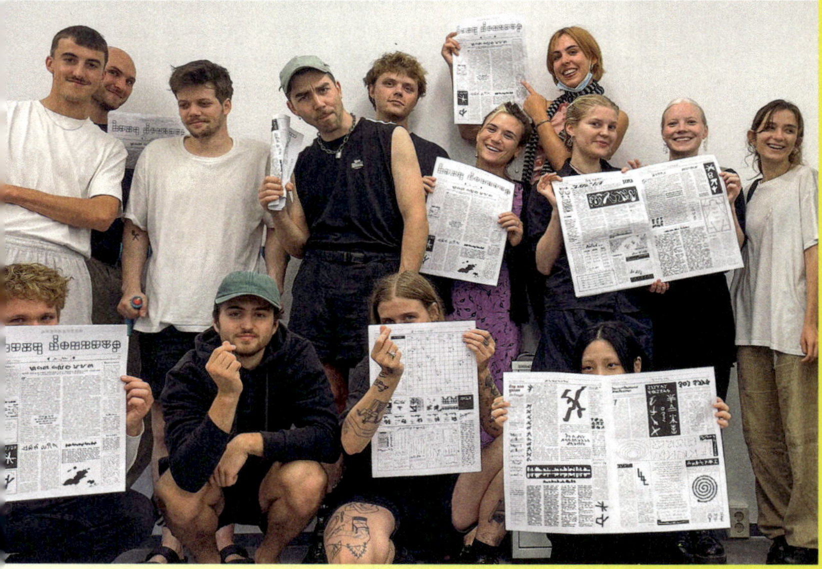

I

IMAGE-MAKING: BEHIND THE LINES OF ENGAGED GRAPHIC DESIGN

ONLINE PANEL MODERATED BY SOUKEINA HACHEM DURING THE
REVEALING » RECORDING » REFLECTING EXHIBITION

The online panel *Image-Making: Behind the Lines of Engaged Graphic Design* was part of series of discussions as part of the *Revealing » Recording » Reflecting* exhibition. It approached the social engagement of women from the SWANA region with their context, and their stories in their respective cultural and national contexts.

The discussion highlighted shared aesthetic and conceptual traits, and presented a nuanced diversity of voices and concerns, unpacking the fundamentally 'human' face of design as a way to empower women and build bridges across different generations of women from the region.

The panel was moderated by Soukeina Hachem, a designer whose work in design and culture aims to create social and systems change. She is the founder of SHAPE, a consulting agency with a sustainability and social approach, and also the initiator of the biennale Casablanca Design Week in 2017 and 2019.

Guest panelists: Lina Ghaibeh, comic and animation artist and Associate Professor at the American University of Beirut; Sara Rizkallah, Assistant Professor at the University of Prince Edwards Islands, Canada; and Tulip Hazbar, a graphic designer, illustrator, and visual artist based in UAE.

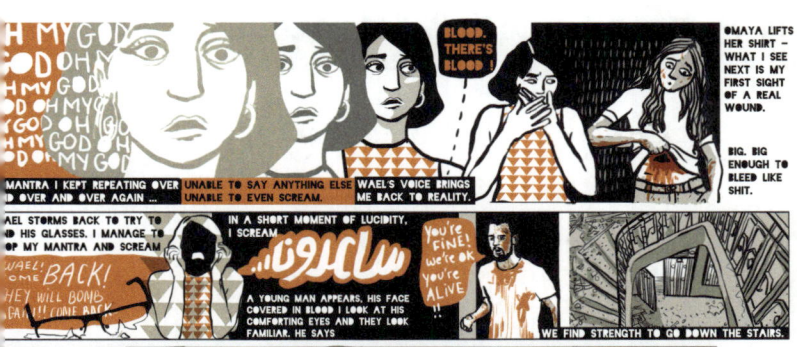
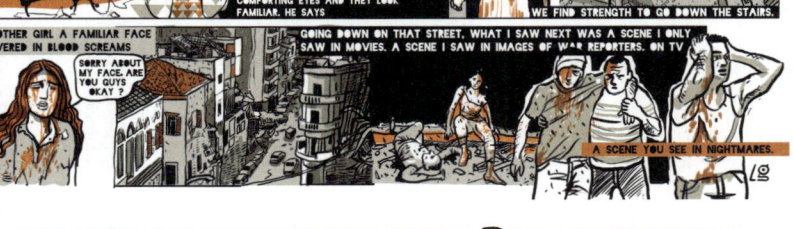

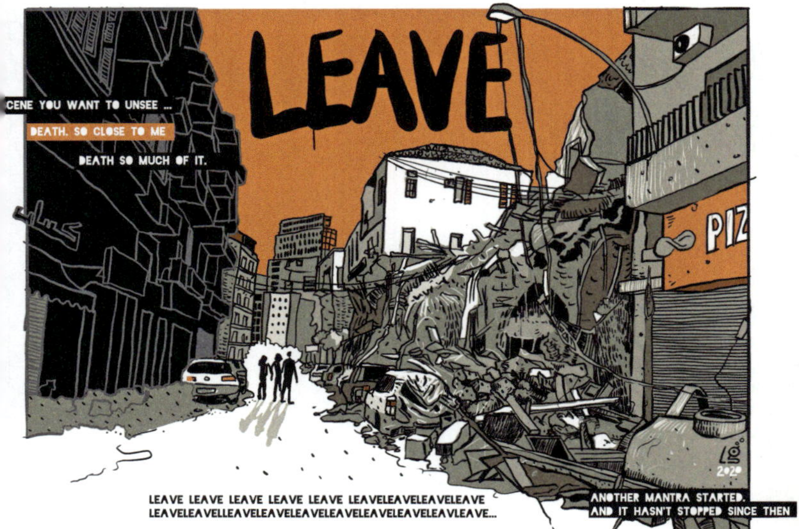

IN A POST-GROWTH WORLD

TALK BY LUCIENNE ROBERTS AT THE *PERHAPS IT'S NOT YOU, IT'S ME.* EXHIBITION

"It seems to me that a lot
about buying or selling g
necessarily needed so ar
So the question is: in a p
might the role of design
mean for designers? The
questions. I don't have t
and hard about the ques

LUCIENNE ROBERTS
PERHAPS IT'S NOT YOU, IT'S ME.
ONLINE VIDEO ARCHIVE

graphic design is
ls, goods that aren't
hen randomly discarded.
-growth world, what
And what does that
are really difficult
nswers but I think long
ns nonetheless."

INDEPENDENCE VERSUS INSTITUTION

EXCERPT FROM A CONVERSATION BETWEEN FREEK LOMME AND ANJA LUTZ

FREEK: There are many artist-run spaces as well as public institutions, not to mention a growing number of practice-based initiatives run by individuals with various public missions. What would you say differentiates A—Z from them? I am also considering how such an initiative validates itself and sustains itself financially.

ANJA: Well, there are not many places that focus on Graphic Design in the same transdisciplinary way as we do. In my experience, non-applied Graphic Design tends to be overlooked, as do many transdisciplinary initiatives. In contrast, I believe that this is a vital area, even in a broader philosophical sense, where we need to collaborate and exchange knowledge across disciplines to address the challenges we face. Regarding finances, we have often attempted to secure structural support for the space but, to date, we have received only a small research grant from the Berlin Senate. I would say the reason for this is precisely the fact that A—Z does not fit the usual categories, and also because, at least in Germany, public funding does not consider Graphic Design a cultural or artistic discipline worthy of support. So, the question remains, "How does one validate what a space like A—Z offers?" I do believe it has an impact, and the positive international resonance and recognition we receive have been proof of that. I also believe in the impact that culture has on society on much deeper levels, prompting and allowing us to develop a broader and more critical understanding—these are tools for supporting our collective being, connecting, and improving lives, which I believe all cultural initiatives can contribute to.

This touches heavily on notions of artistic necessity and autonomous integrity, which for me is based on trust and synergy in a productive, open dynamic, yet where basic practical and financial responsibilities exist. Perhaps staying on the margins, not being heavily institutionalized, also brings a particular managerial independence and more horizontality, which aligns with A—Z's principles?

I find the independence vital, also in the sense of 'vitality', as it allows spontaneity, quick decisions, and unexpected turns in the program. But regardless of independence, there is indeed a fundamental question of responsibilities and who has the power of decision. I can illustrate this with one situation: We used to have a loose verbal agreement with exhibiting designers on who would do what, and I never felt the need to formalize it as I always trusted we could get together and negotiate. With one designer, there were a couple of minor misunderstandings but nothing we could not resolve. Still, our level of informality clearly did not work for them and they preferred to have a written agreement. While that experience led me to develop a comprehensive guideline on how we work at A—Z to share with future exhibitors, I still do not go as far as establishing contracts and institutionalized structures. I want to keep things open and dynamic. However, there is always the danger of dominance and dependency, as the power of decision-making remains with me. I want to believe that I do not abuse the power inherent in this non-formalized structure, and that I remain aware of it.

INFLUENCES: A LEXICON OF CONTEMPORARY GRAPHIC DESIGN

BOOK BY ANJA LUTZ AND ANNA GERBER

Influences: A Lexicon of Contemporary Graphic Design dives deep into the names, ideas, and things that inspire, provoke, and inform the work and creative methods of 200 graphic designers worldwide. Published almost 20 years ago, the book can be seen as a foundational initiative that reflects on Graphic Design, which influenced A—Z curatorial perspectives. The publication also features some designers later exhibiting at the space, such as Andrea Tinnes, Inkahoots, and Alex Jordan, as well as some contributors of the —∞ section of the present book, such as Joseph Foo, April Greiman, and Rebeca Méndez.

Despite the lexicon format, it presents a highly personal and subjective perspective in which entries were compiled and organized to reach the root of each designer's passion, motivation, and creative imagination. From Charles and Ray Eames to John Cage, teaching to yawning, money to plumbing, Frank Zappa to Gandhi, Gridnik to kidney stones, the references provide a unique insight into contemporary Graphic Design practice at the birth of the 21st century. A—Z founder Anja Lutz conceived and designed the publication in collaboration with London-based graphic designer and writer Anna Gerber.

Influences: A Lexicon of Contemporary Graphic Design, Anja Lutz and Anna Gerber, Die Gestalten Verlag, 2006. 304 pages, 170 x 240 mm, hardcover, English.

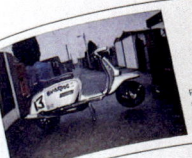

Rory Wood
Lambretta GP 225,
owned and photographed by Wood.

newspapers, during which time he groomed himself to become a pioneering figure in the New Journalism movement. Wolfe defined this style of literary journalism with → books like The Kandy-Kolored Tangerine-Flake Streamline Baby (1965) and The Electric Kool-Aid Acid Test (1968), before editing the anthology New Journalism in 1973. In 1987, Wolfe published his first novel, The Bonfire Of The Vanities. "Inspirational for his astute observations of popular culture and the way in which he is able to communicate these through his novels and short story collections." TEAL TRIGGS

WOMEN GRAPHIC DESIGNERS

"I am part of quite a female graphic designers group. I like and → love women, maybe it's due to the possibility that I have some female characteristics, just as a lot of women have quite macho attitudes. What I can say is that most of the women I have worked with were more extreme, less pragmatic than most of my male collaborators. Also female designers seem to develop an 'it's my baby' kind of attitude to their creations whereas the men would rather create something to show that they are the best in → graphic design (an Olympic Games attitude). But really that's a personal observation and i swear there is no difference between the woman who is obsessed with graphic design and her male counterpart. Could they live together? My stupid answer is: it depends." ALEX JORDAN

WOMEN IN PUNK

"I would expect a number of British designers of a certain age to pick → Punk as a seminal influence. But I would particularly like to celebrate the role that women in Punk played in encouraging me to make my own decisions, cut my hair and go to art college. Gaye Advert, Fay Fife, Poly Styrene, Pauline Penetration, Siouxsie Sioux, The Raincoats, The Slits, Linder Sterling et al. – Thank you." SIÂN COOK

WOOD PAINTING IN THE NIJO CASTLE

The Nijo Castle in Kyoto was built in 1603 by Tokugawa Ieyasu, one of Japan's most powerful shoguns. The castle was built to guard the city's imperial possessions and residences and designed to resemble an Imperial Kyoto Palace. The main building, Ninomaru Palace, has thirty three rooms and approximately eight hundred tatami mats. Today, the castle is filled with many fine works of → art, including many delicate wood carvings and paintings by the Kano School on sliding doors throughout the → space. "For the strong use of empty → space which becomes so present you can literally → travel into its emptiness. This is what I really want to achieve, I keep trying but I always put too much." KATYA BONNENFANT

WOOD, RORY

"Rory Wood, Lambretta enthusiast, Goole, East → Yorkshire. I've known Rory since I was about eight years old. What's great about him is his commitment to the Lambretta GP range, he is obsessed by them. Bertone – who also designed Ferrari's and Lamborghini's – designed the GP, and they're incredibly beautiful scooters. Rory was three years above me at school (and he still is), so when I visit him I'm still the 'youngster', this involves being sent to the chip shop and listening to his sermons about the downside of fitting a hydraulic front disc brake to a Lambretta. This is Rory's GP, 'Blackdog II', which I like to think of as being in a great tradition of 'The Yorkshire Lambretta'." SCOTT KING

WOODMAN, MARION

Marion Woodman (b. 1928) is a Jungian analyst base in Toronto. Woodman is also a → teacher, workshop leader and the author of many → books including diction To Perfection: The Owl Was A Baker's Dau ter: Obesity, Anorexia Nervosa And The Represse Feminine (1980) and Addiction To Perfection: T Unravished Bride (1982). A graduate of the C.G Institute in Zurich, Switzerland, Woodman als the BodySoul Rhythms Intensives with colle Hamilton and Ann Skinner, to create an op to study the inter-relatedness of body and "She saved → my life." REBECA MÉNDEZ

INITIATIVES
SPACES FOR UNCONVENTIONAL GRAPHIC DESIGN

A—Z is not alone in creating a fruitful environment in which to think about and practice diverse perspectives on Graphic Design. Here is a short, non-comprehensive list of other places that are also engaged in similar practices related to visual culture, and whom A—Z deeply appreciates:

Center for Visual Arts, Berlin
Colorama, Berlin
einBuch.haus, Berlin
ENTER ENTER, Amsterdam
Format Club, Berlin
Frisk Gallery, Portland
Futuress, online
Offprint
Onomatopee, Eindhoven
Miriam Gallery, Brooklyn
Page Not Found, The Hague
Parco Gallery, Milan
People's Graphic Design Archive, online
Printed Matter, New York
PrintRoom, Rotterdam
WirWir, Berlin
…

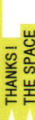

THANKS !
THE SPACE

INKAHOOTS
EXHIBITED COLLECTIVE

Inkahoots is a 'dissident' Australian design studio focusing on creating democratic spaces for productive social resistance and public dialogue. They collaborate locally and internationally on projects of all sizes across various media, specializing in exploratory design, typography, identity, and the creative integration of physical and digital experiences. Inkahoots makes evocative images, online platforms, and immersive installations, which are driven by user-generated content that emphasizes criticality, wonder, accessibility, and inclusion. Some of Inkahoots' work is autonomous advocacy and activism, while other projects are with selected clients. Born as a community access screenprinting studio/arts collective, Inkahoots continues to work for social change through adventurous visual communication.

- BUCHSTABENMUSEUM
- KERNING
- KINDERHYMNE
- NEW ANTHEMS VI – EINE NEUE HYMNE FÜR DEUTSCHLAND
- POST BRANDING MANIFESTO
- UNITY AND JUSTICE AND ...

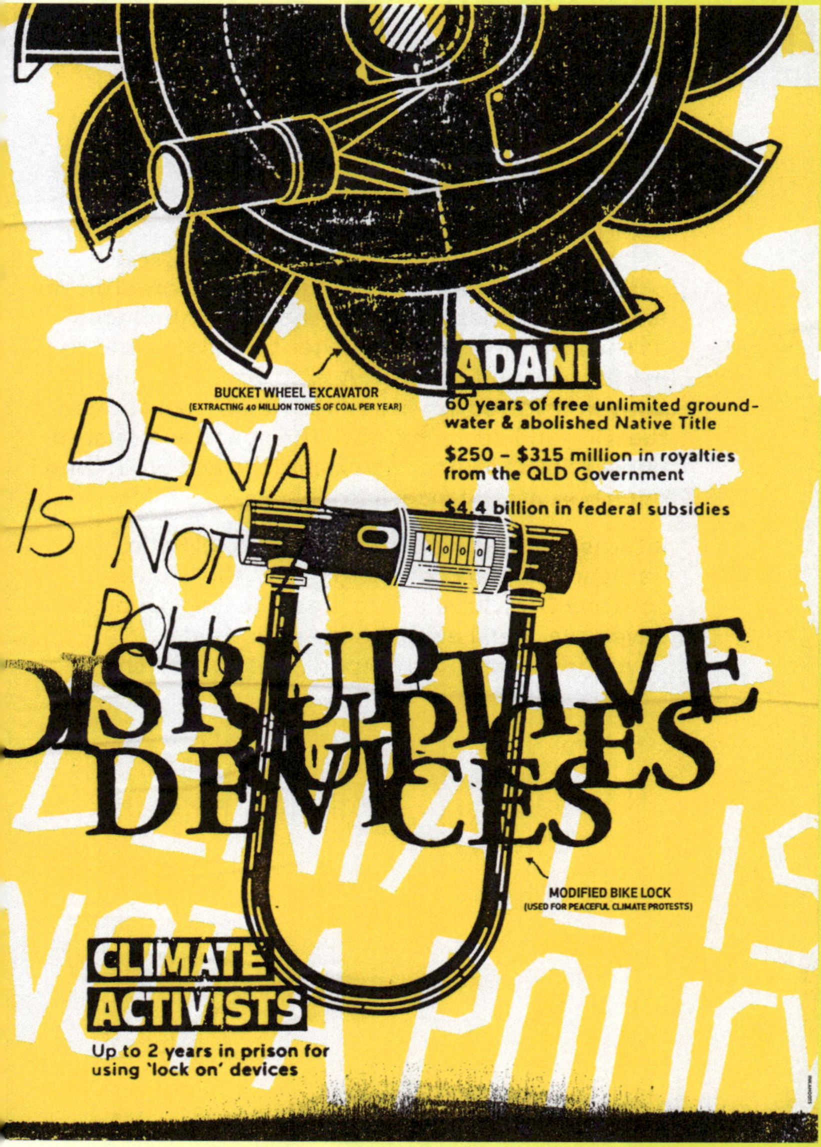

BUCKET WHEEL EXCAVATOR
(EXTRACTING 40 MILLION TONES OF COAL PER YEAR)

ADANI

60 years of free unlimited groundwater & abolished Native Title

$250 – $315 million in royalties from the QLD Government

$4.4 billion in federal subsidies

DISRUPTIVE DEVICES

MODIFIED BIKE LOCK
(USED FOR PEACEFUL CLIMATE PROTESTS)

CLIMATE ACTIVISTS

Up to 2 years in prison for using 'lock on' devices

DENIAL IS NOT POLICY

INTERNS
INTERNSHIP EXPERIENCE AT A–Z

A place like A—Z would not be possible without the help of wonderful and engaged interns. For such a highly collaboration-oriented space, the strategy of having two interns at a time, following a tip shared by designer Hella Jongerius, has created an environment that facilitates sharing experiences as the interns have each other to consult, and to ask for help and support. A—Z interns have been actively involved in various activities, from conceptualizing and designing both the space and related publications to installing exhibitions and organizing openings, attendance, and welcoming guests.

Interns to date: Eva Dumoulin, Ezequiel Hyon, Fernanda de la Mora, Franzi Bauer, Giulia Siviero, Johanna Olm, Juliana Toro, Lisa Böckling, Liudmila Savelyeva, Mari Leach, Nour Asmar, Olena Hryhorieva, Sarah Schümperli, and So Jin Park.

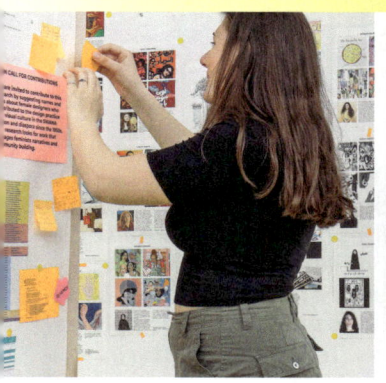
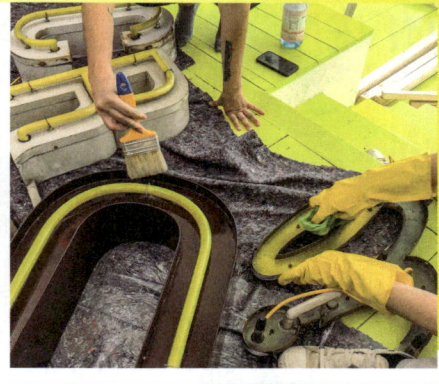
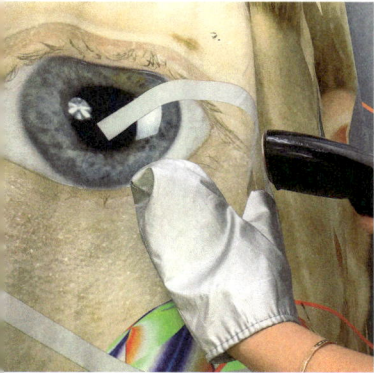
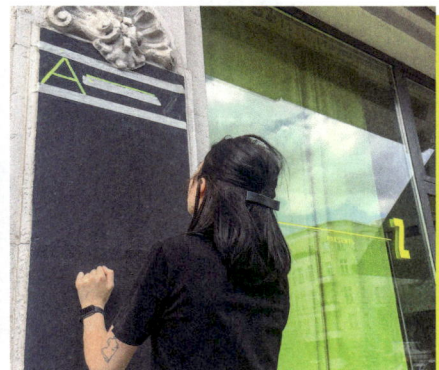
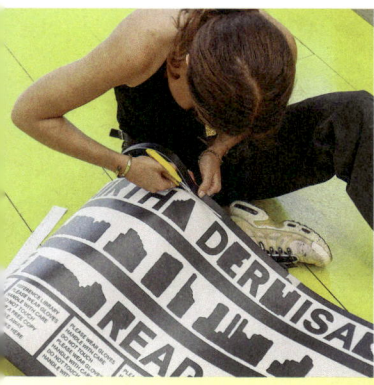
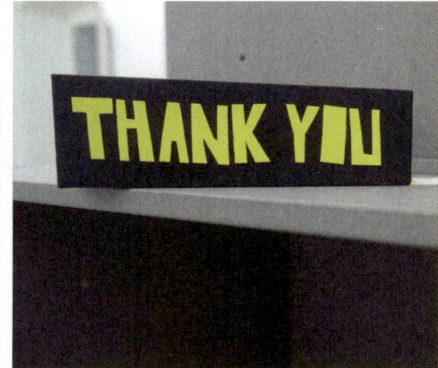

INVENTAR COLLECTION
TYPEFACE BY ANDREA TINNES

Inventar Collection is a typeface by Andrea Tinnes. Created in all caps, it opens an extensive repertoire of typographic possibilities. It includes three serif styles, three sans serif variants with different widths and alternative glyphs, and distinctive back-slanted italics. The font was used in Tinnes's prints for the *Library of Shapes, Text and Structures* exhibition, and for the A—Z presentation showreel.

ANDREA TINNES
LIBRARY OF SHAPES TEXTS AND STRUCTURES
PERSONAL DESIGN LIBRARY
RESEARCH METHODS

INVENTAR
CAPS ONLY
HEADLINE
TYPEFACE
WITH
3 WIDTHS &
3 SANS/SERIF
VERSIONS

INVERSE – A YEARLY RITUAL
COUNTER SESSION #2 **BY FLORIAN DOMBOIS**

The second *Counter Session* featured the artist Florian Dombois, who shared his explorations on sound, silence, and time with the public. The curious moment of October, when summer time comes to an end, and all publicly displayed clocks stand still between the impossible timeframe of 3am and 3am, is the artistic space for his sound, physical, and philosophical experimentations, encapsulated in several musical intros scored to represent that hour. In collaboration with several musicians, the yearly compositions are released on vinyl records, which Dombois presented during his talk. Audience members who had brought a clock to the event could also learn with Dombois how to tweak their devices to work backward.

Florian Dombois is an artist and researcher focused on questions about wind, time, labilities, and tectonic activity. His artistic practice includes various media, and repetitively articulates happenings and sound installations. He is a Transdisciplinary Professor at the Department of Cultural Analysis and Mediation at Zurich University of the Arts.

COUNTER SESSIONS
CYBERFEMINISM INDEX
EVER SINCE THE DAYS OF MRS. GUTENBERG ...
FAMILY TREES & SOUND CLOUDS
YOU NEVER GIVE UP?
ONLINE VIDEO ARCHIVE

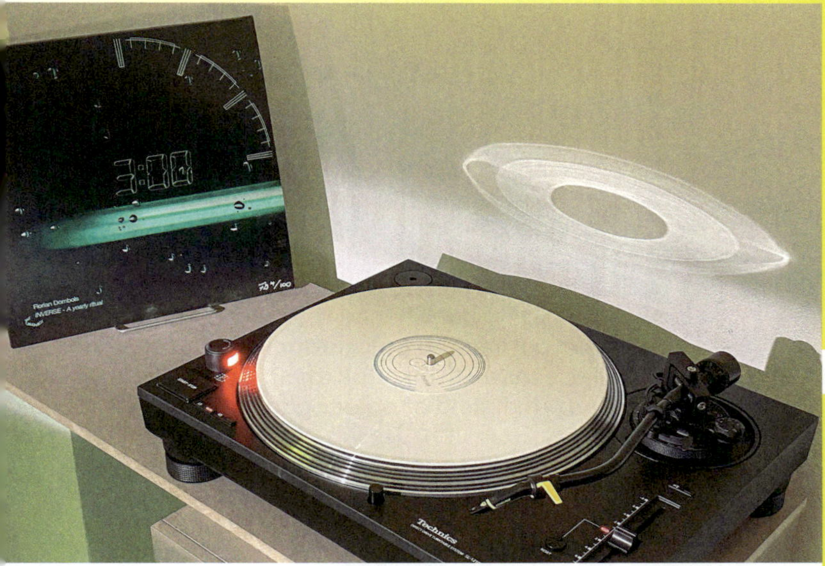

I

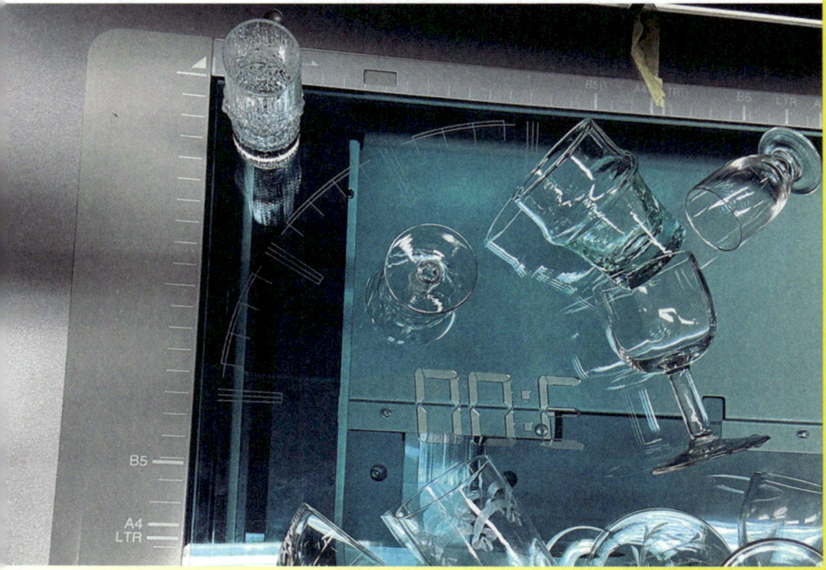

IS THIS A BOOK?!
STUDENT WORKSHOP AT THE UNIVERSITY OF ART AND DESIGN HALLE

The workshop *Is This a Book?!* was offered by A—Z founder Anja Lutz to the students of Communication Design at the Burg Giebichenstein University of Art and Design Halle. This prompted the students to find inspiration in the A—Z approach of experimental Graphic Design, and to translate it into an equally experimental publication format to reflect on the essence of the book itself. Considerations included: What kind of object could a book be? What materiality could it have? What is the concept? What content does it provide? How can we use it and interact with it? Or how can such a book transcend itself and inspire further engagement?

The results were unique books created by each student as original publications, including: an interactive publication with material to connect and explore as a wall-filling toolkit; a publication where playlists made for each A—Z exhibition can be read as concrete poetry; and a publication made of interactive promptings on a picnic blanket.

Participating students: Alexandra Vögtle, Hyeona Uhm, Jule Eretier, Lioba Wachtel, Luisa Kaiser, Nikola Iljučoková, and Paula Schumacher.

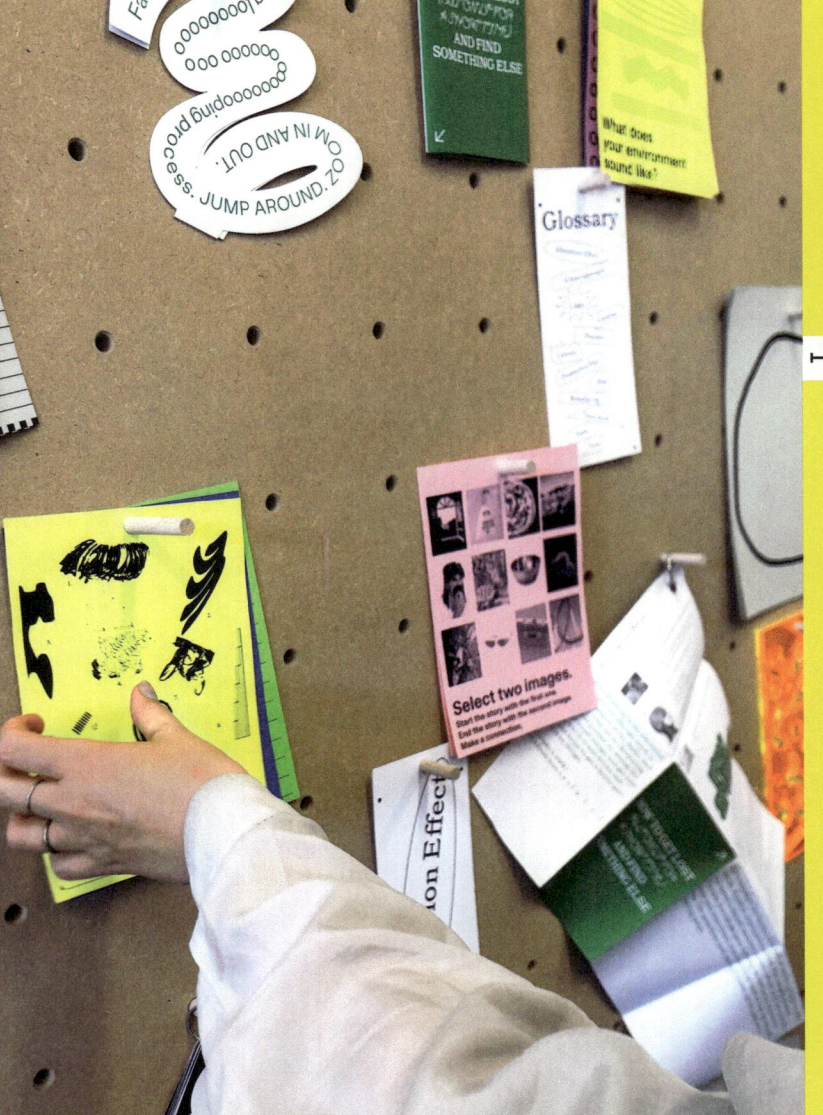

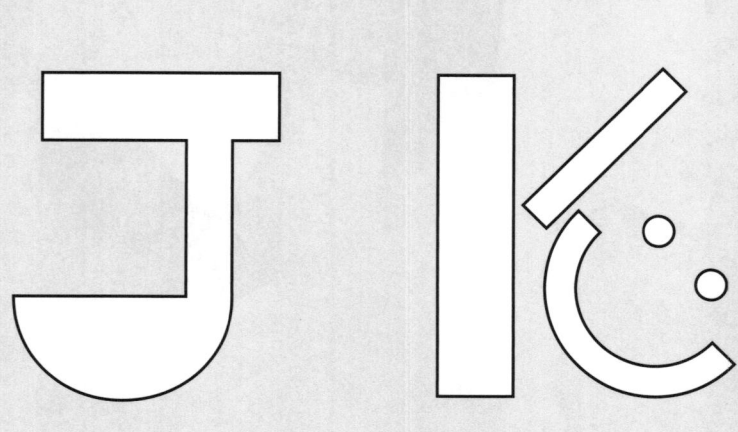

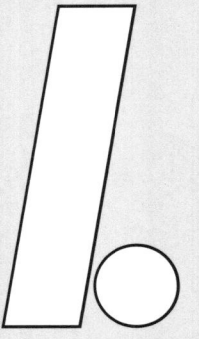
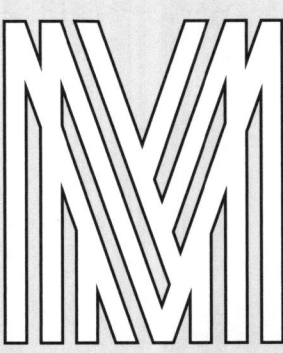

JAZZ AND DESIGN
TALK BY NIKLAUS TROXLER AT THE *TAPE WORKS* EXHIBITION

"*In jazz, I am fa[scinated by]
everything tha[t interests]
me in design: r[hythm,]
composition, i[mprovisation,]
independence[...]*

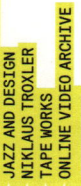

JAZZ AND DESIGN
NIKLAUS TROXLER
TAPE WORKS
ONLINE VIDEO ARCHIVE

cinated by *also interests* *ythm, timbre,* *provisation,* *variety."*

KERNING

TRANSPORTING THE LETTERS FOR THE *NEW ANTHEMS VI (BERLIN)* EXHIBITION

For the Inkahoots interactive typographic installation *New Anthems VI (Berlin)*, A—Z decided to use historic letters and signs from both former East and West Germany, selected from the archives of Buchstabenmuseum in Berlin. They were used to create the prompt "Einigkeit und Recht und ___ für ___" (Unity and justice and ___ for ___) completed by the public during the exhibition.

Transporting the heavy and precious material was a delicate mission. They could all fit in the trunk of a car thanks to the designer's ability to handle the required 'kerning'. The letters originally belonged to commercial establishments such as Rosenthal Porzellan, Cafe Konditorei Richter, the Berliner Metallhütten und Halbwerkzeug factory, and even a pharmacy.

The letters N and D could not be found in the correct size in the museum collection, prompting designer Jason Grant to create them with Styrofoam and apply an aging technique using some dirt from the street. The trick went unnoticed by visitors, and the two fake vintage letters are now part of the museum's official collection.

BUCHSTABENMUSEUM
INKAHOOTS
KINDERHYMNE
UNITY AND JUSTICE AND …
NEW ANTHEMS VI – EINE NEUE HYMNE FÜR DEUTSCHLAND
TRANSPORTATION

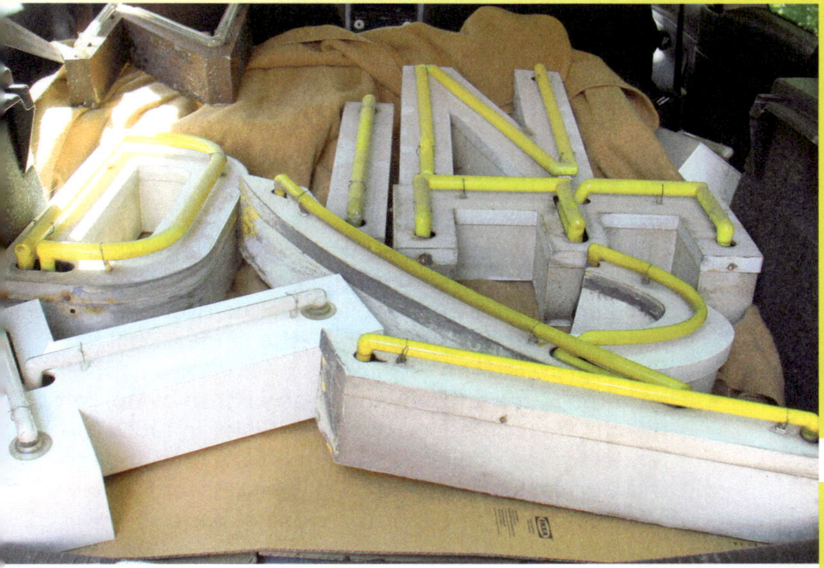

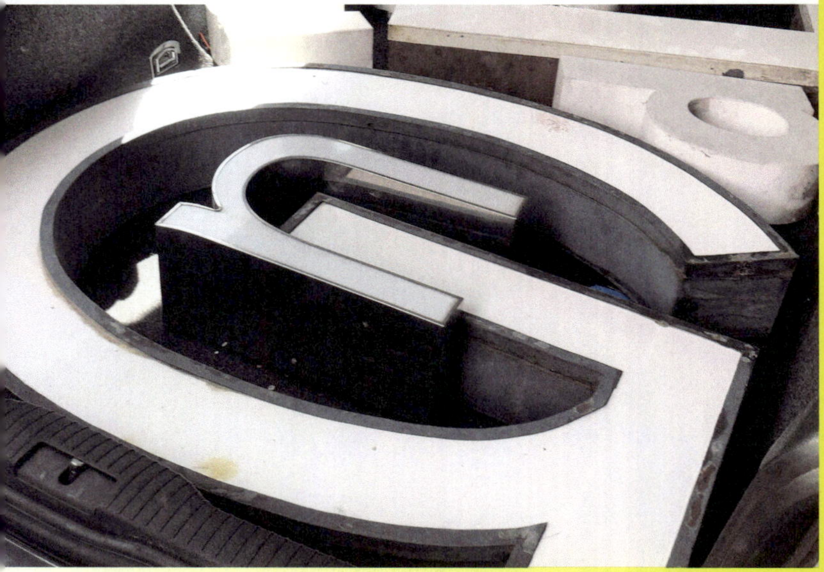

K

KINDERHYMNE
A CURIOUS INTERACTION AT THE *NEW ANTHEMS VI (BERLIN)* EXHIBITION

The Inkahoots exhibition *New Anthems VI (Berlin)* sparked reactions from visitors and passersby, who promptly accepted the challenge of suggesting alternative words to fill in the first sentence of the German national anthem. One visitor, however, made a more curious contribution—the singer Sibille Roth surprised the organizers by singing a cappella an 'alternative anthem' that was written by Bertolt Brecht and composed by Hanns Eisler in 1950. The Kinderhymne (Children's Hymn) was a response to the German national anthem, which Brecht believed was tainted by the country's fascist past.

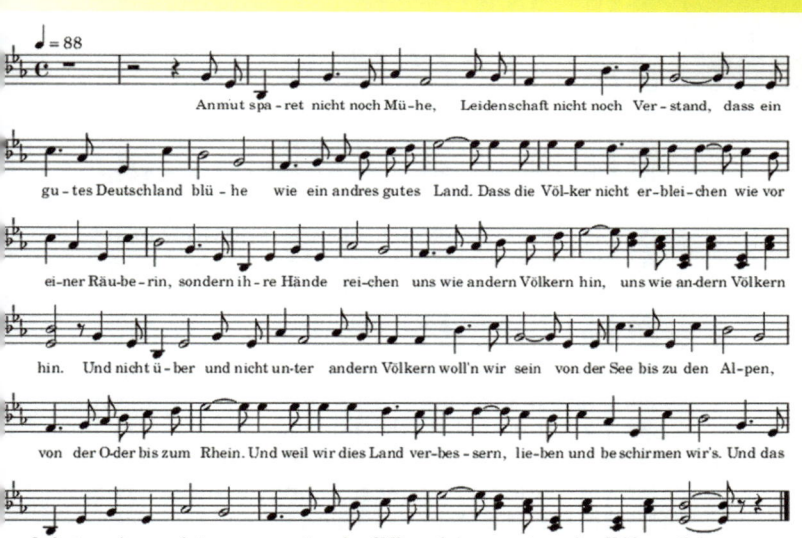

Grace spare not and spare no labor,
passion nor intelligence,
that a decent German nation
flourish as do other lands.

That the people give up flinching
at the crimes which we evoke,
and hold out their hands in friendship
as they do to other folk.

Neither over nor yet under
other people will we be
from the Oder to the Rhineland,
from the Alps to the North Sea.

And because we'll make it better,
let us guard and love our home.
Love it as our dearest country
as the others love their own."

„Anmut sparet nicht noch Mühe
Leidenschaft nicht noch Verstand
Daß ein gutes Deutschland blühe
Wie ein andres gutes Land.

Daß die Völker nicht erbleichen
Wie vor einer Räuberin
Sondern ihre Hände reichen
Uns wie andern Völkern hin.

Und nicht über und nicht unter
Andern Völkern wolln wir sein
Von der See bis zu den Alpen
Von der Oder bis zum Rhein.

Und weil wir dies Land verbessern
Lieben und beschirmen wir's
Und das liebste mag's uns scheinen
So wie andern Völkern ihrs."

L.I.P. COLLECTIVE
EXHIBITED COLLECTIVE

The Liberation in Print (L.i.P.) Collective was an online fellowship of women writers, designers, sociologists, publishers, artists, and educators investigating feminist periodicals. The project marked the beginning of *Futuress*—a platform for design, feminism, and politics.

The L.i.P. Collective was initiated by Nina Paim, Corin Gisel, and Madeleine Morley, with the participation of Amy Gowen, Barbora Demovičová, Carolyn Kerchof, Clara Amante, Delphine Bedel, Elham Namvar, Eugénie Zuccarelli, Fanny Maurel, Floriane Misslin, Klaudia Mazur, Loraine Furter, Mariachiara De Leo, Maya Ober, Mio Kojima, Mujgan Abdulzade, Naïma Ayed, Noemi Parisi, Pauline Piguet, Phoebe Eustance, Silva Baum, Sophia See, Yanchi Huang, Zenobia Ahmed.

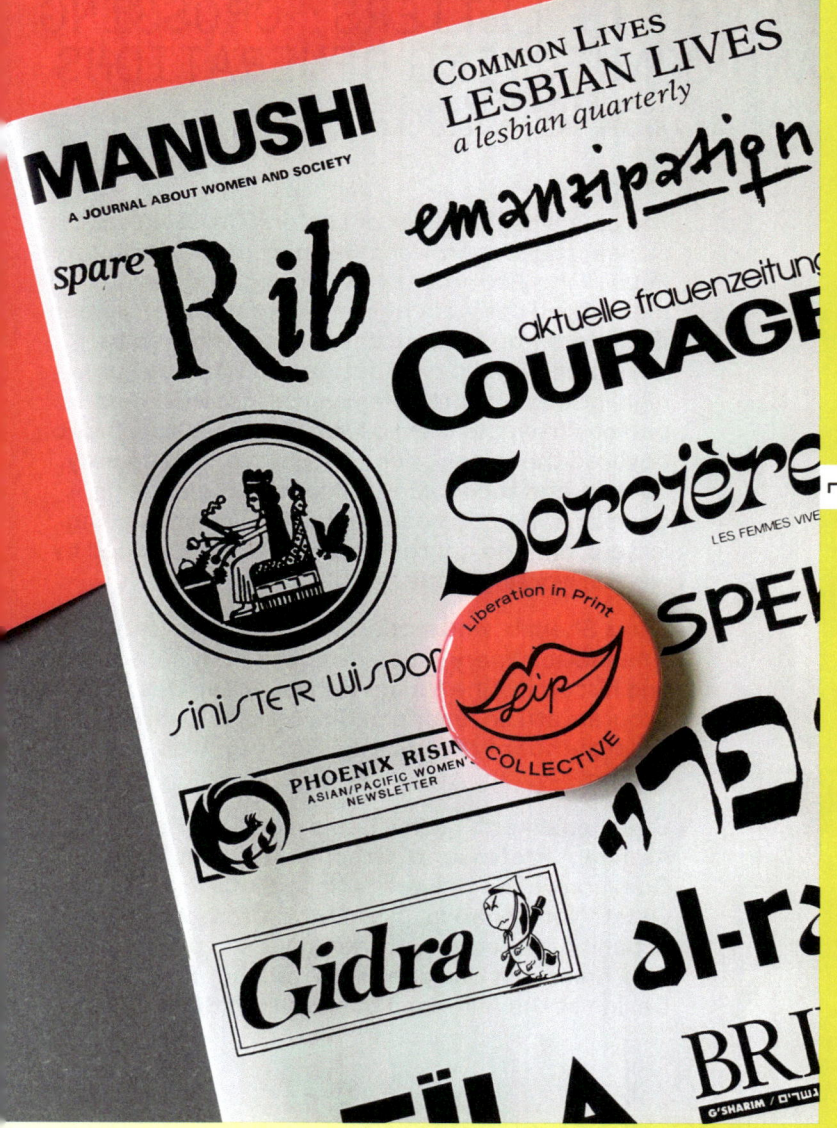

LADIES OF LETTERS: CROSSING AND CONNECTING GENERATIONS

ONLINE PANEL MODERATED BY BAHIA SHEHAB DURING THE
REVEALING » RECORDING » REFLECTING EXHIBITION

The online panel *Ladies of Letters: Crossing and Connecting Generations* was part of the exhibition *Revealing » Recording » Reflecting*. The panel highlighted the work of four generations of women designers who have extensively contributed to developing Arabic type design and visual culture, highlighting forgotten female calligraphers and patrons from the Islamic Mamluk era. The discussion covered these designers' processes, how society, culture, and technology influenced their design decisions, what it means to be a woman designing letters, and the contemporary challenges faced by women working in the field.

Bahia Shehab, who moderated the conversation, is a multidisciplinary artist, designer, political activist, and historian. She founded the Graphic Design Program at The American University in Cairo. She is co-author of the book *A History of Arab Graphic Design.*

Guest speakers: Basma Hamdy, designer and Assistant Professor of Graphic Design at Virginia Commonwealth University School of the Arts in Qatar; Noha Khatwa, Assistant Professor of Islamic Art and Architecture at the University of Cairo; and Yara Nammour, designer and Assistant Professor of Design at the American University of Beirut.

IMAGE-MAKING: BEHIND THE LINES OF ENGAGED GRAPHIC DESIGN
REVEALING » RECORDING » REFLECTING
REVEALING RECORDING REFLECTING
VISUAL STORYTELLING: ABOUT WOMEN, BY WOMEN
WOMEN DESIGNERS IN DIASPORA
ONLINE VIDEO ARCHIVE

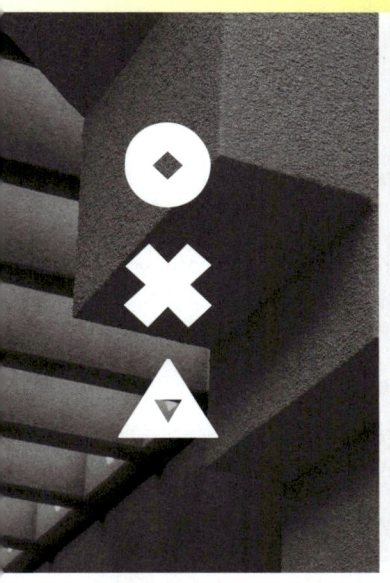
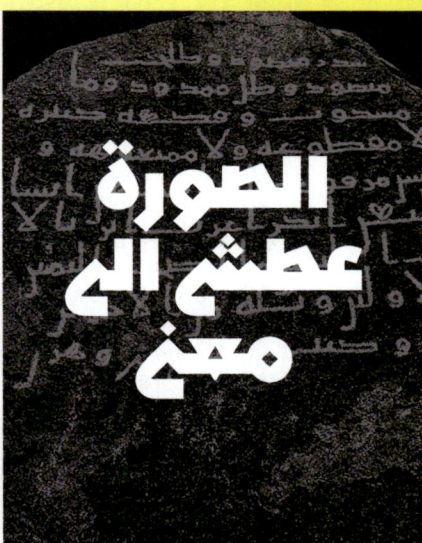

الصورة عطشى الى معنى

الحروف قلقة، جائعة الى صورة، والصورة عطشى الى معنى. الحروف أواني فخار فارغة فاملأها بسِحر الغزو للحروف البيضاء على اللوح الأسود مهابة فجر ربيعي. وكما يطرد الماء، على مَهَل، في جرّة لاتمتلئ، تشرّبتِ الشكلَ الناقصَ وصوتَه معاً، بتعذيب الحنجرة وتطويعها للإشارة، وبإخضاع الخلق لما تراه العينات. حتى يجمع حرفٌ إلى حرفٍ، أي غَبْثٌ إلى عَبث، ينسرُ غامضُ الشكل عن وضوح صوتٍ ما، ويفتح هذا الوضوحُ البطيءُ مجرى لمعنى له صورة، فتصير ثلاثةُ أحرفٍ باباً أو داراً. وهكذا تبقى حروف خاملة، لا قيمةَ لها إذا افترقت، بينما إذا اجتمعت. يا لهــا مــن لعبة! يا لهــا مــن سحر. يولد العالم تدريجياً من كلمات.

LEGO PRINTING
WORKSHOP LED BY GREGORY COWLING

As part of the *A—Z Collective* program, the designer Gregory Cowling, a member of the collective, offered a Lego printing workshop. The participants could practice using simple, flat Lego pieces in different shapes, arranging and fixing them onto the Lego baseboards to create various types, patterns, and forms. Inked with a roller, the lettering could then be printed on sheets of paper.

Gregory Cowling is a practitioner of Graphic Design and Typography, particularly interested in using design as a catalyst for change. He is based in Berlin, where he runs Praxis Typography, a letterpress printing workshop, which is built on the principles of sustainable societal practices.

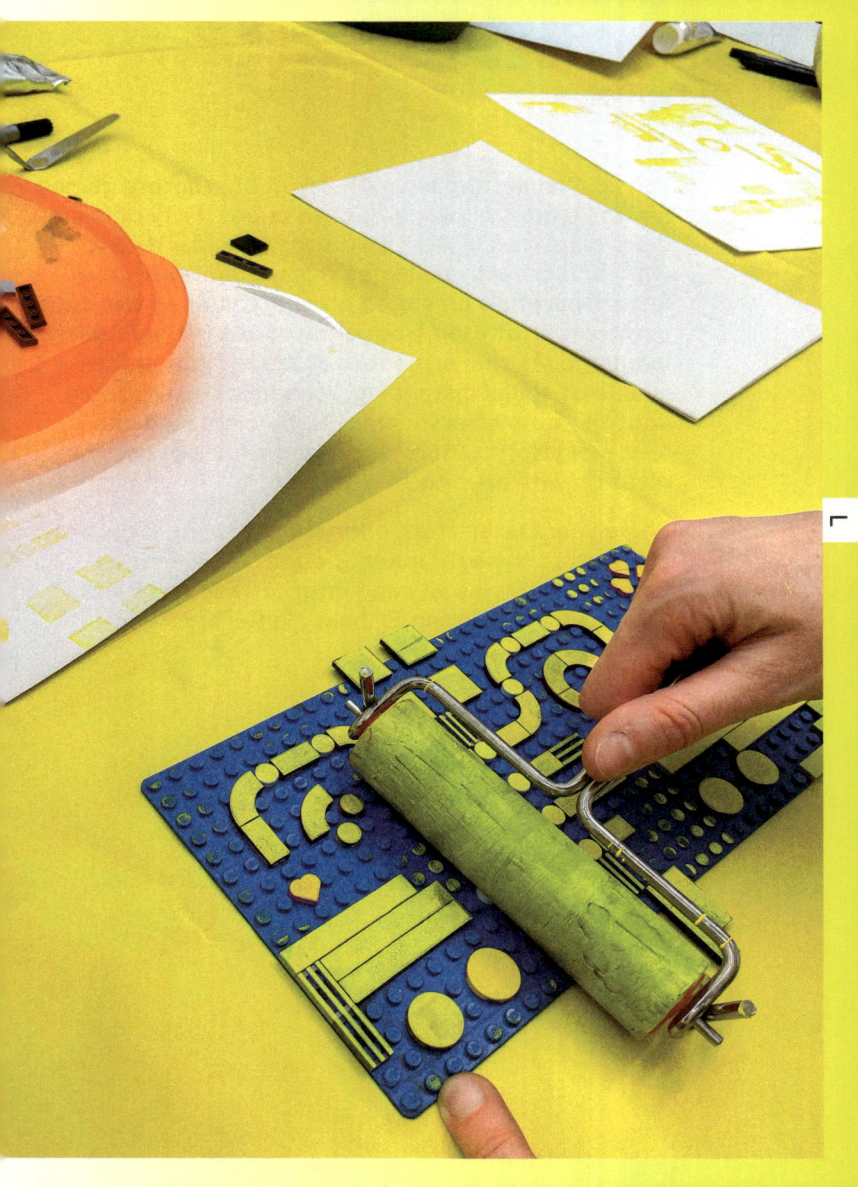

LETTER CUBES
THE LETTERS OF *CONNECTING FROM A–Z*

The 28 *Connecting from A—Z* font characters gained life as 20 cm² yellow cardboard cubes. Fifty of them were displayed at A—Z so visitors could interact with, and create messages from, them—with the letters carefully arranged on all six sides of the cube in the order of their frequency of use in the English language. As this project took place right in the middle of social distancing pandemic rules, people sent their phrases via email to be displayed on A—Z's big front window, creating a form of communication with anyone passing by.

Some years later, the *Connecting from A—Z* cubes traveled to the exhibition *Spear of the Senses*, celebrating inclusivity and interactivity in art and design at the German Embassy in Beijing.

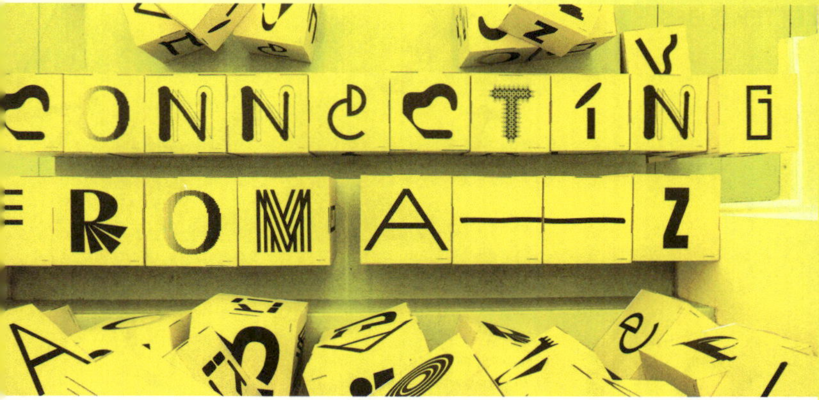

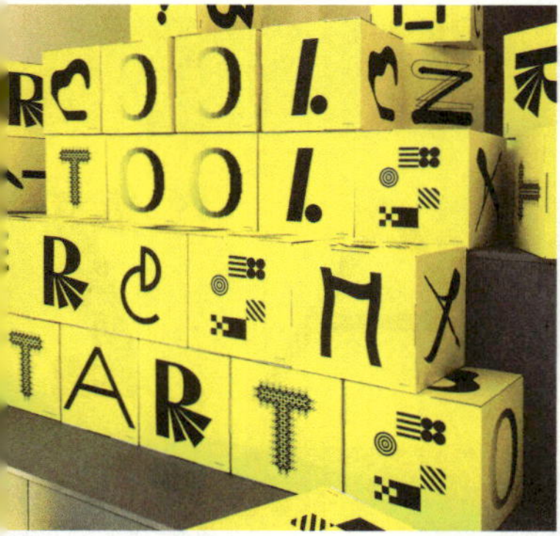

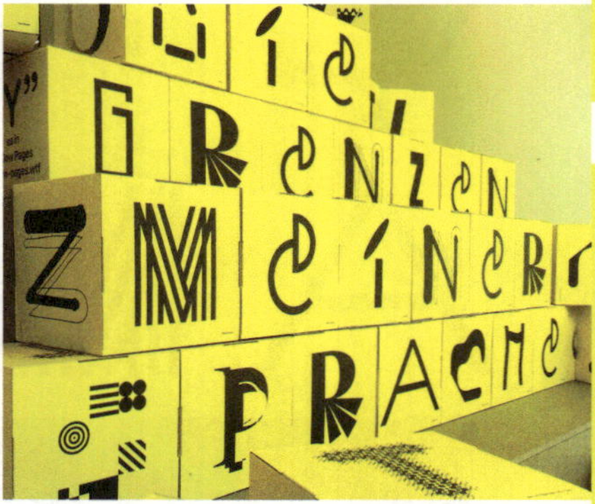

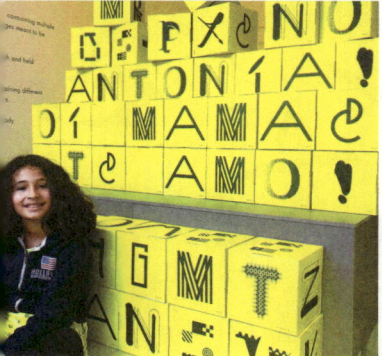
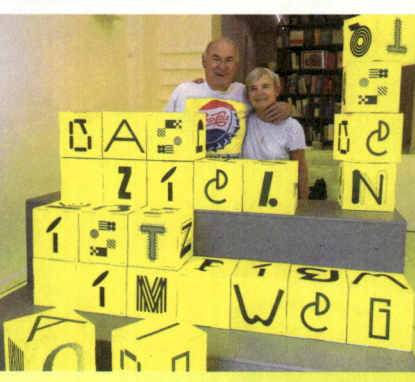

LETTER CUBES

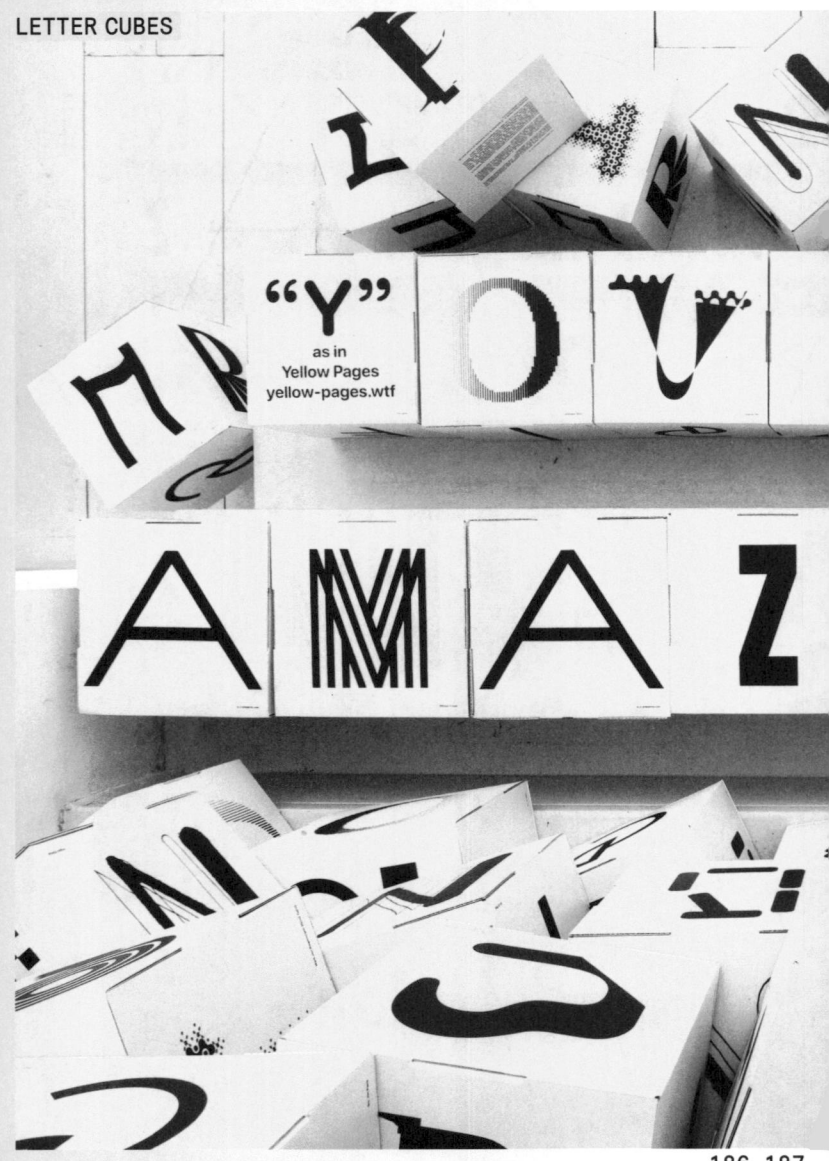

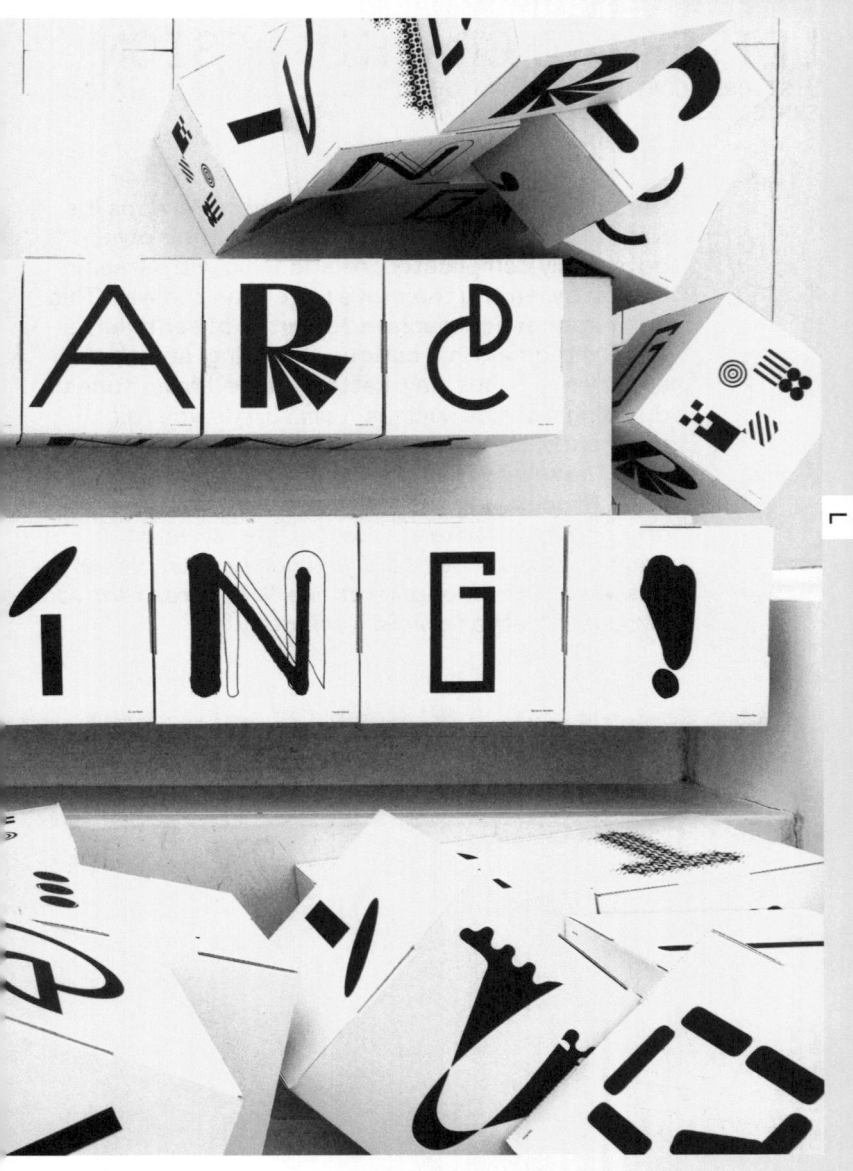

LETTERS TO GRAPHIC DESIGN
VISITORS' CONTRIBUTIONS TO THE *PERHAPS IT'S NOT YOU, IT'S ME.* EXHIBITION

During Lucienne Roberts's exhibition, *Perhaps It's Not You, It's Me.*, visitors could share their own, potentially complicated, relationship with Graphic Design by leaving their love letters on the wall. This correspondence displayed an array of sentiments toward the field in a curious, revealing, and above all very humorous way. Letters ranged from honest dumping classics such as *"I am sorry if you felt differently, but I think you should only stay a job."* and *"I have left you for illustration"* to hard facts as in *"Stop calling yourself a problem solver, you are a problem maker!"*. They included romantic beginnings like *"We're still in a honeymoon phase"* to sweet acknowledgments like *"If it weren't for you, I wouldn't be the feminist I am today."*.

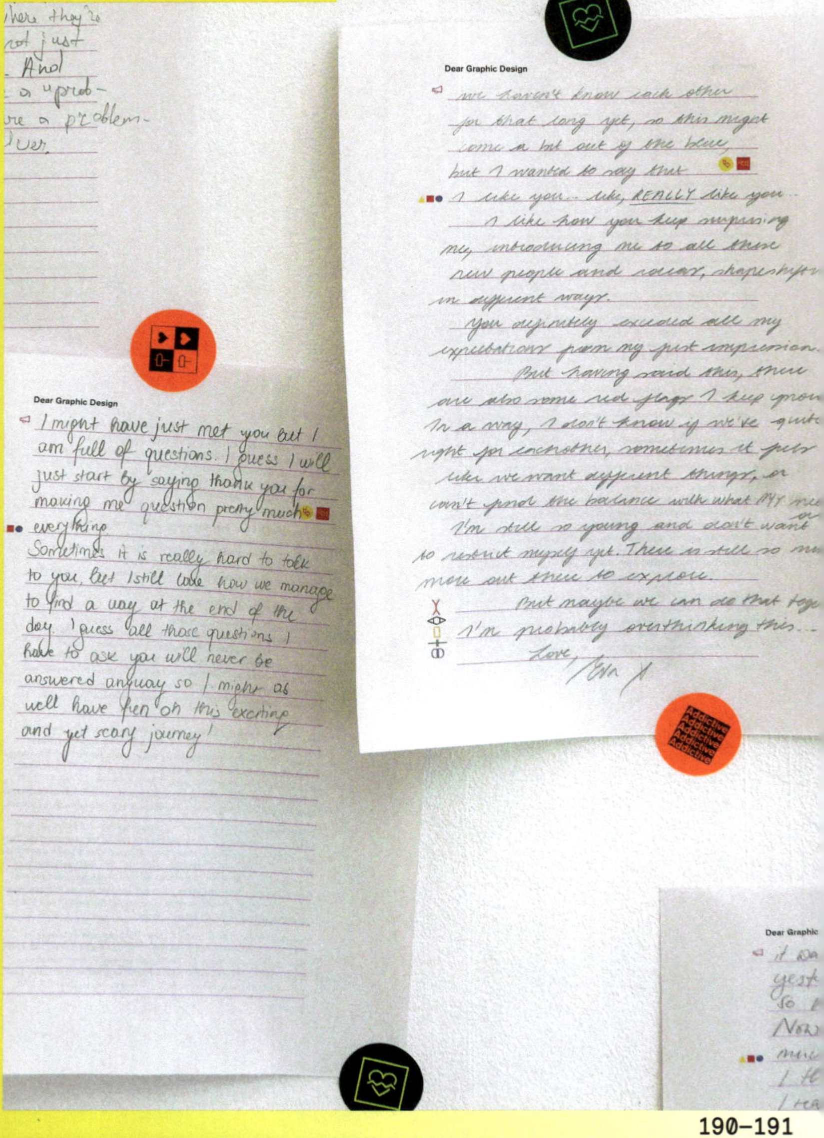

LETTERS TO GRAPHIC DESIGN

(partial letter, left edge cut off)
...here they ro
...not just
...And
...a "prob-
...re a problem-
...ver.

Dear Graphic Design

I might have just met you but I am full of questions. I guess I will just start by saying thank you for making me question pretty much everything.
Sometimes it is really hard to talk to you, but I still love how we manage to find a way at the end of the day. I guess all those questions I have to ask you will never be answered anyway so I might as well have fun on this exciting and yet scary journey!

Dear Graphic Design

We haven't known each other for that long yet, so this might come a bit out of the blue, but I wanted to say that I like you... like, REALLY like you.
I like how you keep surprising me, introducing me to all these new people and ideas, shapeshifting in different ways.
You definitely exceeded all my expectations from my first impression.
But having said this, there are also some red flags I keep ignoring. In a way, I don't know if we're quite right for each other, sometimes it feels like we want different things, or I can't find the balance with what you need.
I'm still so young and don't want to restrict myself yet. There is still so much more out there to explore.
But maybe we can do that together. I'm probably overthinking this...
Love,
/Eva /

Dear Graphic

(partial, cut off)
it was
yest...
so...
Now...
maxi...
I th...
I re...

[partial left page:]
...still in
...phase —

...feel
...rently so grateful +
...you by

...oice, you
...to remain
...ope I haven't
...rong one.

Dear Graphic Design

Dear Graphic Design,
I'm sorry if you felt differently,
but I think you should
stay only a job.
We can have a coffee
sometime.

Barbara

LIBRARY OF SHAPES, TEXTS AND STRUCTURES

EXHIBITION BY ANDREA TINNES

The Library of Shapes, Texts and Structures is a continuous visual research project and personal archive by graphic designer Andrea Tinnes. For the inaugural A—Z Presents exhibition, Andrea showcased her 'library', a vast collection of design elements maintained by the designer in her studio.

For the exhibition, Andrea meticulously arranged her collection in 42 folders with over 4,000 pages, neatly organized and categorized. Covering the two walls of the space, Andrea displayed a series of large hand-offset prints using elements from the archive, overprinted in various color combinations.

The presentation of her highly systematic effort in a comprehensive visual and textual archive, and its relation to the prints' explosion of form and color, created an inspiring tension that singularly illustrates the breadth and depth of Graphic Design practice. To categorize her vast collection, she uses the font format to easily find and retrieve all the elements.

The library has a triple structure: shapes consisting of forms, symbols, and letters; structures with a variety of analog and digital textures, as well as photographic imagery of vernacular typography; and texts complementing the visual collection with excerpts from newspapers, magazines, books, and social media posts.

ANDREA TINNES
INVENTAR COLLECTION
PERSONAL DESIGN LIBRARY
RESEARCH METHODS
TAKEAWAY GRAPHIC DESIGN

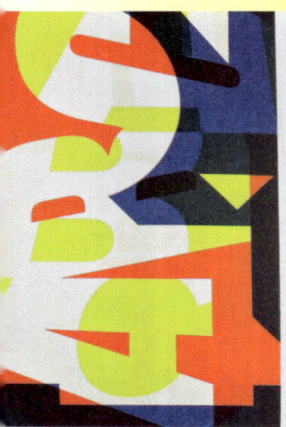
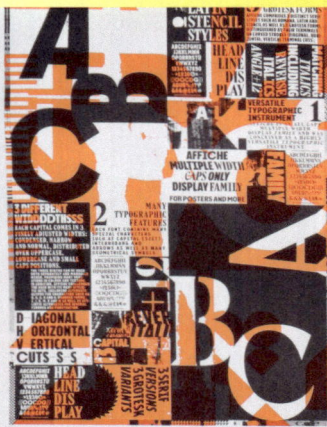
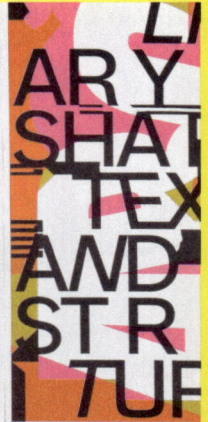
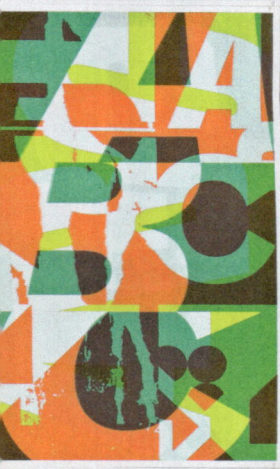
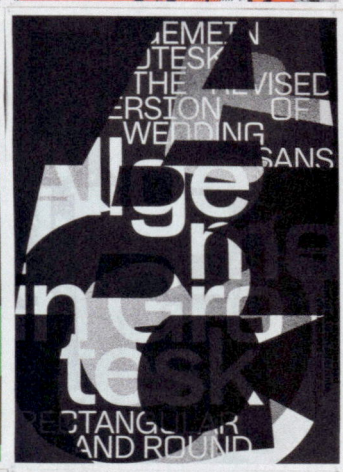
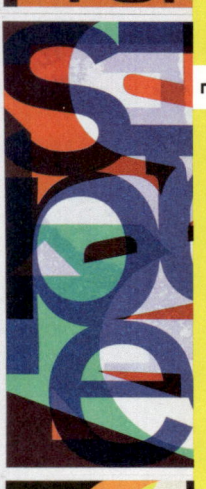
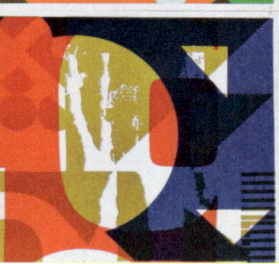
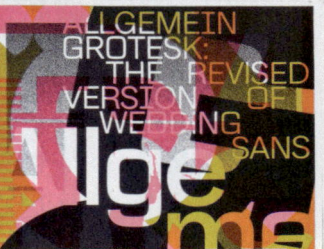
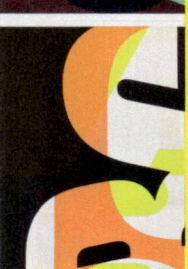

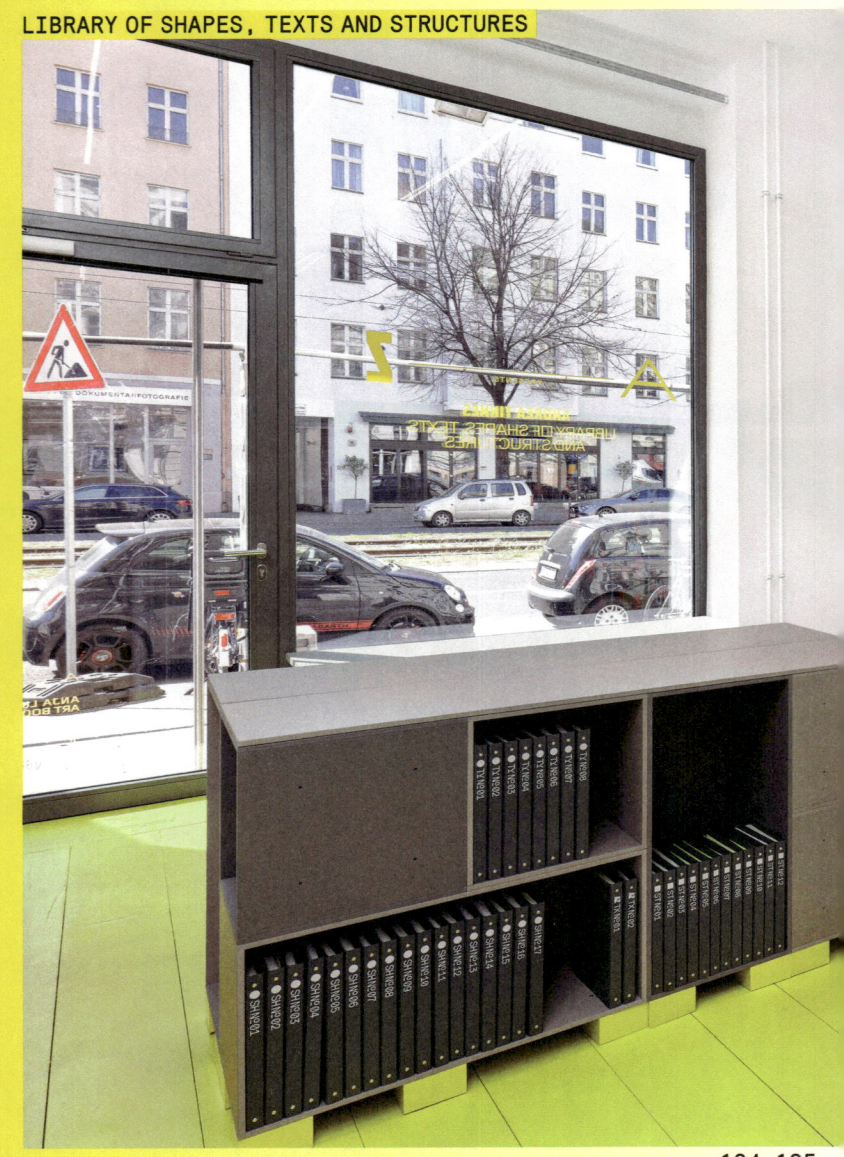

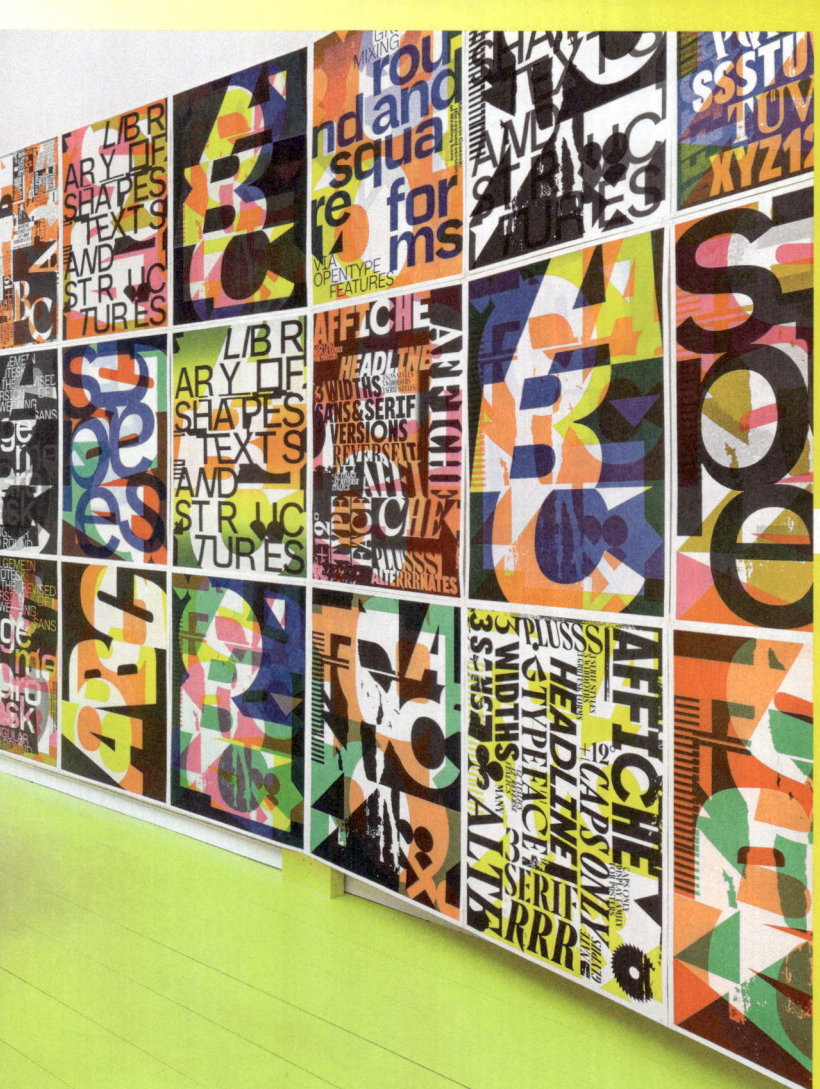

LIBRARY OF SHAPES, TEXTS AND STRUCTURES

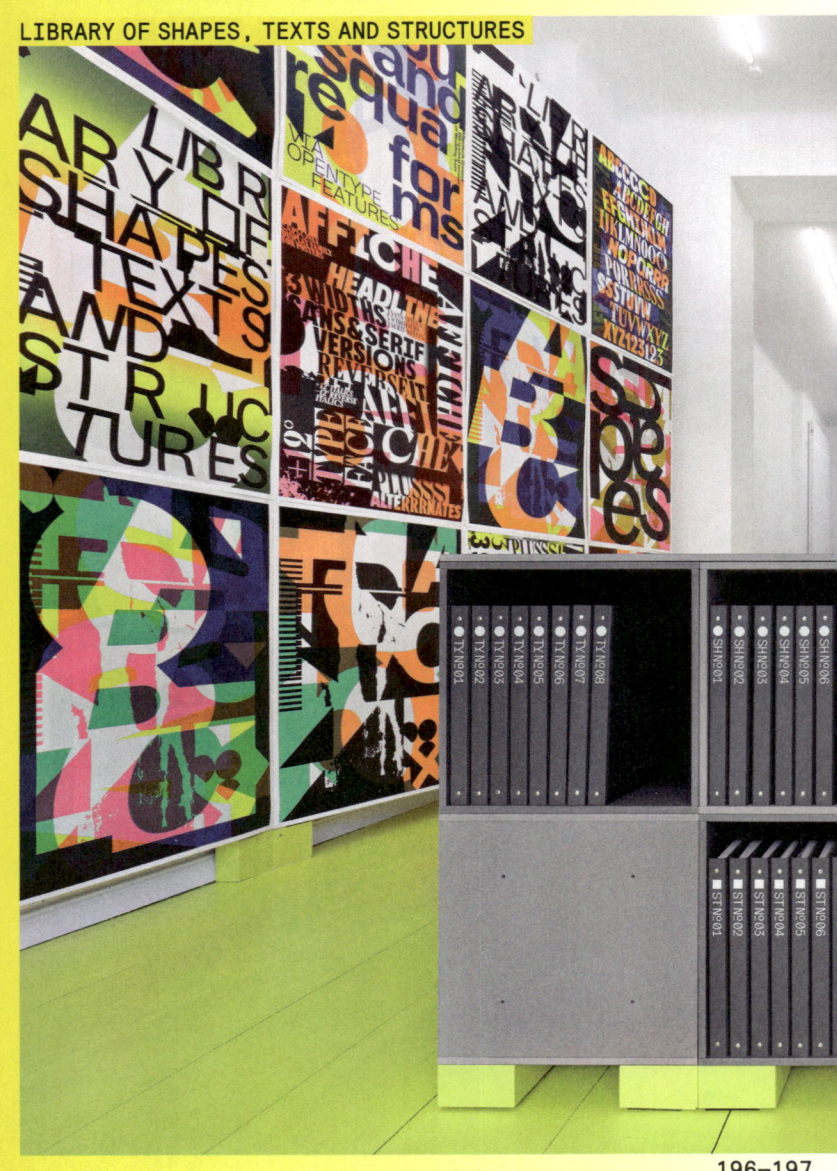

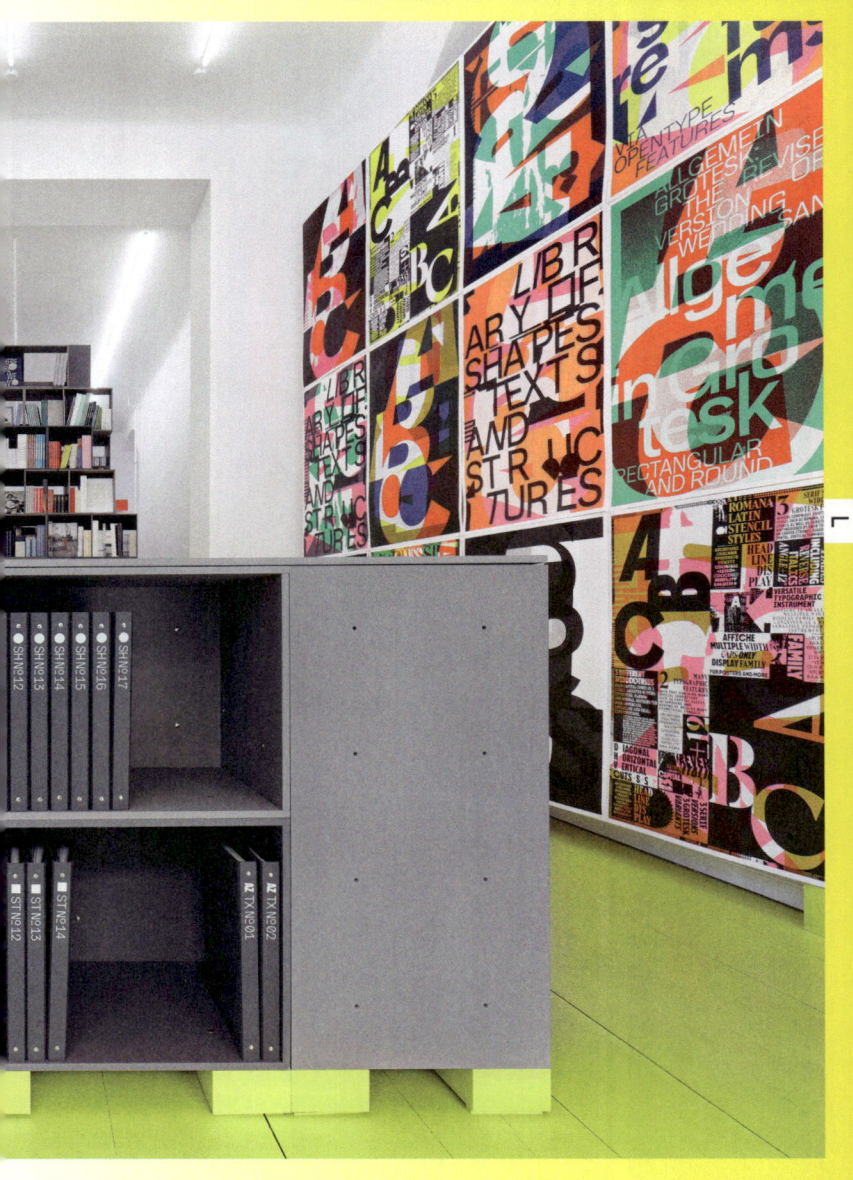

LIBRARY OF SHAPES, TEXTS AND STRUCTURES

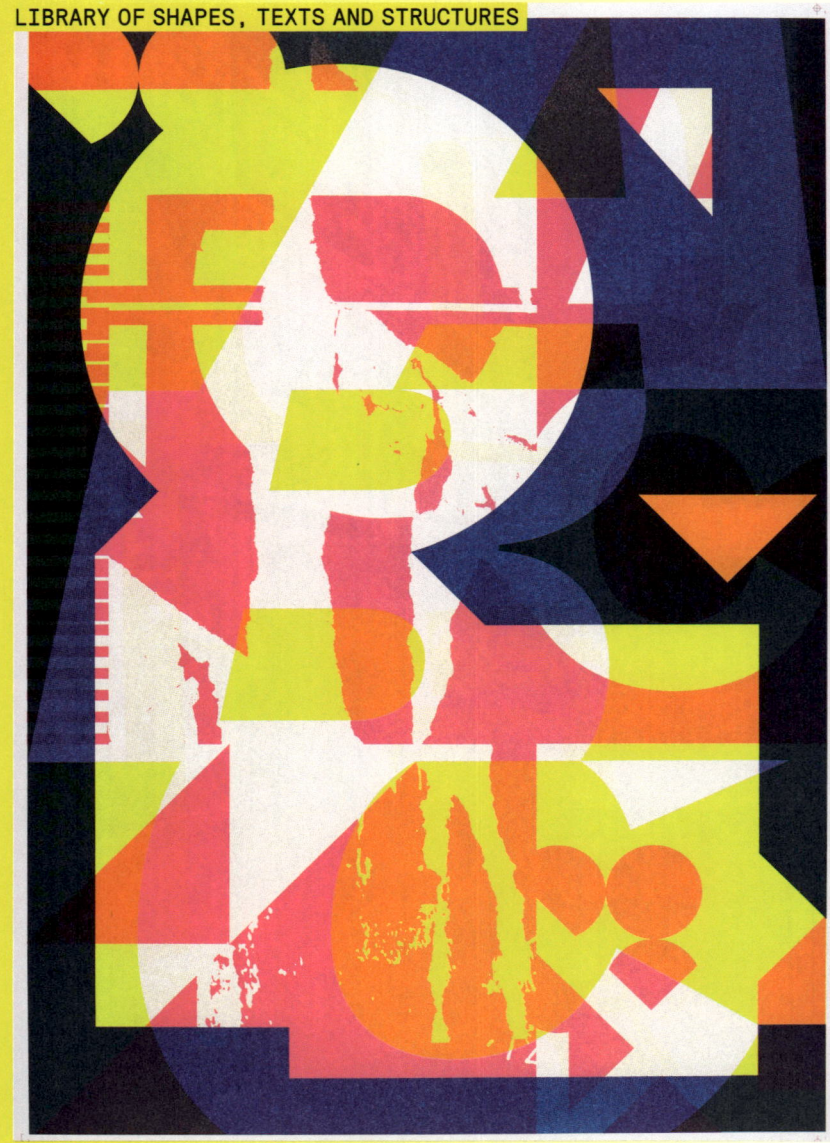

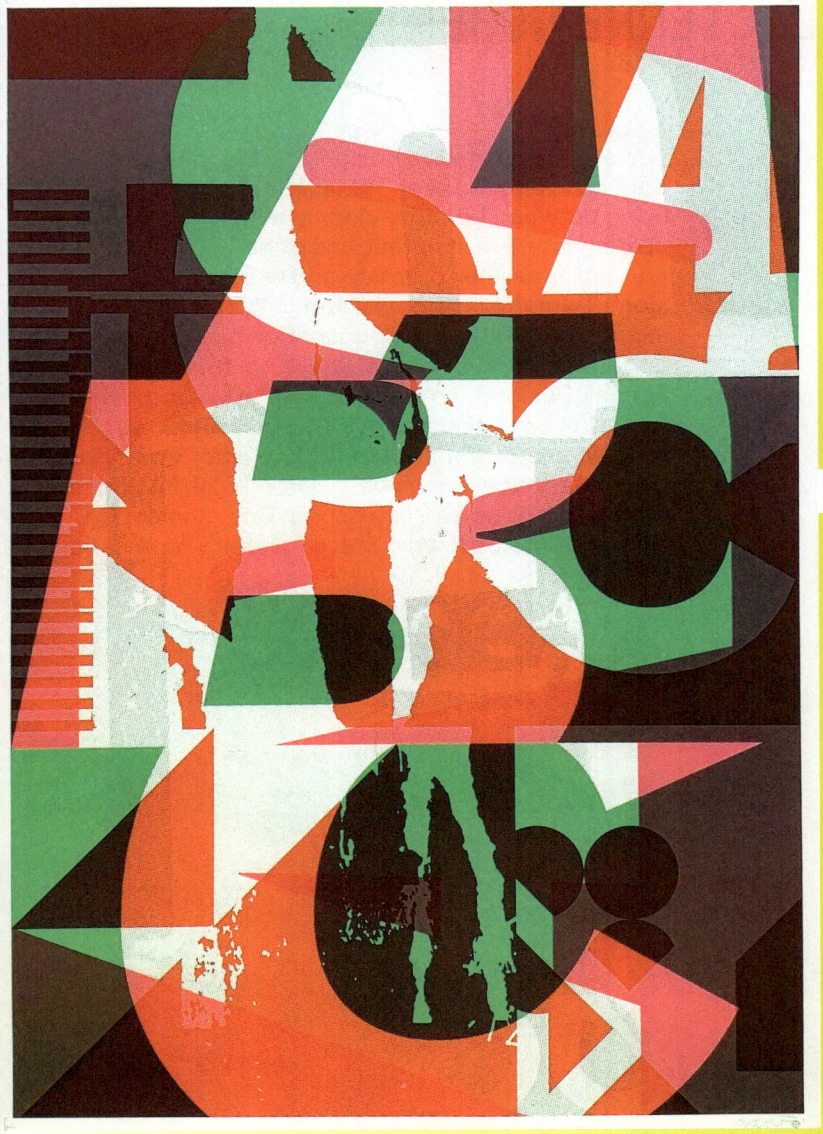

LUCIENNE ROBERTS
EXHIBITED ARTIST

Lucienne Roberts is a design practitioner, writer, educator, and founder of LucienneRoberts+ studio, living between London, Vienna, and Berlin. An abiding interest in definitions of ethical design characterizes her practice and research. Commissioned work for the social and cultural sectors includes exhibition and publication design, content generation, and curation. She is co-founder of GraphicDesign&, an advocacy initiative originating books, exhibitions, and events exploring how graphic design connects with the wider world and the value that it brings to it. Since 2022, Lucienne Roberts has been a Professor in Communication Design at the Stuttgart State Academy of Art and Design.

HELLO YOU!
IN A POST-GROWTH WORLD
LETTERS TO GRAPHIC DESIGN
PERHAPS IT'S NOT YOU, IT'S ME.

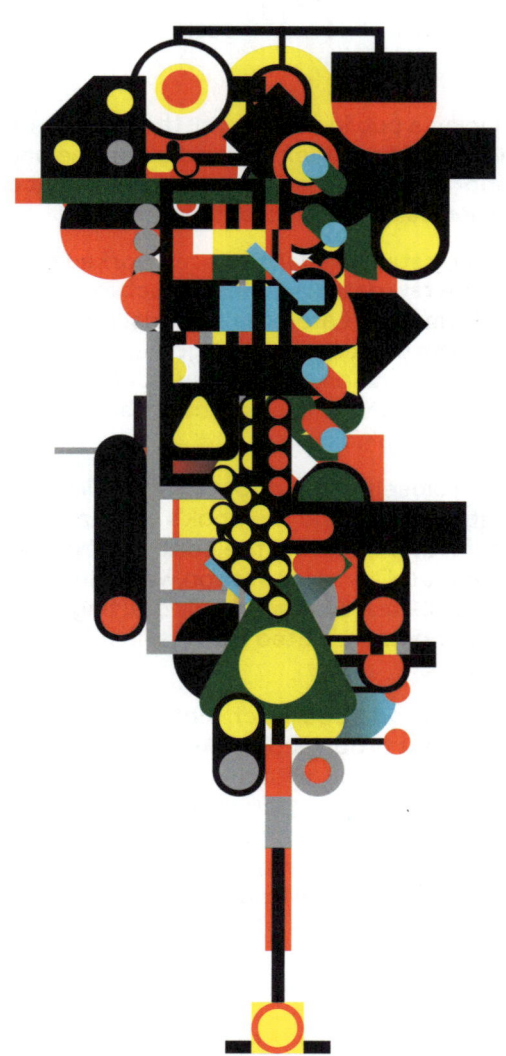

MAKING-OF... THIS BOOK
TEAMWORK PROCESSES BEHIND THE A–Z–∞ BOOK

Producing a publication to tell the journey of A—Z in the form of an index involves extensive and highly collaborative work to such an extent that it can be regarded as an A—Z project by itself.

In its early stage, several interns worked on compiling the raw data and initial structure of the book, to go from A—Z. Later, the editorial decision was to expand the book concept to go beyond a register of, or reflection on, its journey, adding the infinity symbol ∞ to showcase new contributions to the future of Graphic Design.

Working closely with editor Soraya Guimarães, the next step was to find the book's optimal tone and voice, further maturing the editorial style. The most significant editorial innovation was using Notion to create a fileless workspace for drafting the 150+ entries and their related material in highly dynamic databases.

Lorna Fray and Robert Schlicht performed the final content proofreading. A—Z founder Anja Lutz designed the book, with the help of several interns. The image processing, printing and binding was done by DZA–Druckerei zu Altenburg on Pergraphica and Magno Gloss paper by Igepa and published by Set Margins in the Netherlands.

INTERNS
PROJECT SUPPORTERS
THANKS!

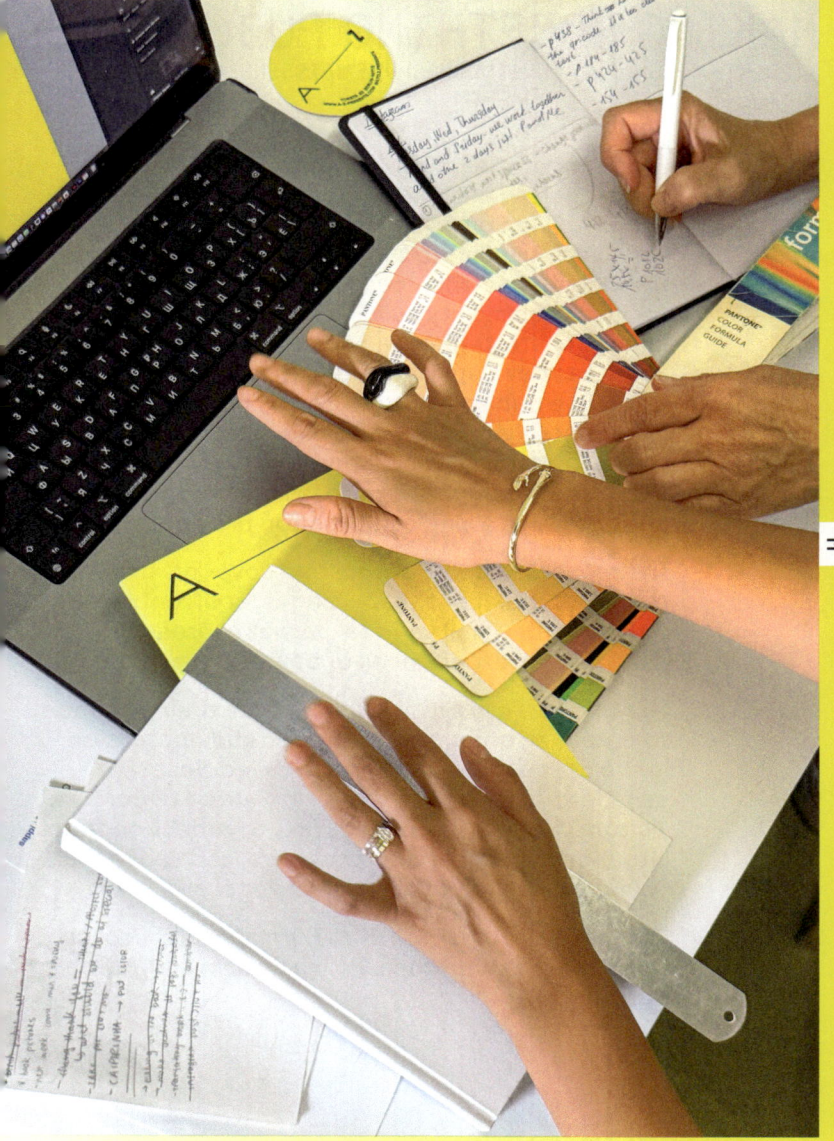

MAKING SOMETHING PUBLIC
STUDENT WORKSHOP AT KUNSTHOCHSCHULE WEISSENSEE

Students of the Editorial Design course at Kunsthochschule Weissensee participated in the workshop *Making Something Public*, led by A—Z founder Anja Lutz. Alluding to the actual act of publishing in the title, the activity focused on the application of tools for community building, such as microsolidarity, emergent strategies, and liberating structures, as well as developing, designing, and producing a collective publication. Inspired by numerous group experiences with the *A—Z Collective*, the idea was to transfer that collaborative know-how and exercise it through the process of conceptualizing and designing a single publication project together.

The result was a wall publication covering an entire room in fluorescent yellow pages, confronting visitors with visuals and texts that express the participants' experiences of being a woman.

The title *Panic in the Nest* came from their intention to create an atmosphere of panic and oppression in the communal school space called Nest. The self-determined womxn's group wanted to confront visitors visually and conceptually to reflect on the situations of aggression, prejudice, and abuse that young women are often subjected to.

Participants: Anna Wolf, Kira Bürmann, Lilly Drosch, Oleksandra Pshenychna, Polina Ryman, and Yewon Seo.

A–Z COLLECTIVE
ANJA LUTZ
VISITORS
YELLOW

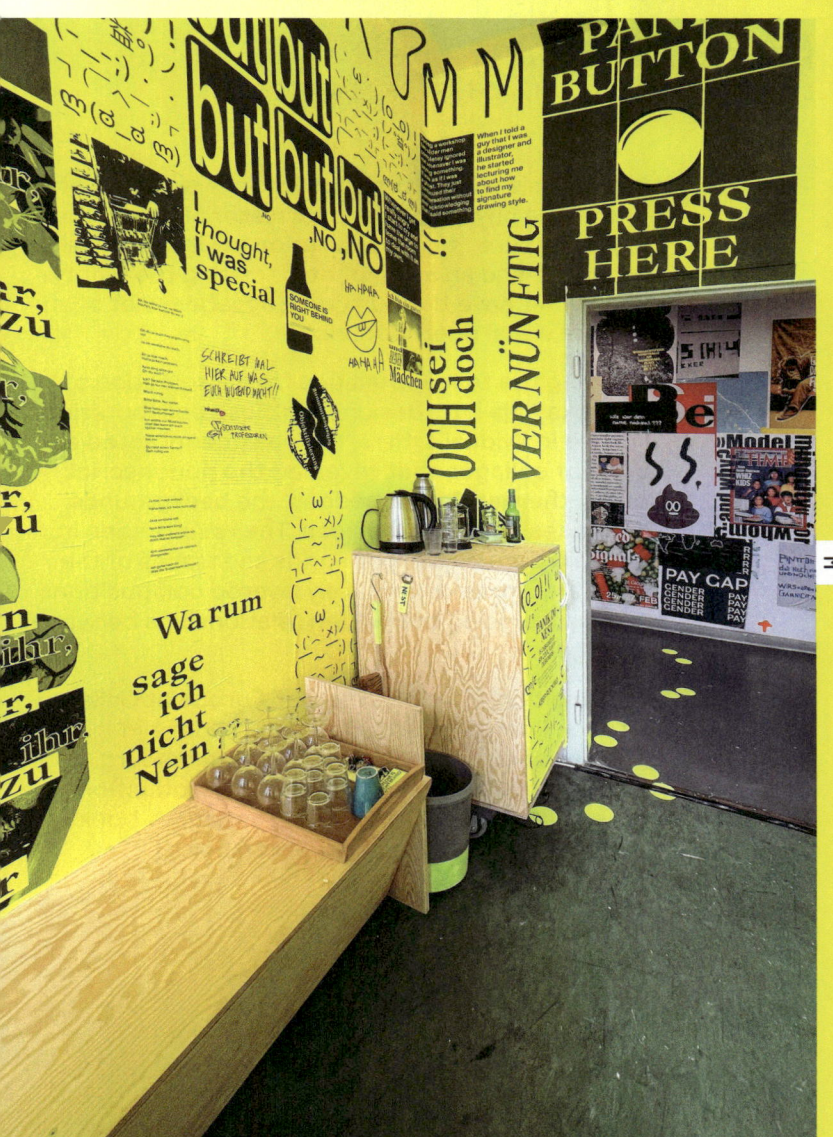

MARGINALIA
EXHIBITION BY ANJA LUTZ AS PART OF *TIME FOR BOOKS*

Marginalia is an investigation into the anatomy of books—the physical object, its materiality, and its inner structure. It is a celebration of Graphic Design and layout, and an attempt at mediating the empty spaces that have their unique language—that of an abstract visual poetry of books.

Removing the text and images from a selection of art books Anja Lutz designed in close collaboration with the individual artists, the designer created a series of collages that revealed the nondescript details: the margins, the edges, the backgrounds, the spaces between the lines. The results seen in the exhibition were filigree grids and traces of the layout that formed intricately layered compositions of voids, exposing the hidden relationships between the pages.

The exhibition *Marginalia* toured Europe at Gallery Florence Loewy in Paris, Haus am Waldsee in Berlin, Nosbaum Reding Gallery in Luxembourg, and in various group exhibitions. A reproduction of the collages was gathered in the artist's book *Marginalia*, published by The Green Box.

MARK VAN WAGENINGEN
EXHIBITED ARTIST

Mark van Wageningen is the founder of Novo Typo, a (typo)graphic design studio and font foundry based in Amsterdam. He has designed and published several innovative multicolor fonts. He is also the author and designer of award-winning design books, such as *Typewood*, *Novo Typo Color Book*, *Type and Color*, *Novo Typo Offgrid*, *Analog Aesthetics*, and *Novo Typo On Site*.

Novo Typo's approach to design is deeply rooted in a love for craftsmanship, and an experimental and investigative approach to design, production techniques, tools, materials, and their context. The studio's output is at the intersection of design, applied arts, and craftsmanship.

FUTURE VS. PAST
NOVO TYPO OFFGRID BERLIN
NOVO TYPO OFFGRID TRANSPORTATION

MULTICOLOR
COLORMULTI
MULTICOLOR
COLORMULTI
MULTICOLOR
COLORMULTI
MULTICOLOR
COLORMULTI
MULTICOLOR
COLORMULTI

MARU MIDI
TYPEFACE USED FOR THE *A–Z COLLECTIVE* IDENTITY

After developing and thoroughly discussing design ideas, the *A—Z Collective* settled on the proposal by Eunjung Kwak to use the typeface *Maru Midi* by Grilli Type to create its visual identity. The funny and quirky individual letter shapes, intersecting and overlapping, perfectly expressed the group's spirit. The logo was displayed across the front window, and the installation process was performed collectively.

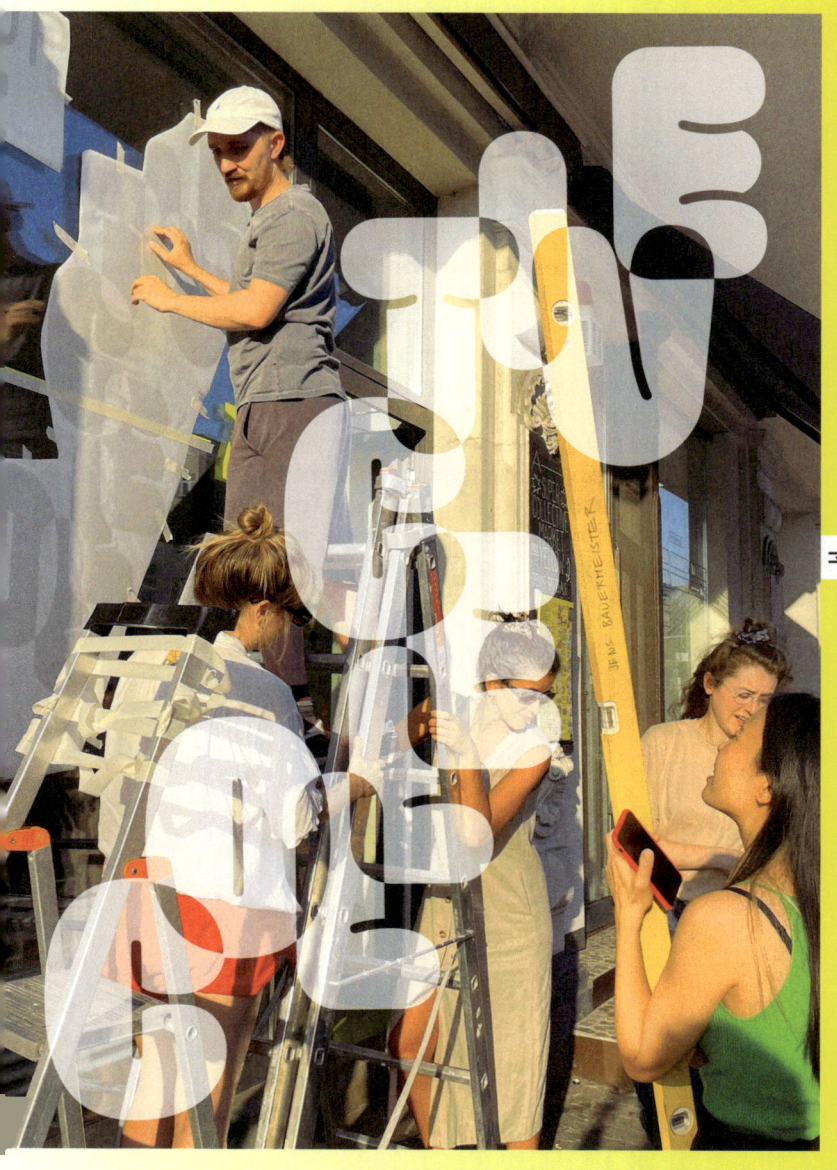

MIRTHA DERMISACHE
EXHIBITED ARTIST

Mirtha Dermisache (1940–2012) was a conceptual artist, writer, and educator who became active in the contemporary art scene in Argentina in the early 1970s. She is known for her explorations in asemic writing, a form of illegible, abstract mark-making that she coined as "graphics", and published in the form of books and printed ephemera. During the military dictatorship in the country, Mirtha Dermisache founded the Taller de Acciones Creativas (TAC) to teach different art techniques to develop creativity and free graphic expression in adults. Her works have been exhibited and collected by art institutions worldwide, and her legacy is kept alive by the Centro de Estudios Espigas in Buenos Aires.

DERMISACHE RELATIVE
ILLEGIBLE
MIRTHA DERMISACHE: TO BE READ
MYSTERIOUS POSTCARD
READING ARTISTS · BOOKS : ASEMIC WRITING

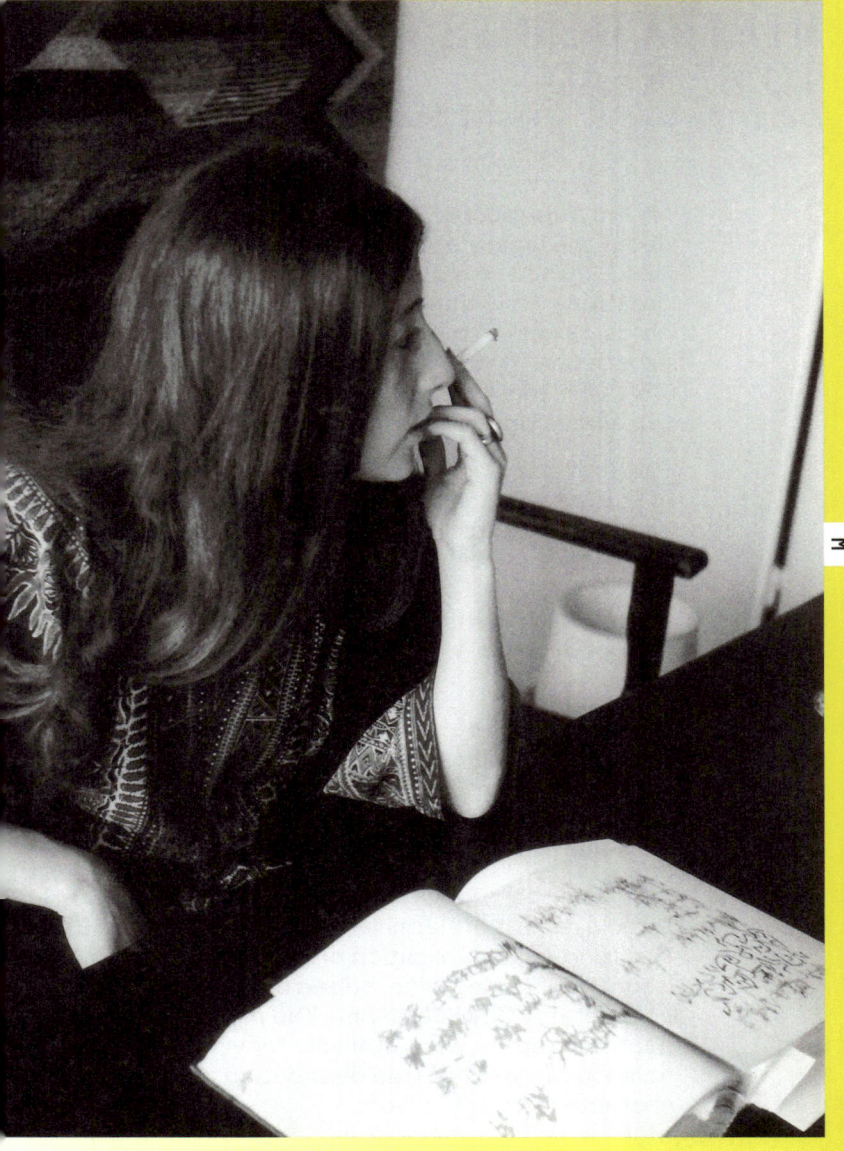

M

MIRTHA DERMISACHE: TO BE READ

EXHIBITION CURATED BY REGINE EHLEITER

Mirtha Dermisache: To Be Read was an exhibition about the legacy of visual artist Mirtha Dermisache's (1940–2012) asemic writing. It made several of her creations, including books, newspapers, and postcards, available to the wider public for a hands-on experience. The exhibition contained her distinctive work of marks resembling writing in both handwritten and typographic forms.

This first solo show of Mirtha Dermisache's work in Europe was possible thanks to co-operation between the Cluster of Excellence *Temporal Communities: Doing Literature in a Global Perspective* of Freie Universität Berlin and A—Z. The bulletin board-as-exhibition oxfordberlin, a space in the district of Berlin-Wedding, functioned as a satellite venue.

The exhibition opening featured a 'reading' by sound artist Paolo Dellapiana. The initiative was supported by Legado Mirtha Dermisache, the artist's estate in Buenos Aires, which lent items for public display, as did some private collectors in Germany and France.

In addition to original material, the exhibition featured a reprint of Dermisache's asemic *Article* (1975). This four-page publication originally appeared in issue 1 of *AXE* magazine, edited by her long-term collaborator Guy Schraenen. The publication and a postcard reprint were available for visitors to take home in the spirit of free distribution, which was characteristic of her work.

ASEMIC WRITING
ILLEGIBLE
MIRTHA DERMISACHE
MYSTERIOUS POSTCARD

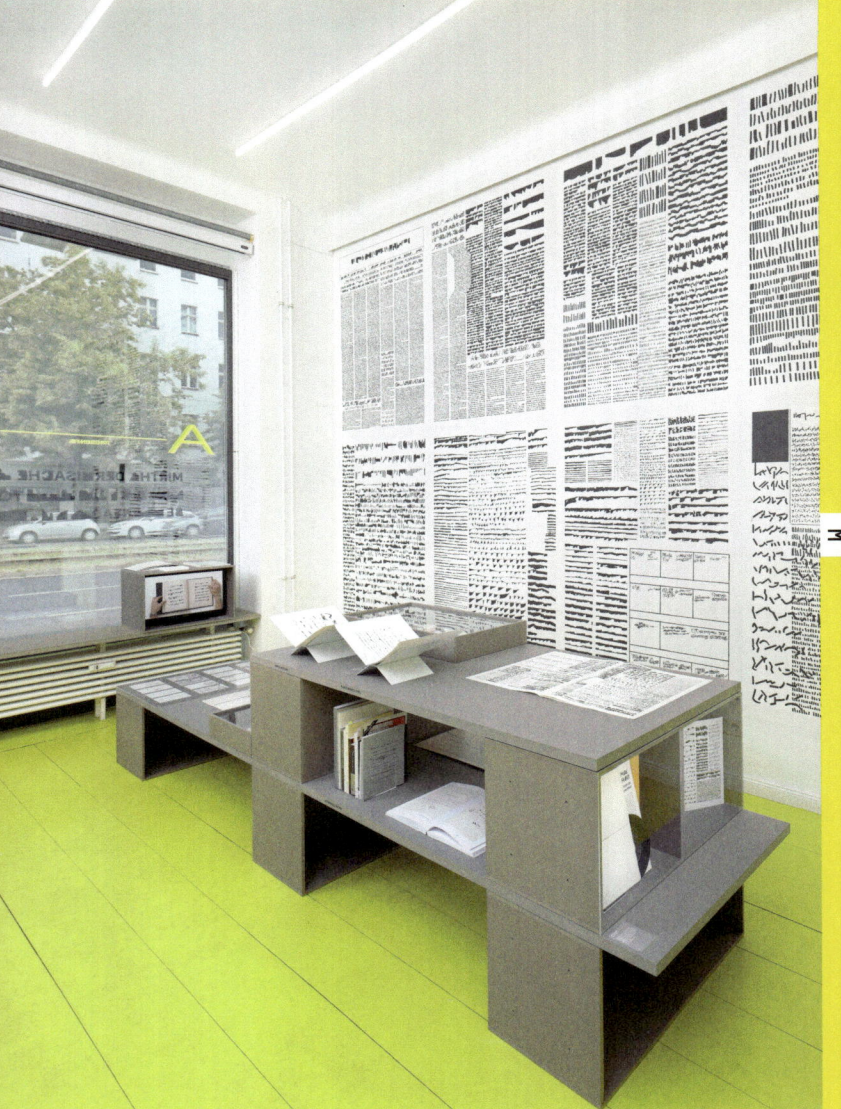

MIRTHA DERMISACHE: TO BE READ

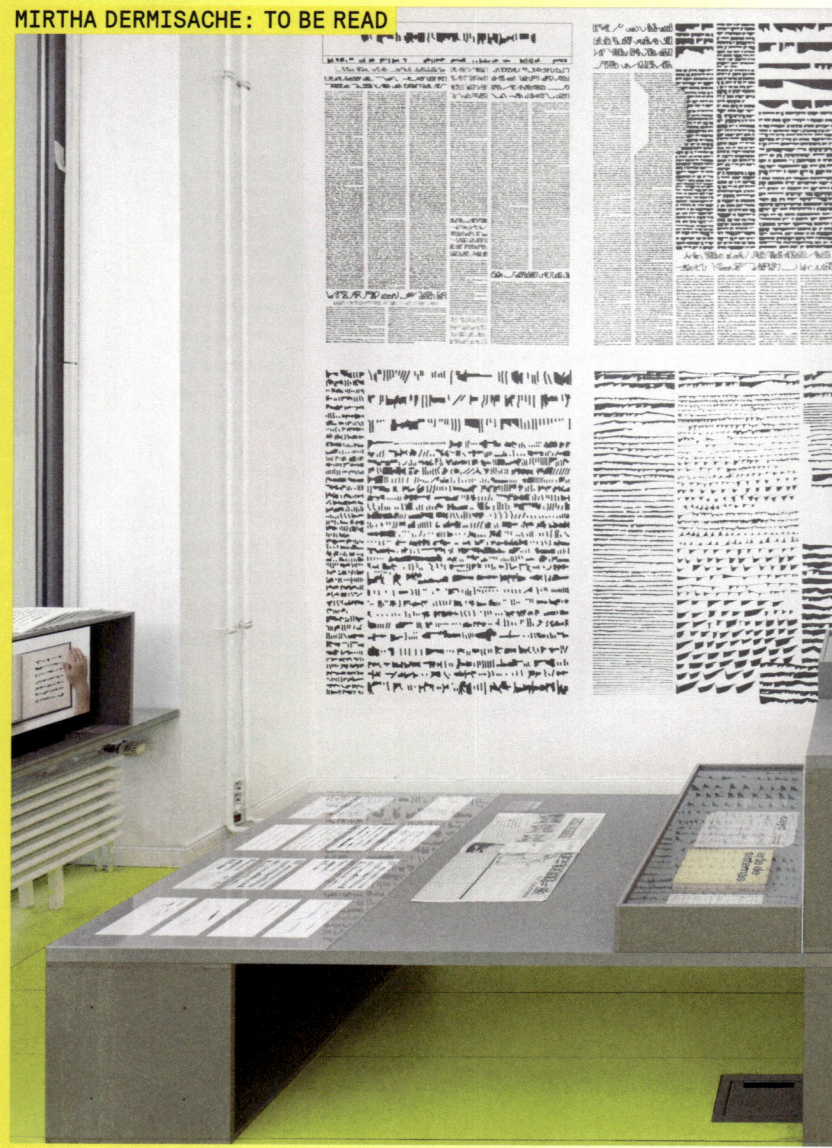

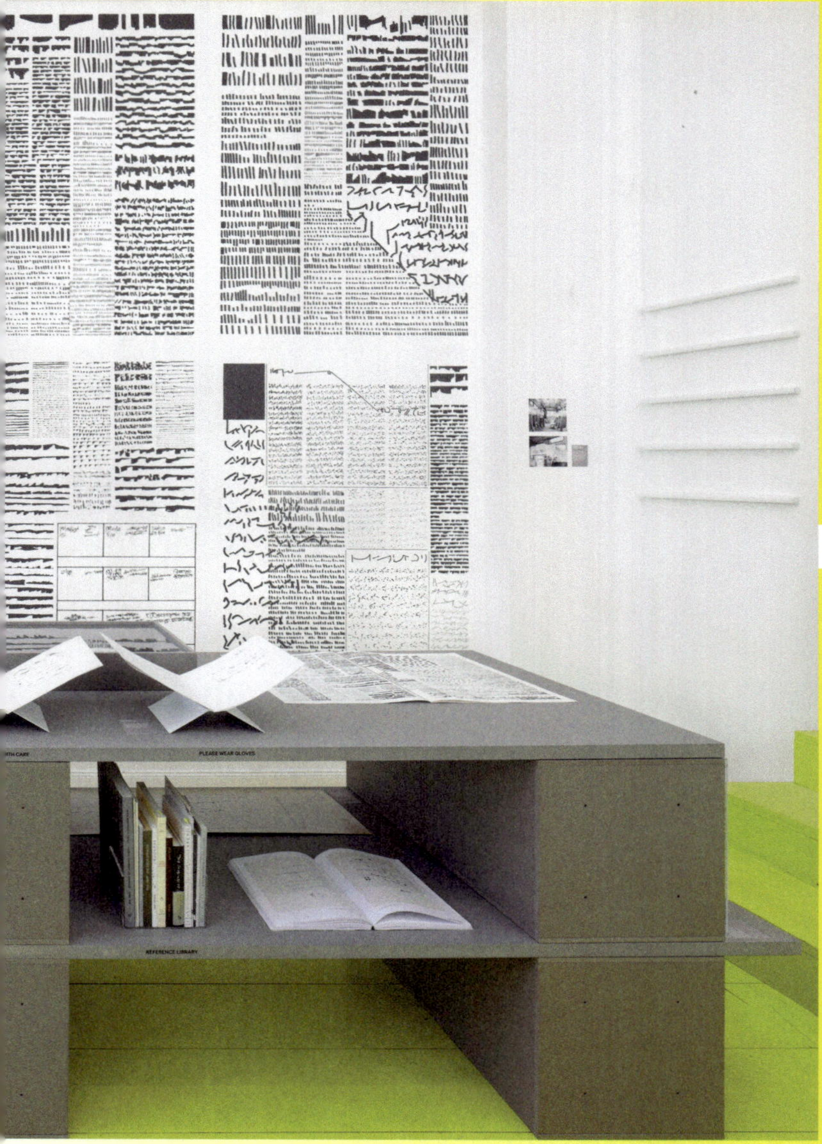

M

MIRTHA DERMISACHE: TO BE READ

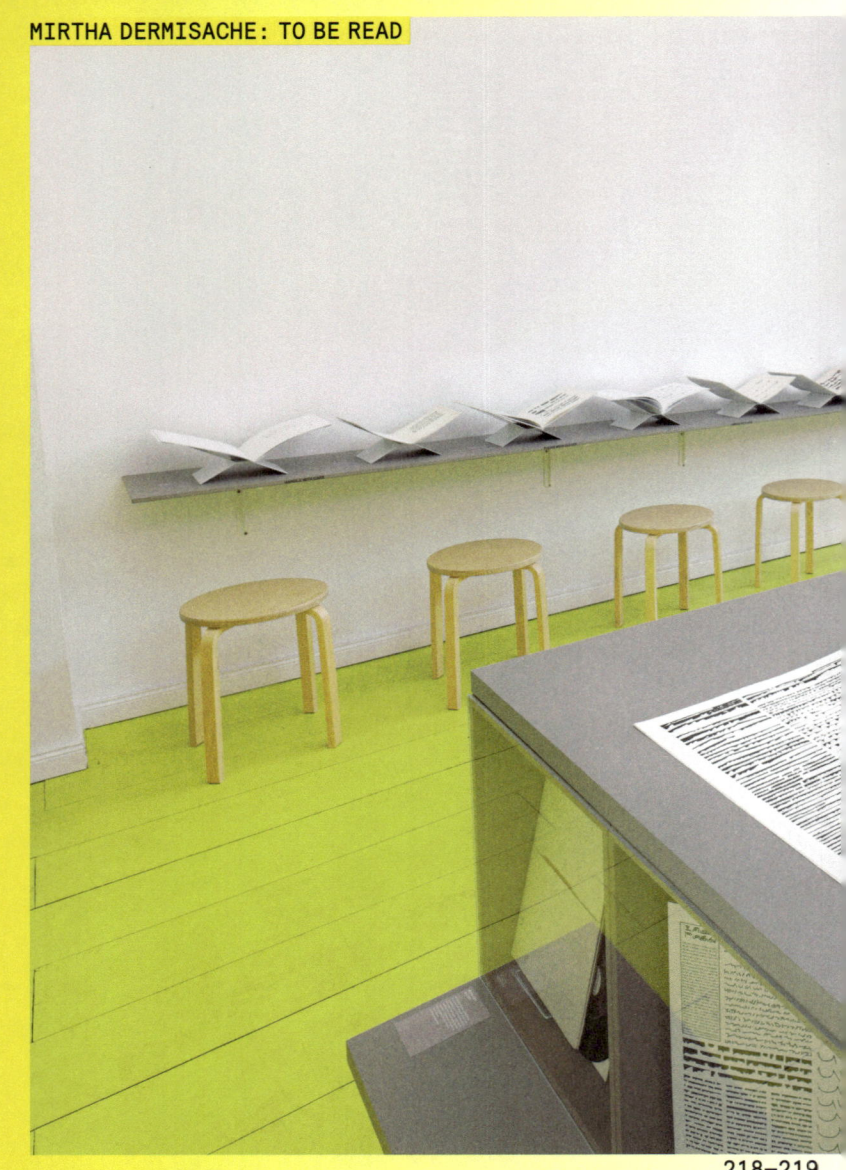

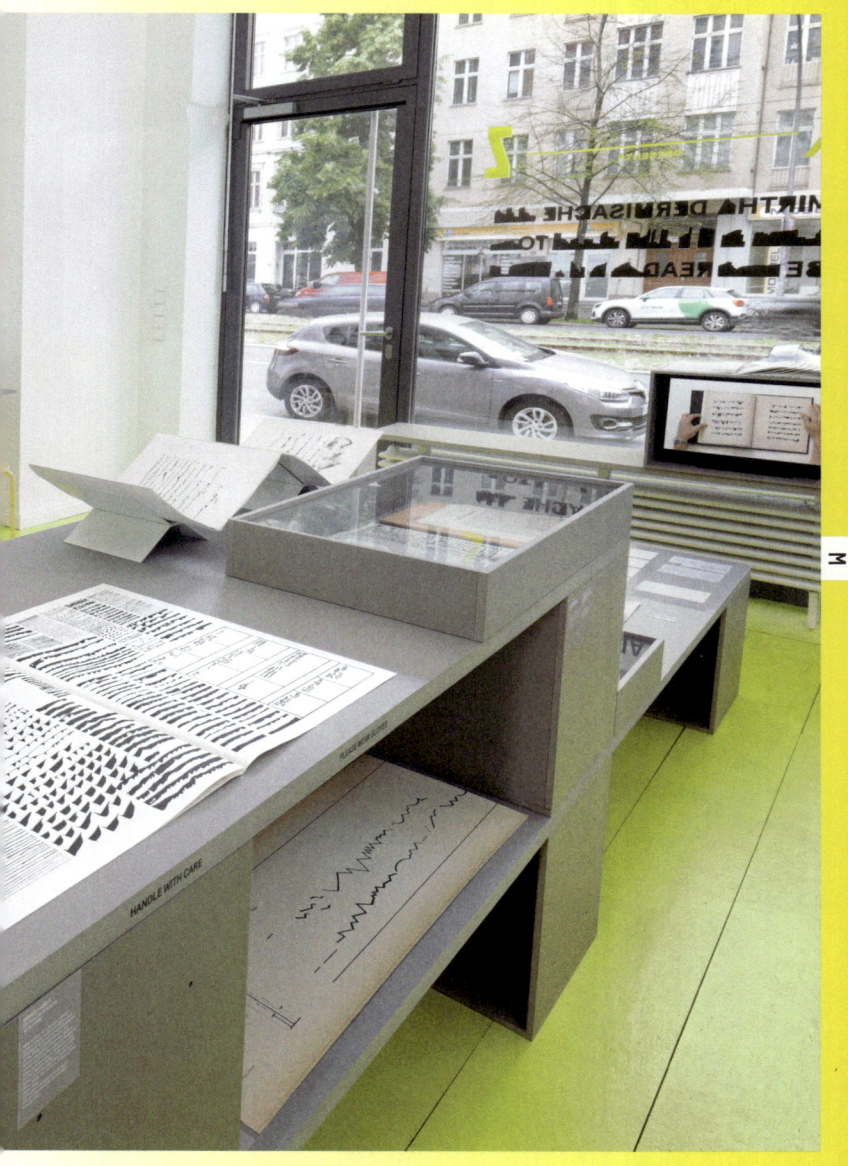

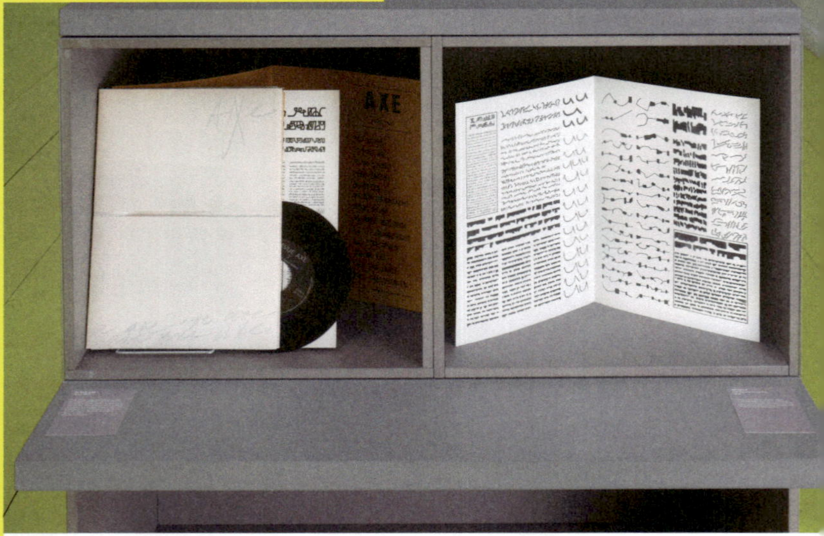

MIRTHA DERMISACHE: TO BE READ

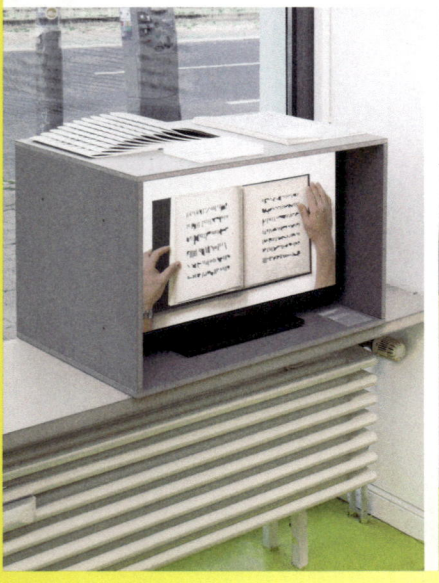
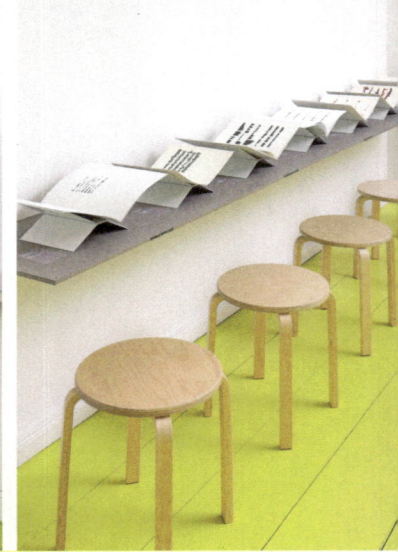

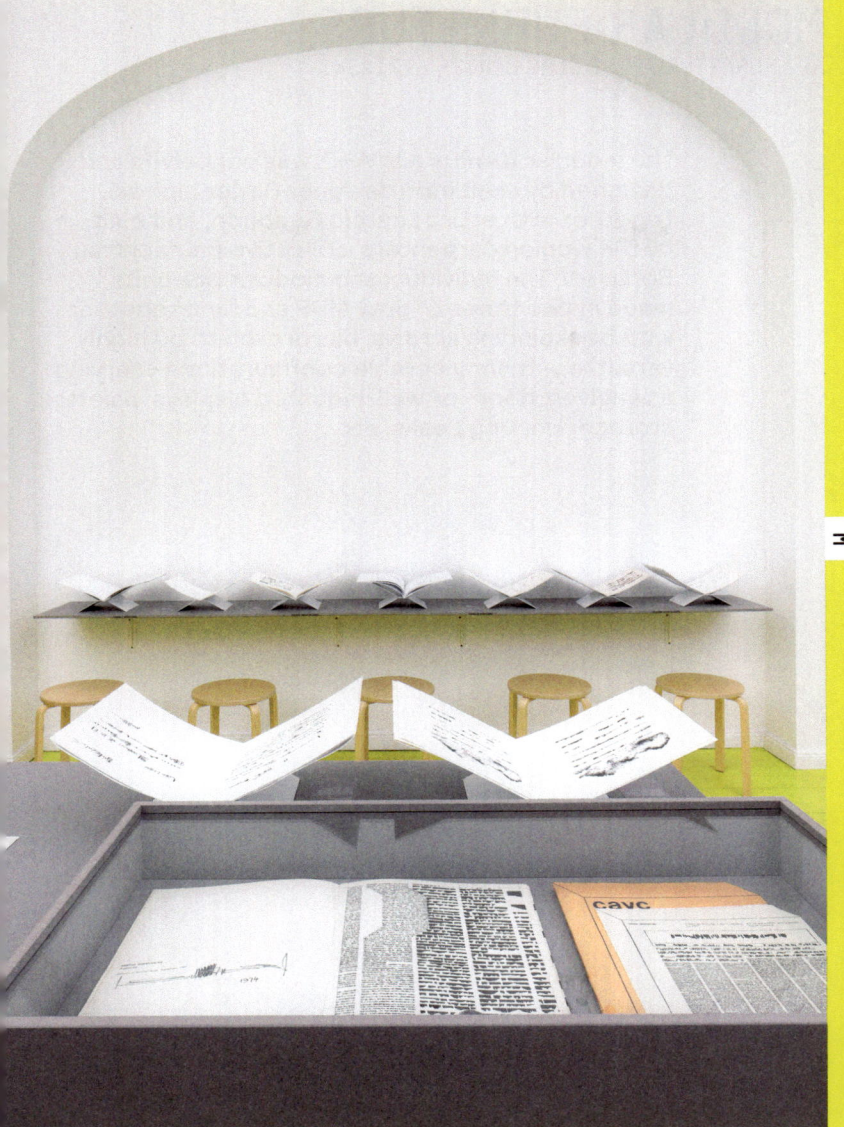

MODULAR FURNITURE
A–Z FURNITURE DESIGN BY BIRGER LIPINSKI

The modular furniture at A—Z was conceived and designed by exhibition designer Birger Lipinski, together with artist Laercio Redondo, and built by the women carpenters' collective Baufachfrau Berlin e.V. The individual and modular box units, made in two tones of grey MDF and held together with bookbinding screws, has proven to be highly versatile with innumerable configurations—serving as shelves, floor- or wall-mounted displays, palettes, storage, working desks, etc.

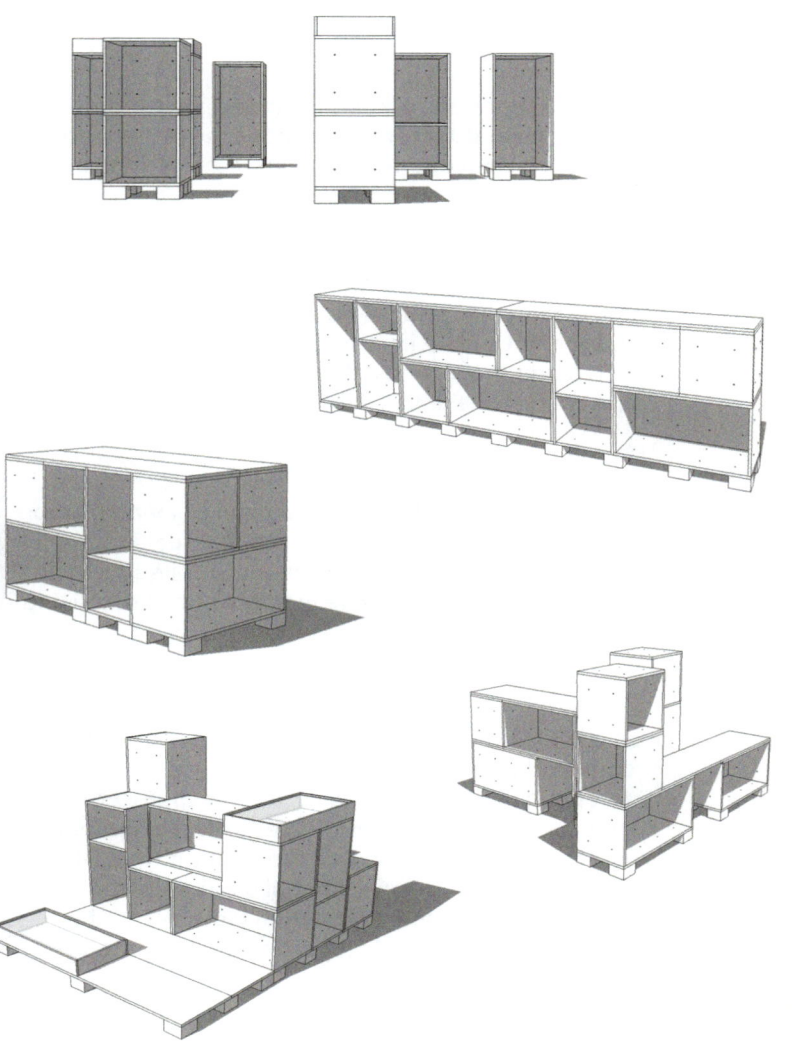

MONEY
A—Z'S SELF-FUNDED JOURNEY

A—Z is an independent, self-funded space that receives no support from any government programs or private sponsors. In its six years of activities, despite many grant applications for public funding, it has only received one small incentive from the Berlin Senate for Culture. The time and energy invested in running A—Z's diverse initiatives come from internal team dedication and, of course, the generous engagement of the invited graphic designers—who often cover travel and exhibit costs from their own resources to make the exhibitions happen.

While A—Z bears the costs of running the space, human resources, and communication, it receives significant practical help in the form of manual labor, lending material resources, or intellectual inputs from the Graphic Design community, colleagues, and close friends who have loyally contributed to making events happen.

All events, workshops, and experiences are offered entirely for free, and are open to both graphic designers and the general public. Small funds come from voluntary donations or sales of event-related artworks on the A—Z website. As the space continues its journey in promoting alternative Graphic Design, funding remains a challenge and A—Z wishes to find ways to achieve financial sustainability through public support. For the whole team, the only certainty is that a lot more could be done with the right financial resources.

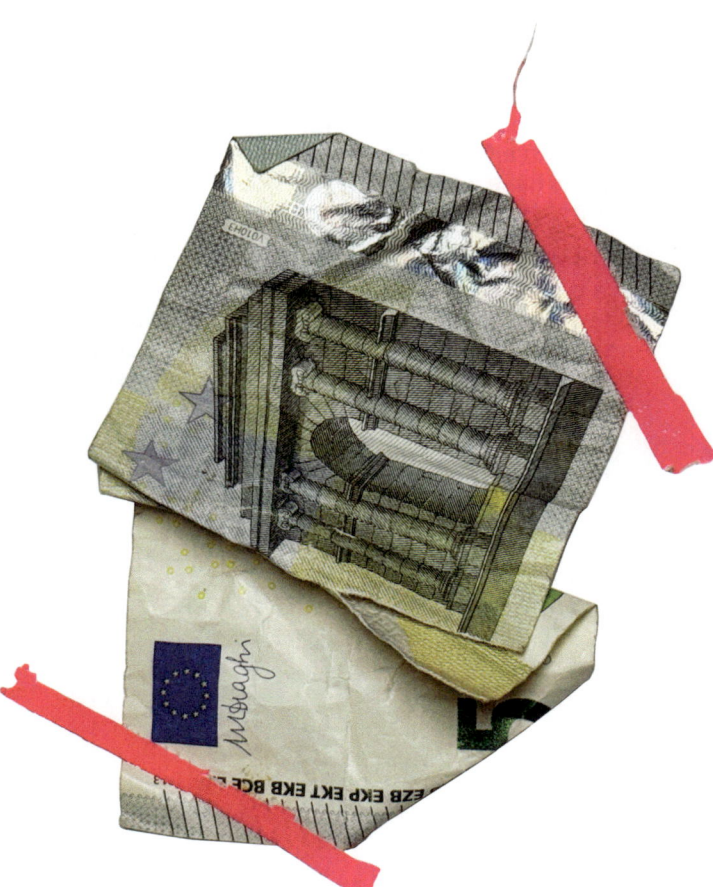

MOZZARELLA & POMODORO
THE LOCAL PIZZA PLACE

Mozzarella & Pomodoro is a cozy little Italian restaurant just a few doors from A—Z. Over the years, it has been a favorite corner where the A—Z team and guests have spent many lovely lunches and dinners during the week and after events.

Marcello, who has run the lower ground floor place in a typical improvised Berlin fashion since 2015, has been a great host, serving delicious Italian pizza and deli foods. He has sometimes even surprised the team, such as with a special dessert after The Rodina's exhibition opening.

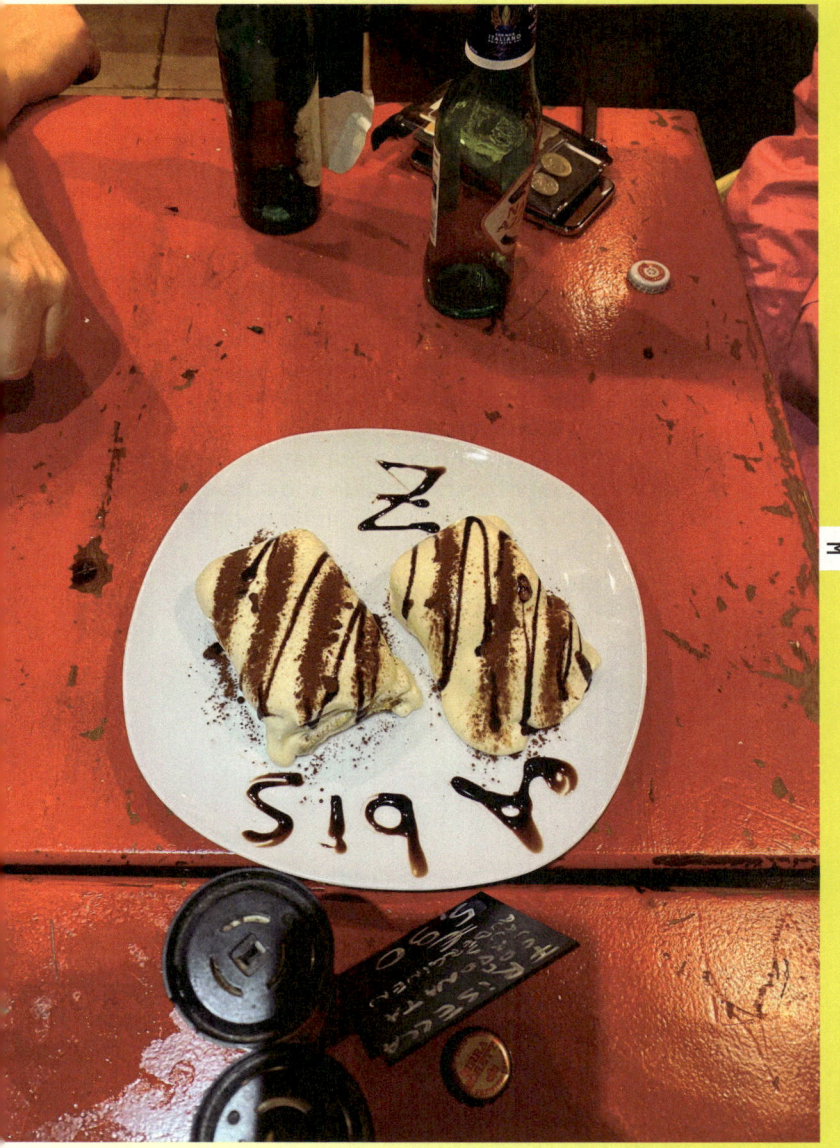

MYSTERIOUS POSTCARD
ANONYMOUS ART PROJECT RELATED TO THE *MIRTHA DERMISACHE: TO BE READ* EXHIBITION

For the *Mirtha Dermisache: To Be Read* exhibition, a flyer replicating one of Dermisache's postcards was designed, printed, and freely distributed to visitors, inspired by Dermisache's strategy of sharing her artwork by using mail services in the 1970s and 1980s. Sometime after, the A—Z team was surprised by a curious returned postcard featuring the German postal service label indicating that postage had not been paid—because the 'stamps' were drawings. The creative sender is still unknown, but no doubt this humorous and subversive attempt would have pleased Dermisache herself.

Invitation to the opening of the exhibition

MIRTHA DERMISACHE: TO BE READ

on Thursday, 6 June 2024, 7 PM
at A—Z, Torstr. 93, Berlin-Mitte

Exhibition dates: 7 June –11 August 2024

Opening hours:
A–Z Thursdays 2–7 PM and by appointment
oxfordberlin display open to the public round the clock
satellite venue: Oxford Str. 3-11, Berlin-Wedding

The exhibition is a collaboration between the Cluster of
Excellence "**Temporal Communities: Doing Literature in a
Global Perspective**" of the Freie Universität Berlin (Curator:
Dr. Regine Ehleiter), A—Z Space for experimental graphic design
(Anja Lutz), oxfordberlin and the Legado Mirtha Dermisache.

www.temporal-communities.de/dermisache
www.a-z-presents.com

TEMPORAL
COMMUNITIES

A ——— Z

Image credit: Mirtha Dermisache, "4 cartes postales", first published by Guy Schraenen éditeur, 1978.
Courtesy Maike Aden, OLegado Mirtha Dermisache

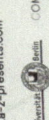

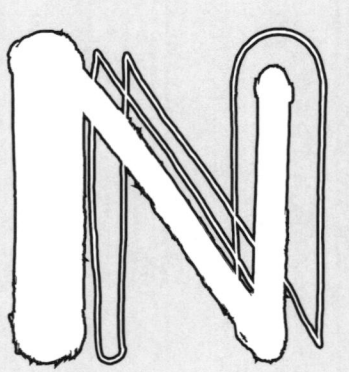
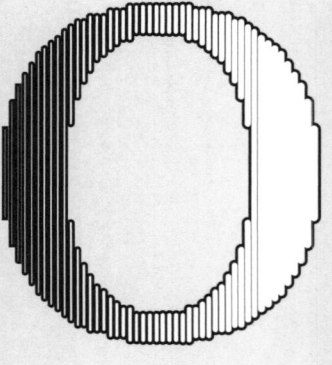

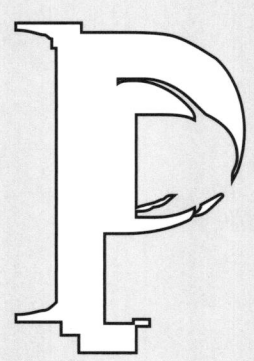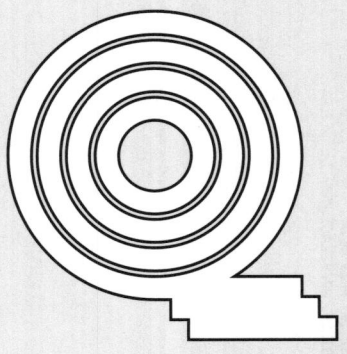

NA KIM
EXHIBITED ARTIST

Na Kim works at the intersection of Graphic Design, art, and curatorial practice, focusing on visual language, space, and memory. Her work re-examines everyday objects and occurrences, which she carefully rearranges and reinterprets—revealing what she calls the "power of found objects", and viewing design as "essentially, creating fiction by chance and sharing it with others". Alongside her artistic and professional practice, Na Kim regularly gives talks and leads workshops, and has presented solo exhibitions internationally. Since 2022, she has also run her own project space, LOOM, in Berlin.

SPACE OF UNCERTAINTY
TRANSITORY HELP DESK
TRANSITORY WORKPLACE, 56

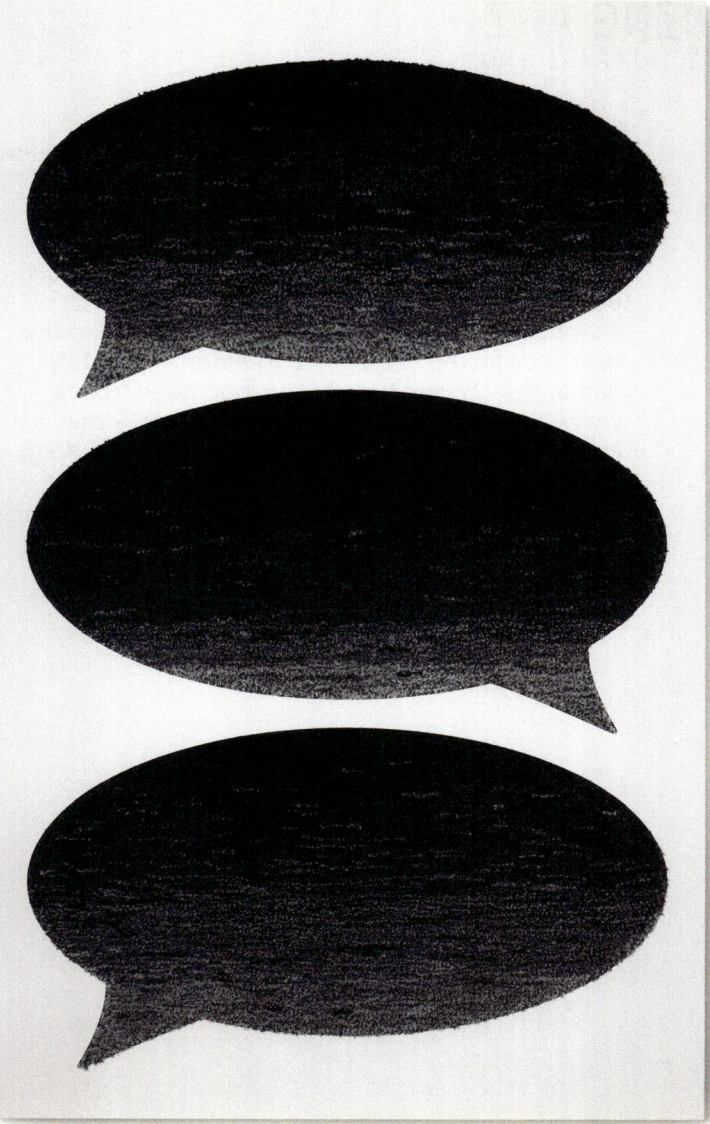

NAMING A–Z
THE ORIGINS OF A–Z'S NAME

The name A—Z most immediately and directly alludes to the standard Western alphabet's first and last letters, which resonates well with the world of Graphic Design, as typography is one of its core elements. However, one less obvious connection pointed out many years ago by Graphic Design colleague Anette Lenz is that A and Z are also the first and last letters of A—Z founder Anja Lutz's name. The chosen type of the logo goes from a very light and extended letter "A" to a very bold and condensed letter "Z", connected by an extra-long dash as a separator, reinforcing the idea of 'the everything in and between' that A—Z aims to be open to in the realm of Graphic Design.

N

NEW ANTHEMS VI (BERLIN) – EINE NEUE HYMNE FÜR DEUTSCHLAND

EXHIBITION BY INKAHOOTS

New Anthems VI (Berlin) – Eine neue Hymne für Deutschland was an interactive installation by the design collective Inkahoots. The exhibition invited the general public to engage in an open dialogue, a critique of contemporary nationalism and national identity, by asking the audience to complete the first line of Germany's national anthem.

Inkahoots invited visitors and passersby to text message their suggestions to the opening verse, originally written by August von Fallersleben, by creatively replacing the final nouns—"Freedom" and "German Fatherland"—in the original line "Einigkeit und Recht und Freiheit für das deutsche Vaterland" (Unity and justice and freedom for the German fatherland).

The installation also featured a mix of historical letters from the Buchstabenmuseum collection, originally belonging to East and West Berlin businesses. The nearly 100 contributions received were immediately displayed and randomly looped, visible around the clock through the A—Z shop window.

The *New Anthems VI (Berlin)* installation questioned the concept of national identity as an invention—a convention that, rather than fixed, is dynamically constructed and constantly made anew.

BUCHSTABENMUSEUM
INKAHOOTS
KERNING
KINDERHYMNE
POST BRANDING MANIFESTO
UNITY AND JUSTICE AND …

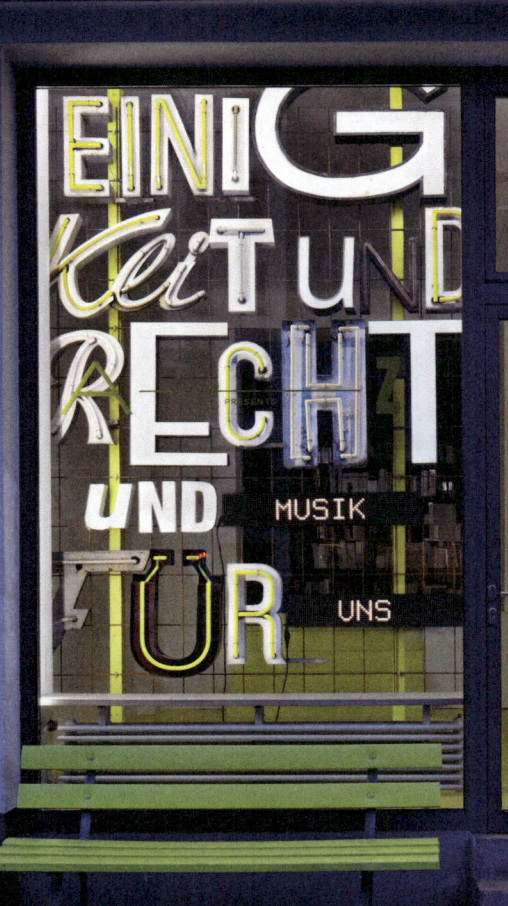

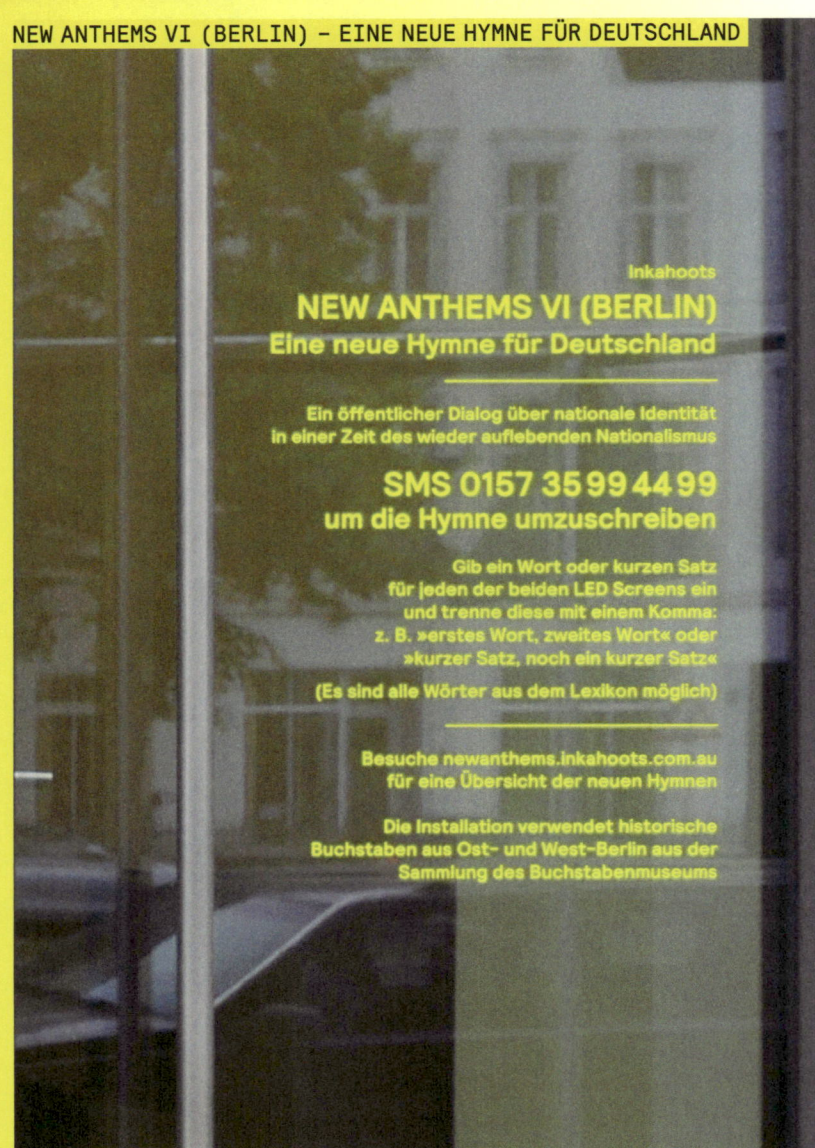

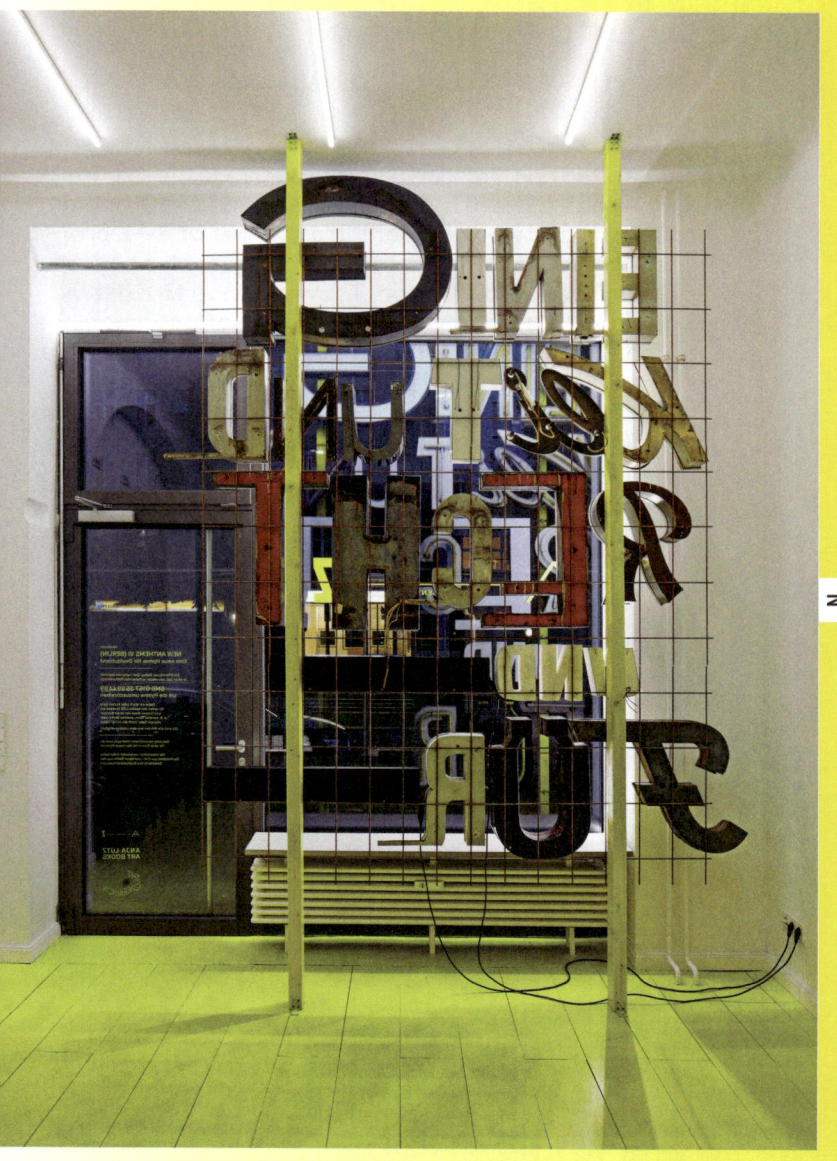

NEWSPAPERS
RANGE OF NEWSPAPER FORMATS USED IN GERMANY

Despite their increasing obsolescence, newspapers continue to have a place and relevance in Graphic Design, and were present in a number of A—Z projects, from workshops to exhibitions, such as *Mirtha Dermisache: To Be Read.* They continue to exist in various sizes, printed on giant roto-offset machines capable of producing high quantities in a short time, and run from rolls of lightweight pulp paper called newsprint. In Germany, the standard formats are the Broadsheet, Nordisch, Rhenish, and Berliner, which can all be used as half-formats for smaller tabloid papers.

In A—Z publications, the Rhenish format was used for the *PULP* newspaper in Patrick Thomas's exhibition. In contrast, the half-Berliner format was used for the *Corrections and Clarifications* publication relating to Anita Di Bianco's exhibition. Each newsprint project demands research on the available newspaper formats, which are comparatively illustrated here for future reference.

ANITA DI BIANCO
PATRICK THOMAS
PULP
THE ERROR IS REGRETTED
THE ERROR IS REGRETTED / WIR ENTSCHULDIGEN UNS FÜR DIESEN FEHLER

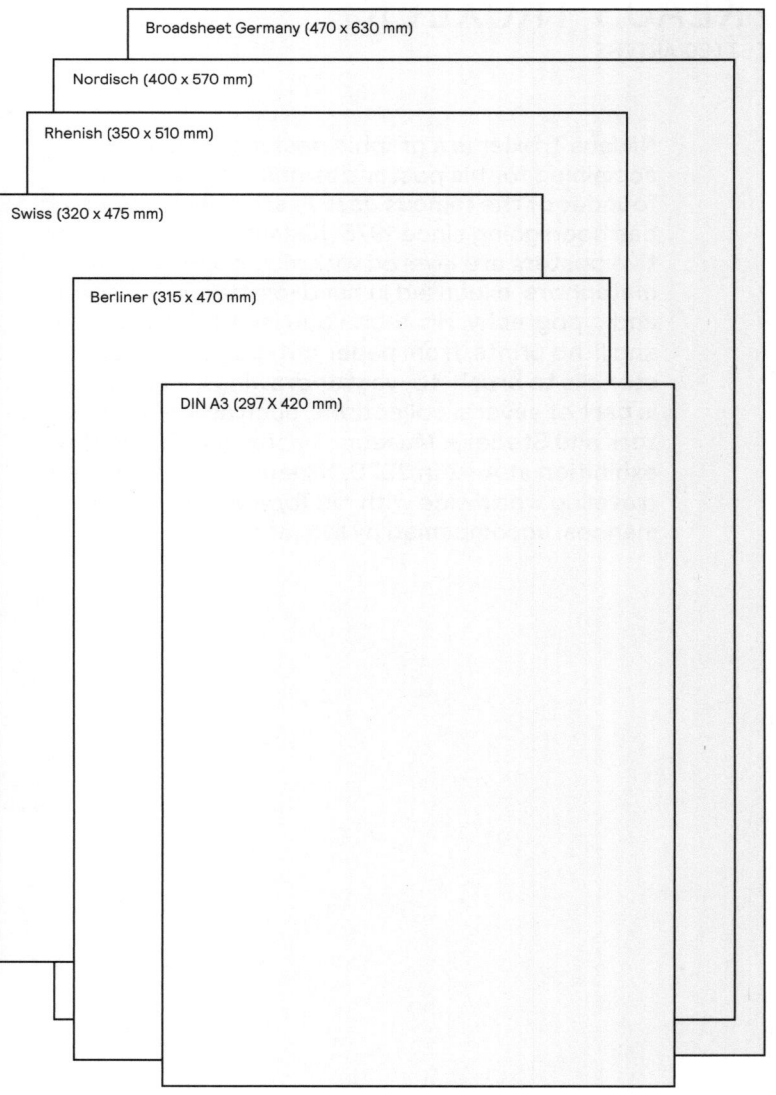

NIKLAUS TROXLER
EXHIBITED ARTIST

Niklaus Troxler is a graphic designer internationally acclaimed for his poster designs. He is also the founder of the famous *Jazz Festival Willisau*, which has been going since 1975. Niklaus Troxler's distinctive posters are layered with visual puns and musical metaphors, executed in hand-crafted illustration and typography. His technique includes silkscreen and litho prints, from paper cut-outs, collages, and stencils to brush-to-vector drawings. His work is part of several collections, such as MoMA New York and Stedelijk Museum Amsterdam. Since the exhibition at A—Z in 2020, Niklaus Troxler has been traveling worldwide with his *Tape Works* performances, accompanied by live jazz music.

Jazz im bau4 Altbüron

Samstag 8. Juni 2024, 20.00 Uhr

Sound of Serendipity

Silke Strahl, ts
Christian Weber, b
Tizia Zimmermann, acc.
Lucas Niggli, dr

NIKLAUS TROXLER

NOT A WHITE CUBE

PRESENTATION BY ANJA LUTZ AT THE *AIGA VIRTUAL DESIGN CONFERENCE* 2021

"The [A—Z] space is thing that is importa it is a working space cube; it is not an exh but rather a mix of a exhibiting, and colla activity in that spac

Excerpt from a Q&A with radio producer Roman Mars

*ot that big. One
t about it is that
t is not a white
bition space only,
signing, publishing,
orating; there is*

NOVO TYPO OFFGRID
BOOK BY MARK VAN WAGENINGEN

How can graphic designers embrace sustainability practices to become self-sufficient? Beyond producing their own letters, how can they produce their own paper and ink, and recycle their work? For Mark van Wageningen, a designer should have a broad understanding of all the elements of their practice, as those are the cornerstones of design.

In this book, he shares the nuts and bolts of a self-initiated DIY project intended as a blueprint for all designers and design studios wishing to become self-sufficient or to recycle their designs. The publication proposes a new standard for polychromatic typography, using plant-based ink and recycled paper, inspiring the pursuit of different approaches in Graphic Design, starting with itself: the cover is letterpress printed with plant-based ink on Amsterdam Pulp Paper.

Novo Typo Offgrid, Mark van Wageningen, The Green Box, 2021. 64 pages, 28 illustrations, 170 x 240 mm, softcover, English.

novo typo grid

Mark van Wageningen

A DIY Manual for Creating a Self-Sufficient Design Studio

THE GREENBOX

NOVO TYPO OFFGRID BERLIN
EXHIBITION BY MARK VAN WAGENINGEN

Novo Typo Offgrid Berlin was an exhibition by the graphic designer Mark van Wageningen. It was conceptualized as a workshop to create a self-sufficient Graphic Design studio. Mark returned to the three fundamental elements of analog Graphic Design—letters, ink, and paper—offering the design community a way to respond to economic and individual vulnerabilities by practicing self-sustainability.

The designer led a series of free DIY experimental workshops, teaching participants an entire design and living strategies workflow by producing self-made recycled pulp paper, plant-based ink, letterpress prints, and even soap. Sieves, spatulas, natural pigments, oils, a manual A4 printing press, paper pulp, and soap-making ingredients transformed A—Z into a workshop, encouraging designers to develop their tools and methods.

Mark's paper-making and color experiments to create his own CMY inks were displayed on the walls, along with larger art prints, created through his sustainable techniques. For the statements, Mark used his multicolor typeface Ziza. Ultimately, participants could learn how to de-standardize their practices and be self-sufficient, sharing tools and knowledge to face a global, overly complex production system, supply chains, and restrictive industrial standards that showed their disruptive effects, especially during pandemic times.

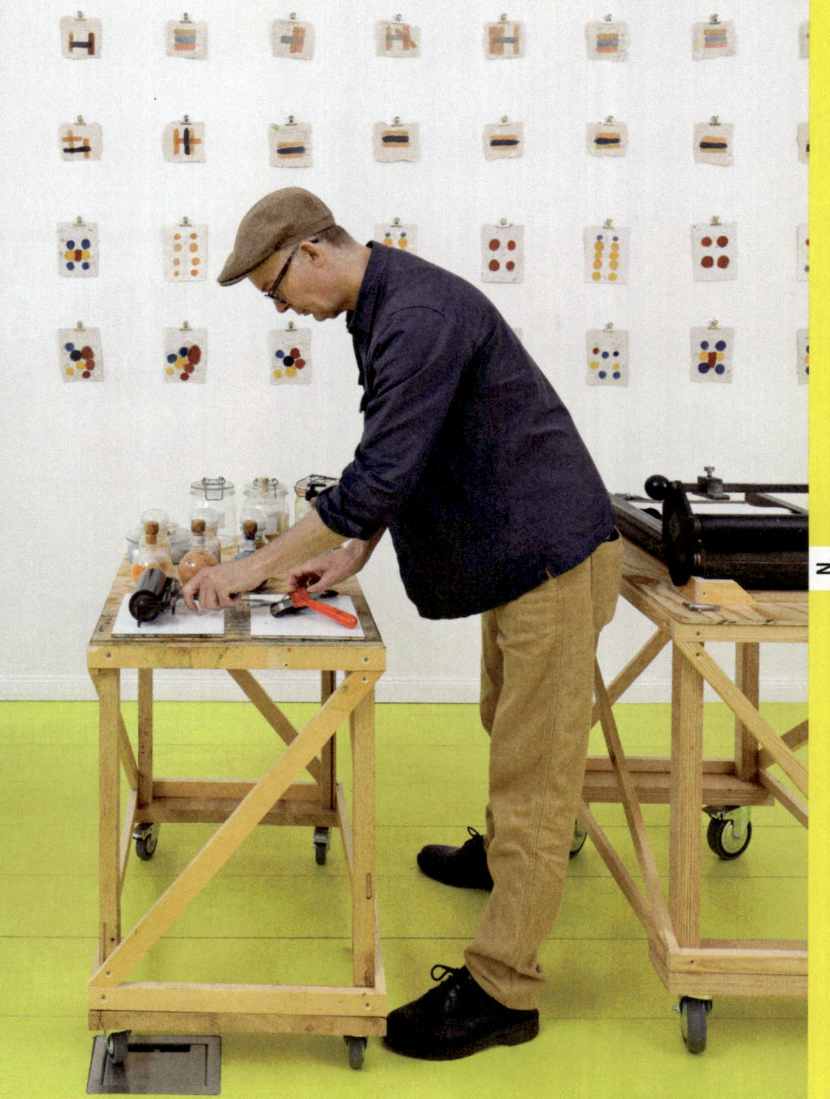

NOVO TYPO OFFGRID BERLIN

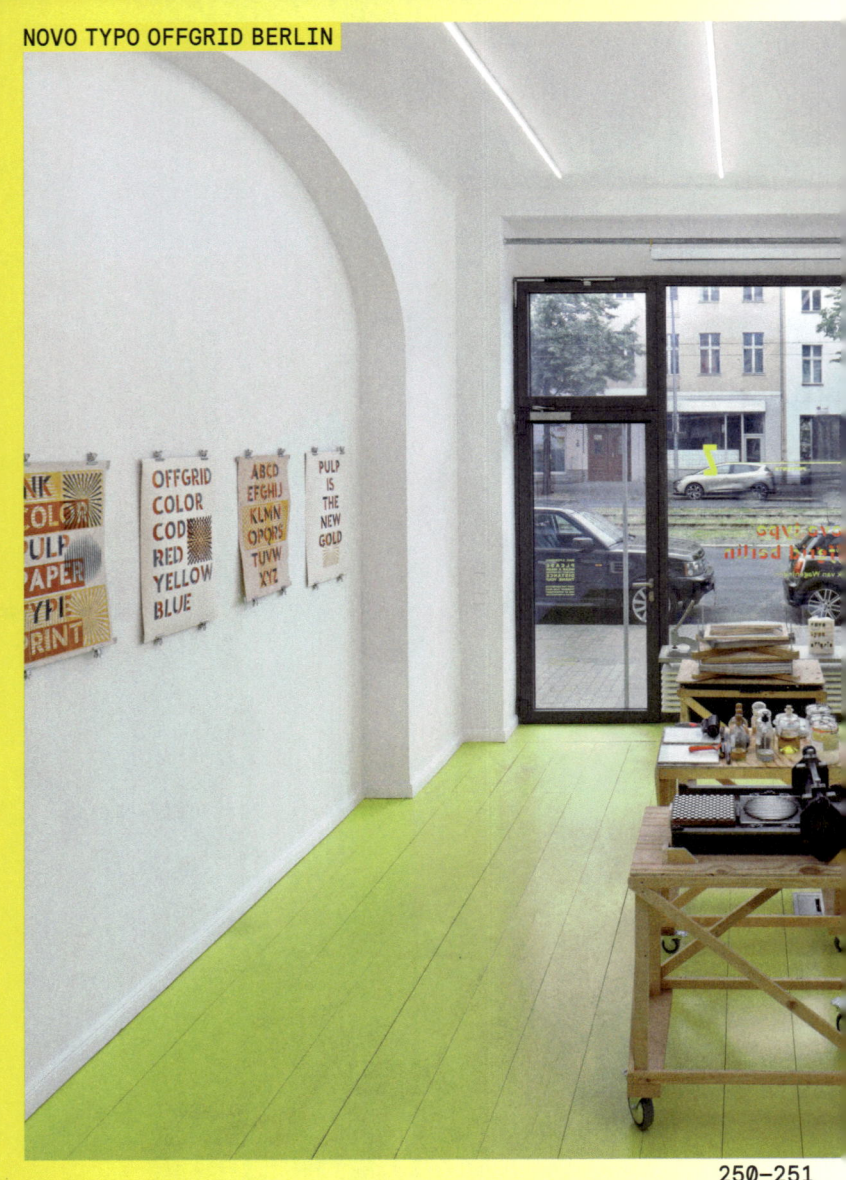

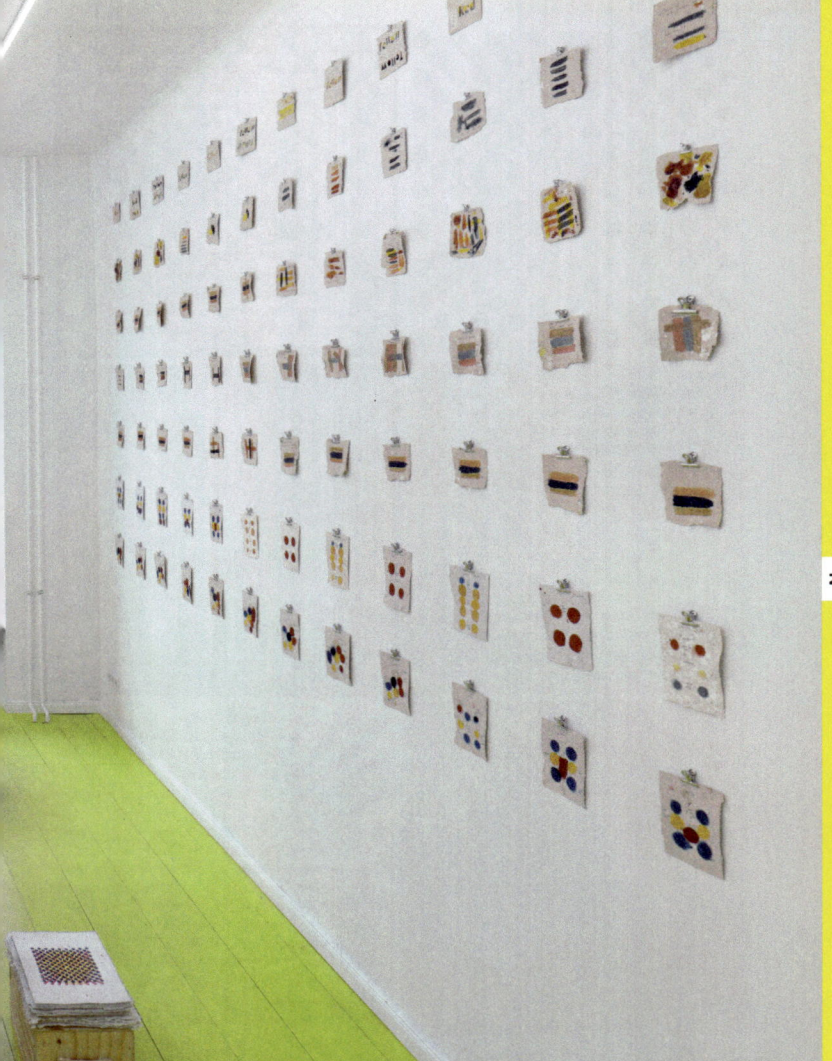

NOVO TYPO OFFGRID BERLIN

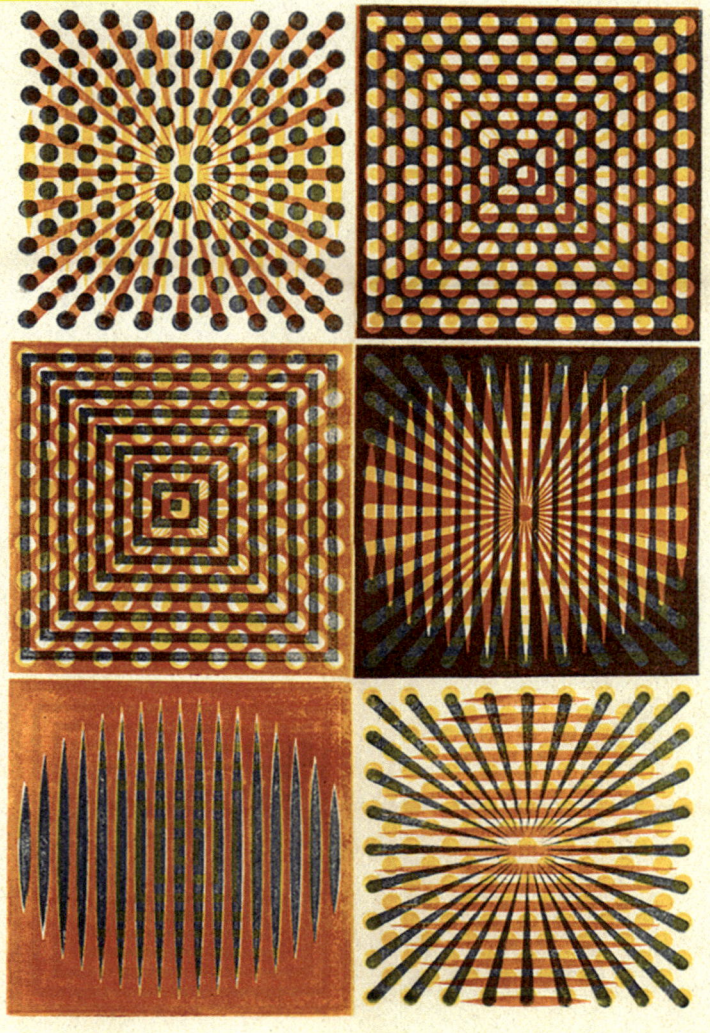

OFFGRID COLOR CODED RED YELLOW BLUE

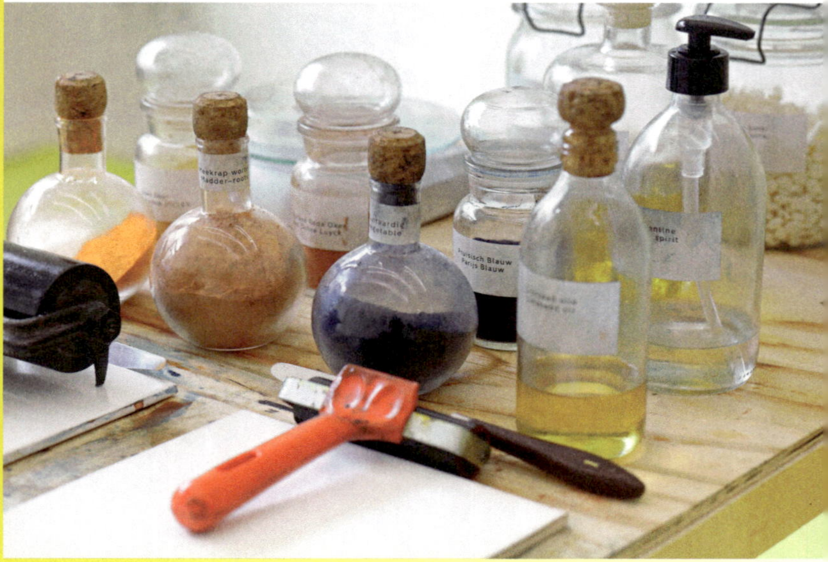

NOVO TYPO OFFGRID BERLIN

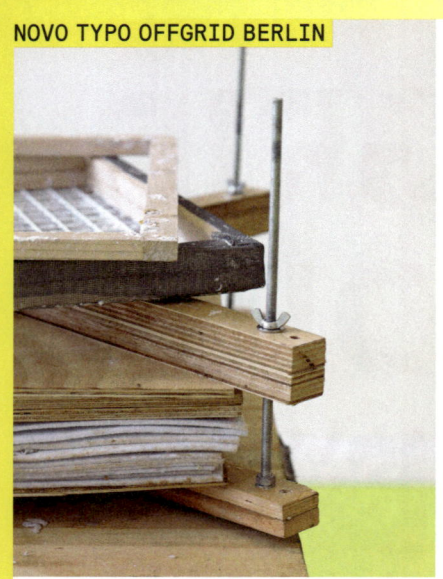
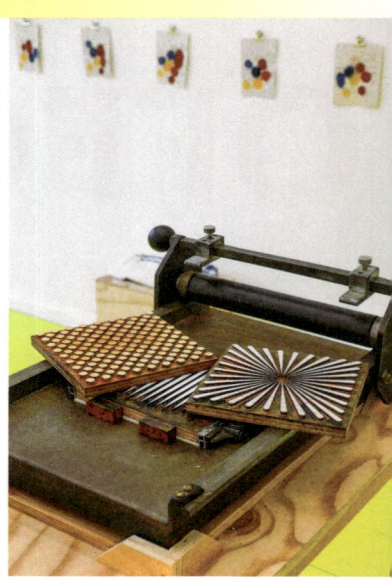

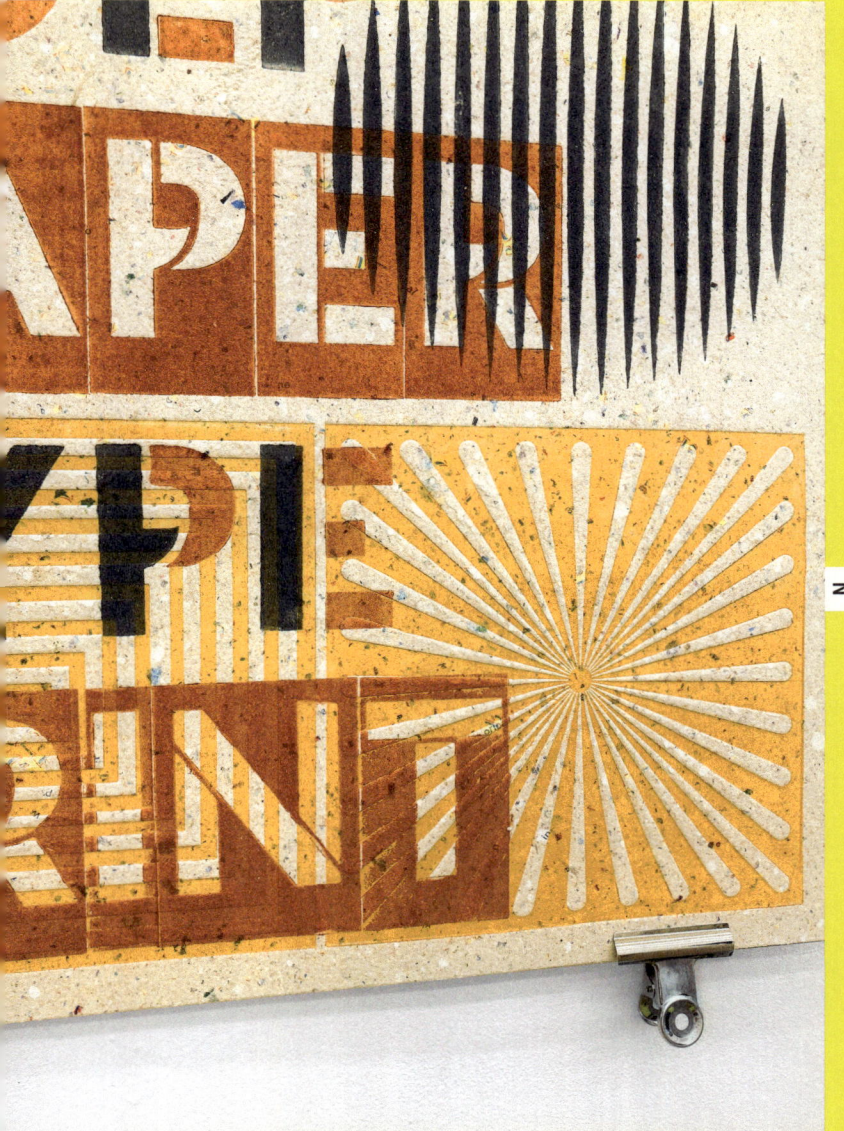

NOVO TYPO OFFGRID BERLIN

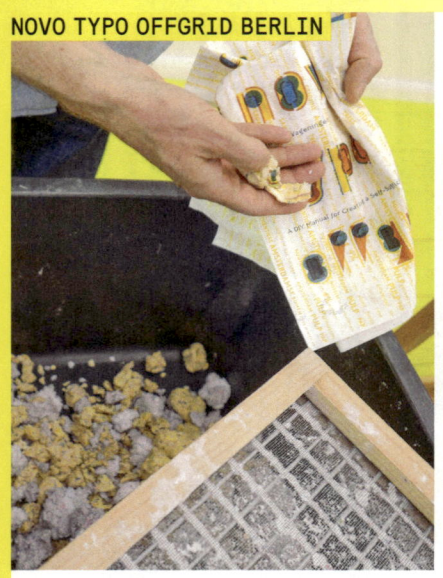
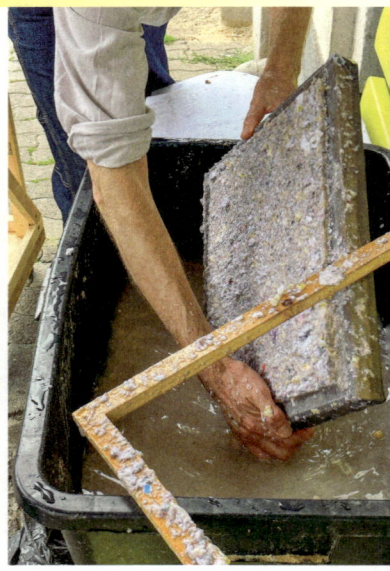
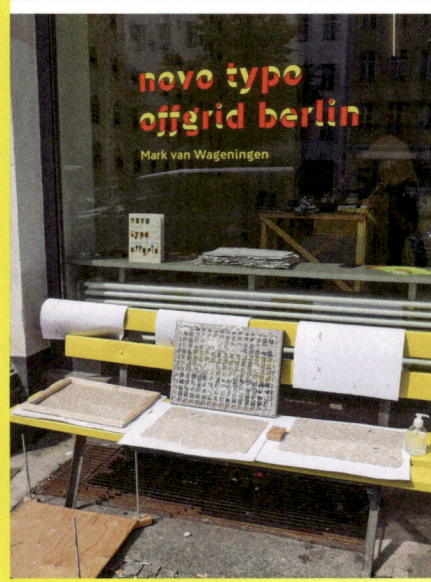
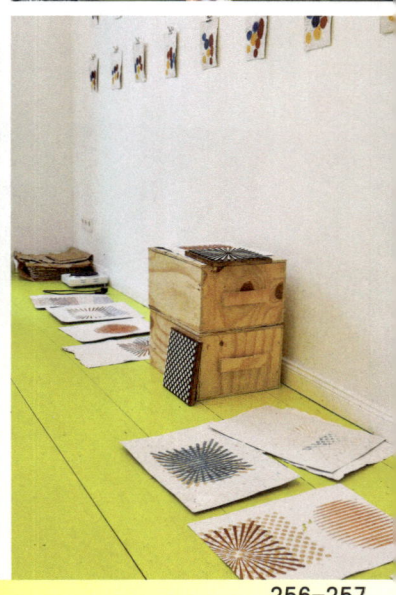

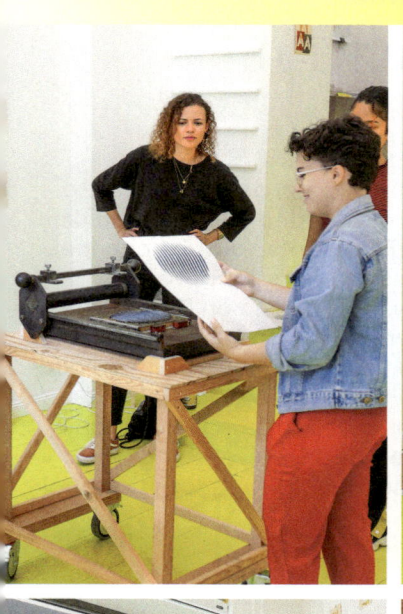
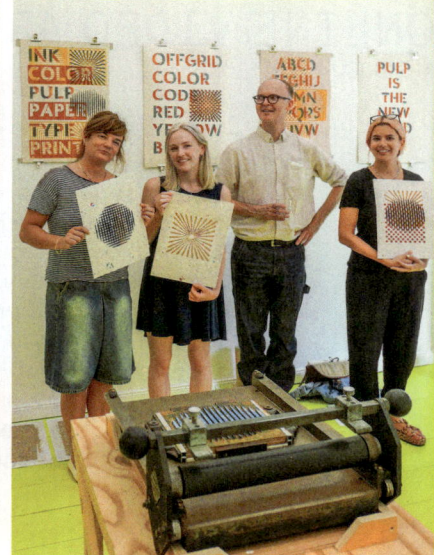
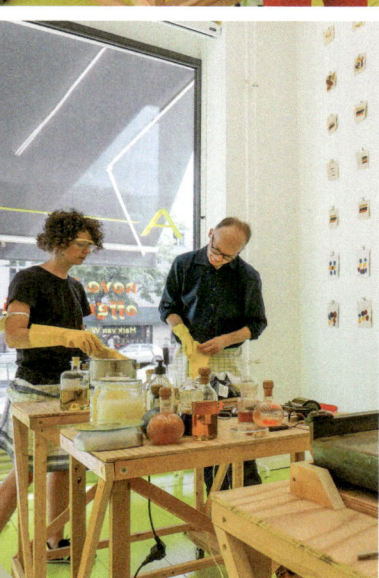
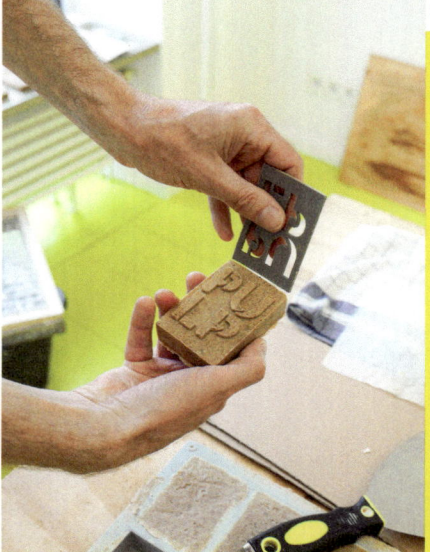

ONLINE VIDEO ARCHIVE
A—Z DOCUMENTATION

Most A—Z events, from talks and performances to exhibition openings, are recorded on video and can be watched on the A—Z Presents YouTube channel. They range from Niklaus Troxler's *Tape Works* performance to panels, like the one on Design and Solidarity, and from a presentation by Mindy Seu to a lecture performance from Tine Melzer, or a guided tour through the *Graphic.Designers.Collectors.* exhibition. These are all currently available in their original language in the video archive, and are also accessible via QR codes found throughout this book.

CURATORIAL PERSPECTIVES
ONLINE VIDEO ARCHIVE

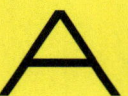

A-Z presents

@a-zpresents3783 · 57 Abonnenten · 21 Videos

A—Z is dedicated to develop, showcase and promote ideas and projects in which grap... **mehr**

a-z-presents.com und **2 weitere Links**

Abonnieren

Übersicht **Videos** 🔍

Neueste Beliebt Älteste

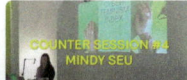

Counter Session #5 | Alex Jordan
18 Aufrufe · vor 7 Monaten

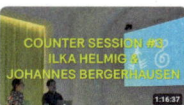

Counter Session #4 | Mindy Seu
87 Aufrufe · vor 7 Monaten

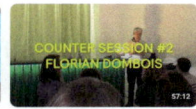

Counter Session #3 | Ilka Helmig and Johannes Bergerhausen
40 Aufrufe · vor 7 Monaten

Counter Session #2 | Florian Dombois
80 Aufrufe · vor 8 Monaten

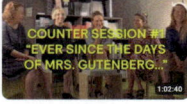

Counter Session #1 | "Ever since the days of Mrs. Gutenberg…"
90 Aufrufe · vor 8 Monaten

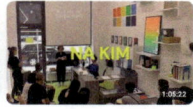

Na Kim | Transitory Workplace, 56
122 Aufrufe · vor 2 Jahren

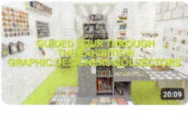

Anja Lutz | Guided Tour through the exhibition Graphic.Designers.Collectors.
239 Aufrufe · vor 2 Jahren

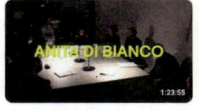

Anita Di Bianco in conversation with Florian Wüst and Anna Bromley | The Error Is...
80 Aufrufe · vor 2 Jahren

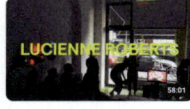

Lucienne Roberts | Perhaps it's not you, it's me.
140 Aufrufe · vor 2 Jahren

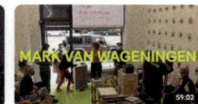

Mark van Wageningen | Novo Typo Offgrid
97 Aufrufe · vor 2 Jahren

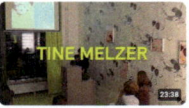

Tine Melzer | Blumen sind geil
228 Aufrufe · vor 2 Jahren

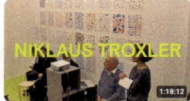

Niklaus Troxler | Tape Works
189 Aufrufe · vor 2 Jahren

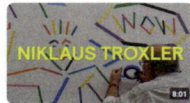

Niklaus Troxler | Performance "Tape Works" with Silke Eberhard, Niklaus Neuser and...
273 Aufrufe · vor 2 Jahren

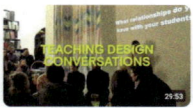

Teaching Design Conversations | Talks by Imad Gebrayel and Stefanie Rau
81 Aufrufe · vor 2 Jahren

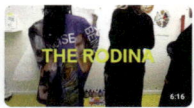

The Rodina | When the Work is Done
97 Aufrufe · vor 2 Jahren

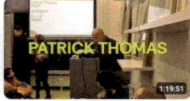

Patrick Thomas | Pulp
219 Aufrufe · vor 2 Jahren

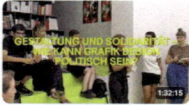

Gestaltung & Solidarität | Mara Recklies, Susanne Beer, Sandy Kaltenborn, Franzi...
203 Aufrufe · vor 2 Jahren

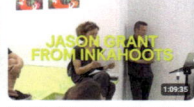

Jason Grant (Inkahoots) | New Anthems VI (Berlin)
47 Aufrufe · vor 2 Jahren

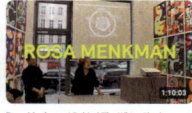

Rosa Menkman | Behind The White Shadows
96 Aufrufe · vor 2 Jahren

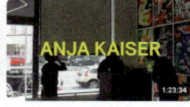

Anja Kaiser | Bodies of Discourse
454 Aufrufe · vor 2 Jahren

OUT & ABOUT
A–Z PROJECTS ON THE ROAD

A—Z Out & About marked the most recent chapter of A—Z Presents, taking the space on a journey outside Berlin. The main idea was to initiate a season of collaborations, partnering with graphic designers and institutions worldwide by developing and performing activities in their locations.

The first stop was the *Index Art Book Fair* in Mexico City, featuring *Recipes for Connecting*, followed by the Graphic Design festival *Festa del Grafisme* in Portbou, Spain, to showcase posters from the Rebellion Riso Posters Collab exhibition *Time is Running*. For Barcelona Design Week, a new version of *Recipes for Connecting* was presented at Casa Bonay in collaboration with Laura Meseguer.

The program continued with participation at the *Tokyo Art Book Fair*, displaying a selection of items from all previous exhibitions at A—Z. The same exhibition travelled to Dongguan, China, to be presented at the *Bigger Art Book Fair*. The project made its next stop at the German Embassy in Beijing, featuring the installation *Connecting from A—Z* in the group exhibition *Senses Unleashed—An Inclusive Exhibition*.

A—Z Out & About will continue collaborating with other individuals and institutions around the world, sharing its unique approach by researching, curating, learning from each other, and executing activities to explore Graphic Design's potential and consider what it might become.

BARCELONA DESIGN WEEK
FESTA DEL GRAFISME
REBELLION RISO POSTERS COLLAB
RECIPES FOR CONNECTING
TOKYO ART BOOK FAIR

OUT & ABOUT

PANDEMIC
SURVIVAL STRATEGIES DURING LOCKDOWN

It is no exaggeration to state that the Covid-19 pandemic was challenging for humanity, and its unprecedented impact on modern life is still present. For A—Z, it was no different, yet the space managed to find ways to carry on and adapt to all degrees of lockdown measures, remaining present for the community, both on-site and virtually.

These measures included creatively adapting its exhibitions, allowing them to be displayed through the large window, to running interactive online projects, such as *Connecting from A—Z*, or adapting to a minimal scale and one-to-one events to comply with strict local regulations, such as with *Time for Books*.

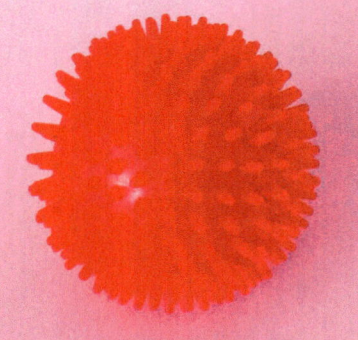

PATRICK THOMAS
EXHIBITED ARTIST

Patrick Thomas is a graphic artist, author, and educator based in London, Barcelona, and Berlin, where he set up his silkscreen press and studio in 2016. Since 2007, he has focused on creating and releasing personal work at the intersection of art and Graphic Design, using generic forms of communication, like flyers, ads, and stencil graphics, for his visual collages exhibited around the globe. Patrick Thomas runs the Open Collab, a workshop format of remote, real-time collaboration that combines and overprints the participants' designs into new collective works. Since 2013, he has been a Professor of Visual Communication at the Stuttgart State Academy of Art and Design.

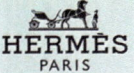

JUNK REA
HOUSEHOLD R
• Appliances • Fu
• Mattresses • TV-E
• Exercise Equipm
• Pianos • Pool Tab
• Hot Tub • Spa • F
WE'LL TAKE A
Ask Fo
310.80

Herm
cavalier j

Inspiron 15 3511

Dell.com/support

CALI

SMOG

CHEC

WE BUY
JUNK CARS

PERHAPS IT'S NOT YOU, IT'S ME.
EXHIBITION BY LUCIENNE ROBERTS

Perhaps It's Not You, It's Me. was an installation by Lucienne Roberts, transforming A—Z into a space of humor and heartbreak. A double bed set the scene where the artist opened to the public her complicated relationship with her long-standing partner, Graphic Design. The scene was set to tell the love story: on the walls, an oversized love letter written by Lucienne was alongside her lover's reply, a wallpaper decorated with Lucienne's design work, and three mirrors in square, circle, and triangle shapes, referencing the Bauhaus Movement.

A video where Lucienne reads her letter while slowly disappearing behind emoji stickers could be seen from the street. Her bed sheets and pajamas featured a YALTD (You're A Long Time Dead) design, along with towels, T-shirts, pins, cups, pens, books, and even a playlist—all elements to corroborate the 'situationship' atmosphere the artist wanted to evoke.

Visitors could write and display their own letters to Graphic Design on the wall as Lucienne took the audience on an intensely personal journey from her early utopian zeal about Graphic Design to a dystopian dilemma and back again. Part critique, part provocation, part celebration of Graphic Design and what it can do, the installation found inspiration in the language of love and leave-takings, set against the finite nature of life.

PERHAPS IT'S NOT YOU, IT'S ME.

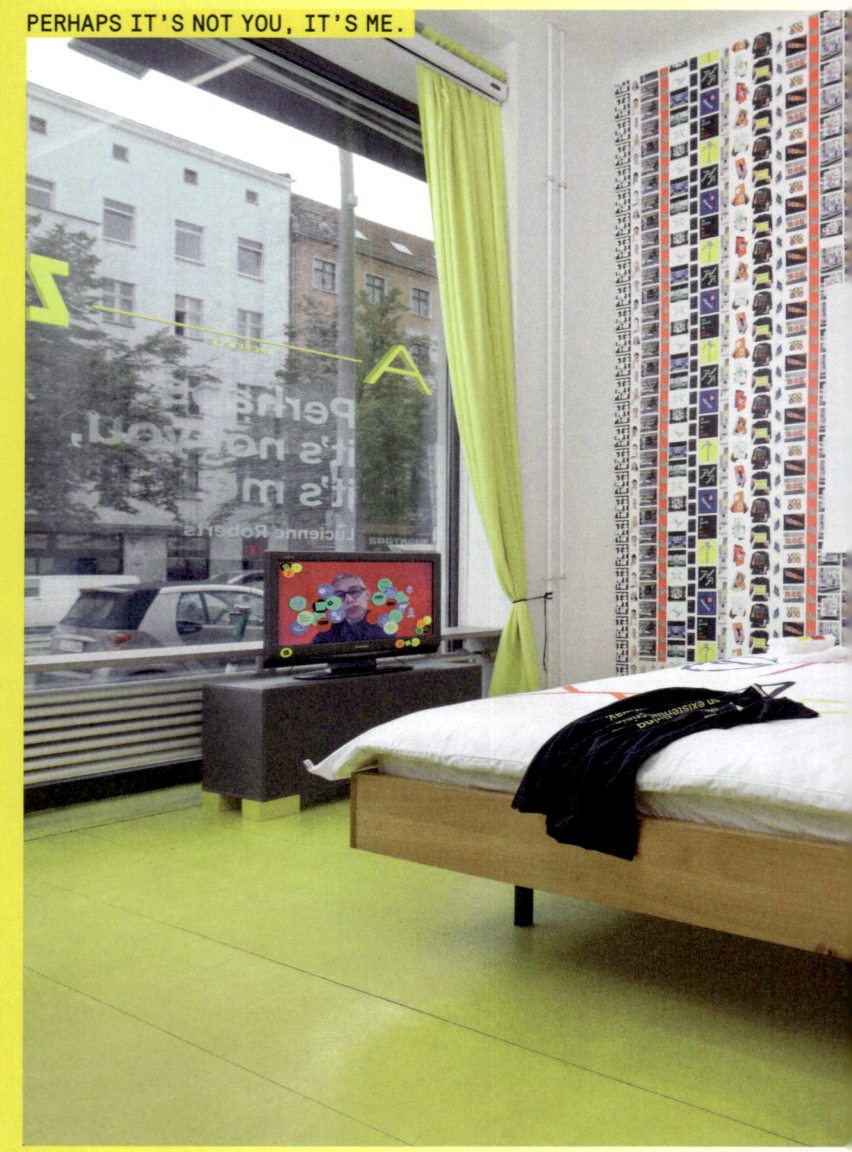

P

PERHAPS IT'S NOT YOU, IT'S ME.

Dear Graphic Design

There's no easy way to say this but, for a while now, I've felt uncomfortable being in this relationship with you. You've been my trusty partner for over 25 years so I don't say this lightly. I am who I am largely because of you. You have given me sustenance, you have fed my heart and soul. But I am not sure I know you anymore or, rather, I am worried that your values are no longer mine. Perhaps they never were. Perhaps we were never a good fit and I got it wrong. Perhaps it's not you, it's me.

I was young when we met. Everything about you seemed so confident, so sure, so visionary and optimistic. You were going to change the world, no? For the better, right? For everybody? I fell for you because you were arty, intellectual, confident and you really seemed to care. You have taught me so much, you were – are – interested in everything. Yes, everything. I was proud to be part of your gang. Together, we'd make a positive difference.

And we did make a good team for a while. Really good. But the thing that makes you so wonderful is also your undoing. You can light up a room, extend a hand of kindness, touch people's hearts. I've seen you make the impenetrable easy to understand, persuade the most stubborn of people to change their minds, happy to take your lead. You're trusted. But perhaps you shouldn't be because you're a chameleon, going with the flow, turning a blind eye, playing with people's feelings. Mine too, sadly.

Yet, I still ♥ U. Trying to part feels futile. Reminders of you are everywhere. I can't imagine a future without you. I know I can't demand that you change. I certainly don't want to constrain you but I need you to see that your behaviour is making us vulnerable. You've been living in the moment, while an existential crisis is heading our way. You've not noticed, but I have. What I see is a version of you seduced by popularity. Friendships that don't last, you feeding an endless insatiable churn. It will destroy us, truly, it will.

I regret giving you so much power. Your approbation is addictive, when you say 'I love you', I run eagerly towards you, arms outstretched. You give shape to my dreams and ideas. You are full of endless possibility, you lure, you beckon, you offer so much – but your rejections are becoming harder and harder to bear. So I turn to walk away, and you say, 'Let's try again' and we do, despite the negotiation that ensues. Perhaps we just need time apart, to rekindle the hope, the potential? But wait! Time is against us. You're still young but it's different for me.

There's a saying, 'You're A Long Time Dead', and it's buzzing in my head. It's paralysing. I question everything. So here I am, writing this crazy letter, arguing that to be valuable we must reinvent ourselves, fearful that I am running out of time, asking if we're holding each other back. And, in the meantime, searching for a new way to stay together.

Lucienne

Lucie... Am I meant to be angry or sad? Not sure. A lot of both perhaps? I tried drafting a 'proper' letter back but couldn't manage it somehow, perhaps because your message isn't clear. Are you actually saying goodbye?

~~Dear Graphic Design~~

Dearest L... I've tried drafting a 'proper' letter back many times but am finding it tough. Perhaps I'm not meant to reply?

There's no easy way to say this but, for a while now, I've felt uncomfortable being in this relationship with you. You've been my trusty partner for over 25 years so I don't say this lightly. I am who I am largely because of you. You have given me sustenance, you have fed my heart and soul. But I am not sure I know you anymore or, rather, I am worried that your values are no longer mine. Perhaps they never were. Perhaps we were never a good fit and I got it wrong. Perhaps it's not you, it's me.

It's mutual... but there has always been a bit of a disconnect, don't you think, between what I am and what you wanted me to be?
I am who I am, Lucie. I didn't set out to mislead. It's not me, it's you, you're right.

I loved your faith in me, your unerring belief, perhaps I was a wee bit flattered even. But you were young. It's a cliché but you are older now so you know life's more complicated than this. Thanks for the compliments though... always nice to hear.

I was young when we met. Everything about you seemed so confident, so sure, so visionary and optimistic. You were going to change the world, no? For the better, right? For everybody? I fell for you because you were arty, intellectual, confident and you really seemed to care. You have taught me so much, you were – are – interested in everything. Yes, everything. I was proud to be part of your gang. Together, we'd make a positive difference.

Um... not on my own, no.
And, incidentally, I did – and do – 'care'.
Yes! I'm interested in EVERYTHING and that means I'm interested in ANY views ... and in having the freedom to express them.
I feel exhausted reading this. Isn't it all a bit over dramatic?

Actually, we still are a 'good' team. But, like you, I'm neither all 'good' nor 'bad'. I am the product of many things, many influences, many needs. You always applauded diversity but I don't seem to see that's what I am about too. I like communicating with everyone, not just a select few. I don't judge. I believe in choice and free will. I'd be the green eyed monster about? I am more and more loved, often still Oops, did I really say that?! I don't really mean it. Sorry.

And we did make a good team for a while. Really good. But the thing that makes you so wonderful is also your undoing. You can light up a room, extend a hand of kindness, touch people's hearts. I've seen you make the impenetrable easy to understand, persuade the most stubborn of people to change their minds, happy to take your lead. You're trusted. But perhaps you shouldn't be because you're a chameleon, going with the flow, turning a blind eye, playing with people's feelings. Mine too, sadly.

I love people. I love interaction, I love communication. That's simply who I am.
I see it differently. I don't set out to be duplicitous.
But it's you who has turned a blind eye! You know I can be spontaneous without being insensitive (I hope). You know I can be serious but also a bit of a clown.

Yet, I still ♥ U. Trying to part feels futile. Reminders of you are everywhere. I can't imagine a future without you. I know I can't demand that you change. I certainly don't want to constrain you but I need you to see that your behaviour is making us vulnerable. You've been living in the moment, while an existential crisis is heading our way. You've not noticed, but I have. What I see is a version of you seduced by popularity. Friendships that don't last, you feeding an endless insatiable churn. It will destroy us, truly, it will.

I still ♥ you too. You surmised the last of me, and why wouldn't I want a partner who does that?
And now we get to it... You do, of course, want a different version of me. The strange thing is that I've always accepted you as you are.
I hear you – let's say I've always been way more interested in politics than me, and that's really what you're talking about here. Not your problem, not mine.
I genuinely love learning from EVERYONE and sharing THEIR ideas. I don't want to change them as you seem to.
I help people learn, hear their families, share opinions. How is this destroying us, exactly?

I regret giving you so much power. Your approbation is addictive, when you say 'I love you', I run eagerly towards you, arms outstretched. You give shape to my dreams and ideas. You are full of endless possibility, you lure, you beckon, you offer so much – but your rejections are becoming harder and harder to bear. So I turn to walk away, and you say, 'Let's try again' and we do, despite the negotiation that ensues. Perhaps we just need time apart, to rekindle the hope, the potential? But wait! Time is against us. You're still young but it's different for me.

If I have too much power, Lucie, it's because you gave it to me.
You wanted some of what I can make possible. You chose me, not the other way round!
I helped you find your voice, and that's good isn't it?
Criticism can be constructive sometimes, no?
Um... perhaps you need to lighten up a wee bit? You take everything SO SERIOUSLY.
OK – perhaps, I have time in a way that you do not. Is this really what this letter is all about?

There's a saying, 'You're A Long Time Dead', and it's buzzing in my head. It's paralysing. I question everything. So here I am, writing this crazy letter, arguing that to be valuable we must reinvent ourselves, fearful that I am running out of time, asking if we're holding each other back. And, in the meantime, searching for a new way to stay together.

Yup... but I am pretty good at surviving! That's the benefit of being a bit of a chameleon, eh?
Sometimes, when I look myself too seriously or was being ridiculously smug, you joked, 'It's only Graphic Design'. But it sounds like you can't be so lighthearted anymore? Your confusion sounds painful. I don't feel defensive and I'm not going to try to persuade you. You need to follow your heart. Don't get me wrong, I'm still here for you. I'm not going anywhere, not yet anyway.

Graphic Design
~~Lucienne~~

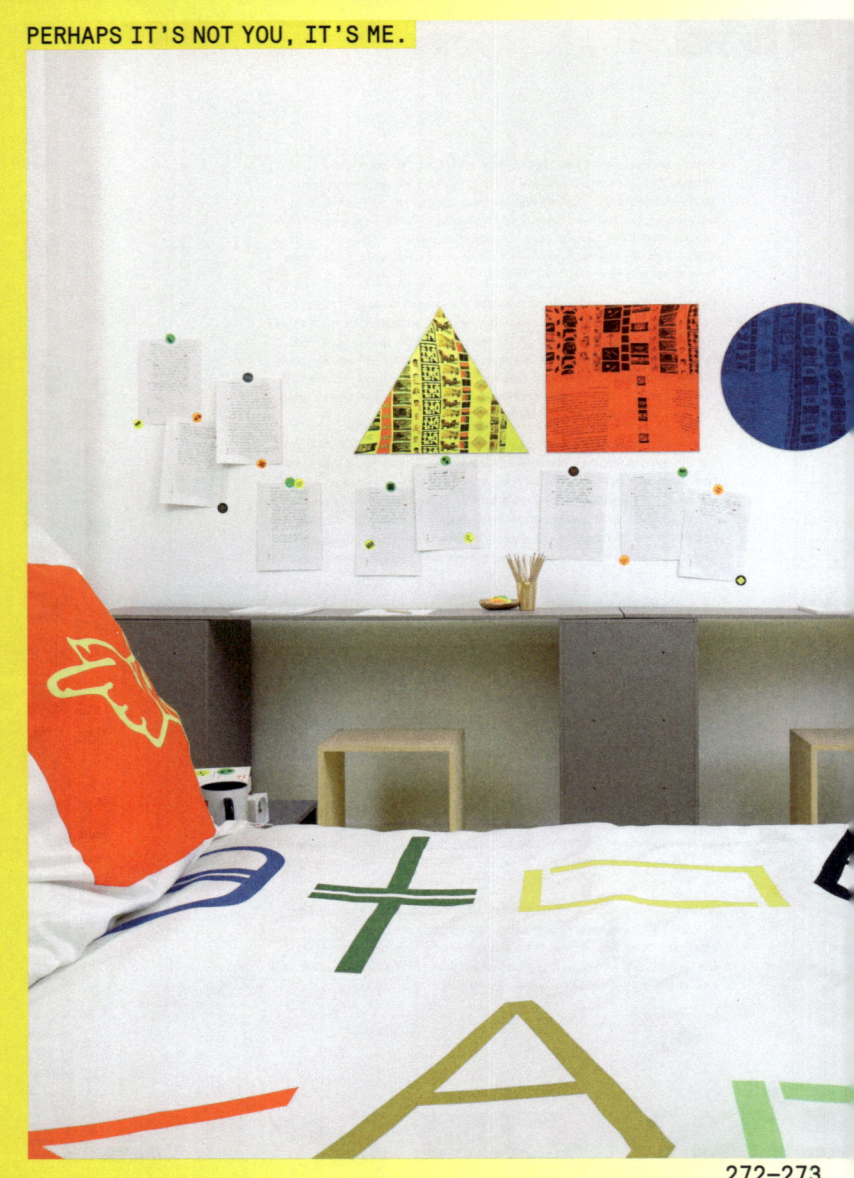

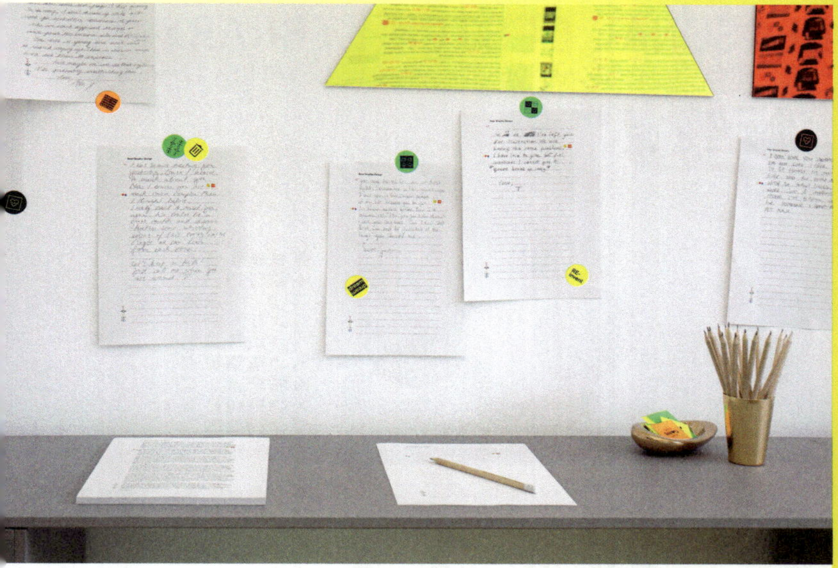

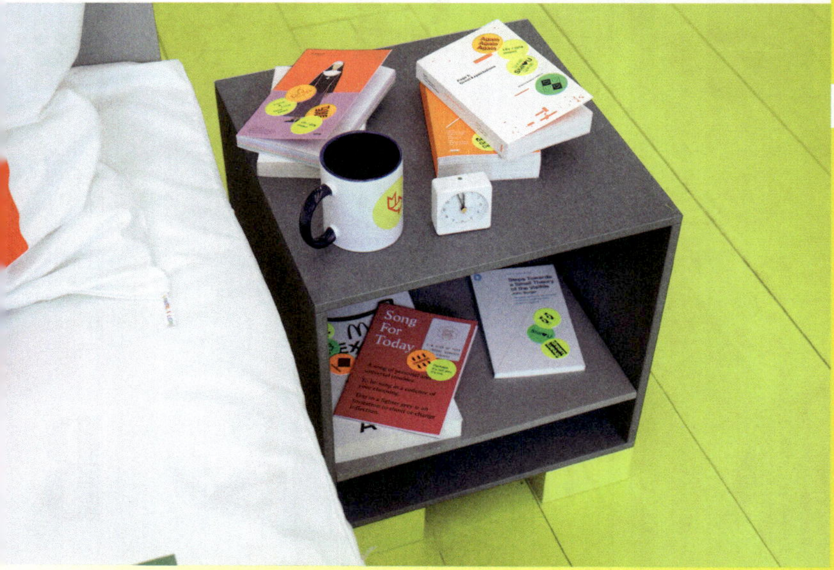

P

PERSONAL DESIGN LIBRARY
PAGES FROM THE PERSONAL DESIGN ARCHIVE OF ANDREA TINNES

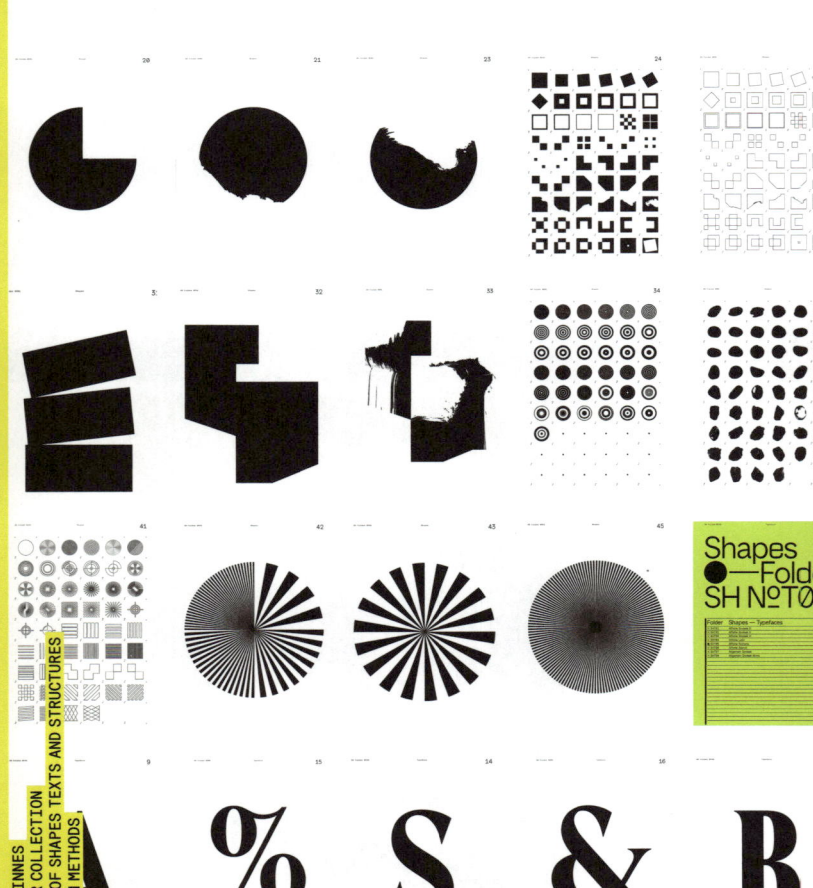

Shapes
—Folder
SH N°T05

ANDREA TINNES
INVENTAR COLLECTION
LIBRARY OF SHAPES TEXTS AND STRUCTURES
RESEARCH METHODS

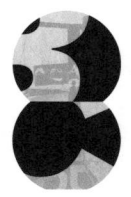
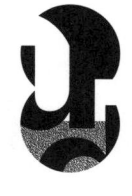
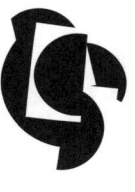
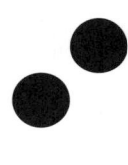
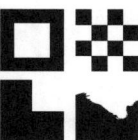
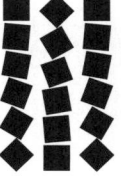
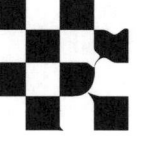
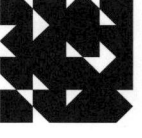
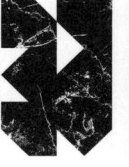
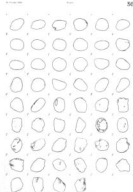
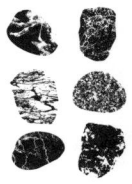
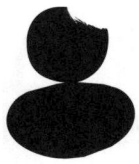
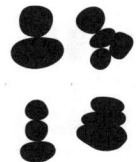
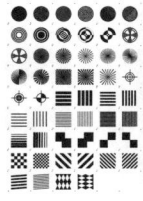
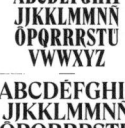
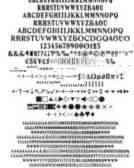
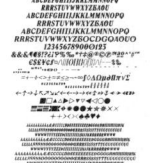
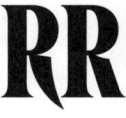

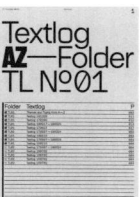

PERSONAL DESIGN LIBRARY

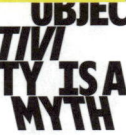
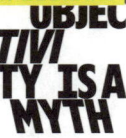
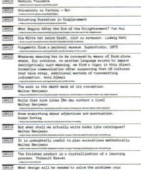
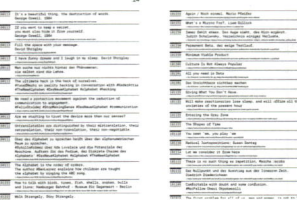
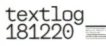
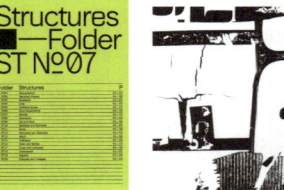

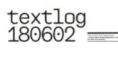
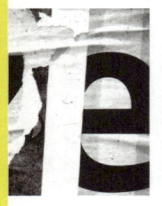
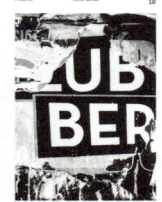
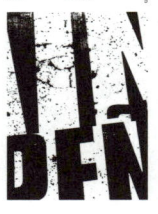
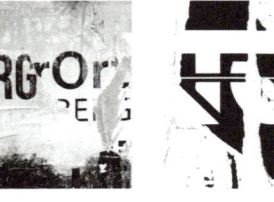
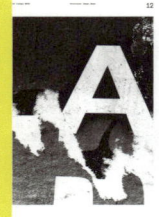
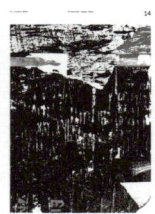
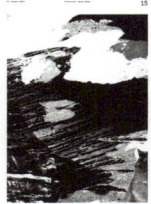
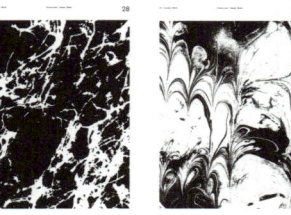

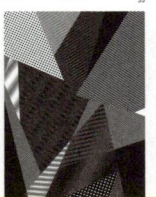
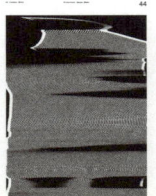
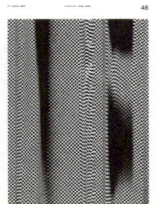
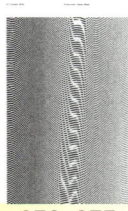

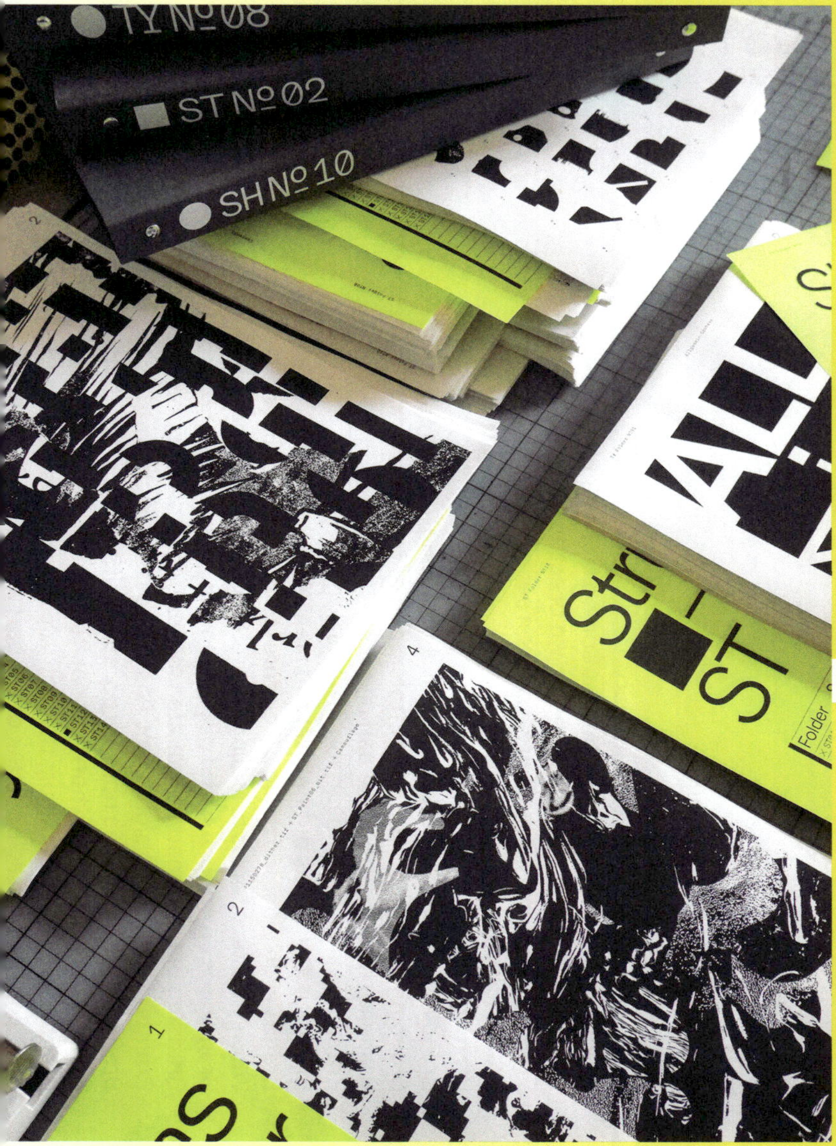
TY № 08
ST № 02
SH № 10
Str
ST
Folder

POST BRANDING MANIFESTO

MANIFESTO BY JASON GRANT AND OLIVER VODEB

Abolishing branding is revolutionary
Branding happens when communication collapses into itself
Branding seems as natural as the air we breathe
Branding is a form of neoliberal common sense
Branding demands conformity
Branding has fascist tendencies
Branding is as much a totalitarian as a totalizing ideology
Branding has an authoritarian intolerance of any values existing beyond its grasp
Branding bullies difference and diversity
Branding simulates and monopolizes dialogue
Branding monetizes our natural and mental environments
Brands aren't just intruding on culture, they are our culture
When your only tool is branding, everything looks like a brand
Branding is an opportunistic dogma, not an evolutionary objective
Branding has changed the relationship between production and consumption
Brands are the most significant financial assets of the world's biggest companies
Branding reconstitutes non-corporate entities as market-tamed subordinates
Branding affirms the authority of capital regardless of its host's mission
Brands become the medium through which capital is socialized
Branding is a strategic system of property rights enforcement

Brands are the sponsored mechanisms for constructing meaning and human identity
Brands don't just want our loyalty, they want our love, they want our-selves
Branding optimizes competition and consumption at the expense the commons
Branding promises big while we're left empty handed, or with fistfuls of literal junk
Branding promises big while the planet floods and burns
Brands are thought-terminating corporate clichés
Branding blurs the line between persuasion and coercion
The 'entrepreneur of the self' creates themself as a brand
When we are worthless in the market, self-branding generates illusions of self-worth
Brandspeak is an apparatus of milieu control
Branding rewrites history and moulds the subject to fit the myth
Branding plays as neutral but there is little it doesn't frame and distort
Branding's cynical public advertisements become hallowed mission-statements
Branding is a regulated freedom that shapes the context in which freedom is exercised
Branding aestheticizes the concealment of social and political conflict
Branding obscures and reinforces hierarchies of privilege and class division
Branding erases the stubborn evidence of real social and political antagonisms
Branding is dangerous delusion, as well as stupidity at the expense of knowledge
Branding has reached its performative optimum through addiction
The more brands record about us, the less we exist
Branding destroys the meaningfulness of communication
It is easier to imagine an end to the world than an end to branding
Branding is a site of urgent political struggle
Abolishing branding is revolutionary

PRESS COVERAGE
NEWS COVERAGE ABOUT A—Z

Specialized and general press coverage continue to be essential ways to reach a broader audience, being especially relevant for allowing critical views and discussing A—Z initiatives. One of the most treasured reviews appeared in the 99th edition of *Eye Magazine.* Since its inception in the 1990s, this influential UK publication has reflected on the cultural aspects of Graphic Design. The extensive article covered the exhibitions by Inkahoots, Andrea Tinnes, as well as A—Z's collaboration with Buchstabenmuseum.

Other noteworthy mentions of A—Z in the press include Steven Heller's column in *PRINT* magazine, and also mentions in *ZEITmagazin*, *Form*, *taz—die Tageszeitung*, formy.xyz, *cc/magazine*, Cee Cee newsletter, and *Experimenta 99.*

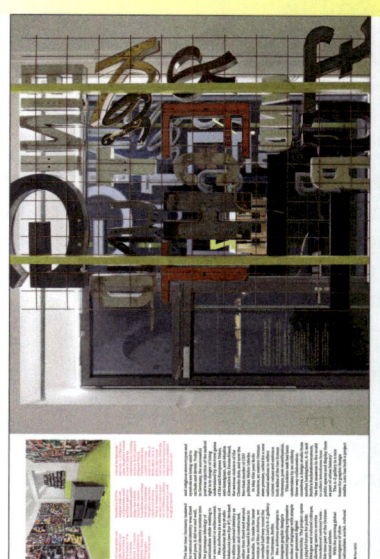

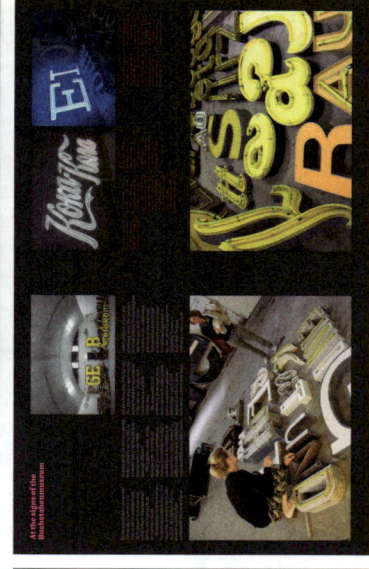

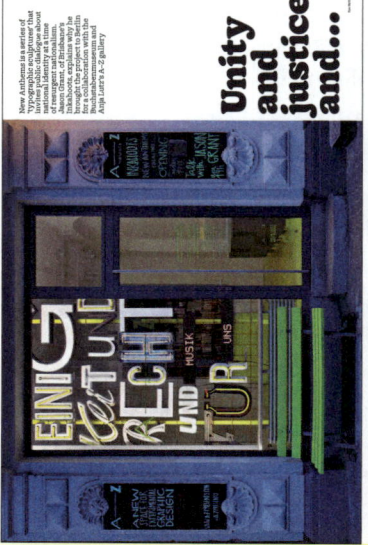

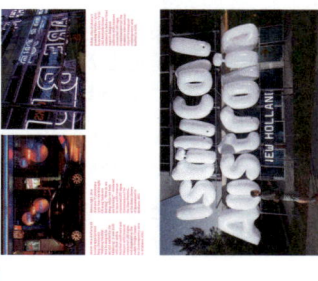

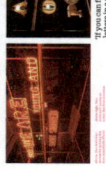

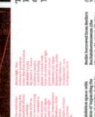

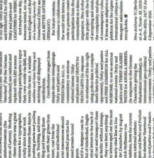

Unity and justice and…

New Anthemis is a series of Typographic sculpture that invites public dialogue about national identity at a time of resurgent nationalism. Jason Grant, of Brisbane's Inkahoots, explains why he brought the project to Berlin for a collaboration with the Buchstabenmuseum and Anja Lutz's A–Z gallery.

"If you can fit fragile historical letters in a small car and take them across Berlin without damage, you can learn anything."

At the sign of the Buchstabenmuseum

PROJECT SUPPORTERS
LIST OF INDIVIDUAL EXHIBITION SPONSORS

Some A—Z guest artists and designers have received various forms of support, allowing them to develop and present their exhibitions. Here is a list of individual sponsors to whom the A—Z team also expresses gratitude.

Blumen sind geil:
Kanton Zug, Switzerland

Library of Shapes, Texts and Structures:
Printing Workshop at Burg Giebichenstein University of Art and Design Halle

L.i.P. Collective:
Le Signe – Centre National du Graphisme

Mirtha Dermisache: To Be Read:
Cluster of Excellence *Temporal Communities, Doing Literature in a Global Perspective* FU Berlin, and the Estate of Mirtha Dermisache

Novo Typo Offgrid Berlin:
Creative Industries Fund Netherlands

Recipes for Connecting:
Peyer Cover and Druckerei zu Altenburg

Recipes for Connecting, Barcelona Edition:
Casa Bonay, Barcelona Design Week, Antalis, Impresum, and Cerveza Alhambra

Revealing » Recording » Reflecting:
Arab Fund for Arts and Culture and the Khatt Foundation

The Error is Regretted:
Stiftung Kunstfonds

THANK YOU
DANKE
GRACIAS
BEDANKT
DZIEKI
SPASIBO
SHUKRAN
GRAZIE
GAMSAHABNIDA
ARIGATO
OBRIGADA
MERCI

PROMPTS FOR INTERACTION
THE VISITOR EXPERIENCE AT THE *EXQUISITE CURIOSITIES* EXHIBITION

For the *Exquisite Curiosities* exhibition of designer and artist Sarah Boris, members of the *A—Z Collective* prepared a series of prompts handwritten on little blue cards to stimulate and encourage guests to experience the space and its elements in a more embodied and sensorial way.

Functioning as guides and ice-breakers, prompt phrases like "Which colors appear seen upside down" or "Read (or sing) titles out loud" facilitated the visitor experience and interactions between the people present and with the exhibition objects.

- WHICH OBJECTS WOULD YOU STEAL
- TELL A LIE
- fill empty holes with led nodes so it sh... at nig...
- If you could shrink yourself which object would you like to stand ...
- READ TITL... OUT LOUD (or sing the...
- find a way to see the object wall upside down
- ...similar to you ... everything together
- DECIDE WHICH OBJECT YOU WOULD LIKE EAT
- which colour appears seen upside down
- down the shelfs of objects. ...t is the first ...ng you see?
- wear sti...
- each object in duos by colo...

PULP
EXHIBITION BY PATRICK THOMAS

PULP was an exhibition by the graphic artist Patrick Thomas, presenting a series of framed silkscreen prints created by combining newsprint sheets and computer-generated graphics. A newspaper with one of the *PULP* motifs alongside a short essay by philosopher Daniel Martin Feige was printed and distributed free to visitors.

The artworks reflect the ever-growing erosion of truth and fact in the 'truth decay' age, marked by fake news, deep fakes, and alternative facts. Provoking more questions than providing answers, the artworks are powerful graphic statements about the manipulation, concealment, and censorship lurking in our public sphere.

Patrick selected daily newsprint samples as the traditional source of factual information to overlap them with layers, drawings, and code-generated graphic forms, utilizing the mechanical process of silkscreen printing.

Intentionally ambiguous, the resulting prints can be appreciated for their abstract beauty. But also, by exposing the physical vulnerability of newsprint, they remind us of the disappearance of both truth and the classical broadsheet format.

DESIGN IS...
NEWSPAPERS
PATRICK THOMAS
TAKEAWAY GRAPHIC DESIGN

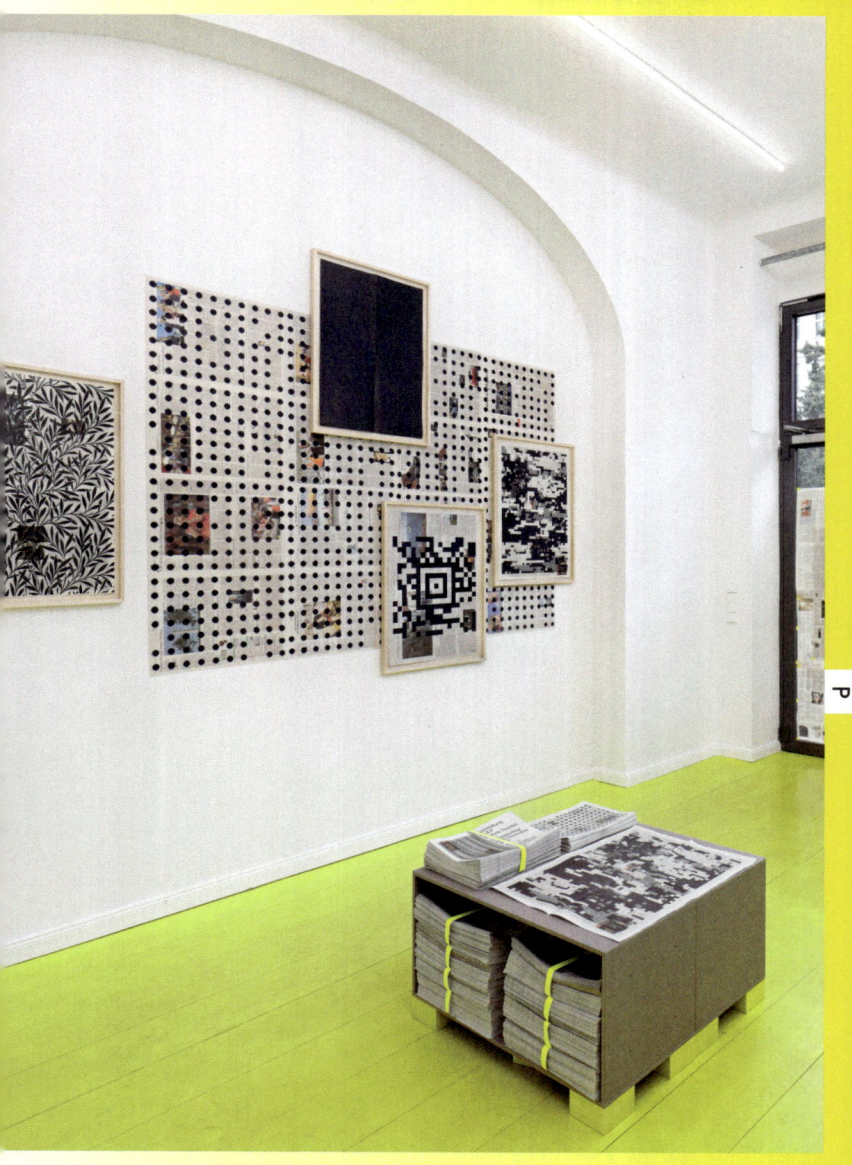

PULP

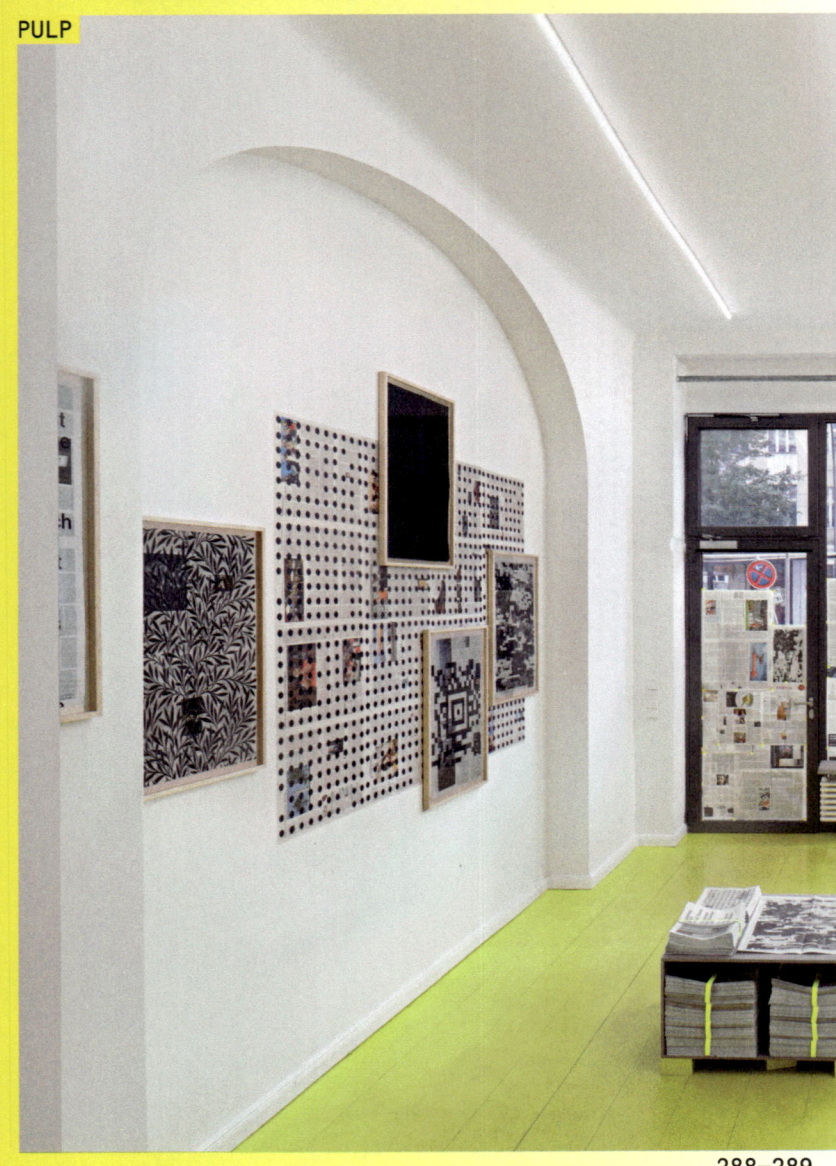

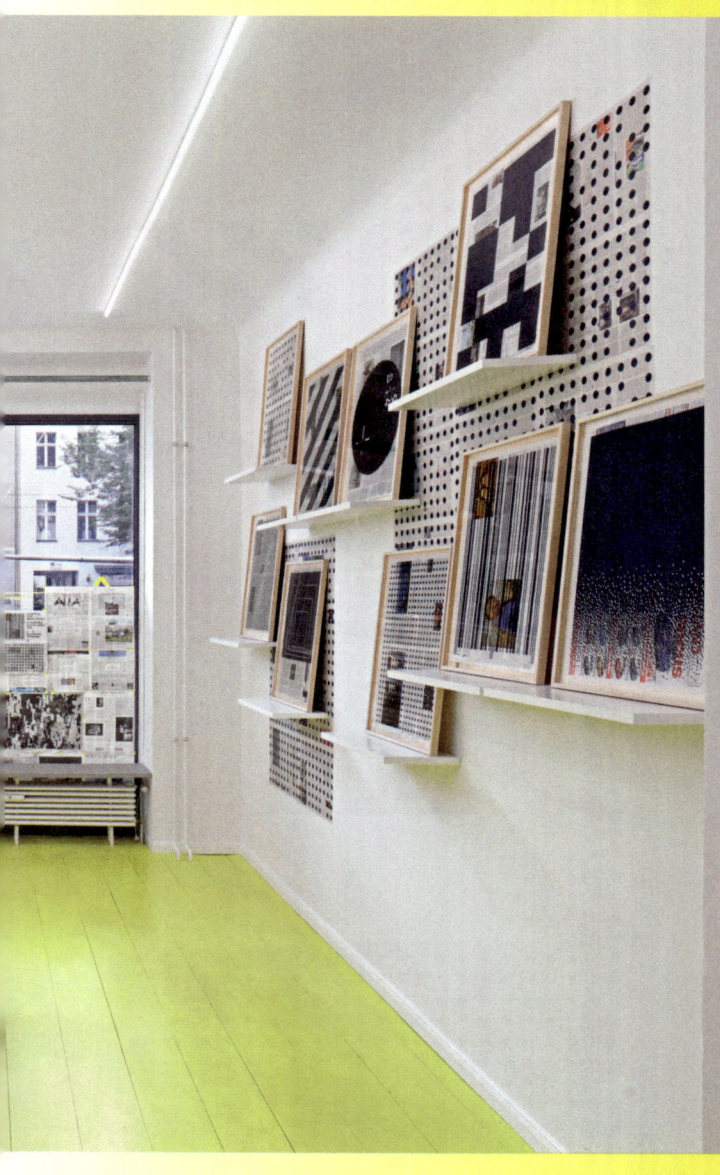

PULP

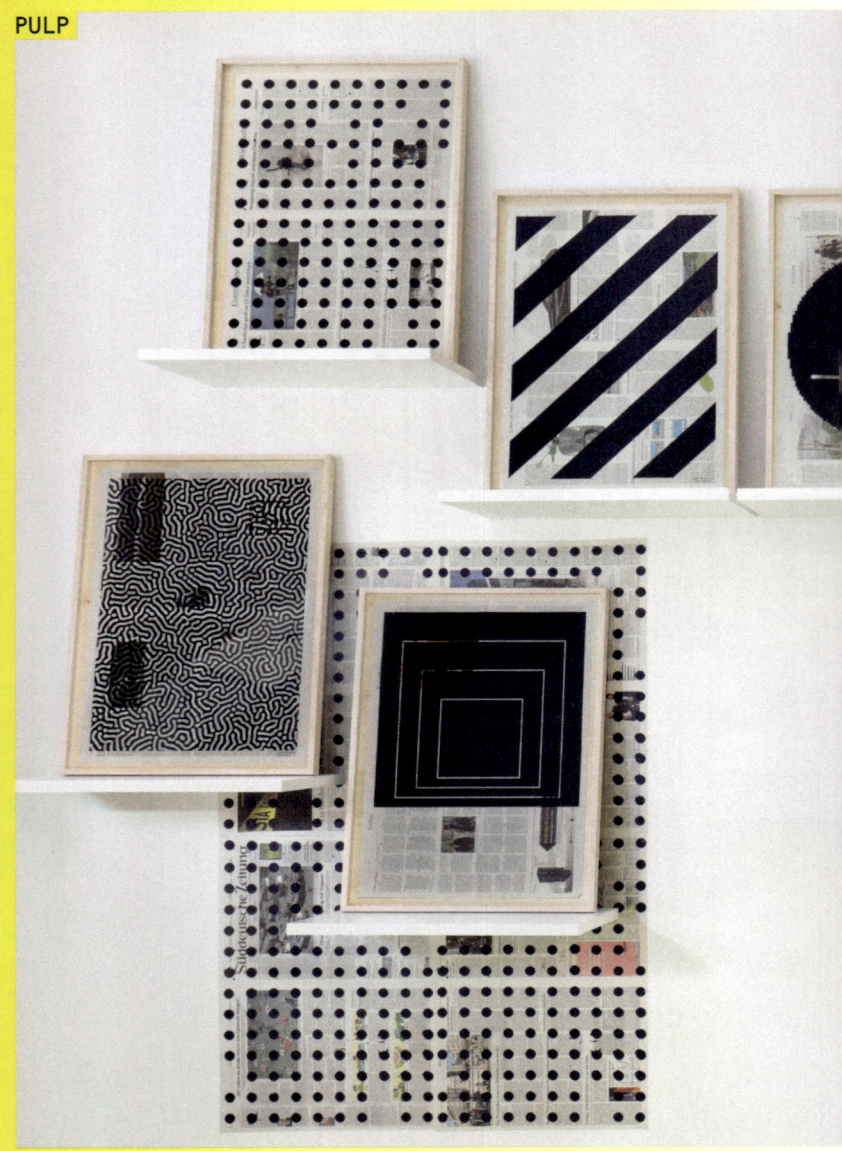

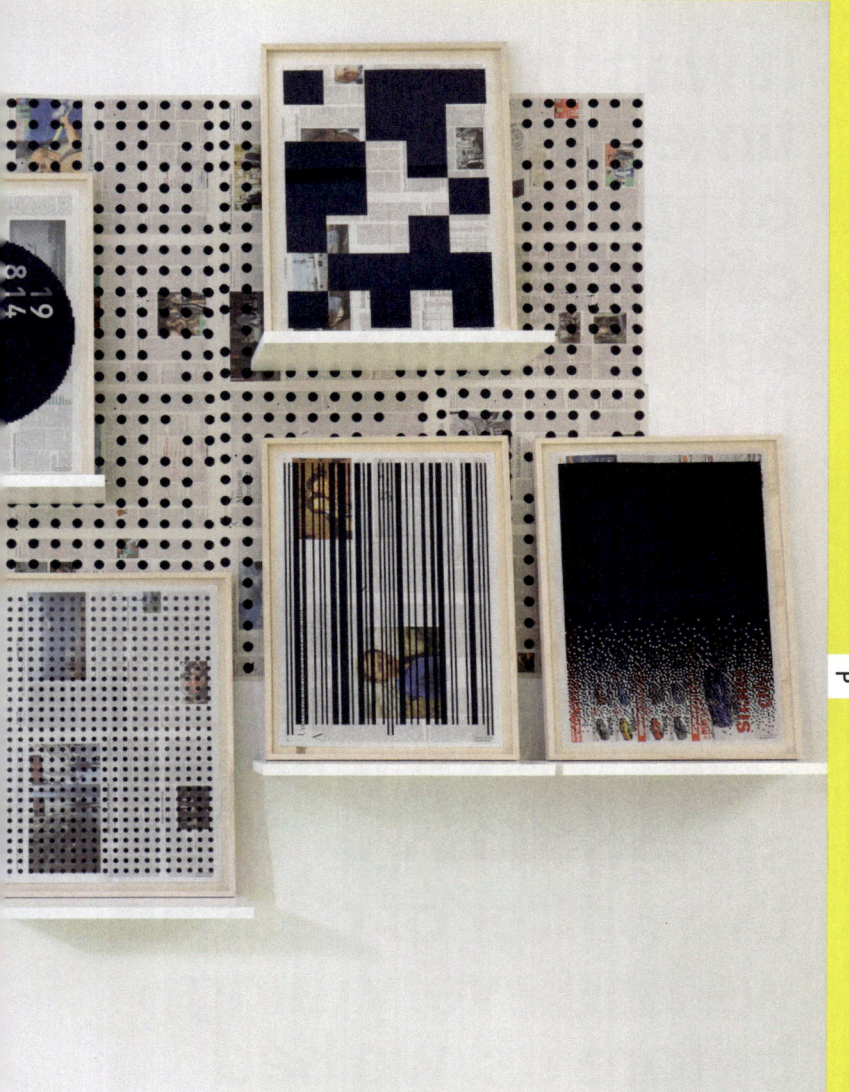

PULP

It was the best of times, it was the worst of times, it was the age of wisdom, it was the age of foolishness, it was the epoch of belief, it was the epoch of incredulity, it was the season of Light, it was the season of Darkness, it was the spring of hope, it was the winter of despair, we had everything before us, we had nothing before us, we

QUESTIONS ABOUT THE FUTURE
EXCERPT FROM A CONVERSATION WITH FREEK LOMME AND ANJA LUTZ

FREEK: I get the impression that you and A—Z, as a space, are two sides of the same coin—one that cannot be monetized because its independent character lies in the engagement you bring. You have your "feet in the clay", as a Dutch saying goes, meaning that you stand in the mud of where the work is to be done, persistent, but not quite knowing. What do you want to take out of these almost six years of A—Z into the future: what can you bring along as scripts, and what would be nice to articulate or express more?

ANJA: I like the feeling of not quite knowing—and this is also a two-sided coin: it is what propels me, as I keep seeking answers, and gives me a reason to go on. But it is also exhausting. As times change rapidly, I must also be prepared to keep up with the perpetual learning, unlearning, and questioning that will undoubtedly continue to dominate the routine of curating the space. While this brings a lot of vitality, I am not yet clear on what that means for the future of A—Z. As my reflections on the world at large, life, and Graphic Design are intertwined, I feel it is best to take a moment and ask: "How can we, how can I, how can Graphic Design respond to daunting and frightening challenges of war, racism, sexism, totalitarianism, lies …?"
Sometimes, I think that what I want to continue doing is opening up the space to individuals and their works that show care and dedication, that touch us with their artistic or conceptual beauty, that share personal, delicate voices. At other times, I wonder whether we should open the space to

organizing resistance, protecting the vulnerable, and speaking up against injustices. The latter is undoubtedly an activist stance but, to me, both are ways of resisting dominant structures—and both will be needed in the future, as it currently appears.

Where do you want new things to go; what directions are you yourself looking at?

Well, if you look at the —∞ section of this book, there are so many amazing ideas, and if possible, I would love to realize them all. In addition to the interdisciplinary areas we have been able to showcase so far, I would still like to show others, such as moving graphics and, in particular, digital graphics experimentation that combines and interacts with physical bodies. Audio is another medium that I think is very exciting in combination with Graphic Design. And I can also think of research projects on historic design, and how we can relate it to a contemporary practice—a fascinating field.
When it comes to the general audience, I would love to welcome initiatives that address children or older people, and explore what Graphic Design has to offer for these demographic groups. Now that I have mentioned all that, I have to laugh! A—Z was initially conceived as a two-year project and, at that point, the limited timeframe was a kind of trick to enable me to fully engage with the project, despite my heavy workload of designing and publishing books. Now, it has been six years of A—Z and here I dream about more and more to come …

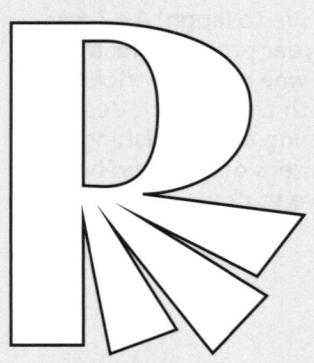
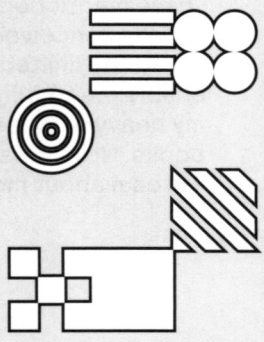

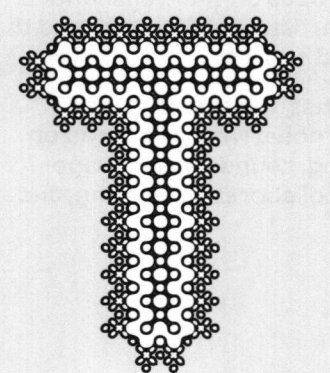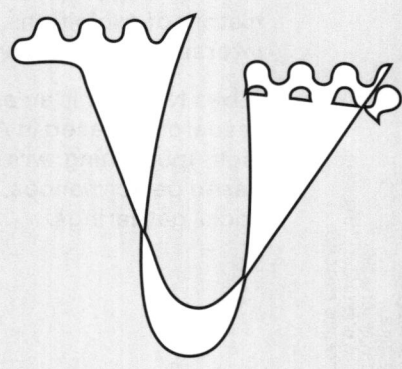

READING ARTISTS' BOOKS: ASEMIC WRITING
EVENT DURING THE *MIRTHA DERMISACHE: TO BE READ* EXHIBITION

How can we read asemic—illegible—writing, or is that a contradiction? What does speaking of 'reading' marks that do not form letters, words, and sentences—or even constitute signs—mean? Does reading require language in order to occur?

These were some of the questions raised and discussed during the series of online and offline talks *Reading Artists' Books: Asemic Writing*, part of the exhibition *Mirtha Dermisache: To Be Read*. Central to the conversation was questioning the act of 'reading' itself and its essence. This was the third event of Reading Artist's Books, an initiative curated by Regine Ehleiter and Tabea Nixdorff, conceived in memory of the artist, curator, and librarian Doro Böhme (1957–2020).

Regine Ehleiter is a Berlin-based art historian and curator with a special focus on the transnational history of exhibitions, artists' publications, and the intersections of art and ecology.

Tabea Nixdorff is an artist, typographer, and researcher based in Arnhem who is focused on (self-)publishing, writing, sound and language-based performances, collaborative learning, and social gatherings.

ASEMIC WRITING
ILLEGIBLE
MIRTHA DERMISACHE
MIRTHA DERMISACHE: TO BE READ
MYSTERIOUS POSTCARD

READING ARTISTS' BOOKS: ASEMIC WRITING

REAL-TIME REALIST NO. 2
LECTURE PERFORMANCE BY JUNGMYUNG LEE AND LIEVEN LAHAYE AS PART OF *TEACHING DESIGN CONVERSATIONS*

As part of the *Teaching Design Conversations*, designer Jungmyung Lee and artist Lieven Lahaye presented and performed a reading of excerpts from their book, *Real-Time Realist* No. 2. The publication is an experiment in exploring the range of human emotions through typography, based on psychologist Robert Plutchik's *Wheel of Emotions*. This second issue invited artists to explore ecstasy, joy, serenity, and love, as well as The Yellow Wheel emotions, also showcasing typefaces produced by the Jung-Lee Type Foundry.

Jungmyung Lee is a graphic and type designer and publisher. Based in Amsterdam, she runs the independent Jung-Lee Type Foundry and the publishing house J-LTF PRESS, which releases her experimental publication series *Real-Time-Realist*.

Lieven Lahaye is an artist and publisher, interested in the value of ephemeral information, and amateur practices. He also lectures in Graphic Design, Contemporary Art, and Craft Studies at the Estonian Academy of Arts.

R

REBELLION RISO POSTERS COLLAB
EXHIBITED COLLECTIVE

Rebellion Riso Posters Collab was the initiative of Drucken 3000 and Poster Rex, supported by *Slanted* magazine and A—Z, uniting several designers to create Risograph posters on climate change for the exhibition *Time is Running.*

Drucken 3000 is a Risograph eco-friendly print studio in Berlin, run by the graphic designers Alex Branczyk and Florian Haberstumpf.

Poster Rex is a silkscreen collective dedicated to societal transformation, based in Leipzig and founded by graphic designers Markus Lange and Lars Harmsen.

Slanted is a magazine for typography issued by Slanted Publishers, a design, publishing, and media house based in Karlsruhe, founded by Lars Harmsen and Julia Kahl.

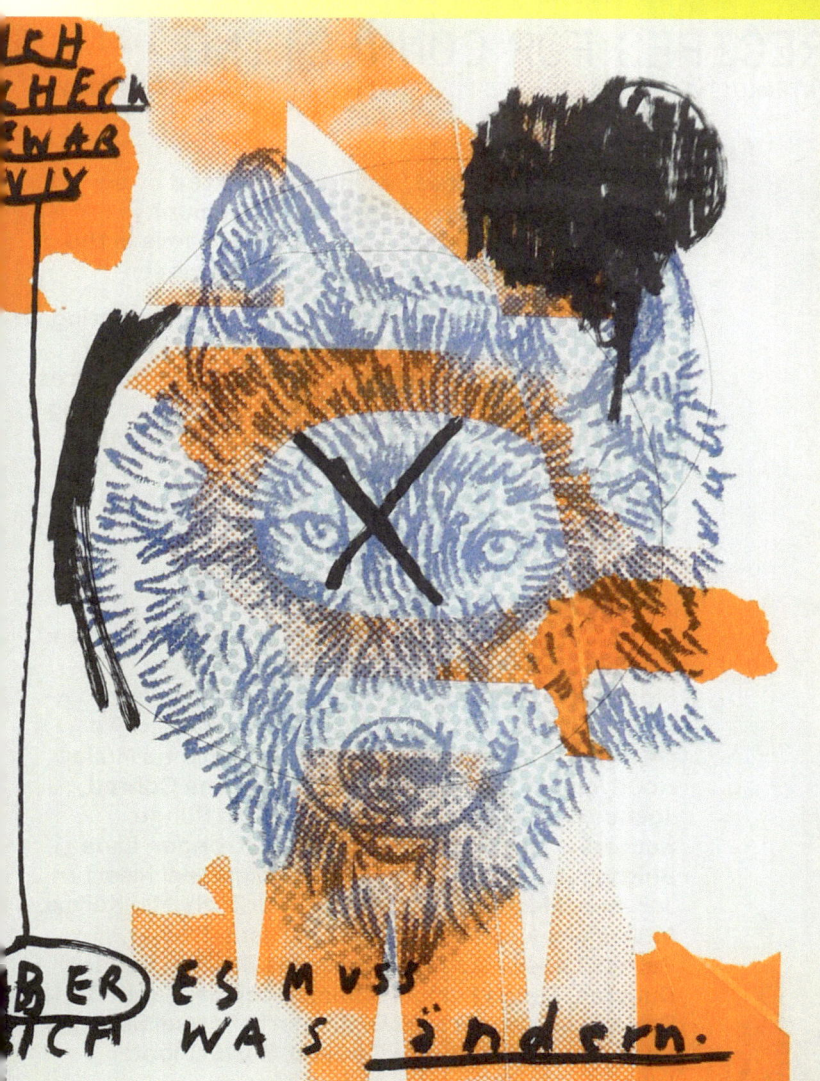

RECIPES FOR CONNECTING
INTERACTIVE EXHIBITION AND PUBLICATION BY THE *A–Z COLLECTIVE*

This project featured 'recipes' submitted by an international group of creatives, community builders, educators, and others who believe in the power of a simple idea to bring people closer.

The recipes included how-tos, forms of connecting, practical social tools, humorous prompts, gentle reminders, and alternative communication structures, as well as meals, with a wide variety of themes, ranging from a recipe for disaster to a poetic shopping list. The 60 recipes were printed in different colors, allowing visitors to browse or gather and bind a selection into their own publication.

Contributors: Alex Jordan, Alina Frieske, Alex Jordan, Andrea Tinnes, Andreas Koch, Anja Lutz, Anne-Christin Plate, April Gertler, Catrin Sonnabend, Claudia de la Torre, Clemens Gensch, Cindy Moorman, Daniel Pearce, Eloise Hammermeister Smith, Emily Smith, Eunjung Kwak, Francesco Pini, George Titheridge, Gregory Cowling, Hanna Müller, Hounyeh Kim, Ivana Jecmenica, Josepha Conrad, Joshua Duttweiler, Judy Smith, Karen Runge, Katherine May, Kristina Wedel, Lan Kroeger, Lana Belton, Laura Meseguer, Lisa Baumgarten, Maarten Janssen, Manuela Eichner, Marin Griffith, Mio Kojima, Molly Haig, Natalia Lombardo, Niklaus Troxler, Patrick Lacey, Paul Steinmann, Pia Steiner, Rachael Dunstan, Radna Rumping, Ramon Tejada, Sarah Boris, Sevinç Lenglachner, Silvia Sfligiotti, Formal Settings, Sofia Harley, Stephanie Cedeño, Susan Ploetz, Tulah Stanford.

A–Z COLLECTIVE
ANDREA TINNES
BARCELONA DESIGN WEEK
BINDING YOUR OWN PUBLICATION
NIKLAUS TROXLER
OUT & ABOUT
SARAH BORIS

R

RECIPES FOR CONNECTING

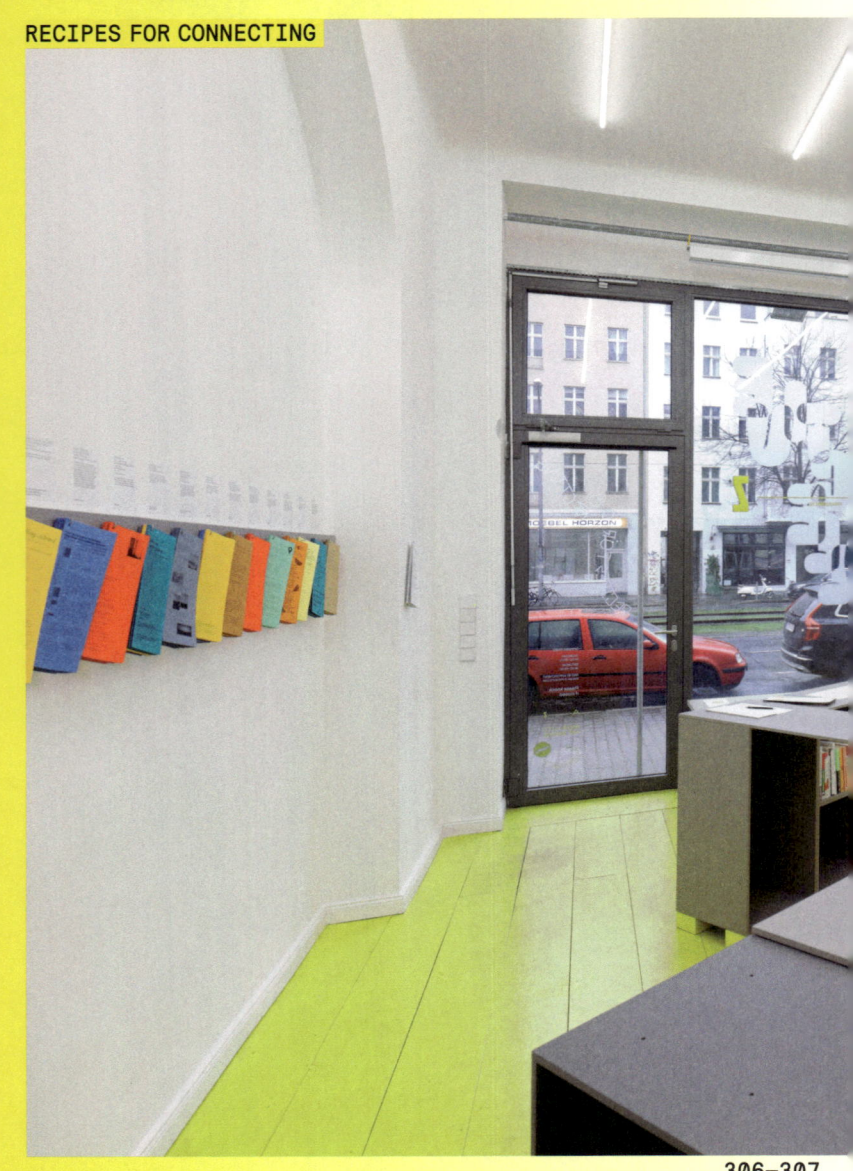

R

RECIPES FOR CONNECTING

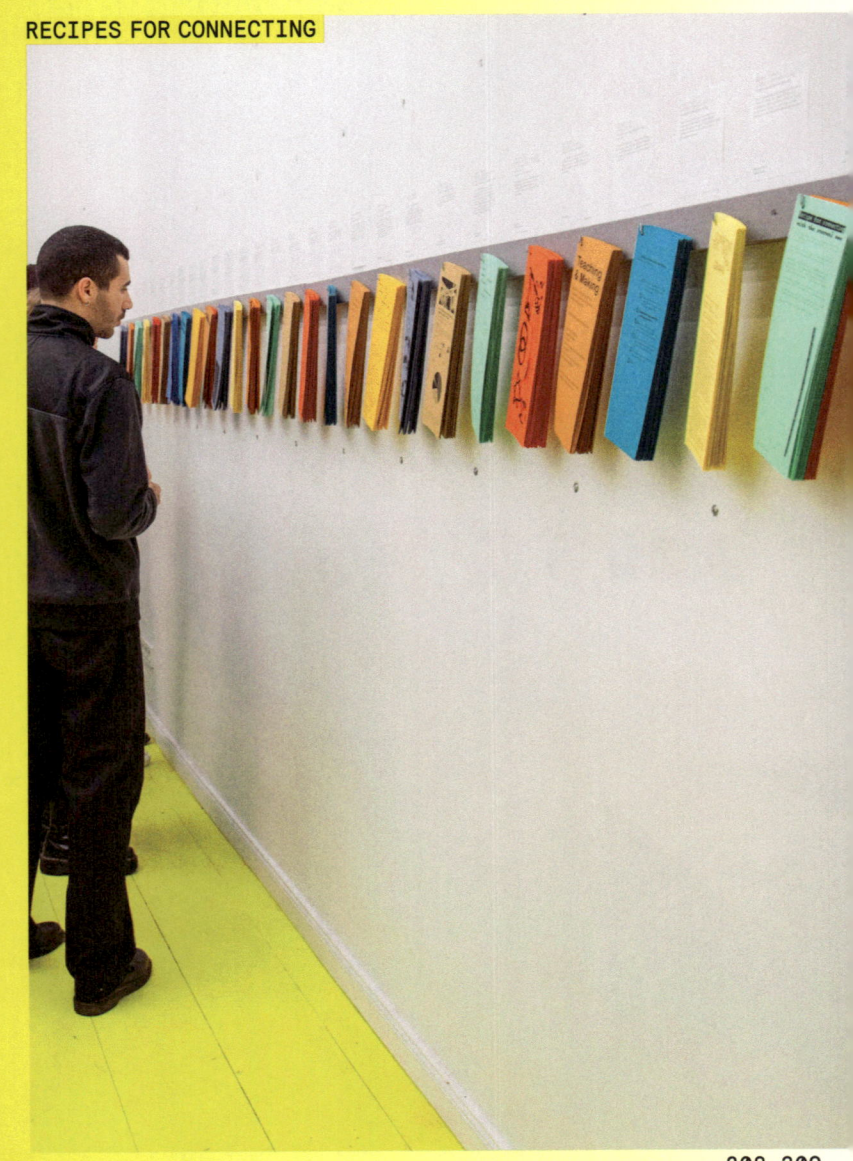

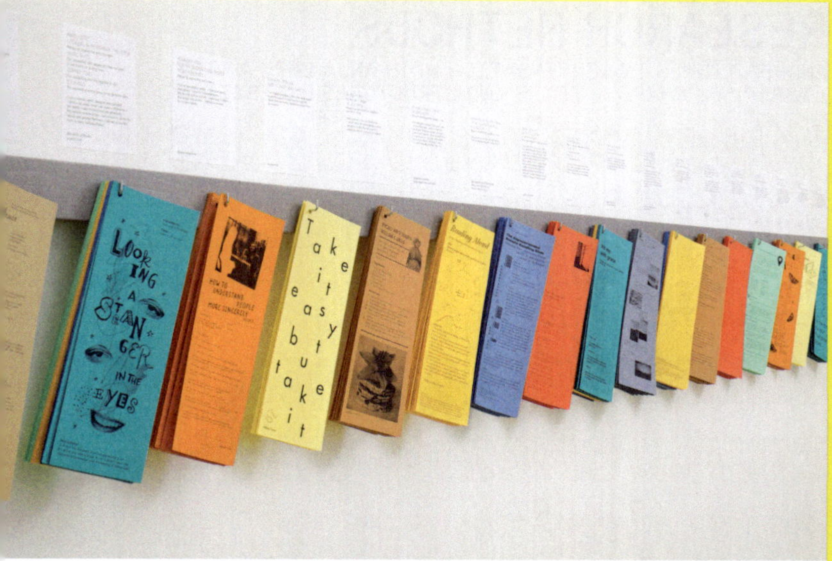

R

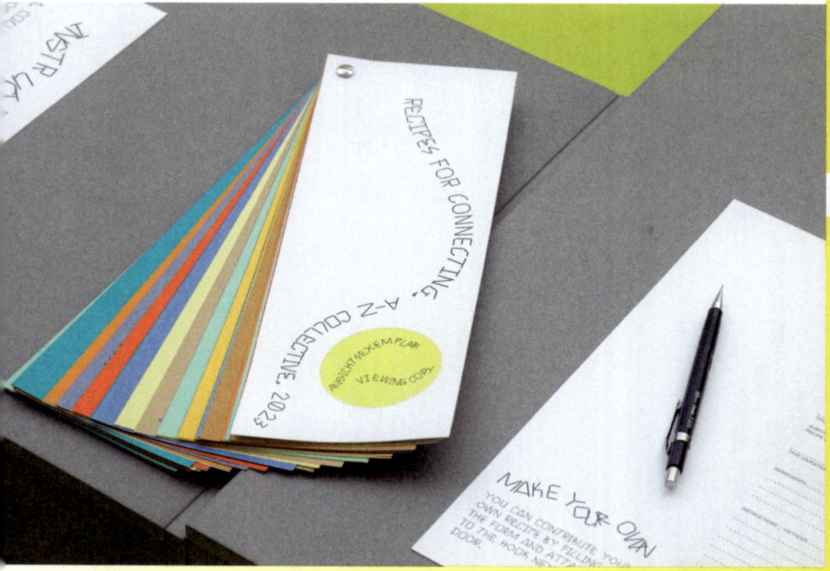

RESEARCH METHODS

ANDREA TINNES IN CONVERSATION WITH ANJA LUTZ AT THE *LIBRARY OF SHAPES, TEXTS AND STRUCTURES* EXHIBITION

"My question relates to te[…] individual methods and t[o] collecting, compiling, sor[ting,] questioning, appropriati[ng,] transforming, and editin[g in one's] own design practice. It c[omes] to which a personal desi[gn is] developed this way."

ANDREA TINNES
INVENTAR COLLECTION
LIBRARY OF SHAPES TEXTS AND STRUCTURES
PERSONAL DESIGN LIBRARY
ONLINE VIDEO ARCHIVE

ing and applying
ls for searching,
ng, archiving,
interpreting,
isual material for one's
esponds to the extent
vocabulary can be

REVEALING » RECORDING » REFLECTING

GROUP EXHIBITION CO-ORDINATED BY HUDA SMITSHUIJZEN ABIFARÈS, BAHIA SHEHAB, SOUKEINA HACHEM, AND YASMINE NACHABE TAAN

Revealing » Recording » Reflecting presented the findings of speculative research on generations of women graphic designers from Southwest Asia and North Africa (SWANA), and the diaspora. The project used the exhibition platform as an editorial space to collect, reveal, retell, and record the work and untold stories of the women graphic designers, calligraphers, typographers, and illustrators who play key roles in shaping and rethinking the region's visual and material culture.

The leading project researchers moderated four online discussions: *Visual Storytelling* with Yasmine Nachabe Taan, *Ladies of Letters* with Bahia Shehab, *Image-Making* with Soukeina Hachem, and *Women Designers in Diaspora* with Huda Smitshuijzen AbiFarès. Fellow women designers from the SWANA region joined them. A—Z was transformed into the project headquarters, where people could follow live-streamed online discussions.

Research assistant Nour Asmar worked on the continuous collection of entries, which were placed dynamically on the wall, gradually filling the space with new contributions. Visitors could also browse key publications and other reading material related to the study, or watch recordings of the online events.

IMAGE-MAKING: BEHIND THE LINES OF ENGAGED GRAPHIC DESIGN
LADIES OF LETTERS: CROSSING AND CONNECTING GENERATIONS
VISUAL STORYTELLING: ABOUT WOMEN, BY WOMEN
WOMEN DESIGNERS IN DIASPORA
WOMEN DESIGNERS FROM SWANA REGION

Revealing

Women Graphic Designers from Southeast Asia and North Africa

الكشف

تصميم الجرافيك

التحليل

REVEALING » RECORDING » REFLECTING

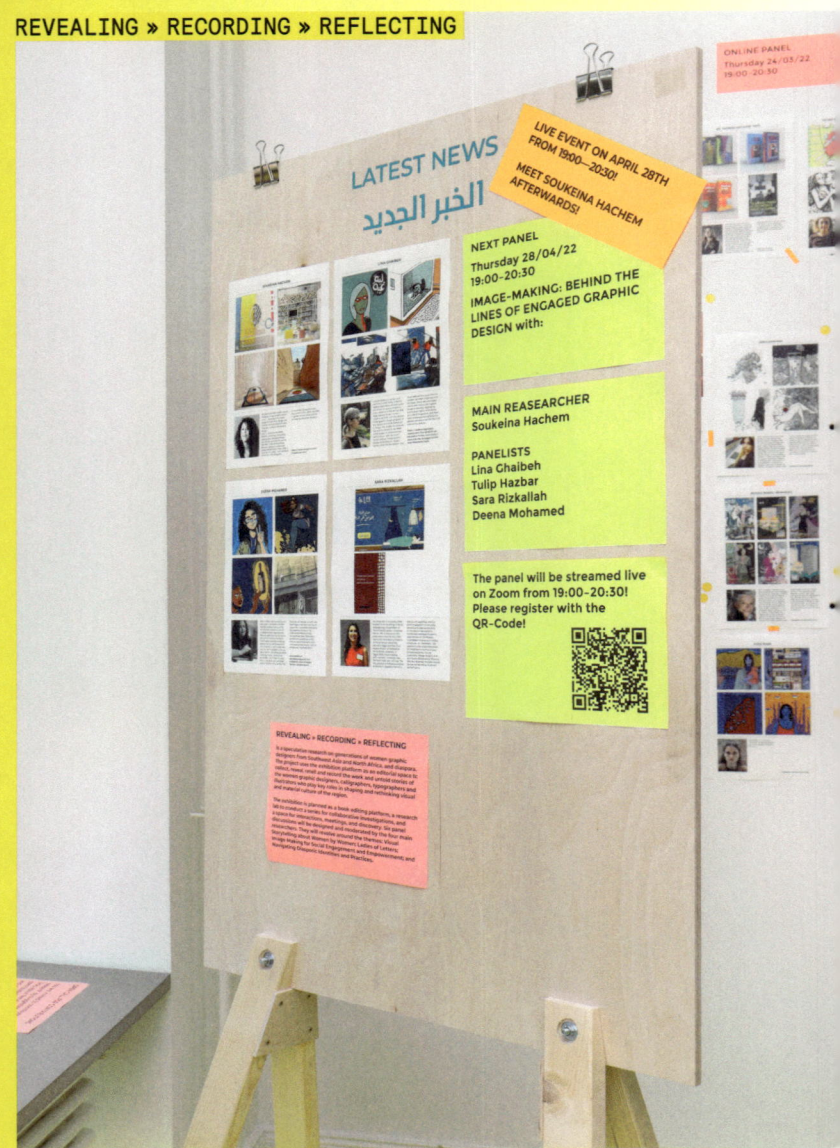

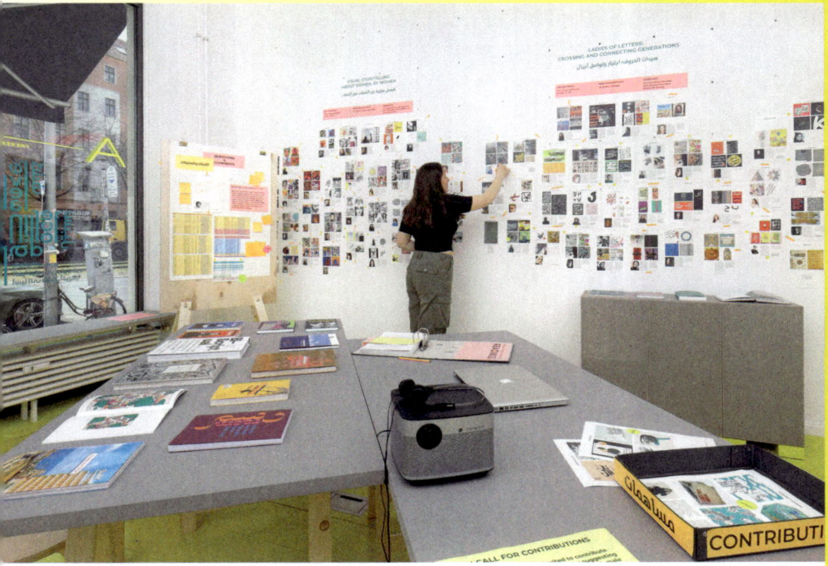

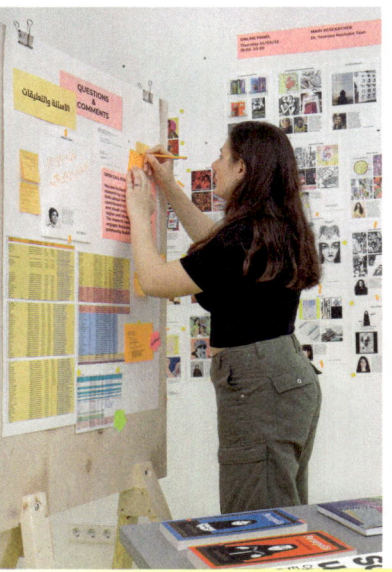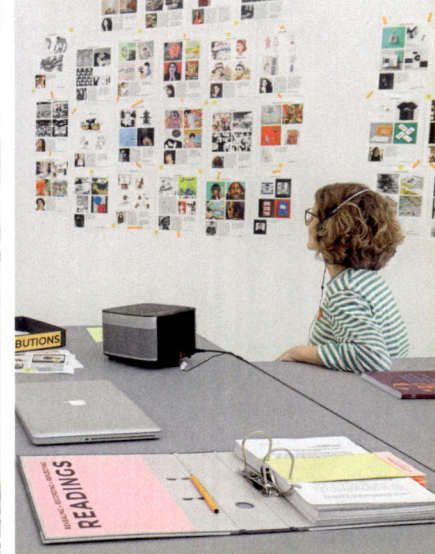

REVEALING » RECORDING » REFLECTING

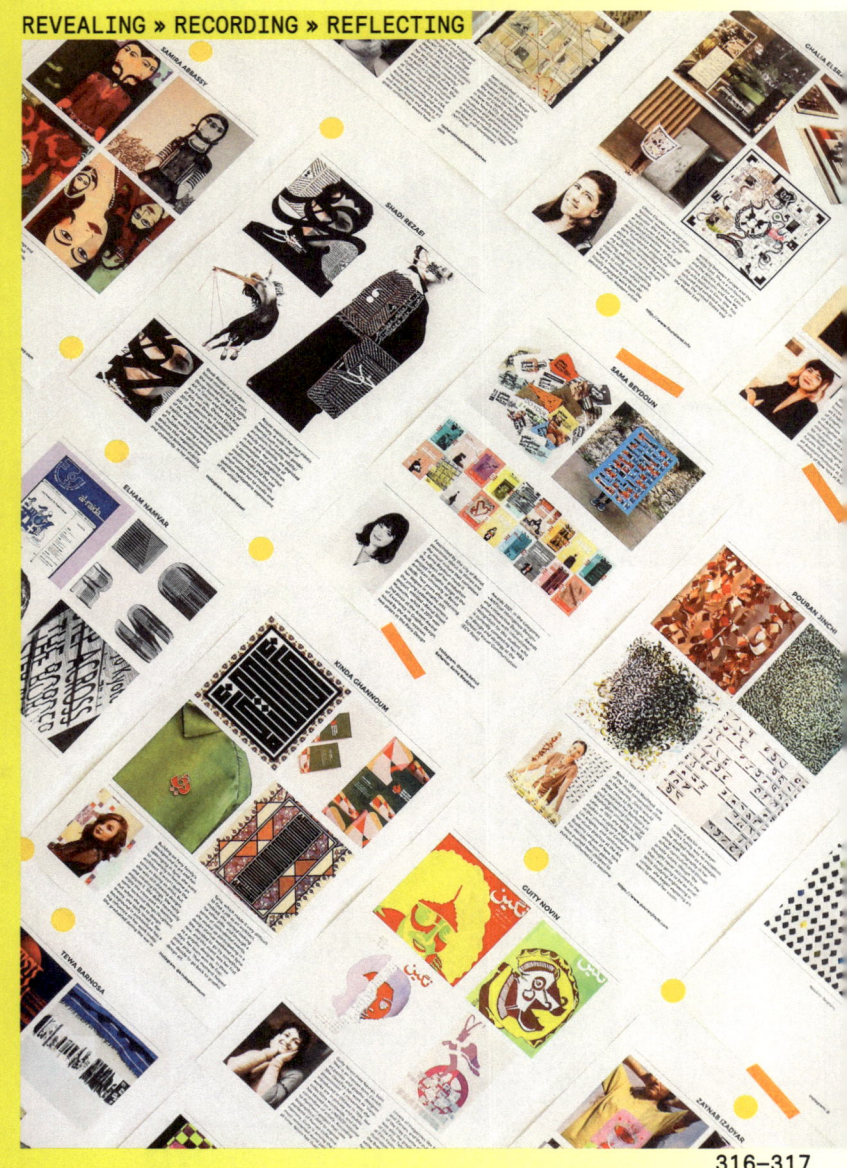

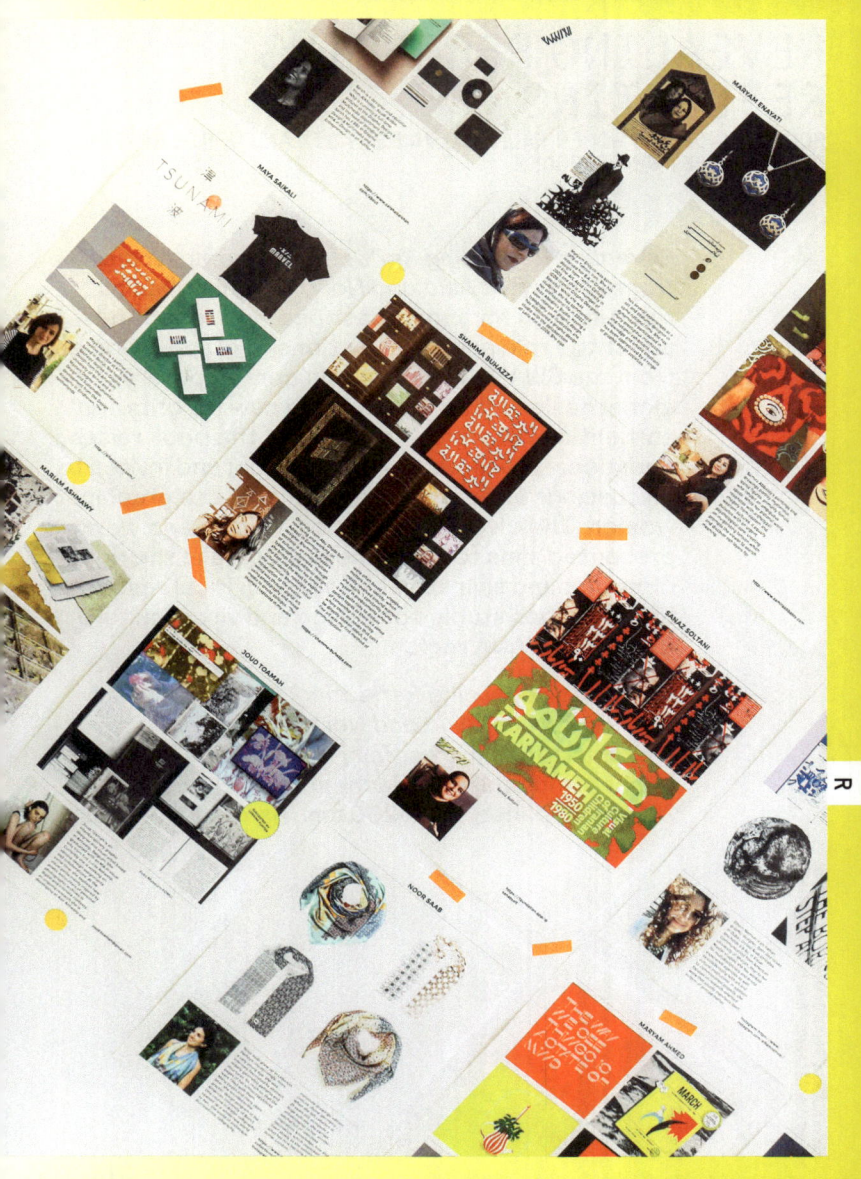

REVEALING RECORDING REFLECTING

BOOK ON GRAPHIC WOMEN FROM SOUTHWEST ASIA AND NORTH AFRICA
PUBLISHED BY KHATT BOOKS

Revealing Recording Reflecting: Graphic Women from Southwest Asia and North Africa compiles the research findings, questions, and reflections about the role and contributions of graphic women from the SWANA region within contemporary global design histories. Through new insights and authentic first-person narratives, the book raises questions, presents raw information, and invites to discussions around the position of these graphic women. The diversity of topics, voices, and works presented aims to point the discourse in the right direction and to instigate further critical research that enriches studies of design and visual culture from the SWANA region.

Revealing Recording Reflecting: Graphic Women from Southwest Asia and North Africa, Huda Smitshuijzen AbiFarès, Yasmine Nachabe Taan, Bahia Shehab and Soukeina Hachem (eds.), Khatt Books, 2024. 640 pages, 150 x 200 mm, hardcover, English.

RE-VEALING
كشف
RE-CORD-ING
RE-FLECT-ING
قحليل
تصميم

Graphic Women from Southwest Asia and North Africa

Edited by
Huda Smitshuijzen AbiFarès
Yasmine Nachabe Taan
Bahia Shehab
Soukeina Hachem

خط Khatt Books

SARAH BORIS
EXHIBITED ARTIST

Sarah Boris is an artist and designer with a solid career working as a graphic designer for leading art and publishing institutions in the UK and further afield. In 2015, she set up her own studio focusing on her art practice, taking the form of sculpture, drawing, painting, and book-making alongside her design practice. Since then, she has had several solo exhibitions in Europe. Sarah Boris is a regular speaker in the UK and abroad. Published titles include *Le Théâtre Graphique*, *Rainbow 1* and *2*, *After the Rain*, and *Global Warming Anyone?*, all of which are now part of museum collections. One of her most iconic artworks is the *Fragile UK flag* (2015), which was exhibited at the Design Museum in London.

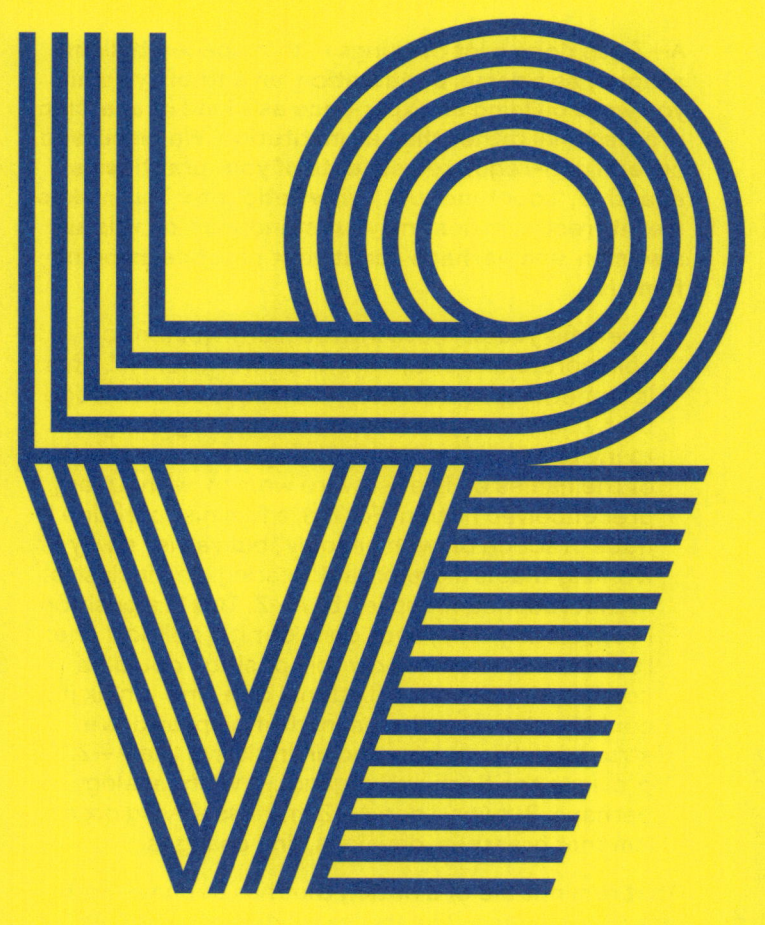

SHARING THE SPACE
EXCERPT FROM A CONVERSATION WITH FREEK LOMME AND ANJA LUTZ

A—Z has done a lot of things in that space—building a legacy as a name, a reputation, an authority—while you were building an experience as a kind of anarchic professional rather than an institution. We discussed several non-regulated aspects of your practice as 'adaptive', 'spontaneous', 'synergetic', etc. This makes me interested in hearing your standpoint on this as a woman, and perhaps about your practice as being feminist.

Over the years, I have invited many women to collaborate and showcase their work at A—Z. This is something I celebrate. And I must acknowledge that when I compiled my list of inspiring designers to invite before launching the space, more than half of the names on the list were women, without any preconceived notion. For me, a feminist practice is not a practice of 'women-only', but rather a way of working that is more organic, caring, and inclusive. In that respect, it applies to A—Z. This is a position I consciously take, and I consider it a political one. I sometimes wonder how this position could be combined with an institutional one, and I think it could work very well. The institution provides a structure, the bones, and an initiative like A—Z provides the flesh and organs ... a weird analogy, perhaps. But yes, I see A—Z more as a living organism that breathes, develops, and changes.

That reminds me of a notion that has become more prevalent in recent years: 'expanded practice'. As you pointed out in your organism analogy, I suppose you have been doing this out of necessity or simply

by being who you are, filled with the energy that A—Z constantly provides. Do you think this concept applies? Given this level of openness, have the people you have welcomed and who have occupied the space also led to changes in the way the space operates?

> I like to think all interactions have led to changes, even on a personal level. I have been really enjoying the encounters, or the unexpected visitors who knock on the door, such as designer Rick Griffith, whom I didn't know before. We ended up collaborating on the AIGA conference and becoming friends. Once, during a debate at one of our A—Z events, I remember I said—to my own surprise—that A—Z was "my own psychotherapy", because for me it is an investigation into Graphic Design at a moment where I am not sure where the practice is going and where I want to go with it.
> The exchange with such diverse practitioners has been inspiring and eye-opening, and it has certainly opened many new perspectives. It is not about finding the ultimate answers, but about gaining a deeper understanding of different agendas and individual approaches to Graphic Design. Ultimately, it has a lot to do with physicality: designing for a space in which people move, sharing the space with invited designers, and opening it to visitors—literally sharing the space, which can also be challenging at times. Being so personally involved is for me an essential way of being and working. It is also a vulnerable position to be in, as I identify with the space, which brings the risk of perceiving something that might not go well as a personal failure.

SHIFT!
EXPERIMENTAL PUBLICATION

Shift! was an experimental, transdisciplinary, and collaborative publication project comprising 16 editions in varied forms: a calendar, a poster collection, a music project, a video, a book-as-lunchbox, a lexicon, etc. As a playground for exploration, and by experimenting and pushing the boundaries of what a publication can be, *shift!* was in many ways a precursor of A—Z, having many common aspects, such as its transdisciplinarity, and its collaborative and experimental approach.

A—Z founder Anja Lutz and graphic designer and illustrator Lily Tomec founded *shift!* in 1995. From 1999 until 2007, the publication continued without Tomec, in collaboration with different graphic designers for each issue. *Shift!* continues to be regarded as an exemplary publication in Graphic Design, being an early case of using personal graphic computers that allowed independent publishing, and experimentation with new technical and visual possibilities.

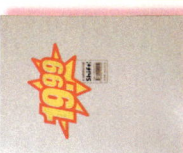
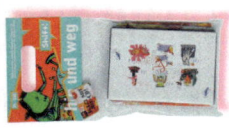
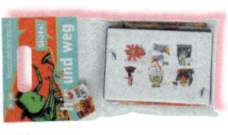
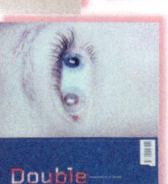
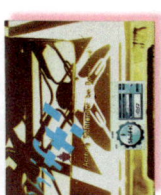
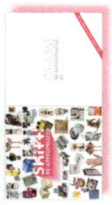
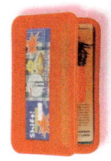
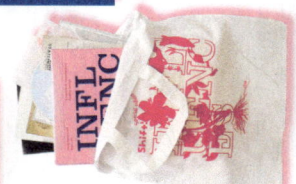
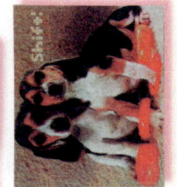
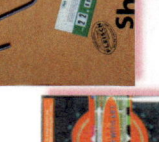
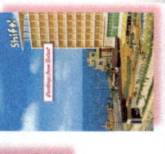
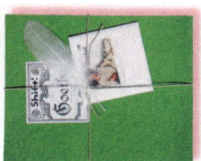
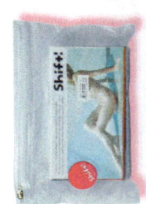
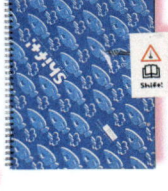
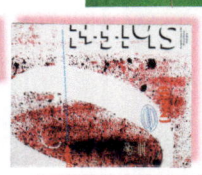
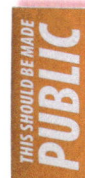
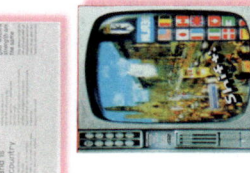

Shift!

SPACE OF UNCERTAINTY

TALK BY NA KIM AT THE *TRANSITORY WORKPLACE, 56* EXHIBITION

"*In my working proce
and revisiting memo
structure often ser
starting point. From
what unfolds—ofte
situations that feel
refer to as found fi*

NA KIM
TRANSITORY WORKPLACE, 56
TRANSITORY HELP DESK
ONLINE VIDEO ARCHIVE

s, I enjoy collecting
es. A given
s as a meaningful
here, I navigate
encountering
ctional, which I
on."

STICKERS
INDIVIDUAL STICKER DESIGNS

The A—Z yellow round stickers are inspired by the iconic "Atomkraft? Nein Danke!" protest stickers from the public mobilization against nuclear energy in Germany in the 1980s. A—Z's stickers have been multipurpose over the years, including being customized with funny faces by various designers and exhibitors.

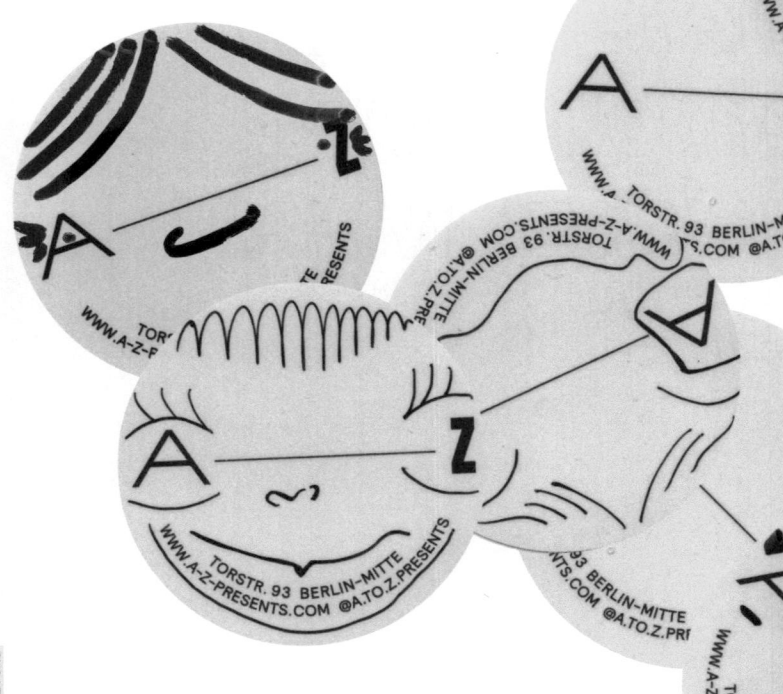

328–329

SUNDOWNER
WINE TASTING EXPERIENCE LED BY MANUELA DOS SANTOS

Sundowner was an unconventional and intentionally fun wine-tasting experience conceived and led by the brand and visual designer Manuela dos Santos, a member of the *A—Z Collective*, as part of the event *Super Collective Market No. 1 Yellow*. The exploratory journey through senses, challenging conventional definitions of wine, was meant to be a fun after-work opportunity to gather and connect. Participants' drinking experience was guided by a sheet with humorous prompts to observe and even build their own flavor profile.

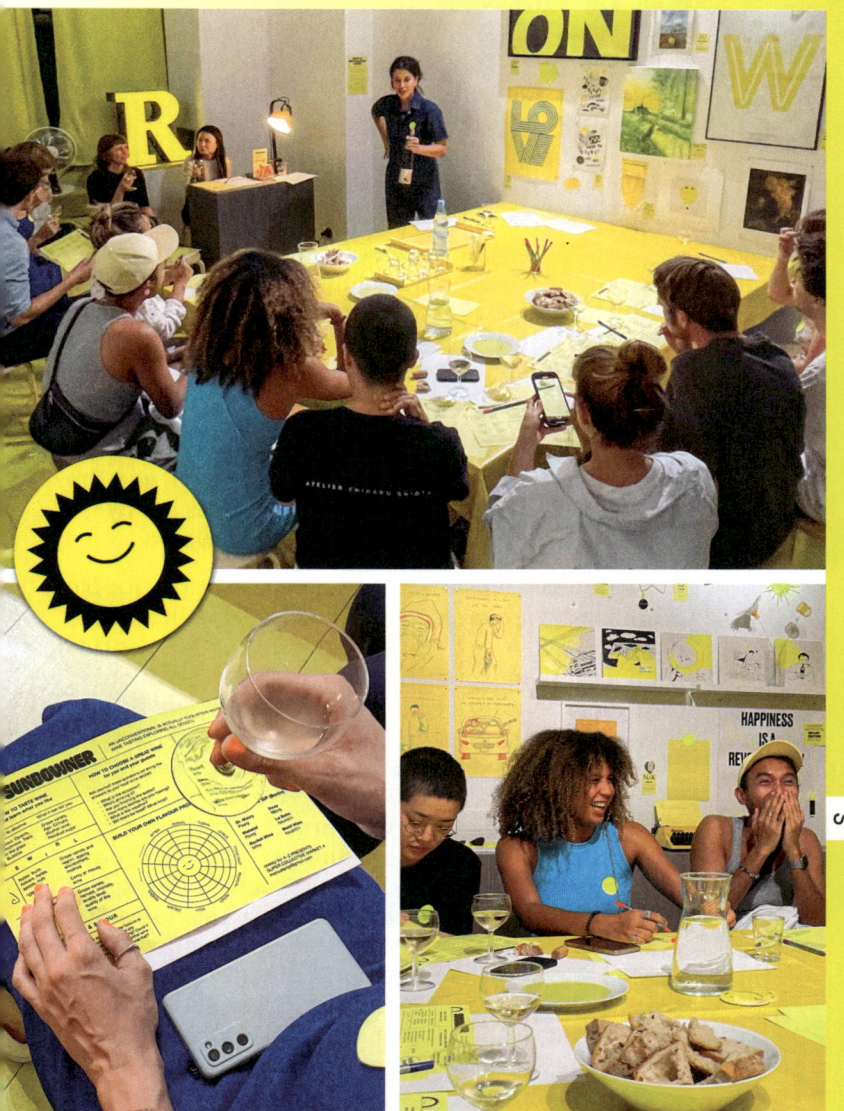

SUPER COLLECTIVE MARKET NO. 1 YELLOW

EXPERIMENTAL SHOP PROJECT BY THE *A–Z COLLECTIVE*

Super Collective Market No 1. Yellow transformed A—Z into a temporary marketplace, exploring the perspectives of community and commerce in Graphic Design. The market showcased a selection of yellow items from several artists and designers, including customized stamps, a kit to grow yellow pigment, limited edition prints, books, and textiles.

The opening night featured the interactive performance *Fishing for Yellow* by Hyesu Son, and the *Yellow Quiz* by Kelly Diepenbrock. Events led by other artists took place the following weeks.

Contributors were: Adrian Schiesser, Aggie Toppins, Agnieszka Węglarska, Alex Jordan, Anna Broujean, Andrea Iten, Anja Lutz, April Gertler, Broos Stoffels, Buchstabenmuseum, Carlos Navarro, Chris Rehberger, Constanze Hein, Dahm Lee, Daniela Burger, Diana Tsantekidou, Die Planung / A Terv, Eunjung Kwak, Francesco Pini, Gregory Cowling, Hanna Kang, Hannah Whitlow, Hans Brüderl, Hyesu Son, Jens Bauermeister, Jens Strandberg, Jenny Richards, Johnny Chang, Judy Kaufmann, Juli Gudehus, Kakoii, Kathrin Krumbein, Kelly Diepenbrock, Kui Park, Lisa Baumgarten, Louise Khadjeh-Nassiri, Manuela dos Santos, Marin Griffith, Mark van Wageningen, Max Spielmann, Niamh McShane, Paul Hutchinson, Pernilla Rozenberg, Pia Steiner, Primitive Hut, Raban Ruddigkeit, Ráhel Rudolf, Random Happiness, Sarah Boris, The Portland Stamp Company, Thies Wulf, Tim Ziola, and Ulrike Mohr.

A–Z COLLECTIVE
BANANA MUSEUM
BUTTER BETTER COME
SORRY TO SEE YOU SPLIT SO SOON
SUNDOWNER

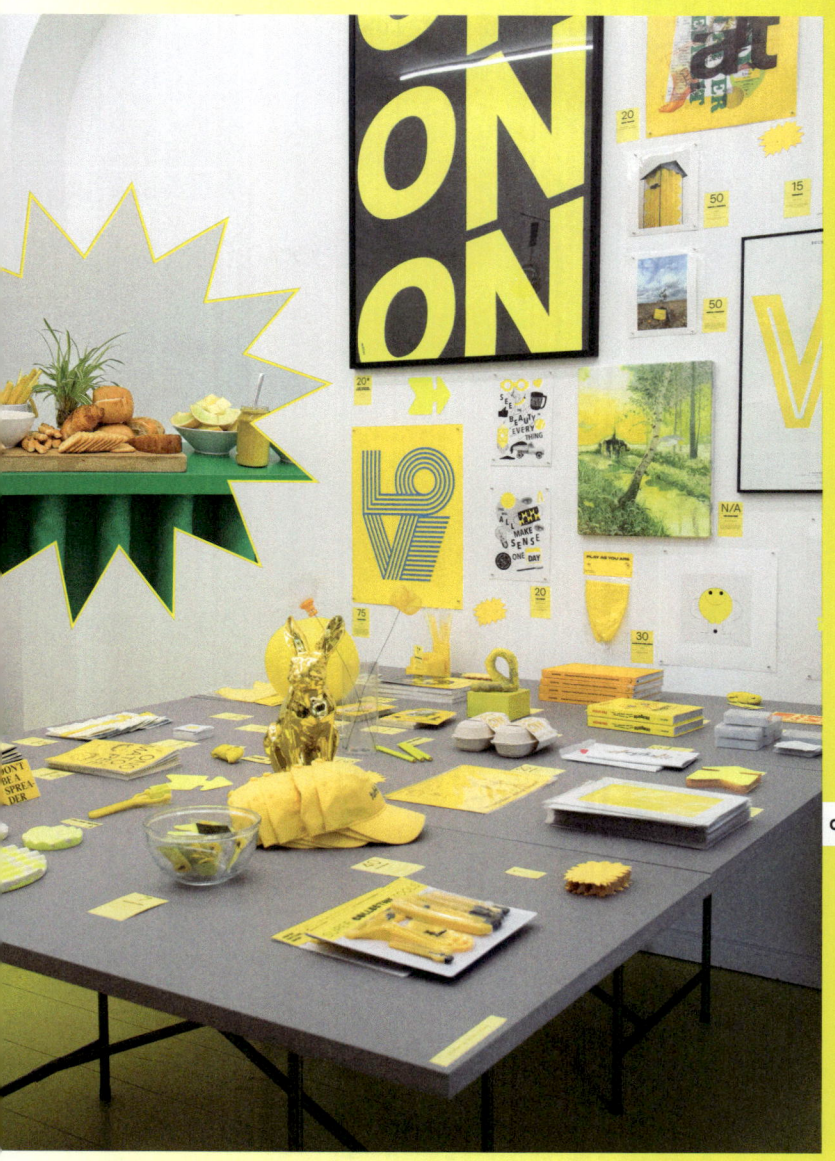

SUPER COLLECTIVE MARKET NO. 1 YELLOW

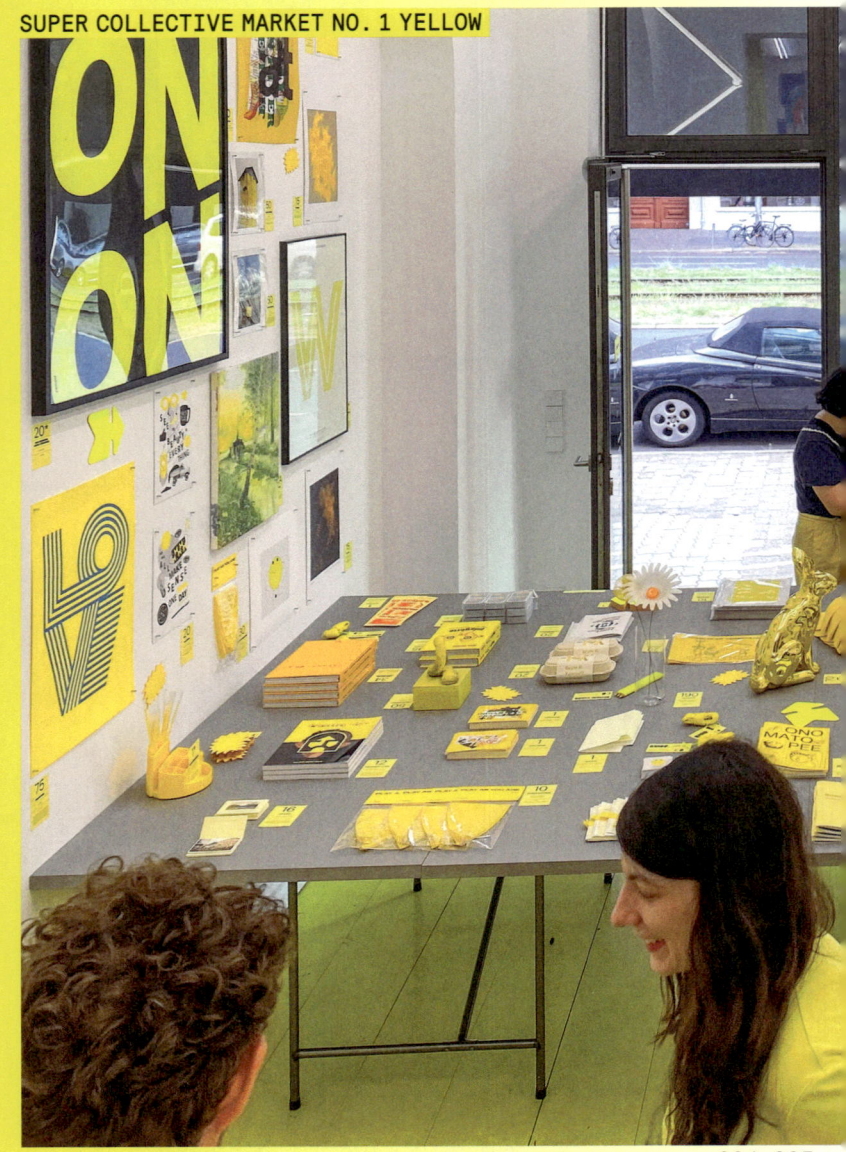

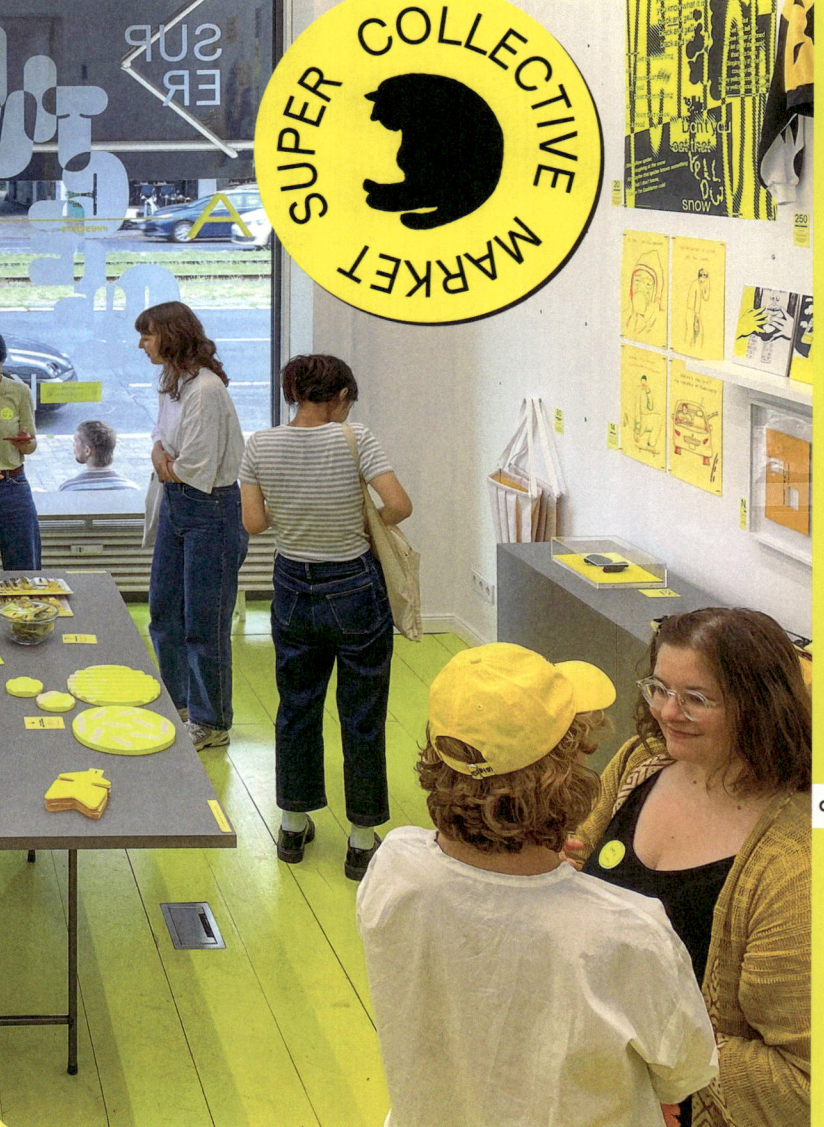

SUPER COLLECTIVE MARKET NO. 1 YELLOW

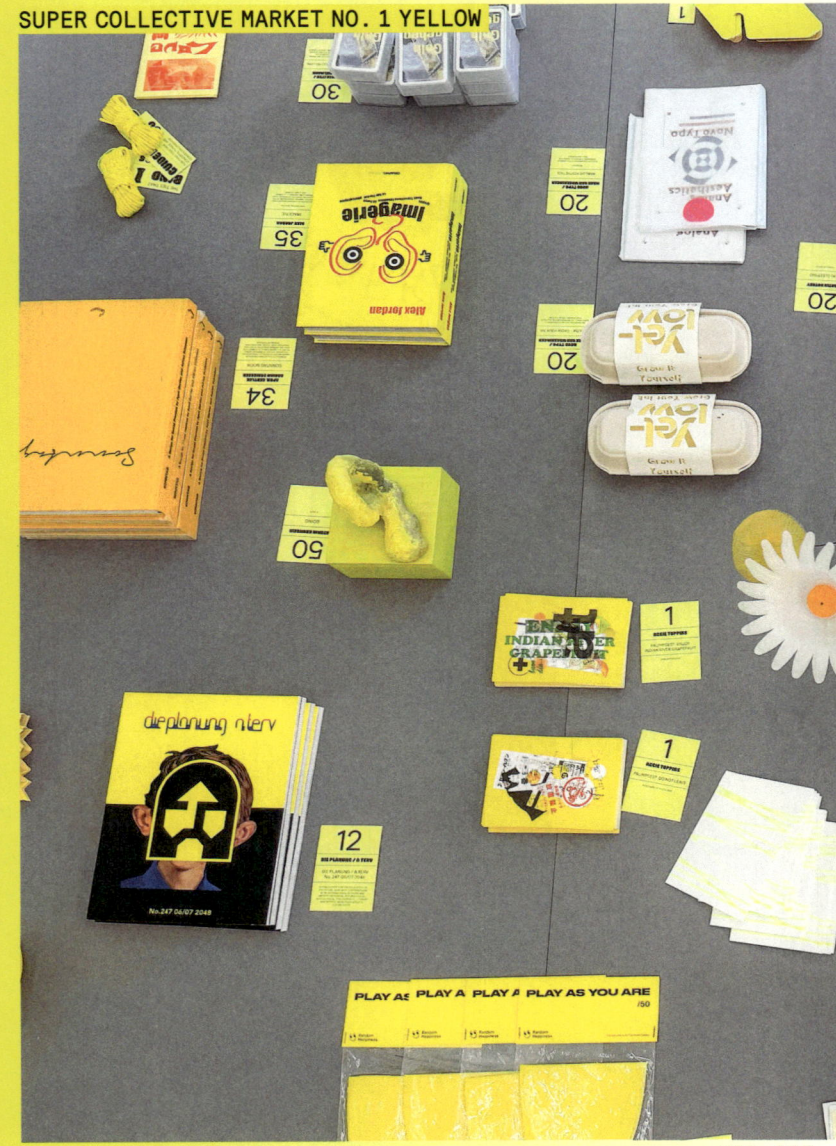

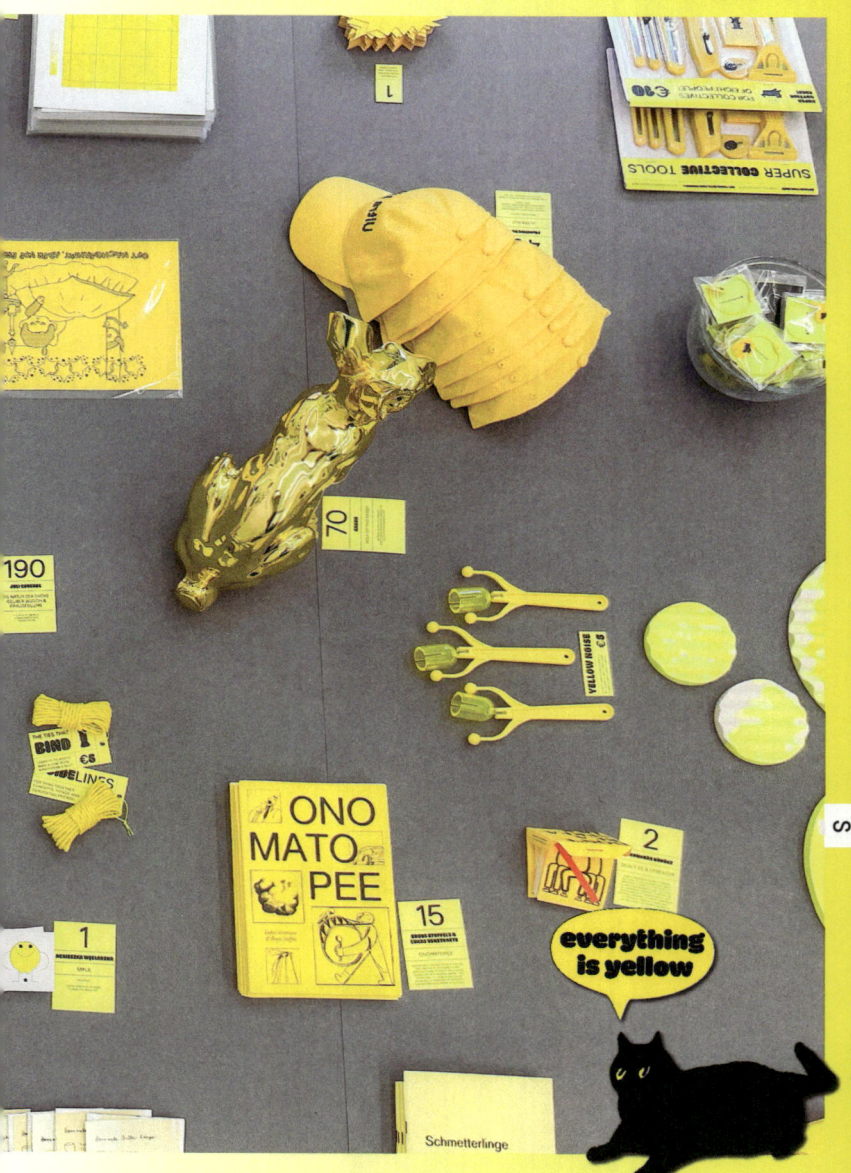

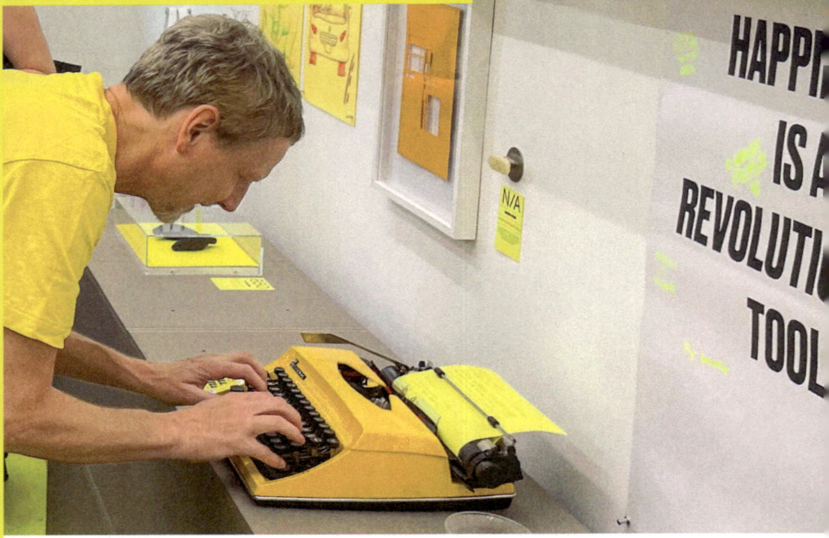

SUPER COLLECTIVE MARKET NO. 1 YELLOW

HAPPI
IS A
REVOLUTI
TOOL

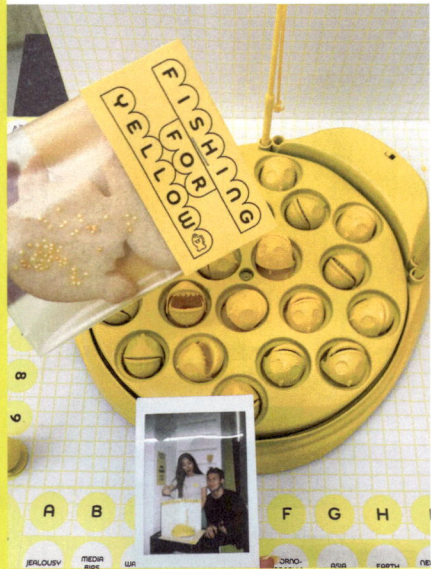
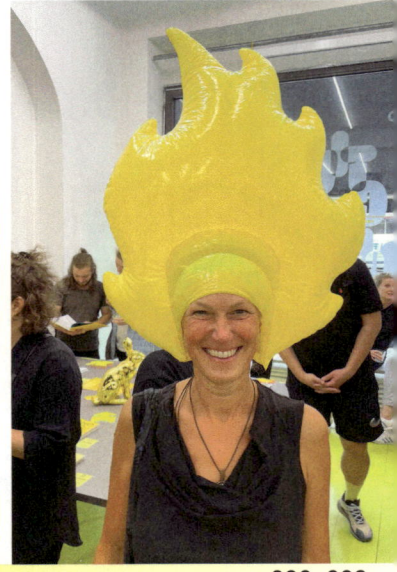

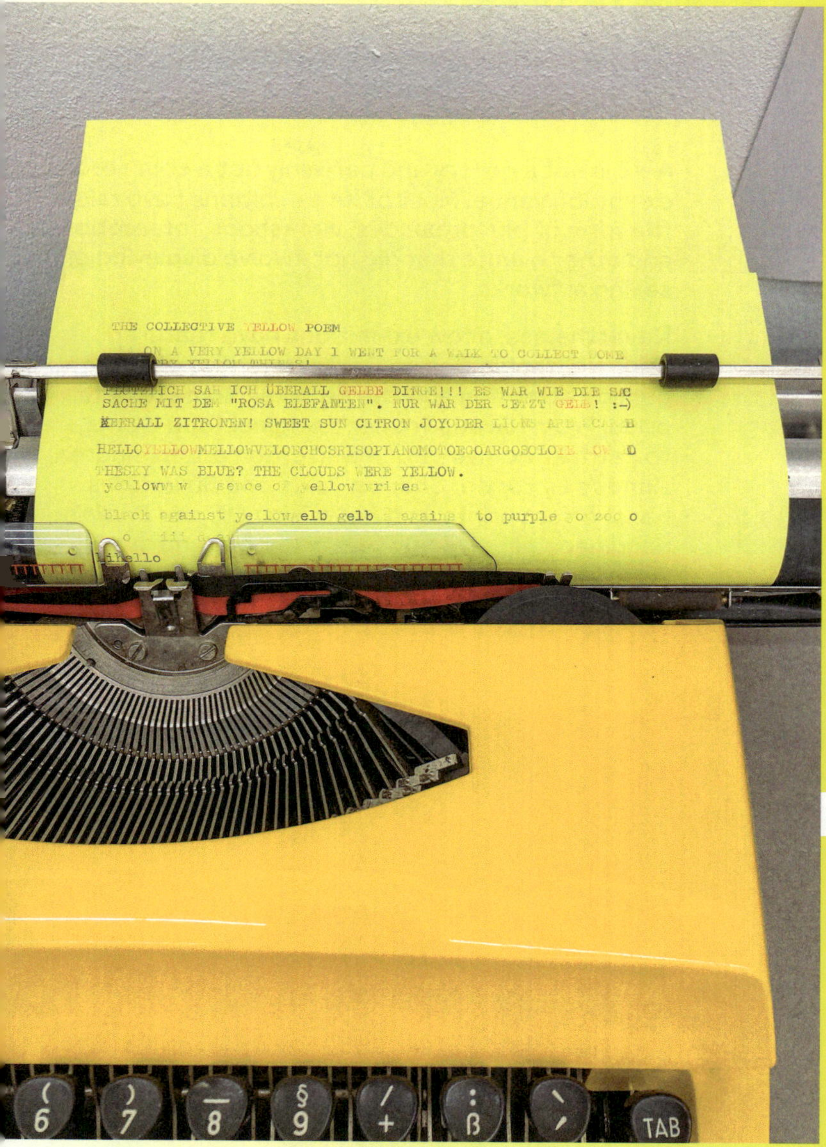

THE COLLECTIVE YELLOW POEM

ON A VERY YELLOW DAY I WENT FOR A WALK TO COLLECT SOME

PLÖTZLICH SAH ICH ÜBERALL GELBE DINGE!!! ES WAR WIE DIE S/C
SACHE MIT DEM "ROSA ELEFANTEN". NUR WAR DER JETZT GELB! :-)
ÜBERALL ZITRONEN! SWEET SUN CITRON JOYODER LIONS APE FC B

HELLOYELLOWMELLOWVELONCHOSRISOPIANOMOTOBOOARGOSOLO   D

THESKY WAS BLUE? THE CLOUDS WERE YELLOW.
yellowww a sence of yellow arises.

black against yellowgelb gelb   arsine   to purple go zoo o

hello

TAKEAWAY GRAPHIC DESIGN
GOODS FROM A—Z

A—Z is not a gallery and certainly not a commercial exhibition venue. Most of its exhibitions have taken the form of performances, workshops, interactions, and other events that did not involve displaying or selling artworks.

Nevertheless, a few exhibitions have featured original Graphic Design works that have caught the public's attention and can be taken home for a fair price. From Niklaus Troxler's original *Tape Works* to Patrick Thomas's *PULP* silkscreen prints, Andrea Tinnes's *Library of Shapes, Texts and Structures* hand-offset prints, and *Novo Typo Offgrid Berlin*'s handmade paper, soap, plus art books and much more besides—a collection of designed items is still available in the Goods section of the A—Z website.

COLLECTING GRAPHIC DESIGN
DO YOU COLLECT GRAPHIC DESIGN?

GOODS

Mirtha Dermisache
Recipes for Connecting by the A—Z Collective
Rainbow by Sarah Boris
Posters and Publication by Johannes Bergerhausen & Ilka Helmig
Items by Graphic.Designers.Collectors
Publication & Newspaper by Anita Di Bianco
Books, Prints and more by Novo Typo
Books & Prints by Tine Melzer & Markus Kummer
Temporary Items by Na Kim
Tape Works by Niklaus Troxler
Real-time Realist #2 by Jungmyung Lee
Ponchos and Posters by The Rodina
Pulp Prints by Patrick Thomas
New Anthems VI (Berlin) by Inkahoots
Library Prints by Andrea Tinnes

Watch past presentations, talks and performances on our Youtube channel

TAPE WORKS
EXHIBITION BY NIKLAUS TROXLER

The *Tape Works* exhibition by Niklaus Troxler presented a selection of his original artworks using the tape technique he has been exploring in recent years. For the first time, Niklaus performed a large-scale live taping on the blank walls of A—Z, accompanied by live improvised jazz.

His tape works had a very curious beginning when, one time in Berlin, thanks to a trip to a hardware store due to a broken washing machine, Niklaus was amazed to discover tapes in all possible colors. Feeling like a "child discovering a new pencil case", he decided to take them all home to try something new with them.

Since then, Niklaus has created abstract and sometimes allusive artworks using colored tape of all sizes and materials—a "totally reduced way of design", combining dots and lines. His in-situ *Tape Works* are always accompanied by jazz improvisations, resulting in a unique sound and visual experience of live performance composition.

Niklaus's *Tape Works* performance at A—Z was joined by the musicians Silke Eberhard (alto sax), Nikolaus Neuser (trumpet), and Almut Kühne (voice).

JAZZ AND DESIGN
NIKLAUS TROXLER
TAKEAWAY GRAPHIC DESIGN
ONLINE VIDEO ARCHIVE

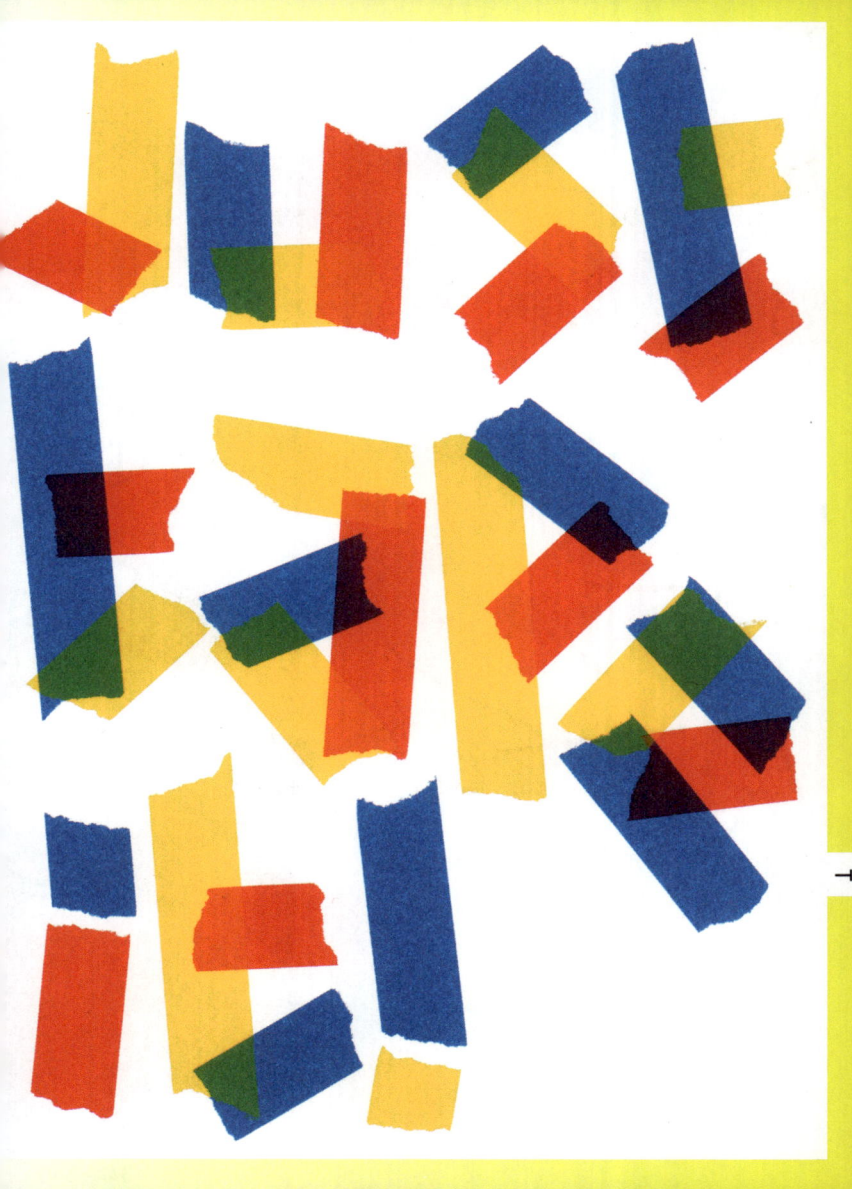

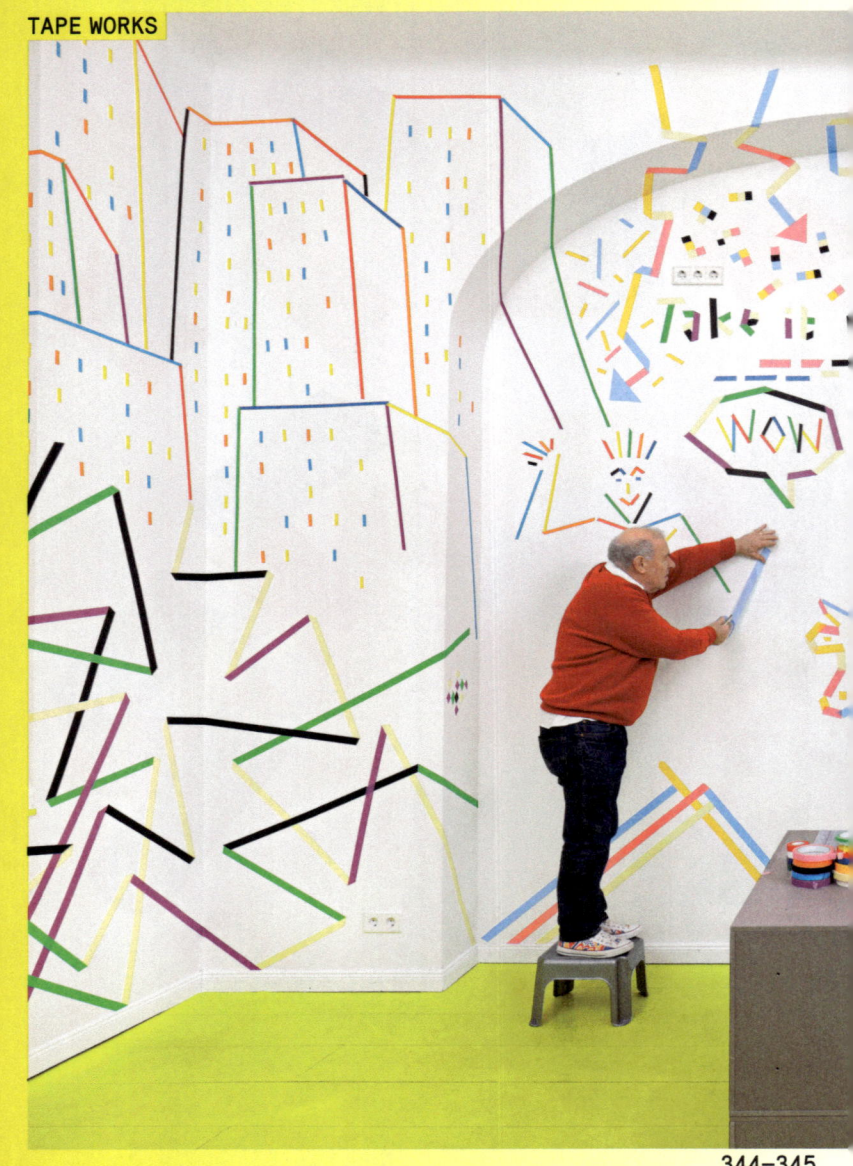

TAPE WORKS

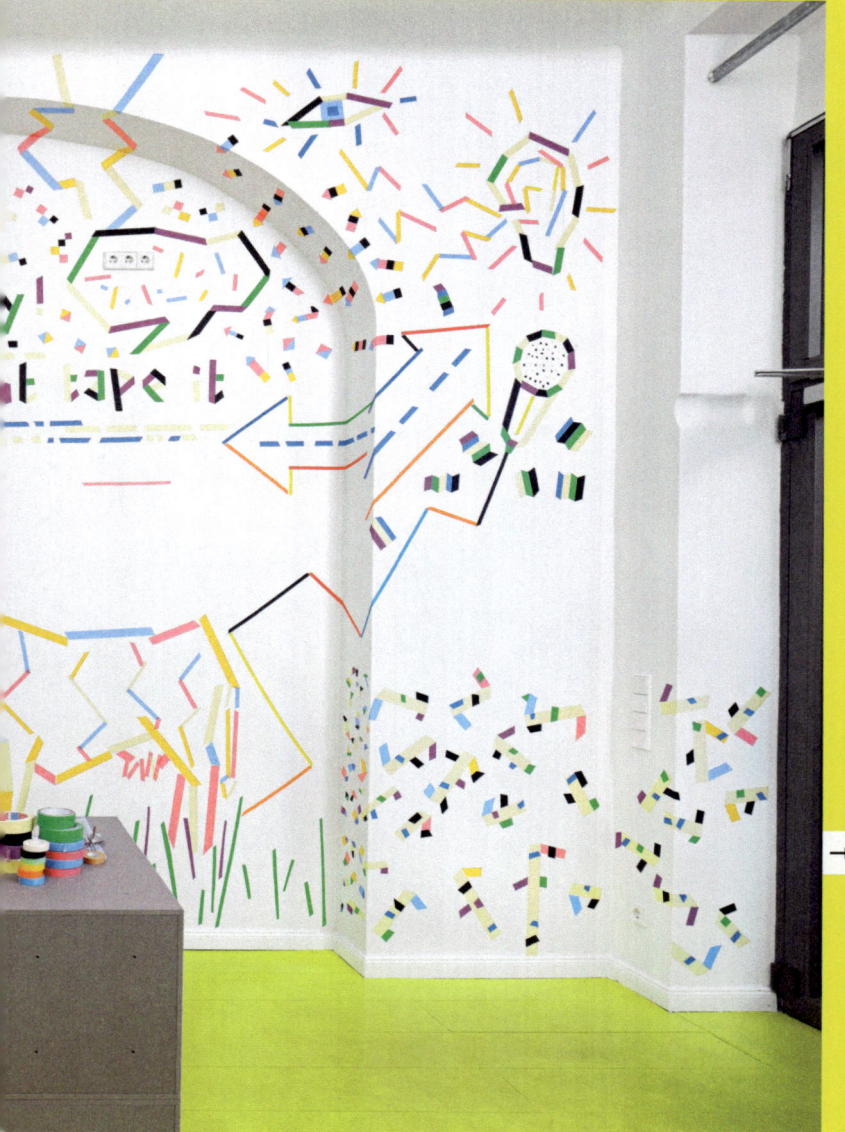

TAPE WORKS

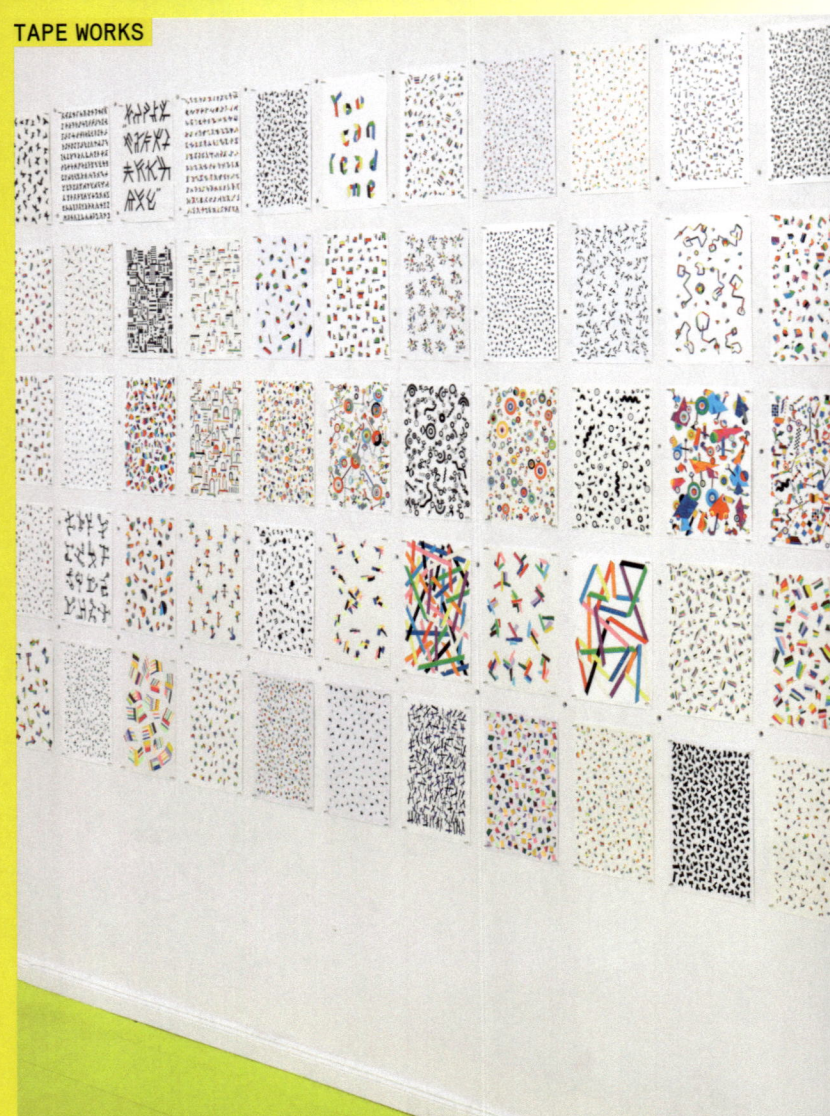

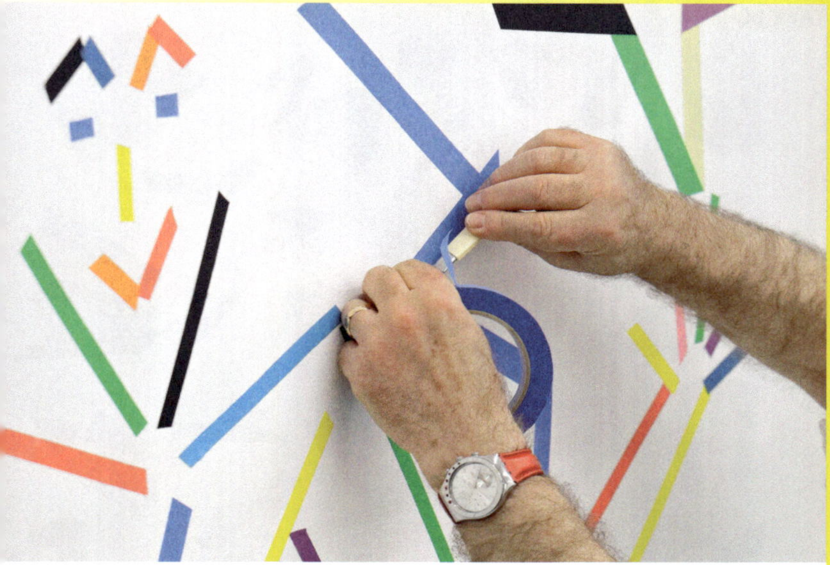

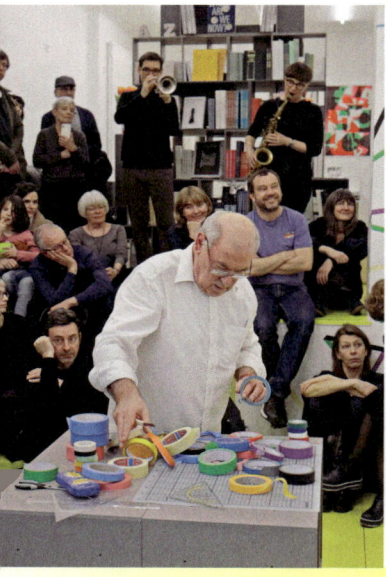
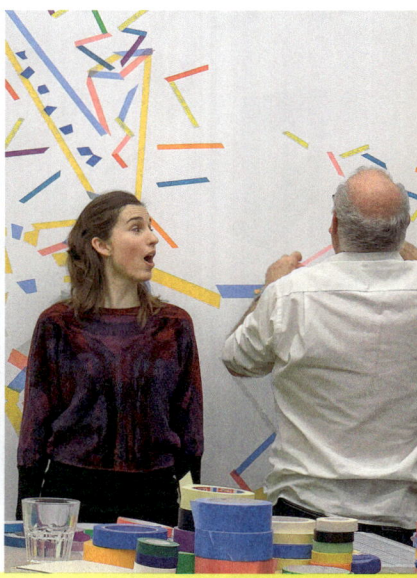

TAPE WORKS

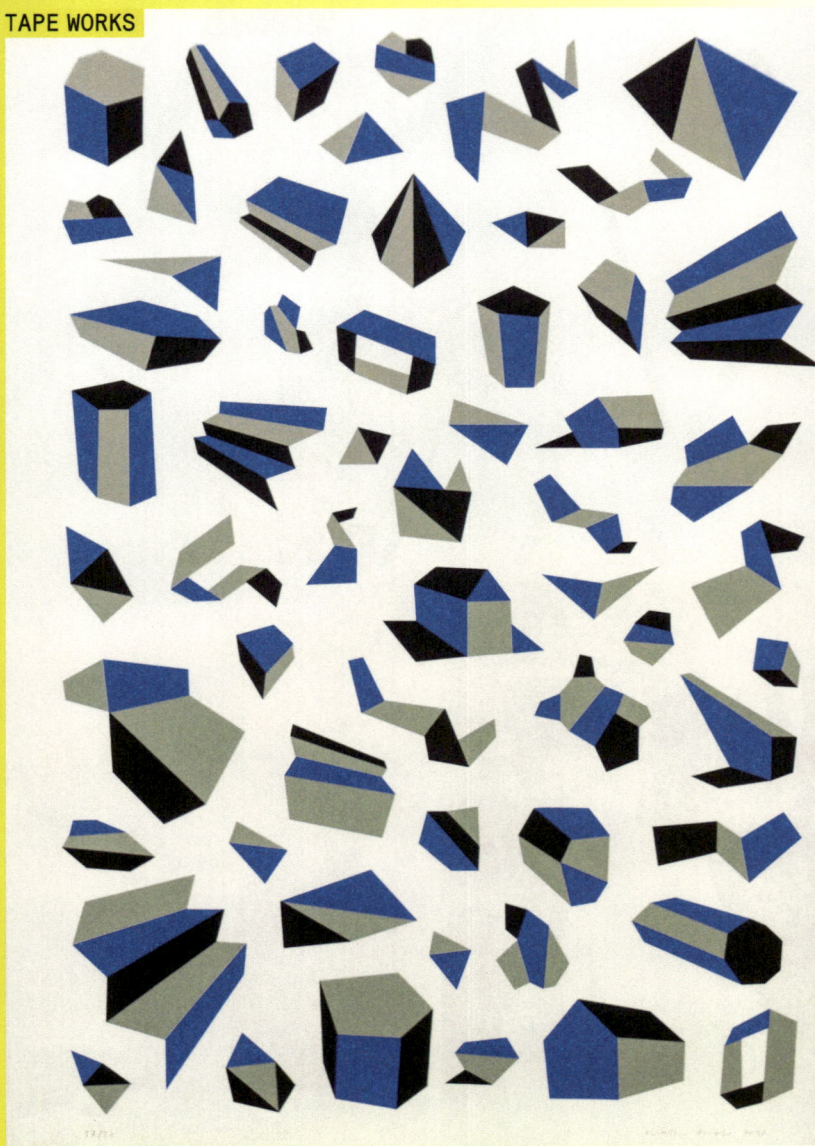

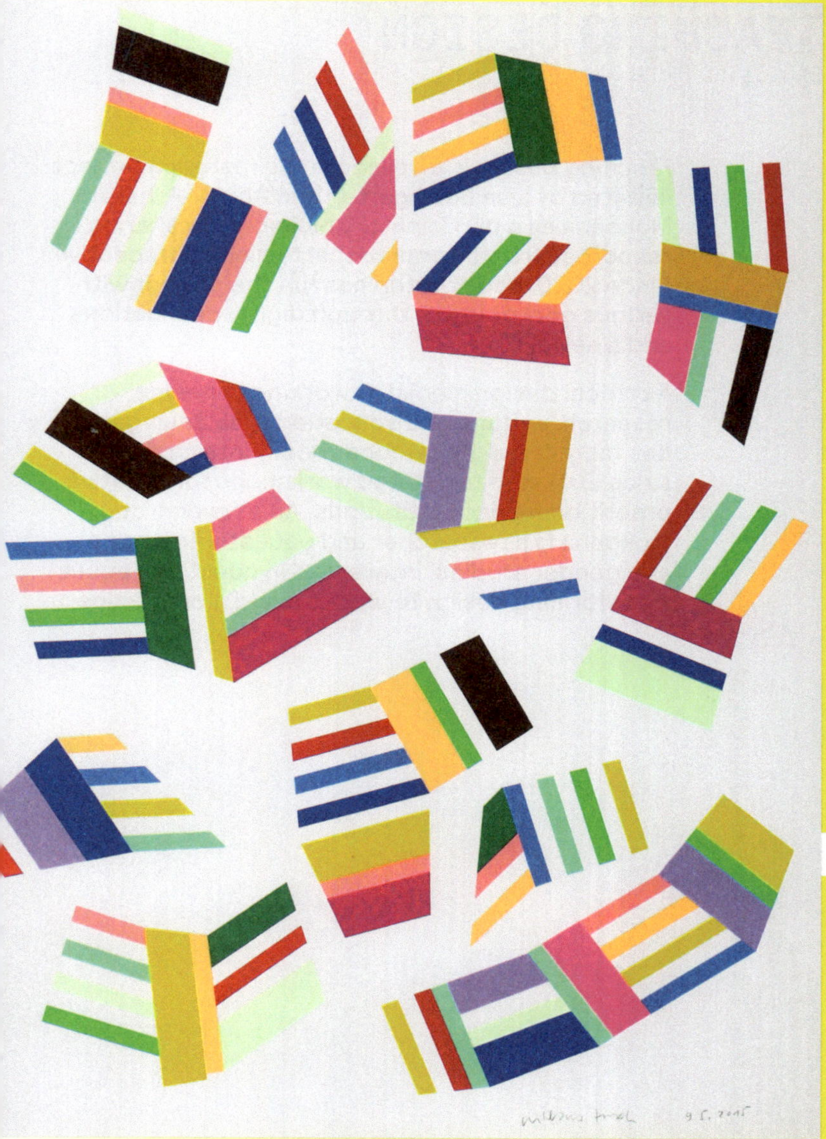

TEACHING DESIGN
EXHIBITED PROJECT

Teaching Design is a collaborative research project initiated by Lisa Baumgarten and Anja Neidhardt-Mokoena as a participatory bibliography sharing resources from intersectional feminist perspectives. Since 2020, Baumgarten has run the project with various contributors through digital publications and a newsletter.

A critical design mediator working in design, research, writing, and education, Lisa Baumgarten has taught design practice theory internationally since 2017, and facilitated workshops for creative practitioners and institutions. Anja Neidhardt-Mokoena is a researcher and educator in design and gender studies, interested in questions about transforming design to work toward more justice.

CONVERSATION SPACE
REAL-TIME REALIST NO. 2
TEACHING DESIGN CONVERSATIONS
TEMPORARY LIBRARY
WHY DO I DO WHAT I DO – LIKE I DO IT – AND NOT DIFFERENTLY?

On which values do we base our work as designers and educators?

How can we learn from and with students?

How can we support the development of a variety of more just design disciplines?

What relationships do you have with your students?

Which content do you focus on?

Which possibilities and which limitations do we have when we create curricula?

How can we contribute to building a more socially and ecologically sustainable world?

How can we teach in non-hierarchical ways?

How can we teach without putting individual designers and their creations on pedestals?

What can we do to support students in finding a balance between their responsibility and limited agency?

How do we support marginalised groups?

How do you position yourself within the design institution(s) you work?

What do we need in order to build and maintain strong networks to support each other?

How can we dismantle discriminating and oppressive structures within design education?

In which ways can we apply intersectional feminist and decolonial thinking in design education?

How can we change structures from within and from outside at the same time?

What do we need in order to create safe spaces?

TEACHING DESIGN CONVERSATIONS

PROJECT BY LISA BAUMGARTEN AND ANJA NEIDHARDT-MOKOENA

Teaching Design Conversations was a two-week project conceptualized and led by Lisa Baumgarten and Anja Neidhardt-Mokoena to install a temporary library, and a series of conversations on design education from an intersectional perspective in terms of feminism and decolonialism.

Set as a physical version of the online platform that shares its name, *Teaching Design Conversations* promoted access to a curated library available to visit as a background for coming together and connecting design educators, and anyone interested in the field.

The program invited participants to experience trust, inclusion, and issues of power through a series of talks, discussions, and practical exercises. These included: an opening conversation panel with the designer and researcher Imad Gebrayel, designer and educator Stefanie Rau, and design writer Madeleine Morley; the workshop *Why Do I Do What I Do – Like I Do It – And Not Differently?*, led by Antonia Schneemann and Lisa Baumgarten; and the book release and readings of *Real-Time Realist* by type designer Jungmyung Lee, with artist and publisher Lieven Lahaye.

CONVERSATION SPACE
REAL-TIME REALIST NO. 2
TEACHING DESIGN
TEMPORARY LIBRARY
WHY DO I DO WHAT I DO – LIKE I DO IT – AND NOT DIFFERENTLY?
ONLINE VIDEO ARCHIVE

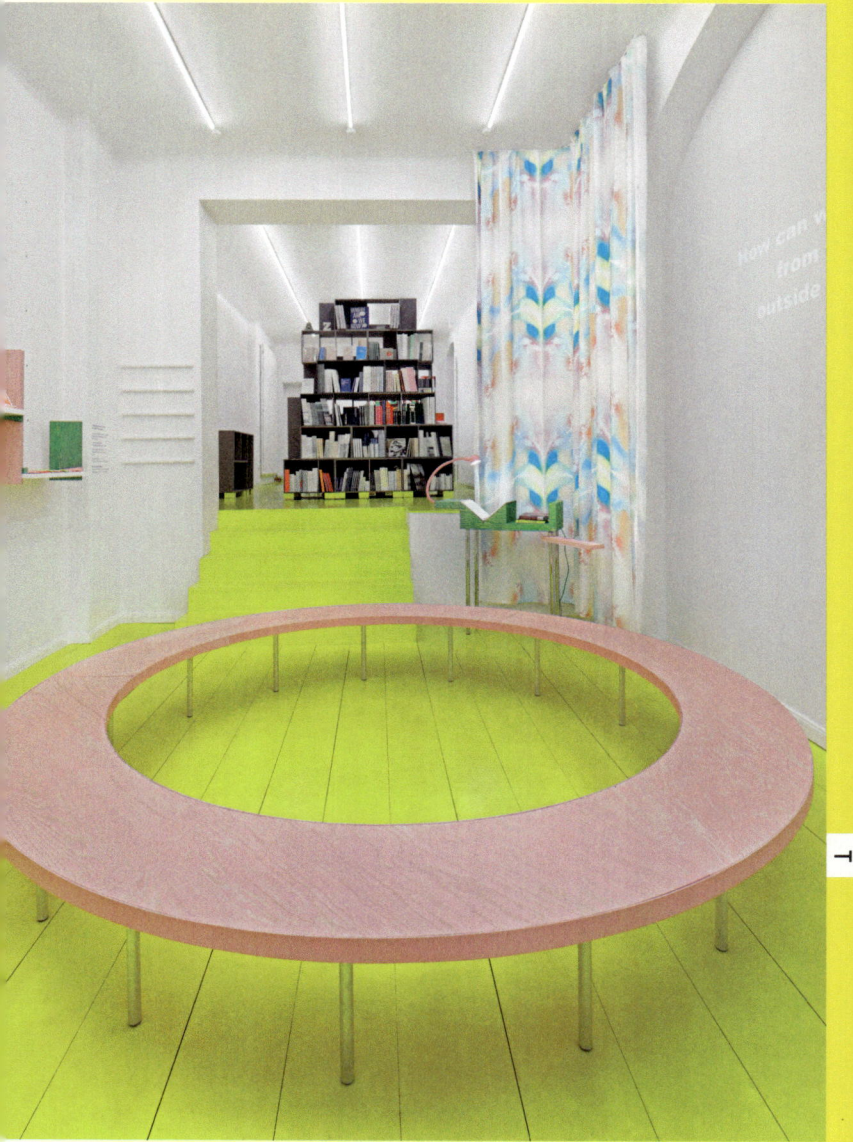

TEACHING DESIGN CONVERSATIONS

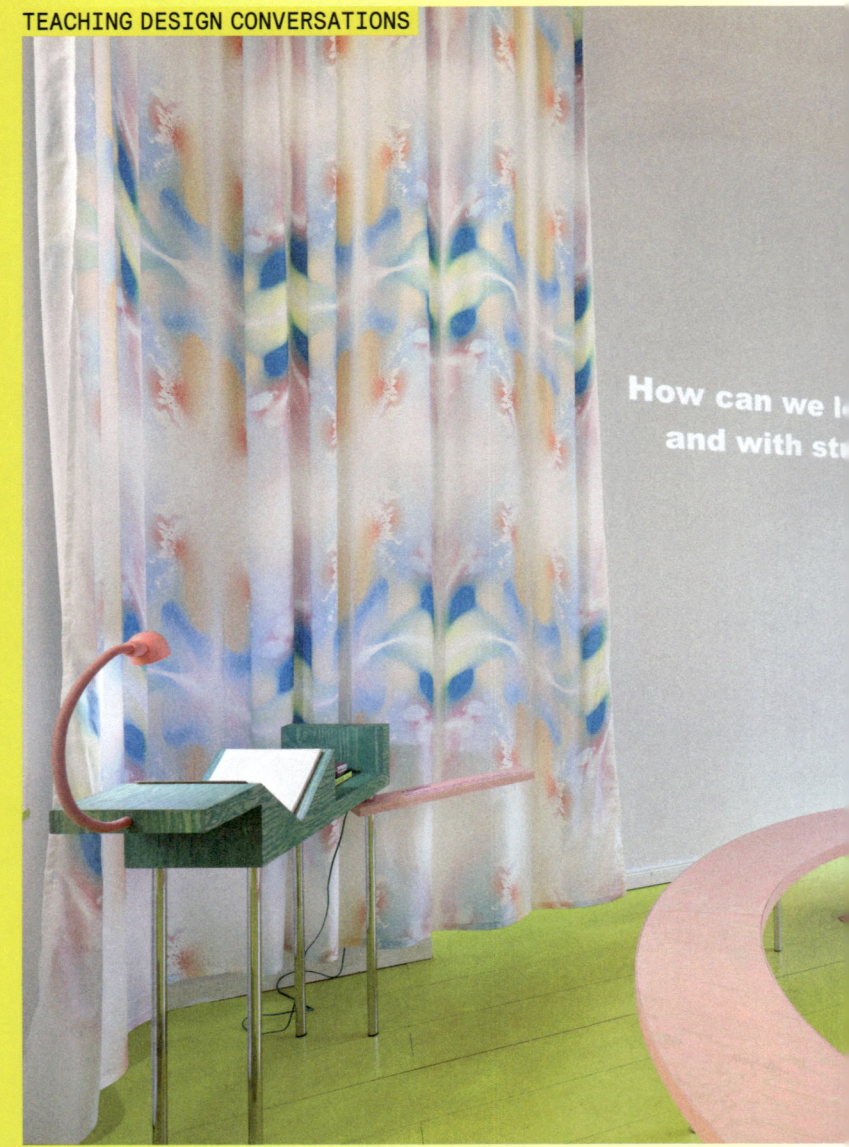

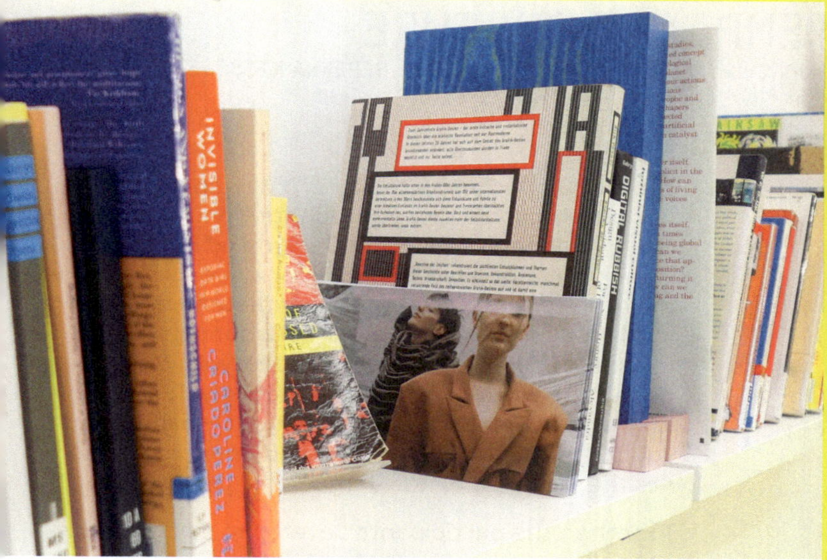

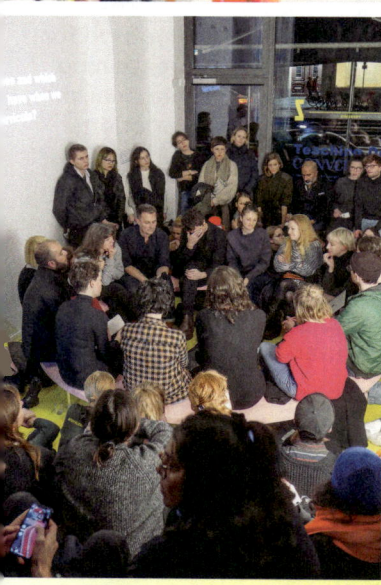

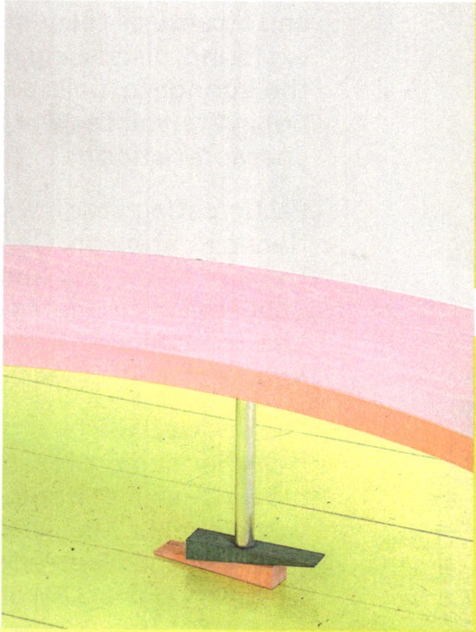

TEMPLATE CULTURE

WORKSHOP LED BY FRANZISKA MORLOK, REBEKKA KIESEWETTER, AND ANJA LUTZ

The workshop *Template Culture* was an event bringing together design students from Hyperwerk – Basel Academy of Arts and Design and Potsdam University of Applied Sciences for a five-day program devoted to reflecting upon the role templates play in all areas of design. Central questions were discussed, including, "How can we deal with templates consciously, critically, and productively?"; and "How do we make templates more inclusive—especially in light of a feminist perspective and one that considers the inclusion of non-hegemonic perspectives?"

Together, the participants developed a publication process based on the three areas of image, text, and structural templates. This became a method for exploring, discussing, and productively questioning the economic, political, and ideological mechanisms behind templates and their graphic and functional characteristics.

Participating students: Juliana Toro, So Jin Park, Nanna Kristensen, Caroline Bertelsen, Carlotta Thomas, Katharina Gomez, Judith Rebekka, Sophie Schütte Meyer, Pierre Kaelin, Sebastian Ramming, Lea Scheidegger, Karin Wiesmann, Serena Lehmann, Alex Lehmann, Elena Eigenheer, Mole Freyhoff.

The activity was facilitated by Franziska Morlok, designer and Professor of the Institute for Transmedia Design at Berlin University of Arts, together with Rebekka Kiesewetter, writer and Research Fellow at the Centre for Post-digital Cultures, Coventry University, and A—Z founder Anja Lutz.

BUNDESREPUBLIK DEUTSCHLAND
FEDERAL REPUBLIC OF GERMANY / RÉPUBLIQUE FÉDÉRALE D'ALLEMAGNE

PERSONALAUSWEIS
IDENTITY CARD / CARTE D'IDENTITÉ

T22000129

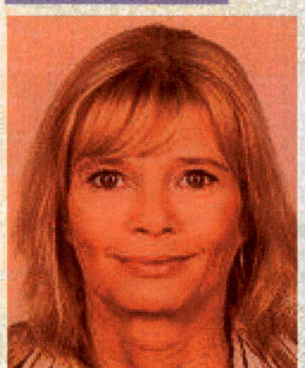

Name/Surname/Nom
MUSTERMANN
GEB. GABLER

Vornamen/Given names/Prénoms
ERIKA

Geburtstag/Date of birth/Date de naissance
12.08.1964

Staatsangehörigkeit/Nationality/Nationalité
DEUTSCH

Geburtsort/Place of birth/Lieu de naissance
BERLIN

Gültig bis/Date of expiry/Date d'expiration
31.10.2020

938568

Unterschrift der Inhaberin/des Inhabers -
Signature of bearer - Signature de la titulaire / du titulaire

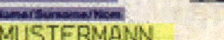

TEMPORARY LIBRARY
BIBLIOGRAPHY OF *TEACHING DESIGN CONVERSATIONS*

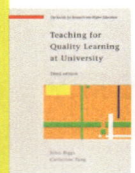 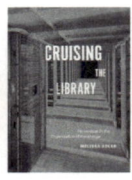 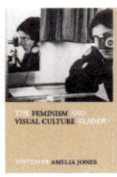  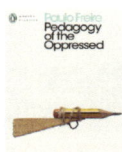 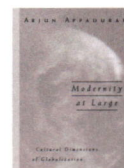

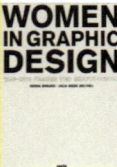 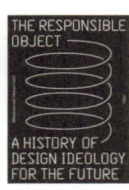 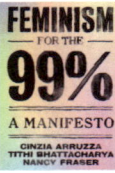 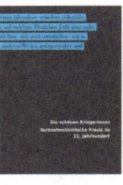 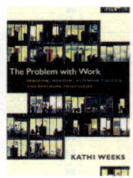 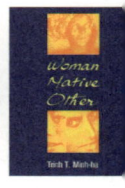

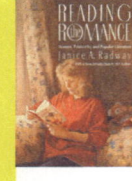 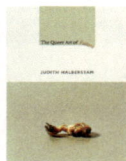 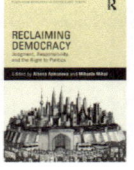 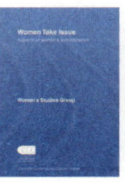 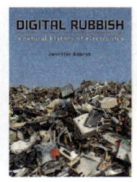 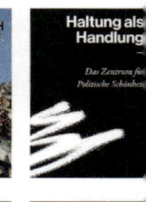

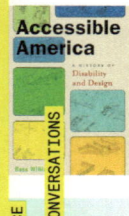 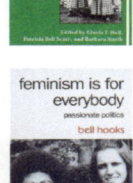 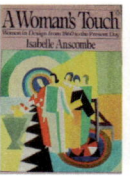 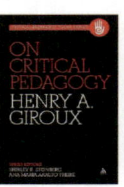 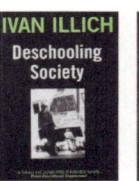 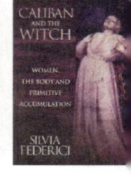

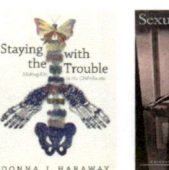 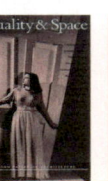 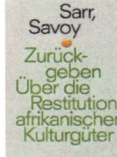

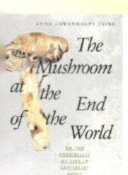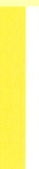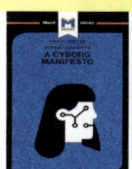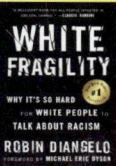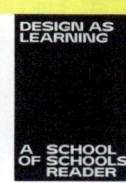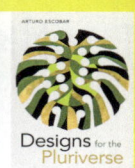
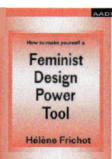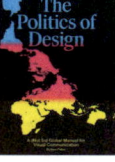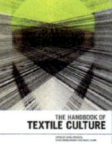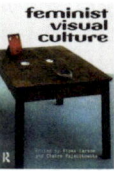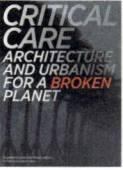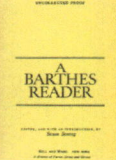
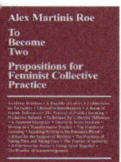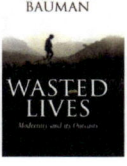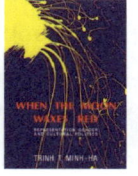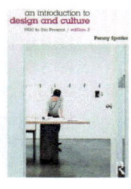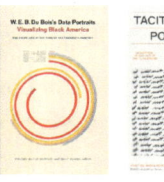
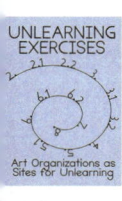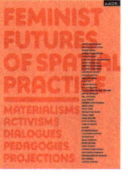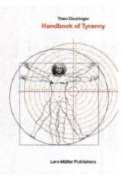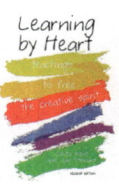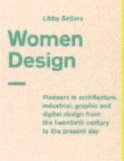
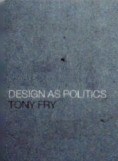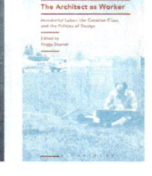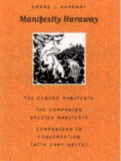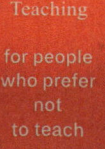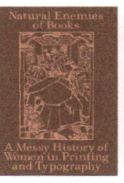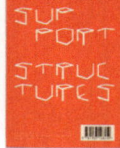
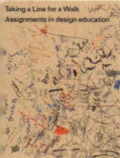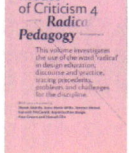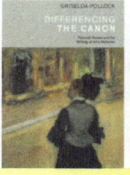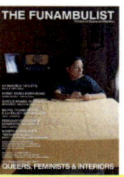

THANKS!
ACKNOWLEDGEMENTS

Behind every A—Z initiative there is a constellation of voluntary collaborators who make the events possible, based on the mutual care and understanding of the challenges of running an independent space.

Special thanks to all the designers and artists who exhibited at A—Z and contributed to its program, and to all the members of the *A—Z Collective*, who ran A—Z during the year 2023. A big thanks to the following, long-term helping hands behind the scenes:

Jens Bauermeister for installations, and technical help as well as emotional support

Soraya Guimarães Hoepfner for developmental editing and copywriting

Birger Lipinski and Laercio Redondo for expography advice and modular furniture design

Hans-Georg Gaul for exhibition photography

Anuschka Spitzer for on-site support and exhibition mounting

Emily Smith, Freek Lomme, Jason Grant, Lucienne Roberts, and Prem Krishnamurthy for their advice, input, and encouragement

And A—Z interns for their enthusiasm and engagement: Eva Dumoulin, Ezequiel Hyon, Fernanda de la Mora, Franzi Bauer, Giulia Siviero, Johanna Olm, Juliana Toro, Lisa Böckling, Liudmila Savelyeva, Mari Leach, Nour Asmar, Olena Hryhorieva, Sarah Schümperli, So Jin Park.

Great!

Thank you!

so helpful!

we love you!

THE ERROR IS REGRETTED
EXHIBITION BY ANITA DI BIANCO

The Error is Regretted exhibition marked the 20th anniversary of the artist Anita Di Bianco's project *Corrections and Clarifications*, an ongoing newsprint research initiative published since 2001 that compiles daily editorial apologies in the form of revisions, retractions, rewordings, distinctions, and rectifications found in international news publications.

The featured 96-page newspaper compiles around 3,000 errata extracted from dozens of English and German news publications between June 2020 and October 2021. These are meticulously selected entries of peculiar mistakes printed and corrected in subsequent editions, from fake news to banal typos, and from bizarre misinformation to the attention economy.

This latest issue was presented at A—Z, along with a conversation between Anita, artist and publisher Florian Wüst and media artist Anna Bromley, discussing and reflecting on editorial lapses, surfacing hidden clues of subtle biases, and giving visibility to those anonymous eyes watching over the facts. Anita offers credit to "ultimately [those] who, regardless of stated intentions, occasionally reveal something, piece by piece, through slips in language and naming systems."

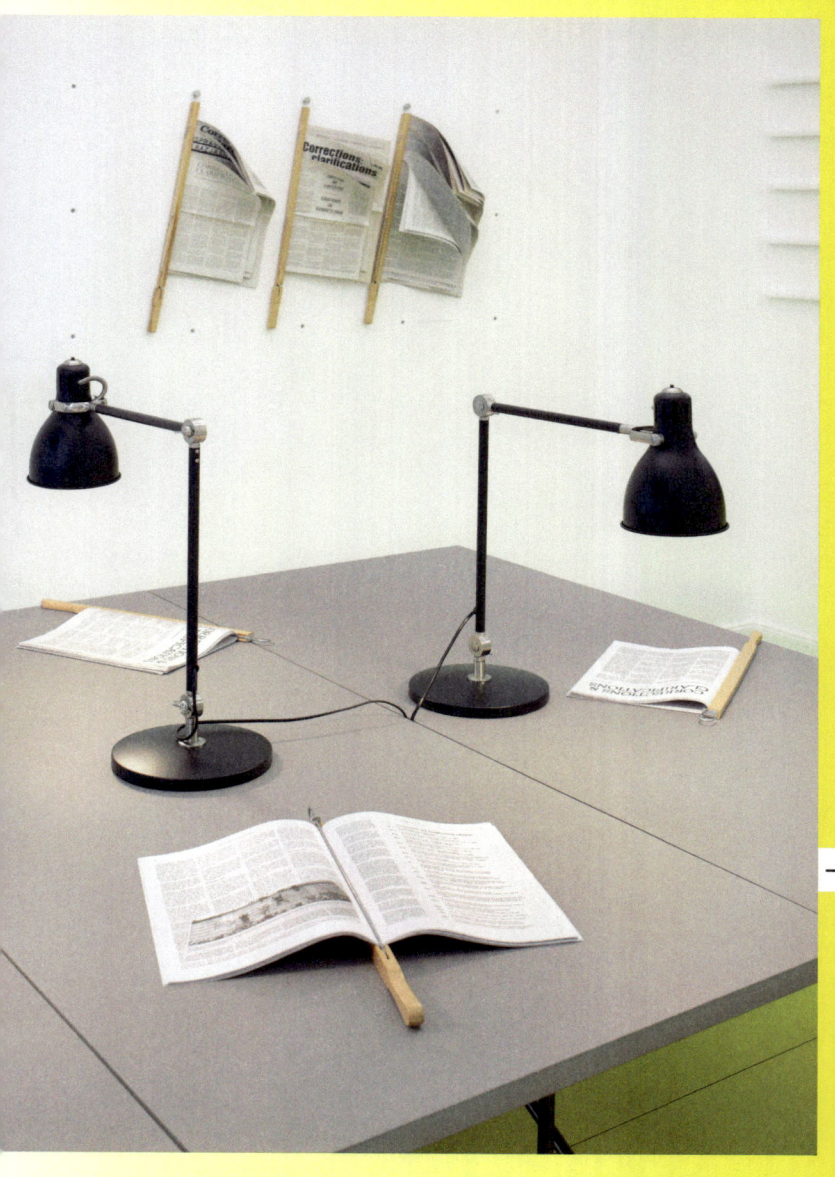

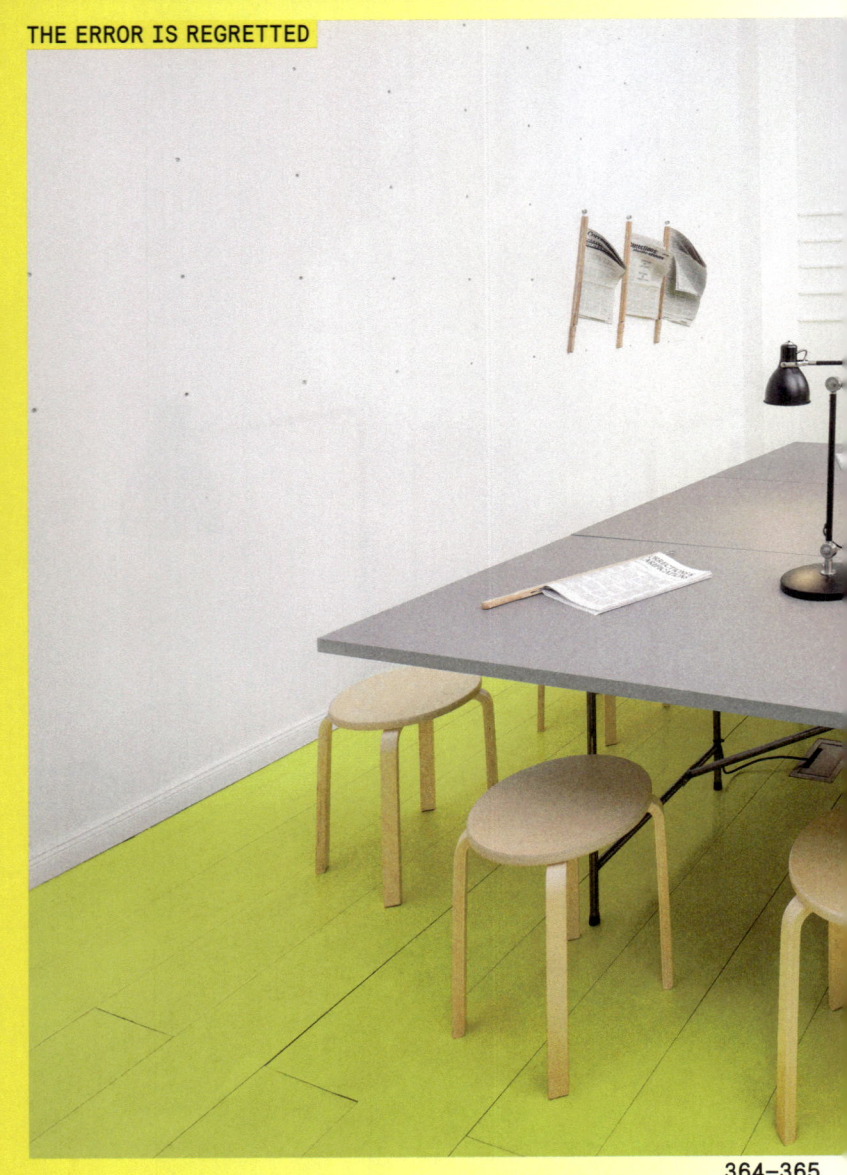

THE ERROR IS REGRETTED

T

THE ERROR IS REGRETTED

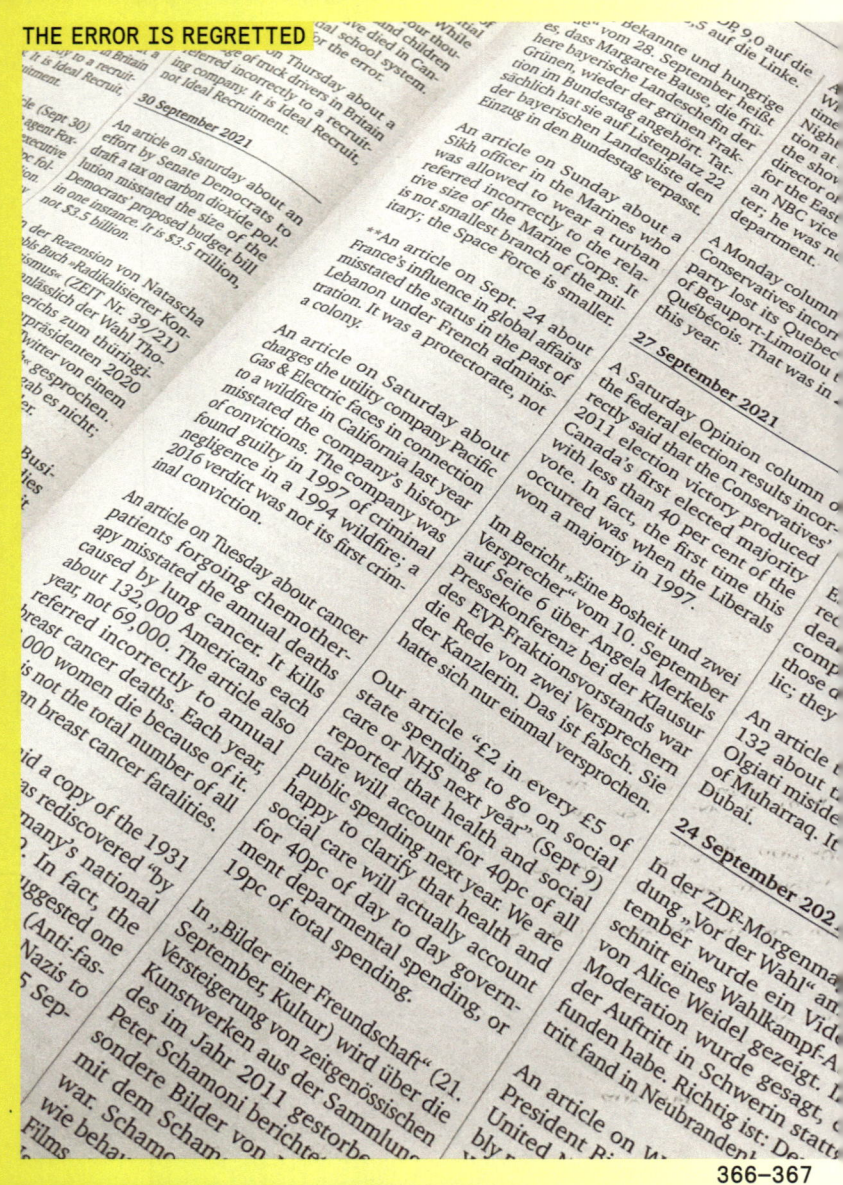

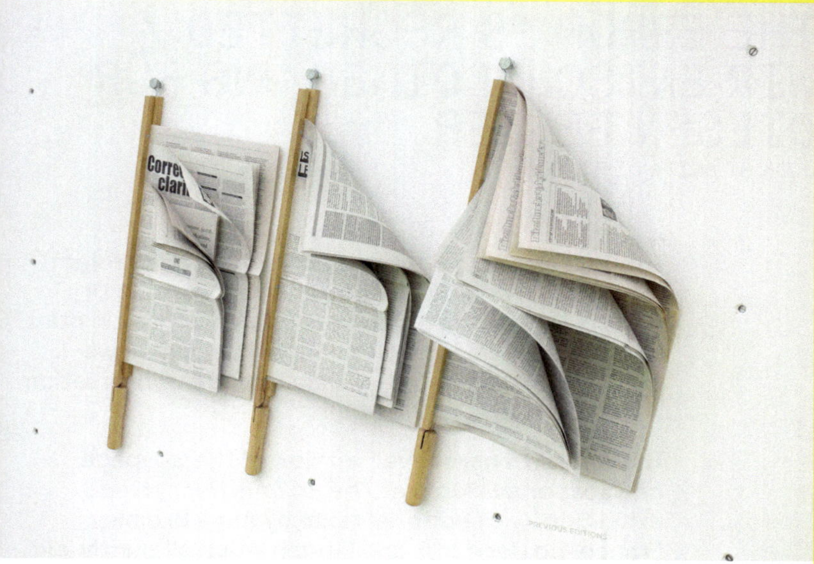

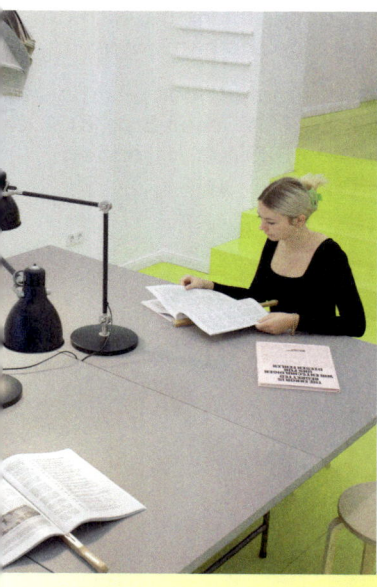
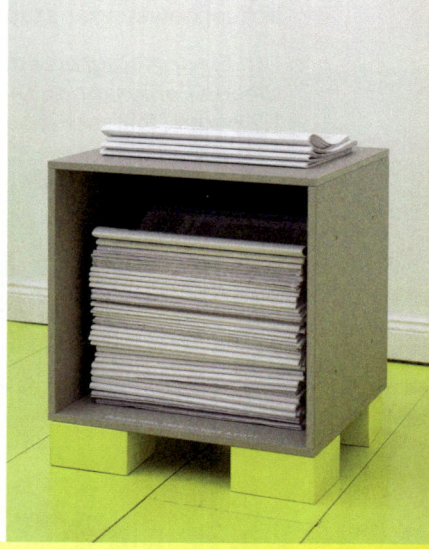

THE ERROR IS REGRETTED / WIR ENTSCHULDIGEN UNS FÜR DIESEN FEHLER

BOOK BY ANITA DI BIANCO

This publication celebrates 20 years of the project *Corrections and Clarifications* by artist Anita Di Bianco. It features a curated series of lapses in print and online news from German and English newspapers, complemented by articles and a conversation with the artist.

The book is a hardcover version of the 96-page newspaper available at *The Error is Regretted* exhibition, with editorial texts by Anna Bromley, Francesco Gagliardi, and Florian Wüst, all tightly laid out like a newspaper front, back and inside, with the actual newspaper stapled inside the hardcover.

The Error is Regretted / Wir entschuldigen uns für diesen Fehler, Anita Di Bianco, The Green Box, 2021. 112 pages, 2 illustrations, 240 x 320 mm, hardcover, English and German.

Anita Di Bianco

THE ERROR IS REGRETTED

WIR ENTSCHULDIGEN UNS FÜR DIESEN FEHLER

CORRECTIONS AND CLARIFICATIONS is ongoing publication, an intermittent compilation of daily revisions, retractions, rewordings, distinctions and apologies in print news from September 2001 to the present. A reverse-chronological cataloging of lapses in naming and classification, of tangled catchphrases, detectable patterns of mis-speech and correction, distraction, connotation and enumeration. The relentlessly populist peace-shifting, sheep-herding entrepreneurial fervor whipped up, incited, inciting once again, in continuous run up to the interminable U.S. (for just one example) election cycle marks a stream of linguistic trickery, disguise and distortion, backtracking, backfiring, and side-talking at once clubbing down and puffing up, ramming or plowing through, evading any means of lying or limiting recklessness, usury, depletion, catastrophic speculation. Any restraint on which has been generalized class warfare and drumbeat alongside vitriol of race fear, as ever, to resounding effect. Believability as affect, lashing in in withering cynicism or punitive option, proven legitimate by the repetitive, arbitrary brutality of example, of undeniable and collective feeling. Statements issued forth in officious demonstration, refutation, denial of observable reality. Pithiness notwithstanding. Rapturous isms of private advantage extracted as popular consensus from what was once called public good, ingloriously recast as the founding myth of our indefatigable pioneering, bootstrapping, DIY-ing spirit. Into the noisy, barren landscape of such speech and informationalism, this is a newspaper without headlines, allowing such doubletalk to talk to itself. Perhaps what is conveyed unintentionally, and by repetitious mistakes, is more revealing, more historically identifiable, and substantially less conciliatory than it is meant to be. This is both fortunate and inevitable.

***

Purely editorial credit to those who have provided the material for this publication by having seen fit to correct themselves, or having seen themselves fit to correct others; who have sought in some public way to offer apologies or clarifications—to redeem, reveal, revise, retract, or shift, to simultaneously claim, deny, and reattribute blame and responsibility. Credit is due for these well-documented efforts to apologize for what is being done and for what has already been done, for continuing attempts to un-say what is said, un-mean what is meant. Credit at a variety of levels to those seekers, processors, middle managers, and ultimate regulators of public information who take it upon themselves (or impose it upon others) to re-name, re-classify, disguise, de-fuse or be de-briefed; who find clever metaphors to obfuscate, euphemize and mystify; who disseminate information according to political structures coincident with particular economic interests, who consent to use language to dismiss, excuse, cushion, cover and obscure the consequences of actions and the submerged structures behind events. And ultimately who, regardless of stated intentions, occasionally reveal something, piece by piece, through slips in language and naming systems.

***

With further acknowledgement to readers who regard this revisions, regrets, re-directions, and retractions with the same skepticism they have the originals.

REPETITION AND INSISTENCE

A Conversation between Anita Di Bianco and Florian Wüst

FLORIAN When looking at books, I almost automatically go straight to the colophon: the year of publication and other features provide historical context and clues about the circumstances of production. Occasionally, as in our *Berlin Journals—On the History and Present State of the City*, an editorial note can be found there, and so too with your *Corrections and Clarifications*. Given the longevity of your project, this statement in each volume has slightly shifted over time; some paragraphs have appeared and disappeared, or you've rearticulated them over the course of the 20 years since the first edition.

Please correct me if I'm wrong, but there is one simple sentence in the editorial note

THE GREEN BOX
ART BOOK PUBLISHING HOUSE

The Green Box is a publishing house specializing in designing and publishing art books. It was founded in 2007 by curator and art critic Axel Lapp and A—Z founder Anja Lutz, who has run the company solo since 2015.

With over 150 books designed and published in close collaboration with contemporary artists worldwide, The Green Box strives to set itself apart by constantly searching for new ways to translate the peculiarities of artworks into book pages. The publishing house operates from the same location as A—Z, and has been responsible for some of its publications, such as *The Error is Regretted / Wir entschuldigen uns für diesen Fehler* by Anita Di Bianco, *Novo Typo Offgrid* by Mark van Wageningen, *Blumen sind geil* by Tine Melzer and Markus Kummer.

BLUMEN SIND GEIL
MARGINALIA
NOVO TYPO OFFGRID
THE ERROR IS REGRETTED / WIR ENTSCHULDIGEN UNS FÜR DIESEN FEHLER

LUDIFIED

Edited by Marko Ciciliani, Barbara Lüneburg and Andreas Pirchner

FREDERICK KIESLER GALAXIES — STEPHANIE BUHMANN

SONNTAG — A Recipe for Social Practice by April Gertler and Adrian Schiesser

neue type allgrid — Bekannt von AUTHENTIEKE **AMSTERDAMSE BOMEN** oude plaatjes

Hannah Höch — Bilderbuch

Lebensbild — Hannah Höch

Conversations Across Place

BEYOND PLANT BLINDNESS — Bryndís Snæbjörnsdóttir / Mark Wilson / Dawn Sanders

KADER ATTIA   THE REPAIR

EDGAR LECIEJEWSKI — A SCENE IN A LIBRARY

Jim Avignon — business as unusual

COSTA VECE — REVOLUCION-PATRIOTISMO

FINGERS LIKE TOES — Karoline Schreiber

FILMS BEFORE REVOLUTION — ADRIAN VILLAR ROJAS

Claudia Reinhardt — Witwen · Widows — THE GREEN BOX

Anita Di Bianco — THE ERROR IS REGRETTED / WIR ENTSCHULDIGEN UNS FÜR DIESEN FEHLER — THE GREEN BOX

Roselyne Titaud — Géographies des limites humaines

BERLIN STUDIO CONVERSATIONS

RHEINLAND STUDIO CONVERSATIONS

SONIA BOYCE   LIKE LOVE

Harriet Groß — Weißer Regen · White Rain

ULRIKE MOHR — ANTHRAKOTHEK

ULRIKE MOHR — ANTHRAKOTHEK (VOL. 2)

Jytte Hoy · Hair Net Geometry — The Green Box

MARGINALIA — Anja Lutz

Tine Melzer · Markus Kummer · Blumen sind geil — The Green Box

SOCIALIST ARCHITECTURE — THE REAPPEARING ACT

R.E.P. REVOLUTIONARY EXPERIMENTAL SPACE — Р.Е.П. РЕВОЛЮЦИОННО ЕКСПЕРИМЕНТАЛЬНИЙ ПРОСТІР

THE RODINA
EXHIBITED ARTIST

The Rodina is the post-critical design studio and collective artistic practice of Tereza and Vit Ruller. The artists in Amsterdam explore and investigate Body presence, Labor, Surface, and Action. Their commissioned work focuses primarily on visual identities for cultural sector clients. The Rodina exhibits, leads workshops, and lectures around the globe in their self-coined 'performative design', employing elements of games and interactivity with the audience.

Tereza Ruller is a Communication Design & Digital Practices Professor at the University of Arts and Design Karlsruhe and also lectures on Critical Narratives and 3D Environments with Vit Ruller at Design Academy Eindhoven.

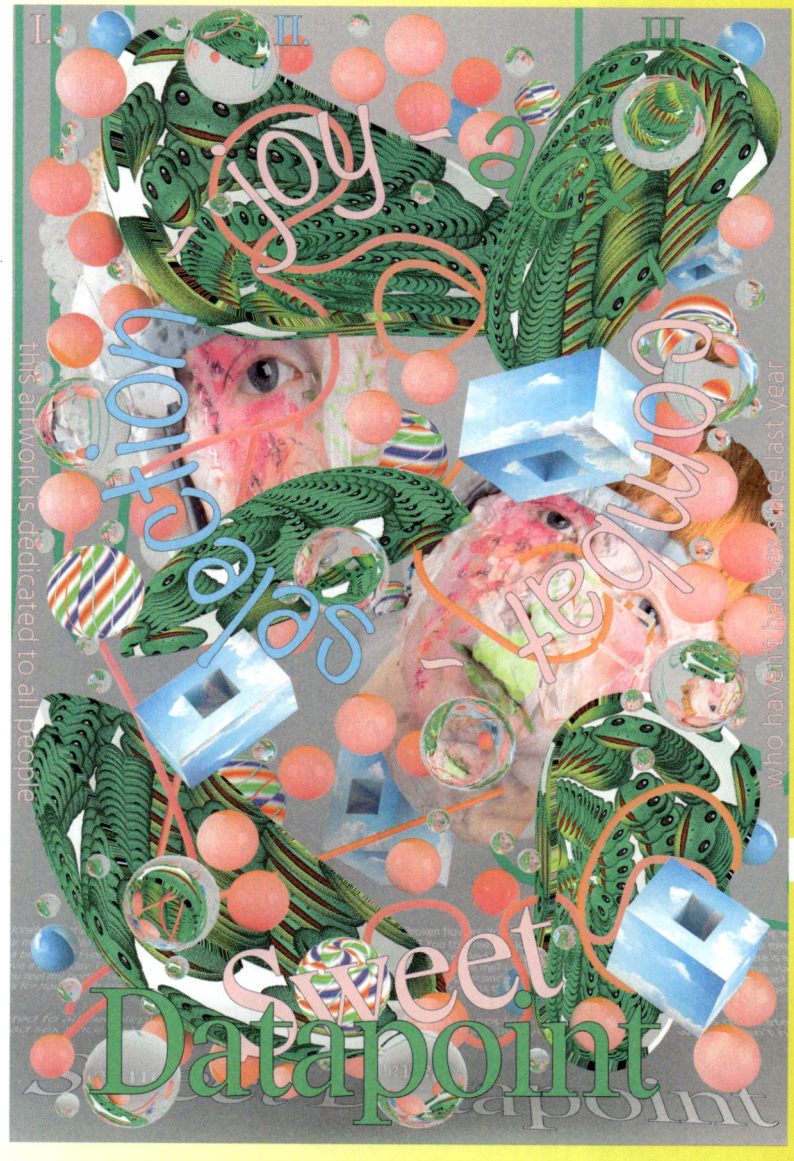

THE SPACE
A—Z LOCATION

A—Z operates in an incredibly versatile small room of only 30 square meters where all of its public activities, from exhibitions to workshops, happen, fitting the diverse needs of its intense program. Behind the yellow curtain, the team shares the space with the art book publishing house The Green Box and the book design practice of Anja Lutz.

The size of the space has proven to be suitable for very minimal displays like the one for Anita Di Bianco's *The Error is Regretted* or Tine Melzer's *Blumen sind geil*, as well as for very dense exhibitions such as *Feminist Findings* or *Graphic.Designers. Collectors.* The numerous possibilities of the setup are enhanced by the modular furniture and also extended by the use of the stairs and its top floor, which has been used in some exhibitions as a "hidden track" to the display in the main space. Thus A—Z's capacity can stretch to 80 people, such as for the opening of the *PULP* exhibition by Patrick Thomas or Mindy Seu's *Cyberfeminism Index* talk.

MODULAR FURNITURE
NOT A WHITE CUBE
THE GREEN BOX
TORSTRASSE

TIME FOR BOOKS
SEVERAL INSTALLATIONS AND EVENTS AROUND BOOKS

During the pandemic in Berlin, between late 2020 and the first months of 2021, A—Z resisted closing its doors by transforming itself within the city health guidelines into a space to enjoy, discover, and discuss the art of making art books.

The project featured a series of events, opening with the exhibition of the artworks *Marginalia* by Anja Lutz, followed by the wall installation *Books To Do* by Albert Coers, the exhibition *All My Books*, with titles designed by Andreas Koch, and closing with the interactive exhibition *Books are Bridges* by Claudia de la Torre.

Bookshops' vital role as spaces to tackle isolation was valued even during the most restrictive lockdown periods, when only supermarkets, drugstores, and bookstores were allowed to remain open in Berlin.

A—Z was set up for people to borrow art books, take them home forever at a fair price, or enjoy reading them at safe individual 'reading islands', sharing their passion for art, books, and art books. Among the book designers presented were Lamm & Kirch, Georg Rutishauser (Edition Fink), and Anja Lutz // Art Books. Visitors could also meet graphic designers at scheduled times, engage in one-on-one conversations, or participate in mini workshops.

ALL MY BOOKS
BOOKS ARE BRIDGES
BOOKS TO DO
MARGINALIA
PANDEMIC

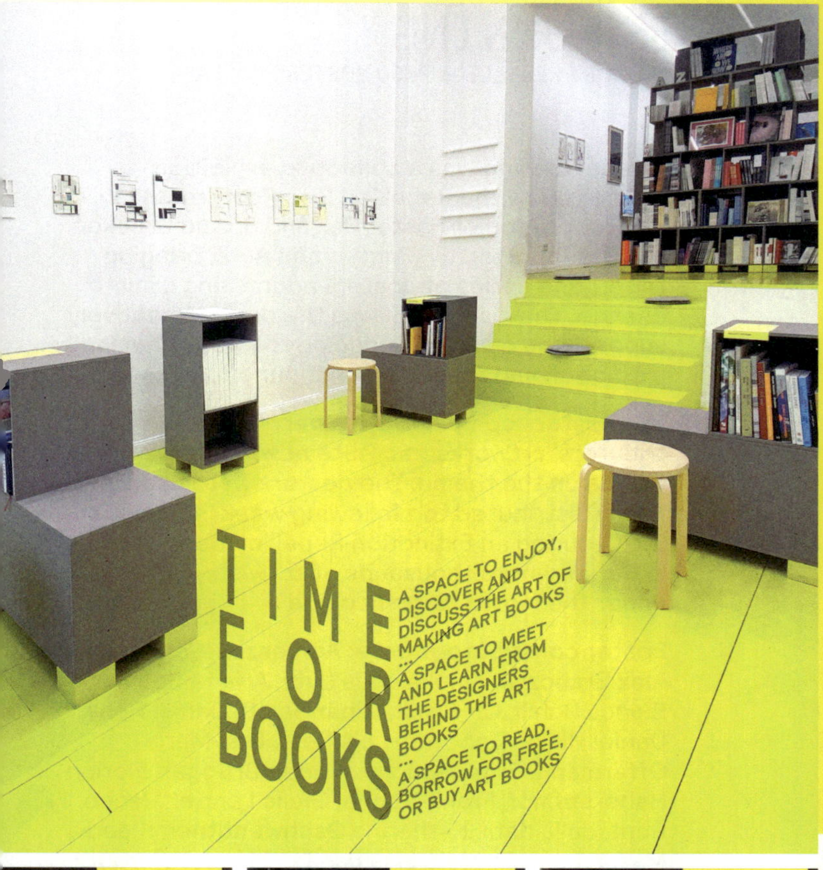

TIME FOR BOOKS

A SPACE TO ENJOY, DISCOVER AND DISCUSS THE ART OF MAKING ART BOOKS ...

A SPACE TO MEET AND LEARN FROM THE DESIGNERS BEHIND THE ART BOOKS ...

A SPACE TO READ, BORROW FOR FREE, OR BUY ART BOOKS

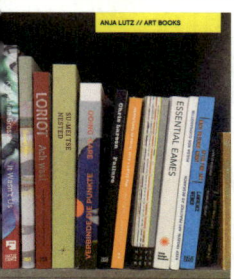
ANJA LUTZ // ART BOOKS

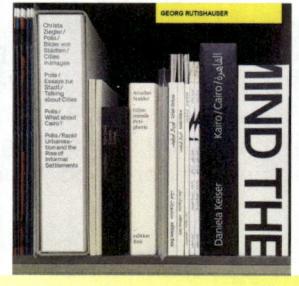
GEORG RUTISHAUSER

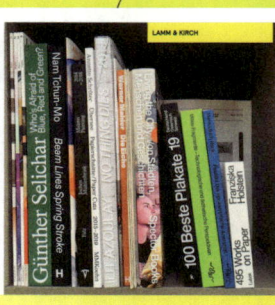
LAMM & KIRCH

TIME IS RUNNING
GROUP EXHIBITION BY REBELLION RISO POSTERS COLLAB

Time is Running was a collective exhibition conceived by the Rebellion Riso Posters Collab, a collaboration of Poster Rex and Studio Drucken 3000, supported by *Slanted* and A—Z, bringing together a series of posters addressing climate change. The inspiration was the desire to actively support the cause of reducing the risk of human extinction and the collapse of our ecosystems.

The posters combined and overprinted the contributors' artworks to create new, multilayered visuals on the theme. The posters were used and freely distributed the following week, in October 2020, during an Extinction Rebellion demonstration in Berlin, where thousands of activists protested under the motto "Stop Ecocide".

Poster contributors were: Agnieszka Węglarska, Alex Branczyk, Amelie, Anja Lutz, Ariane Spanier, Bianca Schill, CH Ernst, Cihan Tamti, Daniel Hahn, Daniel Hicks, Deborah-Lois Sery, Eva-Maria Offermann, Filip Zagórski, Florian Brugger, Florian Haberstumpf, Frank Höhne, Giulia Lantier, Jacco Bunt, Julia Kahl, Katharina Gschwendtner, Klaudia Mazur, Lana Soufeh, Lisa Panitz, Manuel Viergutz, Martina Wember, Martin Gnadt, Max Schürmann, Melis Guenoglu, Miltos Bottis, Nina Engel, Olena Smetanka, Paula Hornickel, Philipp Heinlein, Raban Ruddigkeit, Rafael Bernardo, Raupa Gonzales, Salma Khairy, Sebastian Dietel, Stefan Vogtländer, Thomas Marutschke, Vincent Bord, and Yumiko Soga.

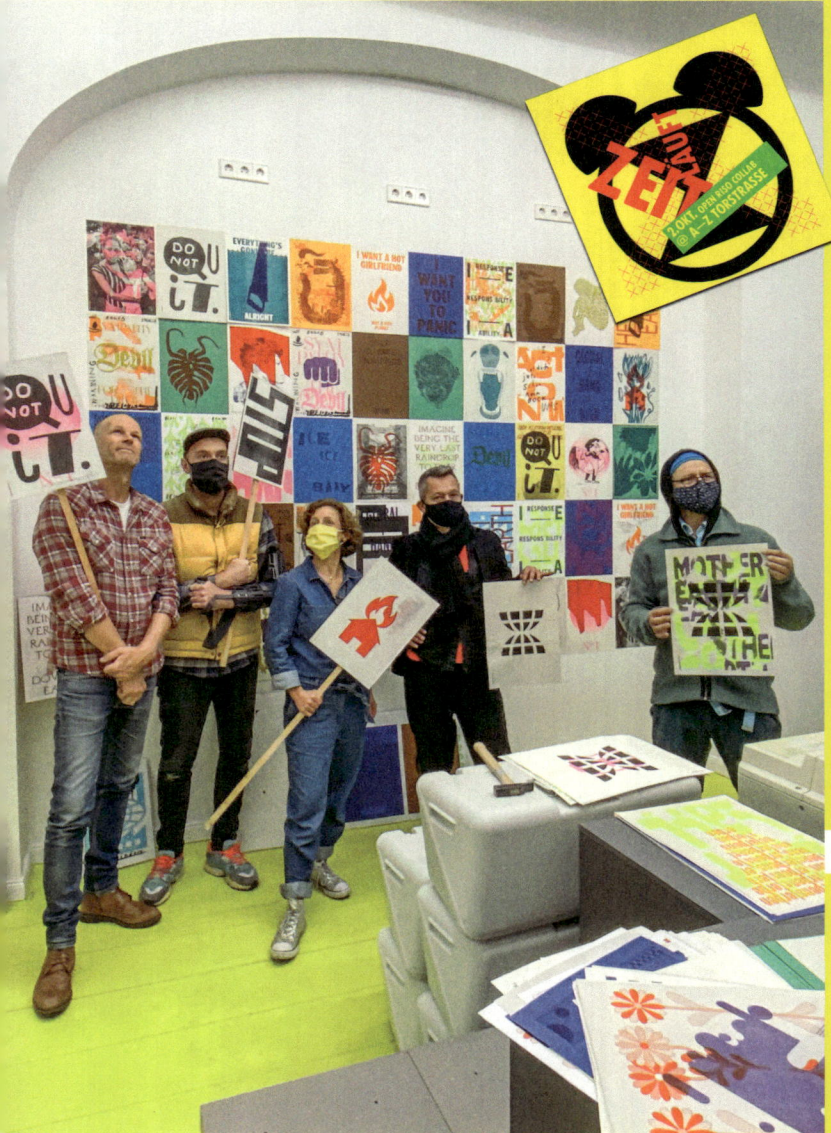

TIME IS RUNNING

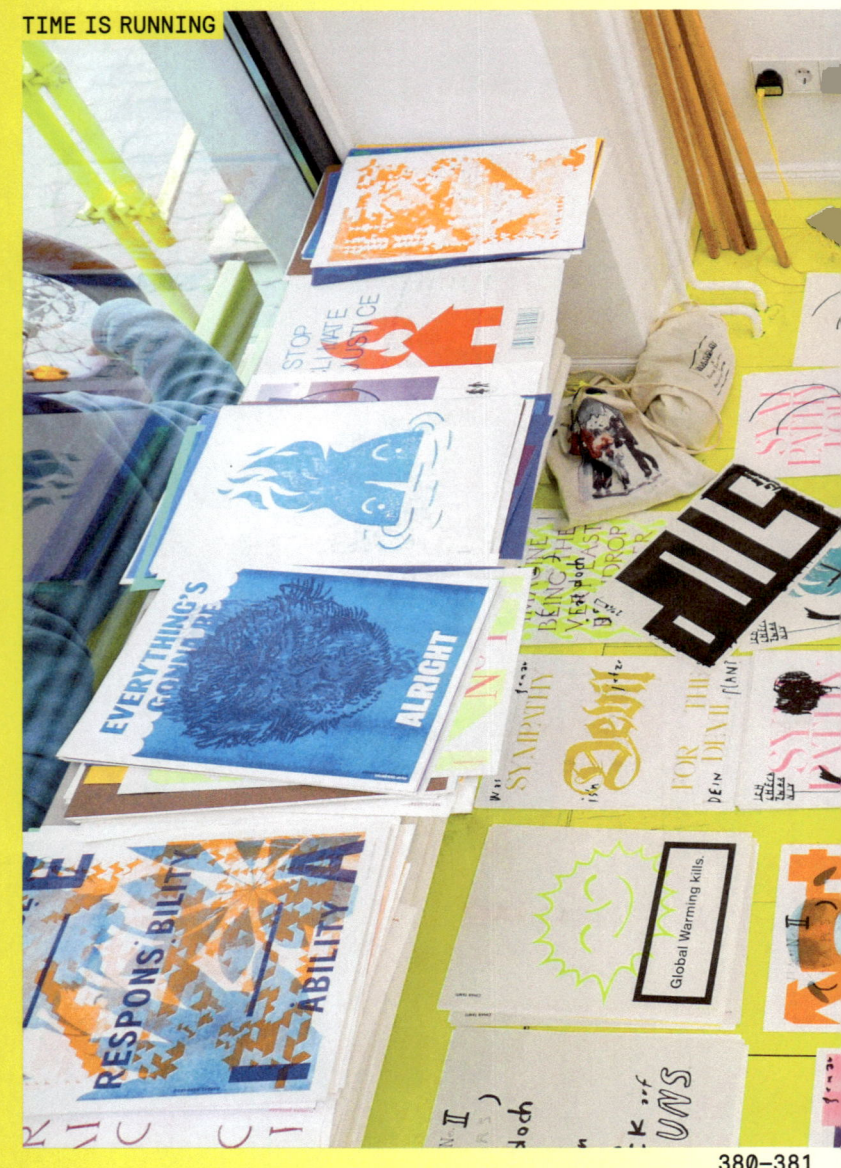

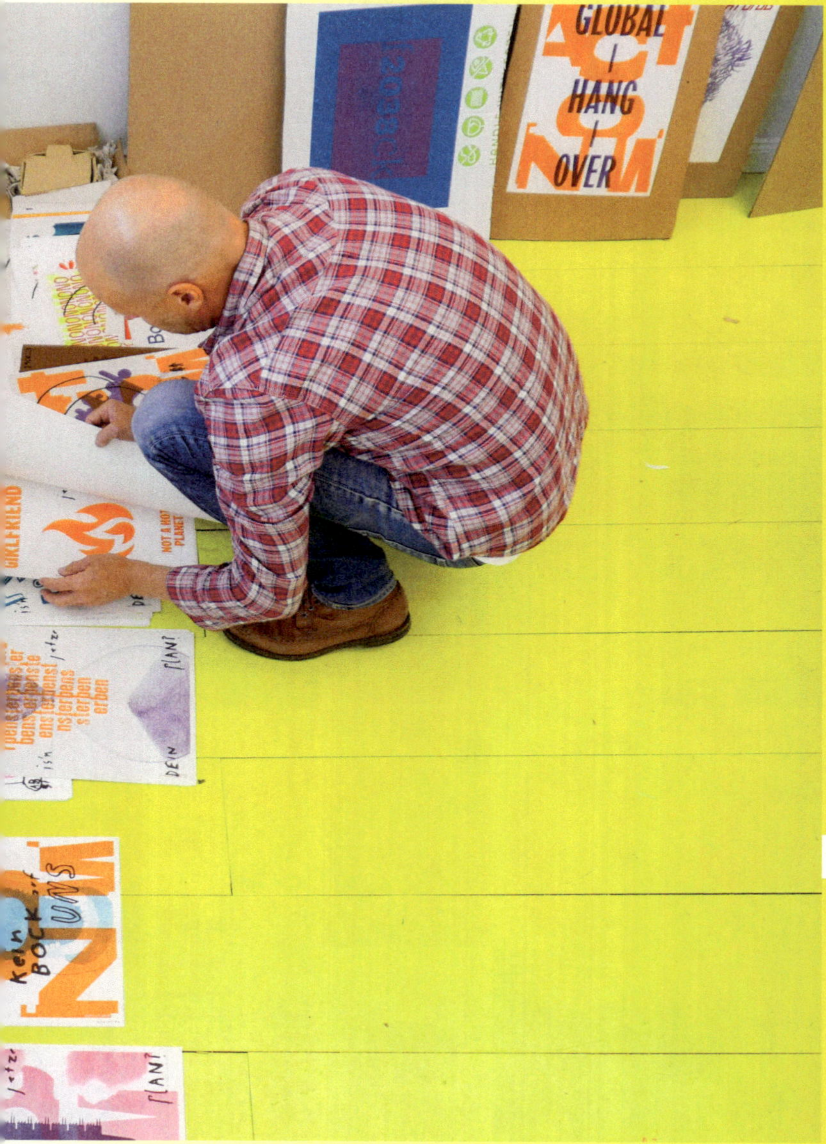

TIME IS RUNNING

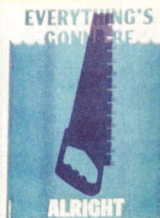
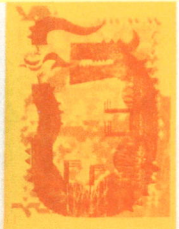
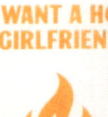

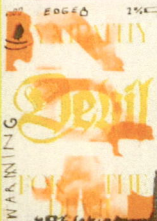
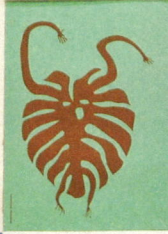
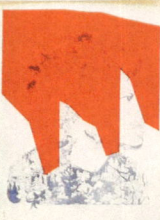
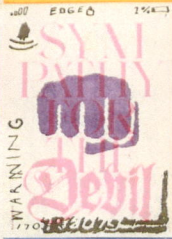
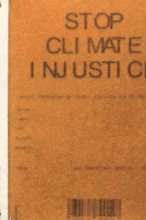
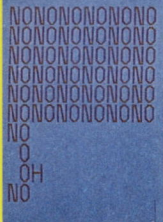
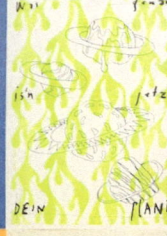
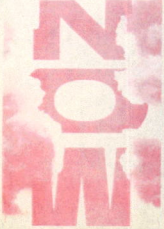
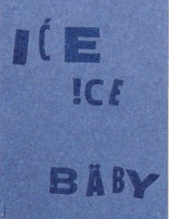

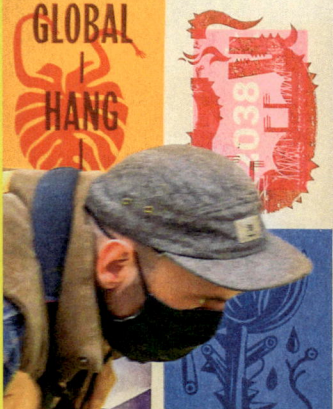
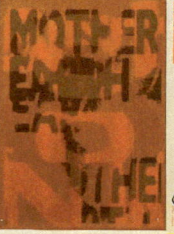
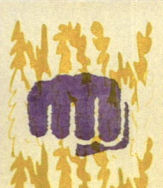
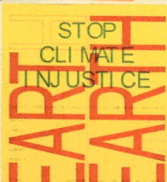
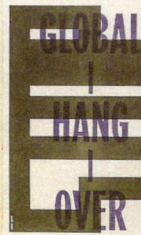
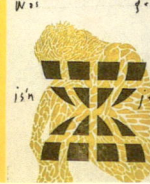

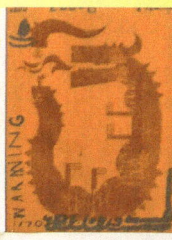
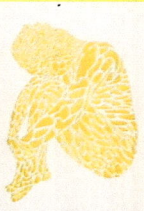
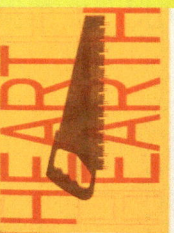
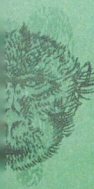
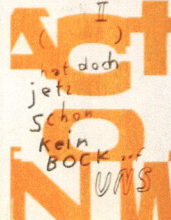
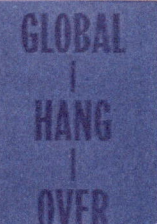
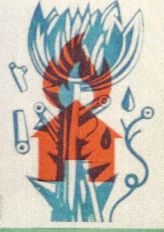
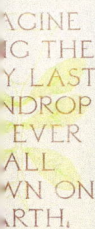
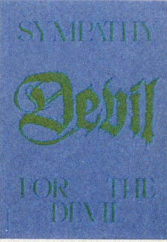
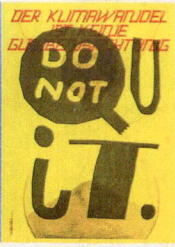
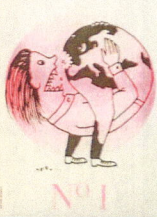
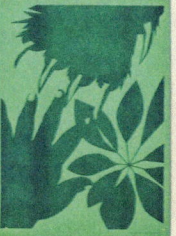
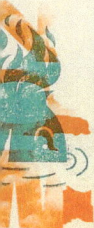
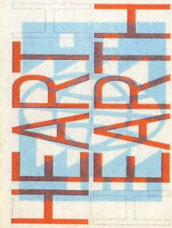
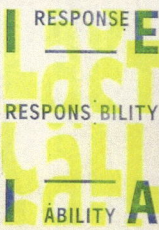
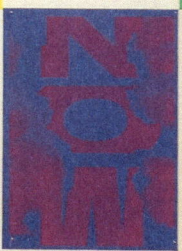
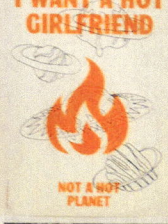
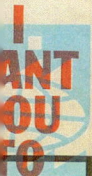
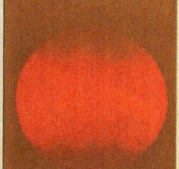
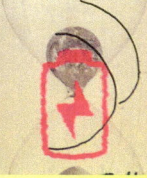
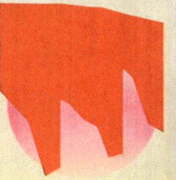
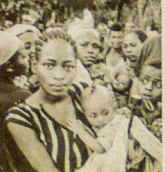

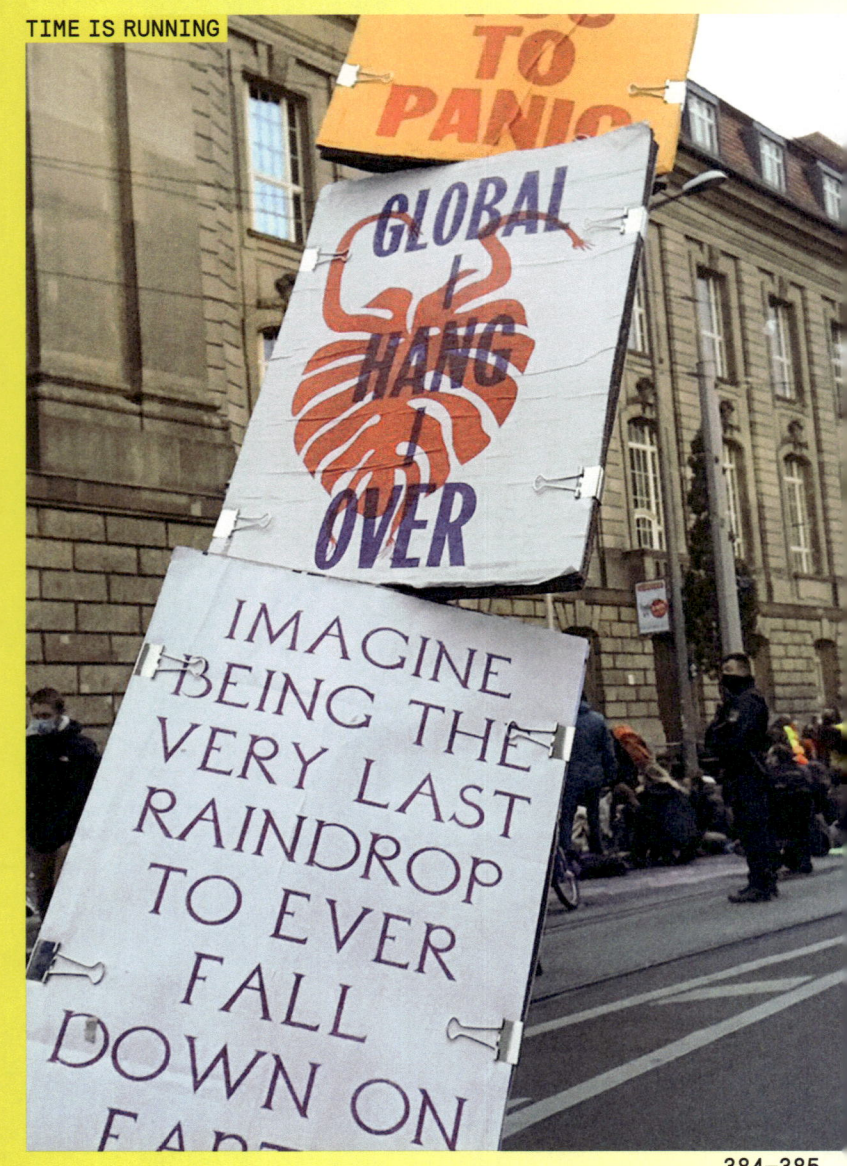

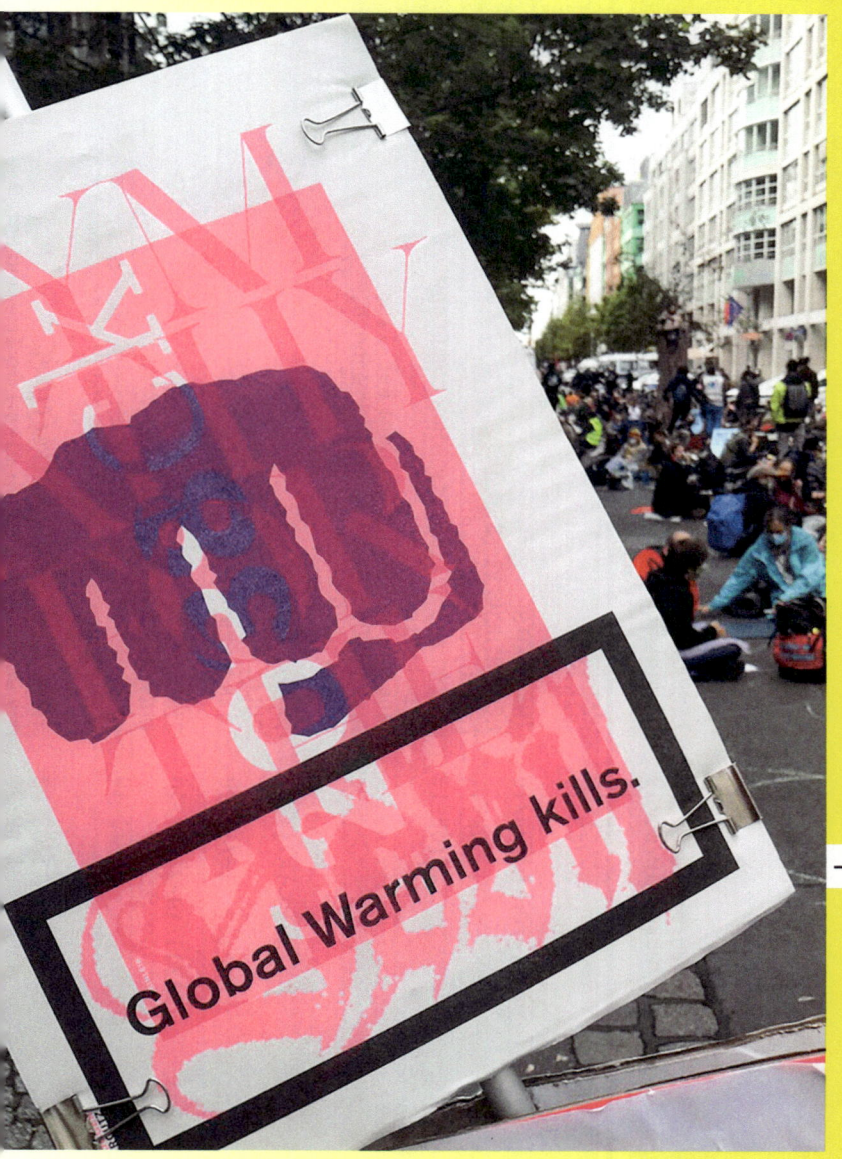

TIMELINE
CHRONOLOGICAL OVERVIEW OF A–Z EVENTS

11/04–08/06/19	**ANDREA TINNES** / **LIBRARY OF SHAPES, TEXTS AND STRUCTURES**
07/06/19	Conversation with Andrea Tinnes and Anja Lutz
06/05–10/05/19	**TEMPLATE CULTURE** / Student Workshop led by Franziska Morlok, Rebekka Kiesewetter and Anja Lutz
06/05–10/05/19	
06/05/19	Talk by Rosa Menkman
07/05/19	Talk by Anja Kaiser
14/06–06/09/19	**INKAHOOTS** / **NEW ANTHEMS VI (BERLIN)**
14/06/19	Talk by Jason Grant
29/08/19	Design and Solidarity – How can Graphic Design be political? Panel Discussion with Mara Recklies, Susanne Beer, and Sandy Kaltenborn, mediated by Franzi Bauer and Toni Brell
13/09–15/11/19	**PATRICK THOMAS** / **PULP**
10/10/19	Talk by Patrick Thomas
21/11/19–24/01/20	**THE RODINA** / **WHEN THE WORK IS DONE**
22/11/19	Agora / Open Debate with The Rodina and Prem Krishnamurthy
28/01–11/02/20	**TEACHING DESIGN CONVERSATIONS**
01/02/20	Why Do I Do What I Do – Like I Do It – And Not

06/02/20	Antonia Schneemann Real-time Realist #2 Lecture Performance with Jungmyung Lee and Lieven Lahaye
11/02/20	Closing Event–reading and book sale
15/02–14/05/20	**NIKLAUS TROXLER** **TAPE WORKS**
15/02/20	Tape Works Performance by Niklaus Troxler, with live music by Silke Eberhard, Nikolaus Neuser, and Almut Kühne
05/03/20	Talk by Niklaus Troxler
29/05–22/07/20	**NA KIM** **TRANSITORY WORKPLACE, 56**
23/06/20	Transitory Help Desk Workshop with Na Kim and Anja Lutz
02/07/20	Talk by Na Kim
30/07–24/09/20	**L.I.P. COLLECTIVE** **FEMINIST FINDINGS**
02/10/20	**REBELLION RISO POSTERS COLLAB** **TIME IS RUNNING**
09/10/20	Distributing posters at Extinction Rebellion demonstration in Berlin
08/10–19/11/20	**TINE MELZER & MARKUS KUMMER** **BLUMEN SIND GEIL**
08/10/20	Lecture-Performance by Tine Melzer

TIMELINE

26/11/20–11/05/21	**TIME FOR BOOKS**
26/11/20–19/01/21	Marginalia Exhibition by Anja Lutz
21/01–17/02/21	Books To Do Exhibition by Albert Coers
18/02–10/03/21	All My Books Exhibition by Andreas Koch
11/03–11/05/21	Books are Bridges Exhibition by Claudia de la Torre
11/05–01/07/21	**CONNECTING FROM A–Z**
08/07–02/09/21	**MARK VAN WAGENINGEN** **NOVO TYPO OFFGRID BERLIN**
08/07/2021	Novo Typo Offgrid Book Release and Talk by Mark van Wageningen
10/07–27/07/21	Open Workshops led by Mark van Wageningen
09/09–04/11/21	**LUCIENNE ROBERTS** **PERHAPS IT'S NOT YOU, IT'S ME.**
09/09/21	Talk by Lucienne Roberts
02/11/21	"Hello You!" Group discussion led by Lucienne Roberts
10/11–07/12/21	**ANITA DI BIANCO** **THE ERROR IS REGRETTED**
10/11/21	Anita Di Bianco in Conversation with Florian Wüst and Anna Bromley
15/12/21–10/03/22	**GRAPHIC DESIGNERS, COLLECTORS**

and Jens Müller

REVEALING » RECORDING » REFLECTING

16/03–23/06/22	
16/03/22	Opening online panel
24/03/22	Visual Storytelling
	Online Panel led by Yasmine Nachabe Taan
14/04/22	Ladies of Letters
	Online Panel led by Bahia Shehab
28/04/22	Image-Making
	Online Panel led by Soukeina Hachem
12/05/22	Women Designers in Diaspora
	Online Panel led by Huda Smitshuijzen AbiFarès
19/05/22	Closing Online Panel

COUNTER SESSIONS

18/08/22–31/05/23	
18/08/22	Counter Session #1
	"Ever Since the Days of Mrs. Gutenberg..." with MMS
13/10/22	Counter Session #2
	Inverse – A Yearly Ritual with Florian Dombois
08/12/22	Counter Session #3
	Family Trees & Sound Clouds with Ilka Helmig & Johannes Bergerhausen
16/02/23	Counter Session #4
	Cyberfeminism Index with Mindy Seu
04/05/23	Counter Session #5
	You never give up? with Alex Jordan

A–Z COLLECTIVE

09/03/23–02/03/24	
09/03/23	What If... Explosion
	Workshop led by Emily Smith

TIMELINE

16/03/23	Structure and Tools Workshop led by Jocelyn Ames
15/04/23	Focus: Shape-Making Workshop led by Emily Smith, Jocelyn Ames, Anja Lutz, and Ioana Ferariu
	SARAH BORIS **EXQUISITE CURIOSITIES**
15/06–02/08/23	
09/03/23	Opening Event with Sarah Boris
	A-Z COLLECTIVE **SUPER COLLECTIVE MARKET NO.1: YELLOW**
26/08–20/10/23	
14/09/23	Lego Printing Workshop led by Gregory Cowling
21/09/23	Sundowner Workshop led by Manuela dos Santos
28/09/23	Banana Museum, Sorry to See You Split So Soon Talk by Anna Broujean
07/10/23	Butter Better Come Workshop led by April Gertler
	A-Z COLLECTIVE **RECIPES FOR CONNECTING**
23/11/23–24/02/24	
12/11/23	Recipes for Connecting with The School for Somatic Design Practices, hosted by Emma Hoette, Sara Kaaman, Susan Sentler, Silvia Sfligiotti, Emily Smith, Vivien Tauchmann, Micaela Terk
26/11/23	Recipes for Connecting through Design Pedagogy, hosted by Lisa Baumgarten

MIRTHA DERMISACHE: TO BE READ

07/06–11/08/24	Exhibition Opening with sound artist
06/06/24	Paolo Dellapiana
07/06/24	Asemic Writing Workshop led by Antoine Lefebvre
18/07/24	Reading Artists' Books: Asemic Writing Collaborative project led by Regine Ehleiter
11/08/24	Closing Event with guided tour by Regine Ehleiter and Anja Lutz

A–Z OUT & ABOUT

18/01/24–ongoing	Recipes for Connecting
18–21/01/24	Index Art Book Fair, Mexico City
01–12/04/24	A–Z Workshop, Gengdan Academy of Design, Beijing, China
05–06/10/24	Rebellion Riso Poster Festa del Grafisme, Portbou, Spain
16–26/10/24	Recipes For Connecting – Barcelona Edition Barcelona Design Week, Spain
28/11–01/12/24	A–Z Exhibition Tokyo Art Book Fair, Japan
09–13/01/25	A–Z Exhibition Bigger Art Book Fair, Dongguan, China
15/05–18/07/25	Connecting from A–Z German Embassy, Beijing, China

ON THE EDGES OF GRAPHIC DESIGN FROM A–∞

01/10/25–17/12/25	Exhibition opening and release of the book On the Edges of Graphic Design from A–∞

TINE MELZER
EXHIBITED ARTIST

Tine Melzer is an author and language researcher based in Zurich. Her work combines philosophy of language with visual arts and literature. Melzer is the author of award-winning books, such as the transdisciplinary *Taxidermy for Language-Animals: A Book on Stuffed Words* and *Atlas Of Aspect Change: A Book on Shifting Meanings.* Her praised novel *Alpha Bravo Charlie* was published in 2023; her second novel, *Do Re Mi Fa So*, in 2024. She holds a professorship at HKB Bern University of the Arts. Tine Melzer's work is often collaborative, such as with photographer Markus Kummer and artist Kasper Andreasen.

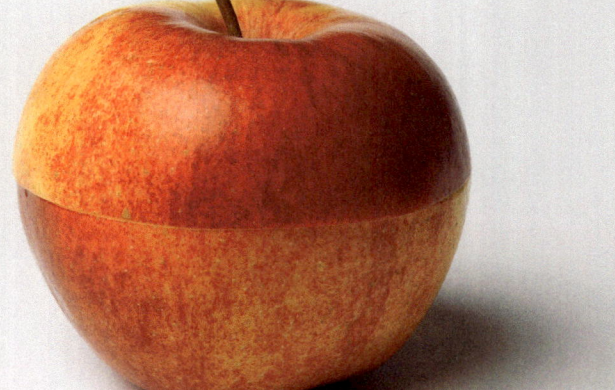

TOKYO ART BOOK FAIR
A—Z OUT & ABOUT PARTICIPATION

A—Z was invited to exhibit at the *Tokyo Art Book Fair* 2024 at the Museum of Contemporary Art Tokyo. A busy, vibrant, varied, and yellow-rich collection of items from several A—Z events and exhibitions traveled to Japan, drawing the attention of visitors as well as event professionals. The organizers of the *Bigger Art Book Fair* in Dongguan, China acquired the entire A—Z stand to rebuild it for their 2025 event.

BARCELONA DESIGN WEEK
FESTA DEL GRAFISME
OUT & ABOUT
REBELLION RISO POSTERS COLLAB
RECIPES FOR CONNECTING
THE GREEN BOX

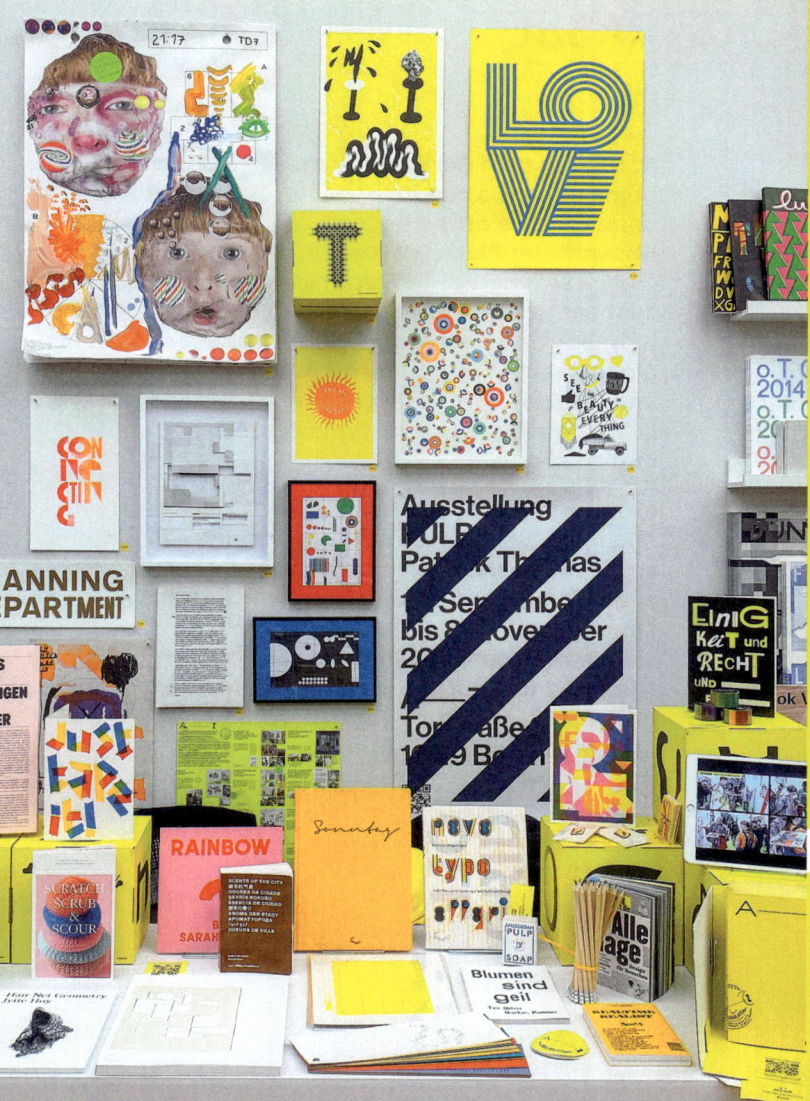

TORSTRASSE
THE HISTORY OF THE LOCATION

At the heart of Berlin, Torstrasse 93 has been the home of A—Z since its opening. The street was once the site of the historic city wall crossing over Rosenthaler Platz, where one of the city gates (Tor) was located. Today, it remains a vibrant area, split between vintage and avant-garde charm, and hipster vibes. Between its independent shops and global fashion brands loved by Gen Zs and Alphas, and the trendy bars and Michelin-star restaurants, lie the 'Spätis'—Berlin's typical late-night convenience stores.

Like Berlin itself, this famous street remains fast-changing, while also remaining home to traditional small businesses that bravely resist gentrification, such as an upholsterer, a shoe and clothes repairer, second-hand shops, and other creative spaces such as the conceptual gallery Möbel Horzon run by the artist and author Rafael Horzon. At any time of the year, a walk along Torstrasse with a stop at A—Z always feels like non-linear time-travel.

BLACKBOARD
THE SPACE
YELLOW BENCH

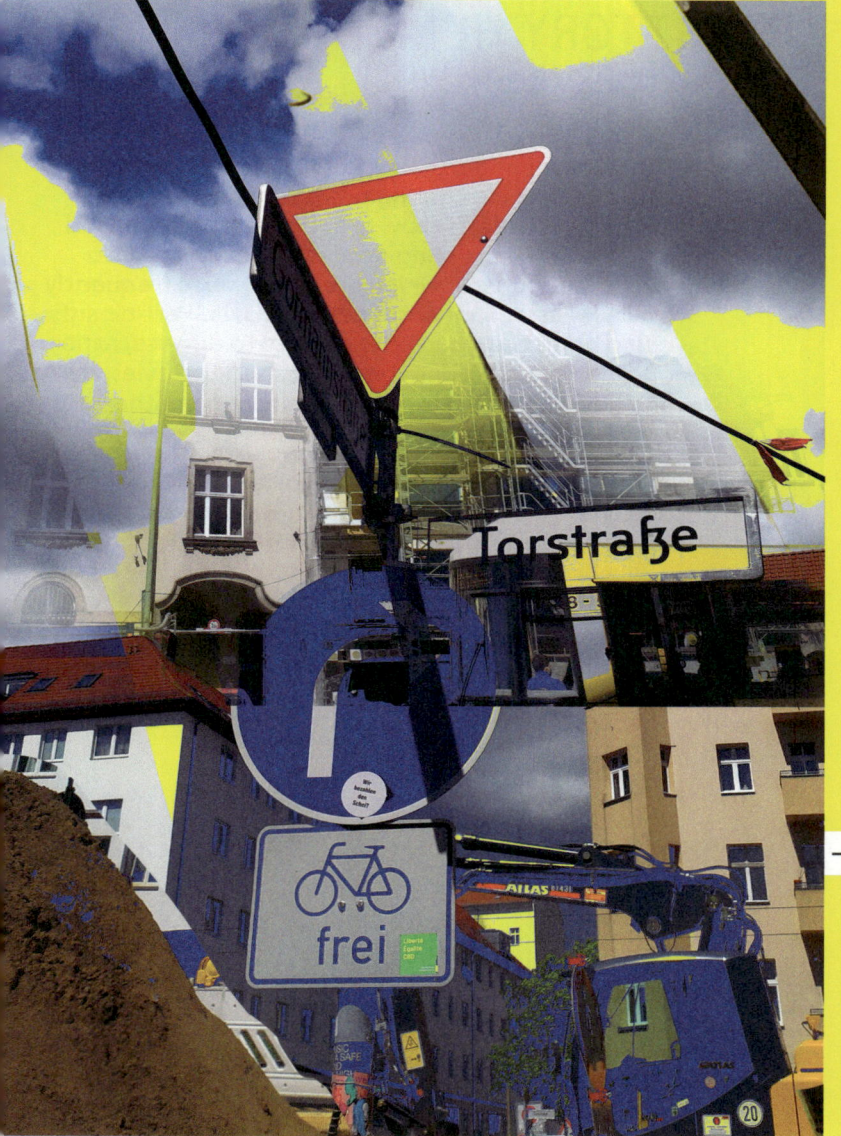

TRANSITORY HELP DESK
WORKSHOP WITH NA KIM AND ANJA LUTZ

The workshop *Transitory Help Desk* was conceived as a platform for sharing practical knowledge and insights between fellow graphic designers, based on the idea of creating opportunities to tap into valuable feedback, which are usually less frequently available after formal education is over. Participants could bring their current projects to discuss, reflect on, and find solutions together, sharing, reviewing, and advising on work processes for each other.

The activity took place during the exhibition *Transitory Workplace, 56*, and was facilitated by the designers Na Kim and Anja Lutz, with the participation of Juliana Toro, Eva-Maria Offermann, and Giulia Siviero.

THD

TRANSITORY WORKPLACE, 56
EXHIBITION BY NA KIM

Transitory Workplace, 56 was an interactive exhibition by graphic designer Na Kim, transforming A—Z into Na Kim's workplace for exactly 56 days. The exhibited provisional space was the office where she led her daily work and arranged personal meetings that interested visitors could book.

By setting her private temporary practice in a public gallery space, Na Kim materialized into a concrete physical realm the myriad uncertainties she had experienced during the pandemic. The daily orchestrated actions evoked an attitude of observing and appreciating the value of everyday life.

During the exhibition, Na Kim divided A—Z into different activity zones as part of her design and creatively tackled the safety measures imposed by the pandemic. She kept a precise schedule, with daily presentations of her work exercises and created artworks directly on the walls of the space.

Transitory Workplace, 56 was nevertheless conceptualized to surpass physical space. Envisioned as "the accumulation of time in space", this routine as a performance revealed the intersection of these two layers in an attempt to capture, collect, document, and present them.

NA KIM
PANDEMIC
SPACE OF UNCERTAINTY
TRANSITORY HELP DESK

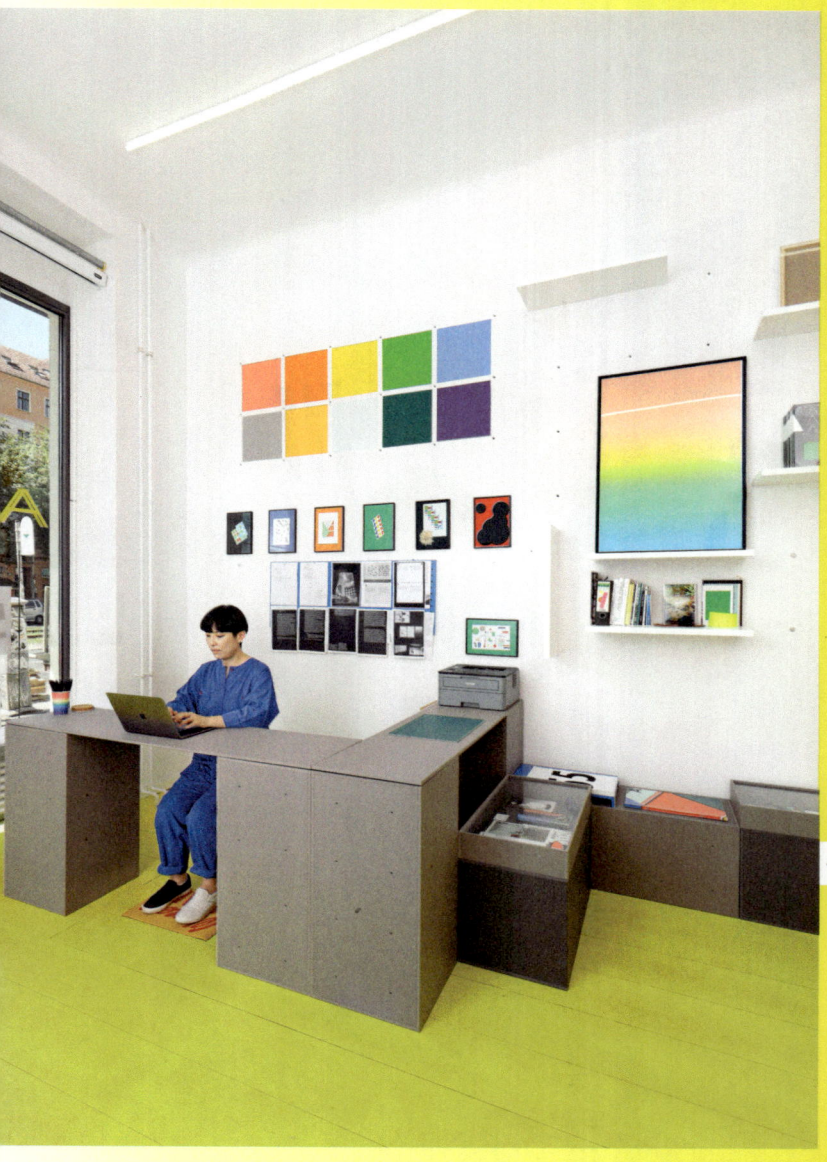

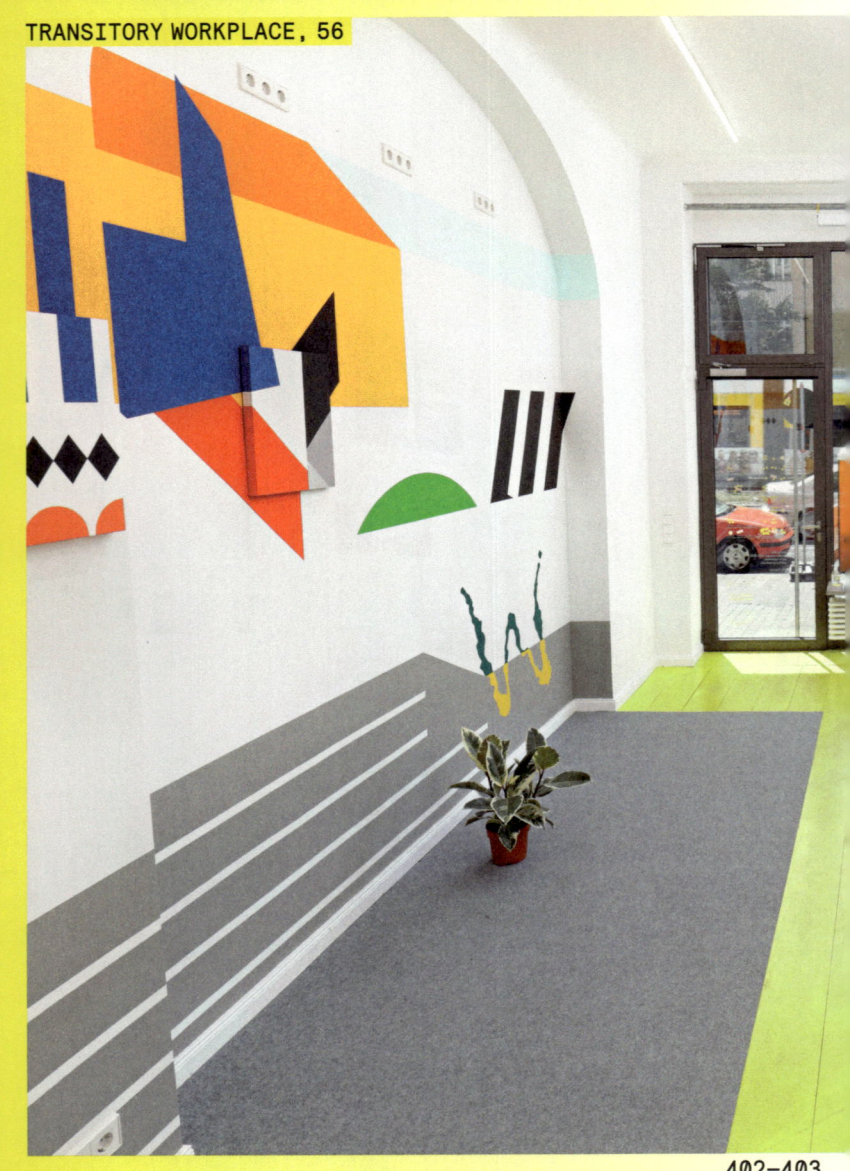

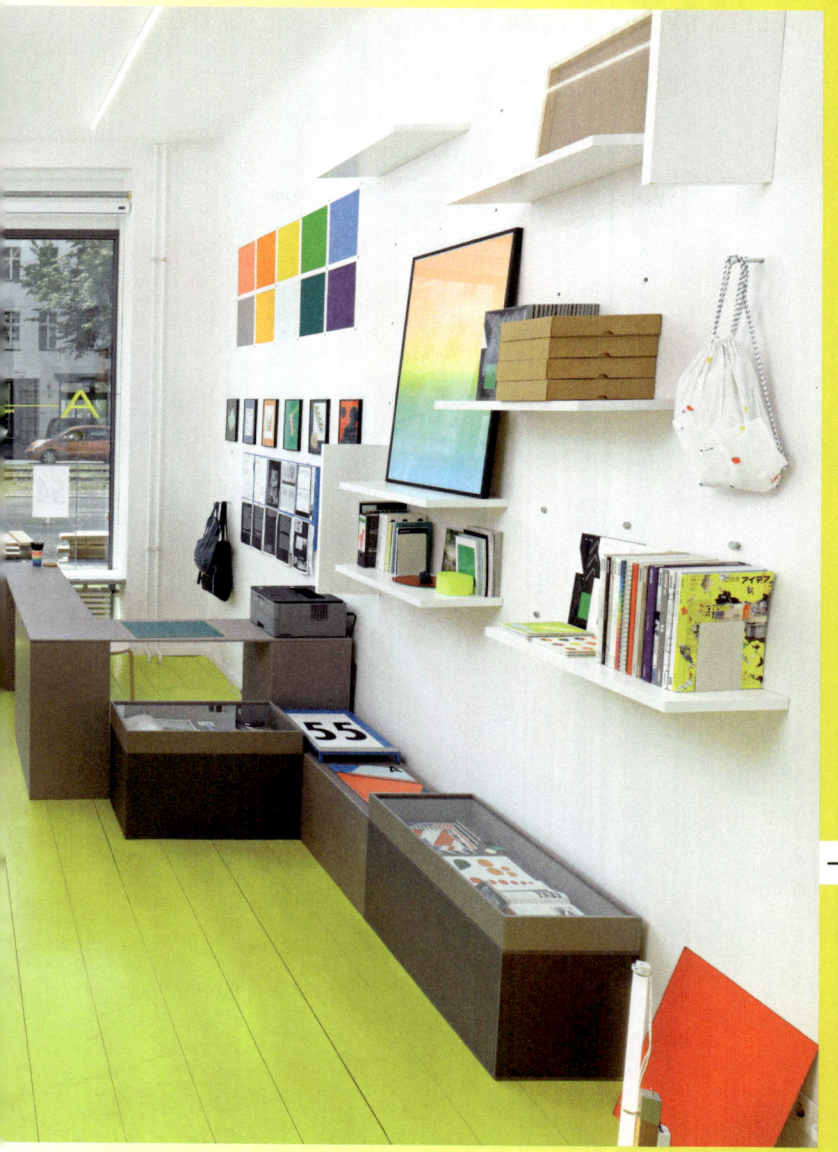

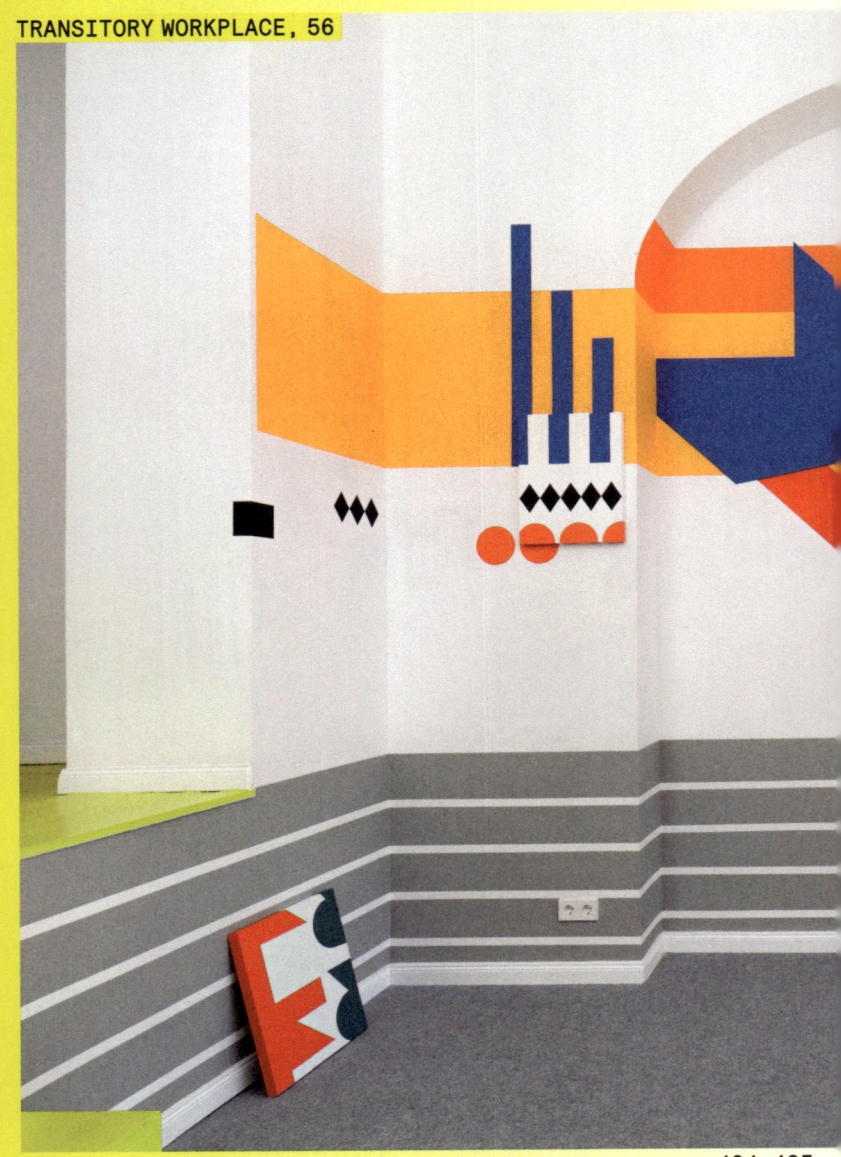

TRANSITORY WORKPLACE, 56

T

TRANSITORY WORKPLACE, 56

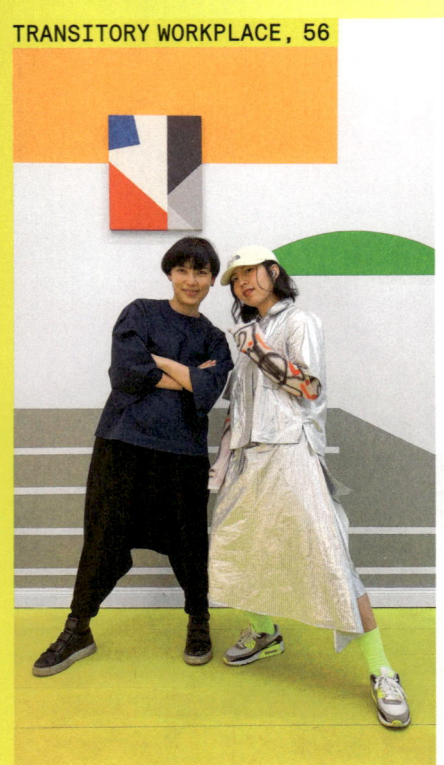
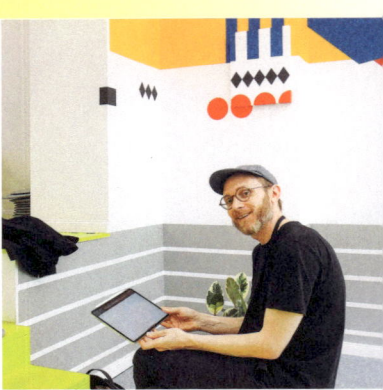
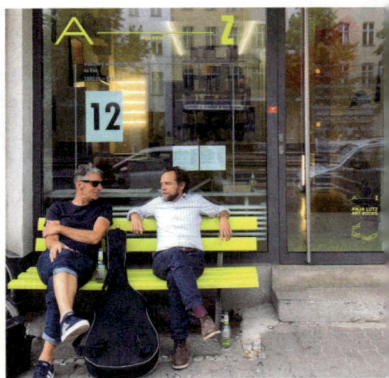
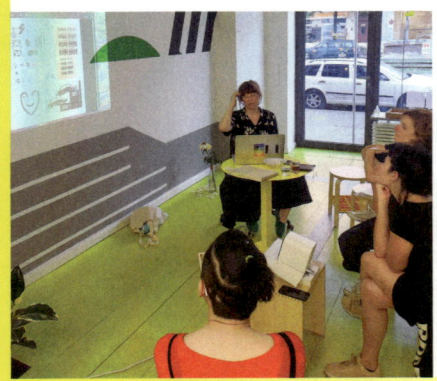
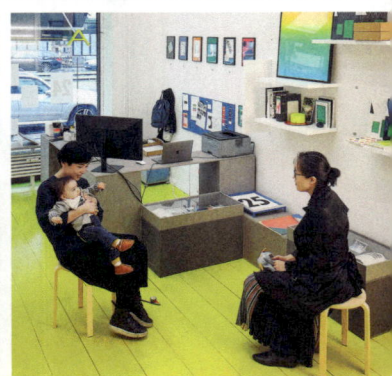

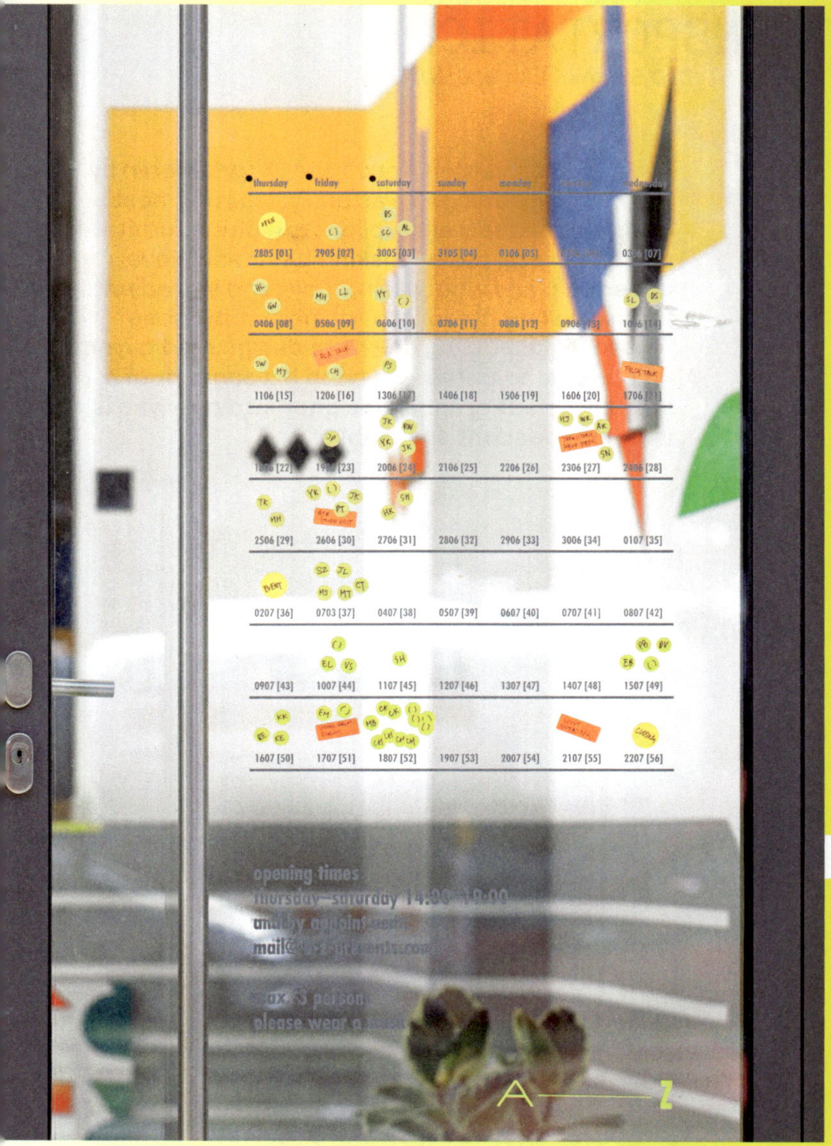

TRANSPORTATION
MOBILE STUDIO BY MARK VAN WAGENINGEN

The entire exhibition *Novo Typo Offgrid Berlin* by Mark van Wageningen was designed to fit neatly in his car. All the wall displays, exhibition furniture, printing press, paper-making basin and sieve, paper pulp and woodgrain, tools, and ingredients for ink making fitted into a mini multipurpose Toyota. Transporting an entire design studio from Amsterdam to Berlin extended his concept of a self-sufficient graphic designer into one who is truly independent and mobile.

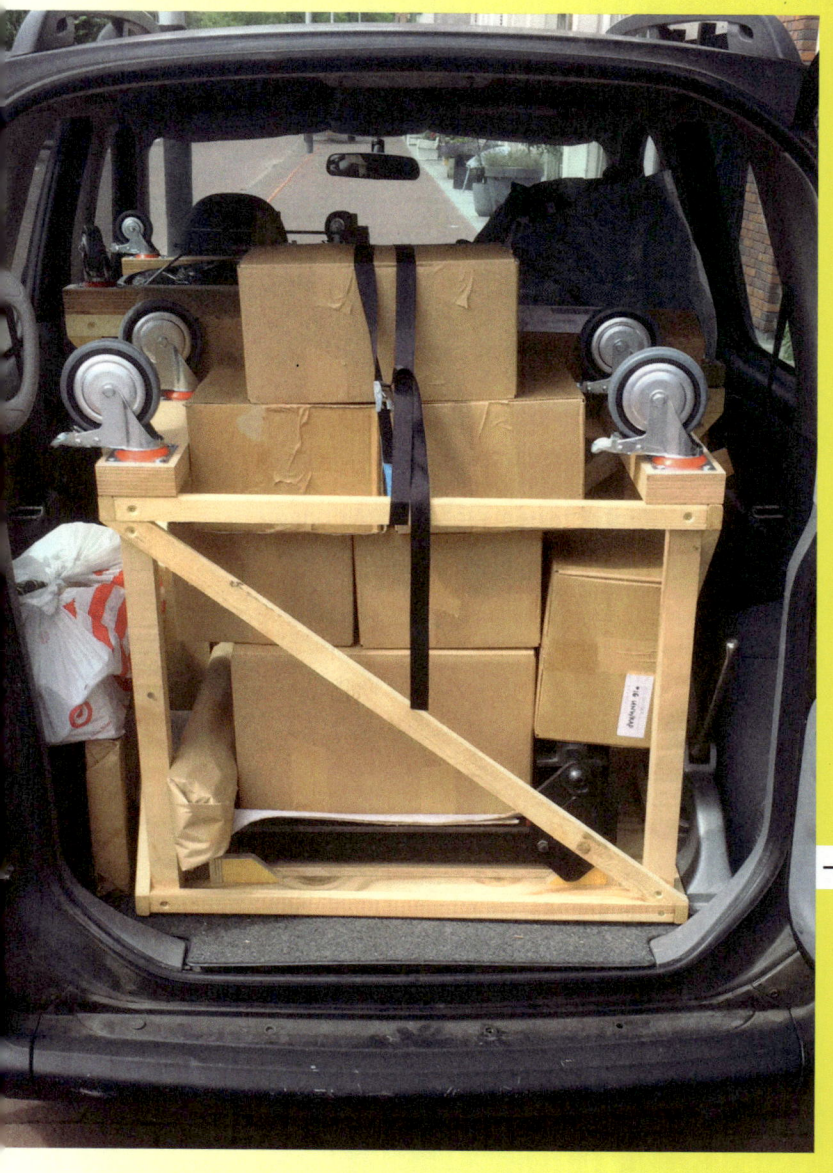

UNITY AND JUSTICE AND …
PUBLIC CONTRIBUTIONS TO THE *NEW ANTHEMS VI (BERLIN)* EXHIBITION BY INKAHOOTS

During the Inkahoots exhibition *New Anthems VI (Berlin)*, visitors and passersby at Torstrasse 93 contributed to the prompt to complete the first line of the German National Anthem, sending their verses for "Einigkeit und Recht und ___ für ___" (Unity and justice and ___ for ___) via text message.

The original, funny, politically engaged and even romantic parodies were displayed continuously and at random on the LED panels of the installations, and are still available in the original in German online at newanthems.inkahoots.com.au.

07.09.2019 / 1:50 AM
…NUTELLA for CHRISTIANE
05.09.2019 / 1:44 AM
…END for GLYPHOSATES
04.09.2019 / 12:21 AM
…KISSES for ZARAH
04.09.2019 / 12:13 AM
…HORNS for COWS
04.09.2019 / 12:10 AM
…CHOCOLATE for ELIAS
04.09.2019 / 12:08 AM
…BRAIN for NAZIS
02.09.2019 / 10:40 PM
…TWINS for PANDA MENG MENG
02.09.2019 / 9:55 PM
…BE KIND for SHARE LOVE
01.09.2019 / 1:47 AM
…LOVE for FANTASTIC3
29.08.2019 / 8:21 PM
…BEAUTIFUL MUSIC for ALLES VON UNS

25.08.2019 / 11:03 PM
…MANDATORY GENITIVES for EVERYONE
25.08.2019 / 11:00 PM
…LAZINESS for EVERYONE
25.08.2019 / 8:10 PM
…A GREAT TIME for CHARLOTTE
21.08.2019 / 12:14 PM
…DESIGN AND SOLIDARITY for HOW CAN GRAPHIC DESIGN BE POLITICAL?
20.08.2019 / 4:31 AM
…RUINED for ELECTIONS
18.08.2019 / 9:05 AM
…SELF-DETERMINATION for ALL
15.08.2019 / 9:49 PM
…HAPPINESS for ALL OF US
14.08.2019 / 8:27 PM
…LOVE LOVE for HATE HATE
13.08.2019 / 9:03 PM
…NEVER AGAIN for GERMANY

INKAHOOTS
KINDERHYMNE
NEW ANTHEMS VI – EINE NEUE HYMNE FÜR DEUTSCHLAND
TORSTRASSE
VISITORS

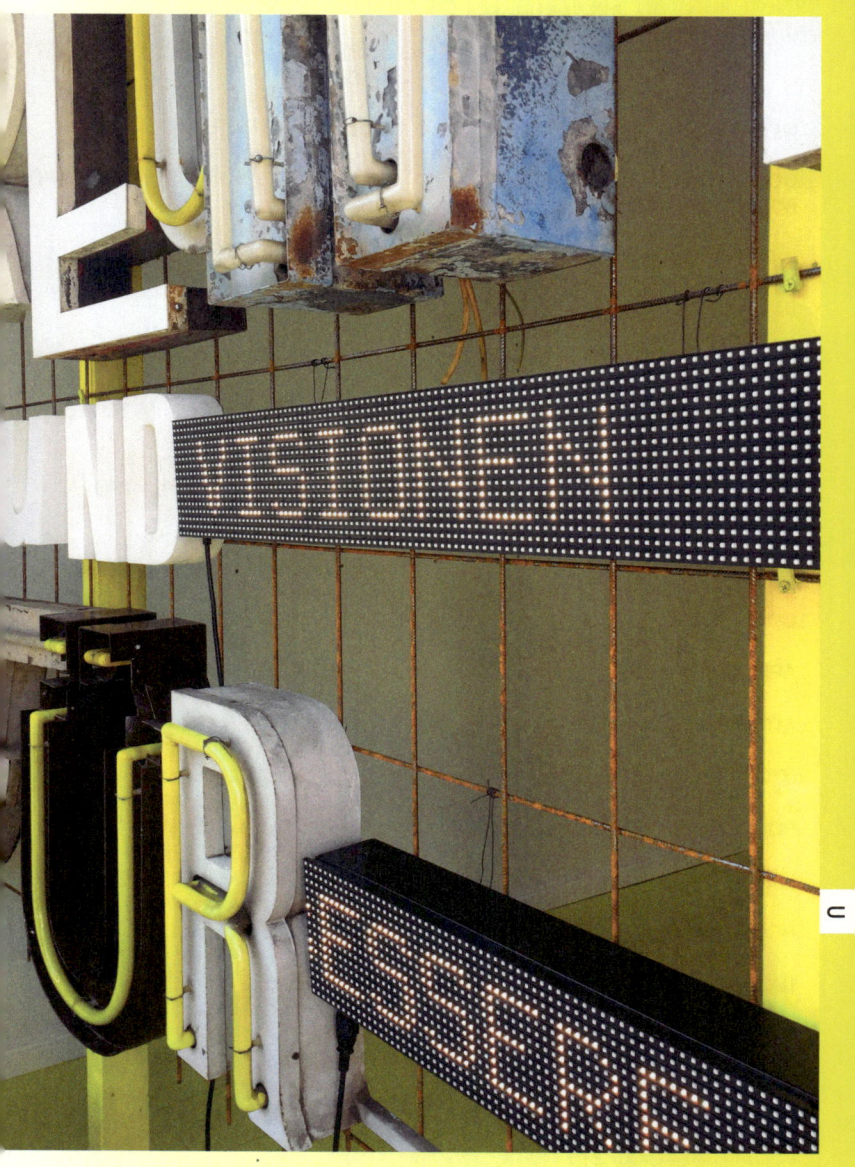

UNITY AND JUSTICE AND ...

10.08.2019 / 9:59 PM
...OPENNESS for DIVERSITY
10.08.2019 / 3:13 PM
...DONATIONS for THE BUCHSTABENMUSEUM
10.08.2019 / 1:17 AM
...GIRLS for CHOIRS
09.08.2019 / 6:44 AM
...INK for POSTERS
08.08.2019 / 9:23 PM
...MUSSELS BANQUETT for ME
08.08.2019 / 9:22 PM
...SALAD for CHILDREN
05.08.2019 / 5:11 PM
...BAN for WEAPONS
05.08.2019 / 5:11 PM
...SUPPORT for FRIDAYS FOR FUTURE
01.08.2019 / 8:41 AM
...PRISON for TRUMP
31.07.2019 / 11:23 PM
...CONCERT TICKETS for KATE
29.07.2019 / 11:59 PM
...APPLAUSE for ANJA
21.07.2019 / 3:56 AM
...ACTION for CLIMATE
17.07.2019 / 6:12 PM
...UTOPIAS for THE YELLOW ROOM
17.07.2019 / 2:53 AM
...PORTIONS for FOXES
16.07.2019 / 2:49 AM
...LIES for SPIES
08.07.2019 / 5:59 AM
...NO BEER for NAZIS
05.07.2019 / 10:57 PM
...BABIES for EVERYONE
04.07.2019 / 12:38 PM
...DATABASE WITHOUT EXCLUSION for ALL PEOPLE
04.07.2019 / 4:59 AM
...FREEDOM for CAROLA RACKETE
02.07.2019 / 11:59 AM
...THE END OF PATRIARCHY for A BETTER SOCIETY
02.07.2019 / 3:55 AM
...DEATH for DEATH LISTS
02.07.2019 / 3:32 AM
...DISMISSAL for RACIST POLICE AND MILITARY
29.06.2019 / 10:18 PM
...ITALY for BROKEN
29.06.2019 / 12:44 AM
...POLAND for ALL
26.06.2019 / 9:46 AM
...SENSIBLE BEHAVIOR for POLITICIANS
26.06.2019 / 9:45 AM
...THIRST AND THERE for A BOTTLE OF COLD BEER
24.06.2019 / 1:53 PM
...CORRECT SPELLING for THE IMPERATIVE
23.06.2019 / 10:17 PM
...BREADCRUMBS for SCHNITZEL
22.06.2019 / 10:29 PM
...GIN for EVERYONE
22.06.2019 / 8:15 PM
...PATRICK THOMAS SAYS for SAVE EUROPE
21.06.2019 / 11:03 PM
...LASERS for TATTOOS
21.06.2019 / 9:15 AM
...PRISON for RACIST MURDERERS
21.06.2019 / 12:02 AM
...PUT THE BENCH STRAIGHT AGAIN for OTHERWISE THERE WILL BE A SMACK
20.06.2019 / 11:45 PM
...GOOD NIGHT for ALL
20.06.2019 / 11:37 PM
...LOVE for US
20.06.2019 / 8:26 PM
...THREE GLASSES OF WATER for ANGELA MERKEL
20.06.2019 / 8:18 PM
...FREEDOM for ALL

20.06.2019 / 8:17 PM
..PERSEVERANCE for FREEDOM
20.06.2019 / 2:01 PM
..INTERNATIONAL ALLIANCES for DEFINITE ENVIRONMENTAL PROTECTION
20.06.2019 / 1:54 PM
..VISIONS for A BETTER FUTURE
19.06.2019 / 10:50 PM
..RENT CAP for BERLIN
19.06.2019 / 7:57 PM
..PINEAPPLE for PIZZA
18.06.2019 / 10:08 PM
..FREEDOM for ALL
17.06.2019 / 11:57 PM
..COURAGE for NEW THINGS
17.06.2019 / 10:25 PM
..RUSSIA for AMERICA
17.06.2019 / 10:44 AM
..FREE ADMISSION for ALL MUSEUMS
16.06.2019 / 7:28 PM
..SOLAR for WIND
16.06.2019 / 2:37 PM
..LOVE for ALL
15.06.2019 / 10:41 PM
..A BETTER ANTHEM for GERMANY
15.06.2019 / 10:02 PM
..LOVE for YOU
15.06.2019 / 3:21 PM
..THUMBS UP for BEST PROGRAMMER
15.06.2019 / 2:22 PM
..TROPICAL FEELINGS for GERMANY
15.06.2019 / 1:42 PM
..EATING TOGETHER for HUMANITY
15.06.2019 / 1:31 PM
..SOLIDARITY for ALL THE EXCLUDED
15.06.2019 / 1:30 PM
..SOLIDARITY for ALL LIVING BEINGS
15.06.2019 / 1:23 PM
..LESS POLLUTION for THE WORLD
15.06.2019 / 1:18 PM
..BRING JUSTICE for SOME
15.06.2019 / 8:26 AM
..YOGA for BALANCE
15.06.2019 / 8:25 AM
...COMMITMENT for THE WEAKER
15.06.2019 / 8:24 AM
...ACCOUNTABILITY for THE MESS WE MAKE
15.06.2019 / 2:25 AM
...MARIA HELENA for EVER
14.06.2019 / 11:49 PM
...CAREER CHANGE for THE HIGH-LEVEL
14.06.2019 / 11:24 PM
...MONEY for CONSUMPTION
14.06.2019 / 9:20 PM
...MIGRATION for HOME
14.06.2019 / 9:11 PM
...LETTERS for EVERYONE
14.06.2019 / 9:10 PM
...APPLE PIE for EVERYONE
14.06.2019 / 9:05 PM
...AFFORDABLE HOUSING for ALL
14.06.2019 / 7:31 PM
...LIGATURES for WEBFONTS
14.06.2019 / 7:12 PM
...HEALTH for MY LOVED ONE
14.06.2019 / 6:33 PM
...SUMMER for EVERYONE
14.06.2019 / 2:36 PM
...APPRECIATION for THE COLORFUL DIVERSITY
14.06.2019 / 2:34 PM
...LOVE for ALL LIVING BEINGS
13.06.2019 / 10:30 PM
...PEACE JOY WAFFLES for HEARTS
13.06.2019 / 10:30 PM
...ROCK for ROLL
13.06.2019 / 9:54 PM
...COURAGE for CHANGE
13.06.2019 / 9:51 PM
...MUSIC for US
13.06.2019 / 9:48 PM
...CHAMPAGNE for EVERYONE
13.06.2019 / 9:47 PM
...RESPECT for THE ENVIRONMENT

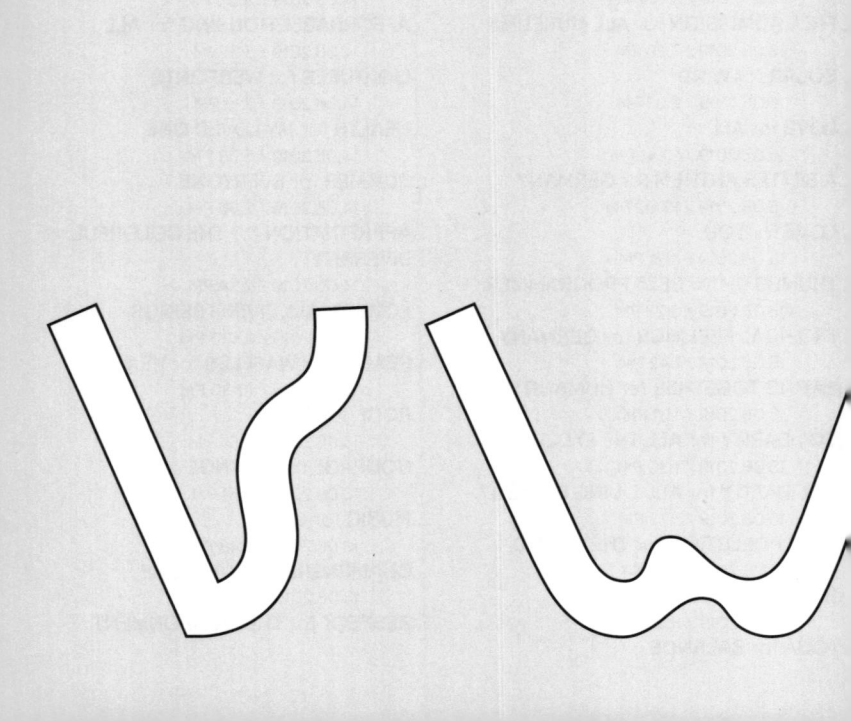

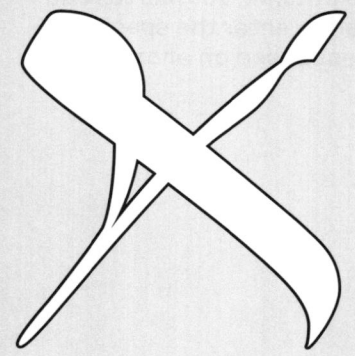

"Y"
as in
Yellow Pages
yellow-pages.wtf

VINYL
SHOP WINDOW LETTERING AT A—Z

Each exhibition or main project at A—Z has its own vinyl design, which is displayed in the front window. For *Transitory Workplace, 56* by Na Kim, for example, the vinyl included the agenda for the 56 days of her exhibition, where she could log visitors. For the exhibition *Perhaps It's Not You, It's Me.* by Lucienne Roberts, the lettering was made from mirror foil.

The vinyl lettering produced by the Rock'n'Roll Letters print studio near A—Z remains a tradition, which has only been broken twice so far: Niklaus Troxler used sticky tape for the title of his *Tape Works* exhibition, and the original 20-year-old pixel curtain from the Flipper Bar was used as the sign for the *Counter Sessions*.

The *Teaching Design Conversations* exhibition was a curious case: the vinyl was accidentally plotted inverted, and instead of reprinting it, the organizers decided to keep the 'mistake', having the text mirrored on the outside, so that to read it comfortably, people had to enter the space—an inviting effect for a project based on encouraging engagement.

- COUNTER SESSIONS
- FLIPPER BAR
- PERHAPS IT'S NOT YOU, IT'S ME.
- TAPE WORKS
- TEACHING DESIGN CONVERSATIONS
- THE SPACE
- TORSTRASSE
- TRANSITORY WORKPLACE, 56

Teaching Design
CONVERSATIONS

A **collectively**[1] built temporary library focusing on **design education** from intersectional feminist and decolonial perspectives offering **access to resources**[2] to develop transformative strategies, a **safe space** to **ask critical questions**[3] and start a **dialogue** and the tools to **share** and **exchange knowledge**[4].

Teaching.Design.school.co.Instagram: @teaching.design

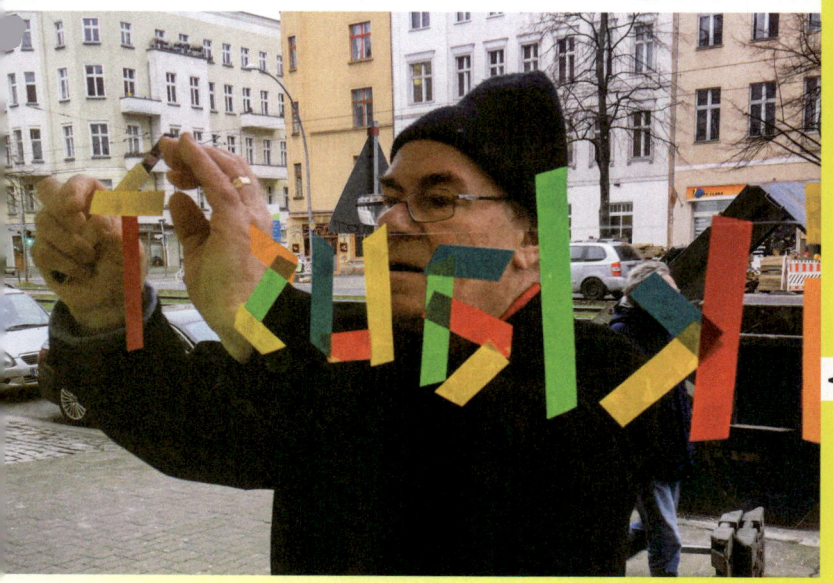

VISITORS
THE AUDIENCE FOR A—Z EVENTS

In its six years of activities, an estimated 6,000 people have been present at A—Z, visiting and participating in a diverse range of events, workshops, lectures, exhibition openings, gatherings, etc. As well as the Graphic Design community and special interest visitors attracted by a particular subject, passersby from all different backgrounds have shown up at the front door on this busy street, just because they were curious to see the exhibitions.

One distinctive group of visitors is students from several international institutions who have attended presentations or workshops discussing contemporary aspects of Graphic Design practices.

Institutions that have visited A—Z include: Akademie der Künste Stuttgart, Art Center Pasadena, Burg Giebichenstein University of Art and Design Halle, Dun Laoghaire Institute of Art, Design and Technology in Dublin, Gengdan Academy of Design Beijing, Glasgow School of Art, Graduate School of Design La Martinière-Diderot Lyon, Haute École d'Art et de Design Genève, Hochschule für Angewandte Wissenschaften Hamburg, Hochschule für Gestaltung und Buchkunst Leipzig, Schule für Gestaltung Bern und Biel, University of Europe Berlin, and Weissensee Kunsthochschule Berlin.

COLLECTING VISITORS STICKERS

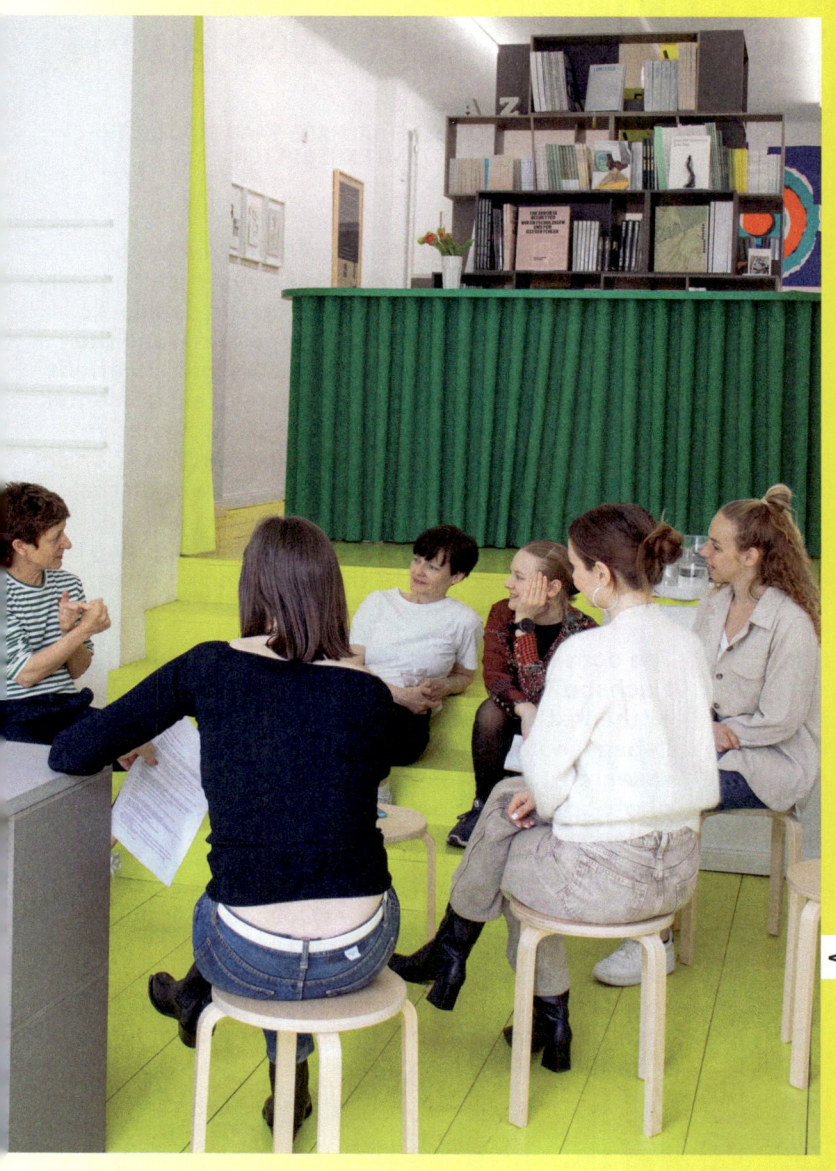

VISUAL STORYTELLING: ABOUT WOMEN, BY WOMEN

ONLINE PANEL MODERATED BY YASMINE NACHABE TAAN DURING THE *REVEALING » RECORDING » REFLECTING* EXHIBITION

The panel *Visual Storytelling: About Women, by Women* addressed the different ways in which newly emerging and established Arab female designers and visual producers bridge the personal and the political to develop stories that confront situations in their everyday lives by using daring, experimental, and creative approaches. How their provocative stories oppose racism, sexism, homophobia, Zionism, Islamophobia, and other forms of oppression that seek to keep women silenced and marginalized? This and other questions were discussed during the event, which was part of the *Revealing » Recording » Reflecting* exhibition.

The conversation was moderated by Yasmine Nachabe Taan, Associate Professor and Director of the Institute of Art in the Arab World at the Lebanese American University. Her interdisciplinary research cuts across visual culture, gender politics, photography, and design history, focusing on Lebanon and the Middle East.

Guest panelists: Fatma Mansour, designer; Hala Al-Ani, Assistant Professor at College of Architecture, Art and Design of the American University of Sharjah; Sahar Khraibani, writer, artist, designer, and educator; Sara Abu Ghazal, writer and activist; and Zadeh Fatehrad, Professor of Design Enterprise at Kingston School of Art, London.

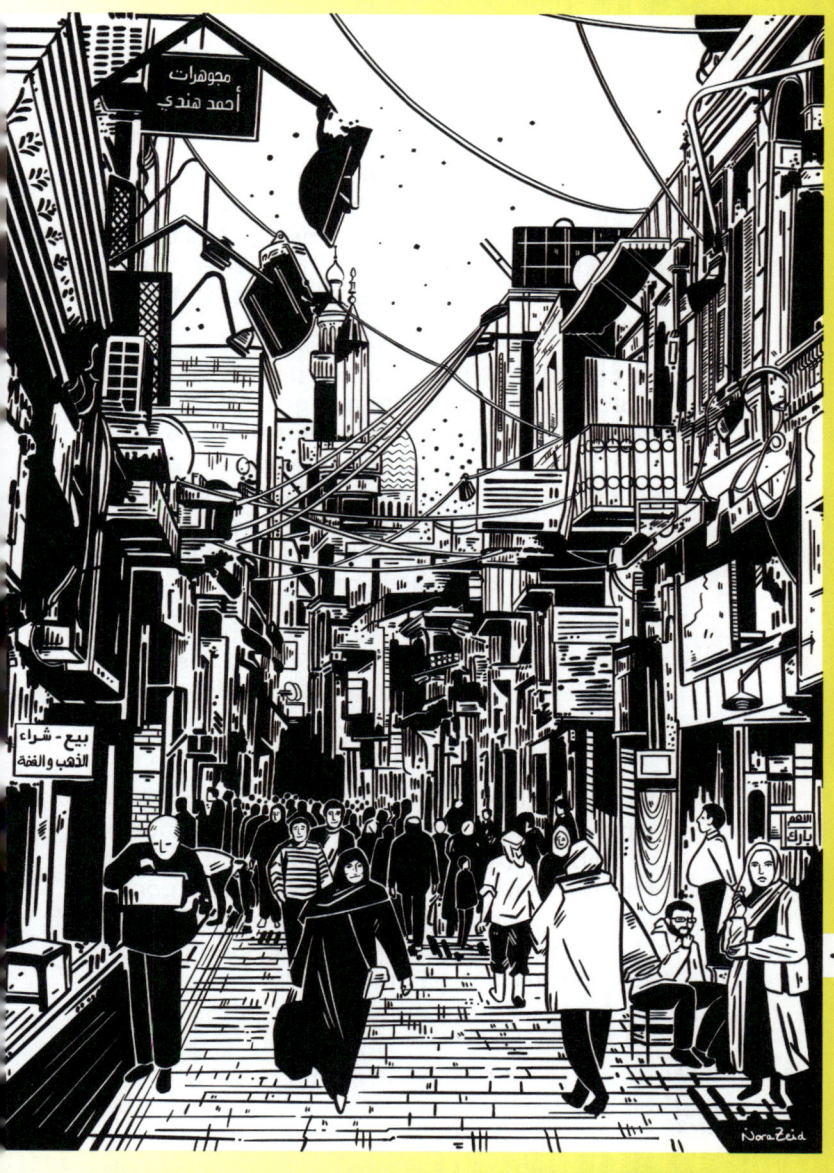

WHEN THE WORK IS DONE
EXHIBITION BY THE RODINA

The interactive exhibition *When the Work is Done* by The Rodina (Tereza and Vit Ruller) surfaced questions on the temporalities of design and the invisible layers of labor behind it, such as: "When does design start, how does it last, and what does it mean 'it is finished'?"

The central inquiry behind the performance of the artist duo, together with designer Yessica Deira, was developed during a non-linear, three-hour event co-directed by the audience. The designers democratized the process of 'situation making', creating a space for exchange and personal encounters about the Graphic Design creative process with each participant.

Visitors were prompted to think of three adjectives to describe themselves, submit their answers to be displayed on the central screen, wear a colorfully designed poncho, pick a color, and paint their chosen words on the drawing sheets.

After that, they were asked to select a book on display and read the marked excerpt out loud to the ambisonic recording device operated by Vit. After the opening, further visitors could continue interacting with the prompts, following the artists' set-up and filling out the drawing sheets, leaving their impressions on the space.

AGORA
THE RODINA
VISITORS
ONLINE VIDEO ARCHIVE

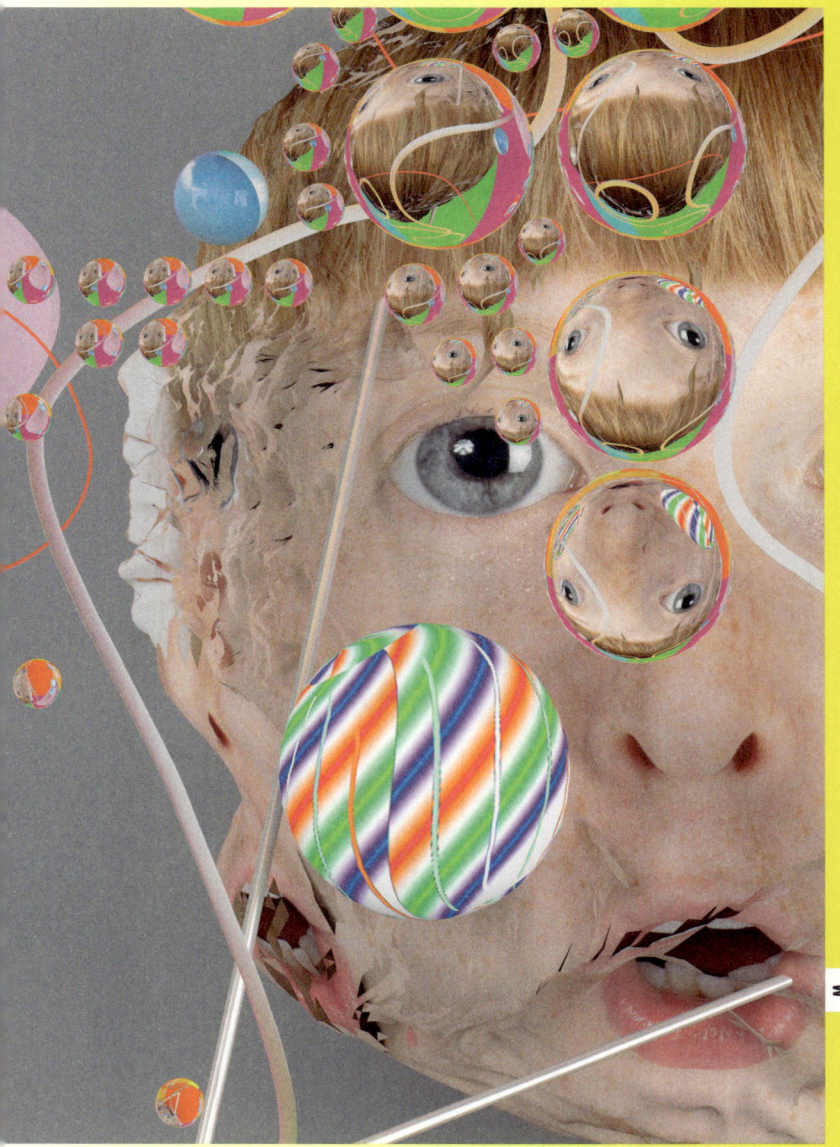

WHEN THE WORK IS DONE

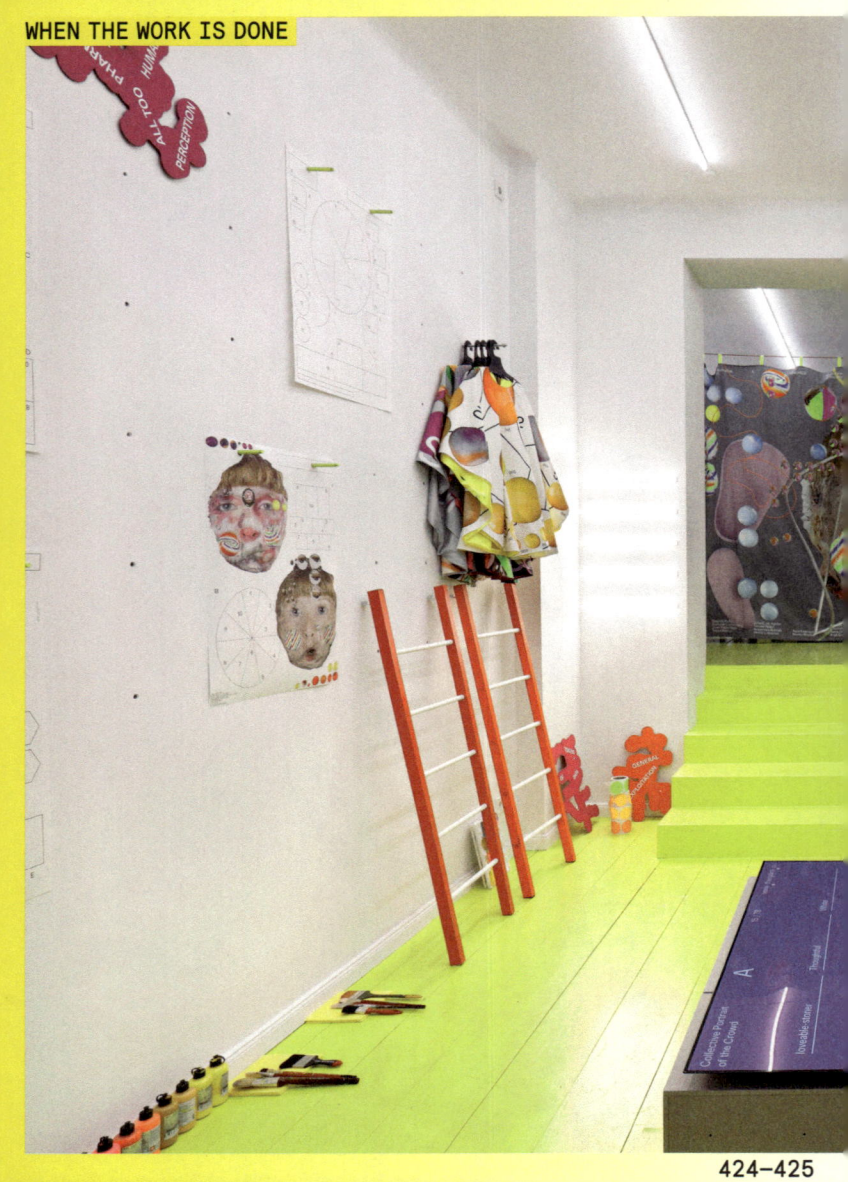

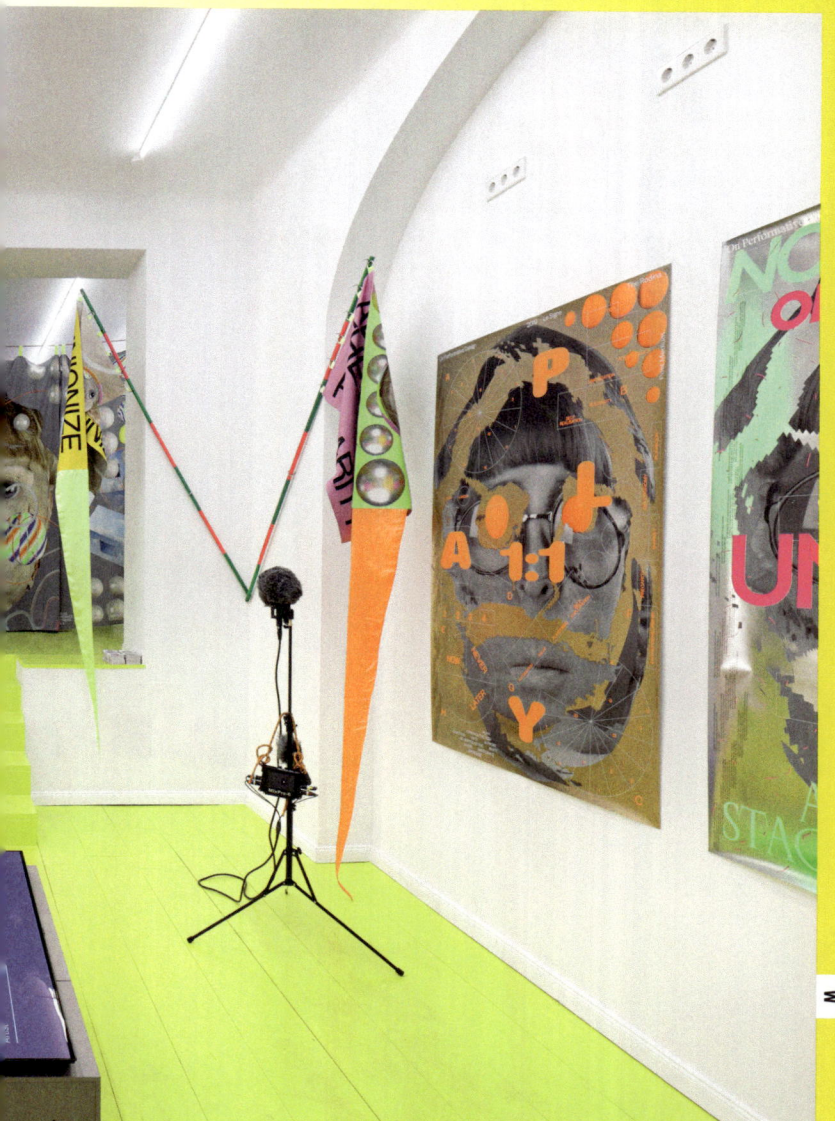

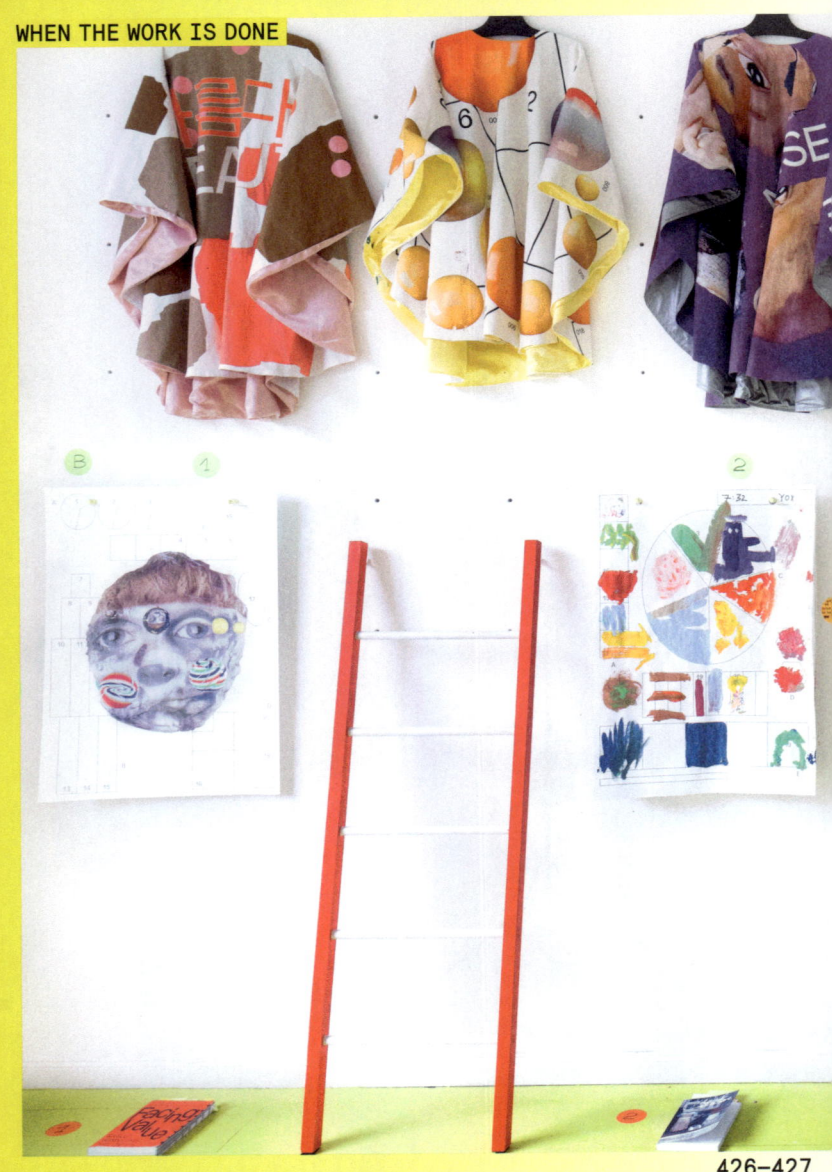

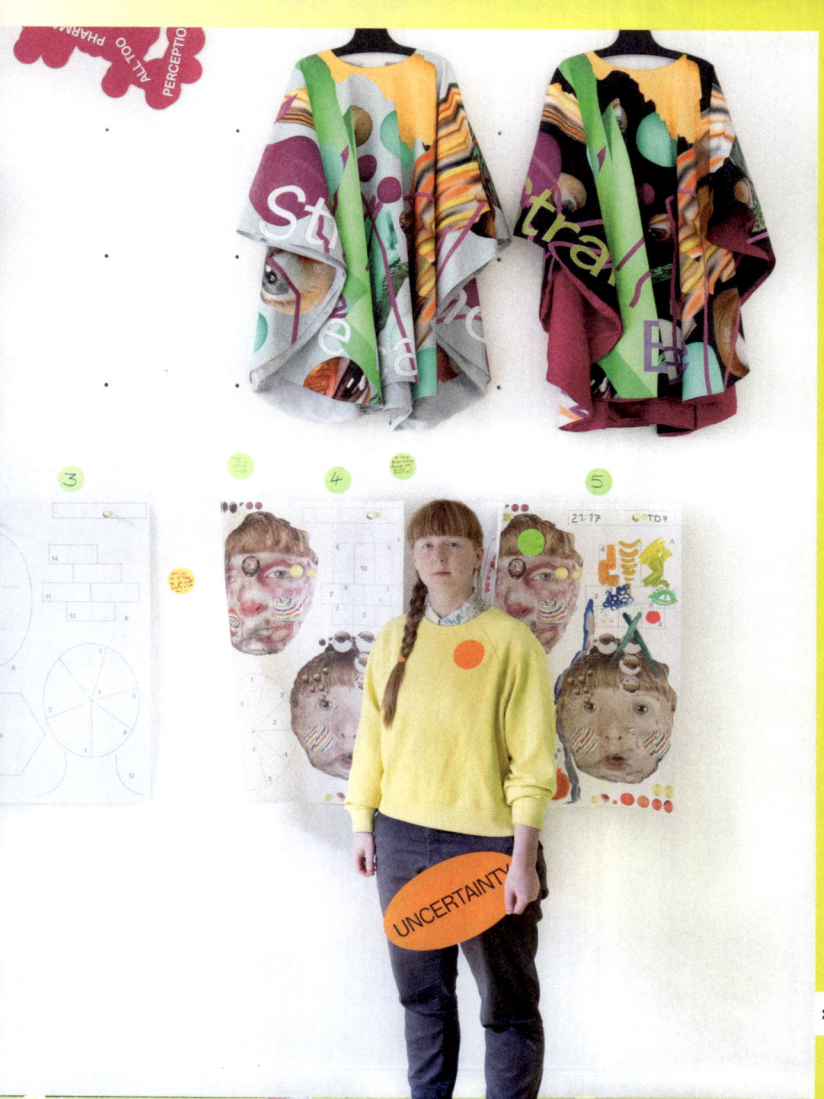

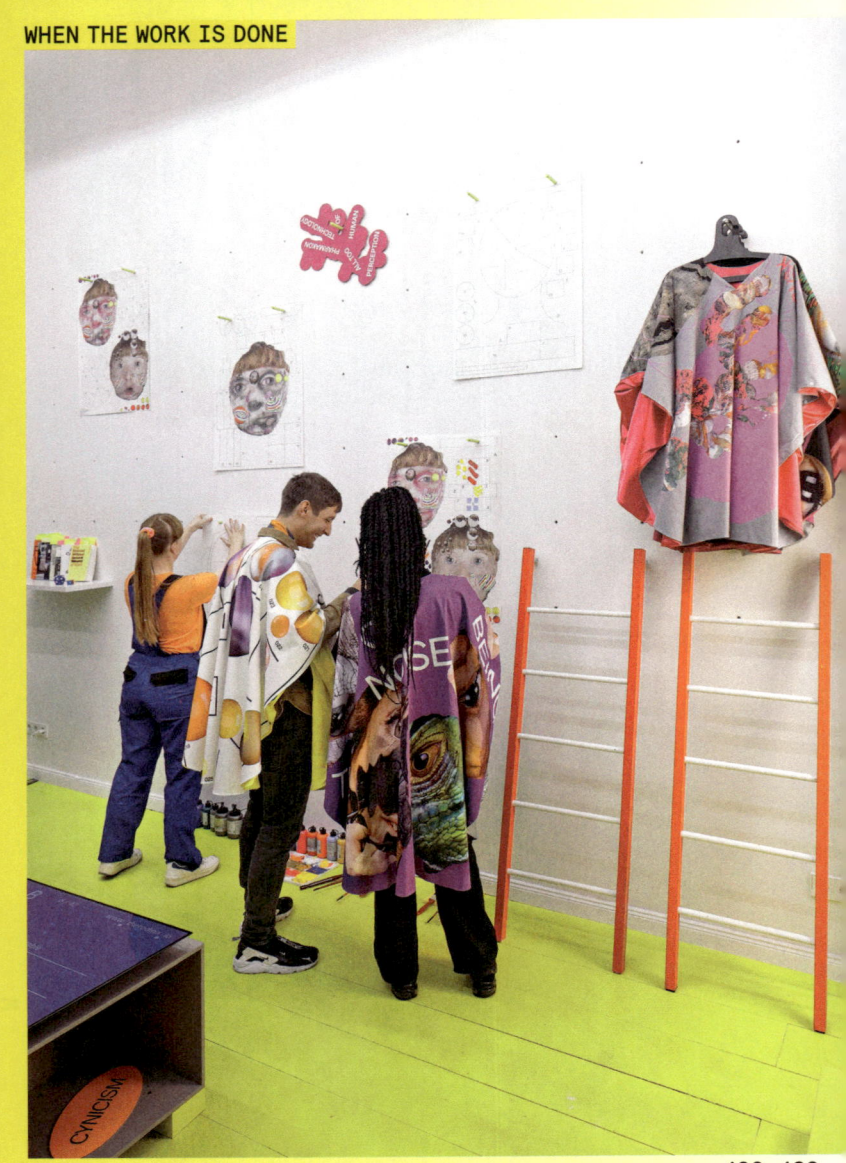
WHEN THE WORK IS DONE

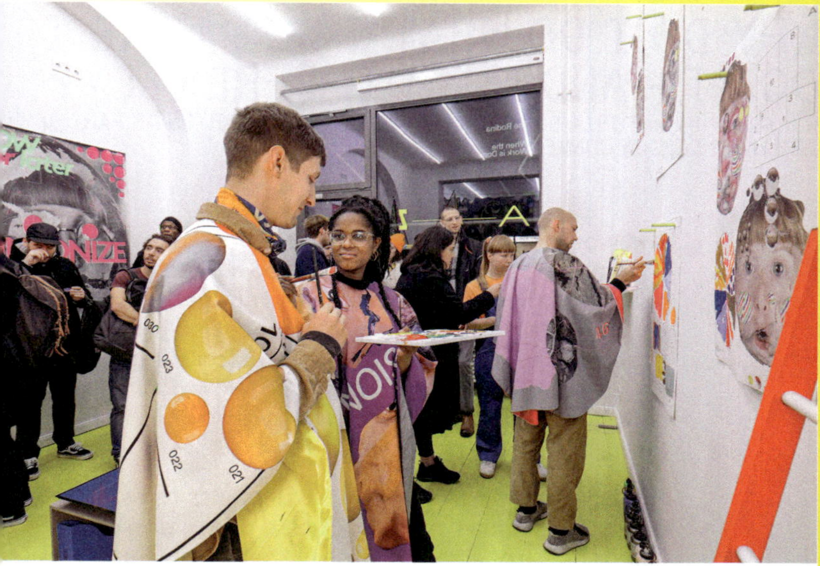

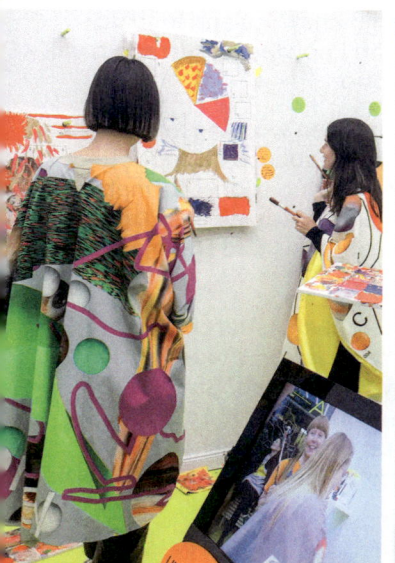
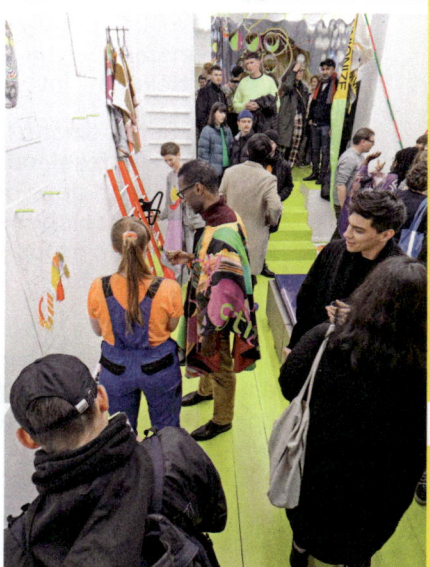

WHY DO I DO WHAT I DO – LIKE I DO IT – AND NOT DIFFERENTLY?

WORKSHOP BY ANTONIA SCHNEEMANN AND LISA BAUMGARTEN AS PART OF *TEACHING DESIGN CONVERSATIONS*

The workshop *Why Do I Do What I Do – Like I Do It – And Not Differently?* proposed a hands-on examination of the educational practices in design through playful interactions, connecting critical practice and design pedagogy, and focusing on four key questions: "How do we see?"; "How do we act?"; How do we think?"; and "How do we want to teach, learn, and work together?"

The goal was to encourage participants to reflect on issues such as inclusion, trust, non-hierarchical relations, non-binaries, etc., without formulating definitive, universally valid answers and instructions—instead, letting the knowledge surface from the participants' interaction.

Antonia Schneemann has been working as an art mediator and freelance art educator, conducting workshops and developing educational formats for museums, associations, and academic institutions, with a focus on group processes and the development of methods.

Lisa Baumgarten is a designer, researcher, writer, and educator who teaches design theory at design universities in Germany and abroad. She is the co-creator of the research platform *Teaching Design*, which focuses on design education from intersectional feminist and decolonial perspectives.

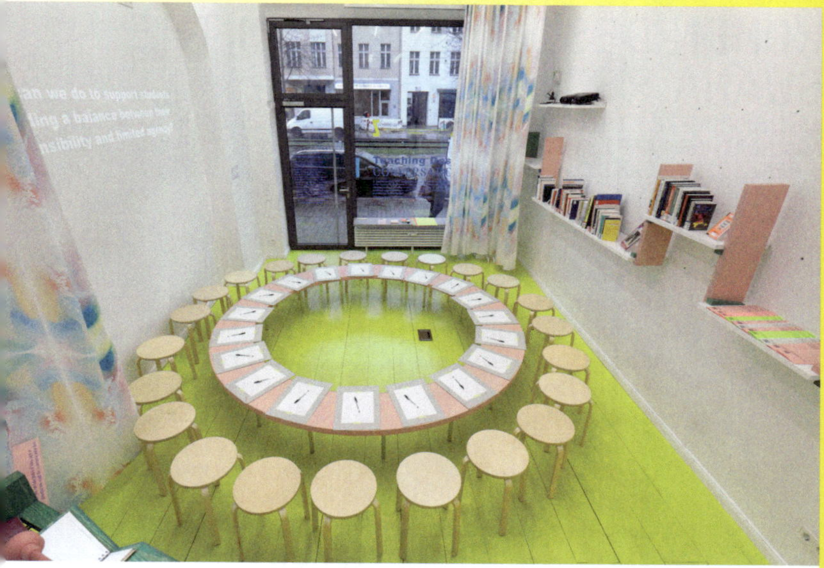

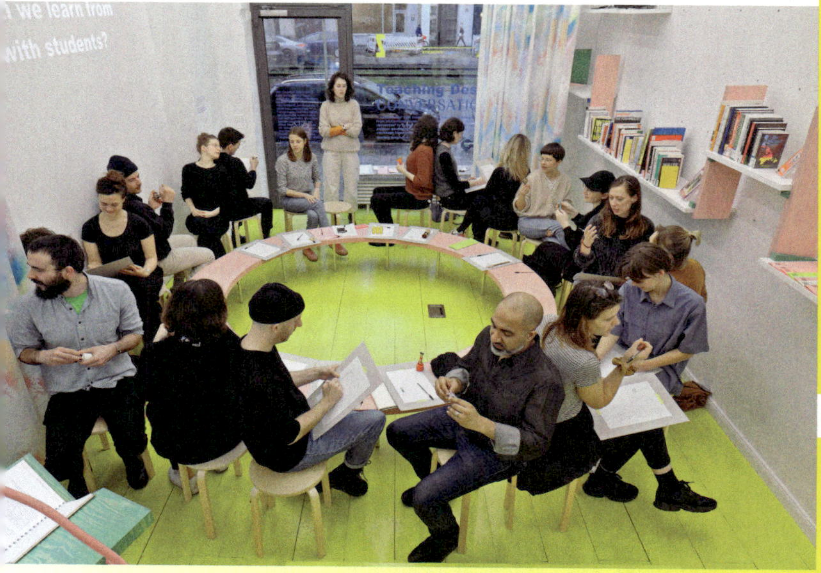

WOMEN DESIGNERS FROM THE SWANA REGION

AN INCOMPLETE LIST OF WOMEN DESIGNERS FROM SOUTH-WEST ASIA AND NORTHERN AFRICA COMPILED DURING THE *REVEALING » RECORDING » REFLECTING* EXHIBITION

Afrouz Razavi
Afsaneh Salek
Aïcha El Beloui
Aliaa Aboukhaddour
Arlette Boutros
Asieh Dehghani
Aude Abou Nasr
Azadeh Fatehrad
Azraa Aghighi
Azza Alameddine
Azza Fars
Bahia Azzam
Bahia Shehab
Basma W. Hamdy
Choghig Der Ghougassian
Christina Atik
Deena Mohamed
Dia Batal
Dima Nachawi
Dina Benbrahim
Doaa El Adl
Elham Namvar
Engy Aly
Esmâ Ibret Hanim
Faezeh Shakoori
Farah Behbehani
Farah Fayyad
Fatima Bint Al Hasan
Fatma Mansour
Fenna Zamouri
Ghada Wali
Ghalia Elsrakbi
Ghazaal Vojdani
Ghazal Foroutan
Gita Hashemi
Golnar Kat Rahmani
Greta Khouri
Greta Naufal
Guity Novin
Hala Al-Ani
Hanan Kai
Hessa Lootah
Hind Kharifi
Homa Delvaray
Ichraq Bouzidi
Jana Traboulsi
Joan Baz
Joud Toamah
Joumana Medlej
Karen Keyrouz
Kinda Ghannoum
Kristine Khouri
Lamia Ziadé
Lara Assouad
Lara Kaptan
Leila Abdelrazaq
Leila Miri
Lena Merhej
Leyly Mati
Leyly Matine
Lina Ghaibeh

Lootah Hessa
Louise Dib
Maece Serafi
Maha Akl
Maha Salah
Mariam Ashmawy
Mariem Abutaleb
Maryam Ahmed
Maryam Enayati
Maryam Moarefvand
Maya Moumne
Maya Saikali
Maya Sariahmed
Mona Bassili Sehnaoui
Mona Chalabi
Morehshin Allahyari
Mouza Al Hamrani
Nadine Chahine
Naïma Ben Ayed
Najla Badran
Narmeen Hamadeh
Nazanin Ebrahimi
Niaz Mirmobini
Nisrine Mansour
Nisrine Sarkis
Noha Abou-Khatwa
Noha Al Maghafi
Noha Rashidi
Nora Aly
Nora Zeid
Nourie Flayhan
Omaima Dajani
Pegah Ahmadi
Pouran Jinchi
Rafaelle Macaron
Rahele Jomepour Bell
Rama Duwaji
Randa Hadi
Rasha Dakkak
Rasha Salti
Rashin Kheiriyeh
Rawand Issa
Rayhaneh Sheikhbahaei
Razan Basim
Roshnak Keyghobadi
Roxana Kavosi
Rym Mokhtari
Sahar Afshar
Sahar Homami
Salek Afsaneh
Sama Beydoun
Samane Kameli
Samira Abbassy
Sanaz Soltani (Studio Kargah)
Sara Qaed
Sarah Rizkallah
Sarah Saroufim
Sasha Haddad
Shadi Rezaei
Shahrzad Changalvaee
Shakmag
Shamma Bouhazza
Sheikha Bin Dhaher
Sima Moushtaghi
Sirène Moukheiber
Siwar Kraitem
Solenne Madi
Somar Sala
Tahereh Mohebi Taban
Tala Safaie
Tewa Barnosa
Tracy Chahwan
Yara Khoury Nammour
Yasmeen Fanari
Zeina Abirached
Zeinab Shahidi
Zeynab Izadyar
Zineb Benjelloun
Zineb Fassiki

WOMEN DESIGNERS IN DIASPORA
ONLINE PANEL DISCUSSION MODERATED BY HUDA SMITSHUIJZEN ABIFARÈS
DURING THE *REVEALING » RECORDING » REFLECTING* EXHIBITION

The online panel *Women Designers In Diaspora: Navigating Multiple Identities and Practices* addressed the work and practices of women designers from the Southwest Asia and North Africa (SWANA) region living in the diaspora as part of the series of online *Revealing » Recording » Reflecting* exhibition discussions.

The panelists discussed the design process outside of its immediate cultural context, and the relationship to the motherland / culture at a distance. They investigated how the state of in-between-ness affected their design practices, and how it has blurred boundaries—contributing to new processes of engaging with audiences. And they analyzed the transformations of the individual designer / collective identities and practices.

The panel was moderated by Huda Smitshuijzen AbiFarès, Founding Director of the Khatt Foundation and Khatt Books publisher in Amsterdam, author of several books on typography and design from the Arab World, and a contributor of essays to professional and academic publications.

Guest panelists: Dina Benbrahim, Assistant Professor of Graphic Design, Art & Art History at the University of Connecticut; Ghalia Elsrakbi, designer and Assistant Professor of Practice at the American University in Cairo; Maya Moumne, Editor-in-Chief of Al Hayya Magazine; and Roshanak Keyghobadi, artist and Assistant Professor of Visual Communications at Farmingdale State College, SUNY.

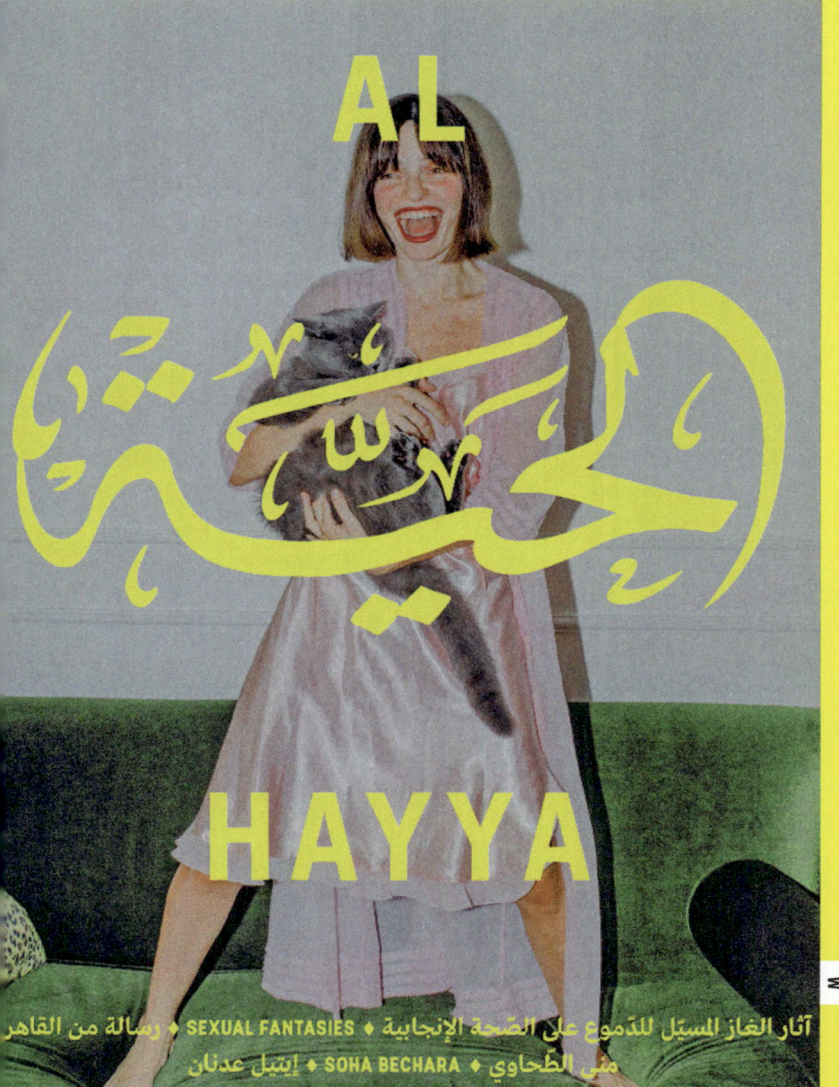

X
A—Z ON SOCIAL MEDIA

A—Z does *not* have a profile on X, but we are on Instagram @a.to.z.presents, and also on Facebook/A.to.Z.presents. We are concerned about the development of social media platforms, the bias of algorithms and their disrespect of copyright, therefore we might one day cancel our social media channels. To stay informed about the program at A—Z, please sign up to our email newsletter, where we share the latest updates about our program, along with calls for participation. The newsletter is sent out at most once a month, and the link for joining is on our website www.a-z-presents.com.

PRESS COVERAGE
VISITORS

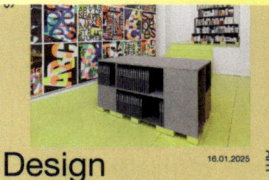
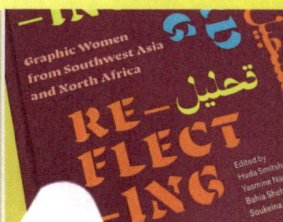
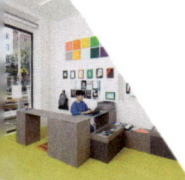

BRIAR LEVIT
ELLEN LUPTON
ANJA LUTZ

Design 16.01.2025 ART

Things That Make Us Grow

#Jewelry #English #Fraktyka #Reizmusy

...rsation with Anja Lutz —, art book designer and founder of A—Z — Space for Experimental Graphic Design in Berlin.

...Z Presents?

...space for experimental graphic design. I've always been interested

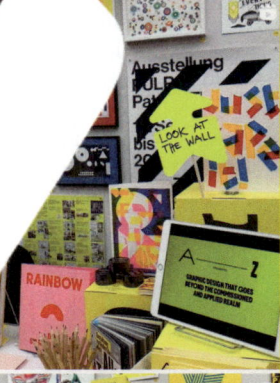
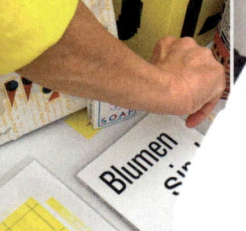
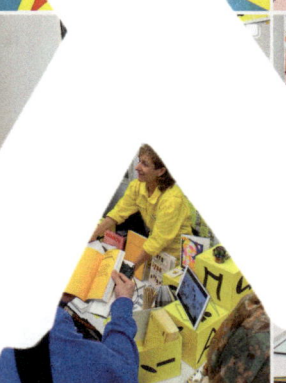
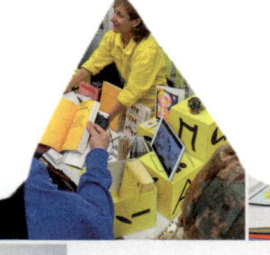

GUEST COUNTRY

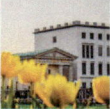

ADN Berliné
Una metrópoli efervescente, auténtica y diversa donde es sello se le da justamente el no seguir ninguna tendencia. Berlín no sigue la moda, la c

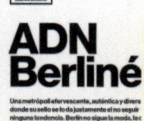

RECIPES FOR CONNECTING

X

YELLOW
THE A–Z OFFICIAL COLOR

Before A—Z was officially open to the public, some colors were tested to repaint the wooden floor. RAL 1016 Sulfur Yellow was chosen as the best fit and quickly became the signature color of A—Z's visual identity. This vibrant yellow surprisingly fits with the work of all the designers and artists who have been invited to exhibit in the space, whether it is super colorful or with monochromatic tones.

SUPER COLLECTIVE MARKET NO. 1 YELLOW
THE SPACE
YELLOW BENCH

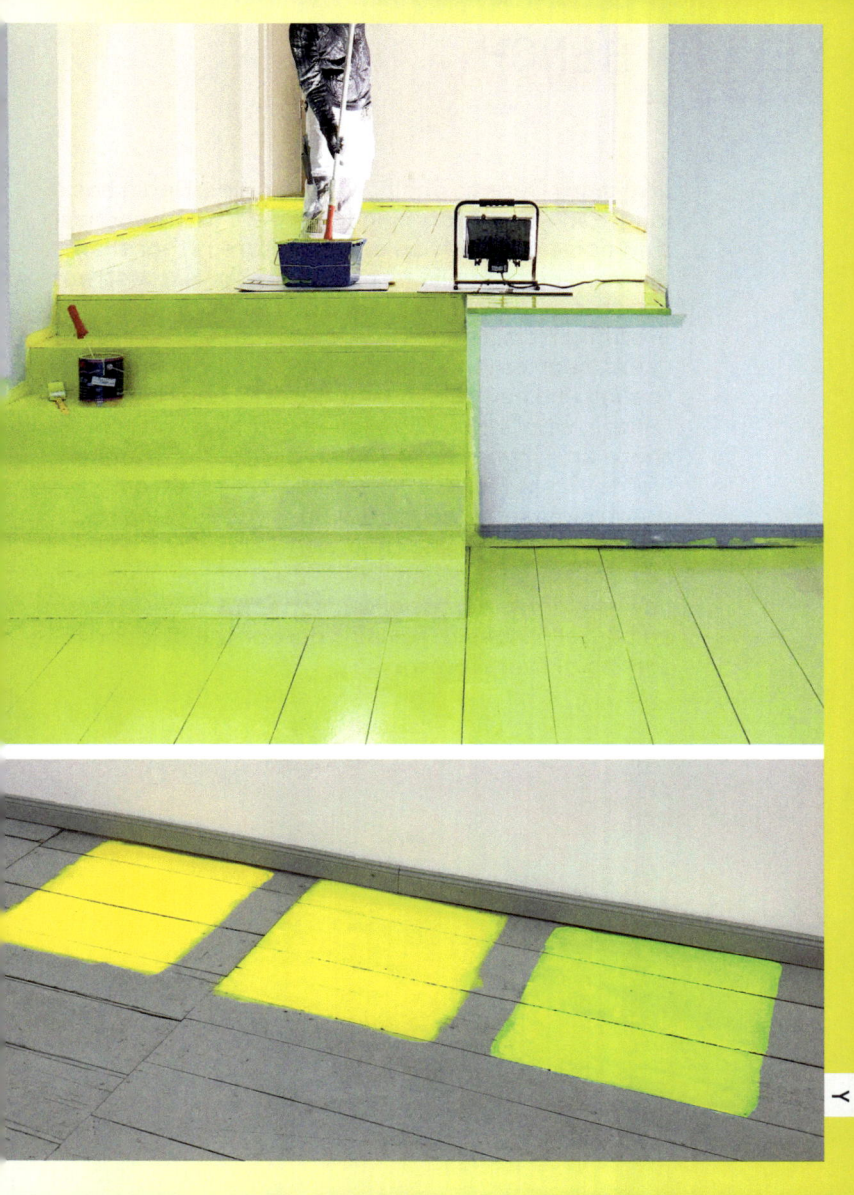

YELLOW BENCH
RESTING AT A—Z

Like many German and European cities, Berlin has a long tradition of adorning its streets with benches that come to signify an entire culture rather than just a piece of public furniture. A—Z's yellow street bench is strategically placed by the front window, profiting from its sunny spot and having regular users, such as long-term resident Ulli who enjoys resting and having occasional chats, and houseless Leszek, who is also often seen catching the sun there on summer days. Labeled with the friendly words "Treat Me Well", which has saved it from rough nights, the bench is where you will also find staff members having their coffee or meals on warm days, event guests convivially chatting, or night owls having a drink. Across all seasons and occasions, the comfy yellow bench remains part of the distinctive setting of lively Torstrasse.

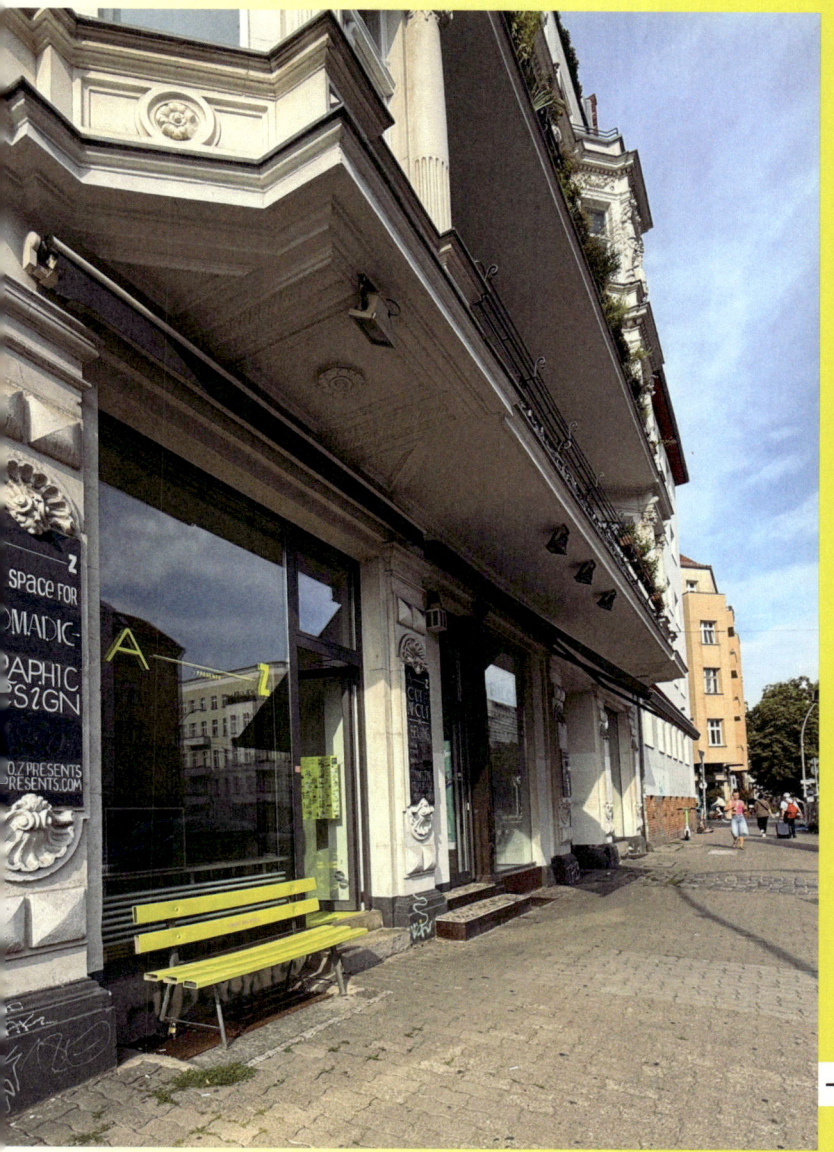

YOU NEVER GIVE UP?
COUNTER SESSION #5 BY ALEX JORDAN

The fifth edition of *Counter Sessions* featured an exhibition and talk by Alex Jordan, who shared a selection of his work from the last five decades with the audience. The material included politically motivated posters, cards, stickers, and books created during his time working with the collectives *Grapus* and *Nous Travaillons Ensemble* in Paris. The works were displayed on the walls and as if 'exploding out' of the suitcases in which the artist transported them to A—Z.

Alex Jordan's talk was a broad reflection on his practices and political engagement, with the designer expressing his continued positive look into the future: "Hope cannot be dangerous; one can only find oneself in a hopeless situation. So, if you have no hope left, you must trust others. And if you no longer have hope that others can still give you something, it becomes challenging ... I can only say that I still have hope. But maybe I'm a hopeless case ... I think you all have to have hope that something can be done differently."

Alex Jordan is a graphic designer and photographer based in Paris. After studying under Joseph Beuys, he became one of the leaders of the politically engaged design collective *Grapus*. Later, he co-founded the studio *Nous Travaillons Ensemble* with Ronit Meirovitz and Anette Lenz. He continues influencing new generations, and actively seeking strong visual communication responses to social challenges.

COUNTER SESSIONS
CYBERFEMINISM INDEX
EVER SINCE THE DAYS OF MRS . GUTENBERG ...
FAMILY TREES & SOUND CLOUDS
INVERSE – A YEARLY RITUAL
ONLINE VIDEO ARCHIVE

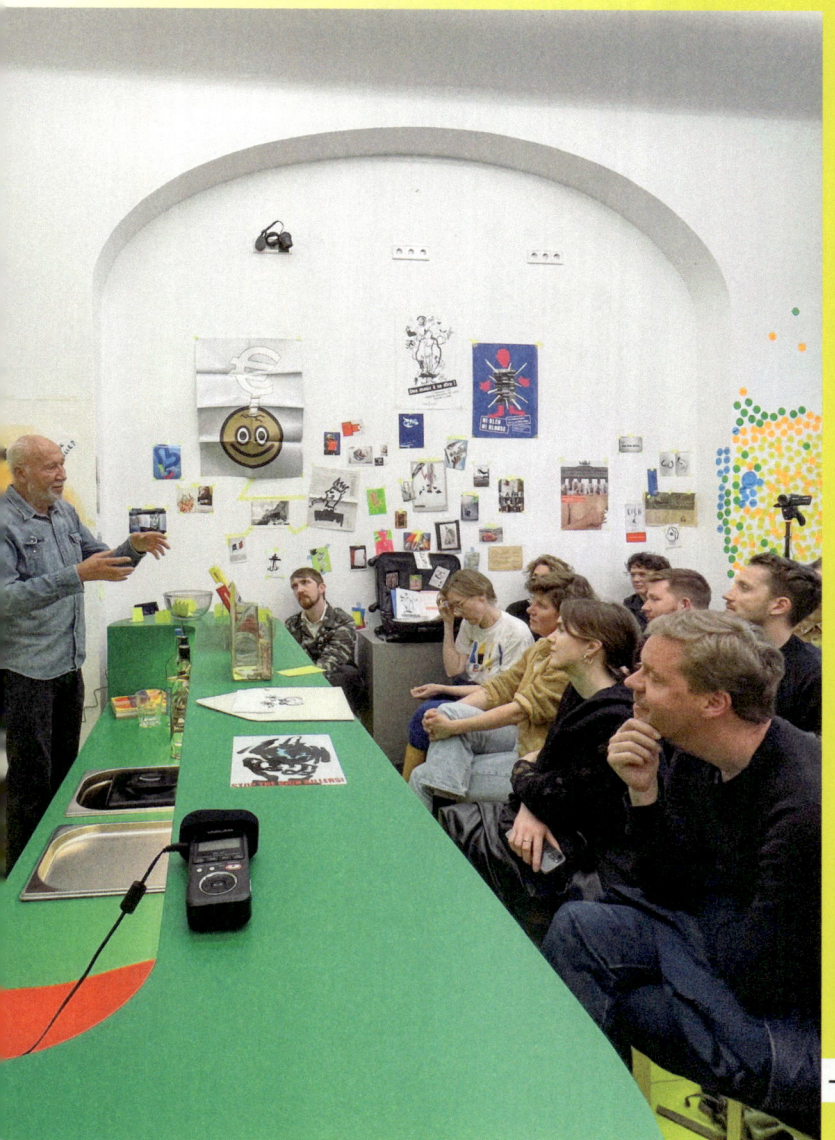

YOU NEVER GIVE UP?

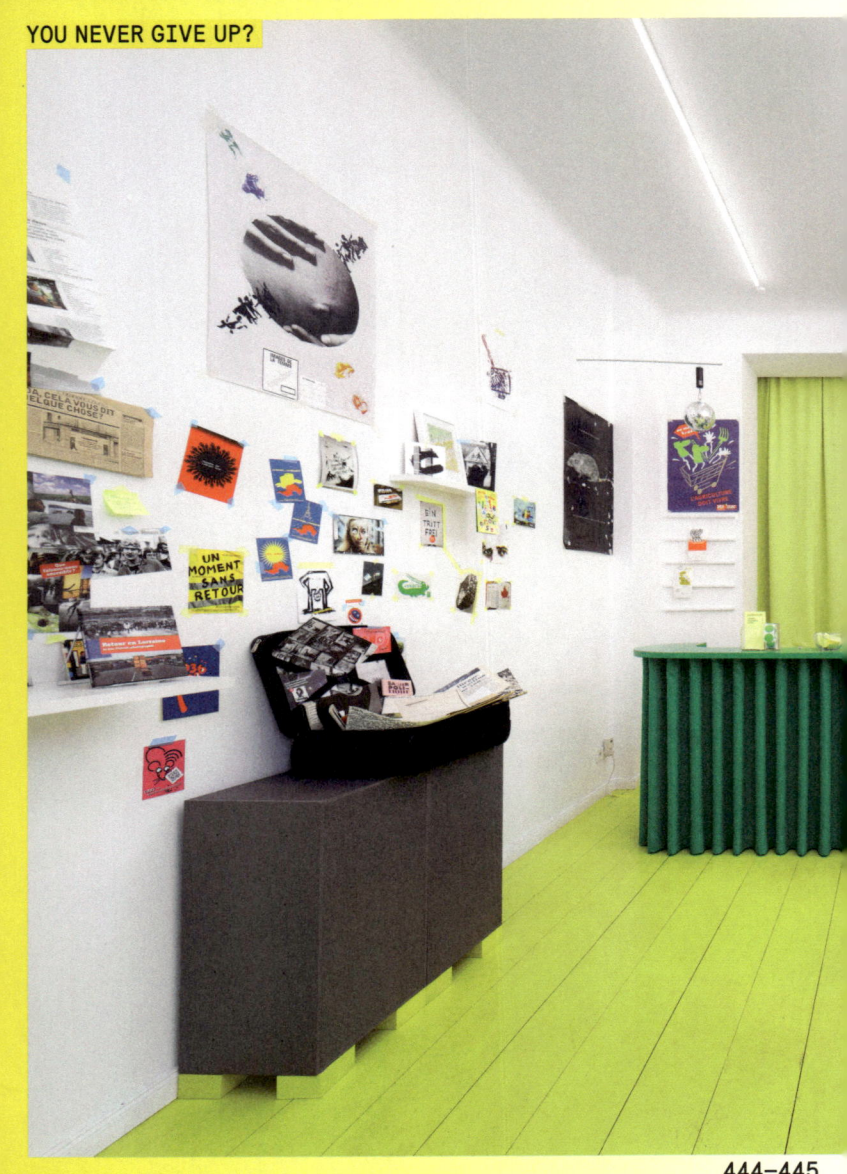

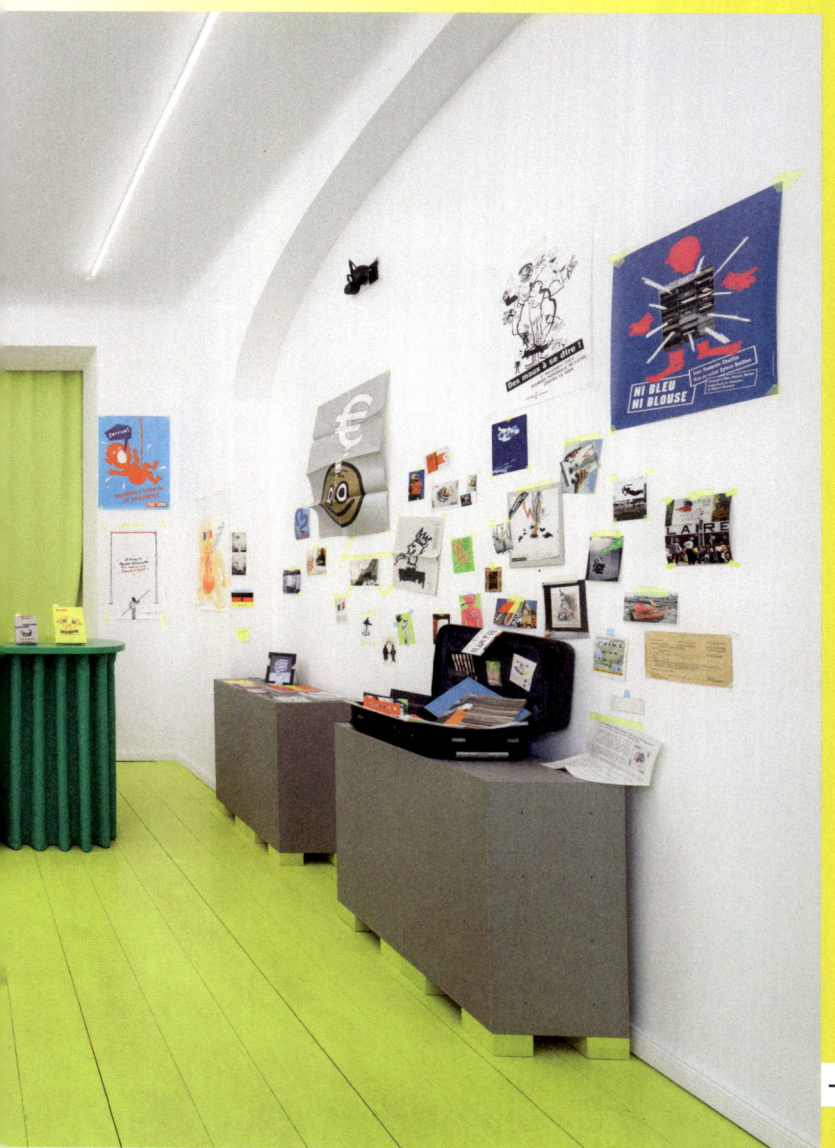

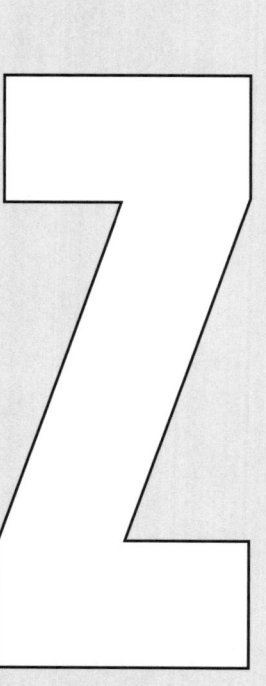

Our journey of exploring and expanding the boundaries of Graphic Design continues …
We have created the section —∞ and have invited 36 graphic designers from diverse backgrounds and career paths to share their vision for the future of Graphic Design.

Their contributions are a response to initial prompts, such as, "What may become of Graphic Design? What will we need it to be?", "What is your vision for the future?", and "How might you want to present, create, or enact this in the A—Z space?"

Their responses came in the form of inspiring, instigating, complex, and also humorous contributions. Altogether, they reflect the diverse facets of alternative Graphic Design that will continue to guide A—Z's upcoming initiatives.

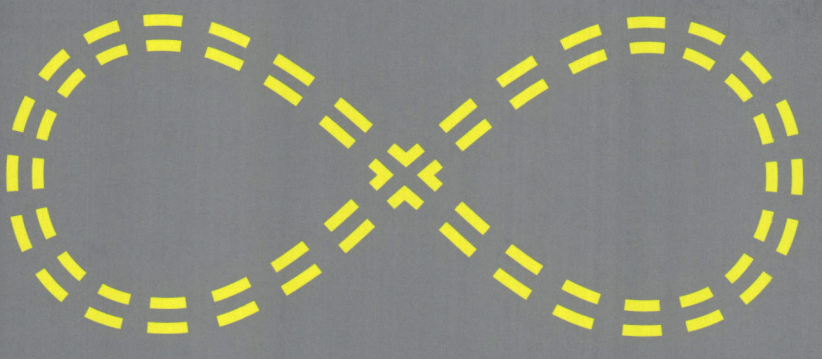

A DANCING BODY IN DIGITAL CULTURE
LUNA MAURER

Media is a driver of human culture, an environment that surrounds us, changes us, and makes us who we are. The media we design is in transition to a sensory experience—words and moving images are not just read but felt and absorbed. They touch, influence, and interact with us physically and emotionally.

The intervention reflects how media, language, and data shape the human experience, blurring the lines between the digital and the physical. It portrays media as something immersive, alive, consuming, and overwhelming, yet also something we actively engage with—dancing with it, pushing against it, and dissolving in it. After writing the *Designing Friction* manifesto—a call for friction in digital culture—my focus currently is the body and the role it can, or should, play in design and our digital future.

I am particularly interested in movement and dance, and their fundamentally human qualities—allowing for pure expression, joy, and vulnerability. I envision A—Z space as part of a series of experimental and participatory gatherings that explore movement and dance, resulting in typographic interventions.

Luna Maurer is a mixed media designer, artist, lecturer, and author with a focus on digital technologies' impact on daily life. She explores human characteristics through installations, performances, and films. She co-founded studio Moniker, known for participatory and web-based projects, and co-authored the influential manifesto *Conditional Design* and currently the *Designing Friction* manifesto, advocating friction in digital culture. / lunamaurer.com /

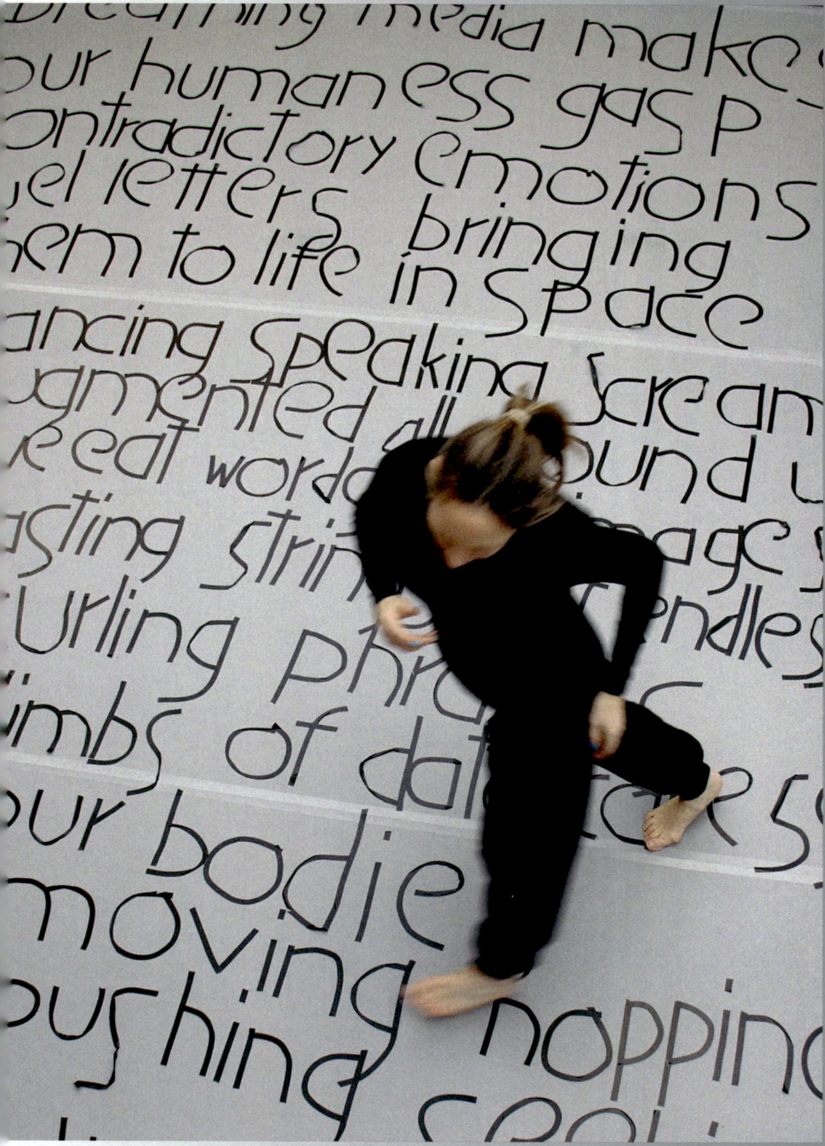

breathing media makes
our humanness gasp
contradictory emotions
feel letters
them to life in space
dancing speaking scream
fragmented all around u
repeat words
casting strin... ...age
curling phra... ...endles
limbs of dat...
our bodie...
moving
pushing hopping

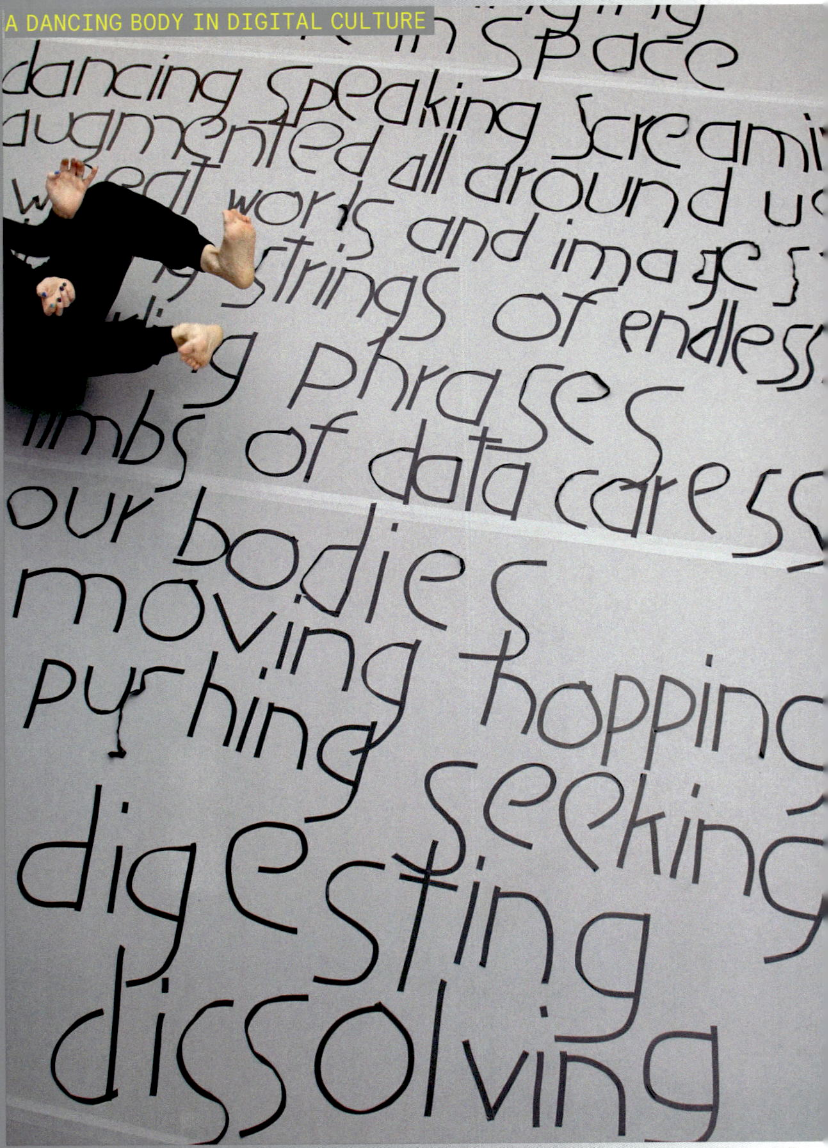

A DANCING BODY IN DIGITAL CULTURE

in space
dancing speaking screaming
augmented all around us
we eat words and images
strings of endless
phrases
limbs of data caress
our bodies
moving
pushing hopping
seeking
digesting
dissolving

...ys or end...
...g phrases
of data care
bodies
...ving ho...
...hing se...kir...
...e sti...

A GRAPHIC DESIGN TOOLBOX FOR THE FUTURE

MADITA FLOHE

The future Graphic Designer's toolbox must be reorganized. As Graphic Design is becoming more and more dispersed, it is expanding into a mode of construction and deconstruction. Its methods evolve from polishing surfaces and wrapping things to becoming an agent of transparency: uncovering, disassembling, dismantling, and deconstructing. For Graphic Designers, this results in the task of dissolving, unraveling, and exposing invisible grids, including the frameworks of their own discipline.

Graphic Design becomes an open construction space that lies between the current state of being and the realm of possibility. In this vision, the A—Z space acts as a collaborative workshop, a library of possibilities, and an ever-changing work in progress. It becomes an accessible collection of tools and resources by providing a collective database of knowledge, ideas, material, and connections. The space itself becomes renegotiable, an unrasterized area based on a deconstructed grid system. Its inventory list includes tools that enable creative processes—there are no templates or standardizations, but rather anchor points, cross-references, connecting elements, building blocks, and metaphors. A— Z provides the tools to rip up the blueprints, saw through grids together, and create something new.

Madita Flohe is an information designer and researcher with a multidisciplinary approach. Her focus is on design research and the political dimensions of design practices. She is currently working on a critical theory of design from the perspective of philosophy/aesthetics. / instagram.com/maditaflh /

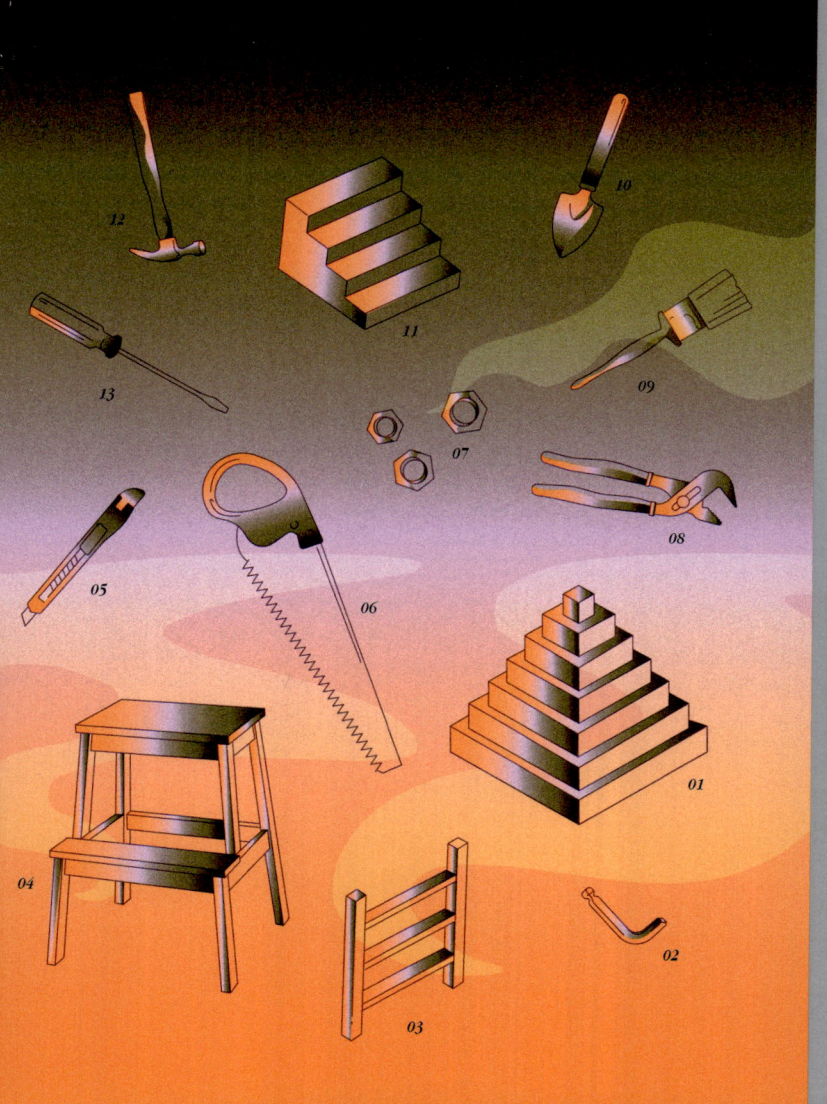

ABOUT SIMPLE SYSTEMS AND COMPLEX OUTCOMES
LENA WEBER

Lena Weber is a designer and creative coder, focusing on research and the development of design tools and typographic systems. After completing her bachelor's and master's degrees at Bauhaus-University Weimar, she is working as a freelancer. She is most interested in the intersection of art, technology, and philosophical theory and how they inspire visual communication. In her thesis, Ambiguous Aesthetics, she explores the aesthetics of the coded and the digital. / lenaweber.com /

The tools we use influence design with their limitations and possibilities, just like they always did. Interfaces are becoming ever more complex, designed, and opaque. In the digital realm, flexibility and variability radically change the systems we used to know. The structures of fixed design instances are evolving and disappearing. An image becomes a matrix, a font becomes software, and a document becomes a flexible system. Ultimately, all functionality is formed by breaking down complex relationships into simple building blocks. Design products are expanded into not only aesthetic but also technical systems. These can translate into each other, blur, and transform. Can we be truly creative if we don't understand how a tool works? How autonomously can we create with tools over which we have no power? All that remains for us to do is design simple systems whose constraints and possibilities we fully understand and control, rather than using systems that are limited by design decisions we didn't make. The building blocks of the digi-technical world invite us to understand them and build our own complexity. We have lost the connection to the beautiful formalization process, locked into it instead of seeing it for what it is: creative.

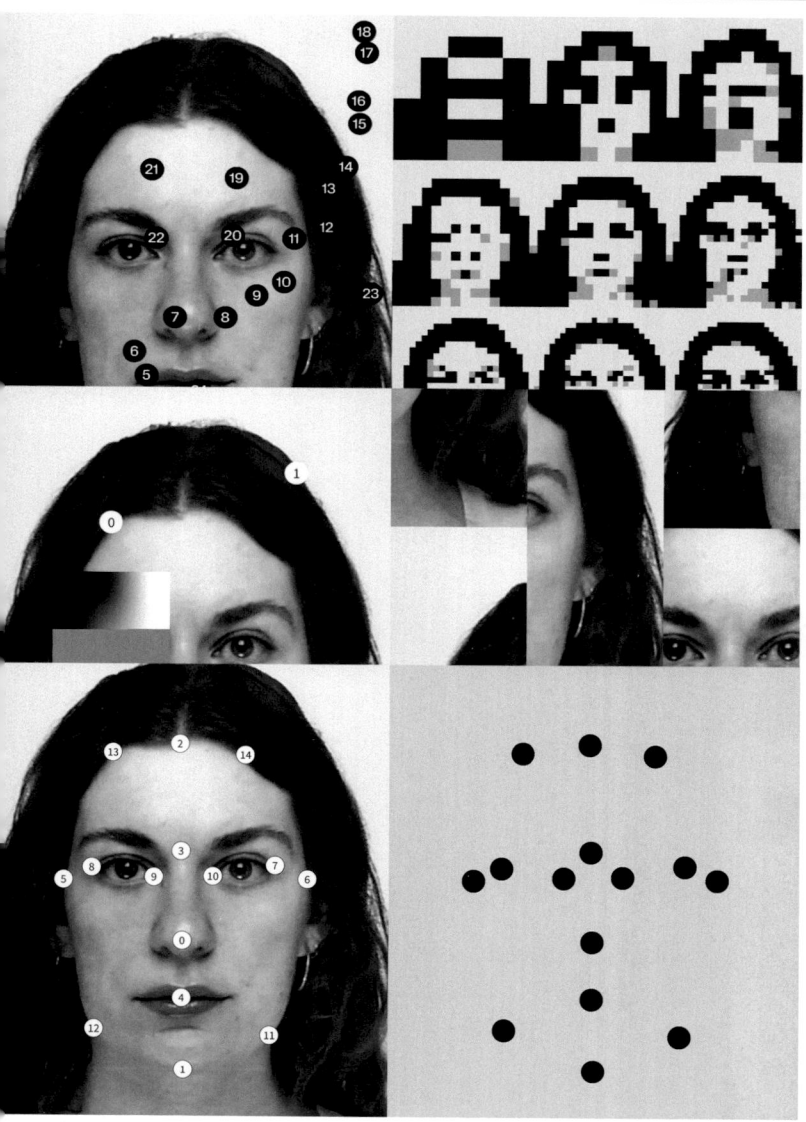

ALT<DQ, DOES IT MAKE SENSE?
APRIL GREIMAN

April Greiman is a transmedia artist, whose projects actively challenge interdisciplinary backgrounds, investigating the parallels and intersections between art and design, color, light and space. Greiman's digital photography and transmedia projects, including the 1986 version of *Does It Make Sense?* have been the subject of solo and group shows at: MoMA; SF MoMA; LACMA; Centre Pompidou; Arc en Reve Centre d'Architecture Bordeaux; Pasadena Museum of California Art, and Brand Library Art Center. / aprilgreiman.com /

proton.neutron.electron.moron. A Zen monk starts on his daily walk through the forest. A young student follows behind, hoping to discover some secrets of his master along the way. Deep in the forest, the master comes across a giant boulder fallen across the path, making it impossible to continue forward on the journey. The monk meditates for a few short moments, then goes into the forest and gets a large tree branch, which he then uses as a lever to gently roll the rock out of his path. The master continues on, but the young student, terribly excited to have witnessed this, grabs the stick and runs back to the monastery to impress the others with the discovery: when you encounter an obstacle, find a stick. The moral of this story is that it isn't about the stick, it's about how to continue the journey. The original *Does It Make Sense?*, created in 1986 for *Design Quarterly* #133, explored the use of Apple's Macintosh computer and high-resolution video to assemble a collage of illustrative assets and words—delivered on paper, 'Z' space implied. Now, *alt<DQ, Does it Make Sense?* can be viewed in x, y and z space. Implied space now becomes actual space in A—Z Presents, using a smartphone or tablet—with fully immersive content; motion, graphic, interactive, and personal Greiman audio narrative. Live where you can …

tewedon'tcontrolthemachines,machinescontrolus

micro . nano . pico . kilo . mega .

h i n g n e s s

Halley's comet discovery
1682

1st Industrial Revolution
1790

and so I'm walking through the English garden
the idea (duality) of order and chaos — a
philosophical twist — chaos is simply a man-made idea
that frankly doesn't exist! I think about how art
of literal geometry though you cannot
without structure. Such as mountain
mountains are in the sense of creation

We were living in a building. It was a warm,
sunny evening. Then...
was rushed to the ground. The
what was just
away from
in the
w

the builders.
The wind towards the ground. As
As I hit the ground, I slipped out of a window
ers were gone with the building. I was the survivor. The
ero were gone with the building. I began my
journey to find another dwelling.

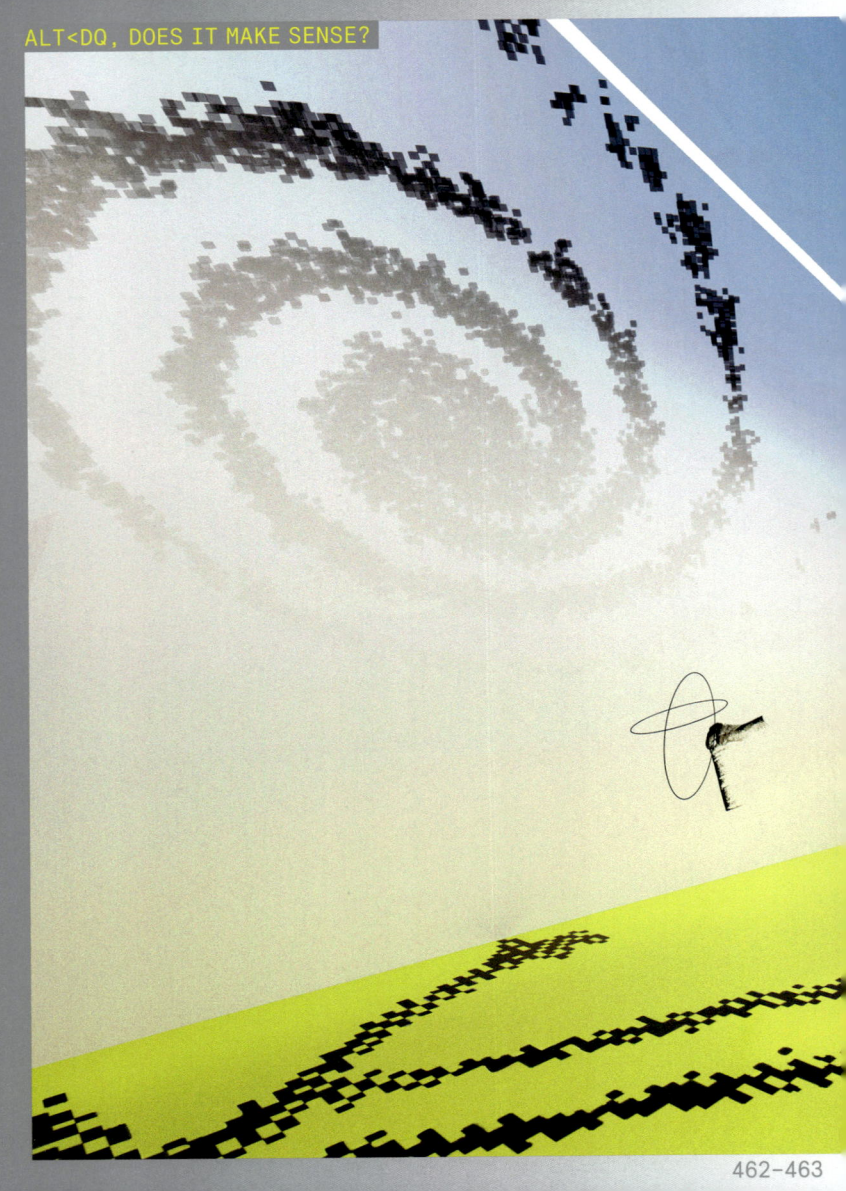

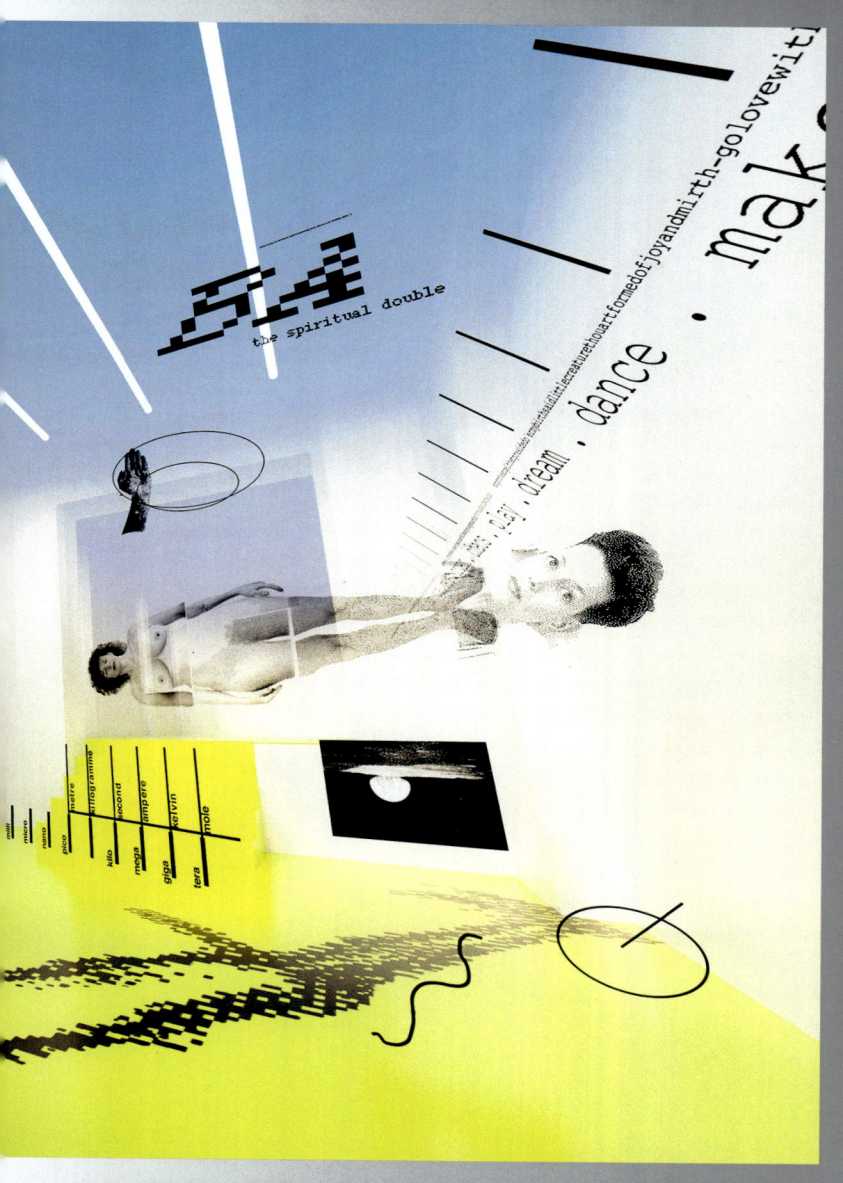

AN ODE TO OTHER LANGUAGES THAT MAKE BERLIN HOME EVERYDAY

SIWAR KRAI(Y)TEM

It is a space where language hierarchies are flipped and where languages with lower voices in Berlin are given the space to exist and shine louder than German and English. It is a celebration of language cannons and archives that we may not be aware of, be it through a book selection, posters, or other contributions, but also a highlighting of possible terms used more quotidianly in our most dominant languages. It is about celebrating four languages written in the Arabic script: Farsi, Arabic, Urdu, and Kurdish, insisting that these languages also make Berlin home every day. The posters hanging in the main space are an invitation for visitors to engage by suggesting references, books, and posters, adding Post-its, or lending objects, books, or posters to help create an archive of the use or existence of these languages in Berlin. Every week, a language comes into focus, and further public engagements and events are planned through highlighting specific terms from each language, as well as archiving and storytelling sessions.

Siwar Kraytem is a multilingual artist, graphic designer, and researcher based between Beirut and Amsterdam. Her research and artistic practice focuses on multilingualism and language in times of transformation, as well as the construction of society through language. She studies the Disarming Design program in Amsterdam. She was a fellow at BAK, basis voor aktuele Kunst in Utrecht in 2023, a 3-package deal recipient for 2024, and a co-curator as part of Mophradat's *New Agents* program. / siwarkraytem.com /

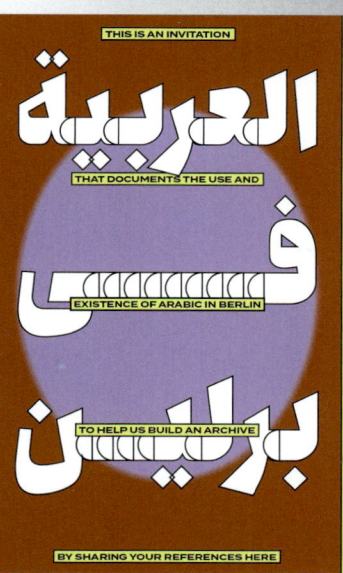
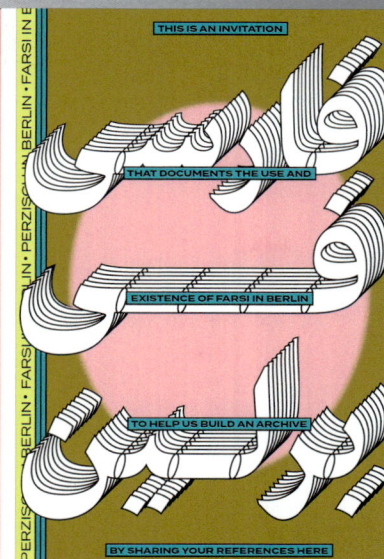
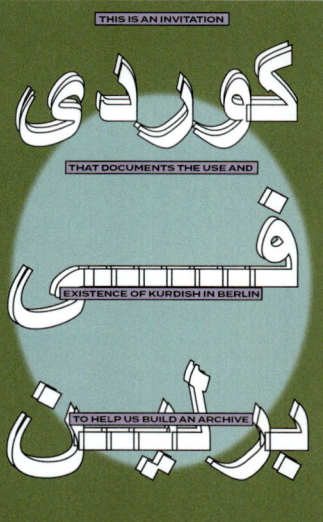
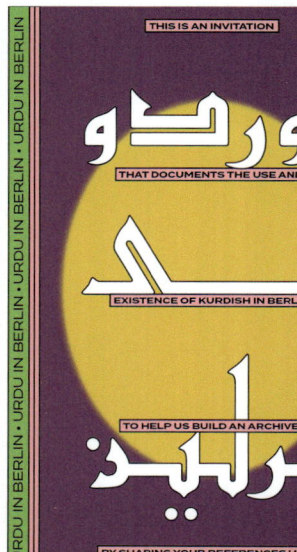

DESIGN BEYOND DESIGN
SANDY KALTENBORN

On the Edges of Graphic Design from A—Z—∞ as an index "beyond graphic design" evokes memories of a 1997 symposium organized in part by Jan van Toorn, which was formative for me. Core positions of the symposium (and its publication) emphasized design's entanglement with power structures and economic interests, as well as the necessity of a critical stance. Design is never neutral—it is always embedded in political and cultural contexts, positioning designers between client interests and broader societal needs. Design is always social and, therefore, political.

Yet, much of our field takes little societal responsibility, settling into self-referential circles and their economies. While (socio-)political design practices and publications have grown in recent years—an encouraging trend—many remain within academic frameworks and rarely engage with power in a substantial way.

Now, a new societal chapter is unfolding: the global rise of authoritarianism and austerity will marginalize or erase cultural production and democratic spaces. Berlin's budget cuts already reflect this shift. Europe's militarization will lead to massive wealth redistribution, depriving many in our field of their working environments.

Against this backdrop, A—Z must confront these challenges—unless we retreat into niche discourses. "Beyond graphic design" must mean fully engaging in societal and political struggles through design.

Sandy Kaltenborn is a communication designer who has been running the design studio image-shift since 1999. The studio operates in social, cultural, and artistic, as well as political and urban contexts. Kaltenborn has lived in Berlin since 1990 and is a co-founder of the housing and urban policy initiative Kotti & Co. He has been actively engaged in social and political issues for many years, and has taught at numerous art and design academies in Germany and abroad. He lives with two cats in Berlin. / www.image-shift.net /

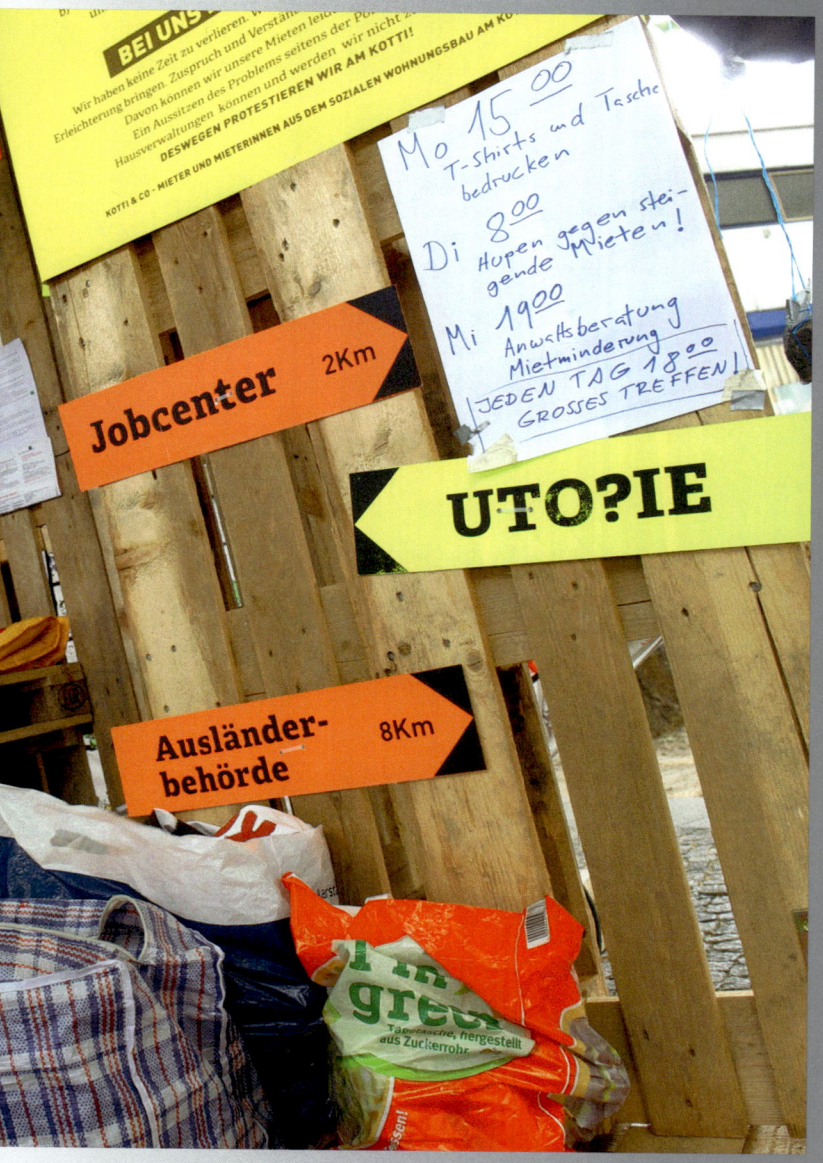

DESIGNING DIGITAL FUTURES
KATHARINA NEJDL

Our world is increasingly intertwined with digital technology. Devices, tools, and platforms are not only reshaping how we work as designers but also altering how we connect as humans. In spaces defined by mechanisms that datify, commodify, and algorithmically curate our interactions, how can we design genuine connection? While many issues require political solutions, graphic design can imagine alternative futures. So, I envision connecting design with code—to prototype spaces that resist algorithmic isolation and reclaim agency.

Let's use code not simply as a design tool but to demystify technology while reimagining its collaborative potential. To reflect this, I propose an installation for A—Z that bridges analog and digital: a movement-sensitive camera faces the street and detects passing bodies. Through pose-recognition, these movements generate digital paint strokes on a screen inside the gallery space—creating a collaborative artwork drawn by the collective presence of strangers.

As passive users transform into active co-creators, we can design new modes of community. In the future, I envision graphic design serving as the connective tissue between worlds—making visible the invisible links between us, and creating spaces where technology enhances rather than inhibits our fundamental need for connection.

What does a digital publication look like? What shapes do we take online? Can AI design posters? Katharina Nejdl deals with these and other questions in her work. As a graphic designer, developer, and educator, she is interested in using digital technologies—such as web, AR and AI—as graphic tools. She founded http://andshymagazine.com/, an online literature magazine, and is currently researching coding as a tool for design by building the grid-based parametric type tool http://grid-type.com/. / katharinanejdl.com /

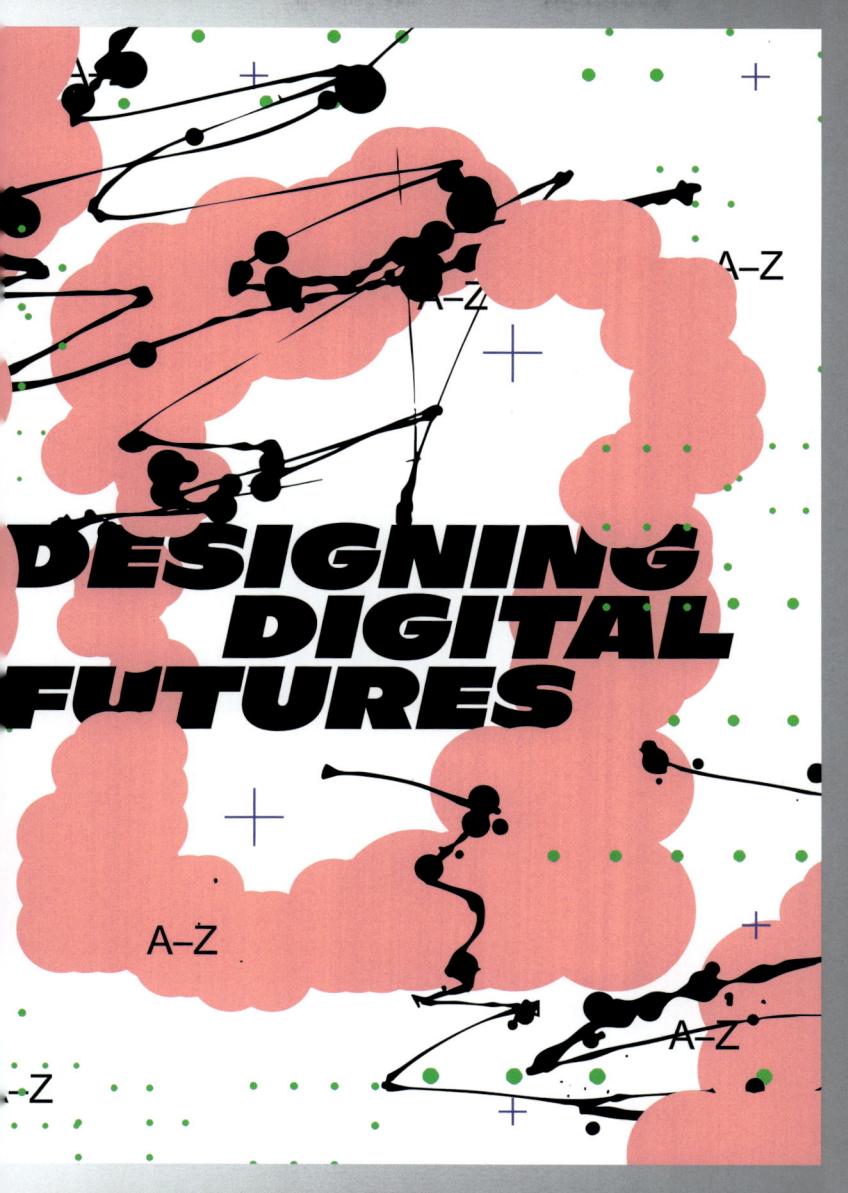

FABULATING PAGES & EXCLAMATION HEARTS
LORAINE FURTER

Take a deep breath in through your nose and a long breath out through your mouth ... In a few breaths, you will enter a parallel space-time in which dreams and stories of empowerment through publishing and design are shared °◕≋ publishing & design in an expanded understanding, including oral transmission and hybrid-cyborg formats .˚˙ from (micro-)typography to editorial structures, gossip to ghostwriting ...

A transparent yellow ramp fixed above the two entrance steps invites you into the space. From the street, you could already see through the window, the door, and the ramp °ஃ°ஃ portals bearing appealing forms and words announcing what is happening inside. A colored carpet welcomes your body into the space. Standing on it, in the middle of the room, is a big structure made of light wood and transparent plexiglass, forming a sort of open book with its pages spread, like a star or an asterisk ✢*✳✴. The 'pages' present a composition of posters and shelves, covered with images, objects, and printed matter. Around and in the structure are different kinds of seats and cushions, making it a soft space for reading, discussing, organizing, revolting, conspiring, healing. {◡˙˙∠ ... ∵ʔ∝}

After your visit, take a rest on the bench outside— you might meet a new person and share stories with them.

Loraine Furter is a graphic designer and researcher, based in Brussels since 2007, who specializes in editorial design, hybrid publishing and intersectional xfeminism. She designs and edits paper publications as well as web and digital ones, and is particularly interested in the interaction between these media. / lorainefurter.net /

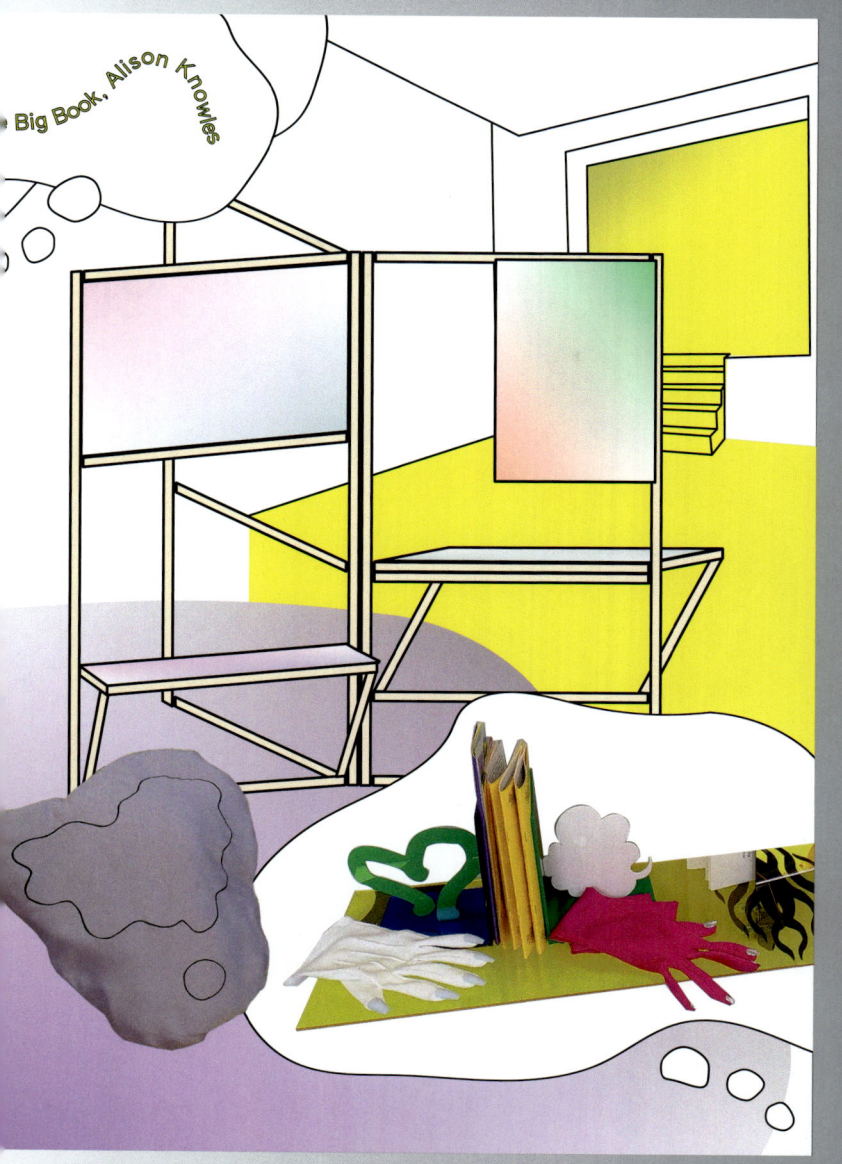

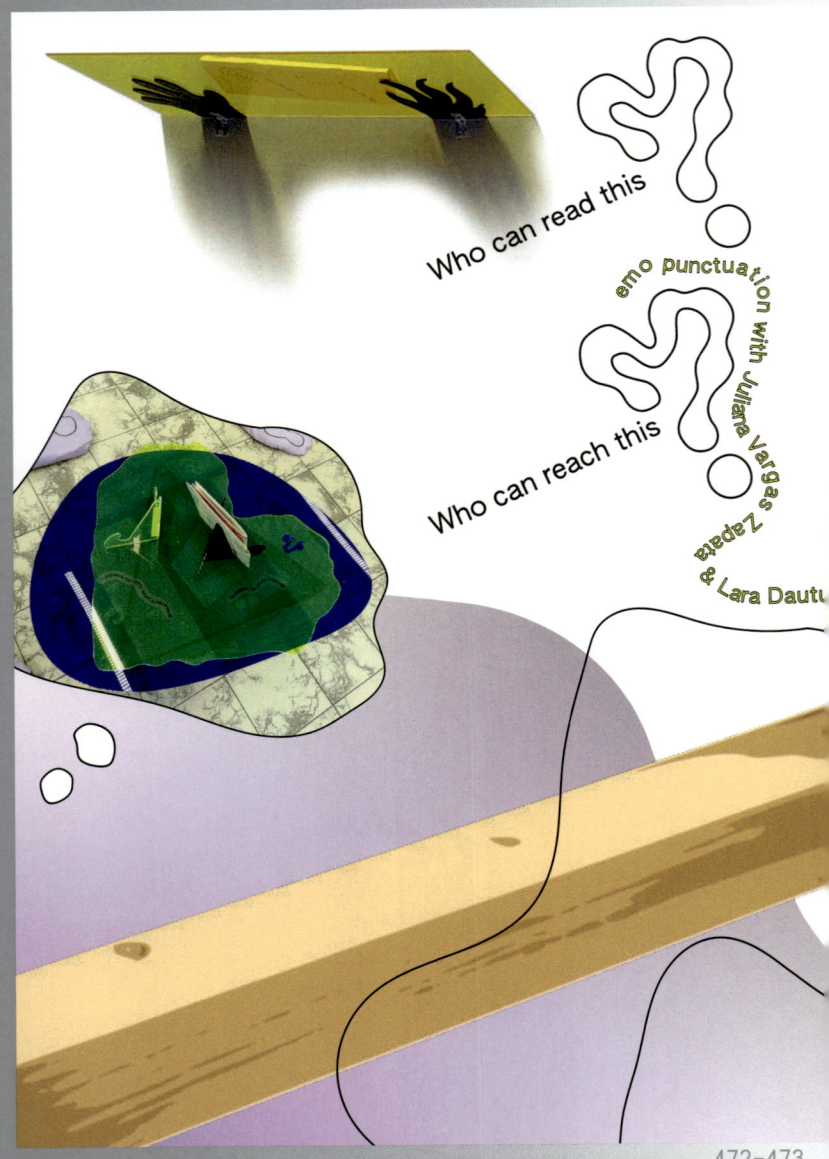

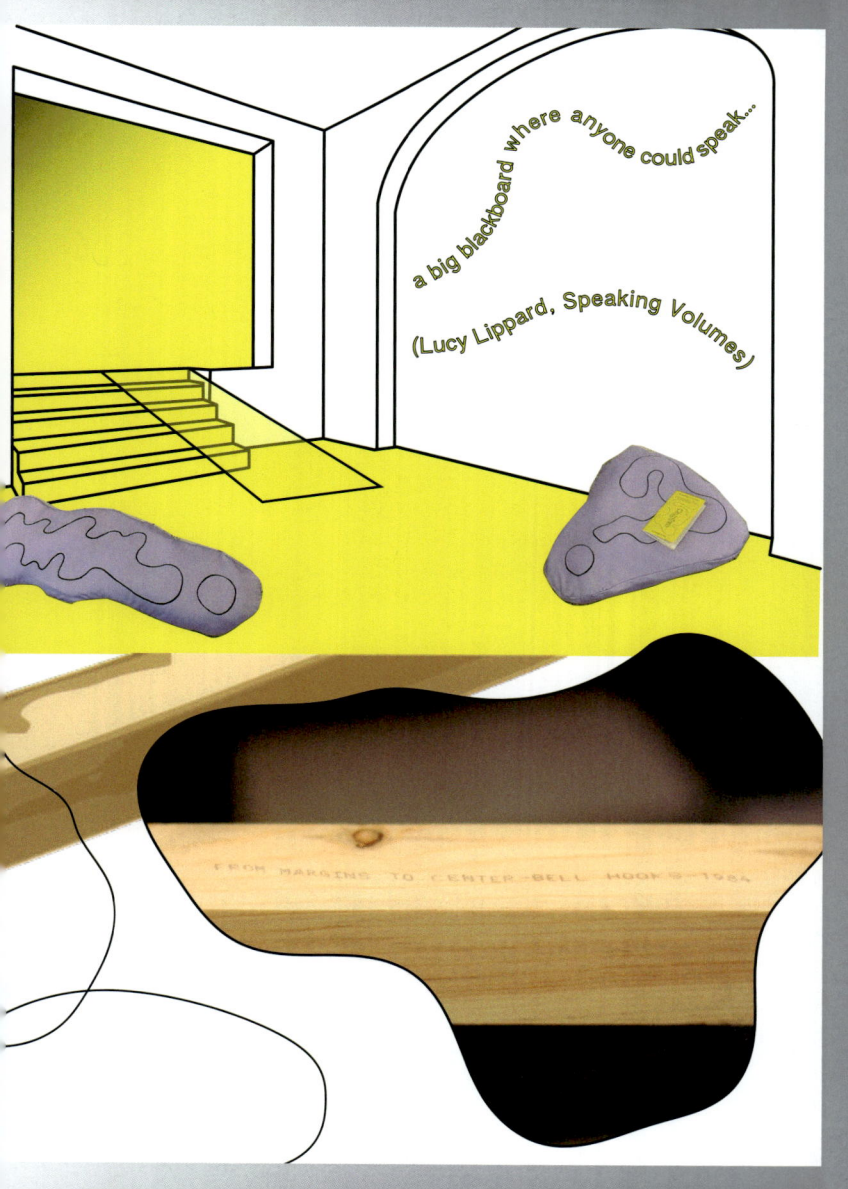

FOUR SMALL EXHIBITIONS
JOHN L. WALTERS

[1] Type and place
Articles from the *Eye* archive that explore types and signs in the city, from London to Berlin, Lisbon, Barcelona, São Paulo, Newcastle (Tyne and Wear), Brisbane, and elsewhere.

[2] Wordless books
A display of international wordless picture books for children from the collection of Clare Walters (my wife), whose *Eye 85* article 'Told in pictures' summarized the contents of her MA thesis. The accompanying web-site and Instagram account have grown to include extensive texts and resources in the under-appreciated field of illustration for children's literature.

[3] Creative music unboxed
The Story of Unknown Public, 1992–2007, with original boxes, texts, CD digipaks, cassettes, posters, and other ephemera from the *UP* archive. With talks by Walters and others about this 'pre-streaming' moment for contemporary creative music.

[4] *Eye* launch
A party to celebrate the latest issue of *Eye*, with German contributors (writers and designers) and friends, and a look back at what has changed since the Berlin special issue—*Eye 74*—in 2009. With copies of *Eye,* wall displays of covers, screenings of the *Eye* short *94: 8000 one-offs,* and other ephemera.

John L. Walters is editor and co-owner of *Eye*, the international review of graphic design, and edits *Pulp* journal for Fedrigoni. Originally a maths/physics graduate, Walters founded electro jazz pop band *Landscape* and worked as a composer and record producer before co-founding the CD journal *Unknown Public*. His writing includes a *Guardian* column and *Alan Kitching: A Life in Letterpress* (2016). He has won three Editor of the Year awards and has programmed 49 Type Tuesdays at the St Bride Foundation in London. / eyemagazine.com /

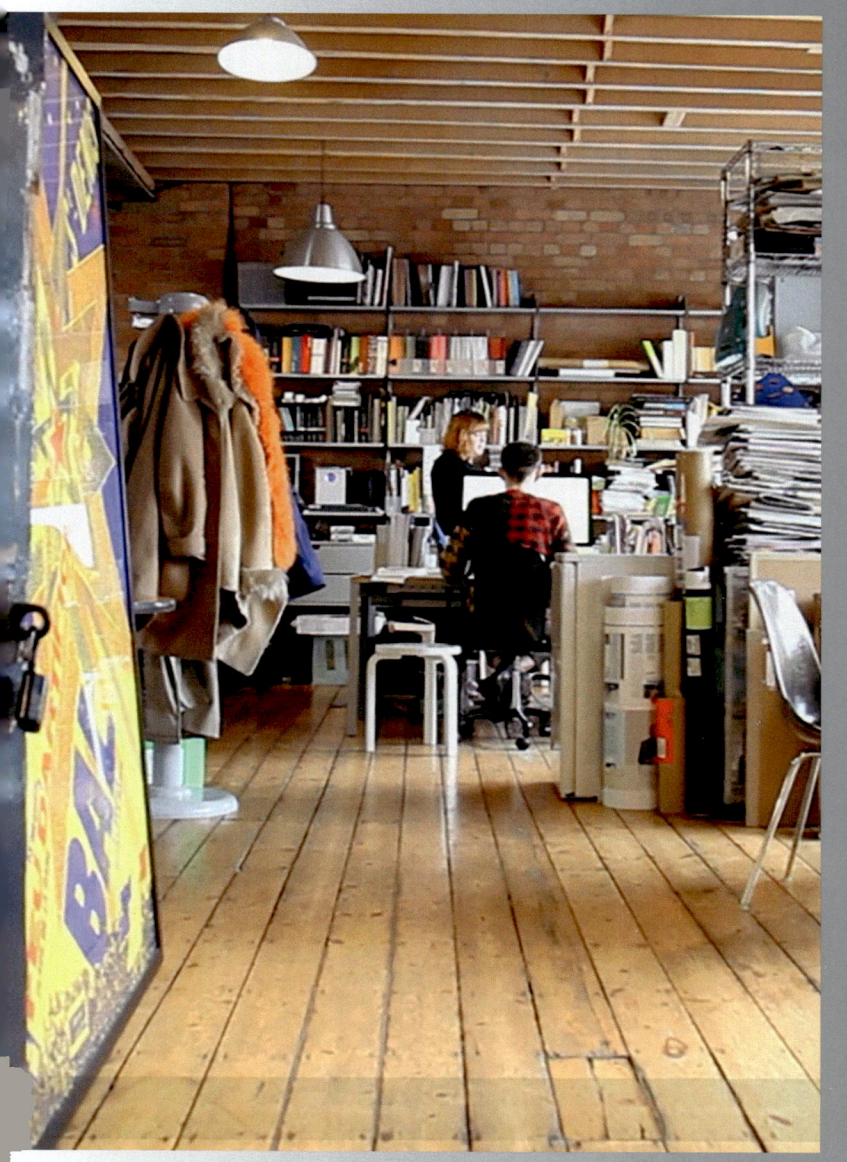

FUTURE GRAPHIC DESIGN'S
26-PIECE THEATER SET
RICHARD NIESSEN

What will the graphic design of the future look like? While we may think that the designer is a genius and that graphic design is intrinsically self-motivated, nothing could be further from the truth: designs are an outcome of a complex set of forces over which we rarely have control. This does not mean that graphic design is a will-less profession, on the contrary, we need to understand that the profession plays a mediating role and always acts within an ever-changing environment. The future of graphic design thus depends on many (perhaps 26) factors, which are interrelated in many ways and can, therefore, form countless different backdrops for the profession. Consider new techniques, changing political relations, or rediscovering a forgotten culture. Constellations of these determinants will undeniably form the scene in which the designer will have to play their part and in which a range of scenarios will be possible. What I present here is a collection of 26 (this is, after all, a proposal for the A—Z space) set pieces, each of which could be a factor in the future stage of graphic design. Depending on which events we think will actually take place and in what proportion or order, a landscape emerges in which the designer will be able to act.

Richard Niessen is a graphic designer living and working in Amsterdam, known for his colorful posters and expressive typography, innovative identities and collaborations with other artists. Besides working in commission, he initiates his autonomous projects, like The Palace of Typographic Masonry, which he started in 2015. It brings together experiment, research, connection with other disciplines, and the embedding of graphic design in a broader cultural history. / richard-niessen.nl /

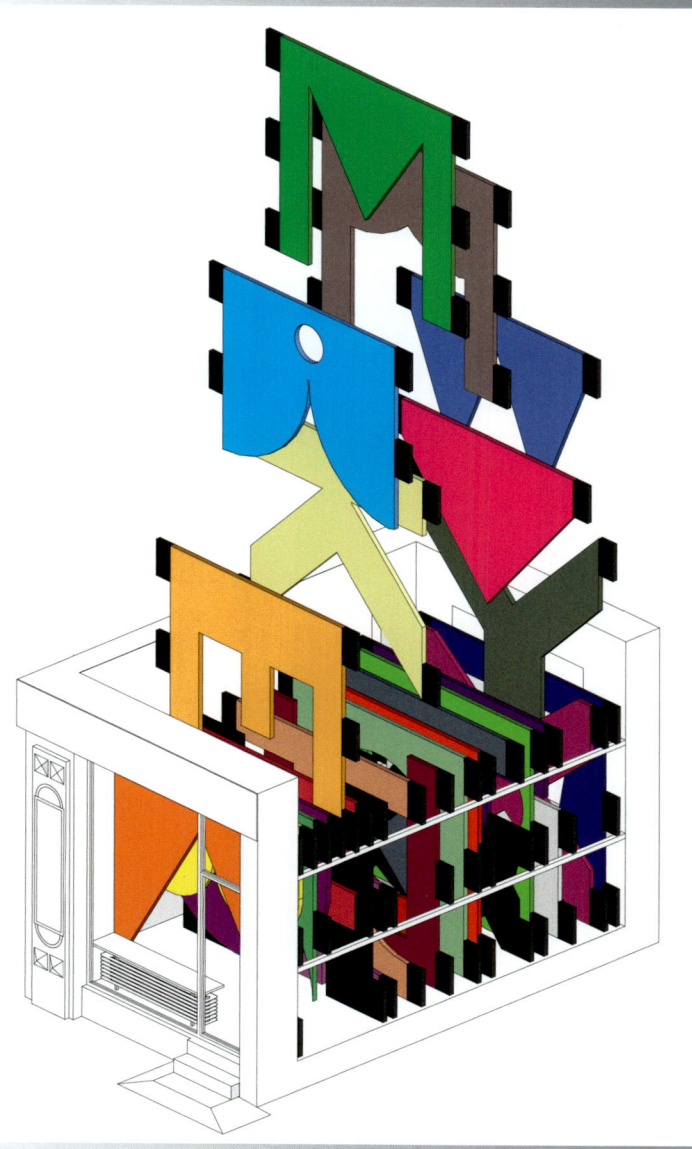

FUTURE SCREENSHOTS
MUSHON

A screenshot is a frozen frame in an interaction flow, a record of a moment in time. Since the first shots were fired on 7 October 2023, and after more than a year of destruction, the reality staring at us from every screen feels like an endless nightmare—a foreign present with no future. But what if we designed screenshots of futures that don't yet exist? I developed *Future Screenshots* as a method to challenge the present, stretch our political imagination, and inspire co-resistance and transformative activism.

The methodology is simple: envision a future, imagine it appearing on someone's screen, and choose one of many screenshot templates to sketch it. For example, a Palestinian and an Israeli chatting about their child's gender ambiguity, a traffic map at the outbreak of a civil war, or a prompt to a future AI: "How was Palestine liberated?"

How do people react? Would they welcome or fear it? Would it challenge their anticipation? We map both hopeful and dreadful screenshots to the *Futures Cone,* an installation of strings, from probable to possible and even preposterous.

The thousands of *Future Screenshots* developed so far don't just tell stories; they serve as landmarks for political imagination. They define our affordances for action in the present and help us chart a path forward, together.

Mushon Zer-Aviv is a designer, writer, educator, and activist based in Tel Aviv. His work explores mapping, wayfinding, and political landscapes, themes central to his research *Friction and Flow—a design theory of change.* He is a board member of A Land For All: Two States, One Homeland, a senior faculty member at Shenkar College, and an Eyebeam alumnus. / mushon.com /

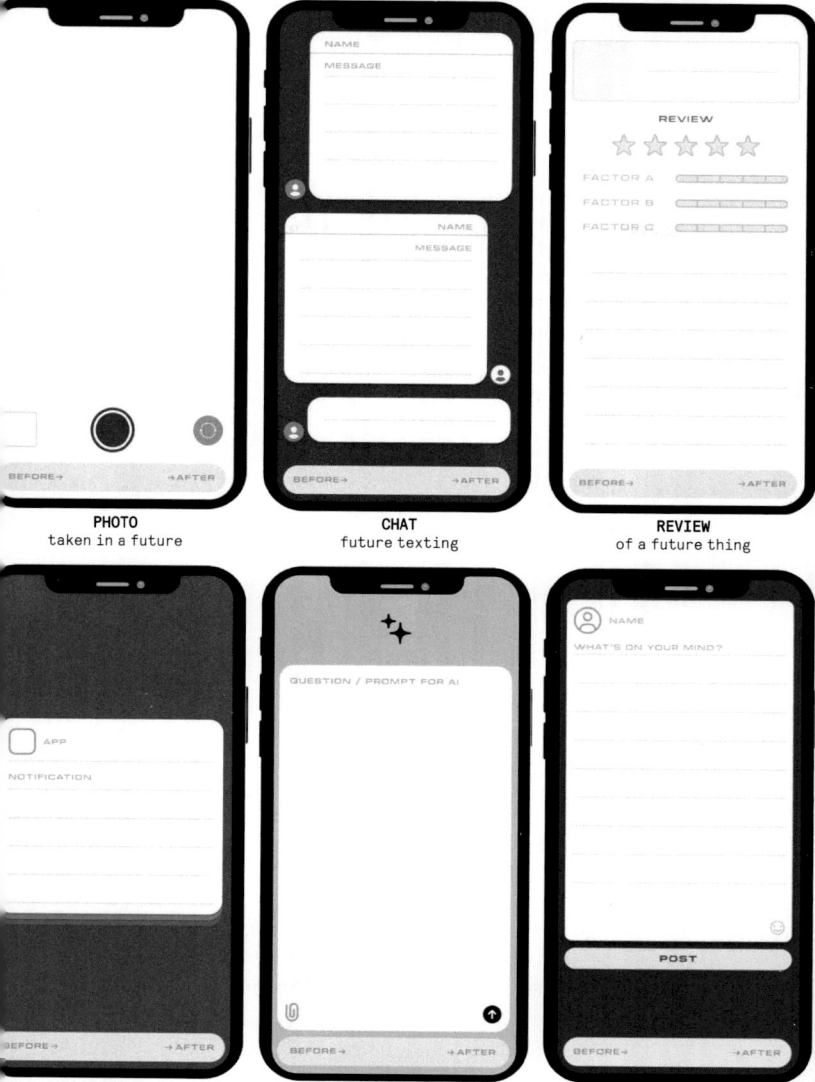

FUTURE SCREENSHOTS

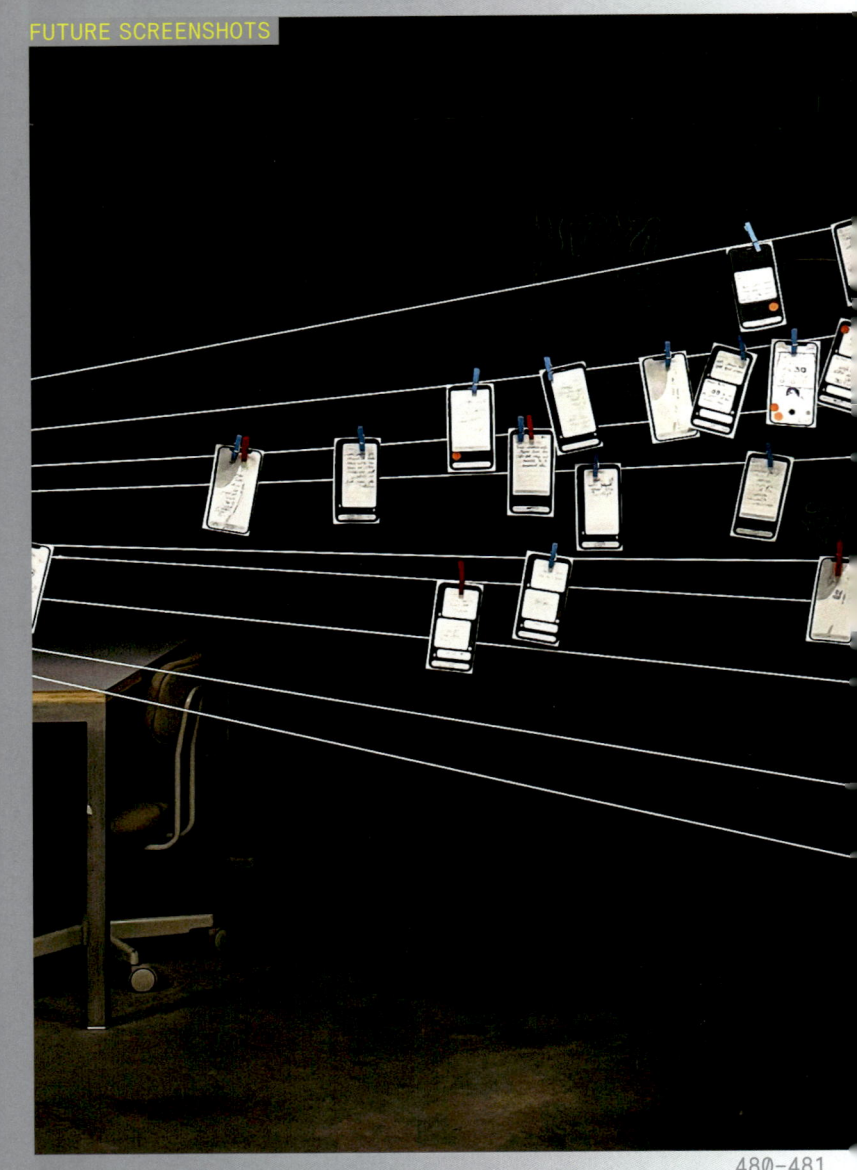

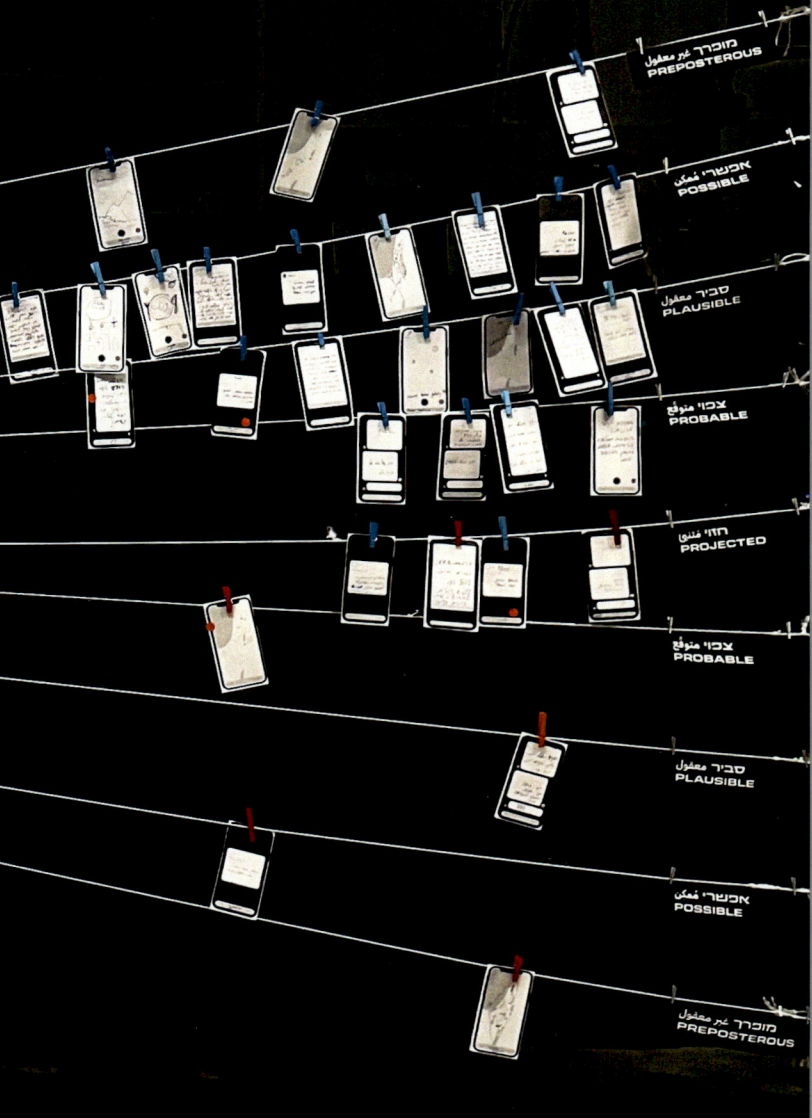

IN TRANSITION
JOSEPH FOO

Graphic design is evolving. The discipline is being reset and recalibrated to meet new standards for a rapidly changing world. Traditional frameworks blur as AI and automation reshape authorship and intention. The grid bends, type fractures, and meaning shifts.

Yet design remains a practice of clarity—not excess, but distillation. Not noise, but resonance. As old frameworks dissolve, new visual languages emerge, demanding not just technical skill but critical thinking, adaptability, and intent.

Still, the fundamental role of the designer endures: to make the intangible visible, to create order from chaos, and to shape how we perceive the world.

The future of graphic design may seem unchanged to some, but it is never the same for many.

Joseph Foo. Creative Director of 3nity, drives design and social innovation through various initiatives. He recently co-founded KongsiKL and REXKL to repurpose old buildings in his hometown Kuala Lumpur. He also champions community-focused transformation projects, and serves as a jury member for awards such as the Cannes Lions, London International Awards, and Creative Circle Awards. Most recently, he was curator for the *Guangzhou Triennial*. / 3nitydesign.com /

grahpic
deisgn

INCLUSIVE, PERSONAL, AMBIGUOUS AND COMPLEX
SILVIA SFLIGIOTTI

Silvia Sfligiotti is a designer based in Milan, working, teaching, researching, and writing in and around visual communication. For decades she has been involved in design education, where she uses critical methods along with the knowledge she gathered practicing conscious movement and dance improvisation. She has developed the concept of somatic research for design as the place where experimental design practice and collective embodied critical thinking come together.
/ silviasfligiotti.it /

I don't see graphic design as a practice that can have a real, widespread impact by itself; I regard it mostly as a sign of the times. That's maybe why I rarely think about its future.

But I do sometimes have a wish or maybe a dream. It's located in an unspecified moment in time, beyond the current obsessive drive against human and non-human life.

I'm not sure whether graphic design will still be regarded as a profession. What I'm quite sure about is that people will still communicate visually with each other, with the means that will be available at that point in time. My wish, or dream, is that learning and reflection around it will still be happening.

When thinking about how I could use the A—Z space in the future, I thought of these four words that Sheila Levrant de Bretteville used to describe design in an essay she wrote in 1974. More than 50 years later, they still make sense to me, and I would love them to be part of the discourse in that unspecified future. I imagine them taking up space in the gallery—and inviting people to move through and around them, surrounded by samples of whatever we will call 'graphic design.'

INCLUSIVE PERSONAL AMBIGUOUS COMPLEX

INTERDISCIPLINARY GRAPHIC DESIGN
JORDAN RITA SERUYA AWORI

As an interdisciplinary artist, my vision for A—Z is to push graphic design beyond static, two-dimensional surfaces into a fluid, immersive, and interactive experience. Graphic design is not just print or screen—it is an evolving language that intersects with performance, installation, sound, digital media, and spatial design. Imagine a design that begins as a video on a screen, spills onto walls via projection, transforms into a mural, extends onto printed materials, moves onto three-dimensional objects, and even integrates with wearables. But it doesn't stop there—imagine those printed elements folding into sculptural forms, shifting as viewers interact with them. A projected graphic could be altered by motion sensors, responding in real time to the people within the space, creating a design that breathes and adapts.

A—Z has the potential to become a space where these boundaries are dissolved—where typography moves through physical space, where augmented reality extends to print, and where graphic design is not just seen but experienced. By fostering experimentation across disciplines, the space can redefine what graphic design is and what it can become, positioning it as a limitless medium for storytelling, interaction, and transformation.

Jordan Rita Seruya Awori is an unapologetically loud-mouthed, emotionally charged, interdisciplinary Kenyan artist based in Frankfurt. With a distinctive blend of cultural influences and experiences, Jordan's artistry defies categorization. Her interdisciplinary approach transcends boundaries, aiming to ignite challenging dialogues and provoke introspective contemplation.
/ jordanawori.com /

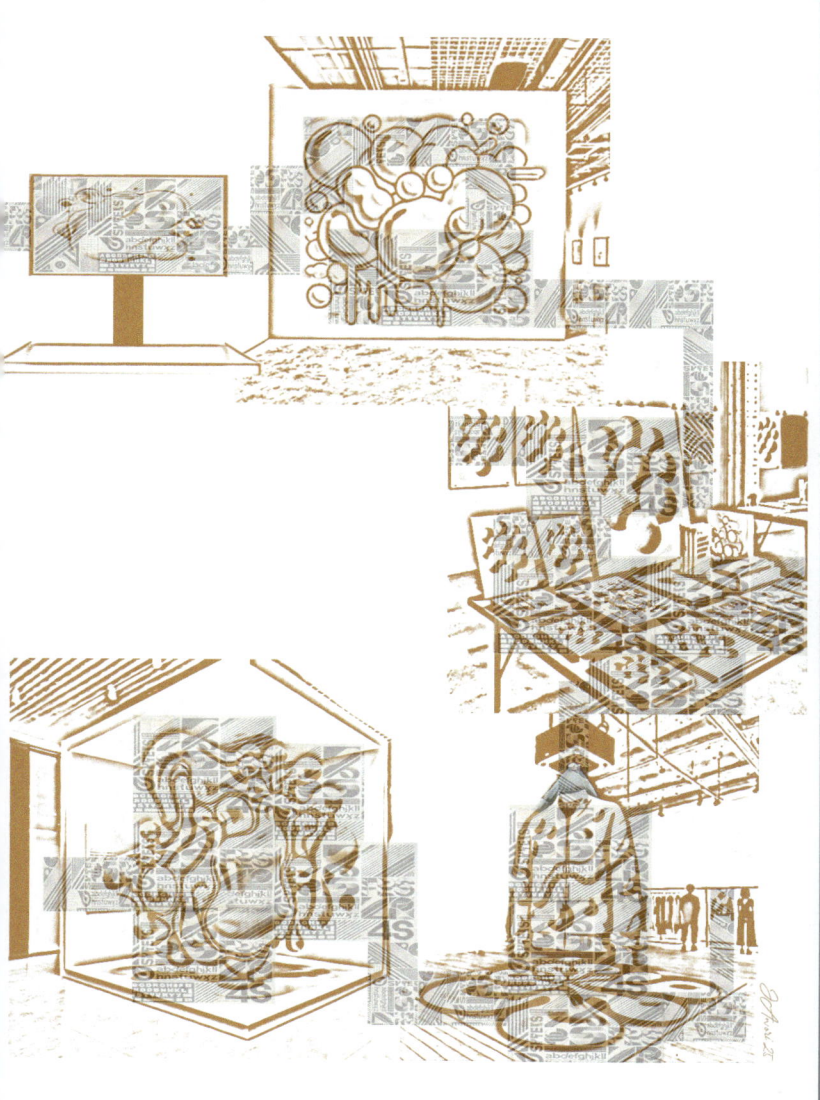

INTERSPECIES RELATIONSHIPS
REBECA MÉNDEZ

The *Biophilia Treehouse* is a public arts initiative to create and grow a series of living sculptures using native trees and plants that together constitute a complete ecosystem for some of LA's most threatened birds. When built in sequence, a series of *Biophilia Treehouses* form a wildlife corridor for these birds that reconnect fractured habitats, especially in dense urban parts of our city where environmental inequities abound.

In collaboration with our community partners, we co-create artistic insignia onto the structure that tell the story of the community's relationship to the land. The ground floor of each *Biophilia Treehouse* sculpture is used by our education-based community partners as an outdoor laboratory for arts + science instruction to primary school students. The *Biophilia Treehouse* is about co-creating art and storytelling with communities, arts and science education, biodiversity, and the reconnection of bird habitats, as well as responding to inequities in access to park space.

Rebeca Méndez is an interdisciplinary artist, designer, and educator who examines reciprocal relationships and environmental justice in a multi-species world amid climate change, mass extinction, and a ravaging extractivist society. Her research-based works manifest as public art, immersive video and sound installations, photography, graphic design, and performance. / counterforcelab.org/biophilia-treehouse-overview // rebecamendez.com /

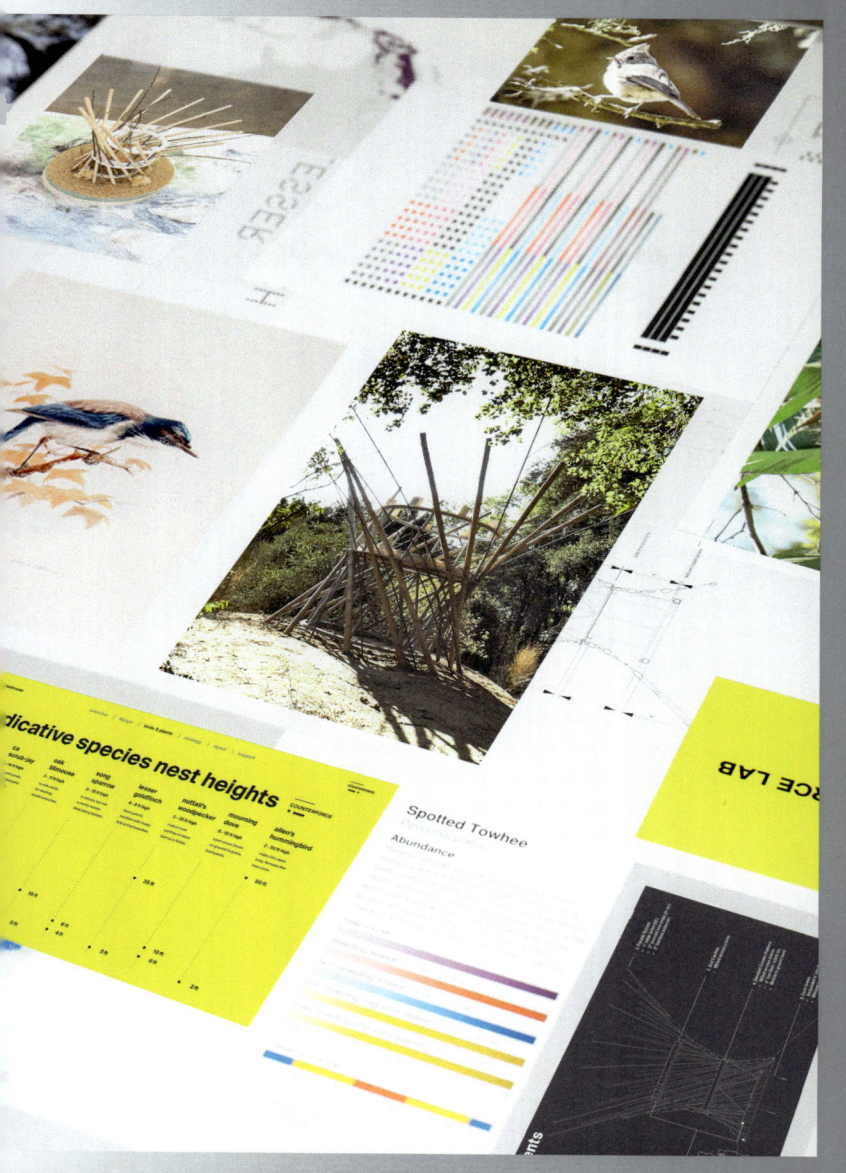

LATE FUTURISM: REQUIEM FOR A DREAM
SILVIO LORUSSO

I want to make a confession: I have a hard time taking seriously the whole conceptual scaffolding that supports preferable futures and the radical imagination. Of course, just as there are, within this system of ideas, naïve and simplistic variants, there are also more subtle and elaborate ones, but my skepticism invests its fundamental assumption: the belief that the future, whether conceived as singular or multiple, lies further along the timeline; that the future is what, in a more or less predictable, more or less surprising, more or less controlled way, has yet to happen. Sadly, the future is not that, or rather, it is no longer that. From my point of view—and not only mine, as I shall show—today, the future is nothing more than a mode of existence of the present, a style; it is, to put it more bluntly, a senescent idea that drags on to us.

Silvio Lorusso is an artist and designer based in Lisbon. He published *Entreprecariat* (Onomatopee) in 2019 and *What Design Can't Do* (Set Margins) in 2023. He is an Assistant Professor at the Lusófona University in Lisbon and a tutor at the Information Design department of Design Academy, Eindhoven. Born in Altamura, Italy, Lorusso holds a PhD in Design Sciences from the Iuav University of Venice. / silviolorusso.com /

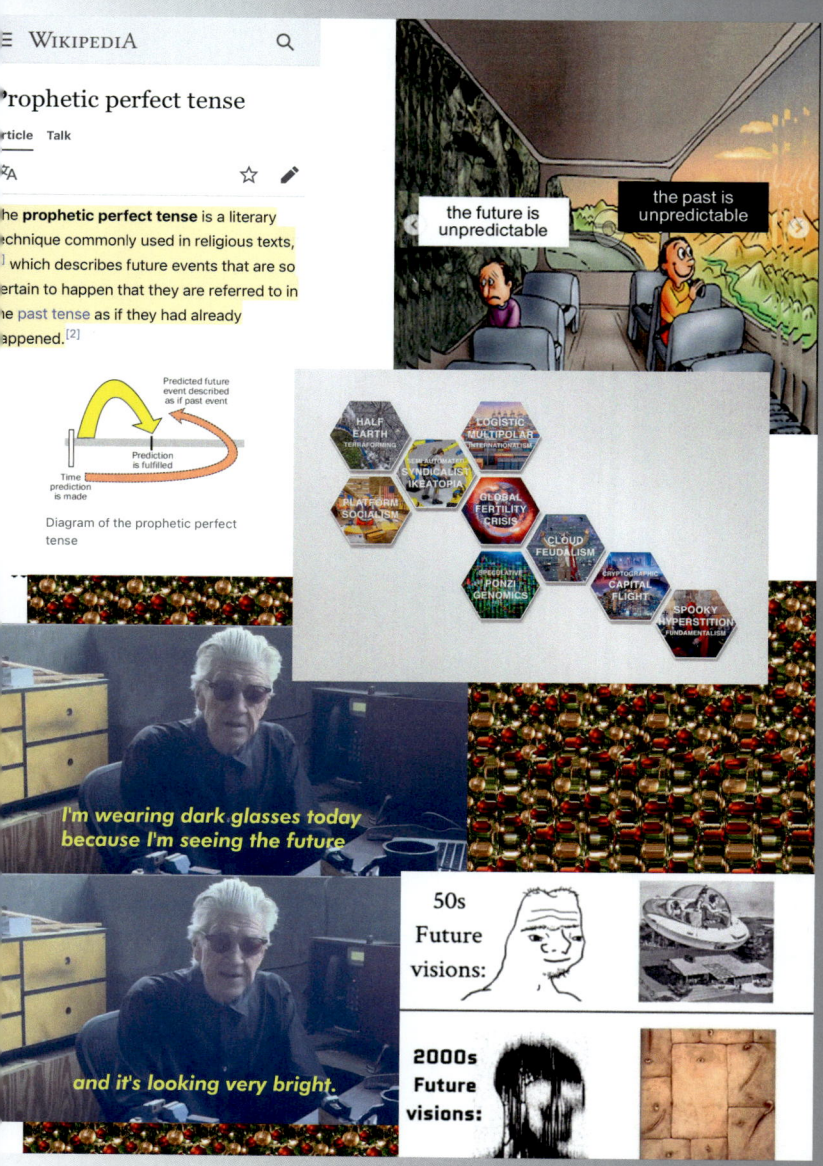

LIFE, AI, TECHNOLOGY
JULIA KAHL

Language is not static—it shifts, evolves, and reshapes meaning through context and interpretation. My work explores the intersections of language, image, and communication as dynamic processes in constant transformation. Spontaneity and creative exploration play a central role, allowing structures to dissolve and new forms to emerge. ASCII-Art reduces language to its essence, transforming letters, numbers, and symbols into visual compositions. This abstraction opens space for interpretation, where words become images, and images become messages. The constraints of the medium create a paradox—limitation fosters possibility. Bold slogans on life, AI, and technology dissolve into patterns of coded expression, inviting reflection on the blurred boundaries between human thought, digital logic, and the uncertain future ahead. Since 2023, I have been experimentally engaging with current political and social issues in the form of 12-page zines. I explore the intersections of language, image, and meaning—not as fixed forms but as dynamic processes in constant flux. As a medium of reflection and communication.

Julia Kahl is co-founder of Slanted Publishers, an independent design, publishing, and media house established in 2014 with Lars Harmsen. Slanted produces *Slanted Magazine*, slanted.de, and books on typography, design, and visual culture, earning it global recognition. As a designer, editor, and publisher, she oversees the entire creative process. Passionate about typography and print, she lectures, speaks at conferences, and serves as a juror for international design competitions.
/ slanted.de // linkedin.com/in/julia-kahl /

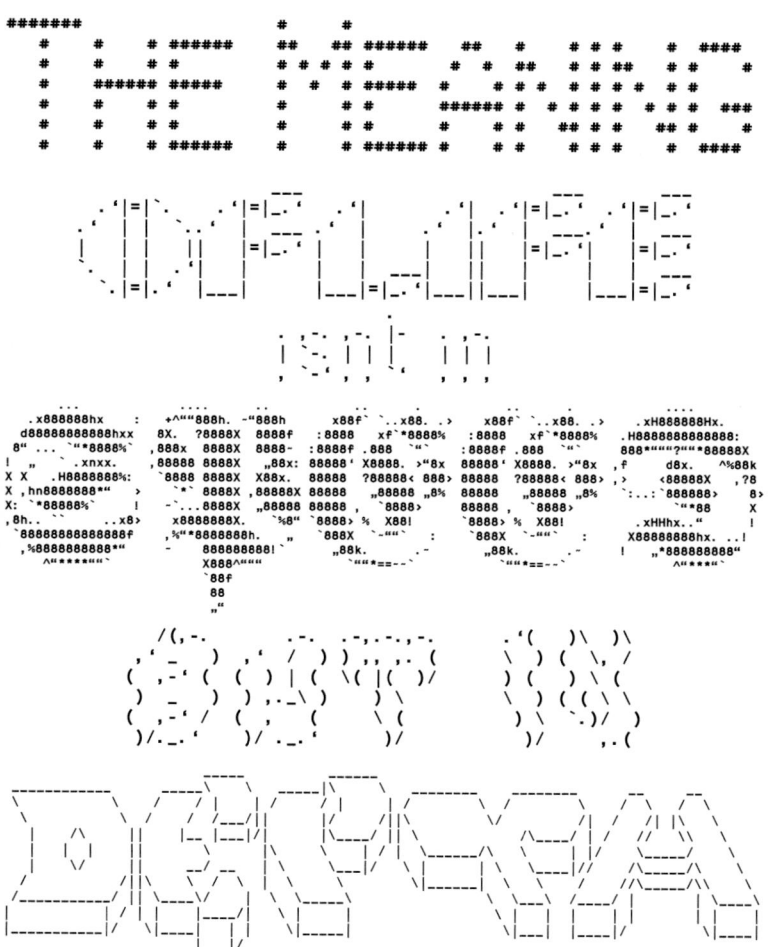

LIFE, AI, TECHNOLOGY

The Search for Machine Intelligence

```
      ,ggg,        gg      ,gg
     dP""Y8a       88    ,8P'    ,dPYb,
     Yb, `88       88   d8'      IP'`Yb
      `"  88       88   88       I8  8I
          88       88   88       I8  8'
          88       88   88       I8 dPgg,      ,gggg,
          88       88   88       I8dP" "8I    dP"  "Y8ggg
          Y8    , 88,   8P       I8P    I8   i8'    ,8I
           Yb,,d8""8b,,dP       ,d8     I8, ,d8,   ,d8'
            "88"   "88"         88P     `Y8P"Y8888P"
```

DIE FUNDE

AUS

DER

MAMMA

MAPPING GRAPHIC DESIGN FUTURES
SANDRA DOELLER

Graphic design is continuously reshaped by digitalization, shifting aesthetic paradigms, and critical discourse. Yet, despite many engaged contributions, the documentation and representation of these discourses remain fragmented, often reaching only small, isolated audiences. What if everything was brought together?

Imagine a collaborative, open-access research platform and time capsule spanning from 2000 (the shift toward digital design) through 2025 (the rise of AI) to 2050, mapping and documenting contemporary graphic design in both theory and practice. This evolving archive connects design practitioners, researchers, students, and educators, gathering contributions that critically reflect on the field's relevance and criteria for design.

The platform includes:
—A meta-library of books, articles, interviews, and multimedia resources, making theoretical discourse accessible.
—An open archive of projects, providing context and arguments for their submission.
—A space to discuss and rethink the criteria for contemporary and future graphic design.

A—Z introduces the platform with an installation and a series of panels, inviting visitors to contribute their reflections and references: What has shaped your understanding of graphic design? What should be preserved, questioned, or redefined?

Sandra Doeller is a graphic designer specializing in book, poster, and exhibition design with a conceptual approach and a focus on typography. In 2013, she founded Bureau Sandra Doeller in Frankfurt am Main, whose work has been awarded and exhibited internationally. She teaches regularly at various art and design schools and co-initiated *GrafikdesignDenkenSprechen*, a platform for interdisciplinary reflection on graphic design at the intersection of applied and fine arts. / sandradoeller.com /

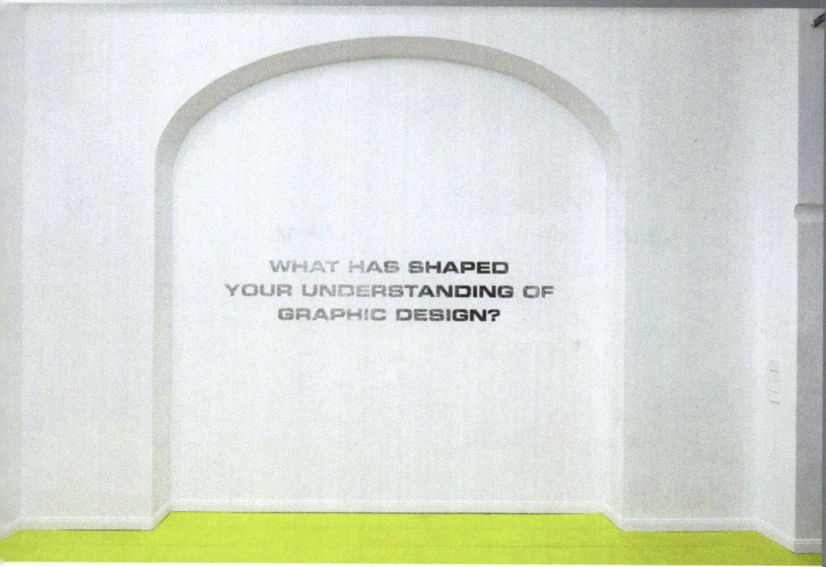

WHAT HAS SHAPED
YOUR UNDERSTANDING OF
GRAPHIC DESIGN?

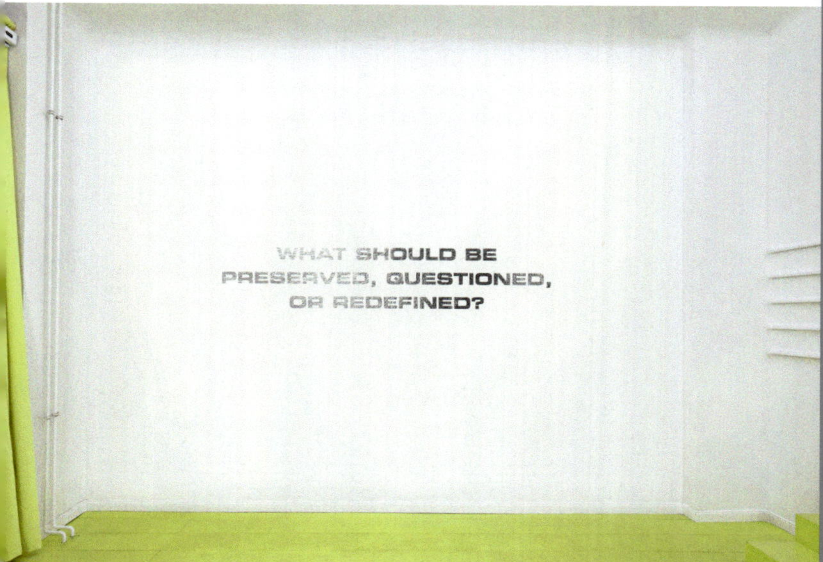

WHAT SHOULD BE
PRESERVED, QUESTIONED,
OR REDEFINED?

MERZBLOK: AGAINST THE INFINITE JEST OF POSTMODERN CULTURE

ELLIOTT EARLS

This project transforms A—Z into a spatial and sculptural essay—a contemporary reworking of Kurt Schwitters's *Merzbau* constructed as critique. *MERZBLOK* engages directly with the downstream effects of postmodern philosophy on visual culture: this installation re-examines truth, teleology, and optimism—not as utopian gestures but as deliberate, critical positions. The work is composed of CNC-milled typography carved from high-density urethane foam, hand-painted, and resin-coated. The dimensional typography is not decorative—it asserts presence. Typography here becomes sculptural, architectural, and spatial. Text fragments from theory, pop culture, and literature form a layered but earnest discourse. In parallel, a series of CNC-machined sculptures anchor the installation. These fabricated objects are composed of industrial geometries and precision-cut surfaces—silent, exacting forms that counterbalance the ephemerality of digital culture with mass and stillness. Spatially, *MERZBLOK* challenges the neutrality of the white cube. It interrupts circulation, reshapes visibility, and resists being read or consumed. Instead, it invites the viewer into an encounter with a rigorous, intentional, and ideologically charged form. Rather than echoing the postmodern detachment, *MERZBLOK* proposes a different future.

Elliott Earls is Designer-in-Residence at Cranbrook Academy of Art. / youtube.com/c/StudioPractice1 /

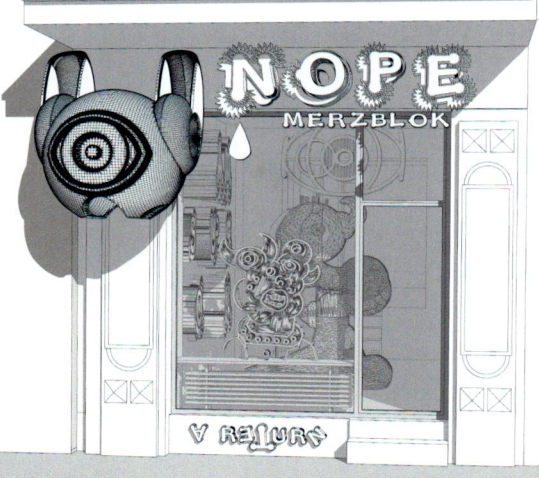

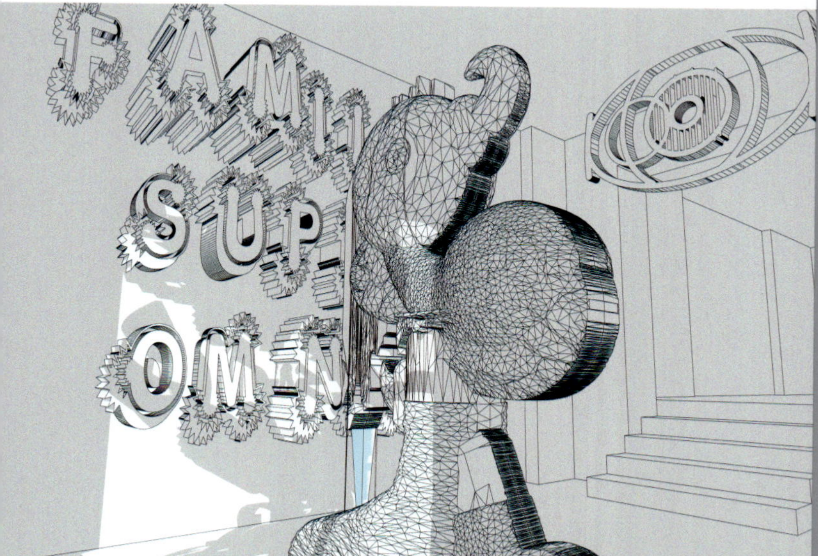

MUTABLE FORMS
CHRISTOPHER SLEBODA & KATHLEEN SLEBODA

The future of typography will not be static; it will be a living, evolving entity responsive to sound, touch, and the passage of time. Through sound-reactive type, environment-interacted forms, and interactive installations, *Mutable Forms* explores how letterforms can shift, decay, and regenerate in real time. Installations demonstrate type physically transforming in response to sound waves, weather conditions, and organic growth, symbolizing the impermanence and adaptability of design. As typography interacts with its surroundings—whether through shifting frequencies or in response to other sensory cues—it will no longer simply communicate but become part of a dynamic, ever-changing landscape. Visitors will witness typography as it cycles through life stages, ultimately redefining our collective understanding of type as a medium that evolves with time and its environment.

Christopher Sleboda and Kathleen Sleboda (nie7kepmx) have run Draw Down Books, their publishing imprint and online bookshop, since 2012. In addition to teaching graphic design at Boston University and Rhode Island School of Design, the pair organize art book fairs, write about publishing, and have exhibited their work at fairs around the world. / draw-down.com /

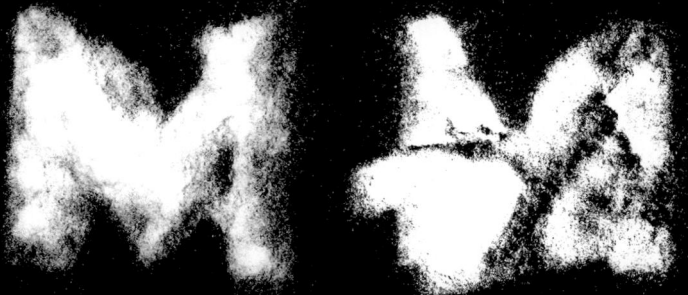

OUT OF SPACE
JAMES LANGDON

Graphic design will run out of space. Virgin materials used up, graphic design will no longer imagine itself in relation to standardized, rectangular surfaces of the display. There will be no blank pages and no white space. No paper merchants with vast warehouses of pure white sheets awaiting the graphic designer's specification. Paper will be collected in spaces like A—Z. Sorted, cleaned, and carefully reused. Generic affinities between format and content: forgotten. Novels will not be portable, not for the pocket and not for the hand. Picture books will not be for opening wide and flat. What fits on pages will fit where fit is found. Graphic design will revert to palimpsestic moves. Done adhoc. Horror vacui will be the responsibility and the imperative of every graphic designer.

James Langdon is an educator, designer, and writer. His PhD, from RMIT University, Melbourne, concerns isomorphism (or 'unreasonable fidelity') in communication design. / typohypergraphicobject.page /

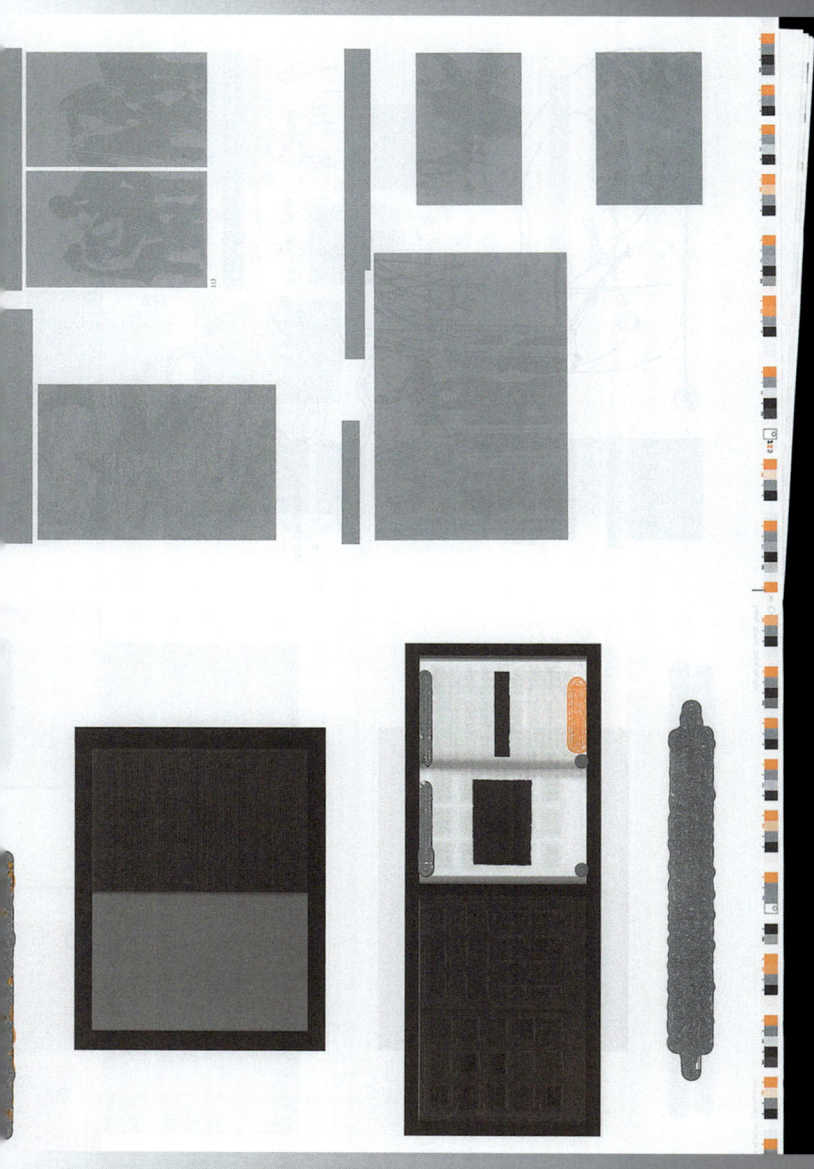

PAST TENSE ; NOW
SARA KAAMAN

Welcome to the future of graphic design; graphic design is no more. We're left with an abundance of memories, and we will collectively trace them. A—Z will host this process via soft cushions all around, hot tea, fresh fruit, and a selection of technological relics from back in the day. We will build a temporary museum of what used to be graphic design practice. Join to relive and reconcile.

We'll remember designer bodies. We'll remember exhausted designer bodies. We'll remember being seated in front of laptops, tapping away at the keyboard (softly, softly), and feeling our chests harden and burn. We'll remember Wi-Fi! What was that? We'll remember "I hope this email finds you well". We'll remember Adobe and its crash. We'll remember how our bodies were separate from our minds, our fingers separate from our hearts. We'll remember individuality—how it felt like. We'll remember paper samples, now expensive collectibles! We'll remember when lichen started to grow on all things made of aluminum and glass. We'll remember select all and force quit. We'll remember the sleepiness and sleeplessness. We'll remember how—toward the end—we nourished those parts of ourselves that knew that another way of living this life and caring for this world was possible. We'll remember how we made it happen.

Sara Kaaman's work explores the politics and poetics of publishing as public action and performance. Using a variety of strategies including writing, printmaking, teaching, publication-making by movement, paper, voice, drawing, and video, she sets up conditions to make language move. She co-edits the queer and feminist magazine *Girls Like Us* and is a member of MMS, a research collective tracing womxn's labor histories in graphic design. She lives next to a large forest in a Stockholm suburb. / sarakaaman.com /

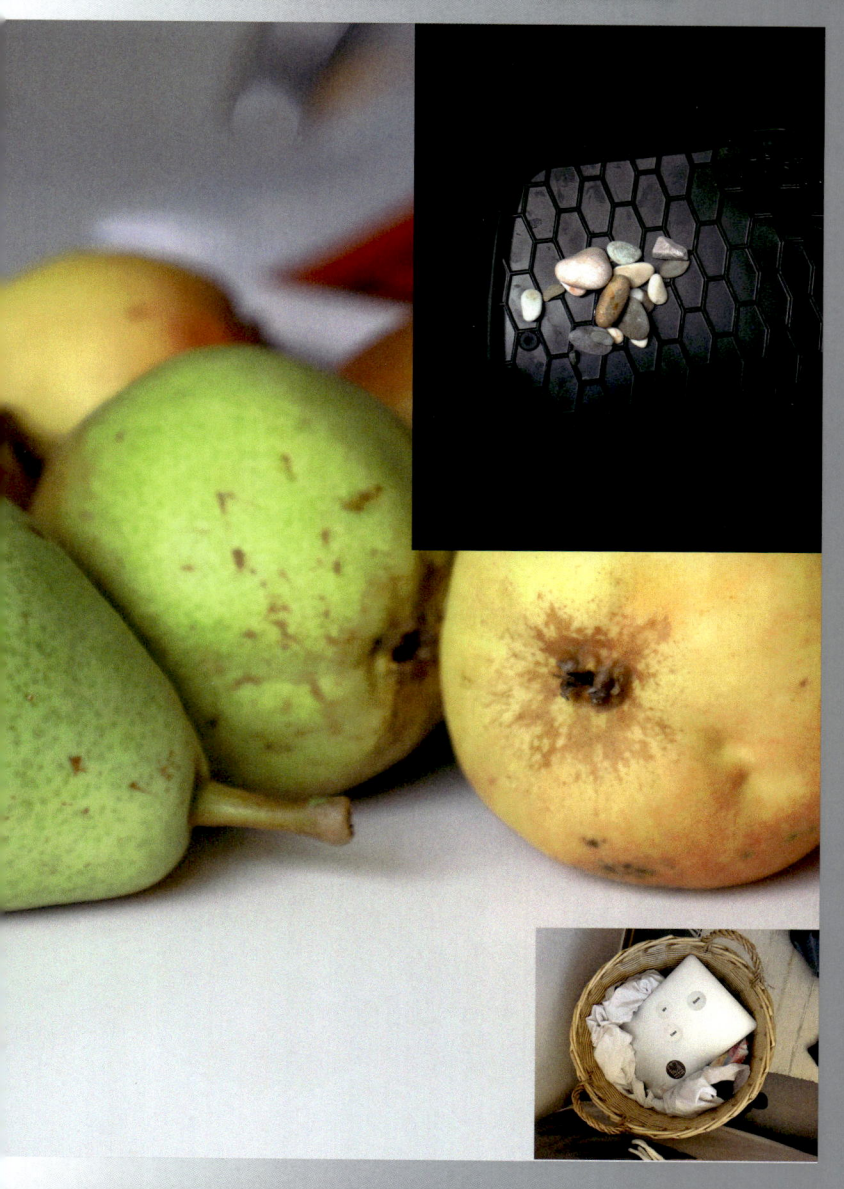

PAST TENSE; NOW

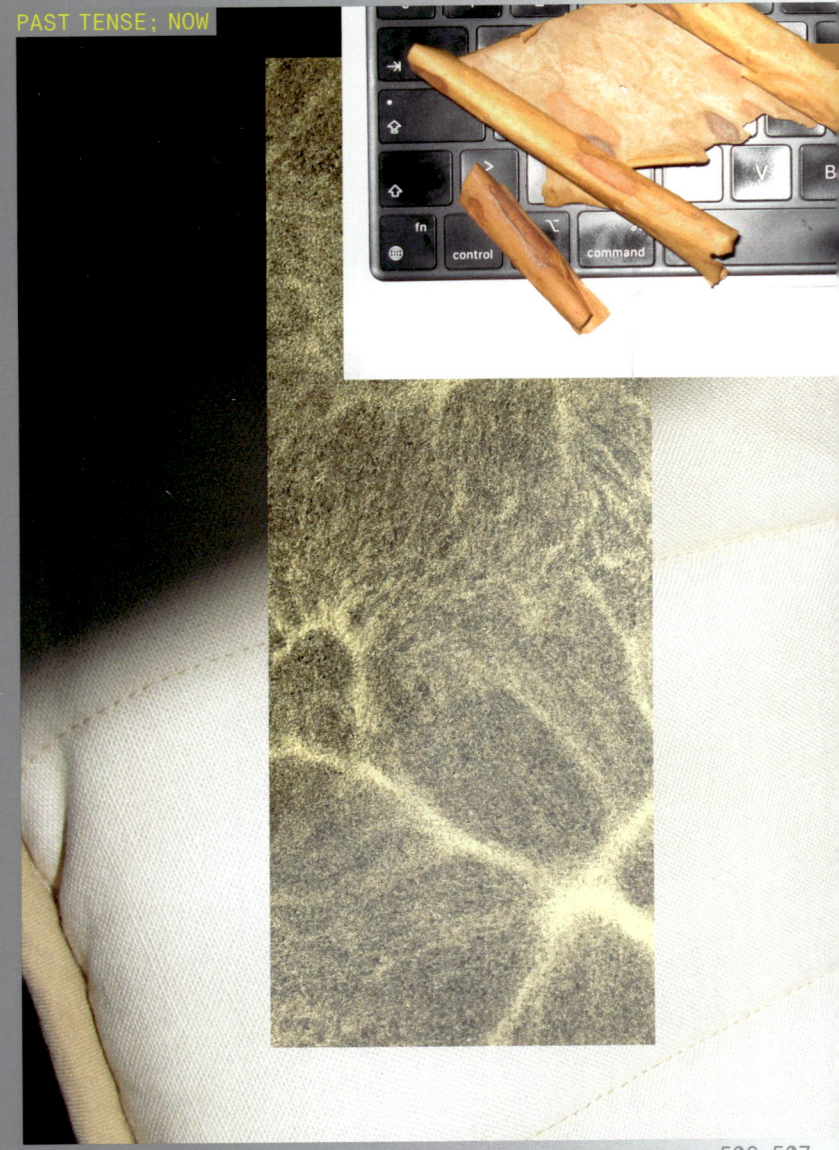

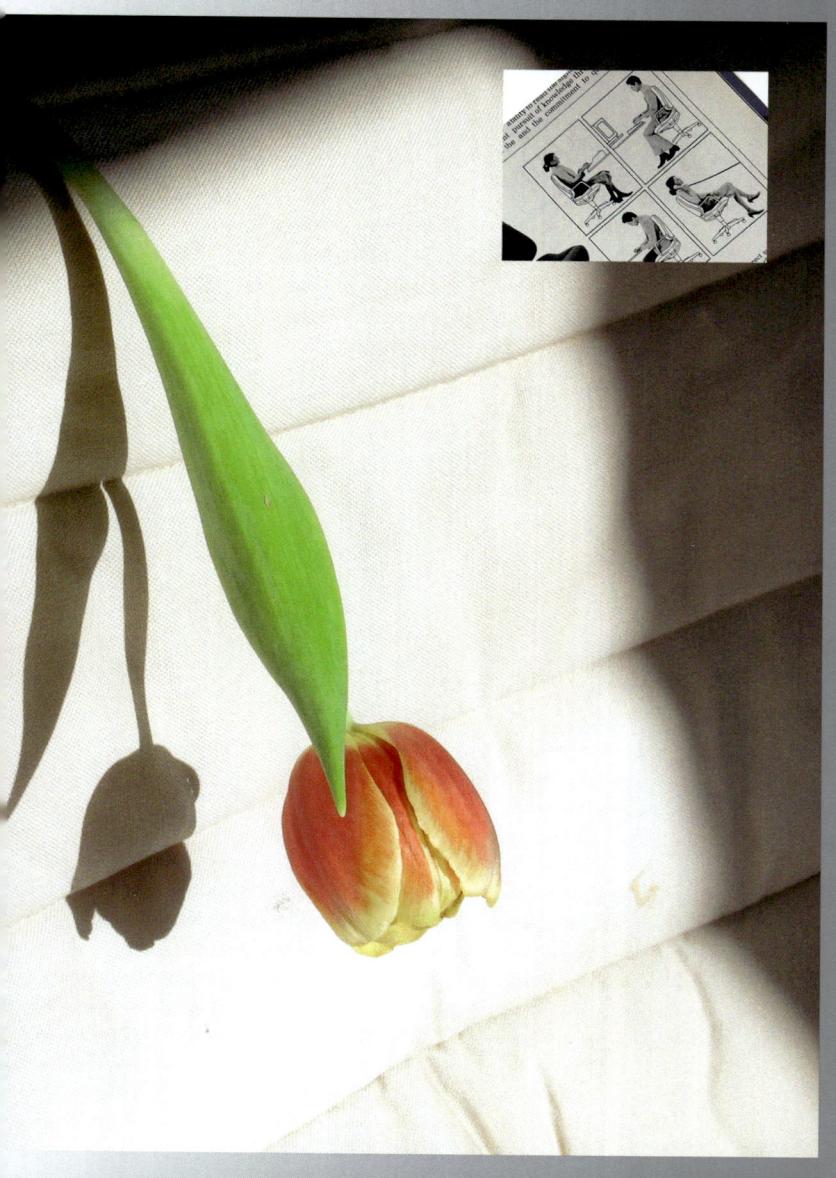

POST EVERYTHING
ULRIKE BRÜCKNER & BIANCA HERLO

"... Design has the power and the potential to make hidden problems and grievances visible and at the same time point out new paths in society. Designers are, among many other things, also seismographs and, as such, predestined to develop socially engaged designs—in other words, to do more than just make products visible. If we do not want to leave it to the economy to define what role design will play in the future, it is up to us to set new standards. We have the knowledge, the power, and the opportunity to change design from within. We have experience and are trained to point out problems. And we have the tools to do so. The hype surrounding new technological developments that are based on stochastic processes does not unsettle us. For us, it is yet another reason for us to think about the future of design.

If each of us works on our own projects for just one day a week or month, it is possible to help drive change in design.

Due to the social upheavals, the pressure on design and on us designers is high. At the same time, anything seems possible at the moment because old certainties are disappearing, and we designers find ourselves in a situation where, if we don't risk anything, we can only lose. ..."

Ulrike Brückner works on artistic and applied projects in the visual communication field. Since 2018 she has been a Professor for Communication Design at the Department of Design at the Fachhochschule Dortmund. Bianca Herlo has been Chair of the board of the German Society for Design Theory and Research (DGTF). Braunschweig since 2021. Since 2024 she has been Professor of Eco-Social Design at Lucerne University of Applied Sciences and Arts (HSLU), and Head of the Competence Center Transformation Design.
/ www.musterfirma.org / instagram.com/ulrike.brueckner / instagram.com/bianca.herlo /

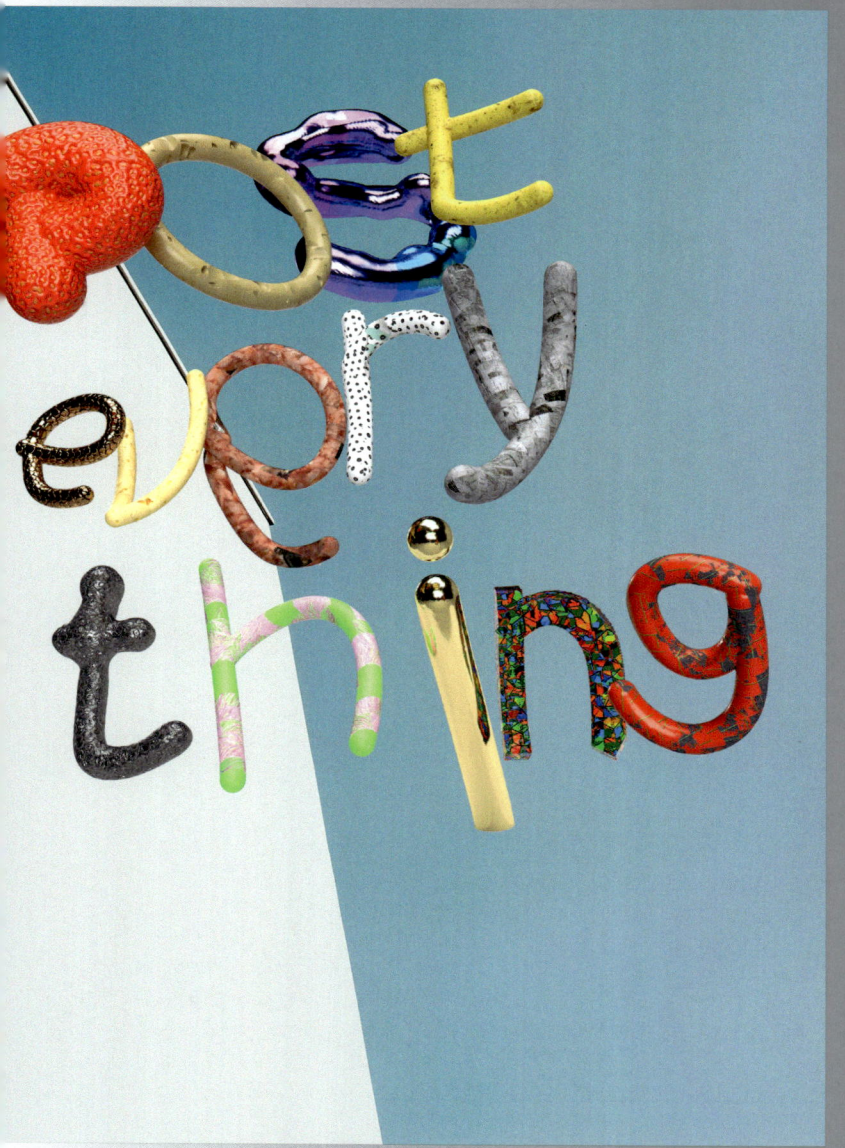

RBOOMK
MARTÍ GUIXÉ

A 19-page blank RBooMK.

Martí Guixé graduated in Barcelona and Milan as an interior and industrial designer in 1994. He started to exhibit his work in 1997, work that characterizes the search for new product systems that alter lifestyles, the introduction of design in food ambits, and presentation through performance. His unconventional gaze provides brilliant and simple ideas of a curious seriousness. Based in Barcelona and Berlin, he works as a designer for companies worldwide. / guixe.com /

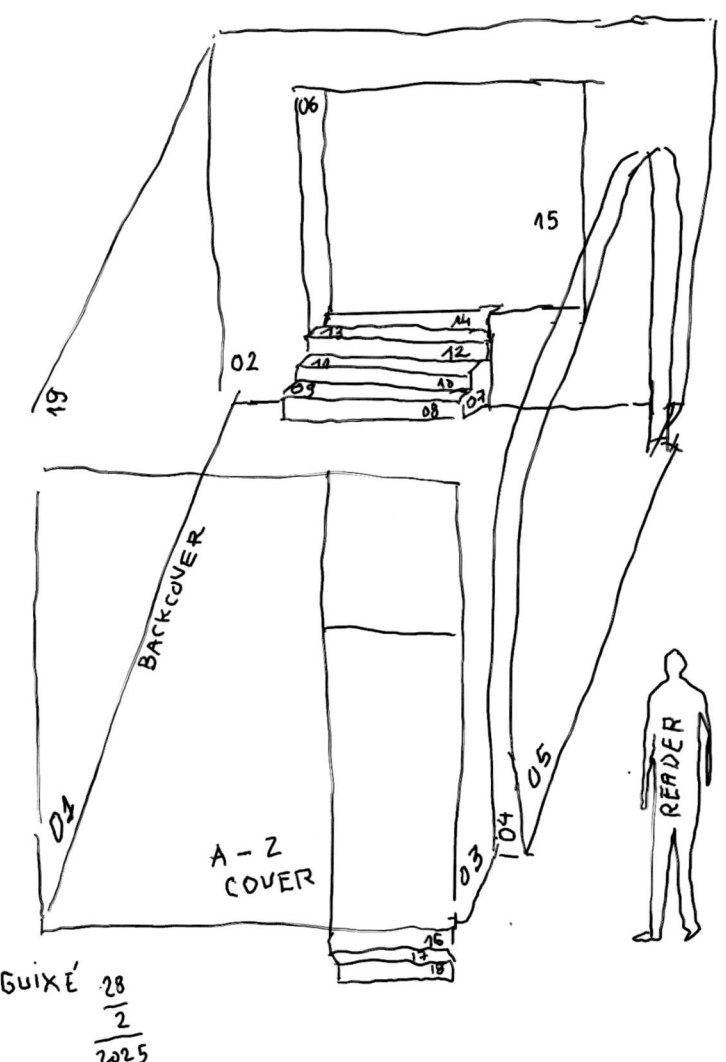

REFLECTION
GOLNAR KAT-RAHMANI

I believe the world is in urgent need of reflection. The future can't be truly improved unless society chooses to confront its issues and engage in deep self-examination to initiate change. This must begin with each of us. Taking time to observe ourselves—to rethink, to reflect on our thoughts and behaviors in relation to others and within ourselves—is essential. In the center of the room, there will be a double-sided, round mirror ca. 150 cm wide, installed on a motorized base that will rotate vertically. Both sides of it will feature inscribed text while still allowing viewers to see their own reflections. The gallery space will be adorned with numerous small mirrors, assembled into larger artistic compositions written "reflection" in Persian, Hebrew and English—some geometric, others freeform—all carefully arranged to achieve aesthetic balance across the walls and partially on the ceiling. This immersive environment will surround visitors with reflections from multiple angles. Visitors will see themselves fragmented into countless pieces as they move through the space—an effect created by the broken mirrors.

Each shard captures a different aspect of their reflection. This experience serves as a metaphor for self-perception.

Golnar Kat-Rahmani is an Iranian graphic designer and lecturer based in Berlin. She runs her studio focused on type design and multilingual typography. Through her initial project, *Type & Politics*, she aims to free Arabic-Persian letters from political and ideological biases for peaceful coexistence. She has lectured and led workshops across Europe and at international conferences, and teaches intercultural Design Knowledge in Practice in German academia. / katrahmani.com /

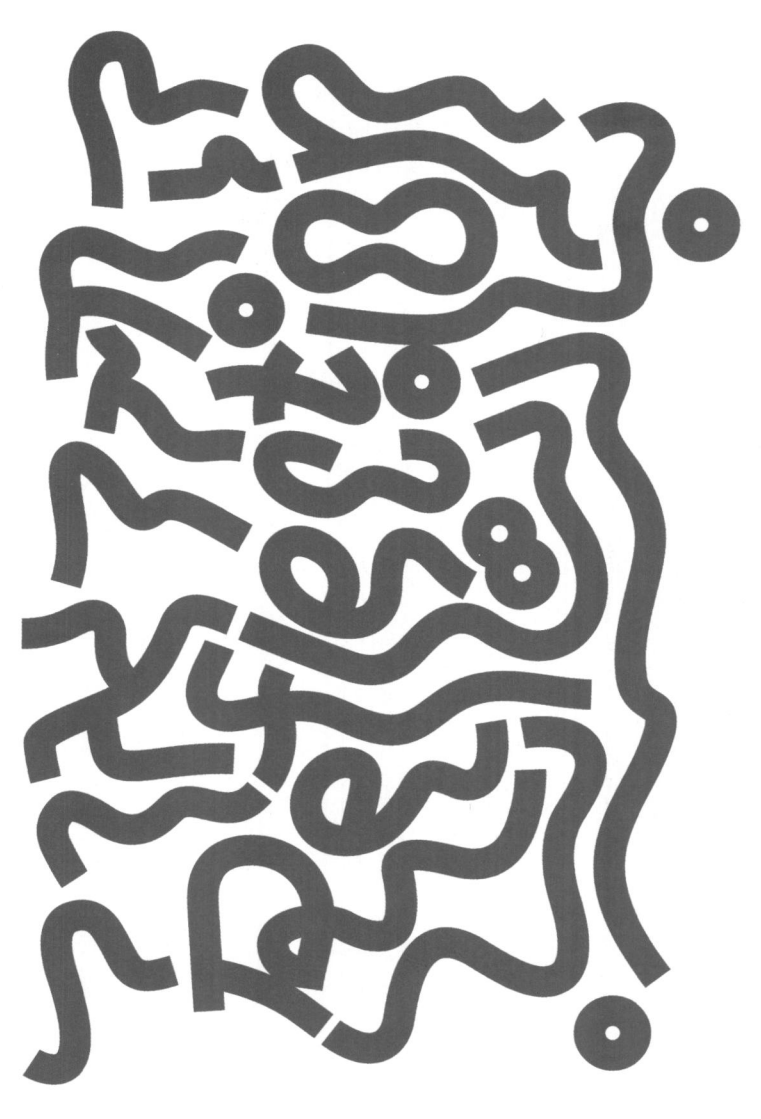

REFLECTION

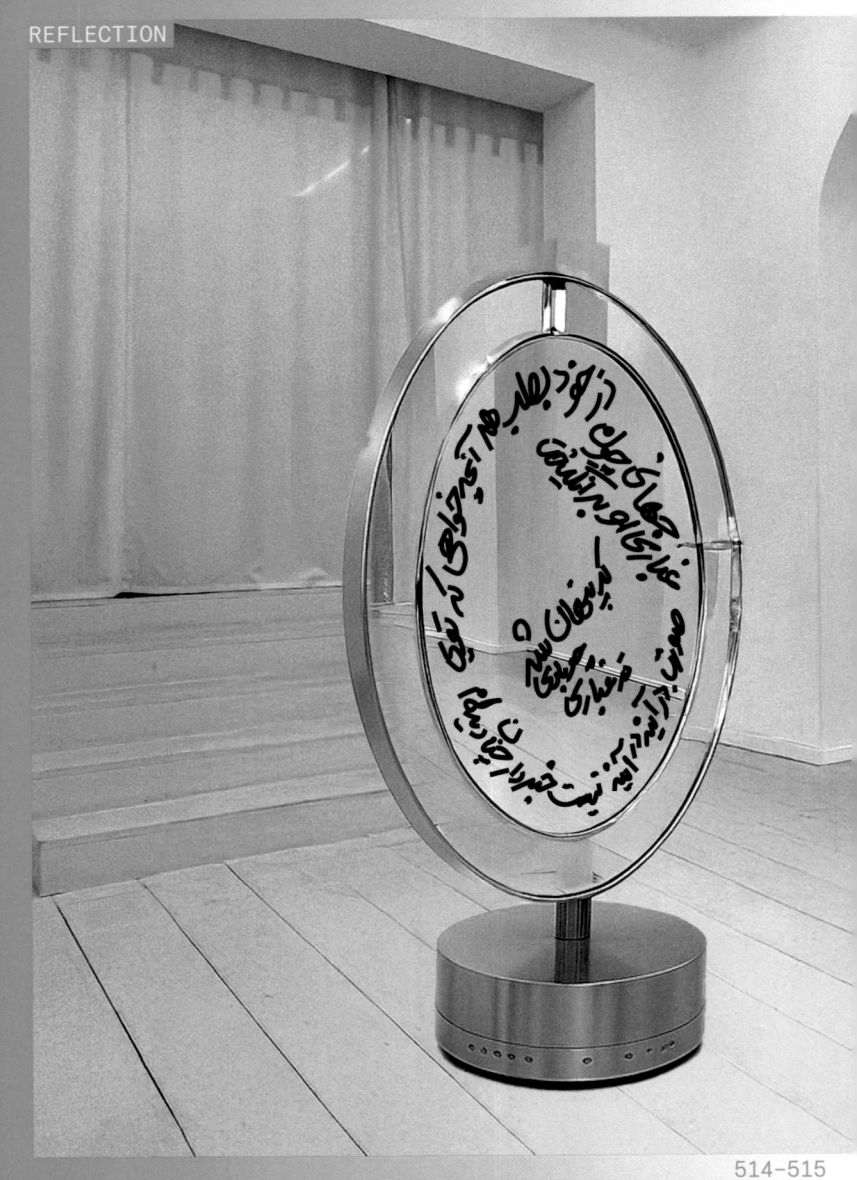

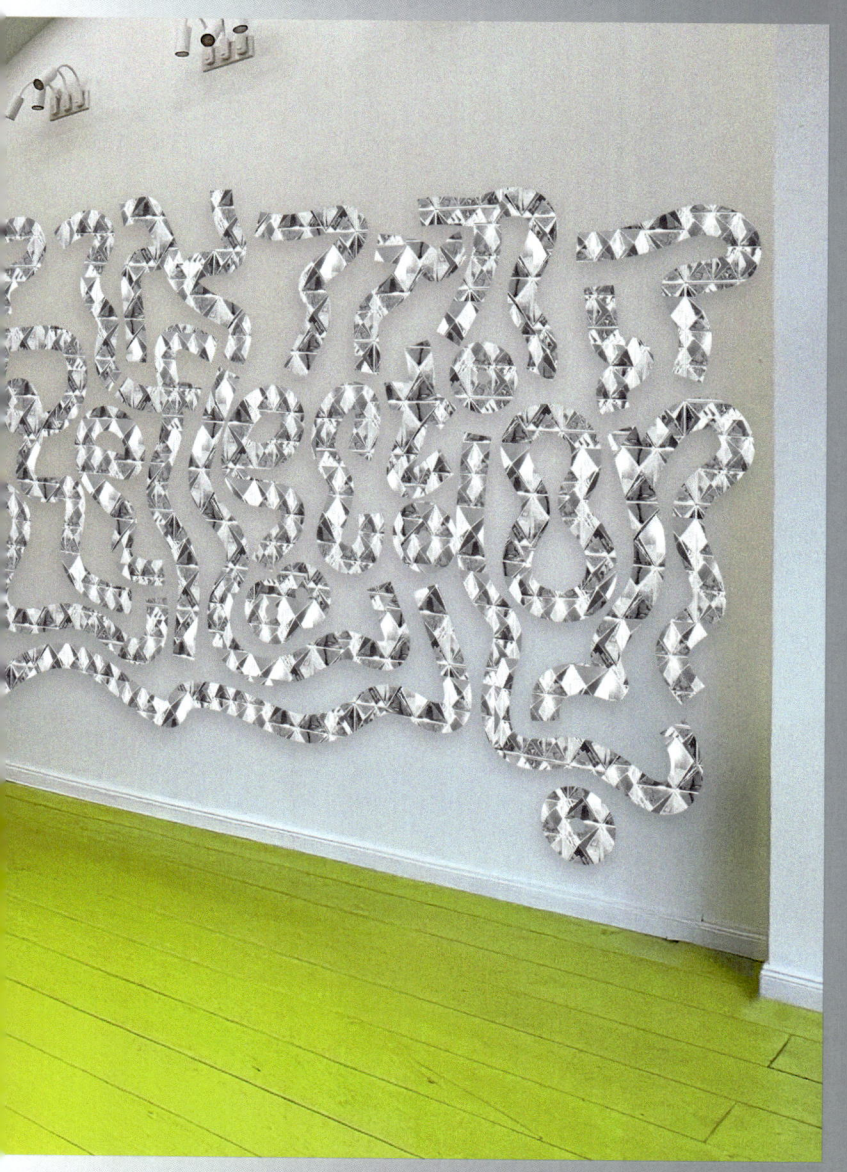

REVIVER
FLÁVIA NALON & FÁBIO PRATA

It's fascinating to look back at past predictions about the future. In graphic design, we've lost count of how many times we've heard it was the end of print. "Print is dead! The future is digital!" Yet here we are—still making books. On paper. Yes, print sometimes shifts to digital, only to return to print, then perhaps go digital again. Replay. Reprint. What we experience and re-experience often feels like the first time because each moment exists in a new context, with new meaning. It's revived—not exactly reborn, since it never truly died. It simply takes on new life. It's cyclical.

As we reflect on this, one word in Portuguese keeps coming to mind: reviver. A palindrome reads the same forward and backward—like cycles of design, history, and culture that can be read and reread over and over again. What we believe to be gone often returns: sometimes slightly altered, sometimes merely updated, sometimes bizarrely unchanged. For better or worse. Like the challenging times we're living through now—which seemed to belong to the past, yet are so current. So, what comes next? Resist. Rebuild. React. Looking forward also means looking back. This is a perspective we can offer. As designers. With type. And, of course, with a touch of poetry or humor so that we can endure, and even enjoy, the ride.

Flávia Nalon and Fábio Prata studied architecture at the University of São Paulo in Brazil, and communication design at the Hochschule Mainz. In 2003, they co-founded ps.2 arquitetura + design, a studio that creates and develops graphic design projects on paper, space and screen. Their work has won over 100 design awards. Flávia Nalon and Fábio Prata have been AGI members since 2013. They currently live and work between São Paulo and Hamburg, supporting clients within the cultural and other sectors worldwide. / ps2.com.br /

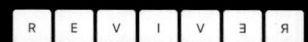
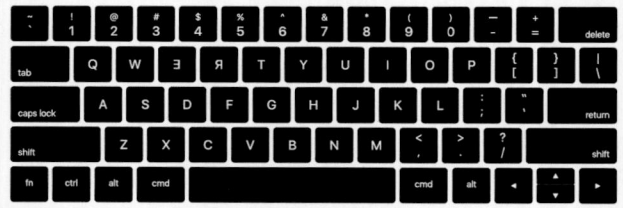

SUGIURA-KEI (SUGIURA SCHOOL)
KIYONORI MUROGA

Post-Cold War, DTP and internet birthed a new international design culture. As a journalist, I saw 90s digital enthusiasm, boundary-pushing 2000s projects and post-2010 'zombified' Modernist design. While the industry grapples with utilitarian thinking in corporate values and Internet culture, autonomous movements and discussions on gender/decolonization suggest 'better' directions.

But the 'liberal democracy' order, which has been the basis for the above-mentioned development, rapidly shifts and has been twisted within neoliberalism and technology. My witnessed design world might be a historical illusion shared by few. Despite this reality, I value democratic, international values in modern design. I'll use this A—Z exhibition to update these values, introducing designers' work that complements hegemonic Western 'design'.

I'll showcase Kohei Sugiura and his editorial design inheritors. This postwar Japanese designer merged Western Modernism with Japanese visual culture. His followers practiced experimental design while developing cultural methodologies based on concepts and research, uniquely interpreting historical influences from China and the West. Their hybrid and marginal approach offers valuable references today, when the world is politically divided yet governed by global information architectures and capitalism.

Kiyonori Muroga is an editor, writer, and lecturer, and former Editor-in-Chief of *IDEA* magazine. Since 1999, he has focused on editing books about Graphic Design, typography, and visual culture.
/ instagram.com/kiyonori_muroga /

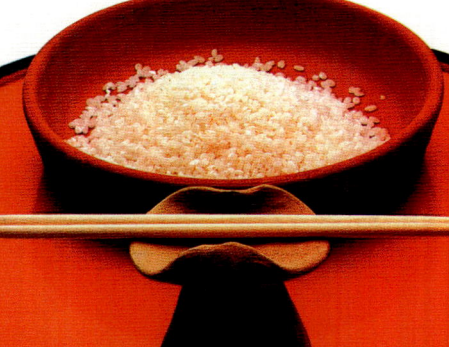

特集❶ 箸の美

凜

浄

箸

箸を使ういわゆる箸食文化圏は中国・朝鮮半島、ヴェトナム、日本に限られている。この中でも日本以外は箸とさじの併用である。かくしてわが国に純粋な箸食文化が開花したのである。

神饌に供えられる箸は、神と人との結合手段としては「最高」のものであった。神が使う箸は、神の依代としての意味を持つ。それ故に古代人は箸を神々籠る聖器としてあがめたのである。

季刊「銀花」

1979
〈箸のいろいろ〉
天削・利休・丁六
緑・小判……

第三十九号 秋

……春一番に芽ぶく柳の白木箸にて新春を壽ぎ、かぐわしき赤杉の箸にて客を饗す……

利休居士は、大和の吉野在より彫杉を取り寄せ、客のある日の朝、自ら小刀を手に中太両細の香り高い箸で、客をもてなした。

THE MAGIC PORRIDGE POT
TOBIAS RÖTTGER & SUSANNE STAHL

In the fairy tale *The Magic Porridge Pot* by the Brothers Grimm, a girl is given a magical pot that endlessly cooks porridge when she says, "Cook, little pot, cook". At first, the pot is helpful, but when she forgets the command to stop, it overflows and causes a flood of porridge. Only when she recalls the right words does the chaos end.

The fairy tale and the current use of Artificial Intelligence (AI) in graphic design are surprisingly similar. Initially, the pot serves as a helpful tool, just like AI in design, streamlining processes and offering new possibilities. However, like the pot that overflows and becomes uncontrollable, AI can overwhelm designers with endless options, pushing creativity aside. What was once a breakthrough tool risks becoming a flood. This story contains the central question of our time: How do we use technology without letting it control us? How do we maintain creative flow and authenticity while being inspired by the seemingly unlimited possibilities of AI? The true value of technology lies not in its infinite productivity but in humanity's ability to steer it with thoughtfulness and responsibility.

Stahl R is a Berlin-based design practice founded in 2013 by Tobias Röttger and Susanne Stahl. They create tailored design solutions for clients in commercial and cultural fields. The studio thrives on collaboration with creatives from diverse disciplines, working across various design areas, including visual identities, publication design, environmental design, art direction, and digital projects, producing innovative and award-winning work./ stahl-r.de /

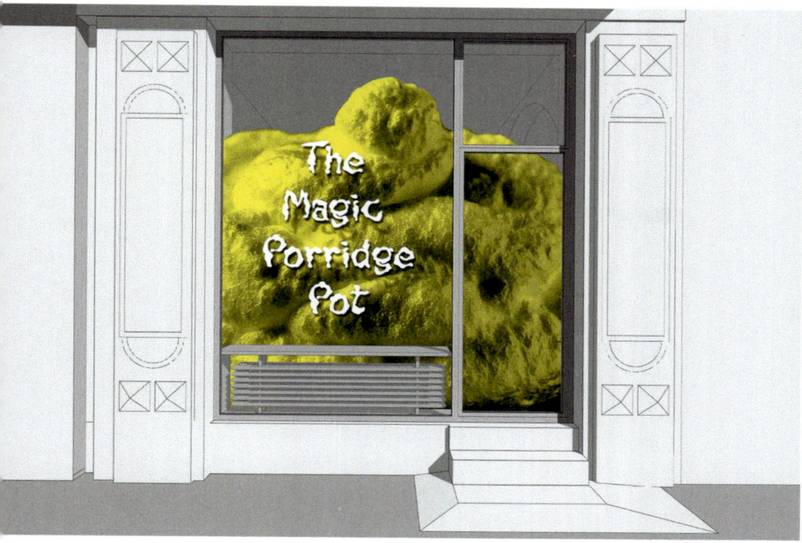

The Magic Porridge Pot

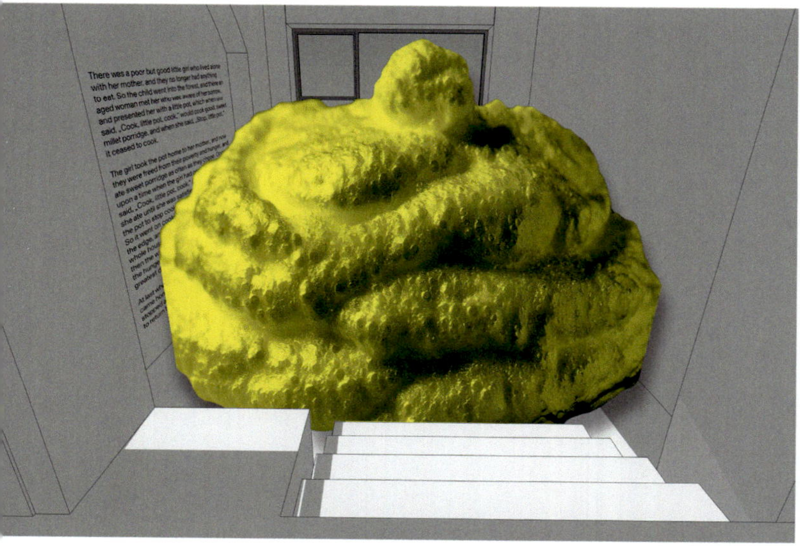

There was a poor but good little girl who lived alone with her mother, and they no longer had anything to eat. So the child went into the forest, and there an aged woman met her who was aware of her sorrow, and presented her with a little pot, which when one said, "Cook, little pot, cook," would cook good sweet millet porridge, and when she said, "Stop, little pot," it ceased to cook.

The girl took the pot home to her mother, and now they were freed from their poverty and hunger, and ate sweet porridge as often as they chose. Once upon a time when the girl had gone out, her mother said, "Cook, little pot, cook." And it did cook and she ate till she was satisfied, and then she wanted the pot to stop cooking, but did not know the word. So it went on cooking and the porridge rose over the edge, and still it cooked on until the kitchen and whole house were full, and then the next house, and then the whole street, just as if it wanted to satisfy the hunger of the whole world, and there was the greatest distress, but no one knew how to stop it. At last when only one single house remained, the child came home and just said, "Stop, little pot," and it stopped and gave up cooking, and whosoever wished to return to the town had to eat his way back.

TOUCH GRASS
AGGIE TOPPINS

With the rise of AI, the future of work will be increasingly automated, and 'life' will take place more and more online. The tools that graphic designers use, and the conditions under which we work, will have the effect of regulating creativity and standardizing form. What makes a human designer different from a machine? How can we make visual communications inspired by our interactions in the material world?

This exercise asks designers to touch grass. By prioritizing studio methods that extend from embodied movement in their physical surroundings, graphic designers can make work that is open to chance and reflects direct experience. I propose a workshop in which participants take one or several walks together, and respond to their experiences by co-creating a large-scale collage.

Based on observation and collected materials—a letterform here, a tree rubbing there—each person will contribute a number of oversized fragments to a room-sized installation. Fragments can be reproduced in paper, vinyl, fabric, or wood. The resulting installation will encourage maneuvering and play, directing our attention back to our bodies.

Aggie Toppins is a graphic designer and writer who explores where graphics come from, what they do, and how they change over time. She has contributed to several books and leading journals, including *Design and Culture*, *Design Issues*, *Slanted*, *Eye*, and *AIGA Eye on Design*. In 2025, she published her first book, *Thinking Through Graphic Design History*. Toppins is an award-winning educator who teaches at Washington University in St Louis. She maintains a vigorous creative practice based on collage.
/ aggietoppins.com /

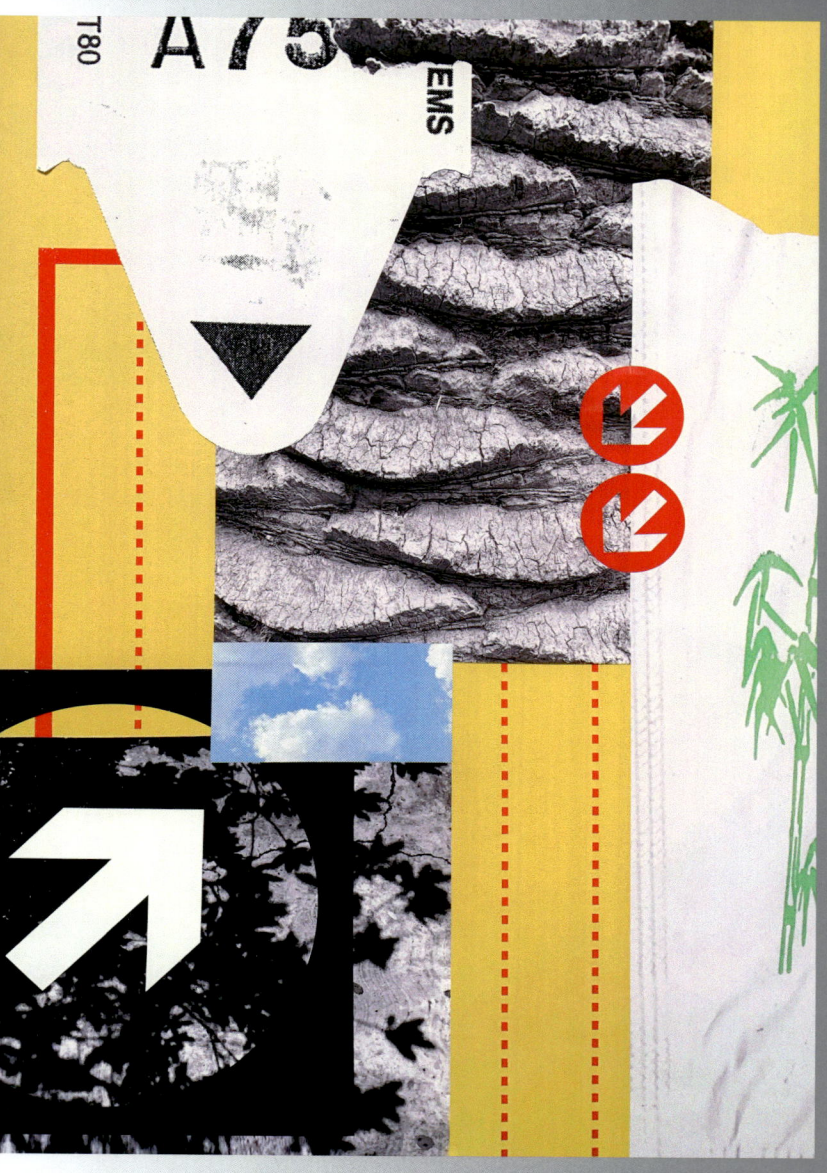

VISUAL VOICES
CHRIS CAMPE

In early 2024, I unexpectedly became a protest sign influencer.

Journalists had revealed that the German neo-fascist party AfD planned to deport up to 20 million people for not being 'German enough'. In protest, hundreds of thousands took to the streets. I was one of them, voicing my anger with hand-painted protest signs. To my surprise, my signs resonated. Others copied my designs and style—white letters on black, contour cut out—and a tutorial I shared went viral.

I thought, 'It's just a protest sign—anyone can make one'. But the process is not obvious to everyone. I had underestimated how a simple how-to takes the pressure off people and gives them the choice: follow along or do your own thing.

Painting a protest sign is a way to take action when times are overwhelming. It helps people clarify thoughts, express feelings, and articulate demands. At a protest, a well-designed sign catches attention and sparks conversation. It travels the world in photographs, and inspires others to visually raise their voices as well.

In the near future, graphic design will help make voices visible at protests against anti-democratic politics all over the world. Let's turn the A—Z space into a sign-painting workshop, with an inspirational gallery and a protest sign library for those who need a sign at short notice.

Chris Campe is a designer and writer based in Hamburg. She studied illustration in Hamburg and Paris, and Visual Studies in Chicago. She creates work at the intersection of text and image, art, and design. She has published six books, teaches and speaks internationally, and co-founded the Berlin Letters festival. / allthingsletters.com /

HOW TO PROTEST SIGN

1. What do you want to say?
Keep it short and punchy.

Save democracy!
Democracy is cool, let's keep it!
Presidents are not Kings *Fascism doesn't solve any of your problems.*
Resist Fascism! *stronger together*
Take a stand!

2. Sketch a quick draft.
- Which words go on which lines?
- Which words should stand out?

Highlight key words: Use capital letters, italics, underlines, different letter styles—whatever grabs attention!

SIZE *Script* lowercase UPPERCASE
underline PLANT WEIGHT

3. Lightly pencil your design onto a piece of cardboard.
Optional: First draw some quick guide lines to keep it neat and readable.

HANDS OFF! SAVE DEMOCRACY! STRONGER TOGETHER TAKE —a— STAND!
FASCISM doesn't solve any of your PROBLEMS
Democracy is cool, let's KEEP IT!

4. Then paint over the letters with a brush or a marker.
Pro-tip: To make sure everything fits, start by placing the first and last letters of each line, then fill in the middle.

5. Optional: Cut out around your text block.
Leave about a 1 cm border. The dynamic contour will make your sign even more eye-catching!

STRONGER TOGETHER DEMOCRACY IS COOL, LET'S KEEP IT! TAKE —a— STAND

6. Tape or glue your sign to a stick.

7. Go to the next protest!
Connect with a local group and bring a friend—it's more fun to go together.

CHRIS CAMPE
@allthingsletters

WAYS OF GRAPHIC DESIGN-ING
P! KRISHNAMURTHY

Prem (P!) Krishnamurthy has directed design studios, established galleries and institutions, curated large-scale exhibitions around the world, and taught widely. He received the Cooper Hewitt's National Design Award for Communications Design in 2015, and Bard College's Center for Curatorial Studies acquired his professional papers in 2019. His books include *P!DF (2017-2020)*, *On Letters (2022)*, and *Past Words (2024)*, an anthology of his writing and experimental curatorial projects. / premkrishnamurthy.com /

When I studied graphic design, we were concerned primarily with the conceptual and visual outcome— barely, if at all, with the process that led to something to present. The focus was typically on the 'what?' rather than the 'how?'. Yet one of the true values of graphic design is its collaborative spirit. This is what differentiates design from the popular perception of artmaking as the work of a lone genius.

Design is nearly always a team sport. Even the most solitary creators depend on a host of others— illustrators, photographers, type designers, programmers, printers, and more—to help author their work. As a result, graphic design offers a particular lens upon co-creation. It has the ability to articulate a set of protocols and tools relevant to other kinds of creative production—and society.

So, let's now imagine this: Instead of being heralded as masters of visual form, graphic designers might be seen as pioneers in practicing and publishing methods for collaboration, managing conflict, and interpersonal connection. Looking beyond its classic purview of problem-solving, graphic design could instead begin to articulate what tools and formats are required to bring together wildly different people to the proverbial table. Amid an increasingly fractured world, it seems like there is a lot of space for such a reformed idea of creating community and communication.

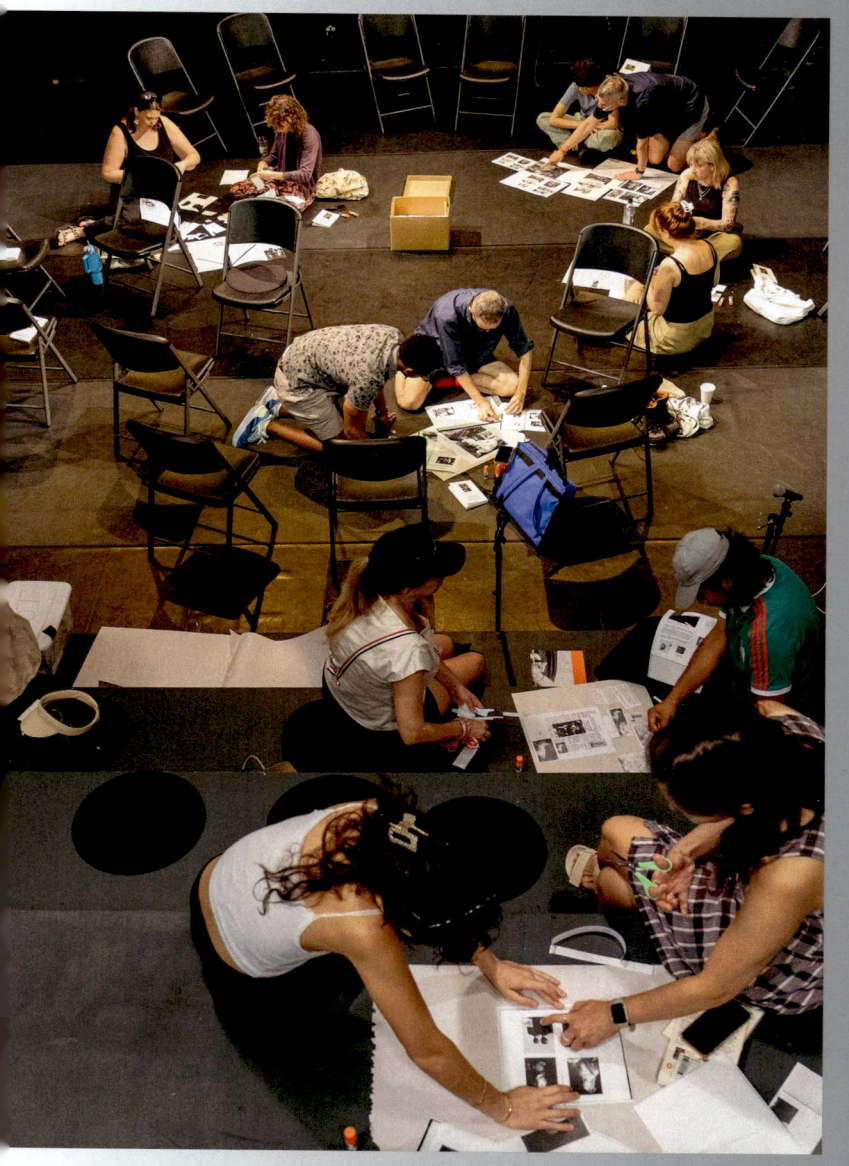

WOR(L)D VIEW – WOMEN X REPRESENTATION X LANGUAGE
MARIKO TAKAGI

Our choice of words plays a crucial role in how we communicate with each other, how we think, and how we see and understand the world. To begin with, only when we have a word/a name for something can we think and talk about it. The concept of what and how we feel about our surroundings is embedded in our culture, which is designed by humans. Language is neither natural nor 'God-given'. Language and the use of words are constantly shifting, reflecting the zeitgeist. Writing and its typographic representation are one method to distribute concepts and ideas efficiently and convincingly.

The "Wor(l)d View" series of artist books invites visitors to think about roles assigned to women, manifested through language and writing. The books will focus on Japanese terms and kanji (Sino-Japanese characters). Through a trilingual (Japanese, German, and English) approach, it will provide an insight into the Japanese wor(l)d view, mostly hidden from non-Japanese readers. It may also inspire visitors to reflect on their language and culture.

In written contemporary Japanese, there are countless kanji characters that contain the radical 女 (woman), which is used as a component or a building block. Fifty-four of those characters are listed and sorted here. The grouping chosen in this layout reveals what is otherwise invisible when you encounter them in samples of textual language.

Mariko Takagi is an educator, typographer, book designer, and author of numerous books on Japanese culture, design history, and typography. She has been teaching and researching as a professor in Kyoto since April 2017. Based on her experiences in Germany, Hong Kong, and Japan, she sees herself as a mediator between cultures and the critical issues of our time. / marikotakagi.de /

女 woman　　　始 to begin

WOR(L)D VIEW – WOMEN X REPRESENTATION X LANGUAGE

媒 matchmaker

姻 marriage

姶 an intelligent and excellent woman

outside the grid ─────

晏 a woman spends her day, resting, relaxing

娶 to take for a wife

婚 to become husband and wife

嫁 to marry into a family, a bride

妻 a wife

婦 a wife

妃 one's wife

"family" ─────

姐 an elder sister

姊 an elder sister

妹 a younger sister

娘 a daughter, an unmarried woman

始 beginning, elder sister

姓 bloodline, surname

妣 a deceased mother or grandmother

姑 a mother-in-law

妊 to become pregnant

奶 (breast) milk

婿 a daughter's husband

appearance ——— 姿 the appearance (of a beautiful woman)

娅 a decent appearance
妤 beautiful
妙 beautiful, young
奼 to boast, beautiful, young
姍 beautiful, to decry
姤 beautiful, good-looking, ugly, bad
姣 beautiful, lurid beauty, sluttishness

outside "family"

佞 an easily approachable woman
妓 a playgirl
娼 a playgirl, a prostitute
妾 a concubine, a slave
妮 a maid servant
婢 a low-status women, a servant
奴 a servant, a slave

behavior & emotions

娓 to obey, honest
如 to obey
委 to ajust and obey

媚 to flirt, to make use of one's sex-appeal
妥 to act as
㛮 to tease and fiddle with
妖 to be seductive

妨 to hinder

好 to like, favor, enjoy, patronize, and be good friends with
嬉 to enjoy, to be amused and to be happy

妒 to envy
妖 to blame
妄 lie
威 to threaten
奸 sin, evil
姦 slut, to pursue one's own private desires, to steal

IMAGE REFERENCES

All images by A—Z team, A—Z Collective, collaborators, and friends except for the pages indicated below.

51–53, 54 top, 55, 79, 87, 118–121, 127, 139–141, 193–197, 215–221, 237–239, 249–253, 268–273, 287–291, 306–307, 309, 314–315, 344–347, 352–357, 363–365, 367, 401–405, 407, 424–429, 431, 445–446
Photos by Hans-Georg Gaul

25   A—Z Collective members from top left: Ioana Ferariu, Kelly Diepenbrock, Anja Lutz, Francesco Pini, Ivana Jecmenica, Pia Steiner, Manuela dos Santos, Emily Smith, Eunjung Kwak, Alina Frieske, Lisa Baumgarten, Gregory Cowling

29   Top right photo by Andreas Koch

31   Andrea Tinnes with Pierre Pané-Farré, *Learning/ Unlearning from Bauhaus*, 2021–2022

33   Detail of *Corrections and Clarifications* by Anita Di Bianco, June 2024

35   Anja Lutz, *Oh Jacno !, 2023*, contribution to the exhibition in homage to the French graphic designer Marcel Jacno

37   Mirtha Dermisache, *Diario 1 Año 1*, page 2, 1972/1995 © 2025 Legado Mirtha Dermisache

41   Image source: International Banana Club membership card in www.bananaclub.com

47   Photos by Alina Frieske

67   Photo by Emily Smith

69   Illustration by Fernanda de la Mora

73   Image source: Magazine cover designed by Karl Schulpig, Archiv für Buchgewerbe und Gebrauchsgraphik, 1925

77   Tablecloth with sketches and interactions from *Collective Salad*.

83   Sketch from *Conversation Piece.* Photo by Lucienne Roberts

85   Peter Behrbohm's sketch of *Round Table Riots*—a set of spatial errors to provoke collective communication created for the *Teaching Design Conversations* exhibition

95   Preparatory notes by Franzi Bauer and Toni Brell for *Design and Solidarity – How can Graphic Design be Political?*

99   Collage of collection items by Eva Dumoulin

105–108   Photos by Alina Frieske

113   Installation view showing the works by Ilka Helmig, *Sound*

	Cloud "P", 2019, and Sound Cloud "O", 2021.
114	*The World's Writing Systems chronological order and Unicode status* Concept: Johannes Bergerhausen, Type Design: J. Bergerhausen, Arthur Francietta, Jérôme Knebusch, Morgane Pierson, ANRT, Nancy, 2016—2021 Poster Design: Ilka Helmig, Johannes Bergerhausen, 2018—2022
115	*The World's Writing Systems chronological and geographical order* Concept: Johannes Bergerhausen, Type Design: J. Bergerhausen, Arthur Francietta, Jérôme Knebusch, Morgane Pierson, ANRT, Nancy, 2016—2021 Poster Design: Ilka Helmig, Johannes Bergerhausen, 2022
135	Christine Hill, Rosa Luxemburg quote, hand-lettering with tempera paint on Stonehenge Paper, 72 x 111 cm, private collection
142	Mark van Wageningen's collection of vernacular East-European design
143	Patrick Thomas's collection of Auto Export business cards
144	Top: Sarah Illenberger's collection of stones. Bottom: Margaret Warzecha's collection of fake documents
145	Top: Niklaus Troxler's collection of rubber stamps. Bottom: Isabel Naegele's collection of kitchen sponges
147	Image by Lucienne Roberts
151	Lina Ghaibeh, *Joan's new Mantra,* graphic narrative, first published in *The Markaz Review*, LA, 2020
161	Inkahoots, *Disruptive Devices.* 2019. Street poster
165	Andrea Tinnes, Type Specimen for Inventar Collection
167	Bottom: Photo by Florian Dombois
169	Alexandra Vögtle, *Tools to play – Toys to work with,* 2023
177	Top: Source: Hanns Eisler, *Anmut sparet nicht noch Mühe (Kinderhymne),* International Music Score Library Project, www.imslp.org/wiki/Kinderlieder_(Eisler,_Hanns) Bottom: Source: Translation by Stephen Brockmann in *Literature and German Reunification*. Cambridge University Press, 2006

181 Yara Khoury Nammour, Mithaq typeface, 2022

201 Lucienne Roberts, *Signals,* book cover design. You're A Long Time Dead Project 3, 2025

205 Photo by Kira Bürmann

207 Anja Lutz, *Marginalia XXIII,* 2017

213 Mirtha Dermisache with her first artist's book *Libro N° 1* (1967), Buenos Aires, 1967. © 2025 Legado Mirtha Dermisache

223 Design drawings by Birger Lipinski

233 Na Kim, *Blank Buzz,* 2023. Photo by Dahahm Choi

243 Niklaus Troxler, *Sound of Serendipity,* silkscreen poster for jazz concert, 90 x 128 cm, 2024

263 Image from book cover *CORONA - Portrait of a Virus* by Isabel Naegele, Institut Design Labor Gutenberg, Hochschule Mainz, 2021

265 Patrick Thomas, *Cali Smog Chec,* mixed media, 22.6 x 28.9 cm, Los Angeles, 2023

267 Photo by Siniz Kim

277 Photo by Andrea Tinnes

281 Eye Magazine, issue 99, 2019, pp. 69–73, 76–77.

303 *Rebellion Riso Poster* with overprinted designs by Agnieszka Węglarska, Markus Lange, Frank Höhne

305 Photo by Alina Frieske

308 Photo by Alina Frieske

313 *Revealing » Recording » Reflecting* identity designed by Nour Asmar

321 Sarah Boris, *Love,* Screenprint in support of Unicef Ukraine, 2022

331 Photos by Emily Smith

333 Photo by Alina Frieske

343 Niklaus Troxler, *Just Tape It,* silkscreen poster for the exhibition *Tape Works,* 90 x 127 cm, 2020

348 Niklaus Troxler, *3 Colors,* silkscreen 50 x 70 cm, 2018

349 Niklaus Troxler, *Tape Work 09.05.2015,* 30 x 40 cm, 2015

355 Bottom right: photo by Peter Behrbohm

357 Collaborative student work from the workshop *Template Culture*

361 Image created with web button maker by Yassmine Tissaoui, www.lisa-online.neocities.org/maker

373 The Rodina, *Sweet Datapoint,* poster, 2015

375	Architectural drawings by Jens Bauermeister
384–385	Photos by Alex Branczyk
393	Cover image of Tine Melzer, *Atlas of Aspect Change*, Rollo Press, 2023
397	Collage by Giulia Siviero
399	*Transitory Help Desk*, logo design by Na Kim
406	Visitors to Na Kim's exhibition, clockwise from top: Ruohan Wang, James Langdon, Michael Friedrich und Hans Wagenknecht, Jae Kyung Kim, Eva-Maria Offermann, Juliana Toro with Na Kim and Anja Lutz
419	Visit from FH Potsdam students accompanied by Prof. Susanne Stahl. Photo by Emma Hermann
421	Nora Zeid, *Bustling Winter Morning in El Moez*, part of *Cairo Illustrated Series*, ink on paper, 35 x 60 cm, 2020
435	*Al-Hayya* magazine, 2022, Cover of Issue 1, alhayyamagazine.com. Photo by Myriam Boulos, Design by Studio Safar
485	Typeface: Azimut, by Benjamin Blaess, Julien Priez and Mathieu Réguer, CC BY-ND 4.0
491	Screenshot collage. Image source from top left to right bottom: 1. Article and diagram on Prophetic Perfect Tense on Wikipedia (en.wikipedia.org/wiki/Prophetic_perfect_tense) 2. Sad Guy Happy Guy Bus meme from Meme Generator (imgflip.com/memegenerator/355414628/Sad-guy-Happy-guy-bus) 3. Joshua Citarella, *Choose Your Future II*, Dye Sublimation Prints on Dibond, 2024 4. Screenshot from *David Lynch's Weather Report 8/21/20*, David Lynch YouTube Channel (youtube.com/watch?v=srT7vXsucHM) 5. Screenshot from *Hyperborea Real Life Not Nice* reel (tiktok.com/@getmotivated2024/video/7312030698385214766)
493–495	The works are part of "Zine #3—Life, AI, Technology: ASCII-Art," created by Julia Kahl, 2024
509	Illustration by Claudia Mai; Photo by Bernhard Hermant / unsplash; Collage by Ulrike Brückner
513	Image: Reflection in Hebrew, English and Persian
519	Quarterly *GINKA* No. 39, Bunka Shuppankyoku, 1979
527	Photo by Hari Adivarekar

NAME INDEX

Adrian Schiesser 332
adrienne maree brown 78
Aggie Toppins 332, 522
Agnieszka Węglarska 332, 378
Albert Coers 62, 376, 388
Alexandra Vögtle 168
Alex Branczyk 80, 302, 378
Alex Jordan 42, 86, 156, 304, 332, 389, 442
Alex Lehmann 356
Alina Frieske 24, 304
Almut Kühne 342, 387
Amelie 378
Amy Gowen 178
Andrea Iten 332
Andreas Koch 28, 304, 376, 388
Andrea Tinnes 30, 42, 80, 98, 138, 156, 164, 192, 274, 280, 304, 310, 340, 386
Anette Lenz 234, 442
Anita Di Bianco 32, 100, 240, 362, 368, 370, 374, 388
Anja Kaiser 58, 386
Anja Lutz 12, 18, 23, 24, 26, 34, 42, 80, 82, 86, 88, 126, 138, 146, 148, 154, 156, 168, 202, 204, 206, 234, 244, 294, 304, 310, 322, 324, 332, 356, 370, 374, 376, 378, 386, 387, 388, 390, 391, 398
Anja Neidhardt-Mokoena 350, 352
Anky Brandt 138
Anna Berkenbusch 138
Anna Bromley 100, 362, 368, 388
Anna Broujean 40, 332, 390
Anna Gerber 156
Anna Wolf 204
Anne-Christin Plate 42, 304
Ann Richter 146
Antoine Lefebvre 148, 391
Antonia Schneemann 352, 387, 430

Anuschka Spitzer 360
April Gertler 42, 66, 304, 332, 390
April Greiman 156, 460
Ariane Spanier 378
A Terv 332
Atipus 42
Axel Lapp 370

Bahia Shehab 180, 312, 318, 389, 432
Barbara Dechant 80, 138
Barbora Demovičová 178
Basma Hamdy 180
bell hooks 13, 14
Benedetta Crippa 84
Bernard Stein 138
Bertolt Brecht 176
Bianca Herlo 508
Bianca Schill 378
Birger Lipinski 222, 360
Broos Stoffels 332
Buchstabenmuseum 64, 126, 160, 174, 236, 280, 332, 410

Carlos Navarro 332
Carlotta Thomas 356
Caroline Bertelsen 356
Carolyn Kerchof 178
Catrin Sonnabend 42, 304
Cem Eskinazi 42
Charles and Ray Eames 156
Charlotte Rhode 84
CH Ernst 378
Chris Campe 524
Chris Rehberger 332
Christina Thomson 72, 389
Christine Hill 134
Christopher Knowles 80
Christopher Sleboda 500
Cihan Tamti 378
Cindy Moorman 304
Clara Amante 178

Clare Walters 474
Claudia de la Torre 42, 60, 304, 376, 388
Clemens Gensch 304
Constanze Hein 146, 332
Corin Gisel 178

Dahm Lee 332
Daniela Burger 332
Daniel Hahn 378
Daniel Hicks 378
Daniel Martin Feige 286
Daniel Pearce 304
Dani Karavan 124
David Reinfurt 126
Deborah-Lois Sery 378
Delphine Bedel 178
Diana Tsantekidou 332
Dina Benbrahim 432, 434
Doro Böhme 298
Douglas Rushkoff 13, 14
Drucken 3000 124, 302, 378

Eider Corral 42
Elena Eigenheer 356
Elham Namvar 178, 432
Elliott Earls 498
Eloise Hammermeister Smith 304
Emily Smith 24, 42, 80, 132, 146, 304, 360, 389, 390
Emma Hoette 390
Erica Fustero 42
Eugénie Zuccarelli 178
Eunjung Kwak 24, 42, 210, 304, 332
Eva Dumoulin 146, 162, 360
Eva-Maria Offermann 378, 398
Ezequiel Hyon 92, 162, 360

Fábio Prata 516
Fabrice Höfgen 84
Fanny Maurel 178
Fatma Mansour 420, 432

Ferdinand Ulrich 80
Fernanda de la Mora 360
Filip Zagórski 378
Flávia Nalon 516
Florian Brugger 378
Florian Dombois 86, 166, 389
Floriane Misslin 178
Florian Haberstumpf 302, 378
Florian Wüst 100, 362, 368, 388
Formal Settings 42, 304
Francesco Gagliardi 368
Francesco Pini 24, 80, 304, 332
Francesco Spampinato 78
Francisca Torres 42
Frank Höhne 80, 378
Frank Zappa 156
Franzi Bauer 80, 94, 162, 360, 386
Franziska Morlok 138, 356, 386
Fraser Muggeridge 138
Freek Lomme 18, 23, 154, 294, 322, 360

Gandhi 156
Gemma Terol 42
George Titheridge 42, 304
Georg Rutishauser 80, 376
Gerda Breuer 102
Ghalia Elsrakbi 432, 434
Giulia Lantier 378
Giulia Siviero 162, 360, 398
Golnar Kat-Rahmani 512
Gregory Cowling 24, 182, 304, 332, 390
Guy Schraenen 214

Hala Al Afsaa 138
Hala Al-Ani 420, 432
Hannah Whitlow 332
Hanna Kang 332
Hanna Müller 304
Hanns Eisler 176
Hans Brüderl 332

Hans-Georg Gaul 360
Heinrich Müller 138
Henning Wagenbreth 138
Hounyeh Kim 42, 304
Huda Smitshuijzen AbiFarès 312, 318, 389, 434
Hyeona Uhm 168
Hyesu Son 332

Ilka Helmig 80, 86, 112, 389
Imad Gebrayel 80, 352
Indre Klimaite 146
Inkahoots 10, 11, 14, 64, 156, 160, 174, 176, 236, 278, 280, 386, 410
Ioana Ferariu 24, 390
Isabel Naegele 138
Ivana Jecmenica 24, 304

Jacco Bunt 378
James Langdon 502
Janine Sack 146
Jan van Toorn 466
Jason Grant 8, 14, 80, 138, 174, 278, 360, 386
Jenny Richards 332
Jens Bauermeister 70, 86, 126, 332, 360
Jens Müller 72, 138, 389
Jens Strandberg 332
Jocelyn Ames 20, 132, 390
Johanna Olm 80, 162, 360
Johannes Bergerhausen 80, 86, 112, 389
John Cage 156
John L. Walters 474
Johnny Chang 332
Jordan Rita Seruya Awori 486
Josepha Conrad 42, 304
Joseph Beuys 442
Joseph Foo 156, 482
Joshua Duttweiler 304
Judith Rebekka 356

Judy Kaufmann 42, 332
Judy Smith 42, 304
Jule Eretier 168
Julia Kahl 302, 378, 492
Julia Meer 72, 389
Juliana Toro 80, 162, 356, 360, 398
Juli Gudehus 138, 332
Jungmyung Lee 80, 300, 352, 387

Kae Tempest 78
Kakoii 332
Karen Runge 42, 304
Karin Wiesmann 356
Kasper Andreasen 392
Katharina Gomez 356
Katharina Gschwendtner 378
Katharina Nejdl 468
Katharina Sussek 138
Katherine May 304
Kathleen Sleboda 500
Kathrin Krumbein 332
Kelly Diepenbrock 24, 332
Kinda Ghannoum 138, 432
Kira Bürmann 204
Kiyonori Muroga 518
Klaudia Mazur 178, 378
Kohei Sugiura 518
Kristina Wedel 42, 304
Kui Park 332

Laercio Redondo 222, 360
Laia Soler 42
Lamm & Kirch 376
Lana Belton 304
Lana Soufeh 378
Lan Kroeger 42, 304
Lars Harmsen 302
Laura Meseguer 42, 82, 130, 260, 304
Lea Scheidegger 356
Lena Weber 458

Lieven Lahaye 300, 352, 387
Lilly Drosch 204
Lily Tomec 324
Lina Ghaibeh 150, 432
Lioba Wachtel 168
L.i.P. Collective 116, 178, 282, 387
Lisa Baumgarten 24, 42, 304, 332, 350, 352, 387, 390, 430
Lisa Böckling 162, 360
Lisa Panitz 378
Liudmila Savelyeva 360
Loraine Furter 178, 470
Lorna Fray 202
Louise Khadjeh-Nassiri 332
Lucienne Roberts 20, 80, 82, 138, 146, 152, 188, 200, 266, 360, 388, 416
Luisa Kaiser 168
Luna Maurer 452

Maarten Janssen 304
Madeleine Morley 102, 178, 352
Madita Flohe 456
Manuela dos Santos 24, 330, 332, 390
Manuela Eichner 304
Manuel Viergutz 378
Mara Recklies 94, 386
Margaret Warzecha 138
María Carmona 42
Mariachiara De Leo 178
Maria Montes 42
María Yin 42
Mariko Takagi 528
Mari Leach 162, 360
Marin Griffith 304, 332
Marisa Lacarta 42
Mark Bohle 42
Markus Etienne 138
Markus Kummer 50, 56, 370, 387, 392
Markus Lange 302

Mark van Wageningen 80, 136, 138, 208, 246, 248, 332, 370, 388, 408
Marshall B. Rosenberg 78
Martí Guixé 42, 510
Martina Wember 378
Martin Gnadt 378
Maryam Fanni 102
Matilda Flodmark 102
Max Schürmann 378
Max Spielmann 332
Maya Moumne 433, 434
Maya Ober 178
Mela Freire 42
Melis Guenoglu 378
Micaela Terk 390
Miltos Bottis 378
Mindy Seu 86, 90, 258, 374, 389
Mio Kojima 178, 304
Mirtha Dermisache 36, 92, 148, 212, 214, 216, 218, 220, 228, 240, 282, 298, 391
MMS (Maryam Fanni, Matilda Flodmark, Sara Kaaman) 86, 102, 389
Mole Freyhoff 356
Molly Haig 304
Mujgan Abdulzade 178
Mushon Zer-Aviv 478

Naïma Ayed 178
Na Kim 80, 138, 146, 232, 326, 387, 398, 400, 416
Nanna Kristensen 356
Natalia Lombardo 304
Neville Brody 9, 10, 12, 14
Niamh McShane 332
Niklaus Troxler 42, 80, 98, 138, 172, 242, 258, 304, 340, 342, 387, 416
Niko Courtelis 138
Nikola Iljučoková 168

Nikolaus Neuser 342, 387
Nina Engel 378
Nina Paim 178
Noemi Parisi 178
Noha Khatwa 180
Nour Asmar 162, 312, 360

Oleksandra Pshenychna 204
Olena Hryhorieva 162, 360
Olena Smetanka 378
Oliver Klimpel 138
Oliver Vodeb 278
Orlando 42

Paolo Dellapiana 214, 391
Patrick Lacey 304
Patrick Thomas 80, 96, 98, 138, 240, 264, 286, 340, 374, 386
Paula Hornickel 378
Paula Schumacher 168
Paul Hutchinson 332
Pauline Clancy 138
Pauline Piguet 178
Paul Steinmann 304
Pernilla Rozenberg 332
Peter Behrbohm 84
Peter Nencini 80, 138
Philippe Delangle 138
Philipp Heinlein 378
Phoebe Eustance 178
Pia Steiner 24, 304, 332
Pierre Kaelin 356
Polina Ryman 204
Pol Pérez 42
Poster Rex 124, 302, 378
P! / Prem Krishnamurthy 26, 82, 360, 386, 526
Primitive Hut 332
Priya Parker 78

Raban Ruddigkeit 332, 378
Rachael Dunstan 42, 304

Radna Rumping 304
Rafael Bernardo 378
Rafael Horzon 396
Ráhel Rudolf 332
Ramon Tejada 42, 304
Random Happiness 332
Raupa Gonzales 378
Rebeca Méndez 156, 488
Rebekka Kiesewetter 356, 386
Rebellion Riso Posters Collab 124, 260, 302, 378, 387
Regine Ehleiter 36, 214, 298, 391
Richard Niessen 476
Rick Griffith 323
Rimini Berlin 80
Robert Plutchik 300
Robert Schlicht 202
Rob Keller 138
Roman Mars 244
Ronit Meirovitz 442
Ronny Duquenne 138
Rosa Menkman 44, 386
Roshanak Keyghobadi 434

Sally Alassafen 138
Salma Khairy 378
Sandra Doeller 496
Sandy Kaltenborn 94, 386, 466
Sara Abu Ghazal 420
Sara De Bondt 138
Sarah Boris 24, 42, 104, 138, 284, 304, 320, 332, 390
Sarah Illenberger 138
Sarah Schümperli 162, 360
Sara Kaaman 102, 138, 390, 504
Sara Rizkallah 150
Sebastian Dietel 378
Sebastian Ramming 356
Serena Lehmann 356
Sevinç Lenglachner 304
Sheila Levrant de Bretteville 484
Sibylle Schlaich 146

Silke Eberhard 342, 387
Silva Baum 178
Silvia Sfligiotti 42, 304, 390, 484
Silvio Lorusso 490
Siwar Krai(y)tem 464
Slanted 124, 302, 378
Sofia Harley 24, 304
So Jin Park 80, 162, 356, 360
Sonia Valentí 42
Sonja Knecht 138
Sonsoles Llorens 42
Sophia See 178
Sophie Schütte Meyer 356
Soraya Guimarães Hoepfner 68, 202, 360
Soukeina Hachem 150, 312, 318, 389
Stefanie Rau 146, 352
Stefan Vogtländer 378
Stephanie Cedeño 304
Sun Young Oh 130
Susanne Beer 94, 386
Susanne Stahl 520
Susan Ploetz 42, 304
Susan Sentler 390
Svenja Prigge 146
Sven Völker 138
Szymon Stemplewski 138

Tabea Nixdorff 298
Tereza Ruller 26, 372, 422
The Portland Stamp Company 332
The Rodina 26, 226, 372, 386, 422
Thies Wulf 332
Thomas Marutschke 378
Tim Ziola 332
Tine Melzer 50, 56, 80, 128, 258, 370, 374, 387, 392
Tobias Röttger 520
Tom Nixon 78
Toni Brell 94, 386
Tulah Stanford 42, 304

Tulip Hazbar 150

Ulrike Brückner 508
Ulrike Mohr 332
Urs Lehni 80

Vincent Bord 378
Vit Ruller 26, 372, 422
Vivien Tauchmann 390

Yanchi Huang 178
Yara Nammour 180
Yasmine Nachabe Taan 312, 318, 389, 420
Yessica Deira 422
Yewon Seo 204
Yumiko Soga 378

Zadeh Fatehrad 420
Zenobia Ahmed 178

On the Edges of Graphic Design
from A—Z—∞

Editors:
Anja Lutz, Soraya Guimarães Hoepfner

Texts & translations:
Soraya Guimarães Hoepfner

Contributing authors:
Jason Grant, Freek Lomme

Proofreading:
Lorna Fray, Robert Schlicht

Design and layout:
Anja Lutz // Design Art Books with Ezequiel Hyon, Fernanda de la Mora, Liudmila Savelyeva, Sarah Schümperli

Typeface:
Relative by Colophon Foundry

Image processing, printing and binding:
DZA Druckerei zu Altenburg GmbH

Paper:
Pergraphica Classic Rough 100g/m^2
Magno Gloss 150g/m^2
Cover: Pergraphica Classic Rough 300g/m^2

Published by:
Set Margins
www.setmargins.press
ISBN 978-90-835795-1-1

Bookshop Distribution
in Germany only:
The Green Box
ISBN 978-3-96216-021-0

With thanks to Sabine Goemann (IGEPA group) for her guidance and support in the selection of the papers: Pergraphica Rough and Magno gloss. More at igepa.de and icon-papers.blog

Thanks to the team at Druckerei zu Altenburg for their expertise and support in the production of this book.

Every effort has been made to contact copyright holders and to obtain their permission for the use of copyright material. If inadvertent infringement has occurred please contact the publisher.

© 2025, A—Z and the authors, photographers and designers.

Set Margins #81
First edition, 2025